Dedicated to the Memory of

HARLAN CHARLES PEDEN

1927 - 1997

Revolutionary Patriots

of

Charles County

Maryland

1775-1783

Henry C. Peden, Jr.

HERITAGE BOOKS
2006

HERITAGE BOOKS
AN IMPRINT OF HERITAGE BOOKS, INC.

Books, CDs, and more—Worldwide

For our listing of thousands of titles see our website
at
www.HeritageBooks.com

Published 2006 by
HERITAGE BOOKS, INC.
Publishing Division
65 East Main Street
Westminster, Maryland 21157-5026

Copyright © 1997 Henry C. Peden, Jr.

All rights reserved. No part of this book may be reproduced or transmitted in any form or by any means, electronic or mechanical, including photocopying, recording or by any information storage and retrieval system without written permission from the author, except for the inclusion of brief quotations in a review.

International Standard Book Number: 978-1-58549-444-5

INTRODUCTION

This book has been compiled for the purpose of serving as a research tool for locating the men and women of Charles County, Maryland, who served in the military, rendered material aid to the army or navy, took the Oath of Allegiance and Fidelity, served in an office or on a committee at the town, county, or state level, or in some fashion contributed and supported the fight for freedom by the American colonies from the rule of Great Britain during the Revolutionary War, 1775-1783.

It is hoped that this book, which is the tenth in a series on Revolutionary War patriots and soldiers in Maryland, will encourage and enable interested persons to become members of such patriotic organizations as The Sons of the American Revolution, The Daughters of the American Revolution, The Sons of the Revolution, and The Society of the Cincinnati.

Information for this book has been gleaned from many primary and secondary sources, which makes this book far more than just a listing of names and ranks. Most of the approximately 4,000 persons named herein have genealogical data included with their respective entries, such as places of residence and dates of birth, death, and marriage, names of wives, husbands, children and other relatives, plus physical descriptions, occupations, and information gleaned from church, military, pension, probate, and other court records, including the "census" of 1778 for Charles County.

Each entry in this book has been documented and a key to that documentation has been implemented within the text to enable the reader to review the cited source. A letter followed by a number is the code used for a source and the page within that source. For example, [Ref: D-555] would indicate that the information can be found on page 555 of Reference D, which is *Archives of Maryland, Volume 18*. The coded sources cited herein are as follows:

A = *Archives of Maryland, Volume XI*. "Journal of the Maryland Convention, July 26, 1775 - August 14, 1775, and Journal and Correspondence of the Maryland Council of Safety, August 29, 1775 -July 6, 1776" (Baltimore: Maryland Historical Society, 1892)

B = *Archives of Maryland, Volume XII*. "Journal and Correspondence of the Maryland Council of Safety, July 7, 1776 - December 31, 1776" (Baltimore: Maryland Historical Society, 1893)

C = *Archives of Maryland, Volume XVI*. "Journal and Correspondence of the Council of Safety, January 1, 1777 - March 20, 1777" and "Journal and Correspondence of the State Council, March 20, 1777 - March 28, 1778" (Baltimore: Maryland Historical Society, 1897)

D = *Archives of Maryland, Volume XVIII*. "Muster Rolls and Other Records of Service of Maryland Troops in the American Revolution, 1775-1783" (Baltimore: Maryland Historical Society, 1900)

E = *Archives of Maryland, Volume XXI*. "Journal and Correspondence of the Council of Maryland, April 1, 1778 - October 26, 1779" (Baltimore: Maryland Historical Society, 1901)

F = *Archives of Maryland, Volume XLIII*. "Journal and Correspondence of the State Council of Maryland, 1779-1780" (Baltimore: Maryland Historical Society, 1924)

G = *Archives of Maryland, Volume XLV*. "Journal and Correspondence of the State Council of Maryland, 1780-1781" (Baltimore: Maryland Historical Society, 1927)

H = *Archives of Maryland, Volume XLVII*. "Journal and Correspondence of the State Council of Maryland, 1781" (Baltimore: Maryland Historical Society, 1930)

I = *Archives of Maryland, Vol. XLVIII*. "Journal and Correspondence of the State Council of Maryland, 1781-1784" (Baltimore: Maryland Historical Society, 1931)

J = *DAR Patriot Index* (Washington, DC: National Society of the Daughters of the American Revolution, Centennial Edition, 1994, 3 volumes)

K = *Revolutionary War Military Collection, Manuscript MS.1814* (Baltimore: Maryland Historical Society, Manuscript Division)

L = Carothers, Bettie. *9000 Men Who Took the Oath of Allegiance and Fidelity to the State of Maryland During the Revolution* (Lutherville, Maryland: Privately Compiled by the Author, 1978)

M = Clements, S. Eugene and Wright, F. Edward. *The Maryland Militia in the Revolutionary War* (Silver Spring, Maryland: Family Line Publications, 1987)

N = Papenfuse, Edward, et al. *An Inventory of Maryland State Papers, Volume I*, "The Era of the American Revolution, 1775-1789" (Annapolis: Hall of Records Commission, 1977)

O = "Some Little Known Data Regarding Maryland Signers of the Oath of Fidelity," by Richard B. Miller, *Maryland Genealogical Society Bulletin*, Volume 27, No. 1, pp. 101-124 (Winter, 1986)

P = Papenfuse, Edward, et al. *A Biographical Dictionary of the Maryland Legislature, 1635-1789* (Baltimore: Johns Hopkins Press, 1979)

Q = Brumbaugh, Gaius M. *Maryland Records: Colonial, Revolutionary, County and Church From Original Sources* (Baltimore: Genealogical Publishing Company, Inc., 1985 reprint, 2 volumes)

R = *Maryland Pension Rolls of 1835: Report from the Secretary of War in Relation to the Pension Establishment of the United States* (Baltimore: Genealogical Publishing Company, Inc., 1968 reprint)

S = *Maryland Society, Sons of the American Revolution* (Original Applications at the University of Baltimore, Langsdale Library)

T = Burns, Annie Walker. *Maryland Soldiers of the Revolutionary, 1812, and Indian Wars Who Drew Pensions While Residing in Kentucky* (Washington, DC: Privately Compiled by the Author, 1939)

U = *National Genealogical Society Quarterly* (as cited)

V = White, Virgil D. *Genealogical Abstracts of Revolutionary War Pension Files* (Waynesboro, Tennessee: The National Historical Publishing Company, 1990, 4 volumes)

W - Newman, Harry Wright. *Maryland Revolutionary Records* (Baltimore: Genealogical Publishing Company, 1980 reprint)

X = *Charles County Militia Lists, 1777* (Maryland Historical Society, Card Catalog No. MF185.H68)

Y = *Calendar of Maryland State Papers, The Red Books, No. 4, Part 1 and Part 2* (Annapolis: The Hall of Records Commission, 1950)

Z = *Maryland Genealogical Society Bulletin* (as cited)

AA = *Charles County Oaths of Allegiance, 1778* (Maryland State Archives, Original Record Book No. X3, pp. 641-651)

BB = *Charles County Court Minutes, 1778-1780* (Maryland State Archives, Original Record Book No. Y3)

CC = *Charles County Court Minutes, 1776-1778* (Maryland State Archives, Original Record Book No. X3)

DD = Barnes, Robert W. "Charles County Depositions," *Maryland Genealogical Society Bulletin*: Vol. 33 No. 4, pp. 693-709 (1992); Vol. 34 No. 1, pp. 8-21 (1993); Vol. 34 No. 2, pp. 170-182 (1993); and, Vol. 34 No. 3, pp. 270-278 (1993)

EE = Jourdan, Elise Greenup. *Colonial Records of Southern Maryland* (Westminster, Maryland: Family Line Publications, 1997)

FF = Barnes, Robert W. *Marriages and Deaths from the Maryland Gazette, 1727-1839* (Baltimore: Genealogical Publishing Co., 1973)

GG = *Charles County Orphans Court Proceedings, 1777-1782* (Maryland State Archives, Original Record Book No. AF-7)

HH = Genealogical Collections of Henry C. Peden, Jr. (1997)

It must be noted that it is not possible to know who all of the patriots were who served in or from Charles County during the entire Revolutionary War period. This is especially true for those who joined the Maryland Line and served in the Continental Army. Due to the constant reorganization of the Maryland troops during the war, it is not easily determinable which soldier served from which county. It is apparent, however, that men from Charles County served in the 1st, 2nd, 3rd, and 5th Maryland Continental Lines.

As may be the case in works such as this, it is possible that some patriots may have been inadvertently omitted. Additional research may be necessary before drawing conclusions. Therefore, one should check the many lists found in the *Archives of Maryland, Volume 18*, for perhaps even more names of soldiers from Charles County.

> Henry C. Peden, Jr.
> Bel Air, Maryland
> July 4, 1997

CHARLES COUNTY, MARYLAND AND ENVIRONS, 1795

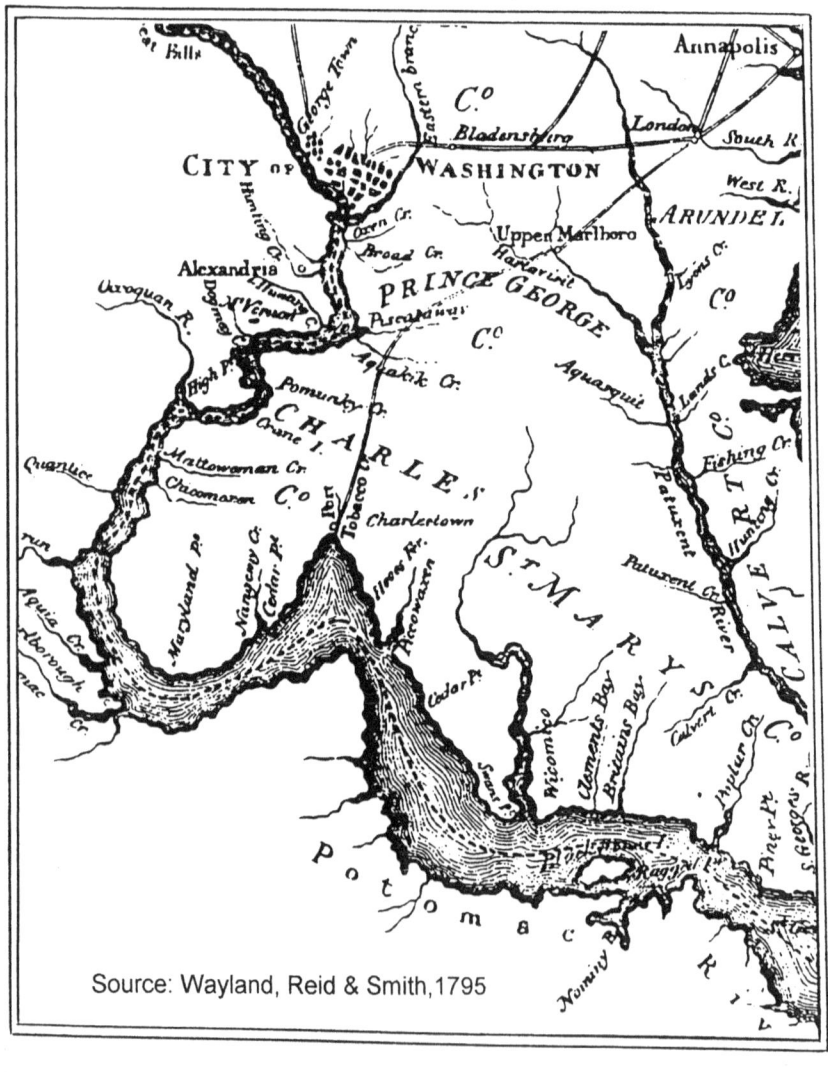

REVOLUTIONARY PATRIOTS OF CHARLES COUNTY, MARYLAND, 1775-1783

ACTON, Barbara. See "Alexander McPherson," q.v.

ACTON, Francis. Second Lieutenant, Militia, 26th Battalion, Capt. Samuel Smallwood's Company, commissioned on May 9, 1778 [Ref: M-47, M-165, E-72]. Took the Oath of Allegiance in 1778 [Ref: L-14, AA-641]. Resident of Port Tobacco Upper Hundred in 1778 [Ref: Q-I:297].

ACTON, Henry. Private, Militia, 12th Battalion, Capt. John Hanson's Company, 1777 [Ref: M-159]. This name appeared twice on the list of those who took the Oath of Allegiance in Charles County in 1778 in addition to Henry Acton, Jr., and Henry Acton, Sr., who are listed herein [Ref: AA-641, J-I:9]. One Henry Acton was a private in the Lower Battalion of Prince George's County in 1776 [Ref: D-35, which misspelled the name as "Aeton"]. One Henry Acton was a resident of Port Tobacco East Hundred in Charles County in 1778 [Ref: Q-I:297].

ACTON, Henry Jr. Took the Oath of Allegiance in 1778 [Ref: L-14, AA-641]. Resident of Port Tobacco Upper Hundred in 1778 [Ref: Q-I:297].

ACTON, Henry Sr. (1709-). Took the Oath of Allegiance in 1778 [Ref: L-14, AA-641]. Aged about 62 as noted in a 1771 deposition [Ref: DD-693]. Resident of Port Tobacco Upper Hundred in 1778 [Ref: Q-I:297].

ACTON, James. Private, Militia, 12th Battalion, Capt. John Hanson's Company, 1777 [Ref: M-158]. Took the Oath of Allegiance in 1778 [Ref: AA-641]. Resident of Port Tobacco East Hundred in 1778 [Ref: Q-I:297].

ACTON, John Jr. Took the Oath of Allegiance in 1778 [Ref: L-14, AA-641]. Resident of Port Tobacco Upper Hundred in 1778 [Ref: Q-I:297].

ACTON, John Sr. Took the Oath of Allegiance in 1778 [Ref: AA-641]. Resident of Port Tobacco Upper Hundred in 1778 [Ref: Q-I:297].

ACTON, John, of John. Private, Militia, 26th Battalion, Capt. Samuel Smallwood's Company, 1777 [Ref: M-165]. Resident of Port Tobacco Upper Hundred in 1778 [Ref: Q-I:297].

ACTON, Joseph. Took the Oath of Allegiance in 1778 [Ref: L-14, AA-641].

ACTON, Osborn. Took the Oath of Allegiance in 1778 [Ref: AA-641]. Rendered patriotic service by providing wheat for the use of the military in August 1782 [Ref: N-538, N-539, which listed the first name as "Osbon"]. Resident of Port Tobacco East Hundred in 1778 [Ref: Q-I:297].

ADAMS, Adam (1762/3-). Private, 1st Maryland Line, enlisted on May 16, 1778 and discharged on May 16, 1781 [Ref: D-78, D-330, D-522]. Resident of William & Mary Lower Hundred in 1778 [Ref: Q-I:297]. In December

1815, the Treasurer of Maryland was directed to pay to "Adam Adams, during his life, a sum of money equal to the half pay of a private, annually in quarterly payments." He was placed on the pension rolls in Charles County as of May 1, 1818, retroactive to March 21, 1818. He applied for a federal pension (S34623) on March 28, 1818, and in 1820 stated he was aged about 57 and had a wife Ann Adams, aged 26 [sic], and these children: Pamelia Adams (aged 14), Eleanor Adams (aged 9), John Adams (aged 8), Robert Adams (aged 6), Richard Adams (aged 4), and Lydia Adams (aged 3 months). [Ref: Q-II:314, R-33, V-I:9].

ADAMS, Ann. See "Adam Adams," q.v.

ADAMS, Benjamin. Private, Militia, 26th Battalion, Capt. William McPherson's Company, 1777 [Ref: M-163].

ADAMS, David Jenifer (1751-1796). Third Lieutenant, 1st Independent Maryland Company under the command of Capt. Rezin Beall on Jan. 2, 1776 [Ref: D-20]. In April 1776, George Dent, Chairman of the Charles County Committee, referred to him as "Lieutenant Jenifer Adams" [Ref: A-305]. Subsequently became a major, married Nancy Hanson, and died in Delaware on Nov. 29, 1796 [Ref: J-I:11].

ADAMS, Eleanor. See "Adam Adams," q.v.

ADAMS, Francis. First Lieutenant, 26th Battalion, Capt. George Dent's Company, commissioned May 9, 1778 [Ref: M-47, E-72]. Resident of Durham Lower Hundred in 1778 [Ref: Q-I:297]. Took the Oath of Allegiance in 1778 [Ref: L-14, AA-641]. Appointed Inspector of Tobacco at Nanjemoy on Aug. 30, 1780 [Ref: F-271]. Francis Adams was aged about 42 (born 1746) as noted in a 1778 deposition and Francis Adams, Jr., was aged about 28 (born 1728) as noted in a 1756 deposition [Ref: DD-693, DD-694].

ADAMS, George. There were at least three men with this name in Charles County during the war. One was a private in the militia, 26th Battalion, Capt. Robert Sinnett's Company, 1777 [Ref: M-164]. One took the Oath of Allegiance in 1778 and one in 1780 [Ref: L-14, AA-641, O-104]. One George Adams petitioned the Council of Maryland in 1783 stating he had not taken the Oath of Allegiance due to any disaffection with the government, but from a variety of incidents, and was unjustly penalized as a non-juror and was fined unfairly; therefore, he asked the Council to consider ordering the County Justices to remit the fines they imposed on him and others who signed the petition. The Council of Maryland, after reviewing his case, indicated they believed the truth of the facts stated in the petition and ordered a remission of the fines and penalties on Sept. 17, 1783 [Ref: I-454]. One George Adams was aged about 50 (born 1729)

as noted in a 1779 deposition [Ref: BB-481, DD-694]. Resident of Port Tobacco East Hundred in 1778 [Ref: Q-I:297].
ADAMS, George, of Andrew. Took the Oath of Allegiance in 1778 [Ref: L-14, AA-641].
ADAMS, Ignatius. Took the Oath of Allegiance in 1778 [Ref: L-14, AA-641]. Private, 1st Maryland Line, Capt. Edward Prall's Company, 1779-1782 [Ref: D-78, D-432]. Rendered patriotic service by providing wheat for the use of the military in May 1783 [Ref: N-598]. In 1778 Ignatius Adams and Ignatius Adams, Sr., resided in Port Tobacco West Hundred and another Ignatius Adams resided in Benedict Hundred [Ref: Q-I:297].
ADAMS, Jacob. Private, Militia, 26th Battalion, Capt. Richard Bennett Mitchell's Company, 1777 [Ref: M-164]. Took the Oath of Allegiance in 1778 [Ref: AA-641].
ADAMS, James. Memorialist and Militiaman, Pomonkey Company, after March 6, 1776 [Ref: M-158, Y-II:26]. Took the Oath of Allegiance in 1778 [Ref: AA-641]. One James Adams was aged about 54 as noted in a 1778 deposition [Ref: DD-694]. Resident of Pomonkey Hundred in 1778 [Ref: Q-I:297].
ADAMS, Jenifer. See "Daniel Jenifer Adams," q.v.
ADAMS, Jeremiah. Private, Militia, Capt. Francis Mastin's Company, 26th Battalion, March 19, 1776 through at least 1777 [Ref: M-158, M-164, K-1814]. Took the Oath of Allegiance in 1778 [Ref: AA-641]. Resident of Durham Lower Hundred in 1778 [Ref: Q-I:297].
ADAMS, John. Private, Militia, 26th Battalion, Capt. Thomas H. Marshall's Company, 1777 [Ref: M-163]. Private (drafted and joined the army), 1st Maryland Line, by Sept. 11, 1778 [Ref: D-330]. Resident of Benedict Hundred in 1778 [Ref: Q-I:297]. See "Adam Adams," q.v.
ADAMS, John. Sergeant, Militia, 12th Battalion, Capt. Peter Wood's Company, 1777 [Ref: M-161]. Took the Oath of Allegiance in 1778 [Ref: L-14, which listed the name as "Addams"]. Resident of Port Tobacco West Hundred in 1778 [Ref: Q-1:297]. See "Adam Adams," q.v.
ADAMS, John Jr. Took the Oath of Allegiance in 1778 [Ref: L-14]. One John Adams was aged about 24 (born 1719) as noted in a 1743 deposition and another John Adams was aged about 23 (born 1747) as noted in a 1770 deposition [Ref: DD-694]. See "Alexander McPherson," q.v.
ADAMS, John B. Sergeant, Militia, 12th Battalion, Capt. John Thomas' Company, 1777 [Ref: M-161]. Took the Oath of Allegiance in 1778 [Ref: L-14, which listed the name as "John R. Adams"]. "John B. Adams" was a resident of Benedict Hundred in 1778 [Ref: Q-I:297].
ADAMS, Josias. Private, Militia, 26th Battalion, Capt. William Winter's Company, 1777 [Ref: M-165]. Petitioned the Council of Maryland in 1783

stating that he had not taken the Oath of Allegiance due to any disaffection with the government, but from a variety of incidents, and was unjustly penalized as a non-juror and fined unfairly; therefore, he asked the Council to consider ordering the County Justices to remit the fines they imposed on him and others who signed the petition. The Council of Maryland, after reviewing his case, indicated they believed the truth of the facts stated in the petition and ordered a remission of the fines and penalties on Sept. 17, 1783 [Ref: I-454]. One Josias Adams was aged about 45 (born 1725) as noted in a 1770 deposition and Josias Adams, Jr., son of Lodwick Adams, deceased, was aged about 24 (born 1747) as noted in a 1771 deposition [Ref: DD-694].

ADAMS, Leonard. Took the Oath of Allegiance in 1778 [Ref: L-14]. Rendered patriotic service by providing wheat for the use of the military in September 1782 [Ref: N-544]. Resident of Port Tobacco Upper Hundred in 1778 [Ref: Q-I:297].

ADAMS, Lodwick. See "Josias Adams," q.v.

ADAMS, Lydia. See "Adam Adams," q.v.

ADAMS, Pamelia. See "Adam Adams," q.v.

ADAMS, Rhody (1745-   ). Son of Lodwick Adams (deceased by 1771). Aged about 26 as noted in a 1771 deposition [Ref: DD-694, which listed his name as "Rhode"]. Private, Militia, 26th Battalion, Capt. William Winter's Company, 1777 [Ref: M-165]. Rendered patriotic service by providing wheat for the use of the military in May 1783 [Ref: N-598, which listed the name as "Rhodah Adams"]. Petitioned the Council of Maryland in 1783 stating that he had not taken the Oath of Allegiance due to any disaffection with the government, but from a variety of incidents, and was unjustly penalized as a non-juror and fined unfairly; therefore, he asked the Council to consider ordering the County Justices to remit the fines they imposed on him and others who signed the petition. The Council of Maryland, after reviewing his case, indicated they believed the truth of the facts stated in the petition and ordered a remission of the fines and penalties on Sept. 17, 1783 [Ref: I-454].

ADAMS, Richard. Private, Militia, 26th Battalion, Capt. Robert Sinnett's Company, 1777 [Ref: M-164]. Took the Oath of Allegiance in 1778 [Ref: L-14, which listed the name as "Addams"]. Resident of Port Tobacco West Hundred in 1778 [Ref: Q-I:297]. See "Adam Adams," q.v.

ADAMS, Robert. See "Adam Adams," q.v.

ADAMS, Samuel. Private, 1st Maryland Line, enrolled and passed on July 25, 1776 [Ref: D-32]. Private, Militia, 12th Battalion, Capt. John Thomas' Company, 1777 [Ref: M-161]. Took the Oath of Allegiance in 1778 [Ref:

L-14]. In 1778 one Samuel Adams resided in Durham Lower Hundred and another Samuel Adams resided in Benedict Hundred [Ref: Q-I:297].
ADAMS, Thomas. Took the Oath of Allegiance in 1778 [Ref: L-14]. Aged about 42 (born 1722) as noted in a 1764 deposition [Ref: DD-694].
ADAMS, William. Ensign, 1st Maryland Line, Capt. Thomas Hanson's Company, July 1776 [Ref: D-31]. See "John Baillie," q.v.
ADDERTON, Joseph. Took the Oath of Allegiance in 1778 [Ref: L-14].
ADDISON, John. See "Samuel Hanson," q.v.
ALBRITTAIN, Charles (1753-   ). Private, Militia, 12th Battalion, Capt. John Parnham's Company, 1777 [Ref: M-160, which listed the name as "Allbritan"]. Took the Oath of Allegiance in 1778 [Ref: L-14, which listed the name as "Allbrittan"]. Aged about 26 as noted in a 1779 deposition [Ref: BB-474, DD-694]. Resident of Newport East Hundred in 1778 [Ref: Q-I:297].
ALBRITTAIN, William (1746-   ). Private, Militia, 12th Battalion, Capt. Henry Clarkson's Company, 1777 [Ref: M-159, which listed the name as "Allbritton"]. Rendered patriotic service by providing wheat for the use of the military in September 1782 [Ref: N-556, which listed the name as "Albritton"]. Took the Oath of Allegiance in 1778 [Ref: AA-641, which listed the name as "Albrittain"]. Aged about 33 as noted in a 1779 deposition [Ref: BB-474, DD-694]. Resident of Newport East Hundred in 1778 [Ref: Q-I:297].
ALEXANDER, James. Took the Oath of Allegiance in 1778 [Ref: L-14].
ALEXANDER, Robert. Rendered patriotic service by providing wheat for the use of the military in May 1783 [Ref: N-597].
ALEXANDER, William. Private, Militia, 26th Battalion, Capt. Thomas H. Marshall's Company, 1777 [Ref: M-163].
ALLDER, Bowles. Private, Militia, 26th Battalion, Capt. Hezekiah Garner's Company, 1777 [Ref: M-162, which listed the name as "Boly Allden"]. Took the Oath of Allegiance in 1778 [Ref: AA-641].
ALLEN, George. Private, Militia, 26th Battalion, Capt. Hezekiah Garner's Company, 1777 [Ref: M-162, which listed the name as "Allin"]. Took the Oath of Allegiance in 1778 [Ref: AA-641].
ALLEN, James. Private, Militia, 26th Battalion, Capt. Hezekiah Garner's Company, 1777 [Ref: M-162, which listed the name as "Allin"].
ALLEN, Jesse. Private, Militia, 26th Battalion, Capt. Hezekiah Garner's Company, 1777 [Ref: M-163, which listed the name as "Allin"]. Private (furnished by class for 9 months), 1st Maryland Line, by Sept. 11, 1778 [Ref: D-330, which listed the name as "Allin"].
ALLEN, Joseph. Private, Militia, 12th Battalion, Capt. Henry Clarkson's Company, 1777 [Ref: M-159].

ALLEN, Joseph Davis. Took the Oath of Allegiance in 1778 [Ref: AA-641]. Resident of Newport East Hundred in 1778 [Ref: Q-I:297].

ALLEN, Levi. Gave a deposition in 1781 pertaining to his inability to perform military service due to poor health [Ref: Z-208].

ALLEN, Samuel. Private, Militia, Capt. Francis Mastin's Company, 26th Battalion, March 19, 1776 [Ref: M-158, K-1814, which listed the name as "Allin"]. Private, Militia, 26th Battalion, Capt. Hezekiah Garner's Company, 1777 [Ref: M-163, which listed the name as "Allin"]. Took the Oath of Allegiance in 1778 [Ref: AA-641].

ALLEN, Thomas. Took the Oath of Allegiance in 1778 [Ref: AA-641]. Resident of Durham Lower Hundred in 1778 [Ref: Q-I:297].

ALLEN, William. Private, Militia, Capt. Francis Mastin's Company, 26th Battalion, March 19, 1776 [Ref: M-158, K-1814, which listed the name as "Allin"]. Took the Oath of Allegiance in 1778 [Ref: AA-641]. See "William Allen, of John," q.v.

ALLEN, William Jr. Took the Oath of Allegiance in 1778 [Ref: L-14].

ALLEN, William, of John. Private, Militia, 26th Battalion, Capt. Francis Mastin's Company, 1777 [Ref: M-164, which listed the name as "William Allen Senr(?)" and X-78, which listed the name as "William Allen, of John(?)"].

ALLEN, William, of William. Private, Militia, 26th Battalion, Capt. Hezekiah Garner's Company, 1777 [Ref: M-162].

ALLEN, Zachariah. Corporal, Militia, 26th Battalion, Capt. Robert Sinnett's Company, 1777 [Ref: M-164]. Took the Oath of Allegiance in 1778 [Ref: L-14].

ALVEY, Mary Ann. See "Richard Mudd," q.v.

ALY, James. Took the Oath of Allegiance in 1778 [Ref: AA-641].

AMERY, Eleanor. See "Zephaniah Swann," q.v.

AMERY, John. See "Samuel Amery," q.v.

AMERY, Mary. See "Samuel Amery," q.v.

AMERY, Samuel (1752-   ). Born on Dec. 23, 1752, son of Samuel Amery (died May 13, 1777) and wife Mary (died Aug. 31, 1787), he married Catherine Matthews on Feb. 14, 1773 in Trinity Parish and had these children: William Amery (born Dec. 17, 1773), Mary Amery (born Aug. 27, 1775), John or Samuel John Amery (born June 29, 1777 and died March 24, 1778), Thomas Amery (born March 2, 1780), and Samuel Amery (born May 22, 1782). [Ref: EE-7, EE-20]. Private, Militia, 12th Battalion, Capt. John Parnham's Company, 1777 [Ref: M-161]. Took the Oath of Allegiance in 1778 [Ref: AA-641]. Resident of Newport East Hundred in 1778 [Ref: Q-I:297].

AMERY, Thomas. See "Samuel Amery," q.v.

AMERY, William. See "Samuel Amery," q.v.
AMMONS, Adolphus. See "Clement Edelen," q.v.
ANDERSON, Edward. Private, Militia, 12th Battalion, Capt. Peter Wood's Company, 1777 [Ref: M-161]. Second Lieutenant, 12th Battalion, Capt. William Wilkinson's Company, commissioned May 9, 1778 [Ref: M-48, E-72]. Took the Oath of Allegiance in 1778 [Ref: L-14]. Resident of Benedict Hundred in 1778 [Ref: Q-I:297].
ANDERSON, James. Private, 1st Maryland Line, drafted from the Charles County militia and in service on June 11 or 12, 1781 [Ref: D-376]. Took the Oath of Allegiance in 1778 [Ref: L-14]. Resident of Bryan Town Hundred in 1778 [Ref: Q-I:297].
ANDERSON, John. See "Samuel Hanson," q.v.
ANDERSON, Joseph. Private, Militia, 12th Battalion, Capt. Peter Wood's Company, 1777 [Ref: M-161]. Justice who administered (and took) the Oath of Allegiance in 1778 [Ref: AA-641]. Rendered patriotic service by providing clothing for the use of the military in February 1778 [Ref: Y-II:234]. Appointed a Justice of the Peace on Nov. 21, 1778 [Ref: E-249]. Resident of Benedict Hundred in 1778 [Ref: Q-I:297].
ANDERSON, Joseph Jr. Private, Militia, 12th Battalion, Capt. Peter Wood's Company, 1777 [Ref: M-161]. Took the Oath of Allegiance in 1778 [Ref: L-14]. Resident of Benedict Hundred in 1778 [Ref: Q-I:297].
ANDERSON, Rebecca Dulaney. See "Thomas Hawkins Hanson," q.v.
ANDERSON, William. Private, 1st Maryland Line, enrolled and passed on July 20, 1776 [Ref: D-33]. Private, Militia, 12th Battalion, Capt. John Parnham's Company, 1777 [Ref: M-161]. Resident of Newport East Hundred [Ref: Q-I:297].
ANDERSON, William. Private, Militia, 12th Battalion, Capt. Peter Wood's Company, 1777 [Ref: M-161]. Resident of Benedict Hundred in 1778 [Ref: Q-I:297].
ANDRUS, Elizabeth. See "Charles Rigg," q.v.
ARMS, John. On Aug. 9, 1781, the Council of Maryland reviewed "the petition of Stacy Arms of Charles County Setting forth that she is a widow and has three children, one a son and the other two Daughters, very small, that her son was Draughted on the 27th of July last, that he is the only support of her and her two Daughters [as verified by John Vardin who hired John Arms last year], and that should he be obliged to march she and her two Daughters must be left in great Distress. It is therefore ordered that John Arms, son of the aforesaid Stacy Arms, be discharged from the Service for which he was Draughted." [Ref: G-552, H-389].
ARMS, Stacy. See "John Arms," q.v.

ARMSTRONG, James. Private, 3rd Maryland Line, enrolled by Capt. Joseph Marbury by May 24, 1780 [Ref: D-333, F-181].
ARNETT, Samuel. Took the Oath of Allegiance in 1778 [Ref: L-14].
ARVIN, Thomas. Rendered patriotic service by providing wheat for the use of the military in December 1782 [Ref: N-575]. Resident of Port Tobacco East Hundred in 1778 [Ref: Q-I:297].
ASH, Charles. Private, Militia, 26th Battalion, Capt. William McPherson's Company, 1777 [Ref: M-163]. Took the Oath of Allegiance in 1778 [Ref: AA-641]. Resident of Port Tobacco Upper Hundred in 1778 [Ref: Q-I:297].
ASHFORD, Butler. Private, Militia, 26th Battalion, Capt. William Winter's Company, 1777 [Ref: M-165].
ASHFORD, John. Private, Militia, 26th Battalion, Capt. William Winter's Company, 1777 [Ref: M-165]. Ensign, 26th Battalion, Capt. George Dent's Company, commissioned May 9, 1778 [Ref: M-49, E-72]. Took the Oath of Allegiance in 1778 [Ref: L-14].
ASHFORD, Thomas. Private, 1st Maryland Line, enrolled and passed on July 25, 1776 [Ref: D-32]. Private, Militia, 26th Battalion, Capt. William Winter's Company, 1777 [Ref: M-165].
ASHTON, Grace. See "Philip Thomas Lee," q.v.
ASHTON, Henry Alexander. See "George Dent," q.v.
ATCHISON, James. Private, Militia, 26th Battalion, Capt. William McPherson's Company, 1777 [Ref: M-163]. Took the Oath of Allegiance in 1778 [Ref: L-14, which listed the name as "Atchinson"]. Resident of Port Tobacco Upper Hundred in 1778 [Ref: Q-I:297].
ATCHISON, Jeremiah. Private, 1st Maryland Line, enlisted May 30, 1777 and died Sept. 23, 1778 [Ref: D-78].
ATCHISON, Joseph. Private, Militia, 26th Battalion, Capt. William McPherson's Company, 1777 [Ref: M-163]. Took the Oath of Allegiance in 1778 [Ref: L-14, which listed the name as "Atchinson"]. Resident of Port Tobacco East Hundred in 1778 [Ref: Q-I:297, which listed the name as "Echison"].
ATCHISON, Joshua. Private, Militia, 26th Battalion, Capt. William McPherson's Company, 1777 [Ref: M-163]. Resident of Port Tobacco Upper Hundred in 1778 [Ref: Q-I:297].
ATCHISON, William. Private, Militia, 26th Battalion, Capt. William McPherson's Company, 1777 [Ref: M-163, which listed the name as "Wm. Atchsion (sic)"]. Private, 1st Maryland Line, enlisted May 31, 1779 [Ref: D-78, which listed the name as "Wm. Atchison, say Hutchinson"]. See "William Etchenson," q.v.
ATHEY, Charles. Private, 1st Maryland Line, drafted from the Charles County militia and in service in June 1781 [Ref: D-376, G-569]. On Sept.

27, 1781, he petitioned Governor Lee stating "May it please Your Excellency, I am a draught from this [Charles] County and belong to Capt. John Mitchell's Company of the 4th Maryland Regiment; and on our march from Annapolis to Virginia obtained a furlough from my Captain for two days to see my friends, in Which time I was Seasd *[sic]* With a pain in one of my hipps Which Was so violent as to Render it out of my power to Rejoin the Regiment, the pain is Still so sevear that I am not able to march, and therefore thought it my duty to inform Your Excellency of my Case, making no doubt But you Will Give some orders in the matter, Which I shall most Gladly Comply With to the utmost of my power." [Ref: H-506, H-607].

ATHEY, Ebenezer. "Ebenezar Athy" was a private in the Lower Battalion of Prince George's County in 1776 [Ref: D-35]. "Ebeazar Athey" was a private in the Charles County Militia, 26th Battalion, Capt. William McPherson's Company, in 1777 [Ref: M-163]. "Ebenezer Athey" was a private (furnished by class for 9 months), 1st Maryland Line, on Sept. 11, 1778 [Ref: D-330]. "Ebenezer Athey" was a private in the 1st Maryland Line, enlisted June 4, 1778 and discharged April 5, 1779 [Ref: D-78].

ATHEY, Elijah (1754-1838). Private, 1st Maryland Line. He married Mary Jane Green and died in Ohio in December 1838 [Ref: J-I:89].

ATHEY, Elisha. Private, Militia, 26th Battalion, Capt. William McPherson's Company, 1777 [Ref: M-163, which listed the name as "Eisha (sic) Athey"].

ATHEY, Hezekiah. Private, Militia, 26th Battalion, Capt. William McPherson's Company, 1777 [Ref: M-163]. Took the Oath of Allegiance in 1778 [Ref: AA-641]. Resident of Port Tobacco Upper Hundred in 1778 [Ref: Q-I:297].

ATHEY, John. Took the Oath of Allegiance in 1778 [Ref: L-14].

ATHEY, William. Memorialist and Militiaman, Pomonkey Company, after March 6, 1776 [Ref: M-158, Y-II:26, which sources all listed the name as "William Aytheay(?)"].

AUD, Lucy. See "Clement Edelen," q.v.

AUD, Susannah. See "Raphael Hagan," q.v.

AUSHUR, John. Private, 1st Maryland Line, enrolled and passed on July 8, 1776 [Ref: D-32].

BACK, James. Took the Oath of Allegiance in 1778 [Ref: L-14].

BADEN, John. Private, Militia, 12th Battalion, Capt. John Thomas' Company, 1777 [Ref: M-161, which listed the name as "Beaden"].

BADEN, John Jr. Took the Oath of Allegiance in 1778 [Ref: L-14].

BADEN, William. Private, Militia, 26th Battalion, Capt. Benjamin Cawood's Company, 1777 [Ref: M-162]. Resident of Port Tobacco Upper Hundred in 1778 [Ref: Q-I:297].

BAGGOTT, Francis Green. Private, 1st Maryland Line, Jan. 24, 1776 [Ref: D-6].

BAGGOTT, Ignatius. Private ("draught who had not yet joined the army"), 1st Maryland Line, Sept. 11, 1778 [Ref: D-330]. Took the Oath of Allegiance in 1778 [Ref: AA-641]. Resident of Port Tobacco East Hundred in 1778 [Ref: Q-I:297]. See "Ignatius Biggott," q.v.

BAGGOTT, Samuel (deceased by November 1779). Took the Oath of Allegiance in 1778 [Ref: L-14, which listed the name as "Baggitt"]. Resident of Bryan Town Hundred in 1778 [Ref: Q-I:297].

BAGGOTT, Samuel. Private, Militia, 12th Battalion, Capt. Alexander McPherson's Company, 1777 [Ref: M-160, which listed the name as "Bggett(?)"]. Rendered patriotic service by providing wheat for the use of the military in December 1781 [Ref: N-462, which listed the name as "Baggot"].

BAILEY, James. Private, 3rd Maryland Line, enrolled by Capt. Joseph Marbury by May 24, 1780 [Ref: F-181, which listed the name as "Baley"].

BAILEY, William. Took the Oath of Allegiance in 1778 [Ref: L-14].

BAILLIE, Andrew. Private, Militia, 26th Battalion, Capt. William Winter's Company, 1777 [Ref: M-165]. Took the Oath of Allegiance in 1778 [Ref: L-14]. See "John Robertson," q.v.

BAILLIE, John. He petitioned the Convention of Maryland prior to July 29, 1775, as follows (verbatim): "The humble petition of John Baillie sheweth that he now lyes under the influence and suffers the extremity of a heavy though just sentance of the Committee of Charles County, for having willfully though in some degree ignorantly broke the Association of the Honourable Continental Congress. Your petitioner is truly sencible that the sentance passed by the Committee is founded in justice, but executed with such rigour, it has been with the most extreme and hazardous difficulty he could obtain the necessary food to support a life rendered miserable by his conduct, and the above mentioned sentence. Your petitioner begs leave to inform this respectable Convention that no one views his conduct in a more odious light than himself, and should you be pleased to forgive your Petitioner his past transgressions and place him in his former state, with respect to the People and Laws of this Province, he most solemnly promises to adhere strictly for the future to the Continental Association, and to do every thing in his power which can any way, or in any manner forward the interest of this Country. Your Petitioner therefor most humbly prays that you will take his case into consideration, and that you will be pleased in your goodness to forgive his past crime, which he will endeavour to atone for, as far as he can, by his future conduct, and your Petitioner as is duty bound will ever pray."

[Petition was signed by H. Davis, John S. Chilton, William G. Adams, and Reuben Dye]. It appears from the record that John Baillie and Patrick Graham had secretly landed and sold goods contrary to the resolves. His petition for relief was read twice in August 1775, but was rejected by the Provincial Convention [Ref: A-6, A-14, A-35, A-37, Y-II:3]. See "Patrick Graham," q.v.

BAKER, Shadrick. Private, Militia, 26th Battalion, Capt. Richard Bennett Mitchell's Company, 1777 [Ref: M-164, which listed the first name as "Shadric"].

BAKER, William. Took the Oath of Allegiance in 1778 [Ref: L-14]. See "Samuel Hanson," q.v.

BALL, William. Took the Oath of Allegiance in 1778 [Ref: L-14].

BARKER, John. Private, Militia, 26th Battalion, Capt. Robert Sinnett's Company, 1777 [Ref: M-164]. Took the Oath of Allegiance in 1778 [Ref: L-14, AA-641]. Resident of Port Tobacco West Hundred in 1778 [Ref: Q-I:297]. One John Barker was aged about 61 as noted in a 1771 deposition and aged about 60 as noted in a 1772 deposition [Ref: DD-695].

BARKER, John Jr. Private, Militia, 26th Battalion, Capt. Robert Sinnett's Company, 1777 [Ref: M-164]. Took the Oath of Allegiance in 1778 [Ref: AA-641, which listed the name without the "Jr."]. Resident of Port Tobacco West Hundred in 1778 [Ref: Q-I:297].

BARKER, Joseph (1721-   ). Took the Oath of Allegiance in 1778 [Ref: L-14]. Aged about 58 as noted in a 1779 deposition [Ref: BB-480]. Resident of Bryan Town Hundred in 1778 [Ref: Q-I:297].

BARKER, Joseph Jr. Private, Militia, 12th Battalion, Capt. John Thomas' Company, 1777 [Ref: M-161, which listed the name without the "Jr."]. Took the Oath of Allegiance in 1778 [Ref: L-14].

BARKER, Samuel. Private, Militia, 26th Battalion, Capt. William McPherson's Company, 1777 [Ref: M-163, which listed the name as "Saml. Borker(?)" and X-74, which listed the name as "Barker"].

BARKER, Shadrick. Took the Oath of Allegiance in 1778 [Ref: AA-641]. Resident of Port Tobacco West Hundred in 1778 [Ref: Q-I:297].

BARKER, William. Ensign, 12th Battalion, Capt. William Winter's Company, by March 7, 1776 [Ref: M-50, A-186, A-206, Y-II:23]. One William Barker was appointed Inspector of the Warehouse at Nanjemoy in Charles County by the Maryland Council of Safety on Oct. 11, 1776 [Ref: B-334]. Resident of Bryan Town Hundred in 1778 [Ref: Q-I:297]. See the other "William Barker," q.v. Additional research may be necessary before drawing conclusions.

BARKER, William. Sergeant, Militia, 12th Battalion, Capt. John Thomas' Company, 1777 [Ref: M-161]. Took the Oath of Allegiance in 1778 [Ref:

L-14]. Ensign, 12th Battalion, Capt. John Gardner's Company, commissioned on Jan. 19, 1781 [Ref: M-50, G-280]. Rendered patriotic service by providing wheat for the use of the military in February 1782 [Ref: N-480]. See the other "William Barker," q.v. Additional research may be necessary before drawing conclusions.

BARNES, Catharine. Rendered patriotic service by providing clothing for the use of the military in January 1778 [Ref: Y-II:230]. Rendered patriotic service by providing wheat for the use of the military in January 1782 [Ref: N-469].

BARNES, Henry. Took the Oath of Allegiance in 1778 [Ref: L-14, AA-641]. See "Walter Hanson," q.v.

BARNES, Matthew (1701-   ). Took the Oath of Allegiance in 1778 [Ref: L-14]. Aged about 55 as noted in a 1756 deposition [Ref: DD-696]. Resident of Port Tobacco West Hundred in 1778 [Ref: Q-I:297].

BARNES, Richard (1726-   ). Justice who administered (and took) the Oath of Allegiance in 1778 [Ref: AA-641]. Rendered patriotic service by providing clothing for the use of the military in January 1778 [Ref: Y-II:230]. Took the Oath of Allegiance in 1778 [Ref: L-14]. Appointed a Judge of the Court of Appeals for Charles County on May 20, 1778 [Ref: E-97]. Appointed a Justice of the Peace on Nov. 21, 1778 and Nov. 19, 1779 and Jan. 17, 1782 [Ref: E-249, F-19, I-45]. Appointed a Judge of the Orphans Court on Dec. 29, 1779 and Jan. 17, 1782 [Ref: F-42, I-46]. Aged about 43 as noted in a 1769 deposition [Ref: DD-696].

BARNES, Robert. See "Matthew Kidwell" and "Gerard Fowke," q.v.

BARNES, William. Second Lieutenant, Militia, 26th Battalion, Capt. Richard Bennett Mitchell's Company, July 27, 1776 [Ref: M-50, M-164, B-127]. Took the Oath of Allegiance in 1778 [Ref: L-14, AA-641]. Rendered patriotic service by providing wheat for the use of the military in May 1783 [Ref: N-599]. Resident of Port Tobacco West Hundred in 1778 [Ref: Q-I:297].

BARNES, William. Sergeant, Militia, 26th Battalion, Capt. Robert Sinnett's Company, 1777 [Ref: M-164]. Rendered patriotic service by providing wheat for the use of the military in May 1783 [Ref: N-598].

BARRON, Abraham. Private, Militia, 12th Battalion, Capt. John Parnham's Company, 1777 [Ref: M-161, which listed the name as "Barrow(?)"]. Took the Oath of Allegiance in 1778 [Ref: L-14]. Resident of Newport East Hundred in 1778 [Ref: Q-I:297].

BARRON, Daniel (1755-1810). Private, 1st Maryland Line, enrolled and passed on July 8, 1776 [Ref: D-32]. Private, Militia, 12th Battalion, Capt. Benjamin Lusby Corry's Company, 1777 [Ref: M-160]. Resident of

Newport West Hundred in 1778 [Ref: Q-I:297]. Daniel Barron married Mary Ann Wilson [Ref: J-I:168].

BARRON, Oliver. Private, Militia, 12th Battalion, Capt. Benjamin Lusby Corry's Company, 1777 [Ref: M-160].

BARRON, Samuel Cooksey (1729-   ). Private, Militia, 12th Battalion, Capt. Benjamin Lusby Corry's Company, 1777 [Ref: M-160]. Took the Oath of Allegiance in 1778 [Ref: L-14]. Aged about 47 as noted in a 1776 deposition [Ref: CC-576, DD-696]. Resident of Newport West Hundred in 1778 [Ref: Q-I:297].

BARRON, Thomas. Took the Oath of Allegiance in 1778 [Ref: L-14]. Resident of Newport East Hundred in 1778 [Ref: Q-I:297].

BARRY, Benjamin. Rendered patriotic service by providing wheat for the use of the military in November 1782 [Ref: N-564].

BARRY, John. Petitioned the Council of Maryland in 1783 stating that he had not taken the Oath of Allegiance due to any disaffection with the government, but from a variety of incidents, and was unjustly penalized as a non-juror and fined unfairly; therefore, he asked the Council to consider ordering the County Justices to remit the fines they imposed on him and others who signed the petition. The Council of Maryland, after reviewing his case, indicated they believed the truth of the facts stated in the petition and ordered a remission of the fines and penalties on Sept. 17, 1783 [Ref: I-454].

BARTLETT, James. Private, Militia, 26th Battalion, Capt. Francis Mastin's Company, 1777 [Ref: M-164].

BARTON, Elizabeth. See "Thomas Smoot," q.v.

BATE (BATES), Benjamin. Took the Oath of Allegiance in 1778 [Ref: AA-641, which listed the name as "Bats"].

BATE (BATES), James. Took the Oath of Allegiance in 1778 [Ref: AA-641 which listed the name as "Bate," and L-14 which listed the name as "Bates"]. Resident of Benedict Hundred in 1778 [Ref: Q-I:297].

BATE (BATES), William. Took the Oath of Allegiance in 1778 [Ref: L-14, which listed the name as "Baett"].

BATEMAN, Benjamin. Private, Militia, 12th Battalion, Capt. Jonathan Yates' Company, 1777 [Ref: M-162]. Took the Oath of Allegiance in 1778 [Ref: AA-641, L-14]. Resident of William & Mary Lower Hundred in 1778 [Ref: Q-I:297].

BATEMAN, Benjamin Jr. Took the Oath of Allegiance in 1778 [Ref: AA-641]. Resident of William & Mary Upper Hundred in 1778 [Ref: Q-I:297].

BATEMAN, Benjamin Sr. Took the Oath of Allegiance in 1778 [Ref: AA-641]. Resident of William & Mary Upper Hundred in 1778 [Ref: Q-I:297].

BATEMAN, Charles. Private, Militia, 12th Battalion, Capt. Jonathan Yates' Company, 1777 [Ref: M-162]. Took the Oath of Allegiance in 1778 [Ref: AA-641]. Resident of William & Mary Upper Hundred in 1778 [Ref: Q-I:297].

BATEMAN, George (1755-   ). Private (furnished by class for 9 months), 1st Maryland Line, June 5, 1778; reenlisted April 5, 1779; discharged Jan. 8, 1780 [Ref: D-82, D-330]. Resident of William & Mary Upper Hundred in 1778 [Ref: Q-I:297]. Sergeant, 1st Maryland Line, Capt. William Rieley's Company, by 1782, and discharged Jan. 8, 1782 [Ref: D-433, D-523]. He was placed on the pension rolls in Charles County on Dec. 8, 1818, retroactive to April 4, 1818 [Ref: R-33, which listed the name as "Batterman"]. He applied for a federal pension (S34635) on April 4, 1818, and in 1820 stated he was "aged 65 and upwards" and resided in William and Mary Parish of Charles County. His sister was aged 35 to 40 (no name given) and lived with him [Ref: V-I:183].

BATEMAN, George Jr. Private, Militia, 12th Battalion, Capt. Jonathan Yates' Company, 1777 [Ref: X-70, but was omitted from the list in Reference M-162]. Took the Oath of Allegiance in 1778 [Ref: AA-641].

BATEMAN, George Sr. Took the Oath of Allegiance in 1778 [Ref: AA-641].

BATEMAN, John. Private, Militia, 12th Battalion, Capt. Jonathan Yates' Company, 1777 [Ref: M-162]. Took the Oath of Allegiance in 1778 [Ref: AA-641, L-14]. Resident of William & Mary Lower Hundred in 1778 [Ref: Q-I:297].

BATEMAN, John (1708-   ). Took the Oath of Allegiance in 1778 [Ref: AA-641]. Aged about 47 as noted in a 1755 deposition [Ref: DD-696]. Resident of William & Mary Lower Hundred in 1778 [Ref: Q-I:297].

BATEMAN, Joseph. Took the Oath of Allegiance in 1778 [Ref: AA-641].

BATEMAN, Nathan. Private, 1st Maryland Line, who was reported killed on June 18, 1781 [Ref: D-527].

BATEMAN, Richard. Private, Militia, 12th Battalion, Capt. Jonathan Yates' Company, 1777 [Ref: M-162].

BATEMAN, Thomas. Took the Oath of Allegiance in 1778 [Ref: AA-641]. Resident of William & Mary Lower Hundred in 1778 [Ref: Q-I:297].

BATES, James. See "James Bate," q.v.

BATES, Benjamin. See "Benjamin Bate," q.v.

BATH, William. Private, Militia, 12th Battalion, Capt. Henry Clarkson's Company, 1777 [Ref: M-159]. Took the Oath of Allegiance in 1778 [Ref: L-19, which misspelled the name as "Rath"]. Resident of Bryan Town Hundred in 1778 [Ref: Q-I:297].

BATIE, Elizabeth. See "Thomas Hanson Marshall," q.v.

BAWNEL, Elijah. Rendered patriotic service by providing wheat for the use of the military in December 1782 [Ref: N-575].

BEALE, Eleanor. Rendered patriotic service by providing wheat for the use of the military in December 1781 and April 1783 [Ref: N-463, N-593, which also listed the name as "Elinor Beal"].

BEALE, Thomas. Corporal, Militia, 26th Battalion, Capt. William McPherson's Company, 1777 [Ref: M-163].

BEALE, William. Private, Militia, 26th Battalion, Capt. William McPherson's Company, 1777 [Ref: M-163]. Took the Oath of Allegiance in 1778 [Ref: AA-641, L-14, which latter source misspelled the name as "Beate"].

BEALL, Amelia. See "Rezin Beall," q.v.

BEALL, Barton. Private, Militia, 26th Battalion, Capt. Hezekiah Garner's Company, 1777 [Ref: M-162, which listed the name as "Bartin Bell"]. Private, 1st Maryland Line, drafted from the Charles County militia on July 27, 1781; determined unfit for service and discharged on Oct. 30, 1781 [Ref: D-377, G-569, G-656].

BEALL, Basil. Private, Militia, 26th Battalion, Capt. William McPherson's Company, 1777 [Ref: M-163, which listed the name as "Basil Beall"]. Took the Oath of Allegiance in 1778 [Ref: AA-641, which listed the name as "Basel (B. B.) Beale"]. Rendered patriotic service by providing wheat for the use of the military in December 1782 [Ref: N-577, which listed the name as "Basil Bell"]. There were three men with this name in Maryland: Basil Beall (1725-1818) was a lieutenant, Basil Beall (1754-1824) rendered patriotic service, and Basil Beall (1751-1819) rendered civil service [Ref: J-I:195]. Additional research will be necessary before drawing conclusions. See "Samuel Hanson, Jr.," q.v.

BEALL, Brice. Took the Oath of Allegiance in 1778 [Ref: L-14].

BEALL, Charles. Took the Oath of Allegiance in 1778 [Ref: AA-641, which listed the name as "Charles Bealle"]. Resident of Port Tobacco Upper Hundred in 1778 [Ref: Q-I:297].

BEALL, Elizabeth. See "William Hanson McPherson," q.v.

BEALL, John Fendall. See "Samuel Hanson, Jr.," q.v.

BEALL, Josias (of Prince George's County). Took the Oath of Allegiance in August 1778 in Charles County [Ref: AA-708].

BEALL, Margery. See "William Loveless," q.v.

BEALL, Mary. See "Zephaniah Swann," q.v.

BEALL, Rezin (1723-1809). Captain of an Independent Company in 1776 [Ref: A-311]. He subsequently became a brigadier general, married first to Amelia Beall, second to Valinda Sheppard, and died on Oct. 14, 1809 [Ref: J-I:197]. See "David Jenifer Adams," q.v.

BEALL, Sarah. See "Samuel Hanson, Jr.," q.v.

BEALL, Thomas. Second Lieutenant, 1st Independent Maryland Company, Jan. 2, 1776 [Ref: D-20, which listed the name as "Beale"]. Took the Oath of Allegiance in 1778 [Ref: L-14, AA-641, which latter source listed the name as "Beall"]. See "Thomas Beale," q.v.

BEALS, Joseph Charles. Took the Oath of Allegiance in 1778 [Ref: L-14].

BEAN, Amelia. See "Henry H. Bean," q.v.

BEAN, Frances. See "Leonard Bean," q.v.

BEAN, Henry H. (1753-1840). "Henry H. Bean" applied for a pension (R663) on June 4, 1832, aged 79, stating he had enlisted in Charles County and was referred to as "Henry Bean, Sr." In 1852 a son, William N. Bean, was living in Bryantown, Maryland [Ref: V-I:199]. "Henry Bean" was a sergeant in the militia, 26th Battalion, Capt. Benjamin Cawood's Company, in 1777 [Ref: M-162]. "Henry Beane" (and several others) petitioned the Council of Maryland in 1783 stating that he had not taken the Oath of Allegiance due to any disaffection with the government, but from a variety of incidents, and was unjustly penalized as a non-juror and fined unfairly; therefore, he asked the Council to consider ordering the County Justices to remit the fines they imposed on him and others who signed the petition. The Council of Maryland, after reviewing his case, indicated they believed the truth of the facts stated in the petition and ordered a remission of the fines and penalties on Sept. 17, 1783 [Ref: I-454]. Resident of Port Tobacco East Hundred in 1778 [Ref: Q-I:297]. Henry H. Bean was born on Oct. 24, 1753, married Amelia ----, and died on May 22, 1840 [Ref: J-I:199].

BEAN, John. Took the Oath of Allegiance in 1778 [Ref: L-14]. Private, 1st Maryland Line, Capt. Edward Prall's Company, by 1782, and discharged on Jan. 22, 1782 [Ref: D-432, D-524]. Resident of Port Tobacco East Hundred in 1778 [Ref: Q-I:297].

BEAN, John Albert. See "Leonard Bean," q.v.

BEAN, Leonard (1758-1851). Private, Militia, 26th Battalion, Capt. Benjamin Cawood's Company, 1777 [Ref: M-162]. Private (substitute for 3 years), 1st Maryland Line, by Sept. 11, 1778; discharged on April 12, 1781 [Ref: D-330, D-524]. On Aug. 10, 1781, the Commissary of Stores delivered "to Leonard Bean, late a soldier in the 3rd Regiment, one suit of cloaths." [Ref: G-553]. He applied for a pension (S35189) in Mason County, Kentucky, on May 5, 1818, stating he served in the Maryland Line and was also in the sea service. In 1820 he was aged 62 with a wife aged about 60 (no name given) and these children: John Albert Bean (aged 28), Leonard Harrison Bean (aged 23), Matilda Bean (aged 18),

Frances Bean (aged 16), and William Gallenous Bean (aged 13). Leonard died on May 29, 1851 [Ref: V-I:200].

BEAN, Leonard Harrison. See "Leonard Bean," q.v.

BEAN, Matilda. See "Leonard Bean," q.v.

BEAN, Thomas. Sergeant, Militia, 26th Battalion, Capt. Benjamin Cawood's Company, 1777 [Ref: M-162]. Resident of Port Tobacco East Hundred in 1778 [Ref: Q-I:297]. Thomas Bean and several others petitioned the Council of Maryland in 1783 stating that he had not taken the Oath of Allegiance due to any disaffection with the government, but from a variety of incidents, and was unjustly penalized as a non-juror and fined unfairly; therefore, he asked the Council to consider ordering the County Justices to remit the fines they imposed on him and others who signed the petition. The Council of Maryland, after reviewing his case, indicated they believed the truth of the facts stated in the petition and ordered a remission of the fines and penalties on Sept. 17, 1783 [Ref: I-454].

BEAN, William G. See "Leonard Bean," q.v.

BEAN, William N. See "Henry H. Bean," q.v.

BEANS, William. See "Samuel Hanson," q.v.

BEAVEN (BEVIN), Basil. Took the Oath of Allegiance in 1778 [Ref: L-14, which listed the name as "Basil Beavner"]. Resident of Bryan Town Hundred in 1778 [Ref: Q-I:297, which listed the name as "Bevin"].

BEAVEN (BEVIN), Benjamin (c1750-c1820). First Lieutenant, Militia, 26th Battalion, Capt. Benjamin Cawood's Company, 1777 [Ref: M-52, M-162, J-I:245]. Rendered patriotic service by providing wheat for the use of the military in November and December 1782 [Ref: N-564, N-573, which listed the name as "Beavin" and "Biven"].

BEAVEN (BEVIN), Benjamin. Private, Militia, 12th Battalion, Capt. John Thomas' Company, 1777 [Ref: M-161, which listed the name as "Bivings"]. Resident of Bryan Town Hundred in 1778 [Ref: Q-I:297, which listed the name as "Bevin"].

BEAVEN (BEVIN), Benjamin, of Richard. Took the Oath of Allegiance in 1778 [Ref: L-14].

BEAVEN (BEVIN), Charles. Private, 1st Maryland Line, enrolled and passed on July 18, 1776 [Ref: D-32]. Private, 1st Maryland Line, drafted from the Charles County militia and reported sick in June 1781 [Ref: D-376, which listed the name as "Beavin"]. Resident of Bryan Town Hundred in 1778 [Ref: Q-I:297, which listed the name as "Bevin"].

BEAVEN (BEVIN), Edward. Private, Militia, 12th Battalion, Capt. Alexander McPherson's Company, 1777 [Ref: M-160].

BEAVEN (BEVIN), Henry (1746-   ). Private, Militia, 12th Battalion, Capt. Alexander McPherson's Company, 1777 [Ref: M-160]. Took the Oath of

Allegiance in 1778 [Ref: L-14]. Aged about 33 as noted in a 1779 deposition [Ref: BB-481, DD-696].

BEAVEN (BEVIN), Ignatius. Private, 1st Maryland Line, enrolled and passed on July 18, 1776 [Ref: D-32].

BEAVEN (BEVIN), James. Took the Oath of Allegiance in 1778 [Ref: AA-641].

BEAVEN (BEVIN), John. Private, Militia, 12th Battalion, Capt. Peter Wood's Company, 1777 [Ref: M-161, which listed the name as "Beavin"]. Took the Oath of Allegiance in 1778 [Ref: L-14, which listed the name as "Beaver" and AA-641, which listed the name as "Beavin"]. Resident of Benedict Hundred in 1778 [Ref: Q-I:297, which listed the name as "Bivings"].

BEAVEN (BEVIN), Joseph. Took the Oath of Allegiance in 1778 [Ref: AA-641, L-14, which listed the name as "Bevan"]. Private, 1st Maryland Line, drafted from the Charles County militia and reported sick on July 27, 1781 [Ref: D-377, which listed the name as "Beavin"].

BEAVEN (BEVIN), Paul. Private, Militia, 12th Battalion, Capt. John Thomas' Company, 1777 [Ref: M-161, which listed the name as "Biving"]. Resident of Bryan Town Hundred in 1778 [Ref: Q-I:297, which listed the name as "Bevin"].

BEAVEN (BEVIN), Richard (1729-   ). Took the Oath of Allegiance in 1778 [Ref: L-14, which listed the name as "Beaver" and AA-641, which listed the name as "Beavin"]. Aged about 50 as noted in a 1779 deposition [Ref: BB-480, which listed the name as "Beavan"]. Resident of Bryan Town Hundred in 1778 [Ref: Q-I:297, which listed the name as "Bevin"].

BEAVEN (BEVIN), Richard. Private, 1st Maryland Line, enrolled and passed on July 20, 1776 [Ref: D-32, which listed the name as "Beavan"]. Private, Militia, 12th Battalion, Capt. Alexander McPherson's Company, 1777 [Ref: M-160]. Took the Oath of Allegiance in 1778 [Ref: L-14]. Resident of Port Tobacco East Hundred in 1778 [Ref: Q-I:297, which listed the name as "Bevin"].

BEAVEN (BEVIN), Richard Jr. Private, Militia, 12th Battalion, Capt. John Thomas' Company, 1777 [Ref: M-161, which listed the name as "Bivings"].

BEAVEN (BEVIN), Richard, of Bar. *[sic]*. Private, Militia, 12th Battalion, Capt. John Thomas' Company, 1777 [Ref: M-161, which listed the name as "Richd. Bivings, of Bar."].

BEAVEN (BEVIN), Walter. Took the Oath of Allegiance in 1778 [Ref: AA-641, L-14, which listed the name as "Bevan"]. Resident of Port Tobacco West Hundred in 1778 [Ref: Q-I:297, which listed the name as "Bibbins"].

BEAVEN (BEVIN), Wheeler. Private, Militia, 12th Battalion, Capt. John Thomas' Company, 1777 [Ref: M-161, which listed the name as "Whealer

Biving"]. Took the Oath of Allegiance in 1778 [Ref: L-14, which listed the name as "Mielers? Beaven"]. Resident of Bryan Town Hundred in 1778 [Ref: Q-I:297, which listed the name as "Bevin"].

BECK, ----. See "William Dunnington," q.v.

BELL, Walter (1720/5-   ). Took the Oath of Allegiance in 1778 [Ref: AA-641, L-14, which latter source listed the name as "Belt"]. Aged about 45 as noted in a 1770 deposition and aged about 51 as noted in a 1771 deposition [Ref: DD-696].

BELL, William. See "John J. S. Keech," q.v.

BELT, John S. Although not a native Charles Countian, he was a captain in the 1st Maryland Line by Jan. 1, 1782 and a number of Charles Countians served under his command [Ref: D-435].

BENNETT, John C. Private, Militia, 26th Battalion, Capt. Thomas H. Marshall's Company, 1777 [Ref: M-163]. Resident of Pomonkey Hundred in 1778 [Ref: Q-I:297].

BENSON, Benjamin. Private, Militia, Capt. Francis Mastin's Company, 26th Battalion, March 19, 1776 through at least 1777 [Ref: M-158, M-163, K-1814]. Took the Oath of Allegiance in 1778 [Ref: L-14, AA-641]. Rendered patriotic service by providing wheat for the use of the military in December 1782 [Ref: N-573].

BENTLY, William. Corporal, Militia, 12th Battalion, Capt. Benjamin Lusby Corry's Company, 1777 [Ref: M-160].

BERRY, Benjamin. Sergeant, Militia, 26th Battalion, Capt. Samuel Smallwood's Company, 1777 [Ref: M-165]. Ensign, commissioned May 9, 1778 [Ref: M-53, E-72]. Took the Oath of Allegiance in 1778 [Ref: L-14, AA-641]. Resident of Port Tobacco Upper Hundred in 1778 [Ref: Q-I:297]. Rendered patriotic service by providing wheat for the use of the military in May 1783 [Ref: N-598].

BERRY, Benjamin, of Humphrey. Private, Militia, 26th Battalion, Capt. Samuel Smallwood's Company, 1777 [Ref: M-165].

BERRY, Henry. Took the Oath of Allegiance in 1778 [Ref: L-14].

BERRY, Hezekiah. Sergeant, Militia, 26th Battalion, Capt. Samuel Smallwood's Company, 1777 [Ref: M-165]. Resident of Port Tobacco Upper Hundred in 1778 [Ref: Q-I:297].

BERRY, Humphrey. Took the Oath of Allegiance in 1778 [Ref: L-14, AA-641]. Resident of Port Tobacco Upper Hundred in 1778 [Ref: Q-I:297].

BERRY, Jeremiah. See "Richard Mudd," q.v.

BERRY, John. Private, Militia, 26th Battalion, Capt. Samuel Smallwood's Company, 1777 [Ref: M-159]. Resident of Port Tobacco Upper Hundred in 1778 [Ref: Q-I:297]. Took the Oath of Allegiance in 1778 [Ref: L-14].

BERRY, John. Private, Militia, 12th Battalion, Capt. Henry Clarkson's Company, 1777 [Ref: M-159, M-165].

BERRY, Joseph. Private, Militia, 26th Battalion, Capt. Samuel Smallwood's Company, 1777 [Ref: M-165]. Took the Oath of Allegiance in 1778 [Ref: L-14, AA-641]. Resident of Port Tobacco Upper Hundred in 1778 [Ref: Q-I:297].

BERRY, Mary. See "Richard Mudd," q.v.

BERRY, Prior (Pryor). Sergeant, Militia, 26th Battalion, Capt. Samuel Smallwood's Company, 1777 [Ref: M-165]. Resident of Port Tobacco Upper Hundred in 1778 [Ref: Q-I:297].

BERRY, Samuel. Private, Militia, 26th Battalion, Capt. Benjamin Cawood's Company, 1777 [Ref: M-162].

BERRY, Samuel (1718-   ). Took the Oath of Allegiance in 1778 [Ref: L-14, AA-641]. Aged about 56 as noted in a 1774 deposition [Ref: DD-696]. Resident of Port Tobacco Upper Hundred in 1778 [Ref: Q-I:297].

BERRY, Thomas. Took the Oath of Allegiance in 1778 [Ref: L-14, AA-641]. Resident of Port Tobacco Upper Hundred in 1778 [Ref: Q-I:297].

BERRY, Thomas, of Humphrey. Private, Militia, 26th Battalion, Capt. Samuel Smallwood's Company, 1777 [Ref: M-165].

BERRY, Thomas, of Samuel. Private, Militia, 26th Battalion, Capt. Samuel Smallwood's Company, 1777 [Ref: M-165]. Died testate by October 1778 [Ref: GG-241].

BEVAN, John. Took the Oath of Allegiance in 1778 [Ref: AA-641].

BIDWELL, Thomas. Took the Oath of Allegiance in 1778 [Ref: L-14, AA-641].

BIER, Robert. See "John Lanham," q.v.

BIGGOTT, Ignatius. Corporal, Militia, 26th Battalion, Capt. Benjamin Cawood's Company, 1777 [Ref: M-162]. See "Ignatius Baggott," q.v.

BIGGS, Benjamin John. Private (recruit), 1st Maryland Line, by Sept. 11, 1778 [Ref: D-330, which listed the name as "Benjamin Jon. Biggs"]. Took the Oath of Allegiance in 1778 [Ref: AA-641, L-14, which latter source mistakenly listed the name as "Benjamin Wm. Biggs"]. Resident of William & Mary Lower Hundred in 1778 [Ref: Q-I:297]. One "John Biggs" was a private in the Maryland Line who died on July 1, 1783 [Ref: D-525]. Additional research may be necessary before drawing conclusions.

BILLINGSLEY, Hezekiah. Corporal, Militia, 12th Battalion, Capt. John Thomas' Company, 1777 [Ref: M-161]. Took the Oath of Allegiance in 1778 [Ref: L-14, AA-641]. Resident of Benedict Hundred in 1778 [Ref: Q-I:297].

BILLINGSLEY, James. Private, Militia, 12th Battalion, Capt. John Thomas' Company, 1777 [Ref: M-161].

BILLINGSLEY, James Jr. Took the Oath of Allegiance in 1778 [Ref: L-14].
BILLINGSLEY, John. Took the Oath of Allegiance in 1778 [Ref: AA-641]. Resident of Bryan Town Hundred in 1778 [Ref: Q-I:297].
BILLINGSLEY, John Jr. Private, Militia, 12th Battalion, Capt. John Thomas' Company, 1777 [Ref: M-161, which misspelled the name as "Billigsley"]. Resident of Bryan Town Hundred in 1778 [Ref: Q-I:297]. One John Billingsley, Jr., migrated to North Carolina [Ref: J-I:255].
BLACK, Ignatius. Private, Militia, 12th Battalion, Capt. Benjamin Lusby Corry's Company, 1777 [Ref: M-160].
BLACK, James. Took the Oath of Allegiance in 1778 [Ref: AA-641, L-14, which latter source mistakenly listed the name as "Block"]. Resident of Newport West Hundred in 1778 [Ref: Q-I:297].
BLACKMAN, Mary. See "John Dent, of John," q.v.
BLAIR, Matthew. Private, Militia, 12th Battalion, Capt. Benjamin Lusby Corry's Company, 1777 [Ref: M-160]. Resident of Newport West Hundred in 1778 [Ref: Q-I:297].
BLANCETT, Benedicta. See "William Fairfax," q.v.
BLAND, George Jr. Private, Militia, 26th Battalion, Capt. Thomas H. Marshall's Company, 1777 [Ref: M-163].
BLANFORD, Charles (1703/5-   ). Took the Oath of Allegiance in 1778 [Ref: L-14, AA-641]. Aged about 61 as noted in a 1764 deposition and aged about 67 as noted in a 1772 deposition [Ref: DD-696]. Resident of Port Tobacco East Hundred in 1778 [Ref: Q-I:297].
BLANFORD, Charles, of Thomas. Private, Militia, 26th Battalion, Capt. Benjamin Cawood's Company, 1777 [Ref: M-162]. Resident of Port Tobacco East Hundred in 1778 [Ref: Q-I:297]. "Charles Thomas Blanford" migrated to Kentucky [Ref: J-I:279].
BLANFORD, Ignatius. Private, 1st Maryland Line, enlisted June 21, 1777. Corporal, July 1, 1779. Sergeant, Dec. 12, 1779 [Ref: D-81]. See "Joseph Blanford," q.v.
BLANFORD, James. Private, Militia, 12th Battalion, Capt. Alexander McPherson's Company, 1777 [Ref: M-160]. Took the Oath of Allegiance in 1778 [Ref: L-14]. Resident of Port Tobacco Upper Hundred in 1778 [Ref: Q-I:297].
BLANFORD, Joseph (1751-1836). "Joseph Blanford or Blandford" applied for a pension (R928) for his services in the Revolutionary War and later died on April 28, 1836, aged 85. His only surviving children were a daughter Elizabeth Dyer (wife of Horatio Dyer) and a son Stanislaw Blanford [Ref: V-I:294]. Although his pension was rejected, both Joseph Blanford and Ignatius Blanford had enlisted in Calvert County on Aug. 23, 1776 [Ref: D-33].

BLANFORD (BLANDFORD), Mary. See "Bennett Mudd," q.v.
BLANFORD, Richard (1756-). Private, 1st Maryland Line, enrolled and passed on July 18, 1776 [Ref: D-32]. Private, Militia, 12th Battalion, Capt. Alexander McPherson's Company, 1777 [Ref: M-160]. Took the Oath of Allegiance in 1778 [Ref: L-14]. "Richard Blanford or Blandford" applied for a pension (S10392) in Bullitt County, Kentucky on Oct. 2, 1832, aged 76, stating he had enlisted in Charles County, Maryland in 1776 and his brother Walter Blandford *[sic]* also lived in Bullitt County and was aged 66 in 1832. "Richard Blansford" received bounty land warrant #10945-100-14 in August 1795, for his service as a private in the Maryland Line [Ref: V-I:204, V-I:295].
BLANFORD, Richard, of Charles. Private, Militia, 26th Battalion, Capt. Benjamin Cawood's Company, 1777 [Ref: M-162]. This might be the Richard Blanford who enlisted in the 1st Maryland Line on June 13, 1779 and was missing after the Battle of Camden in South Carolina on Aug. 16, 1780 [Ref: D-84].
BLANFORD, Stanislaw. See "Joseph Blanford," q.v.
BLANFORD, Thomas (1736-). Took the Oath of Allegiance in 1778 [Ref: L-14]. Aged about 46 as noted in a 1772 deposition [Ref: DD-696]. Resident of Port Tobacco East Hundred in 1778 [Ref: Q-I:297].
BLANFORD, Walter. See "Richard Blanford," q.v.
BLANFORD, William. Private, Militia, 26th Battalion, Capt. Benjamin Cawood's Company, 1777 [Ref: M-162]. Took the Oath of Allegiance in 1778 [Ref: AA-641]. Resident of Port Tobacco East Hundred in 1778 [Ref: Q-I:297].
BLOOR, Harry. Took the Oath of Allegiance in 1778 [Ref: L-14].
BLOXHAM, Samuel. Private, Militia, 12th Battalion, Capt. Peter Wood's Company, 1777 [Ref: M-161].
BOARMAN, Anna. See "Richard Queen," q.v.
BOARMAN, Basil (1757-). Private, Flying Camp, Capt. Bowie's Company, enrolled July 14, 1776; native of Charles County, aged 19, height 6' 3" [Ref: D-36, which listed the name as "Basil Bowman (Bazil S. Boarman"].
BOARMAN, Catharine. See "William Thomas, Jr.," q.v.
BOARMAN, Charles (1751-1819). Private, 1st Maryland Line, enrolled and passed on July 8, 1776 [Ref: D-32]. Took the Oath of Allegiance in 1778 [Ref: L-14]. Resident of Newport West Hundred in 1778 [Ref: Q-I:297]. Charles Boarman married Mary Edelen and died in Washington, D.C. on Dec. 5, 1819 [Ref: J-I:309].
BOARMAN, Charles E. See "Charles Smith," q.v.
BOARMAN, Clement. Took the Oath of Allegiance in 1778 [Ref: L-14]. Resident of Newport West Hundred in 1778 [Ref: Q-I:297].

BOARMAN, Daniel. Private, 2nd Maryland Line, 1778-1780 [Ref: D-83].
BOARMAN, Edward Jr. Sergeant, Militia, 12th Battalion, Capt. Alexander McPherson's Company, 1777 [Ref: M-160]. Ensign, July 5, 1777 [Ref: M-54]. Took the Oath of Allegiance in 1778 [Ref: L-14]. Ensign, Militia, Capt. Henry Boarman's Company, commissioned on Jan. 19, 1781 [Ref: G-280, which listed the name without the "Jr."]. Resident of Bryan Town Hundred in 1778 [Ref: Q-I:297].
BOARMAN, Edward Sr. Private, Militia, 12th Battalion, Capt. Alexander McPherson's Company, 1777 [Ref: M-160]. Took the Oath of Allegiance in 1778 [Ref: L-14]. Assisted the Purchaser of Clothing in Charles County in February 1778 [Ref: Y-II:235]. Resident of Bryan Town Hundred in 1778 [Ref: Q-I:297].
BOARMAN, Eleanor. See "Edward Edelen," q.v.
BOARMAN, Elizabeth. See "James Neale," q.v.
BOARMAN, Garrard. Private, Militia, 12th Battalion, Capt. Benjamin Lusby Corry's Company, 1777 [Ref: M-160]. Took the Oath of Allegiance in 1778 [Ref: L-14]. Resident of Newport West Hundred in 1778 [Ref: Q-I:297]. One Gerrard Boarman, also called Ignatius Gerrard Boarman, was aged 45 as noted in depositions taken in 1773 [Ref: DD-696].
BOARMAN, Henry. Son of James Boarman and Mary Pile, he was of age by 1772, married Theresa Edelen and died without progeny in June 1800. He rendered these patriotic services: First Lieutenant, 1st Maryland Line, Capt. Belain Posey's Company, July 16, 1776 [Ref: B-141, D-31, B-141]. First Lieutenant, Militia, 12th Battalion, Capt. Alexander McPherson's Company, 1777 [Ref: M-54, M-160]. Took the Oath of Allegiance in 1778 [Ref: L-14]. Captain, Militia, 12th Battalion, Feb. 9, 1781 [Ref: M-54, G-307]. Served on the Committee of Observation in 1775. Elected to the Lower House of the Maryland Legislature in 1780, but did not attend and subsequently resigned [Ref: P-I:139]. Resident of Bryan Town Hundred in 1778 [Ref: Q-I:297].
BOARMAN, Henry Jr. Private, 1st Maryland Line, enrolled and passed on July 8, 1776 [Ref: D-32]. Private, Militia, 12th Battalion, Capt. Benjamin Lusby Corry's Company, 1777 [Ref: M-160]. Took the Oath of Allegiance in 1778 [Ref: L-14]. Resident of Newport West Hundred in 1778 [Ref: Q-I:297].
BOARMAN, Ignatius. Private, Militia, 12th Battalion, Capt. Jonathan Yates' Company, 1777 [Ref: M-162]. Took the Oath of Allegiance in 1778 [Ref: L-14]. Resident of William & Mary Lower Hundred in 1778 [Ref: Q-I:297]. See "Garrard Boarman," q.v.
BOARMAN, Ignatius W. See "Charles Smith," q.v.

BOARMAN, James. Private, Militia, 12th Battalion, Capt. Alexander McPherson's Company, 1777 [Ref: M-160]. See "Henry Boarman," q.v.

BOARMAN, John. Private, Militia, 26th Battalion, Capt. Benjamin Cawood's Company, 1777 [Ref: M-161]. Resident of Port Tobacco East Hundred in 1778 [Ref: Q-I:297].

BOARMAN, John. Private, Militia, 26th Battalion, Capt. John Parnham's Company, 12th Battalion [Ref: M-162]. Resident of Newport West Hundred in 1778 [Ref: Q-I:297]. Took the Oath of Allegiance in 1778 [Ref: L-14].

BOARMAN, Joseph. Private, 1st Maryland Line, enrolled and passed on July 8, 1776 [Ref: D-32]. Private, Militia, 12th Battalion, Capt. Benjamin Lusby Corry's Company, 1777 [Ref: M-160].

BOARMAN, Joseph. Private, Militia, 12th Battalion, Capt. Alexander McPherson's Company, 1777 [Ref: M-160]. Took the Oath of Allegiance in 1778 [Ref: L-14]. Resident of Bryan Town Hundred in 1778 [Ref: Q-I:297].

BOARMAN, Leonard (c1725-c1794). Took the Oath of Allegiance in 1778 [Ref: L-14]. Leonard Boarman, Sr., married Elizabeth Jenkins [Ref: J-I:309].

BOARMAN, Marcelino. See "Charles Smith," q.v.

BOARMAN, Mary Rose. See "Charles Smith," q.v.

BOARMAN, Raphael (Ralph). Corporal, Militia, 12th Battalion, Capt. Alexander McPherson's Company, 1777 [Ref: M-160]. "Raphael Boarman, Sr." took the Oath of Allegiance in 1778 [Ref: L-14]. "Ralph Boarman" rendered patriotic service by providing wheat for the use of the military in April 1782 [Ref: N-498]. In 1778 one Ralph Boarman was a resident of Pomonkey Hundred and another Ralph Boarman was a resident of Bryan Town Hundred [Ref: Q-I:297].

BOARMAN, Raphael Jr. Ensign, Militia, 12th Battalion, Capt. Jonathan Yates' Company, Feb. 26, 1776 through 1777 [Ref: M-54, M-162, A-186, A-206, Y-II:23, which latter source listed the name without the "Jr."]. Took the Oath of Allegiance in 1778 [Ref: L-14]. Resident of Newport West Hundred in 1778 [Ref: Q-I:297]. Raphael Boarman, Jr., was also listed as a private in the militia, 12th Battalion, Capt. John Parnham's Company, in 1777 [Ref: M-161]. Additional research may be necessary before drawing conclusions.

BOARMAN, Richard. Private, Militia, 12th Battalion, Capt. Jonathan Yates' Company, 1777 [Ref: M-162]. Took the Oath of Allegiance in 1778 [Ref: L-14, AA-641]. Resident of William & Mary Lower Hundred in 1778 [Ref: Q-I:297].

BOARMAN, Richard Bennett. First Lieutenant, Militia, 26th Battalion, Capt. William Winter's Company, Feb. 26, 1776 [Ref: M-54, A-186, A-206, Y-II:23]. Captain, 12th Battalion, commissioned on Feb. 9, 1781 [Ref: M-54, G-307]. Took the Oath of Allegiance in 1778 [Ref: AA-641, L-14, which sources listed the name as "R. Bennett Boarman"].

BOARMAN, Thomas. Private, 1st Maryland Line, enlisted on June 15, 1779 and taken prisoner at the Battle of Camden in South Carolina on Aug. 16, 1780 [Ref: D-82].

BOARMAN, Thomas James Jr. (c1740-c1814). Private, Militia, 12th Battalion, Capt. Alexander McPherson's Company, 1777 [Ref: M-160]. Resident of Bryan Town Hundred in 1778 [Ref: Q-I:297]. Thomas James Boarman, Jr., married Susanna Semmes [Ref: J-I:309].

BOARMAN, Thomas James Sr. Took the Oath of Allegiance in 1778 [Ref: L-14, AA-641]. Resident of Bryan Town Hundred in 1778 [Ref: Q-I:297].

BOARMAN, Walter. Private, Militia, 12th Battalion, Capt. Benjamin Lusby Corry's Company, 1777 [Ref: M-160]. Took the Oath of Allegiance in 1778 [Ref: L-14]. Resident of Newport West Hundred in 1778 [Ref: Q-I:297].

BOARMAN, William. Private, Flying Camp, Capt. Bowie's Company, enrolled July 12, 1776; native of Charles County, aged 16, height 5' 4 1/2" [Ref: D-36, which listed the name as "Wm. Boomar (Boarman)"]. Rendered patriotic service by providing clothing for the use of the military in February 1778 [Ref: Y-II:234]. Resident of Bryan Town Hundred in 1778 [Ref: Q-I:297]. Two men by this name were privates in the militia, 12th Battalion, in 1777: one in Capt. Alexander McPherson's Company, and one in Capt. Jonathan Yates' Company [Ref: M-160, M-162]. One was a private in the Maryland Line, drafted from the Charles County militia and reported sick with smallpox in June 1781 [Ref: D-376]. Some of this information might pertain to "William Boarman, Jr.," q.v.

BOARMAN, William Jr. Took the Oath of Allegiance in 1778 [Ref: L-14, AA-641]. Resident of William & Mary Lower Hundred in 1778 [Ref: Q-I:297]. See "William Boarman," q.v.

BOARMAN, William Sr. (1710-   ). Took the Oath of Allegiance in 1778 [Ref: L-14, AA-641]. Aged about 45 as noted in a 1755 deposition [Ref: DD-697]. Resident of William & Mary Lower Hundred in 1778 [Ref: Q-I:297].

BOGLE, Ann. See "Samuel Barker Davis," q.v.

BOHANNON, John. Private. Militia, 26th Battalion, Capt. Francis Mastin's Company, 1777 [Ref: M-164].

BOLTON, John. Took the Oath of Allegiance in 1778 [Ref: L-14]. Resident of Port Tobacco East Hundred in 1778 [Ref: Q-I:297].

BOND, Francis. Took the Oath of Allegiance in 1778 [Ref: L-14].

BOND, Richard. On July 30, 1782, the Council of Maryland ordered "that the Treasurer pay to Zephaniah Turner for the use of Richard Bond three thousand two hundred pounds of Tobacco due him per Account passed" agreeable to the Act to adjust the debts (specific nature of his service not stated) due from the State [Ref: I-225].

BOND, Samuel. See "Thomas Hanson Marshall," q.v.

BOND, Thomas. Private, Militia, 12th Battalion, Capt. John Parnham's Company, 1777 [Ref: M-160]. Took the Oath of Allegiance in 1778 [Ref: L-14]. Resident of Newport East Hundred in 1778 [Ref: Q-I:297].

BOONE, Foster. Private, 2nd Maryland Line, enlisted May 28, 1778 and discharged March 8, 1779 [Ref: D-83, which listed the name as "Boon"].

BOONE, James. Private, Militia, 12th Battalion, Capt. Alexander McPherson's Company, 1777 [Ref: M-160, which listed the name as "Boon"]. Took the Oath of Allegiance in 1778 [Ref: L-14]. Resident of Bryan Town Hundred in 1778 [Ref: Q-I:297].

BOONE, John (1758/9-1837). Corporal, 1st Maryland Line, May 26, 1777. Sergeant, July 1, 1779. Ensign, 3rd Maryland Line, Jan. 26, 1780. Lieutenant, March 14, 1780. Apparently discharged on March 26, 1780 and back in service by Jan. 1, 1781 [Ref: D-81, D-363]. Took the Oath of Allegiance in 1778 [Ref: L-14]. In November 1811, the Treasurer of Maryland was directed to pay to "John Boone, of Charles County, a lieutenant in the late Revolutionary Army, $125 annually, in quarterly payments." [Ref: Q-II:321]. "John Boone, sergeant, ensign and lieutenant in the Maryland Continental service" was placed on the pension rolls of Charles County on July 16, 1832, retroactive to March 4, 1831 [Ref: R-47]. He also applied for a federal pension (S8076) on Nov. 26, 1828. His daughter, Mary Jane Boone, stated on Nov. 28, 1853 that she was his only surviving child and he (John Boone) was born in 1758 or 1759 and died on Jan. 31, 1837 [Ref: V-I:323].

BOONE, Mary Jane. See "John Boone," q.v.

BOONE, Michael. Took the Oath of Allegiance in 1778 [Ref: L-14].

BOONE, Nicholas. Private, Militia, 26th Battalion, Capt. Samuel Smallwood's Company, 1777 [Ref: M-165]. Resident of Port Tobacco Upper Hundred in 1778 [Ref: Q-I:297].

BOSSEL, John. Rendered patriotic service by providing wheat for the use of the military in November 1782 [Ref: N-564].

BOSTON, John. Took the Oath of Allegiance in 1778 [Ref: L-14].

BOSWELL, Edward. Two men by this name were privates in the militia, 12th Battalion, in 1777: one in Capt. John Hanson's Company, and one in Capt. Alexander McPherson's Company [Ref: M-159, M-160]. One took the Oath of Allegiance in 1778 [Ref: L-14, AA-641]. Resident of Port Tobacco East Hundred in 1778 [Ref: Q-I:297].

BOSWELL, Elijah. Private, Militia, 12th Battalion, Capt. John Hanson's Company, 1777 [Ref: M-158]. Took the Oath of Allegiance in 1778 [Ref: L-14, AA-641]. Resident of Port Tobacco East Hundred in 1778 [Ref: Q-I:297].

BOSWELL, Elizabeth. See "Jesse Boswell" and "Abraham Murphy," q.v.

BOSWELL, George (1726-c1779). Took the Oath of Allegiance in Charles County in 1778 [Ref: L-14, AA-641]. Resident of Port Tobacco East Hundred in 1778 [Ref: Q-I:297]. Aged about 26 as noted in a 1752 deposition which mentioned his brother John Boswell and their father Michael Boswell [Ref: DD-697]. One George Boswell was a private in the Lower Battalion of Prince George's County in 1776 and died before April 13, 1779 [Ref: D-35, J-I:312].

BOSWELL, Gustavus (c1757-c1837). Private, Militia, 12th Battalion, Capt. John Hanson's Company, 1777 [Ref: M-159]. Took the Oath of Allegiance in 1778 [Ref: AA-641]. Resident of Port Tobacco East Hundred in 1778 [Ref: Q-I:297]. Gustavus Brown married Zeruia Ward and migrated to Alabama [Ref: J-I:312].

BOSWELL, Ignatius. Private, Militia, 12th Battalion, Capt. John Hanson's Company, 1777 [Ref: M-159].

BOSWELL, Jesse (1755-1828). Sergeant, Militia, 12th Battalion, Capt. John Hanson's Company, 1777 [Ref: M-158]. Took the Oath of Allegiance in 1778 [Ref: AA-641, which listed the name as "Bosswell"]. Resident of Port Tobacco West Hundred in 1778 [Ref: Q-I:297]. Jesse applied for a pension on Oct. 27, 1818 in York District, South Carolina, stating he had enlisted at Port Tobacco and served in the Maryland Line. In 1821 he was aged 66 with a wife Mary Boswell (aged 42) and three daughters aged 10, 7 and 5 years (no names given). Jesse married Mary Kelough or Keler on Dec. 24, 1809 or 1810 in York District, South Carolina and died on Nov. 23, 1828. His widow received pension W705 and died on Nov. 12, 1863, leaving three daughters. In 1865 their names and ages were given as Nancy Garvin (aged 53), Elizabeth Boswell (aged 52), and Margaret Boswell (aged 49). [Ref: V-I:330]. Jesse Boswell married first to Elizabeth Carrington and second to Mary Kelough [Ref: J-I:312].

BOSWELL, John (1750-1815). Private, 1st Maryland Line, drafted from the Charles County militia to serve from July 27, 1781 to Dec. 10, 1781; discharged on April 6, 1782 [Ref: D-377, G-569, I-123]. John Boswell married Mary Robey [Ref: J-I:312].

BOSWELL, John (1707-   ). Took the Oath of Allegiance in 1778 [Ref: AA-641]. Resident of Port Tobacco East Hundred in 1778 [Ref: Q-I:297]. Aged about 38 as noted in a 1745 deposition [Ref: DD-697, which listed the name as "Sr."]. See "John Bossell" and "George Boswell," q.v.

BOSWELL, Joseph. Private, Militia, 12th Battalion, Capt. John Hanson's Company, 1777 [Ref: M-159]. Took the Oath of Allegiance in 1778 [Ref: L-14, AA-641]. Resident of Port Tobacco East Hundred in 1778 [Ref: Q-I:297].

BOSWELL, Josias (c1760-c1822). Corporal, Militia, 12th Battalion, Capt. John Hanson's Company, 1777 [Ref: M-158]. Took the Oath of Allegiance in 1778 [Ref: L-14, AA-641]. Resident of Port Tobacco East Hundred in 1778 [Ref: Q-I:297]. Josias Boswell married (wife's name not stated) and migrated to Georgia [Ref: J-I:312].

BOSWELL, Margaret. See "Jesse Boswell," q.v.

BOSWELL, Mary. See "Jesse Boswell," q.v.

BOSWELL, Matthew. Took the Oath of Allegiance in 1778 [Ref: L-14, AA-641]. Rendered patriotic service by providing wheat for the use of the military in December 1782 [Ref: N-573]. Resident of Port Tobacco East Hundred in 1778 [Ref: Q-I:297].

BOSWELL, Richard. Private, Militia, 12th Battalion, Capt. John Hanson's Company, 1777 [Ref: M-159]. Took the Oath of Allegiance in 1778 [Ref: L-14, AA-641]. Resident of Port Tobacco East Hundred in 1778 [Ref: Q-I:297].

BOSWELL, Walter. Rendered patriotic service by providing wheat for the use of the military in September and December 1782 [Ref: N-556, N-573]. Resident of Port Tobacco East Hundred in 1778 [Ref: Q-I:297].

BOSWELL, William (1723-   ). Took the Oath of Allegiance in 1778 [Ref: AA-641]. Aged about 55 as noted in a 1778 deposition [Ref: DD-697]. Resident of Port Tobacco West Hundred in 1778 [Ref: Q-I:297].

BOSWELL, Zepheniah. Took the Oath of Allegiance in 1778 [Ref: L-14].

BOWEN, Mary Ann Queen. See "Marsham Queen," q.v.

BOWERS, Jeremiah (1710-   ). Took the Oath of Allegiance in 1778 [Ref: L-14, AA-641]. Aged about 37 as noted in a 1747 deposition [Ref: DD-697]. Resident of Bryan Town Hundred in 1778 [Ref: Q-I:297].

BOWIE, Rhoda. See "Rhody Bowye," q.v.

BOWLING, Francis. Took the Oath of Allegiance in 1778 [Ref: L-14]. Resident of Bryan Town Hundred in 1778 [Ref: Q-I:297].

BOWLING, John. Private, 1st Maryland Line, enrolled and passed on July 18, 1776 [Ref: D-32]. Private, Militia, 12th Battalion, Capt. Alexander McPherson's Company, 1777 [Ref: M-160, which listed the name as "Boling"]. Took the Oath of Allegiance in 1778 [Ref: L-14]. Resident of Bryan Town Hundred in 1778 [Ref: Q-I:297].

BOWLING, Joseph (c1750-c1790). Took the Oath of Allegiance in 1778 [Ref: L-14]. Resident of Bryan Town Hundred in 1778 [Ref: Q-I:297]. Joseph Bowling married Catharine Queen and died before Oct. 10, 1790 [Ref: J-I:298].

BOWLING, Mary. See "Charles Smith," q.v.

BOWLING, Thomas (1704-   ). Took the Oath of Allegiance in 1778 [Ref: L-14]. Aged about 63 as noted in a 1767 deposition [Ref: DD-697]. Resident of Bryan Town Hundred in 1778 [Ref: Q-I:297].

BOWLING, William (1707-   ). Took the Oath of Allegiance in 1778 [Ref: L-15]. Aged about 60 as noted in a 1767 deposition [Ref: DD-697]. Resident of Bryan Town Hundred in 1778 [Ref: Q-I:297, which listed the name as "Bolling"].

BOWYE, Abraham. Private, Militia, 26th Battalion, Capt. Robert Sinnett's Company, 1777 [Ref: M-164, which listed the name as "Boye"].

BOWYE, Issabel. Rendered patriotic service by providing wheat for the use of the military in May 1783 [Ref: N-598].

BOWYE, James Neal. Took the Oath of Allegiance in 1778 [Ref: AA-641].

BOWYE, Oswell (Oswald). Took the Oath of Allegiance in 1780 [Ref: O-105]. Rendered patriotic service by providing wheat for the use of the military in September 1781 [Ref: N-435, which listed the name as "Oswell Bowry"]. Private, Militia, 26th Battalion, Capt. Robert Sinnett's Company, 1777 [Ref: M-164, which listed the name as "Oswald Boye"].

BOWYE, Rhody (1752-1814). Private, Militia, 26th Battalion, Capt. Hezekiah Garner's Company, 1777 [Ref: M-162, which listed the name as "Rhody Bowie"]. Took the Oath of Allegiance in 1778 [Ref: L-14, AA-641, which latter source listed the name as "Rhoda Bowye"]. "Rhoda Bowie (Bowey)" married Ann Price and died on Aug. 8, 1814 [ref: J-I:322].

BOYEL, Josias. Rendered patriotic service by providing wheat for the use of the military in September 1782 [Ref: N-545].

BRADDOCK, Edward. See "James Craik," q.v.

BRADLEY, Charles Sr. Took the Oath of Allegiance in 1778 [Ref: AA-641]. Resident of Newport West Hundred in 1778 [Ref: Q-I:297].

BRADLEY, Charles. Private, Militia, 12th Battalion, Capt. Jonathan Yates' Company, 1777 [Ref: M-162]. Took the Oath of Allegiance in 1778 [Ref: L-15, AA-641]. Resident of William & Mary Lower Hundred in 1778 [Ref: Q-I:297].

BRADLEY, John. Took the Oath of Allegiance in 1778 [Ref: L-15, AA-641]. Resident of William & Mary Lower Hundred in 1778 [Ref: Q-I:297].

BRADLEY, William. Took the Oath of Allegiance in 1778 [Ref: L-15].

BRADSHAW, Joseph. Private (furnished by class for 9 months), 1st Maryland Line, by Sept. 11, 1778 [Ref: D-330]. Took the Oath of

Allegiance in 1778 [Ref: AA-641]. Resident of Durham Lower Hundred in 1778 [Ref: Q-I:297].

BRADSHAW, Uriah. Took the Oath of Allegiance in 1778 [Ref: L-15]. Resident of Durham Lower Hundred in 1778 [Ref: Q-I:297, which listed the name as "Brandshaw"].

BRADY, Gerard. Private, Militia, 12th Battalion, Capt. John Parnham's Company, 1777 [Ref: M-160, which listed the name as "Garrard Braydy"]. Resident of Newport East Hundred in 1778 [Ref: Q-I:297].

BRADY, John. Private, Militia, 12th Battalion, Capt. John Parnham's Company, 1777 [Ref: M-161, which listed the name as "Braydy"]. Resident of Newport East Hundred in 1778 [Ref: Q-I:297].

BRADY, Owen. Private, Militia, 12th Battalion, Capt. John Parnham's Company, 1777 [Ref: M-161, which listed the name as "Braydy"].

BRAMHALL, Ignatius. Private, Militia, 26th Battalion, Capt. Samuel Smallwood's Company, 1777 [Ref: M-165, which listed the name as "Igns. Brimhall"]. Resident of Port Tobacco Upper Hundred in 1778 [Ref: Q-I:297].

BRAMHALL, James. Private, Militia, 12th Battalion, Capt. Peter Wood's Company, 1777 [Ref: M-161]. Took the Oath of Allegiance in 1778 [Ref: AA-641]. Resident of Benedict Hundred in 1778 [Ref: Q-I:297].

BRAMHALL, Jonathan (1745-c1823). Private, Militia, 12th Battalion, Capt. Peter Wood's Company, 1777 [Ref: M-161]. Resident of Benedict Hundred in 1778 [Ref: Q-I:297]. Jonathan Bramhall was born in 1745 in England, married Thompsa ----, served in the Maryland militia, and died before Oct. 24, 1823 in Kentucky [Ref: J-I:345].

BRAMHALL, Philimon (Philip). "Philimon Bramhall" took the Oath of Allegiance in 1778 [Ref: AA-641]. "Philip Bramhall" was a resident of Bryan Town Hundred in 1778 [Ref: Q-I:297].

BRAMHALL, Thompsa. See "Jonathan Bramhall," q.v.

BRAMHALL, William. Two men by this name were privates in the militia, 12th Battalion, Capt. Peter Wood's Company, 1777 [Ref: M-161]. "Will Bramhall" took the Oath of Allegiance in 1778 [Ref: AA-641]. Resident of Benedict Hundred in 1778 [Ref: Q-I:297].

BRANDT, ----. See "Jacob Latimer," q.v.

BRANDT, Charles. Private, Militia, 12th Battalion, Capt. Jonathan Yates' Company, 1777 [Ref: X-70, but was omitted from the list in Reference M-162]. Took the Oath of Allegiance in 1778 [Ref: L-15, AA-641]. Rendered patriotic service by providing clothing for the use of the military in January and February 1778 [Ref: Y-II:230, Y-II:234]. Resident of William & Mary Lower Hundred in 1778 [Ref: Q-I:297].

BRANDT, Mary. See "William Barton Smoot, of Charles" and "John Nathan Smoot" and "Hendley Smoot," q.v.

BRANDT, Randolph. Private, Militia, 12th Battalion, Capt. Jonathan Yates' Company, 1777 [Ref: M-162]. Took the Oath of Allegiance in 1778 [Ref: L-15, AA-641]. Rendered patriotic service by providing clothing for the use of the military in February 1778 [Ref: Y-II:234]. Resident of William & Mary Lower Hundred in 1778 [Ref: Q-I:297].

BRANDT, Richard. Took the Oath of Allegiance in 1778 [Ref: L-15]. Resident of Pomonkey Hundred in 1778 [Ref: Q-I:297].

BRANNER, Mary Ann. See "Thomas Semmes," q.v.

BRANSON, Leonard. Took the Oath of Allegiance in 1778 [Ref: L-15]. Resident of Benedict Hundred in 1778 [Ref: Q-I:297].

BRAULT, Dorothy Murray. See "Thomas Hussey Luckett," q.v.

BRAWNER, Barton. Private, Militia, 26th Battalion, Capt. Hezekiah Garner's Company, 1777 [Ref: M-163]. Took the Oath of Allegiance in 1780 [Ref: O-106].

BRAWNER, Basil. Took the Oath of Allegiance in 1778 [Ref: AA-641, which listed the name as "Bazel Brawner" and L-16, which misspelled the name as "Drawner"]. Rendered patriotic service by providing wheat for the use of the military in December 1781 and December 1782 [Ref: N-464, N-576, which sources listed the name as both "Brawner" and "Browner"]. Resident of Pomonkey Hundred in 1778 [Ref: Q-I:297].

BRAWNER, Benjamin. Private, Militia, 26th Battalion, Capt. Richard Bennett Mitchell's Company, 1777; listed as an invalid (disabled) soldier [Ref: M-164].

BRAWNER, Benjamin (c1730-   ). Took the Oath of Allegiance in 1780 [Ref: O-106]. Rendered patriotic service by providing wheat for the use of the military in June 1782 and May 1783 [Ref: N-525, N-598]. Aged about 46 or 48 as noted in two depositions taken in 1777 [Ref: CC-581, DD-697]. Resident of Port Tobacco West Hundred in 1778 [Ref: Q-I:297].

BRAWNER, Bennett. Private, Militia, Capt. Francis Mastin's Company, 26th Battalion, from March 19, 1776 through 1777 [Ref: M-158, K-1814]. He was deceased by January 1779 (date of final account). [Ref: GG-269].

BRAWNER, Betsy. See "John Maddox," q.v.

BRAWNER, Edward. Private, Militia, 26th Battalion, Capt. Richard Bennett Mitchell's Company, 1777 [Ref: M-164].

BRAWNER, Esther. See "Henry Brawner," q.v.

BRAWNER, Henry (c1750-c1822). Sergeant, Militia, 26th Battalion, Capt. Richard Bennett Mitchell's Company, 1777 [Ref: M-164]. Took the Oath of Allegiance in 1778 [Ref: AA-641]. Resident of Port Tobacco West Hundred in 1778 [Ref: Q-I:297]. "Henry Brawner, Sr." was born circa

1755, married second to Esther ---- (first wife's name not known), and died before Jan. 12, 1822 [Ref: J-I:350]. Another Henry Brawner died in 1779 [Ref: GG-267].

BRAWNER, Isaac. See "John Maddox," q.v.

BRAWNER, John. Private, Militia, Capt. Francis Mastin's Company, 26th Battalion, March 19, 1776 [Ref: M-158, K-1814]. Private, 1st Maryland Line, enrolled and passed on July 27, 1776 [Ref: D-31].

BRAWNER, John (1722-   ). Took the Oath of Allegiance in 1778 [Ref: AA-641]. Aged about 54 or 55 as noted in two depositions taken in 1777 and aged about 56 as noted in a 1778 deposition [Ref: CC-581, DD-698]. Resident of Port Tobacco West Hundred in 1778 [Ref: Q-I:297].

BRAWNER, Nancy. See "John Maddox," q.v.

BRAWNER, Richard (1736-1783). He married Elizabeth Elder, rendered patriotic service, and died in March 1783 [Ref: J-I:350].

BRAWNER, William. Private, Militia, 26th Battalion, Capt. Hezekiah Garner's Company, 1777 [Ref: M-163]. Rendered patriotic service by providing wheat for the use of the military in February 1782 and May 1783 [Ref: N-481, N-599, which listed the name as "Browner" and "Brawner"]. Took the Oath of Allegiance in 1778 [Ref: AA-641]. Resident of Port Tobacco West Hundred in 1778 [Ref: Q-I:297].

BRAWNER, William (1719-   ). Took the Oath of Allegiance in 1778 [Ref: AA-641]. Aged about 50 as noted in a 1769 deposition [Ref: DD-698]. Resident of Durham Lower Hundred in 1778 [Ref: Q-I:297].

BRENT, Baptist Jr. Sergeant, Militia, 12th Battalion, Capt. John Parnham's Company, 1777 [Ref: M-160, which listed the name as "Babt. Brent Junr.," and X-63, which listed the name as "Robt. Brent, Jr." However, there was already a "Robt. Brent, Jr." who was a private in this same company at the same time].

BRENT, Catherine. See "George Digges," q.v.

BRENT, Eleanor. See "Clement Hill, Jr.," q.v.

BRENT, John. Fifer, 1st Maryland Line, 1780, and died on May 14, 1781 [Ref: D-524].

BRENT, Mary. See "Robert Brent, Sr.," q.v.

BRENT, Richard. Private, Militia, 26th Battalion, Capt. Thomas H. Marshall's Company, 1777 [Ref: M-163].

BRENT, Robert Jr. Private, Militia, 12th Battalion, Capt. John Parnham's Company, 1777 [Ref: M-160]. Took the Oath of Allegiance in 1778 [Ref: L-15]. Resident of Newport East Hundred in 1778 [Ref: Q-I:297]. See "Baptist Brent, Jr.," q.v.

BRENT, Robert Sr. (1734-   ). Born on May 6, 1734, son of Robert and Mary Brent [Ref: EE-1]. Took the Oath of Allegiance in 1778 [Ref: L-15].

Rendered patriotic service by providing wheat for the use of the military in January 1782 and May 1782 [Ref: N-472, N-516, which listed the name without the "Sr."]. Resident of Newport East Hundred in 1778 [Ref: Q-I:297].

BRISCOE, Edward. See "William Mackall Wilkinson," q.v.

BRISCOE, Eleanor Wilson. See "Hendley Smoot," q.v.

BRISCOE, Elizabeth. See "John Compton," q.v.

BRISCOE, James. Took the Oath of Allegiance in 1778 [Ref: L-15]. Rendered patriotic service by providing wheat for the use of the military in October 1782 and May 1783 [Ref: N-563, N-597]. Resident of Pomonkey Hundred in 1778 [Ref: Q-I:297].

BRISCOE, John. Sergeant, Militia, 26th Battalion, Capt. Robert Sinnett's Company, 1777 [Ref: M-164]. Took the Oath of Allegiance in 1778 [Ref: L-15, AA-641]. See "Philip Briscoe" and "Ralph Briscoe," q.v.

BRISCOE, Margaret. See "John Compton," q.v.

BRISCOE, Mary. See "John Nathan Smoot," q.v.

BRISCOE, Mary Hanson. See "Michael Jenifer Stone," q.v.

BRISCOE, Philip (1719-   ). Took the Oath of Allegiance in 1778 [Ref: L-15]. Aged about 36 as noted in a 1755 deposition which mentioned his father John Briscoe, deceased [Ref: DD-698]. Resident of Newport West Hundred in 1778 [Ref: Q-I:297]. Philip Briscoe married Chloe Hanson and died after 1778 [Ref: J-I:369].

BRISCOE, Philip (c1758-c1832). Private (furnished by class for 9 months), 1st Maryland Line, enlisted June 3, 1778, and discharged April 5, 1779 [Ref: D-82, D-330]. Philip Briscoe married Elizabeth Mason and died after 1832 [Ref: J-I:369].

BRISCOE, Ralph (1747-1831). Son of John Briscoe and Anne Wood, he was born in Charles County on Nov. 24, 1747, served as a first lieutenant in Frederick County during the Revolutionary War, and died in Kentucky in 1831 [Ref: EE-7]. For additional information see Henry C. Peden, Jr.'s *Revolutionary Patriots of Frederick County, Maryland, 1775-1783* (p. 49), and Henry C. Peden, Jr.'s *Marylanders to Kentucky, 1775-1825* (p. 18).

BRISCOE, Samuel. Took the Oath of Allegiance in 1778 [Ref: L-15]. Rendered patriotic service by providing wheat for the use of the military in September 1782 [Ref: N-550]. Resident of Newport East Hundred in 1778 [Ref: Q-I:297].

BROADY, Elizabeth. See "John Farrand, of John," q.v.

BROOKE, Baker (1724-   ). Rendered patriotic service by providing clothing for the use of the military in February 1778 [Ref: Y-II:234]. Took the Oath of Allegiance in 1778 [Ref: L-15]. Rendered patriotic service by providing wheat for the use of the military in May and December 1782

[Ref: N-507, N-576, which also listed the name as "Brook"]. Aged about 45 as noted in a 1769 deposition [Ref: DD-698]. Resident of Port Tobacco East Hundred in 1778 [Ref: Q-I:297].

BROOKE, John (1709-   ). Took the Oath of Allegiance in 1778 [Ref: AA-641]. Aged about 36 as noted in a 1745 deposition [Ref: DD-698]. Resident of Newport West Hundred in 1778 [Ref: Q-I:297].

BROOKE, Matthew. Private, 1st Maryland Line, drafted from the Charles County militia on July 27, 1781 [Ref: D-377]. Deemed unfit for the service he was discharged on Nov. 24, 1781 [Ref: I-2, which listed the name as "Brookes"].

BROOKE, Oswell. Private, Militia, 26th Battalion, Capt. Richard Bennett Mitchell's Company, 1777 [Ref: M-165].

BROOKE, Raphael. Took the Oath of Allegiance in 1778 [Ref: L-15].

BROOKE, Walter. Took the Oath of Allegiance in 1778 [Ref: L-15, AA-641]. Resident of Port Tobacco East Hundred in 1778 [Ref: Q-I:297].

BROOKE, William. Took the Oath of Allegiance in 1778 [Ref: L-15, AA-641]. Resident of Port Tobacco East Hundred in 1778 [Ref: Q-I:297].

BROOKS, John (1709-   ). Took the Oath of Allegiance in 1778 [Ref: L-15, AA-641]. Aged about 53 as noted in a 1762 deposition [Ref: DD-698]. Resident of Port Tobacco East Hundred in 1778 [Ref: Q-I:297].

BROOKS, Thomas. Took the Oath of Allegiance in 1778 [Ref: L-15].

BROOKS, Walter. Fifer, Militia, 12th Battalion, Capt. John Hanson's Company, 1777 [Ref: M-158].

BROOKS, William. Private, Militia, 12th Battalion, Capt. John Hanson's Company, 1777 [Ref: M-159].

BROWDER, Sarah R. See "John Compton," q.v.

BROWN, Ann. See "Samuel Hanson" and "Bennett Mudd," q.v.

BROWN, Gerrard. See "Henry Woodward," q.v.

BROWN, Gustavus Richard (1747-1804). Received his medical degree from the University of Edinburgh in 1768 and came to America and practiced medicine in Charles County. Served on the Committee of Correspondence in 1774 and was a County Court Justice in 1776 and 1777. Served at the Constitution Ratification Convention in 1787 and was instrumental in founding the Medical and Chirurgical Faculty of Maryland in 1799. He was also called to the beside of George Washington during his last illness in 1799 [Ref: P-II:787]. Took the Oath of Allegiance in 1778 [Ref: L-15, AA-641]. Resident of Port Tobacco West Hundred in 1778 [Ref: Q-I:297]. Gustavus Richard Brown was born on Oct. 10, 1747, married Margaret Graham, and died on Sept. 30, 1804 [Ref: J-I:391]. He was the brother of Margaret Brown who married Thomas Stone. See "John Robertson" and "Thomas Pickerel" and "William Thompson" and "Thomas Stone," q.v.

BROWN, John. Private, Militia, 12th Battalion, Capt. Walter Hanson's Company, 1777 [Ref: M-159]. Resident of Port Tobacco East Hundred in 1778 [Ref: Q-I:297].

BROWN, Margaret. See "Gustavus Richard Brown" and "Thomas Stone," q.v.

BROWN, Richard. Private, 1st Maryland Line, drafted from the Charles County militia and reported sick or not in service on July 27, 1781 [Ref: D-377]. Resident of Port Tobacco East Hundred in 1778 [Ref: Q-I:297].

BROWN, Tabitha. See "John Lanham," q.v.

BROWN, William. See "John Lanham," q.v.

BROWN, William, of John. Private, Militia, 26th Battalion, Capt. Richard Bennett Mitchell's Company, 1777 [Ref: M-164].

BRUCE, James. Took the Oath of Allegiance in 1778 [Ref: AA-641]. In 1778 one James Bruce was a resident of William & Mary Upper Hundred and another James Bruce was a resident of Port Tobacco Upper Hundred [Ref: Q-I:297].

BRUCE, John. Took the Oath of Allegiance in 1778 [Ref: AA-641]. Rendered patriotic service by providing wheat for the use of the military in May 1783 [Ref: N-599]. Resident of William & Mary Upper Hundred in 1778 [Ref: Q-I:297].

BRUCE, Robert (c1750-1819). In December 1816, the Treasurer of Maryland was directed to pay to "Robert Bruce, an old revolutionary soldier, during his life, quarterly, the half pay of a private, as a further recompense for his meritorious services during the war." In December 1817, the Treasurer of Maryland was directed to pay to "Robert Bruce, of Charles County, quarterly, a sum of money equal to half pay of a trooper, instead of half pay of a common soldier in the line, as was allowed him by the last legislature, and the Treasurer to pay him, or order, a sum of money equal to half pay of a trooper for fifteen months." He was placed on the pension rolls of Charles County as of April 24, 1818 (S34666), retroactive to April 4, 1818, and he died on Aug. 21, 1819 [Ref: Q-II:323, R-33, V-I:439].

BRUCE, Townley. Took the Oath of Allegiance in 1778 [Ref: L-15].

BRUCE, Walter. Took the Oath of Allegiance in 1778 [Ref: AA-641]. Resident of William & Mary Upper Hundred in 1778 [Ref: Q-I:297].

BRUCE, William (1753-1825). Lieutenant, 1st Maryland Line, Dec. 10, 1776; appointed Adjutant, July 6, 1778; promoted to Captain, 1st Maryland Line, Aug. 1, 1779; 5th Maryland Line, Jan. 1, 1781 [Ref: D-80, D-364]. "William Bruce, May 1, 1815, of Charles County, Md., late a Capt. in 1st Md. Cont. Troops, certifies to the service with him by Mark McPherson." [Ref: U-19:4 (1931), p. 110]. He was placed on the pension rolls of Charles County as of April 6, 1818 (S34668), retroactive to March 30, 1818, but was dropped under the Act of May 1, 1820 (reason not stated). He had also received bounty land warrant #233-300-21 in September 1789 [Ref: R-33, V-I:439]. The obituary of Col. William Bruce appeared in the *Maryland Gazette* on Nov. 10, 1825, stating, in part, that he "died 26th ultimate, at his residence in Charles County, in his 73rd year, another soldier of the Revolution gone!" [Ref: FF-22].

BRYAN, Ann. See "George Walker" and "Cornelius Bryan," q.v.

BRYAN, Basil. Took the Oath of Allegiance in 1778 [Ref: L-15, AA-641]. In 1778 one Basil Bryan was a resident of Benedict Hundred and another Basil Bryan was a resident of Bryan Town Hundred [Ref: Q-I:297].

BRYAN, Charles (1752-1838). Private, 2nd Maryland Line, 1778-1780 [Ref: D-83]. He was born on March 17, 1752, married Catharine Stone, and died on May 15, 1838 in Pennsylvania [Ref: J-I:409].

BRYAN, Cornelius (1760-1830). Born in Charles County, Maryland, son od William and Mary Ann Bryan, he married second to Sarah Danford (first wife unknown) and his children were James Bryan, Ann Bryan, Thomas Bryan, Peter Bryan, and Cornelius Bryan, Jr. A resident of Bryan Town Hundred in 1778, he subsequently moved to Jefferson County, Virginia and served in the militia from May 31, 1781 to June 22, 1781 under Capt. Aquilla Whitaker. In 1795 he settled in Noble County, Ohio, where he was a farmer, millwright, justice of the peace, and postmaster [Ref: Q-I:297, HH-1997, citing research by Dave Rummelhart of Ottumwa, Iowa in 1993]. See "William Bryan," q.v.

BRYAN, Elizabeth. See "William Dement," q.v.

BRYAN, Ignatius. Took the Oath of Allegiance in 1778 [Ref: AA-641]. Resident of Bryan Town Hundred in 1778 [Ref: Q-I:297].

BRYAN, James (1712-   ). Took the Oath of Allegiance in 1778 [Ref: L-15]. Resident of Bryan Town Hundred in 1778 [Ref: Q-I:297]. Aged about 62 as noted in a 1774 deposition that was recorded into the county court minutes in 1779 and which also mentioned his father John Bryan [Ref: BB-485, DD-698].

BRYAN, James. Private, 1st Maryland Line, 1780, who was killed on Sept. 15, 1781 [Ref: D-526]. See "William Bryan," q.v.

BRYAN, John. Private, Militia, Capt. Francis Mastin's Company, 26th Battalion, March 19, 1776 [Ref: M-158, K-1814]. Resident of Bryan Town Hundred in 1778 [Ref: Q-I:297]. See "James Bryan," q.v.

BRYAN, Josias. See "William Bryan," q.v.

BRYAN, Mary. See "William Bryan" and "Cornelius Bryan," q.v.

BRYAN, Peter. See "Cornelius Bryan," q.v.

BRYAN, Rebecca. See "William Bryan," q.v.

BRYAN, Thomas. See "Cornelius Bryan," q.v.
BRYAN, William (1728-1795). Took the Oath of Allegiance in 1778 [Ref: L-15]. Born in Berks or Fayette County, Pennsylvania in 1728, he married Mary Ann ---- by 1749 and their children were William Bryan, James Bryan, Cornelius Bryan, Josias Bryan, and Rebecca Bryan. A resident of Durham Lower Hundred in Charles County, Maryland in 1778, he subsequently moved to Monroe (now Noble) County, Ohio where he died in Beaver Township in 1795 [Ref: Q-I:297, HH-1997, citing research by Dave Rummelhart of Ottumwa, Ohio in 1993].
BRYAN, William (1749-   ). Born on June 10, 1749, son of William and Mary Bryan [Ref: EE-2]. Private, 5th Maryland Line, 1779-1780 [Ref: D-186].
BUCHANAN, George. Private, Militia, 26th Battalion, Capt. Francis Mastin's Company, 1777 [Ref: M-164, which listed the name as "Geo. Buchananan (sic)"]. One George Buchanan, possibly the father of George Buchanan the soldier, was aged about 60 as noted in a 1770 deposition and aged about 66 as noted in a 1778 deposition [Ref: DD-698].
BUCHANAN, John (c1760-1785). Drummer and private, 1st Maryland Line, Col. John H. Stone's Regiment, Capt. Samuel McPherson's Company, by Jan. 1, 1782. Wounded on the knee some time in 1782 in North Carolina. Pensioned in Charles County, Maryland beginning Nov. 15, 1783. Died some time in 1785 and his pension ceased on May 15, 1785 [Ref: D-629, which listed the name as "Buckannan" and D-444, which listed the name as "Buckhannan"].
BUCHANAN, William. Private, Militia, 26th Battalion, Capt. Francis Mastin's Company, 1777 [Ref: M-164, which listed the name as "Wm. Buchannon"].
BUCKNER, Elizabeth. See "William Fairfax," q.v.
BULLMAN, Thomas (1742-   ). Private, Militia, 26th Battalion, Capt. Hezekiah Garner's Company, 1777 [Ref: M-163]. Took the Oath of Allegiance in 1778 [Ref: AA-641]. Aged about 24 as noted in a 1766 deposition [Ref: DD-698, which listed the name as "Bulman"].
BURCH, Anne. See "John Burch," q.v.
BURCH, Benjamin (1753-1830). Sergeant (recommended for ensign) in the militia, 12th Battalion, on July 5, 1777 [Ref: M-58]. Took the Oath of Allegiance in 1778 [Ref: AA-641, L-15, which latter source mistakenly listed the name as "Berry Burch"]. Resident of Newport East Hundred in 1778 [Ref: Q-I:297]. Benjamin Burch married first to Mary Matthews on Dec. 9, 1773 in Trinity Parish, second to Mary Townsend, third to Chloe Wedding, and died on Dec. 17, 1830 in Kentucky [Ref: EE-15, J-I:430].
BURCH, Catherine. See "Jonathan Thomas," q.v.

BURCH, Edward. Corporal, Militia, 12th Battalion, Capt. Peter Wood's Company, 1777 [Ref: M-161]. Took the Oath of Allegiance in 1778 [Ref: L-15]. Resident of Benedict Hundred in 1778 [Ref: Q-I:297]. See "Jesse Burch," q.v.

BURCH, Elizabeth. See "John Burch," q.v.

BURCH, Fanney P. See "John Burch," q.v.

BURCH, Francis (1760-). Private, 1st Maryland Line, from March 29, 1777 until discharged on March 29, 1780 [Ref: D-82]. He applied for a pension (S39260) in Campbell County, Virginia on June 22, 1818, aged 58, stating he had enlisted in Charles County, Maryland and served in the Maryland Line [Ref: V-I:464].

BURCH, Gustavus. Private, 1st Maryland Line, enrolled and passed on July 8, 1776 [Ref: D-32].

BURCH, Jesse. Private, Militia, 12th Battalion, Capt. Peter Wood's Company, 1777 [Ref: M-161]. Resident of Bryan Town Hundred in 1778 [Ref: Q-I:297].

BURCH, Jesse (1728-). Took the Oath of Allegiance in 1778 [Ref: L-15]. Aged about 43 as noted in a 1771 deposition which mentioned his father Edward Burch [Ref: DD-698]. Resident of Bryan Town Hundred in 1778 [Ref: Q-I:297].

BURCH, John (1759-1834). Private, Militia, 26th Battalion, Capt. Samuel Smallwood's Company, 1777 [Ref: M-165]. Took the Oath of Allegiance in 1778 [Ref: L-15]. Resident of Port Tobacco Upper Hundred in 1778 [Ref: Q-I:297]. He applied for a pension on Dec. 17, 1832 in Barren County, Kentucky, stating he was born on Jan. 18, 1759 in Prince William County, Virginia and moved with his father (not named) when quite young to Charles County, Maryland. There he served in the war and afterwards moved back to Virginia, where he lived in Fauquier and Amherst Counties for 33 years before moving to Barren County, Kentucky. He died on March 1, 1834 and his widow Elizabeth Burch applied for a pension (W5238) on Nov. 13, 1850, aged 71. They were married in 1796 in Loudoun County, Virginia and had the following children: Robert B. Burch (born July 11, 1797); Margaret F. Burch (born June 21, 1799); Landon I. Burch (born Aug. 9, 1801); Anne Burch (born Sept. 20, 1803); Fanney P. Burch (born Dec. 19, 1806); William D. Burch (born Dec. 9, 1809); and, John Burch (born Feb. 12, 1816). [Ref: V-I:465].

BURCH, Jonathan. Private, Militia, 12th Battalion, Capt. Henry Clarkson's Company, 1777 [Ref: M-159]. Ensign, Militia, Capt. Thomas A. Dyson's Company, commissioned on Jan. 19, 1781 [Ref: M-58, G-280].

BURCH, Joseph. Private, 2nd Maryland Line, enlisted Feb. 28, 1778; promoted to corporal and demoted to private several times; still in service in November 1780 as a private [Ref: D-83].
BURCH, Justinian (1714-   ). Took the Oath of Allegiance in 1778 [Ref: L-15, AA-641]. Aged about 53 as noted in a 1767 deposition [Ref: DD-699].
BURCH, Justinian (c1742-c1806). He married Behethland Dade, rendered patriotic service, and died before June 6, 1806 [Ref: J-I:430].
BURCH, Justinian Thomas. Private, Militia, 12th Battalion, Capt. John Parnham's Company, 1777 [Ref: M-161, which listed the name as "Jestinian Thos. Benet(?)," and X-64, which listed the name as "Justinian Thos. Burch"]. Resident of Newport East Hundred in 1778 [Ref: Q-I:297].
BURCH, Landon I. See "John Burch," q.v.
BURCH, Leonard. Corporal, Militia, 26th Battalion, Capt. Samuel Smallwood's Company, 1777 [Ref: M-165].
BURCH, Margaret F. See "John Burch," q.v.
BURCH, Martha. See "Hezekiah Dent," q.v.
BURCH, Oliver (1713-   ). Took the Oath of Allegiance in 1778 [Ref: L-15]. Aged about 62 as noted in a 1775 deposition [Ref: DD-699]. Resident of Bryan Town Hundred in 1778 [Ref: Q-I:297].
BURCH, Rebeccah. Rendered patriotic service by providing wheat for the use of the military in September 1782 [Ref: N-556].
BURCH, Richard. Private, Militia, 12th Battalion, Capt. Benjamin Lusby Corry's Company, 1777 [Ref: M-160]. "Richard Burch, a draft from Charles County, discharged unfit for service" on June 24, 1778 [Ref: E-148]. Rendered patriotic service by providing wheat for the use of the military in September 1782 [Ref: N-556]. Took the Oath of Allegiance in 1778 [Ref: AA-641]. Resident of Bryan Town Hundred in 1778 [Ref: Q-I:297].
BURCH, Robert B. See "John Burch," q.v.
BURCH, Susan. See "Thomas Latimer," q.v.
BURCH, Susannah. See "Notley Maddox," q.v.
BURCH, Walter. Private, Militia, 12th Battalion, Capt. Alexander McPherson's Company, 1777 [Ref: M-159]. Resident of Benedict Hundred in 1778 [Ref: Q-I:297].
BURCH, Walter. Private, Militia, 12th Battalion, Capt. Henry Clarkson's Company, 1777 [Ref: M-160]. Took the Oath of Allegiance in 1778 [Ref: L-15]. Resident of Newport East Hundred in 1778 [Ref: Q-I:297].
BURCH, William. Private, Militia, 12th Battalion, Capt. Henry Clarkson's Company, 1777 [Ref: M-159]. Took the Oath of Allegiance in 1778 [Ref: L-15]. Rendered patriotic service by providing wheat for the use of the

military in September 1782 [Ref: N-550]. Resident of Newport East Hundred in 1778 [Ref: Q-I:297].
BURCH, William D. See "John Burch," q.v.
BURCHILL, Charles. Took the Oath of Allegiance in 1778 [Ref: L-15]. Resident of Durham Lower Hundred in 1778 [Ref: Q-I:297].
BURGESS, Anna. See "Edward Ward," q.v.
BURGESS, Thomas. Took the Oath of Allegiance in 1778 [Ref: AA-641]. Resident of Port Tobacco East Hundred in 1778 [Ref: Q-I:297].
BURK, Benjamin. Sergeant, Militia, 12th Battalion, Capt. John Parnham's Company, 1777 [Ref: M-160].
BURK, James. Private, Militia, 26th Battalion, Capt. Thomas H. Marshall's Company, 1777 [Ref: M-163].
BURK, Mary. See "Lawrence Simpson," q.v.
BURK, Peter. See "Lawrence Simpson," q.v.
BURKE, Thomas. Took the Oath of Allegiance in 1778 [Ref: AA-641].
BURN, Walter. Private, Militia, 26th Battalion, Capt. William McPherson's Company, 1777 [Ref: M-163].
BURNETT, John. Private, 1st Maryland Line, enrolled and passed on July 8, 1776 [Ref: D-32].
BURNETT, John C. Took the Oath of Allegiance in 1778 [Ref: AA-641].
BURRAGE, Ninian. Private, Militia, 12th Battalion, Capt. Jonathan Yates' Company, 1777 [Ref: M-162]. Took the Oath of Allegiance in 1778 [Ref: AA-641]. Resident of William & Mary Upper Hundred in 1778 [Ref: Q-I:297]. Rendered patriotic service by providing wheat for the use of the military in December 1782 [Ref: N-578, which listed the first name as "Nian"].
BURRELL, Allen. Took the Oath of Allegiance in 1778 [Ref: L-15]. Resident of Bryan Town Hundred in 1778 [Ref: Q-I:297].
BURRIS, Thomas. Took the Oath of Allegiance in 1778 [Ref: L-15].
BURROUGHS, Benjamin. On Jan. 23, 1782, the Council of Maryland ordered "that the Treasurer pay to Daniel Jenifer forty one pounds eight shillings of [the Bills emitted under the Act of] Emission to be delivered over to Benjamin Burroughs for a Certificate passed by the Auditor General" for supplying provisions for the use of the military [Ref: I-53].
BURROUGHS, Elisha. Private, 1st Maryland Line, from St. Mary's County who married Margaret P. Swann on Nov. 30, 1793 in Charles County, Maryland. The pension application (R1503) of widow Margaret P. Burroughs (or Burrows or Burris) was rejected and both she and Elisha were deceased by 1852. The only surviving heirs were sons John H. Burroughs and P. H. Burroughs, both of Charles County, Maryland in 1853 [Ref: V-I:486, W-111].

BURROUGHS, John (1714-   ). Took the Oath of Allegiance in 1778 [Ref: L-15, which listed the name as "Burrus"]. Aged about 50 as noted in a 1764 deposition which also mentioned his father Richard Burroughs [Ref: DD-699]. Resident of Port Tobacco East Hundred in 1778 [Ref: Q-I:297].
BURROUGHS, John H. See "Elisha Burroughs," q.v.
BURROUGHS, Jonathan. Private, Militia, 12th Battalion, Capt. Peter Wood's Company, 1777 [Ref: M-161]. Took the Oath of Allegiance in 1778 [Ref: L-15].
BURROUGHS, Margaret P. See "Elisha Burroughs," q.v.
BURROUGHS, P. H. See "Elisha Burroughs," q.v.
BURROUGHS, Richard. Took the Oath of Allegiance in 1778 [Ref: L-15]. Resident of Benedict Hundred in 1778 [Ref: Q-I:297]. See "John Burroughs," q.v.
BURROUGHS, William. Private, 1st Maryland Line, enrolled and passed on July 20, 1776 [Ref: D-32].
BURROUGHS, Zephaniah. Private, 1st Maryland Line, enrolled and passed on July 20, 1776 [Ref: D-33]. Private, Militia, 12th Battalion, Capt. John Thomas' Company, 1777 [Ref: M-161, which misspelled the name as "Barrough"]. Took the Oath of Allegiance in 1778 [Ref: L-15]. Resident of Benedict Hundred in 1778 [Ref: Q-I:297].
BURTEN, James. Took the Oath of Allegiance in 1778 [Ref: AA-641].
BURTLES, Benjamin. Private, Militia, 12th Battalion, Capt. Benjamin Lusby Corry's Company, 1777 [Ref: M-160]. Took the Oath of Allegiance in 1778 [Ref: AA-641, L-15, which latter source mistakenly listed the name as "Bery Bustles"]. Resident of Newport West Hundred in 1778 [Ref: Q-I:297, which misspelled the name as "Burttes"].
BURTLES, William Sr. Took the Oath of Allegiance in 1778 [Ref: AA-641, L-15, which latter source misspelled the name as "Bustles"]. Resident of Newport West Hundred in 1778 [Ref: Q-I:297, which misspelled the name as "Burttes"].
BURTLES, William Jr. Took the Oath of Allegiance in 1778 [Ref: AA-641, L-20, which latter source misspelled the name as "Rustles"]. Resident of Newport West Hundred in 1778 [Ref: Q-I:297, which misspelled the name as "Burttes"].
BUSH, Ann Catherine. See "Ignatius Hamilton," q.v.
BUSH, John. Ensign, Militia, 26th Battalion, Capt. William Winter's Company, 1777 [Ref: M-165]. Second Lieutenant, 26th Battalion, commissioned May 9, 1778 [Ref: M-58, E-72]. Took the Oath of Allegiance in 1778 [Ref: L-15].

BUTLER, Henry. Private, 1st Maryland Line, drafted from the Charles County militia on July 27, 1781 and discharged on Dec. 3, 1781 [Ref: D-377, G-569, I-10].

BUTLER, John. Private, Militia, 26th Battalion, Capt. Robert Sinnett's Company, 1777 [Ref: M-164]. Took the Oath of Allegiance in 1778 [Ref: AA-641].

BUTLER, John. Took the Oath of Allegiance in 1778 [Ref: AA-641]. Private (drafted and joined the army), 1st Maryland Line, enlisted June 4, 1778 and died Sept. 1, 1778 [Ref: D-82, D-330].

BUTLER, Joseph. Private, 1st Maryland Line, discharged on Dec. 3, 1781 [Ref: I-10].

BUTLER, Matthias. Took the Oath of Allegiance in 1778 [Ref: AA-641, L-15, which latter source mistakenly listed the name as "Matthew Butler"]. Resident of Bryan Town Hundred in 1778 [Ref: Q-I:297].

BUTTS, Clement. Took the Oath of Allegiance in 1778 [Ref: L-15]. Rendered patriotic service by providing wheat for the use of the military in May 1783 [Ref: N-599]. Resident of Port Tobacco West Hundred in 1778 [Ref: Q-I:297].

BYASS, Ignatius. See "John Robertson," q.v.

BYASS, James. Private, 3rd Maryland Line, enlisted Jan. 1, 1777 [Ref: D-85]. Private, 1st Maryland Line, Capt. John S. Belt's Company, Jan. 1, 1782 [Ref: D-436].

CAHILL, Roger. Took the Oath of Allegiance in 1778 [Ref: L-15]. Resident of Bryan Town Hundred in 1778 [Ref: Q-I:297].

CAHOE, Ignatius. Private, Militia, 12th Battalion, Capt. Henry Clarkson's Company, 1777 [Ref: M-159, which listed the name as "Cohoe"]. Took the Oath of Allegiance in 1778 [Ref: L-15, AA-641, which latter source listed the name as "Cohoe"]. Resident of Bryan Town Hundred in 1778 [Ref: Q-I:297, which listed the name as "Caho"].

CAHOE, James. Private, Militia, 26th Battalion, Capt. Benjamin Cawood's Company, 1777 [Ref: M-162, which listed the name as "Cohoe"].

CAHOE, Thomas Jr. (1745-1823). Fifer, 6th Maryland Line, enlisted by October 1780, served in the southern campaign with the 2nd Maryland Line in North Carolina from November 1780 through 1783 [Ref: D-195, D-347, D-439, D-528]. In November 1812, the Treasurer of Maryland was directed to pay to one "Thomas Cahoe or Kahoe, of Charles County, late a private in the Maryland Line in the Revolutionary War, half pay of a private, as a remuneration for meritorious service." He was placed on the pension rolls of Charles County as of Oct. 18, 1819 (retroactive to Aug. 31, 1818) and died on Feb. 15, 1823 [Ref: Q-II:325, R-33]. He applied for a federal pension (S34681) on Nov. 10, 1820, aged 75, and mentioned his wife (not named) who was also aged 75 [Ref: V-I:510].

CAHOE, Thomas Sr. Private, 6th Maryland Line, enlisted July 29, 1777, served in the southern campaign with the 2nd Maryland Line in North Carolina in November 1780, was listed as being on furlough on Dec. 29, 1781, and served into 1783 [Ref: D-193, D-349, D-440, D-528]. Resident of Bryan Town Hundred in 1778 [Ref: Q-I:297, which listed the name as "Caho"]. See "Thomas Cahoe, Jr.," q.v.

CALARY, James. See "James Coley," q.v.

CAMBRON, Henry. Took the Oath of Allegiance in 1778 [Ref: L-15]. Resident of Bryan Town Hundred in 1778 [Ref: Q-I:297]. Private, Militia, 12th Battalion, Capt. Alexander McPherson's Company, 1777 [Ref: M-160, which listed the name as "Camron"].

CAMRON, James. Private, Militia, 12th Battalion, Capt. Alexander McPherson's Company, 1777 [Ref: M-160]. Rendered patriotic service by providing clothing for the use of the military in February 1778 [Ref: Y-II:234]. Resident of Bryan Town Hundred in 1778 [Ref: Q-I:297].

CAMBRON, John Baptist (c1725-1815). Took the Oath of Allegiance in 1778 [Ref: L-15]. Private, Militia, 12th Battalion, Capt. Alexander McPherson's Company, 1777 [Ref: M-160, which listed the name as "John B. Camron"]. Resident of Bryan Town Hundred in 1778 [Ref: Q-I:297]. He married (wife's name not stated) and migrated to Kentucky where he died on May 8, 1815 [ref: J-I:474].

CAMBRON, John Williams. Private, Militia, 12th Battalion, Capt. Alexander McPherson's Company, 1777 [Ref: M-160, which listed the name as "Camron"].

CAMBRON, Thomas. Private, Militia, 12th Battalion, Capt. Alexander McPherson's Company, 1777 [Ref: M-160, which listed the name as "Camron"]. Took the Oath of Allegiance in 1778 [Ref: L-15]. Resident of Bryan Town Hundred in 1778 [Ref: Q-I:297].

CAMPBELL, Gustavus. Private, Militia, 12th Battalion, Capt. Walter Hanson's Company, 1777 [Ref: M-159]. "Gustavus B. Campbell" took the Oath of Allegiance in 1778 [Ref: L-15].

CAMPBELL, Isaac. Took the Oath of Allegiance in 1778 [Ref: L-15]. Resident of Benedict Hundred in 1778 [Ref: Q-I:297]. See "Isaac Campbell, Jr." and "William Campbell," q.v.

CAMPBELL, Isaac Jr. (1761-). Born on Jan. 3, 1761, son of Isaac and Mary Campbell [Ref: EE-8]. Private, Militia, 12th Battalion, Capt. Benjamin Lusby Corry's Company, 1777 [Ref: M-160].

CAMPBELL, James. Took the Oath of Allegiance in 1778 [Ref: AA-641]. Resident of Benedict Hundred in 1778 [Ref: Q-I:297].

CAMPBELL, Jane. See "William Campbell," q.v.
CAMPBELL, Jos. (or Jsa.?). Took the Oath of Allegiance in 1778 [Ref: AA-641].
CAMPBELL, Mary. See "Isaac Campbell, Jr.," q.v.
CAMPBELL, William. Captain, Militia, 26th Battalion, 1776 [Ref: Y-II:23]. It was recommended to the Maryland Convention on Jan. 27, 1776, that since he and Capt. Belain Posey "had behaved themselves in the cause of Liberty so as to gain the good wishes of their County [they were recommended] to any place that may happen to be vacant in the regular Battalion or Regular Independent Company, they being desirous of serving their Country in either." [Ref: A-111]. One William Campbell, son of Rev. Isaac and Jane Campbell, was born on Aug. 28, 1756 [Ref: EE-9]. See "Hugh Gardiner," q.v.
CANTER, Isaac. Private, Militia, 12th Battalion, Capt. Peter Wood's Company, 1777 [Ref: M-161]. Took the Oath of Allegiance in 1778 [Ref: AA-641]. Resident of Benedict Hundred in 1778 [Ref: Q-I:297].
CANTER, James. Private, Militia, 12th Battalion, Capt. Peter Wood's Company, 1777 [Ref: M-161]. Resident of Benedict Hundred in 1778 [Ref: Q-I:297].
CANTER, James Jr. Took the Oath of Allegiance in 1778 [Ref: AA-641].
CANTER, Jonathan. Private, Militia, 26th Battalion, Capt. Samuel Smallwood's Company, 1777 [Ref: M-165, which listed the name as "Cantor"].
CANTER, William Jr. Took the Oath of Allegiance in 1778 [Ref: AA-641, L-15, which latter source listed the name as "Canters"]. Resident of Benedict Hundred in 1778 [Ref: Q-I:297].
CANTER, William Sr. Took the Oath of Allegiance in 1778 [Ref: AA-641]. Resident of Benedict Hundred in 1778 [Ref: Q-I:297].
CAREY, Daniel. Took the Oath of Allegiance in 1778 [Ref: L-15].
CAREY, Henry. Took the Oath of Allegiance in 1778 [Ref: L-15].
CARPENTER, Humphrey. Private, 1st Maryland Line, enlisted in June 1780 and was taken prisoner at the Battle of Camden in South Carolina on Aug. 16, 1780 [Ref: D-92].
CARPENTER, John. Private, Militia, 26th Battalion, Capt. William Winter's Company, 1777 [Ref: M-165]. Resident of Durham Lower Hundred in 1778 [Ref: Q-I:297].
CARPENTER, Mary. See "Francis Clinkscales," q.v.
CARPENTER, William. Private, Militia, 26th Battalion, Capt. Hezekiah Garner's Company, 1777 [Ref: M-163]. Took the Oath of Allegiance in 1778 [Ref: L-15, AA-641]. Rendered patriotic service by providing wheat for the use of the military in September and November 1781, and May

1783 [Ref: N-438, N-455, N-598]. Resident of Durham Lower Hundred in 1778 [Ref: Q-I:297].

CARRICOE, Bartholomew. Took the Oath of Allegiance in 1778 [Ref: L-15, AA-641].

CARRICOE, Catharine. See "Peter Carricoe," q.v.

CARRICOE, James, of James. Took the Oath of Allegiance in 1778 [Ref: L-15, AA-641].

CARRICOE, James, of John. Took the Oath of Allegiance in 1778 [Ref: L-15]. Resident of Bryan Town Hundred in 1778 [Ref: Q-I:297].

CARRICOE, James Sr. Took the Oath of Allegiance in 1778 [Ref: L-15]. Resident of Bryan Town Hundred in 1778 [Ref: Q-I:297].

CARRICOE, Joseph. Private, Militia, 26th Battalion, Capt. William McPherson's Company, 1777 [Ref: M-163, which misspelled the name as "Carries"]. Took the Oath of Allegiance in 1778 [Ref: L-15, AA-641]. Rendered patriotic service by providing wheat for the use of the military in December 1782 [Ref: N-573, which listed the name as "Carrico"]. Resident of Bryan Town Hundred in 1778 [Ref: Q-I:297].

CARRICOE, Katherine. See "Joseph Waters, of James," q.v.

CARRICOE, Peter (c1743-c1803). Private, Militia, 12th Battalion, Capt. Peter Wood's Company, 1777 [Ref: M-161]. Took the Oath of Allegiance in 1778 [Ref: AA-641, L-15, which latter source listed the name as "Carrico"]. Resident of Benedict Hundred in 1778 [Ref: Q-I:297]. Peter Carrico married Catharine ---- and died in Virginia after May 6, 1803 [Ref: J-I:499].

CARRICOE, Sarah. See "Lawrence Simpson," q.v.

CARRICOE, Thomas Ignatius. He married Elizabeth ----, rendered patriotic service in Maryland and migrated to Kentucky where he died after May 5, 1813 [Ref: J-I:499].

CARRINGTON, Elizabeth. See "Thomas Ignatius Carricoe" and "Jesse Boswell," q.v.

CARRINGTON, John (1731-   ). Took the Oath of Allegiance in 1778 [Ref: AA-641]. Rendered patriotic service by providing wheat for the use of the military in December 1781 [Ref: N-463]. Aged about 40 as noted in a 1771 deposition which also mentioned his father Timothy Carrington [Ref: DD-699]. Resident of Port Tobacco East Hundred in 1778 [Ref: Q-I:297].

CARRINGTON, Samuel (1754-1818). Private, Militia, 12th Battalion, Capt. John Hanson's Company, 1777 [Ref: M-159]. Samuel Carrington married Milly McDonald and migrated to Kentucky where he died on May 6, 1818 [Ref: J-I:500].

CARRINGTON, Timothy (1723-   ). Took the Oath of Allegiance in 1778 [Ref: AA-641]. Aged about 48 as noted in a 1771 deposition (which also mentioned his father Timothy Carrington) and aged about 55 as noted in a 1778 deposition [Ref: CC-697, DD-699]. Resident of Port Tobacco East Hundred in 1778 [Ref: Q-I:297]. See "John Carrington," q.v.

CARROLL, Christopher (1713-   ). Took the Oath of Allegiance in 1778 [Ref: L-15, which mistakenly listed the name as "Charles Carroll" and AA-641, which listed the name as "Chris: Carrell"]. Aged 59 as noted in a 1772 deposition [Ref: DD-700, which listed the name as "Christopher Carroll"]. Resident of Durham Lower Hundred in 1778 [Ref: Q-I:297].

CARROLL, James. Private, Militia, 12th Battalion, Capt. Peter Wood's Company, 1777 [Ref: M-161]. Took the Oath of Allegiance in 1778 [Ref: L-15].

CARROLL, John (1754-c1840). Private, Militia, 26th Battalion, Capt. William Winter's Company, 1777 [Ref: M-165, which listed the name as "Carrall"]. Private (furnished by class for 9 months), 1st Maryland Line, by Sept. 11, 1778 [Ref: D-330]. Took the Oath of Allegiance in 1778 [Ref: L-15]. One John Carroll applied for and received a pension (S30913) in Jessamine County, Kentucky on Aug. 20, 1832, aged 78, stating that he lived in Charles County, Maryland at the time of his enlistment in the Revolutionary War. He married Frances Hamilton and died after 1840 in Kentucky [Ref: T-53, J-I:500, V-I:554].

CARROLL, John Jr. "John Carroll, Jr." was a private (furnished by class for 9 months), 1st Maryland Line, by Sept. 11, 1778 [Ref: D-330]. "John Carroll" was a private in the Maryland Line who died on Jan. 13, 1782 [Ref: D-527].

CARROLL, Richard. Private, Militia, 26th Battalion, Capt. William Winter's Company, 1777 [Ref: M-165]. Private (draught who had not yet joined the army), 1st Maryland Line, by Sept. 11, 1778 [Ref: D-330].

CARROLL, Samuel. Sergeant, Militia, 26th Battalion, Capt. William Winter's Company, 1777 [Ref: M-165].

CARROLL, William. Private, Militia, 26th Battalion, Capt. William Winter's Company, 1777 [Ref: M-165]. Resident of Durham Lower Hundred in 1778 [Ref: Q-I:297].

CARTWRIGHT, Gustavus. Private, Militia, 12th Battalion, Capt. Benjamin Lusby Corry's Company, 1777 [Ref: M-160, which listed the name as "Cartright"]. Took the Oath of Allegiance in 1778 [Ref: L-15]. Rendered patriotic service by providing wheat for the use of the military in September 1782 [Ref: N-556, which listed the name as "Chartwright"]. Resident of Newport East Hundred in 1778 [Ref: Q-I:297].

CARTWRIGHT, Judith. See "Lancelot Chunn," q.v.

CARVOLL, John. Private, 1st Maryland Line, enrolled and passed on July 25, 1776 [Ref: D-32].

CARY, Francis. Took the Oath of Allegiance in 1778 [Ref: L-15].
CATO, George (1753-   ). Private, Virginia Line. Applied for a pension (R1814) in Charles County, Maryland on June 2, 1818, aged 65, and in 1820 he and his wife (not named, aged about 56) and two sons (not named, one aged 19 and the other "a few years younger") were living with their daughter (not named). [Ref: V-I:678].
CATO, William (c1750-1781). Private, 2nd Maryland Line, enlisted Jan. 12, 1777; promoted to sergeant on Jan. 1, 1780; demoted to private on Sept. 15, 1780; promoted to sergeant by Nov. 1, 1780; died on June 18, 1781 [Ref: D-92, D-527, which latter source listed the name as "Sgt. William Cata"].
CAUSIN, Gerard Blackstone. Son of John Causeen and grandson of Ignatius Causine, he married Jane Pope and had three children: Nicholas Causin, Nathaniel Pope Causin (married Elizabeth Stone), and Rose Causin (married Luke Francis Matthews). Gerard Causin rendered the following patriotic services: Sergeant, Militia, 12th Battalion, Capt. Walter Hanson's Company, 1777 [Ref: M-159, which listed the name as "Gerrard B. Causeen"]. Rendered patriotic service by providing clothing for the use of the military in February 1778 [Ref: Y-II:234, which listed the name as "Gerrard Blackiston Causin"]. Ensign, May 28, 1779 [Ref: M-60, E-427, which listed the name as "Gerard Blackstone Causin"]. Rendered patriotic service by providing wheat for the use of the military in January, September, and December 1782 [Ref: N-545, N-575, I-53, which listed the name as "Gerrard B. Causin, Esq."]. Served in the Lower House of the Maryland Legislature, 1780 to 1782, was Commissioner of the Tax in Charles County from 1783 to at least 1790, and died after 1800 [Ref: P-I:204]. "G. B. Causeen" took the Oath of Allegiance in 1778 [Ref: AA-641]. Resident of Port Tobacco East Hundred in 1778 [Ref: Q-I:297]. See "Walter Hanson Jenifer," q.v.
CAUSIN, Ignatius. See "Gerard Blackstone Causin," q.v.
CAUSIN, John. Took the Oath of Allegiance in 1778 [Ref: AA-641, L-15, which latter source listed the name as "Causon"]. Resident of Port Tobacco East Hundred in 1778 [Ref: Q-I:297]. See "Gerard Blackstone Causin," q.v.
CAUSIN, Nathaniel Pope. See "John Hoskins Stone" and "Gerard Blackstone Causin," q.v.
CAUSIN, Nicholas. See "Gerard Blackstone Causin," q.v.
CAUSIN, Rose. See "Gerard Blackstone Causin," q.v.
CAWOOD, Benjamin. Captain, Militia, 26th Battalion, 1777 [Ref: M-60, M-162]. Elected Sheriff of Charles County and a commission was issued on Oct. 12, 1779 [Ref: E-554].

CAWOOD, Benjamin Jr. Took the Oath of Allegiance in 1778 [Ref: AA-641]. Resident of Port Tobacco Upper Hundred in 1778 [Ref: Q-I:297].
CAWOOD, Mary. See "Samuel Hanson, Jr." and "Benjamin Davis," q.v.
CAWOOD, Stephen. Private, Militia, 26th Battalion, Capt. Samuel Smallwood's Company, 1777 [Ref: M-165, which listed his first name as "Stepan"]. Resident of Port Tobacco Upper Hundred in 1778 [Ref: Q-I:297]. Petitioned the Council of Maryland in 1783 stating that he had not taken the Oath of Allegiance due to any disaffection with the government, but from a variety of incidents, and was unjustly penalized as a non-juror and fined unfairly; therefore, he asked the Council to consider ordering the County Justices to remit the fines they imposed on him and others who signed the petition. The Council of Maryland, after reviewing his case, indicated they believed the truth of the facts stated in the petition and ordered a remission of the fines and penalties on Sept. 17, 1783 [Ref: I-454].
CAWOOD, William. Private, Militia, 26th Battalion, Capt. Samuel Smallwood's Company, 1777 [Ref: M-165]. Took the Oath of Allegiance in 1778 [Ref: L-15, AA-641]. Resident of Port Tobacco Upper Hundred in 1778 [Ref: Q-I:297]. Private, 1st Maryland Line, enlisted Sept. 30, 1782 [Ref: D-418].
CHANDLER, Ann. See "Edward Smoot," q.v.
CHANDLER, Elizabeth. See "Chandler Ford," q.v.
CHANDLER, Henry. Private, Militia, 12th Battalion, Capt. Jonathan Yates' Company, 1777 [Ref: X-70, but was omitted from the list in Reference M-162]. Took the Oath of Allegiance in 1778 [Ref: L-15, AA-641]. Resident of William & Mary Lower Hundred in 1778 [Ref: Q-I:297].
CHANDLER, John. Private, Militia, 12th Battalion, Capt. Walter Hanson's Company, 1777 [Ref: M-159].
CHANDLER, John (1713-). Took the Oath of Allegiance in 1778 [Ref: AA-641]. Aged 56 as noted in a 1769 deposition [Ref: DD-700]. Resident of Port Tobacco East Hundred in 1778 [Ref: Q-I:297].
CHANDLER, Samuel. Private, 1st Maryland Line, enrolled and passed on July 27, 1776 [Ref: D-31]. Corporal, Militia, 12th Battalion, Capt. Walter Hanson's Company, 1777 [Ref: M-159]. Took the Oath of Allegiance in 1778 [Ref: AA-641]. Resident of Port Tobacco East Hundred in 1778 [Ref: Q-I:297].
CHANDLER, Stephen (1719-). Rendered patriotic service by providing clothing for the use of the military in January 1778 [Ref: Y-II:230]. Took the Oath of Allegiance in 1778 [Ref: AA-641]. Aged 59 as noted in a 1778 deposition [Ref: DD-700]. Resident of Port Tobacco East Hundred in 1778 [Ref: Q-I:297].

CHANE, Judith. See "Judith Chase," q.v.
CHAPMAN, Anne Hanson. See "Henry Henley Chapman," q.v.
CHAPMAN, Catharine. See "Henry Henley Chapman," q.v.
CHAPMAN, Henry. Private, 1st Maryland Line, enlisted March 11, 1777 and died in June 1777 [Ref: D-91].
CHAPMAN, Henry Henley (1764-1821). Son of John and Catharine Chapman, he married first to Eleanor Hanson (died in 1796) and second to Mary Davidson. They had at least eleven children, including John Henley Chapman (1801-1814) and Anne Hanson Chapman (died in 1796). Henry H. Chapman was an ensign in the 2nd Maryland Line in 1781, lieutenant in 1782, and served until November 1783 (held the rank of major by 1821). Styled "Esquire" in 1795 and was a member of the Society of the Cincinnati, he served in the Lower House of the Maryland Legislature from 1787 to 1815 and was Speaker in 1798-1799 and 1814-1815. He was also a Justice of Charles County from 1789 to 1793, an Associate Justice of the First District in 1792, a Maryland Senate Elector in 1796, 1801, 1811, and served on the Executive Council from 1816 to 1819. He died in Georgetown, D. C. in 1821 [Ref: P-I:211, P-I:212, J-I:538, which latter source stated he was born in Virginia on Jan. 9, 1764 and died in Maryland on Dec. 5, 1821]. The obituary of Major Henry H. Chapman appeared in the *Maryland Gazette* on Dec. 13, 1821, stating he "died in Georgetown, a soldier of the Revolution. He had filled various public offices in the State of Maryland, whence he removed about two years ago. A wife and nine children survive." [Ref: FF-30]. See "Samuel Hanson," q.v.
CHAPMAN, John (1725-   ). Took the Oath of Allegiance in 1778 [Ref: L-15, AA-641]. Aged about 53 in 1778 deposition and aged about 54 in a 1779 deposition [Ref: CC-704, BB-469]. See "Henry Henley Chapman," q.v.
CHAPMAN, John (1758-1790). Rendered patriotic service by providing wheat for the use of the military in September 1781, and September and November 1782 [Ref: N-432, N-544, N-568]. The obituary of Dr. John Chapman appeared in the *Maryland Gazette* on June 10, 1790, stating he "died at his house in Port Tobacco, on the 18th of May, in his 32nd year. He was a tender husband and parent." [Ref: FF-30].
CHAPMAN, John Henley. See "Henry Henley Chapman," q.v.
CHAPMAN, Lucretia. See "Francis Semmes" and "Joseph Semmes" and "Marmaduke Semmes" and Ignatius Semmes," q.v.
CHAPMAN, Pearson. Private, Militia, 26th Battalion, Capt. Thomas H. Marshall's Company, 1777 [Ref: M-163]. Took the Oath of Allegiance in 1778 [Ref: L-15, AA-641, which latter source listed the name as

"Champman"]. Rendered patriotic service by providing wheat for the use of the military in August and October 1782 [Ref: N-539, N-563]. Resident of Pomonkey Hundred in 1778 [Ref: Q-I:297].

CHARK (CLARK?), Elijah. Private, Militia, 26th Battalion, Capt. Hezekiah Garner's Company, 1777 [Ref: M-163]. See "Elijah Clark," q.v.

CHARK (CLARK?), George. Private, Militia, 12th Battalion, Capt. Benjamin Lusby Corry's Company, 1777 [Ref: M-160]. See "George Clark," q.v.

CHASE (CHANE?), Judith. "Judith Chase" rendered patriotic service by providing wheat for the use of the military in November and December 1781 [Ref: N-453, N-456, N-461]. "Judith Chane" rendered patriotic service by providing wheat for the use of the military in December 1782 [Ref: N-575].

CHATHAM, William (1759-   ). Applied for a pension (R1895) on Sept. 13, 1836, aged 77, in Orange County, North Carolina, stating he was born in Charles County, Maryland on June 25, 1760 and enlisted there during the Revolutionary War [Ref: V-I:614].

CHATTAM, James. Private, Militia, 12th Battalion, Capt. John Hanson's Company, 1777 [Ref: M-159]. Took the Oath of Allegiance in 1778 [Ref: AA-641, which listed the name as "Chittam"]. Resident of Port Tobacco East Hundred in 1778 [Ref: Q-I:297].

CHATTAM, John. Corporal, Militia, 26th Battalion, Capt. Robert Sinnett's Company, 1777 [Ref: M-164]. Took the Oath of Allegiance in 1778 [Ref: L-15, AA-641]. In 1778 "John Chatam" was a resident of Port Tobacco West Hundred and "John Chattam" was a resident of Port Tobacco East Hundred [Ref: Q-I:297]. A "John Chittam" was aged 53 as noted in a 1780 deposition [Ref: DD-700].

CHESELDYNE, Dryden. See "James Forbes," q.v.

CHILTON, John. Rendered patriotic service by providing wheat for the use of the military in November 1782 [Ref: N-565]. Resident of Durham Lower Hundred in 1778 [Ref: Q-I:297].

CHILTON, John S. Second Lieutenant, Militia, until Feb. 26, 1776 (resigned). [Ref: E-142, Y-II:23]. See "John Baillie," q.v.

CHILTON, John Steuart. Private, Militia, 26th Battalion, Capt. William Winter's Company, 1777 [Ref: M-165]. Took the Oath of Allegiance in 1778 [Ref: L-15]. Ensign, 26th Battalion, Dec. 6, 1779 [Ref: M-62].

CHING, Samuel. Private (furnished by class for 9 months), 1st Maryland Line, by Sept. 11, 1778 [Ref: D-330, which listed the name as "Chinge"]. Resident of Newport East Hundred in 1778 [Ref: Q-I:297].

CHING, Thomas. Private, Militia, 12th Battalion, Capt. John Parnham's Company, 1777 [Ref: M-160]. Took the Oath of Allegiance in 1778 [Ref: AA-641]. Resident of Newport East Hundred in 1778 [Ref: Q-I:297].

CHITTAM, James. See "James Chattam," q.v.

CHRISMOND, Aaron. Private, Militia, 12th Battalion, Capt. Walter Hanson's Company, 1777 [Ref: M-159, which listed the name as "Chrisman"]. Took the Oath of Allegiance in 1778 [Ref: AA-641, which listed the name as "Crismand"]. Resident of Port Tobacco East Hundred in 1778 [Ref: Q-I:297, which listed the name as "Crismond"].

CHRISMOND, John Mason. Private, Militia, 12th Battalion, Capt. Walter Hanson's Company, 1777 [Ref: M-159, which listed the name as "Chrisman"]. Took the Oath of Allegiance in 1778 [Ref: L-15, which mistakenly listed the name as "Chissmoux" and AA-641, which listed the name as "Crismand"]. Resident of Port Tobacco East Hundred in 1778 [Ref: Q-I:297, which listed the name as "Mason Crismond"]. See "Thomas Pickerel," q.v.

CHRISMOND, Joseph. Private, Militia, 12th Battalion, Capt. John Hanson's Company, 1777 [Ref: M-159, which listed the name as "Chrismond"]. Took the Oath of Allegiance in 1778 [Ref: AA-641, which listed the name as "Crismand" and L-14, which listed the name as "Aismond?"]. Resident of Port Tobacco East Hundred in 1778 [Ref: Q-I:297].

CHRISMOND, Leonard. Fifer, 3rd Maryland Line, enlisted Feb. 3, 1777 and discharged in March 1780, "time expired." [Ref: D-94, which listed the name as "Crismond"].

CHUNN, Benjamin. See "Lancelot Chunn" and "Levi Chunn," q.v.

CHUNN, Eleazer. Private, Militia, 12th Battalion, Capt. John Parnham's Company, 1777 [Ref: M-161]. Took the Oath of Allegiance in 1778 [Ref: L-15, which mistakenly listed the name as "Eliazer Churn"]. Resident of Newport East Hundred in 1778 [Ref: Q-I:297].

CHUNN, Elizabeth. See "Joseph Dyson," q.v.

CHUNN, Henry. Private, Militia, 12th Battalion, Capt. John Parnham's Company, 1777 [Ref: M-161]. Took the Oath of Allegiance in 1778 [Ref: L-15, which mistakenly listed the name as "Henry Churn"]. Resident of Newport East Hundred in 1778 [Ref: Q-I:297].

CHUNN, Jonathan (1754-1777). Born on Nov. 7, 1754, son of Lancelot Chunn and Judith Cartwright [Ref: EE-10]. Private, 1st Maryland Line, enlisted Jan. 24, 1776, reenlisted Dec. 10, 1776, and died on March 6, 1777 [Ref: D-6, D-91].

CHUNN, Judith. See "Lancelot Chunn," q.v.

CHUNN, Lancelot (1723-1809). Took the Oath of Allegiance in 1778 [Ref: L-15, which mistakenly listed the name as "Churn"]. Aged 59 as noted in a 1782 deposition which mentioned his father Benjamin Chunn, deceased [Ref: DD-700]. Resident of Newport East Hundred in 1778 [Ref: Q-I:297]. Lancelot Chunn married Judith Cartwright on May 11, 1753 in Trinity Parish [Ref: EE-10, J-I:563]. See "Jonathan Chunn," q.v.

CHUNN, Lancelot Jr. (1764-1830). Private, 1st Maryland Line, drafted from the Charles County militia on July 27, 1781 and discharged on Dec. 3, 1781 [Ref: D-377, I-10]. "Launcelot Chunn, Jr." was born on Oct. 27, 1764, married Martha Ridgley, and migrated to Alabama where he died on Dec. 29, 1830 [Ref: J-I:563].

CHUNN, Levi (1746-   ). Born on Feb. 23, 1746, son of Benjamin and Rebekah Chunn [Ref: EE-2]. Private, Militia, 12th Battalion, Capt. Jonathan Yates' Company, 1777 [Ref: M-162]. Took the Oath of Allegiance in 1778 [Ref: L-15]. Resident of William & Mary Lower Hundred in 1778 [Ref: Q-I:297].

CHUNN, Rebekah. See "Levi Chunn," q.v.

CHUNN, Winifred. See "Bennett Dyson" and "Gerard Wood," q.v.

CHUNN, Zachariah (c1742-c1804). Second Lieutenant, Militia, 12th Battalion, Capt. John Parnham's Company, July 5, 1777 [Ref: M-62, M-160]. Resident of Newport East Hundred in 1778 [Ref: Q-I:297, which also misspelled the name as "Churm"]. Constable, 1778 [Ref: CC-709]. Appointed Inspector of Tobacco at Piles's Fresh on Aug. 30, 1780 [Ref: F-271]. Zachariah Chunn married first to Charity Courts on Dec. 23, 1762, and second to Deborah Turner on May 30 or 31, 1764 [Ref: EE-11, EE-13, J-I:563].

CHURCH, Elizabeth. See "Richard Smith," q.v.

CHUSICK, Ignatius. Took the Oath of Allegiance in 1778 [Ref: AA-641, L-15, which latter source mistakenly listed the name as "Cheswick"]. Resident of Benedict Hundred in 1778 [Ref: Q-I:297, which listed the name as "Cusick"].

CLAGETT, Hezekiah. Took the Oath of Allegiance in 1778 [Ref: AA-641]. Resident of William & Mary Upper Hundred in 1778 [Ref: Q-I:297, which listed the name as "Hezt. Claggett"].

CLAGETT, James. Rendered patriotic service by providing wheat for the use of the military in December 1782 [Ref: N-576].

CLAGETT, Samuel. See "Samuel Hanson," q.v.

CLARBEN, Samuel. Private, 3rd Maryland Line, 1780, enrolled in Charles County for Capt. Joseph Marbury's Company [Ref: D-333].

CLARK, Evans. Took the Oath of Allegiance in 1778 [Ref: L-15].

CLARK, William. Private, Militia, 12th Battalion, Capt. Peter Wood's Company, 1777 [Ref: M-161]. Took the Oath of Allegiance in 1778 [Ref: AA-641]. Resident of Durham Lower Hundred in 1778 [Ref: Q-I:297].
CLARKE, Draden. See "Zephaniah King," q.v.
CLARKE (CLARK), Elias. Took the Oath of Allegiance in 1778 [Ref: L-15, AA-641, which latter source listed the name as "Clark"]. Private, Militia, 12th Battalion, Capt. Walter Hanson's Company, 1777 [Ref: M-159, which listed the name as "Elias Clerke"]. Resident of Port Tobacco East Hundred in 1778 [Ref: Q-I:297].
CLARKE (CLARK), Elijah (1754-1837). Private, 1st Maryland Line, enrolled and passed on July 27, 1776 [Ref: D-31]. Took the Oath of Allegiance in 1778 [Ref: AA-641, which listed the name "Clarke"]. He applied for and received a pension (S37361) in Laurel County, Kentucky on Oct. 1, 1832, aged 79, stating that he was born in 1754 in Charles County, Maryland and there he enlisted for six months in the Flying Camp during the Revolutionary War. After the war he moved to Virginia, then to Tennessee, and then to Kentucky, where he died on June 22, 1837 [Ref: V-I:644, U-33:1 (1945), p. 29]. See "Elijah Chark," q.v.
CLARKE (CLERK), George. Took the Oath of Allegiance in 1778 [Ref: L-15, AA-641]. Resident of Newport West Hundred in 1778 [Ref: Q-I:297, which listed the name as "Clerk"]. See "George Chark," q.v.
CLARKE, Ignatius. Took the Oath of Allegiance in 1778 [Ref: L-15].
CLARKE (CLARK), Moses. Took the Oath of Allegiance in 1778 [Ref: L-15, AA-641, which latter source listed the name as "Clark"]. Resident of Newport West Hundred in 1778 [Ref: Q-I:297].
CLARKE, Susannah Mackall. See "George Clarke Smoot," q.v.
CLARKSON, Henry. Captain, Militia, 12th Battalion, from 1777 to Jan. 19, 1781 [Ref: M-63, M-159, G-280]. Took the Oath of Allegiance in 1778 [Ref: L-15]. Resident of Newport East Hundred in 1778 [Ref: Q-I:297]. Henry Clarkson married Dorcas Dyson on Feb. 11, 1772 in Trinity Parish [Ref: EE-14].
CLEMENTS, Aquilla. Private, 4th Maryland Line, by Jan. 1, 1782 [Ref: D-461].
CLEMENTS, Basil. Private, Militia, 26th Battalion, Capt. William McPherson's Company, 1777 [Ref: M-163]. Took the Oath of Allegiance in 1778 [Ref: AA-641, L-15, which latter source listed the name as "Clement"]. Resident of Port Tobacco West Hundred in 1778 [Ref: Q-I:297].
CLEMENTS, Benedict. Took the Oath of Allegiance in 1778 [Ref: L-15, which listed the name as "Cleamons" and AA-641, which listed the name as "Clemons"]. Private, 1st Maryland Line, drafted from the Charles

County militia on July 27, 1781 and discharged on Dec. 3, 1781 [Ref: D-377, G-569, I-11, which sources listed the name as "Benedict Clements" and "Bennett Clements"]. See "Edward Miles," q.v.

CLEMENTS, Benjamin Notley (1717-   ). Took the Oath of Allegiance in 1778 [Ref: L-15, AA-641]. Aged 55 as noted in a 1772 deposition [Ref: DD-701]. Resident of Port Tobacco Upper Hundred in 1778 [Ref: Q-I:297].

CLEMENTS, Bennett Hanson (c1754-1804). County Elections were held at his house in August 1776 to elect delegates to the Maryland Convention "for the express purpose of forming a new government." [Ref: Y-I:35]. Private, Militia, 26th Battalion, Capt. William McPherson's Company, 1777 [Ref: M-163]. Private, 1st Maryland Line, 1780; discharged on July 23, 1783 [Ref: D-528]. Took the Oath of Allegiance in 1778 [Ref: AA-641, L-15, which sources listed the name as "Bennett H. Clements"]. Resident of Port Tobacco West Hundred in 1778 [Ref: Q-I:297]. He married (wife's name not stated) and died before Dec. 24, 1804 [Ref: J-I:591]. See "Benedict Clements," q.v.

CLEMENTS, Charles (1739-   ). Private, Militia, 26th Battalion, Capt. Richard Bennett Mitchell's Company, 1777 [Ref: M-164]. Private (substitute for 3 years), 1st Maryland Line, by Sept. 11, 1778 [Ref: D-330]. Took the Oath of Allegiance in 1778 [Ref: L-15, AA-641]. Aged 26 as noted in a 1765 deposition [Ref: DD-701]. Resident of Port Tobacco West Hundred in 1778 [Ref: Q-I:297].

CLEMENTS, Charles, of Walter. Private, Militia, 26th Battalion, Capt. Richard Bennett Mitchell's Company, 1777 [Ref: M-165]. Resident of Bryan Town Hundred in 1778 [Ref: Q-I:297].

CLEMENTS, Clair. Received support from the county in August 1778, due to the absence of her husband (not named) who was "away in the regular service." [Ref: CC-712].

CLEMENTS, Clement. Rendered patriotic service by providing wheat for the use of the military in May 1783 [Ref: N-598]. Took the Oath of Allegiance in 1778 [Ref: AA-641]. Resident of Port Tobacco West Hundred in 1778 [Ref: Q-I:297].

CLEMENTS, Edward. Private, Militia, 12th Battalion, Capt. John Hanson's Company, 1777 [Ref: M-158]. Took the Oath of Allegiance in 1778 [Ref: AA-641]. Resident of Port Tobacco East Hundred in 1778 [Ref: Q-I:297].

CLEMENTS, Edward. Private, Militia, 26th Battalion, Capt. William McPherson's Company [Ref: M-163]. Took the Oath of Allegiance in 1778 [Ref: L-15, AA-641]. Resident of Port Tobacco East Hundred in 1778 [Ref: Q-I:297].

CLEMENTS, Edward. See "William Clements," q.v.

CLEMENTS, Elizabeth. See "William Mudd," q.v.

CLEMENTS, Francis, of Jacob. Private, Militia, 26th Battalion, Capt. Richard Bennett Mitchell's Company, 1777; listed as an invalid (disabled) soldier [Ref: M-164]. Took the Oath of Allegiance in 1778 [Ref: L-15]. Resident of Port Tobacco West Hundred in 1778 [Ref: Q-I:297].
CLEMENTS, George. Private, Militia, 12th Battalion, Capt. John Hanson's Company, 1777 [Ref: M-159].
CLEMENTS, George (1726-   ). Took the Oath of Allegiance in 1778 [Ref: AA-641]. Aged 44 as noted in a 1770 deposition [Ref: DD-701]. Resident of Port Tobacco East Hundred in 1778 [Ref: Q-I:297].
CLEMENTS, Henry. Private, 1st Maryland Line, enlisted April 16, 1777 and discharged Feb. 28, 1780 [Ref: D-91]. Private, 1st Maryland Line, drafted from the Charles County militia on July 27, 1781, and the muster roll noted that he "since enrolled himself a substitute in Prince George's County and joined the Army." [Ref: D-377]. There was also a Henry Clements who was a lieutenant in Capt. William Rieley's Company in the 1st Maryland Line on Jan. 1, 1782 [Ref: D-433]. Additional research may be necessary before drawing conclusions.
CLEMENTS, Ignatius N. See "Archibald Johnson," q.v.
CLEMENTS, James. Private, 1st Maryland Line, enlisted Feb. 28, 1777 and discharged Feb. 28, 1780 [Ref: D-91].
CLEMENTS, John. Private, Militia, 26th Battalion, Capt. Hezekiah Garner's Company, 1777 [Ref: M-163]. Private, 1st Maryland Line, enlisted Feb. 21, 1777 and discharged Feb. 22, 1780 [Ref: D-91]. Private, drafted from the Charles County militia on July 27, 1781 [Ref: D-377, G-569]. One or more men by this name rendered patriotic service by providing wheat for the use of the military in May, August, and September 1782 [Ref: N-511, N-539, N-552]. One John Clements was aged about 44 as noted in a 1778 deposition and another John Clements was aged about 25 as noted in a 1774 deposition [Ref: CC-703, DD-701]. John Clements, Sr., and John Clements II both took the Oath of Allegiance in 1778 [Ref: L-15]. However, John Clements and John Clements, Sr., appear on the original lists, not John Clements II [Ref: AA-641]. In 1778 one John Clements was a resident of Port Tobacco West Hundred, another John Clements was a resident of Port Tobacco Town Hundred, and John Clements, Sr., was a resident of Port Tobacco Upper Hundred [Ref: Q-I:297]. Additional research may be necessary before drawing conclusions. Also see "Edward Miles," q.v.
CLEMENTS, John Sr. See "John Clements," q.v.
CLEMENTS, John, of Francis. Rendered patriotic service by providing clothing for the use of the military in February 1778 [Ref: Y-II:234]. Took the Oath of Allegiance in 1778 [Ref: AA-641, L-15, which latter source

mistakenly listed the name as "John Francis Cleamons"]. Resident of Port Tobacco Upper Hundred in 1778 [Ref: Q-I:297]. Rendered patriotic service by providing wheat for the use of the military in April 1783 [Ref: N-594, which listed the name as "John Clemments, of Francis"].

CLEMENTS, John, of Jacob. Private, Militia, 26th Battalion, Capt. Richard Bennett Mitchell's Company, 1777, and listed as an invalid (disabled) soldier [Ref: M-164, and X-82, which listed the name as "John Clements, of Jack"]. Took the Oath of Allegiance in 1778 [Ref: AA-641, which listed the name as "John Clements, of Jacob"].

CLEMENTS, John, of John. Private, Militia, 26th Battalion, Capt. Samuel Smallwood's Company, 1777 [Ref: M-165]. Took the Oath of Allegiance in 1778 [Ref: L-15]. Resident of Port Tobacco Upper Hundred in 1778 [Ref: Q-I:297].

CLEMENTS, John, of Joseph. Private, Militia, 26th Battalion, Capt. Richard Bennett Mitchell's Company, 1777 [Ref: M-164]. Took the Oath of Allegiance in 1778 [Ref: L-15, AA-641].

CLEMENTS, John, of Joshua. Took the Oath of Allegiance in 1778 [Ref: L-15].

CLEMENTS, John, of William. Private, Militia, 26th Battalion, Capt. William McPherson's Company, 1777 [Ref: M-163]. Took the Oath of Allegiance in 1778 [Ref: L-15].

CLEMENTS, John Adler. Took the Oath of Allegiance in 1778 [Ref: AA-641, L-15, which latter source listed the name as "John Adles Clements"]. "John A. Clements" was a private in the militia, 26th Battalion, Capt. Robert Sinnett's Company, 1777 [Ref: M-164]. Resident of Port Tobacco West Hundred in 1778 [Ref: Q-I:297].

CLEMENTS, John Adlow, of Joseph. Private, 1st Maryland Line, enrolled in the place of Bayne Smallwood around Aug. 11, 1776 [Ref: D-31].

CLEMENTS, John Ensy. Private, 1st Maryland Line, drafted from the Charles County militia and in service on June 11 or 12, 1781 [Ref: D-376].

CLEMENTS, Joseph. Took the Oath of Allegiance in 1778 [Ref: L-15, AA-641]. Resident of Port Tobacco West Hundred in 1778 [Ref: Q-I:297].

CLEMENTS, Justinian, of Francis. Took the Oath of Allegiance in 1778 [Ref: L-15].

CLEMENTS, Leonard. Private, Militia, 26th Battalion, Capt. Richard Bennett Mitchell's Company, 1777; listed as an invalid (disabled) soldier [Ref: M-165]. Resident of Port Tobacco West Hundred in 1778 [Ref: Q-I:297].

CLEMENTS, Leonard (1719-   ). Took the Oath of Allegiance in 1778 [Ref: L-15]. Rendered patriotic service by providing wheat for the use of the military in September 1782 [Ref: N-548]. Aged 56 as noted in a 1775 deposition [Ref: DD-701]. Resident of Pomonkey Hundred in 1778 [Ref: Q-I:297].

CLEMENTS, Mark. Private, 3rd Maryland Line, enlisted March 16, 1778 and reported missing after the Battle of Camden in South Carolina on Aug. 16, 1780 [Ref: D-97].

CLEMENTS, Mary Ann. See "Archibald Johnson," q.v.

CLEMENTS, Priscilla. See "Edward Miles," q.v.

CLEMENTS, Ralph (1754-   ). Private, enrolled in Prince George's County, Lower Battalion, 1776 [Ref: D-35]. Aged 20 as noted in a 1774 deposition in Charles County [Ref: DD-701].

CLEMENTS, Samuel. Memorialist and Militiaman, Pomonkey Company, after March 6, 1776 [Ref: M-158, Y-II:26]. Private, Militia, 26th Battalion, Capt. Thomas H. Marshall's Company, 1777 [Ref: M-163]. Took the Oath of Allegiance in 1778 [Ref: L-15, AA-641]. Resident of Pomonkey Hundred in 1778 [Ref: Q-I:297].

CLEMENTS, Thomas. Rendered patriotic service by providing clothing for the use of the military in February 1778 [Ref: Y-II:234]. Took the Oath of Allegiance in 1778 [Ref: L-15, AA-641]. Rendered patriotic service by providing wheat for the use of the military in December 1781, and September and October 1782 [Ref: N-461, N-546, N-559]. Resident of Port Tobacco Upper Hundred in 1778 [Ref: Q-I:297].

CLEMENTS, Walter. Private, Militia, 26th Battalion, Capt. Richard Bennett Mitchell's Company, 1777; listed as an invalid (disabled) soldier [Ref: M-165]. Took the Oath of Allegiance in 1778 [Ref: L-15]. Rendered patriotic service by providing wheat for the use of the military in April 1783 [Ref: N-593]. Resident of Port Tobacco West Hundred in 1778 [Ref: Q-I:297].

CLEMENTS, Walter, of Jacob. Private, Militia, 26th Battalion, Capt. Richard Bennett Mitchell's Company, 1777; listed as an invalid (disabled) soldier [Ref: M-164]. Took the Oath of Allegiance in 1778 [Ref: L-15]. Resident of Port Tobacco West Hundred in 1778 [Ref: Q-I:297].

CLEMENTS, Walter, of Walter. Took the Oath of Allegiance in August 1778 [Ref: AA-707]. Resident of Pomonkey Hundred in 1778 [Ref: Q-I:297].

CLEMENTS, William. Private, 1st Maryland Line, enlisted Sept. 11, 1779, and in Capt. Edward Prall's Company by Jan. 1, 1782; discharged on July 31, 1783 [Ref: D-92, D-432, D-528]. One "W. Clements" took the Oath of Allegiance in 1778 [Ref: AA-641].

CLEMENTS, William (1709-   ). Took the Oath of Allegiance in 1778 [Ref: L-15, AA-641]. Aged 64 as noted in a 1773 deposition which mentioned his father Edward Clements [Ref: DD-701]. Resident of Port Tobacco East Hundred in 1778 [Ref: Q-I:297].

CLERK, James. See "Philip Thomas Lee," q.v.

CLERKE, Elias. See "Elias Clarke," q.v.

CLINKSCALES, Adam. Private, Militia, 26th Battalion, Capt. Hezekiah Garner's Company, 1777 [Ref: M-162].

CLINKSCALES, Adam (1729-   ). Took the Oath of Allegiance in 1778 [Ref: AA-641]. Aged 43 as noted in a 1772 deposition [Ref: DD-701, which listed the name as "Clinksales"].

CLINKSCALES, Francis (c1739-1837). Sergeant, Militia, 26th Battalion, Capt. Hezekiah Garner's Company, 1777 [Ref: M-162]. Took the Oath of Allegiance in 1778 [Ref: AA-641]. He married first to Mary Franklin, second to Mary Carpenter, and migrated to South Carolina where he died in October 1837 [Ref: J-I:597].

CLINKSCALES, Ignatius. Private, Militia, 26th Battalion, Capt. Hezekiah Garner's Company, 1777 [Ref: M-162].

CLINKSCALES, John. Private, Militia, Capt. Francis Mastin's Company, 26th Battalion, March 19, 1776 [Ref: M-158, K-1814].

CLINKSCALES, Levi. Private, 1st Maryland Line, drafted from the Charles County militia and in service on June 11 or 12, 1781 [Ref: D-376, D-407, which latter source listed the name as "Levy Clinckscales, voucher lost"].

CLINKSCALES, Richard. Private, 1st Maryland Line, enrolled and passed on July 27, 1776 [Ref: D-31, which listed the name as "Clinscales (Clinkscales)"]. Private, Militia, 26th Battalion, Capt. Hezekiah Garner's Company, 1777 [Ref: M-162]. Took the Oath of Allegiance in 1778 [Ref: AA-641].

CLINKSCALES, William (1760-1845). Private, Militia, 26th Battalion, Capt. Hezekiah Garner's Company, 1777 [Ref: M-162]. Private, 1st Maryland Line, drafted from the Charles County militia on July 27, 1781 [Ref: G-569, D-377, D-407, which latter source listed the name as "Clinckscales"]. He was born on Jan. 10, 1760, married Nancy Colbert, and migrated to Missouri where he died on Sept. 11, 1845 [Ref: J-I:597].

CLUB, Sarah. See "George Walls," q.v.

COATS, Benjamin. Took the Oath of Allegiance in 1778 [Ref: L-15, AA-641].

COATS, Caleb. Took the Oath of Allegiance in 1778 [Ref: L-15].

COATS, Charles. Took the Oath of Allegiance in 1778 [Ref: AA-641].

COATS, Mary. See "Zephaniah Swann," q.v.

COE, Marsilva. See "Bayne Smallwood," q.v.

COFFER, Benedicta. See "Thomas Hudson," q.v.

COFFER, Francis. Private (substitute for 3 years), 1st Maryland Line, by Sept. 11, 1778 [Ref: D-330].
COFFER, Jeremiah (alias Douglass). Took the Oath of Allegiance in 1778 [Ref: AA-641].
COHOE, Ignatius. See "Ignatius Cahoe," q.v.
COLBERT, John. Took the Oath of Allegiance in 1778 [Ref: L-15, AA-641].
COLBERT, Nancy. See "William Clinkscales," q.v.
COLE, Sarah. Rendered patriotic service by providing clothing for the use of the military in February 1778 [Ref: Y-II:234]. Rendered patriotic service by providing wheat for the use of the military in October 1782 [Ref: N-563].
COLEMAN, Benjamin Notley. Took the Oath of Allegiance in 1778 [Ref: AA-641, L-15, which latter source listed the name as "Colemen"].
COLEY, James. Private, Militia, 26th Battalion, Capt. William McPherson's Company, 1777 [Ref: M-163, which listed the name as "Calary" and X-74, which listed the name as "Colay"]. Private (furnished by class for 9 months), 1st Maryland Line, by Sept. 11, 1778 [Ref: D-330, which listed the name as "Coley"]. Resident of Port Tobacco West Hundred in 1778 [Ref: Q-I:297].
COLEY, James. Took the Oath of Allegiance in 1778 [Ref: L-15, which listed the name as "Colley"]. Resident of Durham Lower Hundred in 1778 [Ref: Q-I:297, which listed the name as "Colly"].
COLEY, Joseph. Private (furnished by class for 9 months), 1st Maryland Line, by Sept. 11, 1778 [Ref: D-330].
COLEY, Robert. Private (substitute for 9 months), 1st Maryland Line, by Sept. 11, 1778 [Ref: D-330]. Resident of Pomonkey Hundred in 1778 [Ref: Q-I:297, which listed the name as "Coly"].
COLLINS, Carolyn Huebner. See "John Baptist Wathen," q.v.
COLLINS, William. Took the Oath of Allegiance in 1778 [Ref: L-15]. Resident of Durham Lower Hundred in 1778 [Ref: Q-I:297].
COLTART, Antipas. Private, 1st Maryland Line, enrolled and passed on July 25, 1776 [Ref: D-32].
COMBS, Richard. Rendered patriotic service by providing wheat for the use of the military in July 1782 [Ref: N-533].
COMBS, William. See "William Coomes," q.v.
COMPTON, Alexander. See "John Compton," q.v.
COMPTON, Edmund Howard (1759-1838). "Edmund or Edmond Compton" was a lieutenant, 1st Maryland Line, 1781, and 4th Maryland Line, 1782 [Ref: D-356, D-460]. "Edmund H. Compton" was born on June 10, 1759, married first to Susannah ----, married second to Sarah (Foster) Read, served as a lieutenant in the Revolutionary War, and migrated to

Kentucky where he died on March 28, 1838 [Ref: J-I:634]. Edmund Howard Compton, son of Matthew Compton and Rachel Howard, was born on June 11, 1759 [Ref: HH-1997, citing the Compton Bible record copy at the Maryland Historical Society].

COMPTON, Eleanor. See "John Compton," q.v.

COMPTON, John (1747-1803). Born on Feb. 28, 1747 in Charles County, a son of Matthew Compton and Rachel Howard, he married Elizabeth Briscoe (1751-1790) on Feb. 12, 1771 in St. Mary's County and had these children (born in Virginia): Philip Briscoe Compton (1772-1830, married Margaret Briscoe), Eleanor Williamson Compton (1774-1851, married Jeremiah Crabb), Alexander Compton (1777-1796), John Compton, Jr. (1779-1855), Leonard Briscoe Compton (1781-1841), and Samuel Compton (1789-1826). John was a major in the Fling Camp, migrated to Virginia and then by 1800 to Jefferson County, Kentucky where he died on Jan. 10, 1803 [Ref: Information compiled in 1997 by Richard D. Prall of Albuquerque, New Mexico and Sarah R. Browder of The Woodlands, Texas]. See "William Stephen Compton," q.v.

COMPTON, John Wilson. Private, Militia, 12th Battalion, Capt. John Parnham's Company, 1777 [Ref: M-161, which listed the name as "Comton"]. Took the Oath of Allegiance in 1778 [Ref: L-15]. Resident of Newport East Hundred in 1778 [Ref: Q-I:297].

COMPTON, Leonard. See "John Compton," q.v.

COMPTON, Margaret. See "Edward Wilder," q.v.

COMPTON, Matthew. See "William Compton" and "John Compton" and "Edmund Howard Compton," q.v.

COMPTON, Philip. See "John Compton," q.v.

COMPTON, Samuel. See "John Compton," q.v.

COMPTON, Stephen (1735-1785). Private, Militia, 12th Battalion, Capt. Jonathan Yates' Company, 1777 [Ref: X-70, but was omitted from the list in Reference M-162]. Rendered patriotic service by providing clothing for the use of the military in February 1778 [Ref: Y-II:234]. Took the Oath of Allegiance in 1778 [Ref: L-15, AA-641]. Rendered patriotic service by providing wheat for the use of the military in December 1782 [Ref: N-577]. Resident of William & Mary Lower Hundred in 1778 [Ref: Q-I:297]. Born on Dec. 26, 1735 and died in 1785 [Ref: HH-1997, citing the Compton Bible record copy at the Maryland Historical Society].

COMPTON, Susannah. See "Edmund H. Compton," q.v.

COMPTON, William. Private, Militia, 12th Battalion, Capt. Jonathan Yates' Company, 1777 [Ref: M-162]. Took the Oath of Allegiance in 1778 [Ref: L-15]. See the other "William Compton," q.v.

COMPTON, William. Private, Militia, 12th Battalion, Capt. John Parnham's Company, 1777 [Ref: M-160, which listed the name as "Comton"]. Rendered patriotic service by providing wheat for the use of the military in July 1781 [Ref: N-408]. One William Compton was aged 22 as noted in a January 1755 deposition which mentioned his grandfather Matthew Compton [Ref: DD-702]. Resident of Newport East Hundred in 1778 [Ref: Q-I:297].
COMPTON, William Stephen (1758-   ). Born on September 7, 1758, son of John Compton [Ref: HH-1997, citing the Compton file at the Maryland Historical Society]. Private, 1st Maryland Line, enrolled and passed on July 8, 1776 [Ref: D-32]. Took the Oath of Allegiance in 1778 [Ref: L-15, AA-641]. Resident of William & Mary Lower Hundred in 1778 [Ref: Q-I:297].
COMSACH, George. Took the Oath of Allegiance in 1778 [Ref: L-15].
CONAWAY, John. Memorialist and Militiaman, Pomonkey Company, after March 6, 1776 [Ref: M-158, Y-II:26]. Took the Oath of Allegiance in 1778 [Ref: AA-641, L-15, which latter source listed the name as "Conoway"]. Resident of Pomonkey Hundred in 1778 [Ref: Q-I:297].
CONNELLY, Benjamin. Private, 1st Maryland Line, killed in Gates' defeat at the Battle of Camden, South Carolina on Aug. 16, 1780, leaving no issue. His brother John Connelly (1762-1849), of Prince George's County, Maryland, also served in the Maryland Line and subsequently migrated to Boone County, Missouri [Ref: V-I:736, U-33:2 (1945), p. 60].
CONNELLY, John. See "Benjamin Connelly," q.v.
CONNER, Owen. Private, Militia, 26th Battalion, Capt. Thomas H. Marshall's Company, 1777 [Ref: M-163]. Took the Oath of Allegiance in 1778 [Ref: AA-641]. Resident of Pomonkey Hundred in 1778 [Ref: Q-I:297, which listed the name as "Owing Coner"].
CONNER, William. Private, 3rd Maryland Line, 1780, enrolled in Charles County for Capt. Joseph Marbury's Company [Ref: D-333].
CONTEE, Benjamin. See "Philip Thomas Lee," q.v.
CONWAY, Robert. Captain (Commander or Master) of the sloop *Molly* from 1776 to May 15, 1778 [Ref: A-245, D-607, E-84]. On Aug. 28, 1776 the Maryland Council of Safety sent word to the Committee of Charles County that "Captain Conway is just ready to sail and wants one hundred and fifty pounds of Cannon Powder -- be pleased to let him have it, and we will cause it to be replaced." [Ref: B-248]. See "Robert Townsend Hooe," q.v.
COOK, Richard. Took the Oath of Allegiance in 1778 [Ref: L-15].

COOKSEY, Andrew. Private, Militia, 12th Battalion, Capt. John Thomas' Company, 1777 [Ref: M-161]. Took the Oath of Allegiance in 1778 [Ref: AA-641]. Resident of Bryan Town Hundred in 1778 [Ref: Q-I:297].

COOKSEY, Elizabeth. See "Henry Cooksey," q.v.

COOKSEY, Henry (1758-   ). Born on June 8, 1758, a son of Thomas Reed and Elizabeth Cooksey [Ref: EE-8]. Private, Militia, 12th Battalion, Capt. Benjamin Lusby Corry's Company, 1777 [Ref: M-160]. Took the Oath of Allegiance in 1778 [Ref: L-15]. Resident of Newport West Hundred in 1778 [Ref: Q-I:297].

COOKSEY, Hezekiah (c1750-c1820). Private, 1st Maryland Line, enrolled and passed on July 8, 1776 [Ref: D-32]. Private, Militia, 12th Battalion, Capt. Benjamin Lusby Corry's Company, 1777 [Ref: M-160]. Resident of Newport West Hundred in 1778 [Ref: Q-I:297]. Hezekiah Cooksey married second to Elizabeth Grey (first wife's name not known) and migrated to Georgia where he died after 1820 [Ref: J-I:654].

COOKSEY, John (1738-1811). "John Cooksey" was born on March 21, 1738, the son of Justinian and Sarah Cooksey [Ref: EE-4]. Took the Oath of Allegiance in 1778 [Ref: L-15]. Resident of Newport West Hundred in 1778 [Ref: Q-I:297]. "John Baptist Cooksey" was born circa 1740 in Maryland, married Mary ----, and died in Virginia before Jan. 8, 1811 [Ref: J-I:654]. "John Cooksey" was a private in the 2nd Maryland Line from May 8, 1777 until discharged on Jan. 10, 1780 [Ref: D-92].

COOKSEY, Jonathan. Private, Militia, 12th Battalion, Capt. John Thomas' Company, 1777 [Ref: M-161]. Took the Oath of Allegiance in 1778 [Ref: AA-641]. Resident of Benedict Hundred in 1778 [Ref: Q-I:297].

COOKSEY, Justinian (1731-   ). Born on May 8, 1731, son of Justinian and Sarah Cooksey [Ref: EE-4]. Private, Militia, 12th Battalion, Capt. Benjamin Lusby Corry's Company, 1777 [Ref: M-160, which listed the name as "Jestn. Coosey"]. Took the Oath of Allegiance in 1778 [Ref: L-15, which listed the name as "Justinian Cooksey" and AA-641, which listed the name as "Just. S. Cooksey"]. Resident of Newport West Hundred in 1778 [Ref: Q-I:297]. See "John Cooksey," q.v.

COOKSEY, Ledstone Smallwood. Private, 1st Maryland Line, enrolled and passed on July 8, 1776 [Ref: D-32]. Private, Militia, 12th Battalion, Capt. Benjamin Lusby Corry's Company, 1777 [Ref: M-160, which listed the name as "... S Cooksey," and X-59, which listed the name as "Leor. S. Cooksey"]. Took the Oath of Allegiance in 1778 [Ref: L-15, which listed the name as "Leadson S. Cooksley" and AA-641, which listed the name as "Ledstone Sm. Cooksey"]. Resident of Newport West Hundred in 1778 [Ref: Q-I:297].

COOKSEY, Mary. See "John Cooksey," q.v.

COOKSEY, Philip Jr. Private, Militia, 12th Battalion, Capt. John Thomas' Company, 1777 [Ref: M-161]. Resident of Benedict Hundred in 1778 [Ref: Q-I:297].
COOKSEY, Philip Sr. Took the Oath of Allegiance in 1778 [Ref: AA-641]. Resident of Benedict Hundred in 1778 [Ref: Q-I:297].
COOKSEY, Sarah. See "Justinian Cooksey" and "John Cooksey," q.v.
COOKSEY, Thomas (c1745-c1794). He married Elizabeth McPherson, rendered patriotic service, and died before Dec. 30, 1794 [Ref: J-I:654]. See "Thomas R. Cooksey," q.v.
COOKSEY, Thomas R. "Thomas R. Cooksey" was a resident of Newport West Hundred in 1778 [Ref: Q-I:297]. "Thomas Richard Cooksey" took the Oath of Allegiance in 1778 [Ref: L-15]. "Thomas Reed Cooksey" married Elizabeth Matthews in Trinity Parish on March 12, 1757 [Ref: EE-8]. See "Henry Cooksey," q.v.
COOMES, John C. Private, 1st Maryland Line, enrolled and passed on July 25, 1776 [Ref: D-32].
COOMES, Joseph. Private, Militia, 26th Battalion, Capt. William McPherson's Company, 1777 [Ref: M-163]. Took the Oath of Allegiance in 1778 [Ref: L-15, AA-641]. Resident of Port Tobacco Upper Hundred in 1778 [Ref: Q-I:297].
COOMES, Nicholas. Private, Militia, 26th Battalion, Capt. William McPherson's Company, 1777 [Ref: M-163]. Private, 1st Maryland Line, enlisted Sept. 11, 1779 and still in service in November 1780 [Ref: D-92, which listed the name as "Coombs"].
COOMES, Richard. Sergeant, 3rd Maryland Line, enlisted May 10, 1777 and discharged in May 1780 [Ref: D-94].
COOMES, Walter. Private, 1st Maryland Line, enrolled and passed on July 25, 1776 [Ref: D-32].
COOMES, Wharton, of Thomas (1728-   ). Took the Oath of Allegiance in 1778 [Ref: AA-641, L-15]. Aged 35 as noted in a 1763 deposition [Ref: DD-702, which listed the name as "Thos. Wharton Combs"]. Resident of Port Tobacco Upper Hundred in 1778 [Ref: Q-I:297].
COOMES, William. Private (furnished by class for 9 months), 1st Maryland Line, enlisted June 6, 1778 and discharged April 5, 1779 [Ref: D-91, which listed the name as "Coombs" and D-330, which listed the name as "Coombes"]. Private, 1st Maryland Line, who was drafted from the Charles County militia on July 27, 1781 [Ref: D-377, G-569, which listed the name as "Coombe"]. Substitute determined unfit for service and was discharged on Oct. 30, 1781 [Ref: G-657, which listed the name as "Combs"]. Some of this information may pertain to "William Coomes, Jr.," q.v. Additional research may be necessary before drawing conclusions.

COOMES, William Jr. Took the Oath of Allegiance in 1778 [Ref: L-15, AA-641]. Rendered patriotic service by providing wheat for the use of the military in October 1781 [Ref: N-449]. Resident of Port Tobacco East Hundred in 1778 [Ref: Q-I:297].
COOMES, William Sr. (1700-   ). Took the Oath of Allegiance in 1778 [Ref: L-15, AA-641]. Aged 62 as noted in a 1762 deposition [Ref: DD-702, which listed the name as "Combs"]. Resident of Port Tobacco East Hundred in 1778 [Ref: Q-I:297].
COOMES, William, of Joseph. Private, Militia, 26th Battalion, Capt. William McPherson's Company, 1777 [Ref: M-163]. Took the Oath of Allegiance in 1778 [Ref: L-15, AA-641]. Resident of Port Tobacco Upper Hundred in 1778 [Ref: Q-I:297].
COOPER, John. Private, Militia, 26th Battalion, Capt. William Winter's Company, 1777 [Ref: M-165]. Resident of Durham Lower Hundred in 1778 [Ref: Q-I:297].
CORBET, Eliza. See "Jacob Corbet," q.v.
CORBET, Jacob (1758-1842). Private, 1st Maryland Line, enlisted at Port Tobacco on March 2, 1777, served under Capt. John Stone, and was discharged on March 2, 1780 [Ref: D-91, which listed the name as "Corbett"]. He applied for and received a pension (S35852) in Washington County, Kentucky on Sept. 25, 1826, aged 68, with a wife (no name given) aged 59 and these children: Mary Corbet (aged 21 in March 1826), Julia Ann Corbet (aged 29 in June 1826), James Corbet (aged 17 in April 1826), and Eliza Corbet (aged 12 in February 1826). Jacob Corbet died on June 15, 1842 and on March 22, 1844 his children applied for any balance due from his pension [Ref: T-56, V-I:764].
CORBET, James. See "Jacob Corbet," q.v.
CORBET, John. Private, Militia, 12th Battalion, Capt. John Hanson's Company, 1777 [Ref: M-159]. Resident of Port Tobacco East Hundred in 1778 [Ref: Q-I:297, which listed the name as "Corbut"].
CORBET, Julia Ann. See "Jacob Corbet," q.v.
CORBET, Mary. See "Jacob Corbet," q.v.
CORBETT, Patrick. Private, 1st Maryland Line, enlisted March 13, 1778 and reportedly "deserted" on Feb. 25, 1779 [Ref: D-91].
CORNISH, John. See "Henry Woodward," q.v.
CORRY, Benjamin Lusby (deceased by June 1779). First Lieutenant, Militia, 12th Battalion, July 5, 1777 [Ref: M-65, which listed the name as "Benjamin Lesly Corry"]. Took the Oath of Allegiance in 1778 [Ref: L-15, AA-641, which listed the name as "Benjamin Lesly Corry"]. Captain, Militia, 12th Battalion, 1777 [Ref: M-160, which listed the name as "Benj. Lusby Curry"]. He is listed as "Benjamin Lusby Corry" in a land

transaction in Charles County in 1772 [Ref: Harry Wright Newman's *Charles County Gentry*, p. 140].

CORRY, Margaret. See "Belain Posey," q.v.

COTTON, Sarah. See "Hezekiah Murphy," q.v.

COTTRELL, Benjamin. Took the Oath of Allegiance in 1778 [Ref: AA-641]. Resident of William & Mary Upper Hundred in 1778 [Ref: Q-I:297].

COTTRELL, Burford. Second Lieutenant, Militia, 12th Battalion, Capt. Benjamin Philpott's Company, Feb. 26, 1776 [Ref: M-65, A-186, A-206, Y-II:23]. Took the Oath of Allegiance in 1778 [Ref: AA-641, L-15, which latter source listed the name as "Cottell"]. Resident of William & Mary Lower Hundred in 1778 [Ref: Q-I:297, which listed the name as "Cattrell"]. See "John Warren," q.v.

COTTRELL, James. Rendered patriotic service by providing clothing for the use of the military in February 1778 [Ref: Y-II:234]. Took the Oath of Allegiance in 1778 [Ref: AA-641]. Resident of William & Mary Upper Hundred in 1778 [Ref: Q-I:297].

COTTRELL, Thomas. Took the Oath of Allegiance in 1778 [Ref: AA-641]. Resident of William & Mary Upper Hundred in 1778 [Ref: Q-I:297]. Gave a deposition in 1781 pertaining to his inability to perform military service due to family obligations and poor health [Ref: Z-208].

COURTS, Charity. See "Zachariah Chunn," q.v.

COURTS, Elizabeth. See "William Courts," q.v.

COURTS, John. Private, 3rd Maryland Line, enrolled by Capt. Joseph Marbury by May 24, 1780 [Ref: F-181].

COURTS, Richard Hendley. First Lieutenant, Militia, Charles County, Feb. 26, 1776 [Ref: Y-II:23]. Took the Oath of Allegiance in 1778 [Ref: AA-641, which listed the name as "R. H. Courts"]. Resident of Newport East Hundred in 1778 [Ref: Q-I:297]. First Lieutenant, Militia, Montgomery County, Jan. 24, 1779 [Ref: M-65, A-206].

COURTS, Robert Hendley (1733-1778). "Robert Courts" took the Oath of Allegiance in 1778 [Ref: L-15, which mistakenly listed the name as "Counts"]. "Robert Henley Courts" was aged 14 as noted in 1747 when he chose William Courts as his guardian [Ref: DD-702]. "Robert Hendly Court" was deceased by September 1778 (date of account). [Ref: GG-232].

COURTS, William. Son of William Courts (died in 1758) and wife Elizabeth Courts, he also had a wife Elizabeth and a son William (plus a daughter, name not known). Took the Oath of Allegiance in 1778 [Ref: L-15, AA-641]. Rendered patriotic service by providing wheat for the use of the military in December 1782 and May 1783 [Ref: N-577, N-599]. Served in the Lower House of the Maryland Legislature, 1782-1783. Died on Sept. 28, 1792 [Ref: P-I:238]. See "Robert Courts," q.v.

COUSIN, N. P. See "John Hoskins Stone," q.v.
COWARD, Benjamin Jr. Took the Oath of Allegiance in 1778 [Ref: L-15].
COWLEY, James. Took the Oath of Allegiance in 1778 [Ref: L-15].
COWLEY, Robert. Private, Militia, 12th Battalion, Capt. Peter Wood's Company, 1777 [Ref: M-161]. Took the Oath of Allegiance in 1778 [Ref: L-15].
COX, Abram. Took the Oath of Allegiance in 1778 [Ref: L-15].
COX, Ann. See "Thomas Hussey Luckett" and "Marcus Latimer," q.v.
COX, Benjamin. Private, 1st Maryland Line, enrolled and passed on July 8, 1776 [Ref: D-32]. Took the Oath of Allegiance in 1778 [Ref: L-15]. Resident of Port Tobacco Town Hundred in 1778 [Ref: Q-I:297].
COX, Francis. Private, Militia, 12th Battalion, Capt. Walter Hanson's Company, 1777 [Ref: M-159].
COX, Hugh. Private, Militia, 12th Battalion, Capt. Walter Hanson's Company, 1777 [Ref: M-159]. Resident of Port Tobacco East Hundred in 1778 [Ref: Q-I:297]. See "Thomas Pickerel," q.v.
COX, James. Private, 1st Maryland Line, enrolled and passed on July 8, 1776 [Ref: D-32].
COX, John (1726-   ). Rendered patriotic service by providing wheat for the use of the military in November 1782 [Ref: N-564, which listed the name as "Cocks"]. Aged 49 as noted in a 1775 deposition [Ref: DD-703]. Resident of Port Tobacco Upper Hundred in 1778 [Ref: Q-I:297].
COX, John. Private, Militia, 12th Battalion, Capt. Walter Hanson's Company, 1777 [Ref: M-159]. Took the Oath of Allegiance in 1778 [Ref: AA-641]. See "John Cocks," q.v.
COX, John. Private, Militia, 26th Battalion, Capt. William McPherson's Company, 1777 [Ref: M-163]. Took the Oath of Allegiance in 1778 [Ref: AA-641, L-15]. See "Thomas Pickerel," q.v.
COX, John Jr. Took the Oath of Allegiance in 1778 [Ref: AA-641]. Resident of William & Mary Upper Hundred in 1778 [Ref: Q-I:297].
COX, Richard ("talor"). Took the Oath of Allegiance in 1778 [Ref: AA-641].
COX, Richard. Private, Militia, 26th Battalion, Capt. Thomas H. Marshall's Company [Ref: M-163]. Took the Oath of Allegiance in 1778 [Ref: AA-641]. Resident of Port Tobacco East Hundred in 1778 [Ref: Q-I:297].
COX, Richard. Private, Militia, 12th Battalion, Capt. Walter Hanson's Company, 1777 [Ref: M-159]. Took the Oath of Allegiance in 1778 [Ref: L-15, AA-641]. Resident of Pomonkey Hundred in 1778 [Ref: Q-I:297].
COX, Samuel. Private, Militia, 12th Battalion, Capt. Walter Hanson's Company, 1777 [Ref: M-159]. Took the Oath of Allegiance in 1778 [Ref: AA-641].

67

COX, Thomas. Took the Oath of Allegiance in 1778 [Ref: L-15]. Rendered patriotic service by providing wheat for the use of the military in April 1783 [Ref: N-593].
COX, William. Private, 1st Maryland Line, enrolled and passed on July 19, 1776 [Ref: D-31]. Private, Militia, 26th Battalion, Capt. William McPherson's Company, 1777 [Ref: M-163]. Resident of Port Tobacco Town Hundred in 1778 [Ref: Q-I:297].
COX, William. Private, Militia, 12th Battalion, Capt. Walter Hanson's Company, 1777 [Ref: M-159]. Took the Oath of Allegiance in 1778 [Ref: L-15, AA-641]. Resident of Port Tobacco East Hundred in 1778 [Ref: Q-I:297].
COX, William, of Abram. Took the Oath of Allegiance in 1778 [Ref: L-15].
CRABB, Jeremiah. See "John Compton," q.v.
CRACKLES, Thomas. Took the Oath of Allegiance in 1778 [Ref: AA-641, L-15, which latter source misspelled the name as "Crockett"]. Resident of Port Tobacco Town Hundred in 1778 [Ref: Q-I:297]. He was accused, but not officially charged, of concealing his horses from Daniel Jenifer, Contractor of Horses for Charles County, in June 1781 [Ref: H-324, which listed the name as "Crackels"].
CRAGAIN (CREGAN), Dennis. Private (substitute during the war), 1st Maryland Line, enlisted May 14, 1778; transferred to invalids corps on April 26, 1780, but later returned to the 1st Maryland Regiment on July 14, 1781; discharged on Sept. 18, 1783 [Ref: D-92, D-330, D-529].
CRAIG, John (of Dorchester County). Took the Oath of Allegiance in February 1778 in Charles County [Ref: AA-620].
CRAIK, James (1730-1814). Physician, graduated from the University of Edinburgh, emigrated to America from Scotland, accompanied George Washington on an expedition against the French and Indians in 1754, and was with Edward Braddock in 1755. He was Director General of the hospital at the siege of Yorktown in 1781. After the Revolutionary War he was invited by Washington to settle near Mount Vernon. He served as Washington's physician and died in Fairfax County, Virginia on Feb. 6, 1814. His wife was Marianne Ewell (1739-1815) and a son William Craik was born on Oct. 3, 1761 in Charles County, married Hannah Hall on Nov. 9, 1796 in Allegany County, and died prior to 1814. William Craik served in the Lower House of the Maryland Legislature, 1789-1792, and served on the Constitution Ratification Committee in 1788. He was Chief Justice of the Fifth Judicial District of Maryland, 1793-1796, 1801-1802, and a United States Congressman, 1796-1799 [Ref: P-I:242, J-I:694].
CRAIK, William. See "James Craik," q.v.

CRAIN, Elizabeth. Rendered patriotic service by providing clothing for the use of the military in February 1778 [Ref: Y-II:234].

CRAIN, Peter W. See "Lawrence Simpson," q.v.

CRAWFORD, Nehemiah (1760-   ). Private, Virginia Line, who was placed on the pension rolls of Charles County, Maryland as of May 16, 1822, retroactive to March 16, 1820 [Ref: R-33]. He applied for a federal pension (S34718) on March 31, 1820, stating he was "aged about 60" and enlisted in Charles County, Maryland, serving in the Maryland Line [Ref: V-I:810]. He was a sergeant in Col. Grayson's Regiment and on Oct. 6, 1783 received depreciation pay through March 10, 1780 [Ref: D-603].

CRAYCROFT, Charity. Rendered patriotic service by providing wheat for the use of the military in May 1783 [Ref: N-597, which listed the name as "Craycraft"].

CRAYCROFT, Clement. Private, Militia, 12th Battalion, Capt. Jonathan Yates' Company, 1777 [Ref: M-162]. Took the Oath of Allegiance in 1778 [Ref: L-15, AA-641]. Resident of William & Mary Lower Hundred in 1778 [Ref: Q-I:297].

CRAYCROFT, Nicholas (1736-   ). Private, Militia, 26th Battalion, Capt. Robert Sinnett's Company, 1777 [Ref: M-164]. Took the Oath of Allegiance in 1778 [Ref: L-15, AA-641]. Aged about 42 as noted in a 1778 deposition [Ref: CC-703, DD-703]. Resident of Port Tobacco West Hundred in 1778 [Ref: Q-I:297, which misspelled the name as "Crancroft"].

CRAYCROFT, Thomas. Sergeant, Militia, 26th Battalion, Capt. Thomas H. Marshall's Company, 1777 [Ref: M-163]. Took the Oath of Allegiance in 1778 [Ref: L-15]. Resident of Pomonkey Hundred in 1778 [Ref: Q-I:297]. Constable, 1778 [Ref: CC-709]. Rendered patriotic service by providing wheat for the use of the military in April 1782 [Ref: N-498].

CRISMAND, Aaron, et al. See "Aaron Chrismond," q.v.

CROMILL, William. Private, Militia, 26th Battalion, Capt. Thomas H. Marshall's Company, 1777 [Ref: M-163, and X-76, which listed the name as "Cromell"].

CROSS, John. Took the Oath of Allegiance in 1778 [Ref: L-15, AA-641].

CROWN, Samuel. Private, Militia, 26th Battalion, Capt. Thomas H. Marshall's Company, 1777 [Ref: M-163]. Took the Oath of Allegiance in 1778 [Ref: L-15]. Resident of Pomonkey Hundred in 1778 [Ref: Q-I:297].

CURNIGAN, Lewis. Took the Oath of Allegiance in 1778 [Ref: AA-641].

CURRY, Benjamin Lesly. See "Benjamin Lusby Corry," q.v.

CURTAIN, Anthony. See "Anthony Kearton," q.v.

CURTAIN, Dennis. Private, Militia, 26th Battalion, Capt. Samuel Smallwood's Company, 1777 [Ref: M-165]. Resident of Port Tobacco East Hundred in 1778 [Ref: Q-I:297].
CURTAIN, Edward. Private, Militia, 26th Battalion, Capt. Thomas H. Marshall's Company, 1777 [Ref: M-163].
CURTAIN, William. Private, Militia, 26th Battalion, Capt. Thomas H. Marshall's Company, 1777 [Ref: M-163].
CUSICK, Ignatius. See "Ignatius Chusick," q.v.
CUTTS, Charles. Private, Militia, 12th Battalion, Capt. Jonathan Yates' Company, 1777 [Ref: M-162].
DADE, Behethland. See "Justinian Burch," q.v.
DAILY, John. Took the Oath of Allegiance in 1778 [Ref: L-15, which listed the name as "Daly"]. Resident of Port Tobacco East Hundred in 1778 [Ref: Q-I:297].
DAILY, Samuel. Private, 1st Maryland Line, enrolled and passed on July 18, 1776 [Ref: D-32].
DAILY, Thomas. Took the Oath of Allegiance in 1778 [Ref: L-15, AA-641, which latter source listed the name as "Dailey"].
DALRIMPLE, George. Took the Oath of Allegiance in 1778 [Ref: L-15, which listed the name as "Dalrymple"]. Resident of Durham Lower Hundred in 1778 [Ref: Q-I:297].
DANFORD, Sarah. See "Cornelius Bryan," q.v.
DANIEL, John Moncure. See "Thomas Stone," q.v.
DANIEL, Travers Jr. See "Thomas Stone," q.v.
DARNALL, Benjamin. Private, Militia, 26th Battalion, Capt. Benjamin Cawood's Company, 1777 [Ref: M-162]. Resident of Bryan Town Hundred in 1778 [Ref: Q-I:297].
DARNALL, Benjamin, of William. Took the Oath of Allegiance in 1778 [Ref: AA-641, which listed the name as "Darnal"].
DARNALL, Samuel. Private, Militia, 26th Battalion, Capt. Benjamin Cawood's Company, 1777 [Ref: M-162]. Resident of Port Tobacco East Hundred in 1778 [Ref: Q-I:297, which listed the name as "Darnal"].
DARNALL, Thomas. See "Thomas Darnall, Jr.," q.v.
DARNALL, Thomas Jr. Private, Militia, 26th Battalion, Capt. Benjamin Cawood's Company, 1777 [Ref: M-162]. He was probably the son of Thomas Darnall who was aged about 60 as noted in a 1779 deposition [Ref: BB-480, DD-703]. "Thomas Darnal, Jr." and "Thomas Darnal, Sr." were residents of Port Tobacco East Hundred in 1778 [Ref: Q-I:297].
DATON, John Sr. Took the Oath of Allegiance in 1778 [Ref: L-15].
DAVIDSON, Mary. See "Henry Henley Chapman," q.v.
DAVIES, William. See "Samuel Wright," q.v.

DAVIS, Abraham. Took the Oath of Allegiance in 1778 [Ref: AA-641]. Resident of William & Mary Upper Hundred in 1778 [Ref: Q-I:297].
DAVIS, Ann. See "Samuel B. Davis" and "Cornelius Davis," q.v.
DAVIS, Aquilla. Corporal, Militia, 12th Battalion, Capt. Henry Clarkson's Company, 1777 [Ref: M-159, which listed the name as "Davies"].
DAVIS, Benjamin. Corporal, Militia, 12th Battalion, Capt. Henry Clarkson's Company, 1777 [Ref: M-159, which listed the name as "Davies"]. Rendered patriotic service by providing wheat for the use of the military in November 1782 [Ref: N-564].
DAVIS, Benjamin. Took the Oath of Allegiance in 1778 [Ref: AA-641]. Resident of Newport East Hundred in 1778 [Ref: Q-I:297]. See "Benjamin Davis, Jr.," q.v.
DAVIS, Benjamin Jr. (1758-   ). Born on April 13, 1758, son of Benjamin Davis and Mary Cawood, of Trinity Parish, who were married on May 26, 1757 [Ref: EE-14]. Took the Oath of Allegiance in 1778 [Ref: L-15, AA-641]. Resident of Newport East Hundred in 1778 [Ref: Q-I:297].
DAVIS, Benjamin, of Richard. Private, Militia, 26th Battalion, Capt. Robert Sinnett's Company, 1777 [Ref: M-164, which listed the name as "Benjamin Davies, of Richard"]. Took the Oath of Allegiance in 1778 [Ref: AA-641, which listed the name as "Benjamin Davis"].
DAVIS, Bennett. Private, Militia, 12th Battalion, Capt. Henry Clarkson's Company, 1777 [Ref: M-159, which listed the name as "Davies"].
DAVIS, Charity. See "Randolph Davis" and "George Davis," q.v.
DAVIS, Charles (1737-   ). Sergeant, Militia, 12th Battalion, Capt. Henry Clarkson's Company, 1777 [Ref: M-159, which listed the name as "Davies"]. Took the Oath of Allegiance in 1778 [Ref: AA-641]. Resident of Port Tobacco West Hundred in 1778 [Ref: Q-I:297]. Aged about 42 as noted in a 1779 deposition [Ref: BB-474, DD-703].
DAVIS, Charles. Private, Militia, 26th Battalion, Capt. Robert Sinnett's Company, 1777 [Ref: M-164, which listed the name as "Davies"]. Took the Oath of Allegiance in 1778 [Ref: L-15, which listed the name as "Davies"]. Resident of Newport East Hundred in 1778 [Ref: Q-I:297].
DAVIS, Cornelius (1744-   ). Born on Dec. 7, 1744, son of Luke Davis and Ann Hunt who were married on Feb. 26, 1737/8 in Trinity Parish [Ref: EE-5]. Private, 1st Maryland Line, raised from the militia in 1781 [Ref: D-407].
DAVIS, David (1712-   ). Took the Oath of Allegiance in 1778 [Ref: AA-641]. Aged 61 as noted in a 1773 deposition [Ref: DD-703]. Resident of Newport East Hundred in 1778 [Ref: Q-I:297].

DAVIS, David. Private, 1st Maryland Line, drafted from the Charles County militia to serve from July 27, 1781 to Dec. 10, 1781 and was discharged on April 6, 1782 [Ref: D-377, G-569, I-123].

DAVIS, Eanus. Private (drafted and joined the army), 1st Maryland Line, by Sept. 11, 1778 [Ref: D-330, which listed the name as "Enious Davice"]. Resident of Newport East Hundred in 1778 [Ref: Q-I:297].

DAVIS, Edward. "Edward Davies" appeared twice on the list of privates in the militia, 12th Battalion, Capt. Henry Clarkson's Company, 1777 [Ref: M-159]. One "Edward Davis" took the Oath of Allegiance in 1778 [Ref: L-16, AA-641]. Resident of Newport East Hundred in 1778 [Ref: Q-I:297]. See "Peter Davis," q.v.

DAVIS, Eleazer. Private, Militia, 12th Battalion, Capt. John Parnham's Company, 1777 [Ref: M-161]. Took the Oath of Allegiance in 1778 [Ref: L-16, AA-641]. Resident of Newport East Hundred in 1778 [Ref: Q-I:297].

DAVIS, Elias. Private, Militia, 12th Battalion, Capt. Henry Clarkson's Company, 1777 [Ref: M-159, which listed the name as "Davies"].

DAVIS, Elizabeth. Rendered patriotic service by providing wheat for the use of the military in December 1782 [Ref: N-573]. See "James Davis" and "Samuel Smoot," q.v.

DAVIS, George. Private, Militia, 12th Battalion, Capt. John Thomas' Company, 1777 [Ref: M-161]. Took the Oath of Allegiance in 1778 [Ref: AA-641]. Resident of Port Tobacco East Hundred in 1778 [Ref: Q-I:297]. One George Davis, son of Peter and Charity Davis, was born on Aug. 22, 1751 [Ref: EE-10].

DAVIS, George. Private, Militia, 12th Battalion, Capt. Henry Clarkson's Company, 1777 [Ref: M-159]. Took the Oath of Allegiance in 1778 [Ref: L-15]. Both sources listed the name as "Davies."

DAVIS, Gerrard. Private, 1st Maryland Line, enrolled and passed on July 20, 1776 [Ref: D-32, which listed the name as "Davies"].

DAVIS, Gustavus. Private, Militia, 12th Battalion, Capt. John Parnham's Company, 1777 [Ref: M-160]. Took the Oath of Allegiance in 1778 [Ref: AA-641]. Resident of Newport East Hundred in 1778 [Ref: Q-I:297].

DAVIS, H. M. See "Thomas Davis," q.v.

DAVIS, Henry (1723-). Took the Oath of Allegiance in 1778 [Ref: L-16, AA-641, which latter source listed the name only as "H. Davis"]. Aged 55 as noted in a 1778 deposition [Ref: DD-703]. Resident of Durham Lower Hundred in 1778 [Ref: Q-I:297]. See "John Baillie," q.v.

DAVIS, Isaac. See "Thomas Davis," q.v.

DAVIS, James (1751-). Born on Aug. 2, 1751, son of Thomas and Elizabeth Davis [Ref: EE-9]. Private, Rawlings Regiment, 1st Maryland Line, enlisted March 27, 1779 [Ref: D-105].

DAVIS, Jeremiah. Private, Militia, 26th Battalion, Capt. Hezekiah Garner's Company, 1777 [Ref: M-162].
DAVIS, Jesse. Private, Militia, 26th Battalion, Capt. Hezekiah Garner's Company, 1777 [Ref: M-162]. Took the Oath of Allegiance in 1778 [Ref: L-16]. Resident of Bryan Town Hundred in 1778 [Ref: Q-I:297]. Private, 1st Maryland Line, drafted from the Charles County militia on July 27, 1781, and determined unfit for service and discharged on Oct. 30, 1781 [Ref: D-377, G-656].
DAVIS, Jesse. Private, Militia, 12th Battalion, Capt. Henry Clarkson's Company, 1777 [Ref: M-159, which listed the name as "Davies"].
DAVIS, John (1736-). Sergeant, 4th Maryland Line, 1776-1780 [Ref: D-105]. Rendered patriotic service by providing wheat for the use of the military in December 1782 [Ref: N-573]. In November 1812, the Treasurer of Maryland was directed to pay to "John Davis, of Charles County, late a sergeant in the Revolutionary War, or order during his life, in quarterly payments, half pay of a sergeant." [Ref: Q-II:333]. One John Davis was aged 42 as noted in a 1778 deposition [Ref: DD-703].
DAVIS, John W. See "Thomas Davis," q.v.
DAVIS, Joseph. See "Notley Davis," q.v.
DAVIS, Luke. Took the Oath of Allegiance in 1778 [Ref: L-16]. Resident of Benedict Hundred in 1778 [Ref: Q-I:297]. See "Cornelius Davis," q.v.
DAVIS, Mary. See "Notley Davis" and "Benjamin Davis, Jr.," q.v.
DAVIS, Notley (1747-). Born on Feb. 9, 1747, son of Joseph and Mary Davis [Ref: EE-3]. Private, 9th Company of Infantry, enlisted June 7, 1776 [Ref: D-20].
DAVIS, Peter. Private, Militia, 26th Battalion, Capt. Richard Bennett Mitchell's Company, 1777 [Ref: M-165]. Resident of Pomonkey Hundred in 1778 [Ref: Q-I:297].
DAVIS, Peter (1715-). Took the Oath of Allegiance in 1778 [Ref: L-16]. Aged 65 as noted in a 1780 deposition which mentioned his father Edward Davis [Ref: DD-704]. See "Randolph Davis" and "George Davis," q.v.
DAVIS, Philip. Took the Oath of Allegiance in 1778 [Ref: L-15, which listed the name as "Davies"]. Resident of Newport East Hundred in 1778 [Ref: Q-I:297]. Philip Davis married Chloe Poston on Feb. 10, 1770 in Trinity Parish [Ref: EE-15].
DAVIS, Randolph (1747-). Born on Feb. 20, 1747, son of Peter and Charity Davis [Ref: EE-6]. Private, Militia, 12th Battalion, Capt. Henry Clarkson's Company, 1777 [Ref: M-159, which listed the name as "Davies"]. Resident of Newport East Hundred in 1778 [Ref: Q-I:297]. Rendered patriotic service by providing wheat for the use of the military in September 1782 [Ref: N-556]. Randolph Davis petitioned the Council

of Maryland in 1783, stating that he had not taken the Oath of Allegiance due to any disaffection with the government, but from a variety of incidents, and was unjustly penalized as a non-juror and fined unfairly; therefore, he asked the Council to consider ordering the County Justices to remit the fines they imposed on him and others who signed the petition. The Council of Maryland, after reviewing his case, indicated they believed the truth of the facts stated in the petition and ordered a remission of the fines and penalties on Sept. 17, 1783 [Ref: I-454].

DAVIS, Richard (1753-   ). Private, Militia, 26th Battalion, Capt. Hezekiah Garner's Company, 1777 [Ref: M-163]. Resident of Newport East Hundred in 1778 [Ref: Q-I:297]. Aged about 26 as noted in a 1779 deposition [Ref: BB-472]. He may have been the son of Richard Davis, aged 76, who was also deposed in 1779 [Ref: BB-473, DD-704].

DAVIS, Samuel. Private, Militia, 26th Battalion, Capt. William Winter's Company, 1777 [Ref: M-165].

DAVIS, Samuel Barker (1757-1840). Private, Virginia Line, enlisted in Fairfax County on July 10, 1775. He was born in Charles County, Maryland and removed with his father (not named) to Virginia circa 1769 or 1770. They moved to Loudoun County in 1778, Prince William County in 1785, and Hampshire County in 1787. Samuel applied for a pension on Feb. 2, 1833, aged 75, stating he enlisted in the war in Fairfax County and also in Loudoun County. According to the pension application (W1728) of his widow Ann Davis (maiden name was Bogle) on June 26, 1852, she was born in 1777 and they were married on Dec. 7, 1814 by Rev. John Johnson. Samuel died on April 16, 1840 and Ann was still living in 1855 (bounty land application) and the land she was entitled to was assigned to William Mosely on July 27, 1856 (Register's Office, Plattsburg, Missouri). [Ref: V-I:909, U-41:2 (1953), pp. 67-68].

DAVIS, Thomas (1753-1840). Sergeant, Militia, 12th Battalion, Capt. Peter Wood's Company, 1777. Drafted into the 4th Maryland Line on July 27, 1781 and served as an Orderly Sergeant for Gen. Smallwood. He was in the siege of Yorktown and was discharged on Nov. 29, 1783 [Ref: M-161, D-377]. Thomas was born on Nov. 8, 1753 in Durham Parish, Charles County, Maryland, married Joannah Whitten or Johanna Whitler on Jan. 2, 1786, and died on Sept. 22, 1840 in Knox County, Ohio. His widow applied for a pension (W6974) on Nov. 23, 1840, stating she was born on Feb. 21, 1764. Also mentioned were Isaac Davis (Acting Justice of the Peace), John W. Davis (Clerk of the Court), and H. M. Davis, but no relationships were given [Ref: V-I:910, W-113, U-36:3 (1938), p. 35]. Took the Oath of Allegiance in 1778 [Ref: L-15, which listed the name as "Davies"]. Resident of Benedict Hundred in 1778 [Ref: Q-I:297].

DAVIS, Thomas. Private, Militia, 26th Battalion, Capt. Hezekiah Garner's Company, 1777 [Ref: M-163]. Took the Oath of Allegiance in 1778 [Ref: L-16]. See "James Davis," q.v.

DAVIS, William. Private, Militia, 12th Battalion, Capt. John Parnham's Company, 1777 [Ref: M-161]. William Davis, of Mattawoman, petitioned the Council of Maryland in 1783 stating that he had not taken the Oath of Allegiance due to any disaffection with the government, but from a variety of incidents, and was unjustly penalized as a non-juror and fined unfairly; therefore, he asked the Council to consider ordering the County Justices to remit the fines they imposed on him and others who signed the petition. The Council of Maryland, after reviewing his case, indicated they believed the truth of the facts stated in the petition and ordered a remission of the fines and penalties on Sept. 17, 1783 [Ref: I-454]. Resident of Port Tobacco West Hundred in 1778 [Ref: Q-I:297]. See "Samuel Wright," q.v.

DAVIS, William. Private, Militia, 26th Battalion, Capt. Richard Bennett Mitchell's Company, 1777; listed as an invalid (disabled) soldier [Ref: M-165]. Resident of Durham Lower Hundred in 1778 [Ref: Q-I:297].

DAVIS, William Jr. Took the Oath of Allegiance in 1778 [Ref: L-16]. Resident of Newport East Hundred in 1778 [Ref: Q-I:297].

DAVIS, William Sr. Took the Oath of Allegiance in 1778 [Ref: L-16, AA-641, which listed the name without the "Sr."]. Resident of Newport East Hundred in 1778 [Ref: Q-I:297].

DAVIS, Zachariah. Private, 1st Maryland Line, enrolled and passed on July 25, 1776 [Ref: D-32]. Private, Militia, 26th Battalion, Capt. William Winter's Company, 1777 [Ref: M-165]. Took the Oath of Allegiance in 1778 [Ref: L-16]. Resident of Durham Lower Hundred in 1778 [Ref: Q-I:297].

DAVIS, Zaccheus. "Zaccheus Davis" took the Oath of Allegiance in 1778 [Ref: AA-641]. Resident of Bryan Town Hundred in 1778 [Ref: Q-I:297]. "Zacchius Davis" married Margaret Stone on April 15, 1759 in Trinity Parish [Ref: EE-12].

DAWSON, Benjamin. Private, Militia, 26th Battalion, Capt. Thomas H. Marshall's Company, 1777 [Ref: M-163]. Took the Oath of Allegiance in 1778 [Ref: L-16]. Resident of Pomonkey Hundred in 1778 [Ref: Q-I:297].

DAWSON, George. Private, Militia, 26th Battalion, Capt. Thomas H. Marshall's Company, 1777 [Ref: M-163]. Took the Oath of Allegiance in 1778 [Ref: L-16]. Resident of Pomonkey Hundred in 1778 [Ref: Q-I:297].

DAWSON, Henry. Private, Militia, 26th Battalion, Capt. Thomas H. Marshall's Company, 1777 [Ref: M-163].

DAWSON, Richard. Memorialist and Militiaman, Pomonkey Company, after March 6, 1776 [Ref: M-158, Y-II:26]. Corporal, Militia, 26th Battalion, Capt. Thomas H. Marshall's Company, 1777 [Ref: M-163].
DAWSON, Robert. Private, Militia, 12th Battalion, Capt. Peter Wood's Company, 1777 [Ref: M-161]. Took the Oath of Allegiance in 1778 [Ref: L-16]. Resident of Benedict Hundred in 1778 [Ref: Q-I:297].
DAWSON, William. See "Philip Thomas Lee," q.v.
DAY, Benjamin. Took the Oath of Allegiance in 1778 [Ref: AA-641]. Resident of Port Tobacco West Hundred in 1778 [Ref: Q-I:297].
DEAKINS, Ambrose. Took the Oath of Allegiance in 1778 [Ref: L-16]. Resident of Durham Lower Hundred in 1778 [Ref: Q-I:297].
DEAKINS, Edward. Private, Militia, 12th Battalion, Capt. John Hanson's Company, 1777 [Ref: M-159]. Took the Oath of Allegiance in 1778 [Ref: L-16, AA-641]. Resident of Port Tobacco East Hundred in 1778 [Ref: Q-I:297].
DEAKINS, Francis. Took the Oath of Allegiance in 1778 [Ref: L-16].
DEAN (DEEN), George. Took the Oath of Allegiance in 1778 [Ref: AA-641]. Resident of Port Tobacco West Hundred in 1778 [Ref: Q-I:297].
DELOZIER, George (1710-   ). Took the Oath of Allegiance in 1780 [Ref: O-109]. Aged 68 as noted in a 1778 deposition [Ref: DD-704].
DELOZIER, John. Memorialist and Militiaman, Pomonkey Company, after March 6, 1776 [Ref: M-158, Y-II:26]. Private, Militia, 26th Battalion, Capt. Hezekiah Garner's Company, 1777 [Ref: M-162].
DELOZIER, John. Sergeant, Militia, 26th Battalion, Capt. Thomas H. Marshall's Company, 1777 [Ref: M-163]. Took the Oath of Allegiance in 1778 [Ref: AA-641]. Resident of Pomonkey Hundred in 1778 [Ref: Q-I:297]. Rendered patriotic service by providing wheat for the use of the military in May 1783 [Ref: N-597].
DELOZIER, John Sr. (1700-   ). Took the Oath of Allegiance in 1780 [Ref: O-109]. Aged 69 as noted in a 1769 deposition [Ref: DD-704].
DELOZIER, Thomas (c1745-1811). Private, Militia, 26th Battalion, Capt. Hezekiah Garner's Company, 1777 [Ref: M-162]. Took the Oath of Allegiance in 1780 [Ref: O-109]. Thomas Delozier married Sarah Garner and died on Jan. 19, 1811 [Ref: J-I:811].
DELOZIER, William. Private, Militia, 26th Battalion, Capt. Hezekiah Garner's Company, 1777 [Ref: M-162]. Private (drafted and joined the army), 1st Maryland Line, enlisted June 4, 1778 and discharged Feb. 14, 1779 [Ref: D-101, D-330, which also listed the name as "Delozior"]. Took the Oath of Allegiance in 1780 [Ref: O-109].

DEMAR, Francis. Private, Militia, 12th Battalion, Capt. Peter Wood's Company, 1777 [Ref: M-161]. Took the Oath of Allegiance in 1778 [Ref: AA-641].
DEMAR, Joshua. Private, Militia, 12th Battalion, Capt. Peter Wood's Company, 1777 [Ref: M-161].
DEMENT, Anne. See "James Waters," q.v.
DEMENT, Charles (1743-   ). Memorialist and Militiaman, Pomonkey Company, after March 6, 1776 [Ref: M-158, Y-II:26]. Private, Militia, 26th Battalion, Capt. Thomas H. Marshall's Company, 1777 [Ref: M-163]. Took the Oath of Allegiance in 1778 [Ref: AA-641, L-16, which latter source listed the name as "Dument"]. Resident of Pomonkey Hundred in 1778 [Ref: Q-I:297]. Rendered patriotic service by providing wheat for the use of the military in October 1782 [Ref: N-562]. Aged 27 as noted in a 1770 deposition [Ref: DD-704].
DEMENT, Edward (Jr.). Private, Militia, 12th Battalion, Capt. Henry Clarkson's Company, 1777 [Ref: M-159]. Resident of Newport East Hundred in 1778 [Ref: Q-I:297].
DEMENT, Edward (Sr.). Took the Oath of Allegiance in 1778 [Ref: AA-641]. Resident of Newport East Hundred in 1778 [Ref: Q-I:297].
DEMENT, Elizabeth. See "James Moore," q.v.
DEMENT, John. Private, Militia, 12th Battalion, Capt. Henry Clarkson's Company, 1777 [Ref: M-159]. Rendered patriotic service by providing wheat for the use of the military in September 1782 [Ref: N-556]. Resident of Newport East Hundred in 1778 [Ref: Q-I:297].
DEMENT, John (1713-   ). Took the Oath of Allegiance in 1778 [Ref: AA-641]. Aged 55 as noted in a 1766 deposition [Ref: DD-704].
DEMENT, Susannah. See "William Roby, of Richard," q.v.
DEMENT, William. Private, Militia, 12th Battalion, Capt. Henry Clarkson's Company, 1777 [Ref: M-159]. Took the Oath of Allegiance in 1778 [Ref: L-16, which listed the name as "Demant"]. Rendered patriotic service by providing wheat for the use of the military in October 1782 [Ref: N-563]. Resident of Bryan Town Hundred in 1778 [Ref: Q-I:297]. William Dement, son of John, married Elizabeth Bryan on Aug. 27, 1775 in Trinity Parish [Ref: EE-17]. See "William Roby, of Richard," q.v.
DENNIS, Ezekiel. Took the Oath of Allegiance in 1778 [Ref: L-16, AA-641, which latter source listed the name as "Zekiel Dennis"]. Resident of William & Mary Lower Hundred in 1778 [Ref: Q-I:297].
DENNIS, John. Took the Oath of Allegiance in 1778 [Ref: AA-641].
DENNIS, Peter. Private (substitute for 3 years), 1st Maryland Line, by Sept. 11, 1778 [Ref: D-330].
DENNISON, James. Took the Oath of Allegiance in 1778 [Ref: L-16].

DENT, Ann (Anne). See "John Dent" and "Benjamin Dent" and "William Mackall Wilkinson" and "George Dent" and "John Parnham" and "John Dent, of Hatch" and "Hezekiah Dent" and "Hatch Dent" and "Thomas Swann" and "Peter Dent" and "Theodore Dent," q.v.

DENT, Benjamin Sr. (c1720-1778). Took the Oath of Allegiance in March 1778 and died testate in August 1778 [Ref: Harry Wright Newman's *Charles County Gentry*, p. 68]. Resident of Newport West Hundred in 1778 [Ref: Q-I:297].

DENT, Benjamin Jr. (1750-1835). Private, Militia, 12th Battalion, Capt. Benjamin Lusby Corry's Company, 1777 [Ref: M-160]. Born on June 21, 1750, he married first to Anne Dent, married second to Ann Hancock, and died on Feb. 6, 1835. Jane Dent, a daughter by his first wife, married John Penn [Ref: S-3102, S-3149, J-I:819]. Resident of Newport West Hundred in 1778 [Ref: Q-I:297].

DENT, Chloe. See "Joseph Waters, of James," q.v.

DENT, Dennis. See "George Dent, of John," q.v.

DENT, Eleanor. See "George Dent" and "George Dent, Jr.," q.v.

DENT, Elizabeth. See "George Dent, of John" and "John Dent" and "Richard Harrison" and "Joseph Semmes" and "Hatch Dent" and "Zachariah Dent," q.v.

DENT, George (c1725-1785). Son of George Dent (1690-1754) and Anne Harbert, he married Eleanor Hawkins and had these children: Henry Dent, George Dent (married Elizabeth Yates), Eleanor Dent (spinster), Johanna Greenfield Dent, Jane Dent (spinster), Mary Dent (married first to Henry Alexander Ashton and second to Johannis Storke), and Anne Dent (married Dr. John Parnham). George Dent rendered the following patriotic services: Represented Charles County in the Lower House of the Maryland Legislature from 1757 to 1775 [Ref: P-I:262, P-I:263]. Appointed a Judge of the Orphans Court of Charles County on June 4, 1777 and May 15, 1778 and Nov. 19, 1779 [Ref: C-274, E-84, F-19]. Appointed an Election Judge for Charles County by the Maryland Convention on July 3, 1776 [Ref: Y-I:35]. Took the Oath of Allegiance in 1778 [Ref: L-16]. Resident of William & Mary Upper Hundred in 1778 [Ref: Q-I:297]. Justice who administered (and took) the Oath of Allegiance in 1778 [Ref: AA-641]. Rendered patriotic service by providing clothing for the use of the military in February 1778 [Ref: Y-II:234]. Appointed a Judge of the Court of Appeals for Charles County on May 20, 1778 [Ref: E-97]. Appointed a Justice of the Peace on Nov. 21, 1778 and Nov. 19, 1779 [Ref: E-249, F-19]. Rendered patriotic service by providing wheat for the use of the military in May 1783 [Ref: N-597]. In April 1781, his home was burned by the British. He died in 1785 [Ref: P-I:263]. See "George Dent, Jr." and "John Dent," q.v.

DENT, George Jr. (c1750-1802). First Lieutenant, Militia, 26th Battalion, Capt. William Winter's Company, Feb. 26, 1776. Captain, May 9, 1778 [Ref: M-69, M-165, A-186, A-206, E-72, Y-II:23]. On Aug. 5, 1776 the Maryland Council of Safety ordered the Treasurer to "pay to Lieut. George Dent for the Committee of Observation for Charles County for the Purchase of Arms, two hundred pounds." [Ref: B-170]. Took the Oath of Allegiance in 1778 [Ref: L-16]. Rendered patriotic service by providing wheat for the use of the military in October 1782 [Ref: N-559, which listed him as "Capt. George Dent"]. See "Daniel Jenifer Adams," q.v.

DENT, George, of John (1756-1813). Son of John Dent, of George (1732-1809) and Sarah Marshall, h married Anne Magruder Truman (daughter of James Truman who died in 1789) and had these children: John Herbert Dent (married Elizabeth Anne Harry), James Truman Dent (married Catherine Anne Cooper), George Columbus Dent (1792-1815, killed in a duel), Dennis Dent (married Martha Beall), Sarah Marshall Dent (married first to Edward Briscoe and second to ---- Fendall), Elizabeth Truman Dent (1786-1789), Maria Dent (married John Neilson), and Mary Ann Dent (died young). [Ref: P-I:263]. Resident of Pomonkey Hundred in 1778 [Ref: Q-I:297]. George Dent, of John, rendered the following patriotic services: Second Lieutenant, Militia, Pomonkey Company, after March 6, 1776 [Ref: M-158, Y-II:26]. First Lieutenant, Militia, 26th Battalion, Capt. Thomas H. Marshall's Company, Feb. 26, 1776 [Ref: M-163, Y-II:23, which latter source listed the name without the "of John"]. First Lieutenant, 1st Maryland Line, Capt. Thomas Hanson's Company, July 1776. Captain, 26th Battalion, Militia, commissioned May 9, 1778 [Ref: D-31, M-69, E-72, Y-II:26]. Represented Charles County in the Lower House of the Maryland Legislature, 1782-1790, and in the Senate, 1791-1796. Served as a Court Justice, 1774-1795, and as a United States Congressman, 1793-1801. When he was not appointed to the post of United States Treasurer as he expected because of his ardent support of Thomas Jefferson in the 1801 election, George moved to Georgia in 1802. He died near Augusta on Dec. 2, 1813 as the result of being thrown from a horse [Ref: P-I:263, P-I:264, J-I:819]. See "John Dent," q.v.

DENT, George, of Peter (1755-1812). Private, Militia, 26th Battalion, Capt. Thomas H. Marshall's Company, 1777 [Ref: M-163]. Took the Oath of Allegiance in 1778 [Ref: L-16]. Resident of Pomonkey Hundred in 1778 [Ref: Q-I:297]. He was probably the George Dent who was a private in the 2nd Maryland Line who enlisted on May 25, 1778 and was discharged on April 3, 1779 [Ref: D-102].

79

DENT, George Columbus. See "George Dent, of John," q.v.
DENT, Gideon (c1755-1814). Private, Militia, 12th Battalion, Capt. Henry Clarkson's Company, 1777 [Ref: M-159]. Resident of Newport West Hundred in 1778 [Ref: Q-I:297].
DENT, Hatch (1751-1799). Born on May 20, 1751, son of Hatch and Ann Dent, he married Judith Poston, served as a captain in the 2nd Maryland Line in 1777, and died on Dec. 30, 1799 [Ref: EE-3, J-I:819, D-101]. Rendered patriotic service by providing wheat for the use of the military in December 1782 [Ref: N-575]. See "Zephaniah Waters," q.v.
DENT, Hatch (c1750-1816). Private, Militia, 12th Battalion, Capt. Henry Clarkson's Company, 1777 [Ref: M-159]. He married first to Susanna Edwards, married second to Elizabeth ----, and died before Feb. 26, 1816 [Ref: J-I:819].
DENT, Hatch Sr. (1707-1781). Took the Oath of Allegiance in 1778 [Ref: L-16]. Aged about 72 as noted in a 1779 deposition [Ref: BB-473, DD-704]. Resident of Newport West Hundred in 1778 [Ref: Q-I:297]. He married Anne ---- and died in October 1781 [Ref: J-I:819]. See "John Dent, of Hatch" and "Hezekiah Dent," q.v.
DENT, Henry (c1750-1803). First Lieutenant, Militia, 12th Battalion, Capt. Benjamin Philpott's Company, Feb. 26, 1776 [Ref: M-69, A-186, A-206, Y-II:23]. Took the Oath of Allegiance in 1778 [Ref: L-16, AA-641]. Resident of Newport West Hundred in 1778 [Ref: Q-I:297]. Captain, 12th Battalion, commissioned on Feb. 9, 1781 [Ref: M-69, G-307]. See "George Dent," q.v.
DENT, Henry (c1755-1815). Private, Militia, 12th Battalion, Capt. Henry Clarkson's Company, 1777 [Ref: M-159]. Took the Oath of Allegiance in 1778 [Ref: AA-641]. Resident of William & Mary Upper Hundred in 1778 [Ref: Q-I:297].
DENT, Hezekiah (1747-1792). Born on Aug. 2, 1747, son of Hatch and Ann Dent [Ref: EE-3]. Second Lieutenant, Militia, July 5, 1777, and First Lieutenant, Militia, 12th Battalion, Capt. Benjamin Lusby Corry's Company, Oct. 22, 1777 [Ref: M-69, M-160, C-401]. Captain, May 28, 1779 [Ref: E-427]. Resident of Newport West Hundred in 1778 [Ref: Q-I:297]. Rendered patriotic service by providing wheat for the use of the military in December 1782 [Ref: N-575]. Hezekiah Dent married first to Catherine Poston on Nov. 2, 1769 in Trinity Parish, married second to Martha Burch, and died on Sept. 8, 1792 [Ref: EE-15, J-I:819].
DENT, James Truman. See "George Dent, of John," q.v.
DENT, Jane. See "Benjamin Dent" and "George Dent," q.v.
DENT, Johanna Greenfield. See "George Dent," q.v.
DENT, John. Private, 1st Maryland Line, enrolled and passed on July 20, 1776 [Ref: D-32]. Private, Militia, 26th Battalion, Capt. Thomas H.

Marshall's Company, 1777 [Ref: M-163]. Took the Oath of Allegiance in 1778 [Ref: L-16, AA-641]. Resident of Pomonkey Hundred in 1778 [Ref: Q-I:297]. He was probably the John Dent who was a private in the 2nd Maryland Line, enlisted on May 20, 1778 and "died in Town" (exact date not stated). [Ref: D-102].

DENT, John Sr. Took the Oath of Allegiance in 1778 [Ref: L-16]. Resident of Newport West Hundred in 1778 [Ref: Q-I:297]. See "John Dent, of John," q.v.

DENT, John, of George (1732-1809). Son of George Dent (1690-1754) and Anne Harbert, he was born on July 11, 1732, married Sarah Marshall (1735-1795) on Feb. 27, 1753/4 and had these children: George Dent (c1758-1813), Thomas Marshall Dent (1761-1823, married Anne Magruder), Elizabeth Dent (died young), and Anne Herbert Dent (1756-1813, married Capt. William Mackall Wilkinson (1752-1799) on March 24, 1774). John died on Aug. 24, 1809 [Ref: S-3107, S-3134, S-3136, P-I:264, J-I:819]. He rendered the following patriotic services: Delegate to the Maryland Convention from April 24 to May 3, 1775 and July 26 to Aug. 14, 1775 [Ref: A-4, Y-I:1, Y-I:4]. Captain, Militia, Pomonkey Company, Jan. 6, 1776. Resigned and was subsequently appointed Brigadier General of the Flying Camp of Maryland [Ref: A-186, M-69, M-158, Y-II:26, P-I:264]. Appointed by the Maryland Convention on Feb. 2, 1776 to be one of the Collectors of Gold & Silver Coin in Charles County [Ref: A-132]. Appointed a Judge of the Orphans Court of Charles County on June 4, 1777 and Nov. 19, 1779 and Jan. 17, 1782 [Ref: C-274, F-19, F-42, I-46]. Justice who administered (and took) the Oath of Allegiance in 1778 [Ref: AA-641, which listed the name without the "of George"]. Appointed a Justice of the Peace on Nov. 21, 1778 and Nov. 19, 1779 and Jan. 17, 1782 [Ref: E-249, F-19, I-45]. Rendered patriotic service by providing wheat for the use of the military in November 1782 [Ref: N-564]. See "William Mackall Wilkinson" and "Thomas Price" and "John Dent, of John" and "George Dent, of John," q.v.

DENT, John, of Hatch (1729-1778). Born on Dec. 2, 1729, son of Hatch and Ann Dent, and married Margaret Dyson on Feb. 3, 1757 in Trinity Parish [Ref: EE-3, EE-12, J-I:819]. Took the Oath of Allegiance in 1778 [Ref: L-16]. Resident of Bryan Town Hundred in 1778 [Ref: Q-I:297].

DENT, John, of John. Son of John Dent (died in 1791) and Mary Blackman, he married Mary ---- and had two children: John Shelton Dent and Priscilla Elizabeth Dent (who married "John Brewer Dent," q.v.). Took the Oath of Allegiance in 1778 [Ref: L-16]. Resident of Bryan Town Hundred in 1778 [Ref: Q-I:297]. Served in the Lower House of the Maryland Legislature in 1783 and died in 1799 [Ref: P-I:264].

DENT, John Brewer (1759-1838). Private, 1st Maryland Line. He was born on May 9, 1759, married Priscilla Elizabeth Dent, and died on April 24, 1838 [Ref: J-I:819]. See "John Dent, of John," q.v.
DENT, John Herbert. See "George Dent, of John," q.v.
DENT, John Shelton. See "John Dent, of John," q.v.
DENT, Joseph Manning (c1750-1790/5). Sergeant, Militia, 12th Battalion, Capt. Benjamin Lusby Corry's Company, 1777 [Ref: M-160]. Constable, Pomonkey Hundred, 1778 [Ref: CC-709]. Ensign, Militia, 12th Battalion, Capt. Dent's Company, May 28, 1779 [Ref: M-69, E-427]. He married Mary Manning ---- and died between 1790 and 1795, having pre-deceased his father Michael Dent [Ref: J-I:819, and Harry Wright Newman's *Charles County Gentry*, p. 77].
DENT, Letitia. See "Kenhelm Truman Stoddert," q.v.
DENT, Margaret. See "Thomas Hatch Dent," q.v.
DENT, Maria. See "George Dent, of John," q.v.
DENT, Mary. See "George Dent" and "John Dent, of John" and "George Dent, of John" and "Peter Dent," q.v.
DENT, Michael (1713-1795). Took the Oath of Allegiance in 1778 [Ref: L-16]. Resident of Newport West Hundred in 1778 [Ref: Q-I:297]. Aged about 66 as noted in a 1779 deposition [Ref: BB-473, DD-704]. Rendered patriotic service by providing wheat for the use of the military in December 1782 [Ref: N-577, which listed the first name as "Michel"]. He married ---- Manning and died before Oct. 12, 1795 [Ref: J-I:819]. See "Joseph Manning Dent," q.v.
DENT, Peter (1728-1785). Private, Militia, 26th Battalion, Capt. Thomas H. Marshall's Company, 1777 [Ref: M-163]. Resident of Pomonkey Hundred in 1778 [Ref: Q-I:297]. Appointed Inspector of Tobacco at Pomonkey Creek on Aug. 30, 1780 [Ref: F-271]. "Peter Dent, son of Peter" was aged about 41 as noted in a 1771 deposition [Ref: DD-704]. "Peter Dent" was born on Jan. 10, 1728, married first to Mary Eleanor ----, married second to Anne ----, and died before March 26, 1785 [Ref: J-I:819]. See "Theodore Dent," q.v.
DENT, Peter (1717-   ). Took the Oath of Allegiance in 1778 [Ref: L-16]. Resident of Newport West Hundred in 1778 [Ref: Q-I:297]. Aged 46 as noted in a 1763 deposition [Ref: DD-704].
DENT, Priscilla Elizabeth. See "John Dent, of John" and "John Brewer Dent," q.v.
DENT, Rebecca. See "William Harrison," q.v.
DENT, Rhoda. See "William Turner," q.v.
DENT, Richard. Rendered patriotic service by providing wheat for the use of the military in April 1782 [Ref: N-499].

DENT, Samuel. Private, Militia, 12th Battalion, Capt. Henry Clarkson's Company, 1777 [Ref: M-159]. Private, 1st Maryland Line, drafted from the Charles County militia on July 27, 1781 and discharged on Dec. 3, 1781 [Ref: D-377, I-10].

DENT, Sarah. Rendered patriotic service by providing wheat for the use of the military in October 1782 [Ref: N-563].

DENT, Sarah Marshall. See "George Dent, of John," q.v.

DENT, Shadrick. Private, Militia, 12th Battalion, Capt. Benjamin Lusby Corry's Company, 1777 [Ref: M-160]. Took the Oath of Allegiance in 1778 [Ref: L-16, AA-641].

DENT, Theodore (1761-1815). Private, Militia, 26th Battalion, Capt. Thomas H. Marshall's Company, 1777 [Ref: M-163]. Son of Peter and Anne Dent, he married Eleanor Sheid, daughter of Martha Sheid (widow). [Ref: Harry Wright Newman's *Charles County Gentry*, pp. 41-43].

DENT, Thomas (1735-1788/9). Took the Oath of Allegiance in 1778 [Ref: L-16, AA-641]. Resident of Newport West Hundred in 1778 [Ref: Q-I:297]. Thomas Dent married Elizabeth Edelen [Ref: J-I:819]. See "Thomas Dent Hardy" and "Clement Edelen," q.v.

DENT, Thomas Jr. Sergeant, Militia, 12th Battalion, Capt. Henry Clarkson's Company, 1777 [Ref: M-159]. Resident of Newport West Hundred in 1778 [Ref: Q-I:297].

DENT, Thomas Hatch (1760-1817). Born on July 28, 1760, son of John and Margaret Dent [Ref: EE-12]. Private, Militia, 12th Battalion, Capt. Benjamin Lusby Corry's Company, 1777 [Ref: M-160].

DENT, Thomas Marshall. See "John Dent," q.v.

DENT, Titus (c1755-1811). Private, Militia, 12th Battalion, Capt. Benjamin Lusby Corry's Company, 1777 [Ref: M-160]. Resident of Newport West Hundred in 1778 [Ref: Q-I:297].

DENT, Walter (1744-c1820). Private, Militia, 12th Battalion, Capt. Henry Clarkson's Company, 1777 [Ref: M-159]. Took the Oath of Allegiance in 1778 [Ref: L-16]. Resident of Newport West Hundred in 1778 [Ref: Q-I:297]. Walter Dent married Elizabeth Montgomery and migrated to Georgia where he died after 1820 [Ref: J-I:819].

DENT, Walter (Jr.). Eldest son of Walter Dent and Elizabeth Montgomery, he was born on January 7, 1765 and was drafted in 1781 in Major Higgins' battalion for service at Yorktown [Ref: Harry Wright Newman's *Charles County Gentry*, p. 32].

DENT, Warren. Son of William Dent (1706-1757) and Anne Warren, he never married and died without progeny. Warren Dent rendered the following patriotic services: Appointed an Election Judge for Charles County by the Maryland Convention on July 3, 1776 [Ref: Y-I:35]. Justice who administered (and took) the Oath of Allegiance in 1778 [Ref: L-16, AA-641]. Appointed a Justice of the Peace on Nov. 21, 1778 and Nov. 19, 1779 and Jan. 17, 1782 [Ref: E-249, F-19, I-45]. Appointed a Judge of the Orphans Court for Charles County on Nov. 19, 1779 [Ref: F-19]. Rendered patriotic service by providing wheat for the use of the military in December 1782 and May 1783 [Ref: N-577, N-598]. Represented Charles County in the Lower House of the Maryland Legislature, 1778-1781. Served on the Committee of Observation, elected 1774, and was a County Justice, 1771-1794. He died testate on Oct. 24, 1794 [Ref: P-I:266].

DENT, William (1756-1816). Private, Militia, 12th Battalion, Capt. Henry Clarkson's Company, 1777 [Ref: M-159]. Took the Oath of Allegiance in 1778 [Ref: L-16]. Resident of Newport West Hundred in 1778 [Ref: Q-I:297]. William Dent married Margaretta Smoot and died before Aug. 21, 1816 [Ref: J-I:819]. See "Warren Dent," q.v.

DENT, Zachariah (c1755-1828). Sergeant, Militia, 12th Battalion, Capt. Benjamin Lusby Corry's Company, 1777 [Ref: M-160]. Took the Oath of Allegiance in 1778 [Ref: L-16]. Resident of Newport East Hundred in 1778 [Ref: Q-I:297]. Zachariah Dent married Elizabeth ---- and died on Dec. 18, 1828 [Ref: J-I:820].

DESHON, Daniel (Captain). One May 15, 1778 he was issued a Letter of Marque and Reprisal as Master of the sloop *Molly* "mounting ten carriage guns navigated by thirty men belonging to the State of Maryland" (including Charles Countians). [Ref: E-84]. See "Captain Conway," q.v.

DEVIN, James (1756-   ). Private, Flying Camp, Capt. Bowie's Company, enrolled July 13, 1776; native of Charles County, aged 20, height 5' 10" [Ref: D-36, which listed the name as "Deven"]. Private (furnished by class for 9 months), 1st Maryland Line, by Sept. 11, 1778 [Ref: D-330]. Took the Oath of Allegiance in 1778 [Ref: AA-641]. Resident of William & Mary Upper Hundred in 1778 [Ref: Q-I:297, which listed the name as "Diven"].

DEVIN, Joseph. Took the Oath of Allegiance in 1778 [Ref: L-16, AA-641].

DIGGES (DIGGS), Edward. See "John Digges," q.v.

DIGGES (DIGGS), George (1743-1792). Rendered patriotic service at Port Tobacco in December 1781, by offering to supply wheat to Hezekiah Reeder, Commissary of Purchases for Charles County [Ref: N-464]. George Diggs married Catherine Brent [Ref: J-I:837].

DIGGES (DIGGS), Henry. Took the Oath of Allegiance in 1778 [Ref: AA-641, which listed the name as "Diggs" and L-16, which listed the name as "Diggins"]. Resident of Port Tobacco East Hundred in 1778 [Ref: Q-I:297]. Rendered patriotic service by providing wheat for the use of the military in November 1782 [Ref: N-564].

DIGGES (DIGGS), Jane. See "John Digges," q.v.

DIGGES (DIGGS), John. Son of Edward Digges and Mary Neale, he married Ann Hammersley (died in 1805) and they had two children, Edward Digges and Jane Digges [Ref: P-I:271, P-II:939]. Appointed a Justice of the Peace on Nov. 19, 1779 and Jan. 17, 1782, he served in the Lower House of the Maryland Legislature from 1778 to 1780 and died in 1783 [Ref: P-I:271, F-19, I-46].

DIGGES (DIGGS), John. Private, Militia, 12th Battalion, Capt. Jonathan Yates' Company, 1777 [Ref: M-162]. Took the Oath of Allegiance in 1778 [Ref: AA-641, L-16]. Resident of William & Mary Lower Hundred in 1778 [Ref: Q-I:297].

DIGGES (DIGGS), Mary. See "Clement Hill, Sr.," q.v.

DIGGES (DIGGS), William. Rendered patriotic service by providing wheat for the use of the military in December 1782 [Ref: N-577].

DILLARD, Frances. See "Notley Maddox," q.v.

DIXON, Elizabeth. See "Henry Dixon," q.v.

DIXON, Francis (1742-   ). Took the Oath of Allegiance in 1778 [Ref: AA-641]. Resident of Port Tobacco East Hundred in 1778 [Ref: Q-I:297]. Aged 34 as noted in a January 1776 deposition which mentioned his father Jacob Dixon [Ref: DD-704].

DIXON, George Jr. Took the Oath of Allegiance in 1778 [Ref: L-16, AA-641]. Resident of Port Tobacco Upper Hundred in 1778 [Ref: Q-I:297]. Private, 1st Maryland line, Capt. John S. Belt's Company, by Jan. 1, 1782 [Ref: D-437, which listed the name without the "Jr."]. Rendered patriotic service by providing wheat for the use of the military in December 1782 [Ref: N-576].

DIXON, George Sr. Took the Oath of Allegiance in 1778 [Ref: L-16, AA-641]. Resident of Port Tobacco Upper Hundred in 1778 [Ref: Q-I:297]. Rendered patriotic service by providing wheat for the use of the military in May 1783 [Ref: N-597].

DIXON, Henrietta. See "Henry Dixon," q.v.

DIXON, Henry (c1758 - 1784 or 1785). Private (recruit), 1st Maryland Line, by Sept. 11, 1778 [Ref: D-330, which listed the name as "Dickson"]. He married Henrietta Varden, of Port Tobacco, on June 5, 1783 in Charles County, and Henrietta Dixon (widow) married Samuel Mickum on Nov. 24, 1796 at Port Tobacco. When Henrietta Mickum applied for a pension (W23988) in Washington, D. C. on Aug. 31, 1842, aged 82, she stated that Henry Dixon had died either in 1784 or 1785 and she married Samuel Mickum in 1796 and he died in November 1805 or in the spring of 1806. She had a daughter Elizabeth Dixon who married Charles Murphy or Murphey. Elizabeth died in 1808, leaving an infant daughter (not named) and a son Francis J. Murphy. Henrietta had two sons by her second husband, namely William Mickum (who died by 1842) and Samuel Mickum, Jr. (who was aged 45 in 1842). Henrietta Mickum died on Sept. 30, 1842. Her brothers were Joseph Varden and Richard Varden [Ref: V-I:986, W-113, W-119].

DIXON, Jacob. Private, 1st Maryland Line, enrolled and passed on July 8, 1776 [Ref: D-32, which listed the name as "Dixson"].

DIXON, Jacob (1709-   ). Took the Oath of Allegiance in 1778 [Ref: L-16, AA-641]. Aged 62 as noted in a 1771 deposition [Ref: DD-705]. Resident of Port Tobacco East Hundred in 1778 [Ref: Q-I:297]. See "Francis Dixon," q.v.

DIXON, Jeremiah. Took the Oath of Allegiance in 1778 [Ref: AA-641].

DIXON, Joseph. See "Thomas Pickerel," q.v.

DIXON, Richard. Private, 1st Maryland Line, 1780, who died on Dec. 27, 1782 [Ref: D-532].

DIXON, Samuel. Took the Oath of Allegiance in 1778 [Ref: AA-641]. Resident of Port Tobacco East Hundred in 1778 [Ref: Q-I:297].

DIXON, William. Private, Militia, 26th Battalion, Capt. William McPherson's Company, 1777 [Ref: M-163, which listed the name as "Wm. Duxon"].

DODSON, Charles. Took the Oath of Allegiance in 1778 [Ref: L-16]. Resident of Port Tobacco East Hundred in 1778 [Ref: Q-I:297].

DODSON, Charles. Resident of Port Tobacco Town Hundred in 1778 [Ref: Q-I:297]. Constable, 1778 [Ref: CC-709].

DODSON, Helen. See "Isaac Stewart," q.v.

DODSON, Jacob (1730-   ). Rendered patriotic service by providing wheat for the use of the military in December 1782 [Ref: N-575]. Aged about 49 as noted in a 1779 deposition [Ref: BB-466, DD-705]. Resident of Port Tobacco East Hundred in 1778 [Ref: Q-I:297].

DODSON, John. Private, Militia, 12th Battalion, Capt. Walter Hanson's Company, 1777 [Ref: M-159]. Took the Oath of Allegiance in 1778 [Ref: L-16, AA-641]. Resident of Port Tobacco East Hundred in 1778 [Ref: Q-I:297]. See "Thomas Pickerel," q.v.

DODSON, Margaret. See "William Barton Smoot," q.v.

DODSON, William. Private, Militia, 12th Battalion, Capt. John Hanson's Company, 1777 [Ref: M-159]. Resident of Port Tobacco East Hundred in 1778 [Ref: Q-I:297].

DODSON, William Barton. Took the Oath of Allegiance in 1778 [Ref: L-16, AA-641]. See "Thomas Pickerel," q.v.

DONNOLLON, William. Private, 1st Maryland Line, enrolled and passed on July 19, 1776 [Ref: D-31].

DOOLEY, Elizabeth. See "John and Thomas Dooley," q.v.
DOOLEY, James. See "John and Thomas Dooley," q.v.
DOOLEY (DULEY), John (1739-   ). Born on Jan. 8, 1739, son of James and Elizabeth Dooley [Ref: EE-2]. "John Dooley" was aged about 34 as noted in a 1776 deposition [Ref: DD-705]. "John Duley" took the Oath of Allegiance in 1778 [Ref: AA-641]. Resident of William & Mary Upper Hundred in 1778 [Ref: Q-I:297].
DOOLEY (DULEY), Thomas. "Thomas Duley" was a private in the militia, 12th Battalion, Capt. Jonathan Yates' Company, 1777 [Ref: M-162]. Took the Oath of Allegiance in 1778 [Ref: AA-641]. "Thomas Doley" was a resident of William & Mary Lower Hundred in 1778 [Ref: Q-I:297]. "Thomas Read Dooley" was born on Nov. 25, 1740, a son of James and Elizabeth Dooley [Ref: EE-2].
DORA, Thomas. See "Thomas Dory," q.v.
DORRITT, William. Took the Oath of Allegiance in 1778 [Ref: L-16, AA-641]. Resident of William & Mary Lower Hundred in 1778 [Ref: Q-I:297, which listed the name as "Dorrete"].
DORSAY, Josiah. Master of the privateer sloop *Potomack* on July 25, 1777, "mounting twelve carriage guns, eight swivels, navigated with thirty men, belonging to Robert Townsend Hooe & others of Charles County, commissioned of Letter of Marque & Reprisal." [Ref: C-318].
DORSEY, Mary. See "James Farnandis," q.v.
DORSEY, Thomas. Rendered patriotic service by providing wheat for the use of the military in October 1781 [Ref: N-450].
DORTON, John. Private, Militia, 26th Battalion, Capt. Richard Bennett Mitchell's Company, 1777 [Ref: M-164].
DORTON, William. Private, 1st Maryland Line, drafted from the Charles County militia on July 27, 1781 [Ref: D-377].
DORY, Thomas. Took the Oath of Allegiance in 1778 [Ref: L-16, AA-641]. Resident of Newport West Hundred in 1778 [Ref: Q-I:297, which listed the name as "Dora"]. Thomas Dory was deceased by July 1778 (date of inventory). [Ref: GG-189].
DOUGLAS, Ann. Rendered patriotic service by providing clothing for the use of the military in February 1778 [Ref: Y-II:234]. See "Josias Smoot," q.v.
DOUGLAS, Benjamin. Private, Militia, 26th Battalion, Capt. Thomas H. Marshall's Company, 1777 [Ref: M-163]. Resident of Pomonkey Hundred in 1778 [Ref: Q-I:297].
DOUGLAS, Benjamin. Took the Oath of Allegiance in 1778 [Ref: L-16, AA-641]. Resident of Port Tobacco East Hundred in 1778 [Ref: Q-I:297, which listed the name as "Douglass"]. Rendered patriotic service by storing corn

and wheat at Chickamuxon and Pomonkey on the Potomac River for the use of the military from March 1780 to October 1782 [Ref: N-274, N-457, N-563, F-442, which listed the name as "Douglass"]. One "Benjamin Douglas, Jr." was deceased by Nov. 17, 1778 (date of final account). [Ref: GG-249].

DOUGLAS, Charles (1714-   ). Took the Oath of Allegiance in 1778 [Ref: AA-641]. Aged about 53 as noted in a 1767 deposition [Ref: DD-705]. Resident of Port Tobacco East Hundred in 1778 [Ref: Q-I:297].

DOUGLAS, Eleanor. See "Thomas Hussey Luckett," q.v.

DOUGLAS, Elizabeth. See "Henry Smoot," q.v.

DOUGLAS, Jeremiah. See "Jeremiah Coffer," q.v.

DOUGLAS, Jesse (1733-   ). Private, Militia, 26th Battalion, Capt. Robert Sinnett's Company, 1777 [Ref: M-164]. Took the Oath of Allegiance in 1778 [Ref: L-16]. Aged about 45 as noted in a 1778 deposition [Ref: CC-623, DD-705]. Rendered patriotic service by providing wheat for the use of the military in December 1782 [Ref: N-576, which listed the name as "Douglass"].

DOUGLAS, John (1709-c1780). Took the Oath of Allegiance in 1778 [Ref: AA-641]. Aged about 45 as noted in a 1754 deposition [Ref: DD-705]. Resident of Port Tobacco East Hundred in 1778 [Ref: Q-I:297]. John Douglas married Eleanor Howard and died after March 29, 1780 [Ref: J-I:865]

DOUGLAS, John Jr. (died testate in November 1778). Took the Oath of Allegiance in 1778 [Ref: AA-641, which listed the name as "Douglass"]. Resident of William & Mary Upper Hundred in 1778 [Ref: Q-I:297, which listed the name without the "Jr."].

DOUGLAS, Joseph. Took the Oath of Allegiance in 1778 [Ref: AA-641, which listed the name as "Douglass"]. Resident of William & Mary Upper Hundred in 1778 [Ref: Q-I:297].

DOUGLAS, Richard. On March 2, 1781 "Richard Douglass" was appointed Auctioneer for Charles County by the Council of Maryland "in virtue of the Act to Regulate Auctions." [Ref: G-334]. Resident of Port Tobacco East Hundred in 1778 [Ref: Q-I:297]. "Richard Lr. *[sic]* Douglas" took the Oath of Allegiance in 1778 [Ref: AA-641].

DOUGLAS, Samuel. Private, Militia, 12th Battalion, Capt. Walter Hanson's Company, 1777 [Ref: M-159, which listed the name as "Douglass"].

DOUGLAS, Susan. See "Joseph Timms," q.v.

DOUGLAS, Thomas (1730-   ). Private, Militia, 12th Battalion, Capt. Walter Hanson's Company, 1777 [Ref: M-159]. Took the Oath of Allegiance in 1778 [Ref: L-16, AA-641]. Rendered patriotic service by providing wheat for the use of the military in May 1783 [Ref: N-597].

Aged about 45 as noted in a 1775 deposition [Ref: DD-705, which listed the name as "Douglass"]. Resident of Port Tobacco East Hundred in 1778 [Ref: Q-I:297].

DOWNES, William. Private, Militia, 26th Battalion, Capt. Thomas H. Marshall's Company, 1777 [Ref: M-163]. Resident of Port Tobacco Upper Hundred in 1778 [Ref: Q-I:297]. See "William Downs," q.v.

DOWNING, Abednego. Took the Oath of Allegiance in 1778 [Ref: L-16]. Resident of Bryan Town Hundred in 1778 [Ref: Q-I:297, which listed the name as "Dowing"]. Abednago Downing married Milesent Waters on June 30, 1776 in Trinity Parish [Ref: EE-17]. See "Abenego Dunning," q.v.

DOWNING, James (1760-1832). Private, 1st Maryland Line, enrolled and passed on July 18, 1776 [Ref: D-32]. Took the Oath of Allegiance in 1778 [Ref: L-16]. Resident of Bryan Town Hundred in 1778 [Ref: Q-I:297, which listed the name as "Dowing"]. James Downing was born in Scotland in 1760, married Asenath Walters, served in the Revolutionary War in Maryland, and died in Virginia in 1832 [Ref: J-I:870]. See "James Dunning," q.v.

DOWNING, John (1733-   ). Took the Oath of Allegiance in 1778 [Ref: L-16, AA-641]. Aged about 39 as noted in a 1772 deposition [Ref: DD-705, which listed the name as "Dowing"]. See "John Dunning," q.v.

DOWNS, William. Memorialist and Militiaman, Pomonkey Company, after March 6, 1776 [Ref: M-158, Y-II:26]. Private, Militia, 26th Battalion, Capt. William McPherson's Company, 1777 [Ref: M-163]. Took the Oath of Allegiance in 1778 [Ref: L-16, AA-641]. Resident of Pomonkey Hundred in 1778 [Ref: Q-I:297]. Rendered patriotic service by providing wheat for the use of the military in December 1782 [Ref: N-573]. One William Downs was aged about 62 as noted in a 1767 deposition [Ref: DD-705]. See "William Downes," q.v.

DOXON, George Sr. Rendered patriotic service by providing wheat for the use of the military in October 1782 [Ref: N-563].

DOYAL, Martin. Private (substitute for 3 years), 1st Maryland Line, by Sept. 11, 1778 [Ref: D-330].

DOYNE, Charles. Private, Militia, 12th Battalion, Capt. Jonathan Yates' Company, 1777 [Ref: M-162].

DOYNE, Jesse (c1735-1786). Private, Militia, 26th Battalion, Capt. Robert Sinnett's Company, 1777 [Ref: M-164]. Took the Oath of Allegiance in 1778 [Ref: L-16]. Jesse Doyne married Anne King [Ref: J-I:872].

DOYNE, Robert. Took the Oath of Allegiance in 1778 [Ref: L-16, AA-641].

DRUGH, Thomas. Private, 3rd Maryland Line, enrolled by Capt. Joseph Marbury by May 24, 1780 [Ref: F-181].

DRURY, John. Private, 3rd Maryland Line, enrolled by Capt. Joseph Marbury by May 24, 1780 [Ref: F-181].
DRURY, Joseph. Private (furnished by class for 9 months), 1st Maryland Line, by Sept. 11, 1778 [Ref: D-330, which listed the name as "Drurey"]. Resident of William & Mary Lower Hundred in 1778 [Ref: Q-I:297].
DUFFY, Patrick. Private, Militia, 26th Battalion, Capt. Richard Bennett Mitchell's Company, 1777 [Ref: M-164]. Took the Oath of Allegiance in 1778 [Ref: AA-641].
DUFFY, Terrence, Sergeant, 3rd Company, 3rd Maryland Line, Aug. 28, 1781 [Ref: D-393].
DUGGARD, Henry. Private, Militia, 12th Battalion, Capt. Benjamin Lusby Corry's Company, 1777 [Ref: M-160].
DUGGINS (DUGGONS), Robert. Took the Oath of Allegiance in 1778 [Ref: L-16, which listed the name as "Dugend" and AA-641, which latter listed the name as "Dugud"]. Resident of Newport West Hundred in 1778 [Ref: Q-I:297].
DUGGINS (DUGGONS), Henry. Private, 1st Maryland Line, enrolled and passed on July 8, 1776 [Ref: D-32]. Took the Oath of Allegiance in 1778 [Ref: AA-641]. Resident of Newport West Hundred in 1778 [Ref: Q-I:297].
DUKE, Jane. See "John Stone," q.v.
DUKE, Thomas. See "John Stone," q.v.
DULANY, Rebecca. See "Samuel Hanson," q.v.
DULANY, Walter. See "Samuel Hanson," q.v.
DULEY, John. See "John Dooley," q.v.
DULEY, Thomas. See "Thomas Dooley," q.v.
DUNCAN, James. Took the Oath of Allegiance in 1778 [Ref: AA-641].
DUNN, John (1705-). Rendered patriotic service by providing wheat for the use of the military in October 1782 [Ref: N-563]. Aged about 65 as noted in a 1770 deposition [Ref DD-706].
DUNNING, Abednego. Private, Militia, 12th Battalion, Capt. Alexander McPherson's Company, 1777 [Ref: M-160]. See "Abenego Downing," q.v.
DUNNING, Butler. On Feb. 16, 1820, the Treasurer of Maryland was directed to pay to "Butler Dunning, of Charles County, half pay of a private for his Revolutionary War services." [Ref: O-338].
DUNNING, Dennis. Drummer, 2nd Company, 1st Maryland Line, Capt. Edward Prall's Company, Jan. 1, 1782 [Ref: D-431].
DUNNING, James. Private, Militia, 12th Battalion, Capt. Alexander McPherson's Company, 1777 [Ref: M-160]. Private, 1st Maryland Line, drafted from the Charles County militia and in service on June 11 or 12, 1781 and discharged on Dec. 3, 1781 [Ref: D-376, G-569, I-10]. See "James Downing," q.v.

DUNNING, John. Corporal, Militia, 26th Battalion, Capt. Hezekiah Garner's Company, 1777 [Ref: M-162]. Resident of Port Tobacco East Hundred in 1778 [Ref: Q-I:297]. See "John Downing," q.v.

DUNNINGTON, Elijah. Private, Militia, 26th Battalion, Capt. William Winter's Company, 1777 [Ref: M-165]. Took the Oath of Allegiance in 1778 [Ref: L-16]. Resident of Durham Lower Hundred in 1778 [Ref: Q-I:297].

DUNNINGTON, Elizabeth. See "Joseph Manning," q.v.

DUNNINGTON, Francis (1700-   ). Took the Oath of Allegiance in 1778 [Ref: L-16, AA-641]. Resident of Durham Lower Hundred in 1778 [Ref: Q-I:297]. Aged about 74 as noted in a 1774 deposition [Ref: DD-706].

DUNNINGTON, Francis Jr. (1746-1820) Took the Oath of Allegiance in 1778 [Ref: L-16]. Private, 3rd Maryland Line, enrolled by Capt. Joseph Marbury by May 24, 1780 [Ref: D-333, F-181, which latter source listed the name as "Francis Durington"]. Private, 1st Maryland Line, Capt. John S. Belt's Company, by Jan. 1, 1782 [Ref: D-437, which listed the name without the "Jr."]. Francis Dunnington married Margaret E. Perry and died on Nov. 14, 1820 [Ref: J-I:898].

DUNNINGTON, George (1743-   ). Sergeant, Militia, 26th Battalion, Capt. Francis Mastin's Company, March 19, 1776 [Ref: M-158, K-1814]. Took the Oath of Allegiance in 1778 [Ref: L-16, AA-641]. Ensign, 26th Battalion, Capt. Samuel Luckett's Company, recommended on March 20, 1781 and commissioned on April 6, 1781 [Ref: M-72, G-379, H-136]. Aged about 37 as noted in a 1780 deposition [Ref: DD-706].

DUNNINGTON, Hezekiah (1757-1822). Private, 1st Maryland Line, enrolled and passed on July 19, 1776 [Ref: D-31]. Private, Militia, 26th Battalion, Capt. William Winter's Company, 1777 [Ref: M-165]. Took the Oath of Allegiance in 1778 [Ref: L-16]. Resident of Durham Lower Hundred in 1778 [Ref: Q-I:297]. Hezekiah Dunnington was born on Sept. 29, 1757, married Ann McGregor, and died in Virginia in February 1822 [Ref: J-I:898].

DUNNINGTON, James. Took the Oath of Allegiance in 1778 [Ref: L-16, AA-641].

DUNNINGTON, Peter. Sergeant, Militia, 26th Battalion, Capt. Hezekiah Garner's Company, 1777 [Ref: M-162]. Took the Oath of Allegiance in 1778 [Ref: L-16, AA-641]. Rendered patriotic service by providing wheat for the use of the military in May 1783 [Ref: N-598].

DUNNINGTON, William (1740-1802). Private, Militia, 26th Battalion, Capt. William Winter's Company, 1777 [Ref: M-165]. "William Dunnington" took the Oath of Allegiance in 1778 [Ref: L-16]. "William Sone Dunnington" was a resident of Durham Lower Hundred in 1778

[Ref: Q-I:297]. "William Dunnington" was born on April 13, 1740, married ---- Beck, served as a private in the war, and died in 1802 [Ref: J-I:898].
DUNNINGTON, William Jr. Took the Oath of Allegiance in 1778 [Ref: AA-641]. Resident of Durham Lower Hundred in 1778 [Ref: Q-I:297, which listed the name as "William J. Dunnington"].
DUNNINGTON, William Sr. Took the Oath of Allegiance in 1778 [Ref: L-16, AA-641]. See "William Dunnington," q.v.
DUTTON, Gerrard. Took the Oath of Allegiance in 1778 [Ref: AA-641, which listed the name as "Gerald Dutton"]. Resident of William & Mary Upper Hundred in 1778 [Ref: Q-I:297].
DUTTON, Notley (c1734-1801). Rendered patriotic service by providing clothing for the use of the military in February 1778 [Ref: Y-II:234]. Took the Oath of Allegiance in 1778 [Ref: AA-641]. Resident of William & Mary Upper Hundred in 1778 [Ref: Q-I:297]. A substitute for Notley Dutton was certified by County Lieutenant Francis Ware on May 24, 1779 [Ref: N-224, J-I:905, which latter source stated he had also served as a private]. See "Andrew Gray," q.v.
DUTTON, Thomas. Private, Militia, 12th Battalion, Capt. Jonathan Yates' Company, 1777 [Ref: M-162]. Private (furnished by class for 9 months), 1st Maryland Line, by Sept. 11, 1778 [Ref: D-330]. Took the Oath of Allegiance in 1778 [Ref: AA-641]. Resident of William & Mary Upper Hundred in 1778 [Ref: Q-I:297].
DUTTON, Zachariah. Private, Militia, 12th Battalion, Capt. John Parnham's Company, 1777 [Ref: M-160]. Took the Oath of Allegiance in 1778 [Ref: AA-641]. Resident of William & Mary Upper Hundred in 1778 [Ref: Q-I:297].
DYAL, David. Private, 1st Maryland Line, enrolled and passed on July 19, 1776 [Ref: D-31].
DYAL, Joseph. Private, Militia, Capt. Francis Mastin's Company, 26th Battalion, March 19, 1776 [Ref: M-158, K-1814, which listed the name as "Dyall"].
DYAL, William. Took the Oath of Allegiance in 1778 [Ref: AA-641].
DYE, Reuben. Took the Oath of Allegiance in 1778 [Ref: L-16]. See "Reuben Dyer" and "John Baillie," q.v.
DYER, Annacletus (1753-   ). Took the Oath of Allegiance in 1778 [Ref: L-16, which listed the name as "Cletus Dyar"]. Rendered patriotic service by providing wheat for the use of the military in April 1782 [Ref: N-498, which listed the name as "Annaclatus Dyan"]. Aged about 30 as noted in a 1783 deposition [Ref: DD-706, which listed the name as "Annacletus Dyar"]. Resident of Port Tobacco Upper Hundred in 1778 [Ref: Q-I:297, which listed the name as "Annactitus Dyar"].

DYER, Elizabeth. See "Joseph Blanford," q.v.
DYER, George. Private, 2nd Maryland Line, 1782 [Ref: D-443].
DYER, Horatio. See "Joseph Blanford" and "Charles Smith," q.v.
DYER, James. Private, 3rd Maryland Line, 1778 [Ref: D-103].
DYER, Jeremiah. Private, Militia, 12th Battalion, Capt. Alexander McPherson's Company, 1777 [Ref: M-160]. Resident of Port Tobacco East Hundred in 1778 [Ref: Q-I:297].
DYER, John. Private, 1st Maryland Line, Capt. John S. Belt's Company, by Jan. 1, 1782 [Ref: D-437].
DYER, Joseph. Private, Militia, 26th Battalion, Capt. Hezekiah Garner's Company, 1777 [Ref: M-162].
DYER, Reuben. Private, Militia, 26th Battalion, Capt. William Winter's Company, 1777 [Ref: M-165]. Resident of Durham Lower Hundred in 1778 [Ref: Q-I:297]. See "Reuben Dye," q.v.
DYER, Walter. "Walter Dyar" was a private in the Lower Battalion of Prince George's County in 1776 [Ref: D-35]. "Walter Dyer" was a sergeant in the 3rd Maryland Line from June 26, 1777 to Jan. 26, 1780 [Ref: D-103]. "Walter Dyer" was from Charles County and a lieutenant in the Maryland Line in 1782 [Ref: I-81].
DYER, William. Private, Militia, 26th Battalion, Capt. Hezekiah Garner's Company, 1777 [Ref: M-162]. Took the Oath of Allegiance in 1778 [Ref: L-16, AA-641, which sources listed the name as "Dyar"]. Resident of Port Tobacco Upper Hundred in 1778 [Ref: Q-I:297].
DYNE, Jesse. Private, Militia, Capt. Francis Mastin's Company, 26th Battalion, March 19, 1776 [Ref: M-158, K-1814].
DYSON, Aquilla. Took the Oath of Allegiance in 1778 [Ref: L-16]. Resident of Newport East Hundred in 1778 [Ref: Q-I:297].
DYSON, Bennett (1745-   ). Born on Aug. 13, 1745, son of John Baptist Dyson and Mary ----, he married Winifred Chunn on Jan. 27, 1765 in Trinity Parish [Ref: EE-5, EE-12]. First Lieutenant, Militia, 12th Battalion, Capt. John Parnham's Company, July 5, 1777 [Ref: M-72, M-160]. Appointed a Justice of the Peace on Nov. 19, 1779 and Jan. 17, 1782 [Ref: F-19, I-45]. Procured corn for the immediate use of the military and reported same to Governor Lee on June 20, 1780 [Ref: F-518]. Captain, Militia, 26th Battalion, recommended on March 20, 1781 and commissioned on April 6, 1781 [Ref: G-379, H-136].
DYSON, Dorcas. See "Henry Clarkson," q.v.
DYSON, Elizabeth. See "Thomas Andrew Dyson," q.v.
DYSON, George Jr. Sergeant, Militia, 12th Battalion, Capt. Henry Clarkson's Company, 1777 [Ref: M-159]. Second Lieutenant, Militia, Capt.

Thomas A. Dyson's Company, commissioned on Jan. 19, 1781 [Ref: M-72, G-280]. Resident of Newport East Hundred in 1778 [Ref: Q-I:297].

DYSON, George Sr. (1716-1791). Took the Oath of Allegiance in 1778 [Ref: L-16]. Resident of Newport East Hundred in 1778 [Ref: Q-I:297]. George Dyson was aged about 63 as noted in a 1779 deposition and stated that he was the son of Thomas Dyson and nephew of John Dyson [Ref: BB-472, DD-706]. He married (wife's name not given) and died in January 1791 [Ref: J-I:911].

DYSON, Gerrard (c1755-1832). Private, Militia, 12th Battalion, Capt. Henry Clarkson's Company, 1777 [Ref: M-159]. Resident of Newport East Hundred in 1778 [Ref: Q-I:297]. Rendered patriotic service by providing wheat for the use of the military in December 1782 [Ref: N-575]. Gerrard Dyson was born circa 1755, married (wife unknown), and a son Oswell or Oswald Dyson (c1792-1852) married Lucinda Green(?). [Ref: S-3140].

DYSON, John. See "George Dyson, Jr.," q.v.

DYSON, John Baptist. See "Bennett Dyson," q.v.

DYSON, Joseph. See "Thomas Andrew Dyson," q.v.

DYSON, Margaret. See "John Dent, of Hatch," q.v.

DYSON, Mary. See "Bennett Dyson" and "John Maddox," q.v.

DYSON, Thomas. See "George Dyson, Jr.," q.v.

DYSON, Thomas Andrew (1754-   ). Born on Oct. 28, 1754, son of Joseph Dyson and Elizabeth Chunn who were married on April 17, 1752 in Trinity Parish [Ref: EE-10]. Private, 1st Maryland Line, enrolled and passed on July 8, 1776 [Ref: D-32]. Second Lieutenant and then First Lieutenant, Militia, 12th Battalion, Capt. Henry Clarkson's Company, 1777 [Ref: M-72, M-159, which listed the name as "Thomas A. Dyson" and C-401, which listed the name as "Thomas Andrew Dyson"]. Took the Oath of Allegiance in 1778 [Ref: AA-641, L-16, which latter source mistakenly listed the name as "Thomas O. Dyson"]. Resident of Newport East Hundred in 1778 [Ref: Q-I:297]. Recruiting Officer in Charles County, 1779-1780 [Ref: F-54, which listed the name as "Thomas Dyson"]. Captain, 12th Battalion, commissioned on Jan. 19, 1781 [Ref: M-72, G-280, which listed the name as "Thomas A. Dyson"]. Appointed an Ensign in the Maryland Line on Sept. 4, 1781, "date of rank to be determined." [Ref: G-600].

ECHISON, Joseph. See "Joseph Atchison," q.v.

EDELEN, Ann. See "Joseph Benedict Gardiner," q.v.

EDELEN (EDELIN), Basil. Corporal, 3rd Maryland Line, enlisted May 27, 1778 and discharged in 1780, "time out." [Ref: D-107].

EDELEN (EDELIN), Benjamin (c1750-1791). Private, Militia, 26th Battalion, Capt. William Winter's Company, 1777 [Ref: M-165, which listed the name as "Edelin"]. Took the Oath of Allegiance in 1778 [Ref: L-16]. Rendered patriotic service by providing wheat for the use of the military in December 1782 [Ref: N-574]. A son of John and Sarah Edelen, he was born in Prince George's County, rendered patriotic service in Charles County, married Sarah ----, and died in King George County, Virginia (directly across the Potomac River from his ancestral home in Maryland) by December 16, 1791 (date of inventory). [Ref: Harry Wright Newman's *Charles County Gentry*, pp. 199-200].

EDELEN, Catherine. See "Joseph Edelen," q.v.

EDELEN (EDELIN), Clement (1753-1839). Sergeant, 1st Maryland Line, enlisted Dec. 10, 1776 and discharged Dec. 27, 1779 [Ref: D-106]. He was born in Charles County, fought in the battles of White Plains, Germantown and Brandywine during the war, married Anne Simpson in Prince George's County, moved to Breckenridge County, Kentucky after the war, migrated to White County, Illinois where he married secondly at the age of 74 to Lucy Aud ("who was much his junior") and died on May 25, 1839. His widow married Adolphus Ammons and she was still living in February 1862, aged 56 [Ref: Harry Wright Newman's *Charles County Gentry*, p. 215].

EDELEN (EADLIN), Edward (1747-1811). Private, 1st Maryland Line, enlisted Dec. 10, 1776 and discharged Dec. 27, 1779 [Ref: D-106]. Son of James Edelen and Salome Noble, he was a staunch patriot during the Revolutionary War. He and Thomas Dent were among those present who attended a meeting of the Committee of Observation for Prince George's County at Piscataway on August 4, 1775 [Ref: Harry Wright Newman's *Charles County Gentry*, p. 179].

EDELEN (EDELIN), Edward Jr. (1752-1834). Private, Militia, 12th Battalion, Capt. John Parnham's Company, 1777 [Ref: M-161, which listed the name as "Edelin" without the "Jr."]. Took the Oath of Allegiance in 1778 [Ref: L-16]. Resident of Newport West Hundred in 1778 [Ref: Q-I:297]. Rendered patriotic service by providing wheat for the use of the military in May 1783 [Ref: N-598]. Edward Edelen was born in 1752, married Eleanor Boarman, and died testate before Dec. 23, 1834 [Ref: J-I:926].

EDELEN (EDELIN), Edward Sr. (1715/7-1780). Took the Oath of Allegiance in 1778 [Ref: L-16]. Aged about 64 as noted in a 1779 deposition [Ref: BB-477, DD-706]. Resident of Newport West Hundred in 1778 [Ref: Q-I:297, which listed the name as "Edelin"].

EDELEN, Elizabeth. See "Thomas Dent," q.v.

EDELEN (EDELIN), Francis (c1755-1830). Private, 1st Maryland Line, enrolled and passed on July 8, 1776 [Ref: D-32, which listed the name as

"Edilen"]. Private, Militia, 12th Battalion, Capt. John Parnham's Company, 1777 [Ref: M-161, which listed the name as "Frans. Edilin"]. Took the Oath of Allegiance in 1778 [Ref: AA-641, L-16, which listed the name as "Edelin"]. Resident of Newport West Hundred in 1778 [Ref: Q-I:297, which listed the name as "Edelin"].

EDELEN (EDELIN), Francis (c1753-1823). Private, Militia, 26th Battalion, Capt. William McPherson's Company, 1777 [Ref: M-163, which listed the name as "Edelin"]. Resident of Port Tobacco Upper Hundred in 1778 [Ref: Q-I:297]. Rendered patriotic service by providing wheat for the use of the military in January and December 1782 [Ref: N-474, N-573, which also listed the name as "Edelin"].

EDELEN (EDELIN), George. Private, 3rd Maryland Line, enlisted May 30, 1778 and discharged Feb. 13, 1779 [Ref: D-107].

EDELEN (EDELIN), Henry. Private, Militia, 26th Battalion, Capt. William McPherson's Company, 1777 [Ref: M-163, which listed the name as "Edelin"]. Private, 3rd Maryland Line, 1778 [Ref: D-107]. One Henry Edelin died in 1778 [Ref: GG-192].

EDELEN (EDELIN), James. Private, Militia, 12th Battalion, Capt. Alexander McPherson's Company, 1777 [Ref: M-160, which listed the name as "Edilin"]. Took the Oath of Allegiance in 1778 [Ref: L-16, which listed the name as "Edelin"]. Resident of Bryan Town Hundred in 1778 [Ref: Q-I:297]. See "Edward Edelen (Eadlin)" and "Joseph Edelen (Edelin)," q.v.

EDELEN (EADLIN), John. Private, 1st Maryland Line, enlisted Dec. 10, 1776 and discharged Dec. 27, 1779 [Ref: D-106].

EDELEN (EDELIN), John (c1750-1803). Corporal, Militia, 12th Battalion, Capt. John Parnham's Company, 1777 [Ref: M-160, which listed the name as "Edilin"]. Took the Oath of Allegiance in 1778 [Ref: L-16, which listed the name as "Edelin"]. Resident of Newport West Hundred in 1778 [Ref: Q-I:297, which listed the name as "Edelin"]. Rendered patriotic service by providing wheat for the use of the military in November 1781 [Ref: N-457, which listed the name as "Edelin"]. See "Benjamin Edelen," q.v.

EDELEN (EDELIN), Joseph (1757-1833). Rendered patriotic service by providing wheat for the use of the military in Charles County in May 1783 [Ref: N-598]. Took the Oath of Allegiance in 1778 in Prince George's County. Son of James Edelen and Salome Noble, he married Catherine Edelen, daughter of Joseph Edelen and Catherine Queen, and died on Jan. 4, 1833 [Ref: J-I:926, and Harry Wright Newman's *Charles County Gentry*, p. 181].

EDELEN, Mary. See "Charles Boarman," q.v.

EDELEN (EDELIN), Richard. Sergeant, Militia, 26th Battalion, Capt. William McPherson's Company, 1777 [Ref: M-163, which listed the name as "Edelin"]. Took the Oath of Allegiance in 1778 [Ref: L-16, which listed the name as "Edelin"]. Resident of Bryan Town Hundred in 1778 [Ref: Q-I:297].

EDELEN (EDELIN), Richard (1715-1791). Rendered patriotic service by providing wheat for the use of the military in December 1782 [Ref: N-573, which listed the name as "Edelin"]. Richard Edelen was born on Aug. 4, 1715, married Sarah Stonestreet, and died testate by February 1791 in Prince George's County [Ref: J-I:926].

EDELEN (EDELIN), Richard (c1750-1803). Private, Militia, 12th Battalion, Capt. Alexander McPherson's Company, 1777 [Ref: M-160, which listed the name as "Edelin"]. Rendered patriotic service by providing wheat for the use of the military in June 1782 [Ref: N-523].

EDELEN (EDELIN), Richard, of Thomas (1723-1810). Took the Oath of Allegiance in 1778 [Ref: AA-641, L-16, which listed the name as "Edelin"].

EDELEN (EDELIN), Samuel. Took the Oath of Allegiance in 1778 [Ref: L-16, which listed the name as "Edelin"].

EDELEN, Sarah. See "Benjamin Edelen," q.v.

EDELEN (EDELIN), Susannah. Rendered patriotic service by providing wheat for the use of the military in May 1783 [Ref: N-598]. One Susannah Edelen died testate in 1813 in the District of Columbia and another Susannah Edelen died testate in 1818 in Charles County [Ref: Harry Wright Newman's *Charles County Gentry*, p. 214].

EDELEN, Theresa. See "Henry Boarman," q.v.

EDGAR, Sarah. See "John Scott," q.v.

EDMUNDS, William. Took the Oath of Allegiance in 1778 [Ref: AA-641].

EDWARDS, Jesse. Private, 1st Maryland Line, enrolled and passed on July 20, 1776 [Ref: D-33].

EDWARDS, John. Private, Militia, 12th Battalion, Capt. Henry Clarkson's Company, 1777 [Ref: M-159]. Resident of Bryan Town Hundred in 1778 [Ref: Q-I:297].

EDWARDS, Susanna. See "Hatch Dent," q.v.

EGERTON, Lydia. See "William Smallwood, Jr.," q.v.

EGERTON, Peter. Took the Oath of Allegiance in 1778 [Ref: AA-641]. Resident of Port Tobacco East Hundred in 1778 [Ref: Q-I:297].

EILBECK, Sarah. Rendered patriotic service by providing clothing for the use of the military in February 1778 [Ref: Y-II:234].

ELDER, Elizabeth. See "Richard Brawner," q.v.

ELGIN, George. Private, Militia, 26th Battalion, Capt. William Winter's Company, 1777 [Ref: M-165]. Resident of Port Tobacco Upper Hundred in 1778 [Ref: Q-I:297].

ELGIN, George (deceased by September 1778). Took the Oath of Allegiance in 1778 [Ref: L-16]. Resident of Durham Lower Hundred in 1778 [Ref: Q-I:297].

ELGIN, Harrison. Private, Militia, 26th Battalion, Capt. Francis Mastin's Company, 1777 [Ref: M-164]. Private, 1st Maryland Line, drafted from the Charles County militia on July 27, 1781 [Ref: D-377, G-569].

ELGIN, Hezekiah (1762-1814). Private, 1st Maryland Line, drafted from the Charles County militia on July 27, 1781 [Ref: D-377, G-569]. Hezekiah Elgin married Sinai Elgin and migrated to Kentucky where he died before Feb. 22, 1814 [Ref: J-I:941].

ELGIN, John. Two men by this name took the Oath of Allegiance in 1778 [Ref: AA-641, L-16, which latter source only listed one]. One John Elgin was aged about 64 as noted in a 1773 deposition [Ref: DD-706]. Resident of William & Mary Upper Hundred in 1778 [Ref: Q-I:297].

ELGIN, Joseph. Took the Oath of Allegiance in 1778 [Ref: L-16]. Rendered patriotic service by assisting in the purchase of wheat for the use of the military in 1781 [Ref: N-450, N-454, N-456].

ELGIN, Richard. Private, 1st Maryland Line, enrolled and passed on July 25, 1776 [Ref: D-32]. Private, Militia, 26th Battalion, Capt. William Winter's Company, 1777 [Ref: M-165]. Took the Oath of Allegiance in 1778 [Ref: L-16]. Resident of Port Tobacco Upper Hundred in 1778 [Ref: Q-I:297]. Rendered patriotic service by assisting in the purchase of wheat for the use of the military in 1781 [Ref: N-345, N-438, N-440, N-448, N-450, N-457, N-458].

ELGIN, Samuel (1758-1844). Private, 1st Maryland Line, enrolled and passed on July 27, 1776 [Ref: D-31]. Private, Militia, 26th Battalion, Capt. Francis Mastin's Company, 1777 [Ref: M-163]. Took the Oath of Allegiance in 1778 [Ref: L-16, AA-641]. Samuel Elgin was born on July 5, 1758, married Agnes McClanahan, and died in Missouri on Dec. 27, 1844 [Ref: J-I:941].

ELGIN, Sinai. See "Hezekiah Elgin," q.v.

ELGIN, William. Private, Militia, Capt. Francis Mastin's Company, 26th Battalion, March 19, 1776 through at least 1777 [Ref: M-158, M-164, K-1814, which also listed the name as "Edglin"].

ELGIN, William Jr. Took the Oath of Allegiance in 1778 [Ref: L-16].

ELGIN, William Sr. (1732-1794). Took the Oath of Allegiance in 1778 [Ref: L-16]. William Elgin, Sr., married Elizabeth Harrison and died in September 1794 [Ref: J-I:941].

ELLETT, Richard. Took the Oath of Allegiance in 1778 [Ref: L-16].
ELLIOTT, Thomas. Private, 1st Maryland Line, drafted from the Charles County militia on July 27, 1781 [Ref: D-377, G-569].
ELMER, Benjamin. Private, Militia, 26th Battalion, Capt. Thomas H. Marshall's Company, 1777 [Ref: M-163, which listed the name as "Benj. Elmer(?)" and X-76, which listed it as "Benjamin Elmer"].
ENGLISH, James. Fife Major, 3rd Maryland Line, enlisted May 1, 1779 and reported missing at the Battle of Camden in South Carolina on Aug. 16, 1780 [Ref: D-107].
ENGLISH, Joseph. Private, Militia, 26th Battalion, Capt. William Winter's Company, 1777 [Ref: M-165]. Took the Oath of Allegiance in 1778 [Ref: L-16, AA-641]. Resident of Durham Lower Hundred in 1778 [Ref: Q-I:297].
ENGLISH, Samuel. Private, 3rd Maryland Line, 1777-1779 [Ref: D-107].
ENNIS, David. Took the Oath of Allegiance in 1778 [Ref: AA-641]. Resident of William & Mary Upper Hundred in 1778 [Ref: Q-I:297].
ENNIS, George. Private, 1st Maryland Line, 1778, and reportedly "deserted" on June 10, 1778 [Ref: D-106].
ERSKINE, Elizabeth. Rendered patriotic service by providing clothing for the use of the military in January 1778 [Ref: Y-II:230].
ESTEP, Ann. See "James Keech," q.v.
ESTEP, John. Private, Militia, 12th Battalion, Capt. Peter Wood's Company, 1777 [Ref: M-161]. Took the Oath of Allegiance in 1778 [Ref: L-16]. Resident of Benedict Hundred in 1778 [Ref: Q-I:297].
ESTEP, Richard. Ensign, Militia, 12th Battalion, Capt. John Thomas' Company, July 27, 1776 [Ref: B-127, M-74, M-161, which latter source listed the name as "Rich'd Eastip(?)"]. Took the Oath of Allegiance in 1778 [Ref: L-16]. Resident of Benedict Hundred in 1778 [Ref: Q-I:297]. Second Lieutenant, Militia, Capt. John Gardner's Company, commissioned on Jan. 19, 1781 [Ref: G-280].
ETCHENSON, Mary. See "William Etchenson," q.v.
ETCHENSON, William (c1760-1821). Private, 1st Maryland Line. He married Mary Weedin or Weeding on Feb. 23, 1797 in Charles County and died in 1821. Mary Etchenson applied for a pension (R3373) on June 6, 1851, aged 78 [Ref: V-I:1129, W-113, which latter source listed the name as "Etcheson"]. See "William Atchison," q.v.
EVANS, Alexander. Private, Militia, Capt. Francis Mastin's Company, 26th Battalion, March 19, 1776 [Ref: M-158, K-1814, which sources listed the name as "Evens"]. Private, Militia, 26th Battalion, Capt. Francis Mastin's Company, 1777 [Ref: M-164, which listed the name as "Alex. Evens"]. Took the Oath of Allegiance in 1778 [Ref: L-16, AA-641]. Constable, 1778

[Ref: CC-709]. Rendered patriotic service by providing wheat for the use of the military in May 1783 [Ref: N-598, which listed the name as "Evins"].
EVANS, Hezekiah. Private, Militia, 26th Battalion, Capt. Hezekiah Garner's Company, 1777 [Ref: M-162].
EVANS, Jesse. Private, 1st Maryland Line, enrolled and passed on July 19, 1776 [Ref: D-31]. Took the Oath of Allegiance in 1778 [Ref: L-16, AA-641].
EVANS, Joseph (1727-   ). Took the Oath of Allegiance in 1778 [Ref: L-16, AA-641]. Aged about 51 as noted in a 1778 deposition [Ref: CC-699, DD-707].
EVANS, Joshua. Private, Militia, 26th Battalion, Capt. Francis Mastin's Company, 1777 [Ref: M-164].
EVANS, Thomas. Private, Militia, 12th Battalion, Capt. Jonathan Yates' Company, 1777 [Ref: M-162]. Took the Oath of Allegiance in 1778 [Ref: L-16]. Resident of William & Mary Lower Hundred in 1778 [Ref: Q-I:297].
EWELL, Marianne. See "James Craik," q.v.
FAGG, Joel. Private, Militia, 26th Battalion, Capt. Francis Mastin's Company, 1777 [Ref: M-163, which listed the name as "Joell(?) Fagg" and X-76, which listed the name as "Joel Fagg"]. Resident of Durham Lower Hundred in 1778 [Ref: Q-I:297].
FAGG, William. Private, Militia, 26th Battalion, Capt. Francis Mastin's Company, 1777 [Ref: M-164, which listed the name as "Wm. Fagg" and X-78, which listed the name as "William Tagg"]. Resident of Durham Lower Hundred in 1778 [Ref: Q-I:297].
FAIRFAX, Anne. See "Jonathan Gill," q.v.
FAIRFAX, Jonathan. Private, Militia, 26th Battalion, Capt. Francis Mastin's Company, 1777 [Ref: X-78]. Took the Oath of Allegiance in 1778 [Ref: L-16, AA-641]. Resident of Durham Lower Hundred in 1778 [Ref: Q-I:297]. Rendered patriotic service by providing wheat for the use of the military in May 1783 [Ref: N-597].
FAIRFAX, William (c1720-1793). Took the Oath of Allegiance in 1778 [Ref: AA-641]. Rendered patriotic service by providing wheat for the use of the military in July 1782 [Ref: N-531, which listed the name as "Farfax"]. William Fairfax married first to Benedicta Blancett, second to Elizabeth Buckner, and died in Virginia before Dec. 3, 1793 [Ref: J-I:983].
FARMER, James. Took the Oath of Allegiance in 1778 [Ref: AA-641].
FARMER, Sally. See "Thomas Owen," q.v.
FARMER, William. Corporal, Militia, 26th Battalion, Capt. Richard Bennett Mitchell's Company, 1777 [Ref: M-164]. Resident of Port Tobacco West Hundred in 1778 [Ref: Q-I:297].
FARNANDIS, Chloe. See "James Farnandis," q.v.

FARNANDIS, Elenor. Rendered patriotic service by providing wheat for the use of the military in August and December 1782 [Ref: N-538, N-576].

FARNANDIS, James (c1755-1790). First Lieutenant, Militia, 26th Battalion, Capt. Richard Sinnett's Company, until Jan. 20, 1776 when he entered the continental service as a cadet in the 1st Maryland Company [Ref: M-75, Y-II:23, D-5, which latter source listed the name as "Fernandis"]. Ensign, 1st Maryland Line, captured and exchanged on March 24, 1777 [Ref: D-616, which listed the name as "Fernandez"]. Promoted to lieutenant, 1st Maryland Line, effective Dec. 10, 1776, and later to captain; resigned July 15, 1779 [Ref: D-108, C-399, which listed the name as "Farnandes"]. He was paid for being a recruiting officer in January 1780 [Ref: F-54, which listed the name as "Fernandes"]. James Farnandis married first to Anne Elizabeth Wallace and married second to Chloe Farnandis. A son Walter Farnandis (1782-1856) married Mary Dorsey. James died testate before June 7, 1790 (date of probate). [Ref: J-I:989, S-1635].

FARNANDIS, Peter (1740-c1790). First Lieutenant, Militia, 26th Battalion, Capt. Richard Bennett Mitchell's Company, July 27, 1776 [Ref: B-127, M-75, M-164, which latter source listed the name as "Fernandies"]. Took the Oath of Allegiance in 1778 [Ref: AA-641, L-16, which latter source listed the name as "Farnadiz"]. Aged about 35 as noted in a 1775 deposition and aged about 37 as noted in a 1777 deposition [Ref: CC-581, DD-707]. Resident of Port Tobacco West Hundred in 1778 [Ref: Q-I:297, which listed the name as "Fernandis"]. Constable, 1778 [Ref: CC-709]. Rendered patriotic service by providing wheat for the use of the military in December 1782 and May 1783 [Ref: N-576, N-599]. Peter Farnandis married Elizabeth Grant and died after 1789 [Ref: J-I:989].

FARNANDIS, Sarah. See "John Maddox," q.v.

FARNANDIS, Walter. See "James Farnandis," q.v.

FARR, John. Took the Oath of Allegiance in 1778 [Ref: AA-641]. Resident of William & Mary Upper Hundred in 1778 [Ref: Q-I:297].

FARR, William. Rendered patriotic service by providing clothing for the use of the military in February 1778 [Ref: Y-II:234]. Took the Oath of Allegiance in 1778 [Ref: AA-641, which listed the name as "Far"]. Resident of William & Mary Upper Hundred in 1778 [Ref: Q-I:297].

FARRAND, Hezekiah (1752-   ). Born on May 13, 1752, son of John and Mary Farrand [Ref: EE-8]. Took the Oath of Allegiance in 1778 [Ref: L-16]. Resident of Bryan Town Hundred in 1778 [Ref: Q-I:297, which listed the name as "Farran"].

FARRAND, John. Took the Oath of Allegiance in 1778 [Ref: L-16, AA-641, which sources listed the name as "Farrans" and "Farrand"]. "John Farran" was a resident of Bryan Town Hundred in 1778 [Ref: Q-I:297]. "John Farrand" married Mary Stonestreet on May 2, 1743 in Trinity Parish [Ref: EE-5].

FARRAND, John, of John. "John Farran" was a sergeant in the 7th Maryland Line in 1777-1778 [Ref: D-207]. "John Farrand, son of John" married Elizabeth Broady on Dec. 13, 1772 in Trinity Parish [Ref: EE-19]. See "Hezekiah Farrand," q.v.

FARRAND, Mary. See "Hezekiah Farrand" and "John Farrand," q.v.

FARRAND, Timothy. Took the Oath of Allegiance in 1778 [Ref: L-16]. Resident of Bryan Town Hundred in 1778 [Ref: Q-I:297, which listed the name as "Farran"].

FARRELL, Patrick. See "Patrick Ferrell," q.v.

FARRIE, John. See "John Ferrell," q.v.

FEARSON, Attwix (c1710-1792). Took the Oath of Allegiance in 1778 [Ref: AA-641, which listed the name as "Attevix Fearson" and L-16, which misspelled the name as "Alwin Furson"]. Aged about 32 as noted in a 1742 deposition and aged about 66 as noted in a 1774 deposition [Ref: DD-707, which listed the name as "Allwicks Fearson" (and mentioned his father Samuel Fearson) and DD-172, which listed the name as "Attwix Pherson"]. Resident of William & Mary Lower Hundred in 1778 [Ref: Q-I:297]. "Attovix Fearson" was born in 1720 in England, married Pricilla Newman, and died in 1792 in Maryland [Ref: J-I:1000].

FEARSON, Joseph (1758-1832). Private, Militia, 12th Battalion, Capt. Jonathan Yates' Company, 1777 [Ref: M-162]. Joseph Fearson married Elizabeth Shaw and died in Washington, D.C. on Sept. 7, 1832 [Ref: J-I:1000].

FEARSON, Samuel. See "Attwix Fearson" and "Walter Fearson," q.v.

FEARSON, Walter. Private, Militia, 12th Battalion, Capt. Jonathan Yates' Company, 1777 [Ref: M-162]. Took the Oath of Allegiance in 1778 [Ref: AA-641, L-16, which latter source listed the name as "Ferson"]. Resident of William & Mary Lower Hundred in 1778 [Ref: Q-I:297]. One Walter Fearson, son of Samuel, was aged about 37 as noted in a 1743 deposition and mentioned that he married Eleanor Newman, daughter of George Newman [Ref: DD-707].

FENDALL, ----. See "George Dent, of John," q.v.

FENDALL, Benjamin. Private, Militia, 26th Battalion, Capt. Thomas H. Marshall's Company, 1777 [Ref: M-163]. Resident of William & Mary Upper Hundred in 1778 [Ref: Q-I:297]. See "Philip Richard Fendall," q.v.

FENDALL, Benjamin Sr. Took the Oath of Allegiance in 1778 [Ref: L-16]. Resident of Pomonkey Hundred in 1778 [Ref: Q-I:297]. Rendered patriotic service by providing wheat for the use of the military in January and October 1782 [Ref: N-471, N-563].

FENDALL, Elizabeth. See "Philip Richard Fendall" and "Samuel Hanson, Jr." q.v.

FENDALL, Henry. Took the Oath of Allegiance in 1778 [Ref: L-16].

FENDALL, John. See "George Clarke Smoot," q.v.

FENDALL, Philip Richard. Son of Benjamin Fendall (died in 1764) and Eleanor Lee (1710-1759), he married first to Sarah Lettice Lee in 1759 and second to Elizabeth ---- by 1786 (no children mentioned). [Ref: P-I:318]. Philip Richard Fendall rendered the following patriotic services: Clerk of the County Court, 1756-1778. Delegate to the Maryland Convention from July 26 to Aug. 14, 1775. Clerk of the Court of Oyer and Terminer and Gaol Delivery, appointed in 1773 and 1776. Served on the Committee of Observation, elected in 1775. He died after 1798, probably in Virginia [Ref: P-I:319, A-10, Y-I:4].

FENDALL, Samuel. Took the Oath of Allegiance in 1778 [Ref: L-16].

FENDALL, Sarah. See "George Dent, of John" and "George Clarke Smoot" and "John Alexander Smoot," q.v.

FENISUS, James. Private, Militia, 26th Battalion, Capt. Francis Mastin's Company, 1777 [Ref: M-164, which listed the name as "Fenisus(?)" and X-78, which listed the name as "Finisisee"].

FENWICK, Ignatius (Colonel), of St. Mary's County. Took the Oath of Allegiance in August 1778 in Charles County [Ref: AA-708].

FENWICK, Monacy. See "James Hagan," q.v.

FERGUSON, Jonathan. Private, Militia, 12th Battalion, Capt. John Parnham's Company, 1777 [Ref: M-160, which listed the name as "Furguson"]. Resident of Newport East Hundred in 1778 [Ref: Q-I:297].

FERGUSON, Robert Sr. Rendered patriotic service by providing wheat for the use of the military in September 1781, and November and December 1782 [Ref: N-438, N-566, N-573]. The obituary of Robert Ferguson, Sr., appeared in the *Maryland Gazette* on Sept. 17, 1812 stating, in part, that he "died Tuesday, Sept. 1, at Mulberry Grove, Charles County, an old inhabitant of that county, and a native of Scotland. He risked his rising fortunes in the same bottom with (America's) liberties, at the time of the Revolution. He was Chief Judge of the Orphans Court." [Ref: FF-60].

FERRAL, Thomas Kennedy. See "Kennedy Ferrell," q.v.

FERRELL (FARRELL), Charles. Private, Militia, 26th Battalion, Capt. Samuel Smallwood's Company, 1777 [Ref: M-165]. Took the Oath of Allegiance in 1778 [Ref: L-16, which listed the name as "Farroll" and AA-641, which listed the name as "Farrall"]. Resident of Port Tobacco Upper Hundred in 1778 [Ref: Q-I:297].

FERRELL (FARRELL), Elisha. Private, Militia, 12th Battalion, Capt. Benjamin Lusby Corry's Company, 1777 [Ref: M-160]. Took the Oath of Allegiance in 1778 [Ref: L-16, which listed the name as "Ferral" and AA-641, which listed the name as "Ferroll"]. Resident of Newport West Hundred in 1778 [Ref: Q-I:297].
FERRELL (FARRELL), Ignatius. Took the Oath of Allegiance in 1778 [Ref: L-16, which listed the name as "Ferral" and AA-641, which listed the name as "Ferrall"]. Resident of Port Tobacco Upper Hundred in 1778 [Ref: Q-I:297].
FERRELL (FARRELL), James. Private, Militia, 12th Battalion, Capt. Benjamin Lusby Corry's Company, 1777 [Ref: M-160]. Resident of Durham Lower Hundred in 1778 [Ref: Q-I:297]. "Jas. Farrell" was a private in the 2nd Maryland Line, Capt. Samuel McPherson's Company, by Jan. 1, 1782 [Ref: D-444].
FERRELL (FARRELL), James Jr. Took the Oath of Allegiance in 1778 [Ref: AA-641, L-16, which latter source listed the name as "Ferral"]. Resident of Newport West Hundred in 1778 [Ref: Q-I:297].
FERRELL (FARRELL), James Sr. Took the Oath of Allegiance in 1778 [Ref: AA-641, L-16, which latter source listed the name as "Ferral"]. Resident of Newport West Hundred in 1778 [Ref: Q-I:297].
FERRELL (FARRELL), John. Private, 3rd Maryland Line, enrolled by Capt. Joseph Marbury by May 24, 1780 [Ref: F-181]. Took the Oath of Allegiance in 1778 [Ref: AA-641, which listed the name as "Farrell" and L-16, which misspelled the name as "Farrie"]. Resident of Newport West Hundred in 1778 [Ref: Q-I:297].
FERRELL (FARRELL), Kennedy. "Kennedy Ferrell" was a private in the militia, 26th Battalion, Capt. William Winter's Company, 1777 [Ref: M-165]. "Thomas Kennedy Ferral" took the Oath of Allegiance in 1778 [Ref: L-16].
FERRELL (FARRELL), Patrick. Private, Militia, 12th Battalion, Capt. Benjamin Lusby Corry's Company, 1777 [Ref: M-160]. Took the Oath of Allegiance in 1778 [Ref: AA-641, which listed the name as "Farrell" and L-16, which misspelled the name as "Farrie"]. Resident of Newport West Hundred in 1778 [Ref: Q-I:297].
PERRELL (FARRELL), Peter. Private, 1st Maryland Line, 1780, who died on June 18, 1781 [Ref: D-535].
FERRELL (FARRELL), Richard. Private, 1st Maryland Line, enrolled and passed on July 8, 1776 [Ref: D-32].
FERRELL (FARRELL), Robert. Private, 2nd Maryland Line, Capt. Samuel McPherson's Company, by Jan. 1, 1782 [Ref: D-444].

FERRELL (FARRELL), Thomas Jr. Took the Oath of Allegiance in 1778 [Ref: L-16, which listed the name as "Ferrie"].

FERRELL (FARRELL), Thomas Kennedy. Took the Oath of Allegiance in 1778 [Ref: AA-641, which listed the name as "Ferrill" and L-16, which listed the name as "Ferrel"].

FISHER, John (1751-   ). Private, Flying Camp, Capt. Bowie's Company, enrolled on July 17, 1776; native of Germany, aged 25, height 5' 6 1/2" [Ref: D-36].

FITZGERALD, James. Private, Militia, 26th Battalion, Capt. Robert Sinnett's Company, 1777 [Ref: M-164, which listed the name as "Jas. Fitzgerrell"]. Took the Oath of Allegiance in 1778 [Ref: AA-641, which listed the name as "Fitzjarell" and L-16, which misspelled the name as "Fittarell"]. Gave a deposition in 1781 pertaining to his inability to perform military service due to family obligations [Ref: Z-208].

FITZGERALD, John. Private, 1st Maryland Line, enrolled and passed on July 25, 1776 [Ref: D-32]. Private, Militia, 26th Battalion, Capt. William Winter's Company, 1777 [Ref: M-165, which listed the name as "Fitzjarrell"]. Took the Oath of Allegiance in 1778 [Ref: AA-641, which listed the name as "Fitzgerrell"].

FLANIGAN, Barton. Private, Militia, 26th Battalion, Capt. Hezekiah Garner's Company, 1777 [Ref: M-163]. Took the Oath of Allegiance in 1778 [Ref: L-16, which listed the name as "Flannigan" and AA-641, which listed the name as "Flannagin"]. Resident of Durham Lower Hundred in 1778 [Ref: Q-I:297].

FLURRY, Edward. Private (draught who had not yet joined the army), 1st Maryland Line, by Sept. 11, 1778 [Ref: D-330].

FLURRY, Edward Jr. Private, Militia, 26th Battalion, Capt. Robert Sinnett's Company, 1777 [Ref: M-164].

FLURRY, Edward Sr. Took the Oath of Allegiance in 1778 [Ref: AA-641].

FLURRY, John. Private, Militia, 26th Battalion, Capt. Robert Sinnett's Company, 1777 [Ref: M-164]. Rendered patriotic service by providing wheat for the use of the military in October and December 1782 [Ref: N-563, N-571].

FLURRY, Rachael. Rendered patriotic service by providing clothing for the use of the military in February 1778 [Ref: Y-II:234, which listed the name as "Furry"].

FLURRY, William. Private, Militia, 26th Battalion, Capt. Robert Sinnett's Company, 1777 [Ref: M-164].

FOOTE, John. Took the Oath of Allegiance in 1778 [Ref: L-16, AA-641].

FORBES, Charles S. Private, Militia, 12th Battalion, Capt. Peter Wood's Company, 1777 [Ref: M-161]. Took the Oath of Allegiance in 1778 [Ref: L-16].

FORBES, James. Son of John Forbes, of Scotland (who emigrated to St. Mary's County and died by 1732), and wife Dryden Cheseldyne. James Forbes married (name of wife not given) and had a son John Forbes (1757-1804). James was County Justice, 1770-1777, and Commissioner of the Tax, 1777. He provided clothing for the use of the military in February 1778. A Delegate to the Continental Congress, 1777-1780, he died while in office [Ref: P-I:323, Y-II:234].

FORBES, James. Private, Militia, 12th Battalion, Capt. Peter Wood's Company, 1777 [Ref: M-161].

FORBES, John. Private, Militia, 12th Battalion, Capt. Peter Wood's Company, 1777 [Ref: M-161]. See "James Forbes" and "Thomas Hanson Marshall," q.v.

FORBES, John. Second Lieutenant, 1st Maryland Line, Capt. Belain Posey's Company, July 17, 1776 [Ref: B-141, D-31, M-76]. See "James Forbes" and "Thomas Hanson Marshall," q.v.

FORD, Ann. See "Thomas Latimer" and "Jacob Latimer," q.v.

FORD, Chandler (c1755-1799). Sergeant, Militia, 12th Battalion, Capt. Jonathan Yates' Company, 1777 [Ref: M-162]. Took the Oath of Allegiance in 1778 [Ref: AA-641]. Resident of William & Mary Lower Hundred in 1778 [Ref: Q-I:297]. Chandler Ford married Elizabeth Chandler [Ref: J-I:1055].

FORD, Charles. Rendered patriotic service by providing wheat for the use of the military in December 1782 and April 1783 [Ref: N-577, N-593].

FORD, Charles Allison (1712-   ). Took the Oath of Allegiance in 1778 [Ref: AA-641, which listed the name as "Charles Alls Ford" and L-16, which listed the name as "Charles Alvin Ford"]. Resident of William & Mary Lower Hundred in 1778 [Ref: Q-I:297]. Aged about 30 as noted in a 1744 deposition [Ref: DD-708, which listed the name as "Charles Allison Ford"].

FORD, Esther. See "Joseph Warder," q.v.

FORD, Hepzabah (Beall). See "Hezekiah Johnson," q.v.

FORD, John. Took the Oath of Allegiance in 1778 [Ref: AA-641]. Resident of Port Tobacco Upper Hundred in 1778 [Ref: Q-I:297].

FORD, Notley (1731-   ). Private, Lower Battalion, Prince George's County, 1776 [Ref: D-35]. Private, Charles County Militia, 26th Battalion, Capt. Samuel Smallwood's Company, 1777 [Ref: M-165]. Took the Oath of Allegiance in Charles County in 1778 [Ref: L-16, AA-641]. Resident of Port Tobacco Upper Hundred in 1778 [Ref: Q-I:297]. Rendered patriotic service by providing wheat for the use of the military in December 1781 [Ref: N-462]. Aged about 39 as noted in a 1770 deposition [Ref: DD-708].

FORD, Posthuma. See "Edward Smoot," q.v.

FORREST, Uriah. See "Zephaniah Turner," q.v.

FOSTER, William. Private, Militia, 12th Battalion, Capt. John Parnham's Company, 1777 [Ref: M-160]. Resident of Newport East Hundred in 1778 [Ref: Q-I:297].

FOWKE, Gerrard (1724-1783). Private, Militia, Capt. Francis Mastin's Company, 26th Battalion, March 19, 1776 [Ref: M-158, K-1814, which listed the name as "Jerard Fowke"]. Ensign, Capt. Belain Posey's Company, July 27, 1776 [Ref: B-141, D-31, M-76]. Took the Oath of Allegiance in 1778 [Ref: AA-641, L-16, which latter source listed the name as "Gerard Fowkes, Sr."]. The obituary of Capt. Gerard Fowke of Charles County appeared in the *Maryland Gazette* on April 3, 1783, stating he died on March 19, 1783, in his 59th year [Ref: FF-62, and "The Fowke Family of Charles County," by Robert W. Barnes, *Maryland Genealogical Society Bulletin* Vol. 34, No. 2 (Spring, 1993), pp. 158-159].

FOWKE, Gerrard Jr. Private, Militia, 26th Battalion, Capt. Robert Sinnett's Company, 1777 [Ref: M-164]. Took the Oath of Allegiance in 1778 [Ref: AA-641, L-16, which latter source listed the name as "Gerard Fowkes, Jr."].

FOWKE, Richard. Private, 1st Maryland Line, enrolled and passed on July 19, 1776 [Ref: D-31].

FOWKE, Roger. Sergeant, Militia, 26th Battalion, Capt. William Winter's Company, 1777 [Ref: M-165]. Took the Oath of Allegiance in 1778 [Ref: AA-641, L-16, which latter source listed the name as "Rogers Fowkes"]. Second Lieutenant, Militia, Capt. George Dent's Company, commissioned May 9, 1778 [Ref: E-72, M-76]. Resident of Durham Lower Hundred in 1778 [Ref: Q-I:297]. Rendered patriotic service by providing wheat for the use of the military in December 1782 [Ref: N-575].

FOWLER, Henry. Took the Oath of Allegiance in 1778 [Ref: L-16]. Private (furnished by class for 9 months), 1st Maryland Line, by Sept. 11, 1778 [Ref: D-330, which listed the name as "Fouler"]. Resident of William & Mary Upper Hundred in 1778 [Ref: Q-I:297].

FOWLER, Thomas. Took the Oath of Allegiance in 1778 [Ref: L-16].

FRANKLIN, Francis Boucher. First Lieutenant, Militia, 26th Battalion, Capt. Hezekiah Garner's Company, 1777 [Ref: M-162]. Took the Oath of Allegiance in 1778 [Ref: L-16, AA-641, which latter source listed the name as "F. B. Franklin"]. Appointed an Inspector of Tobacco at Chickamuxen Creek on Aug. 30, 1780 [Ref: F-271]. Rendered patriotic service by providing wheat for the use of the military in October 1781, and April and

May 1782 [Ref: N-450, N-501, N-509, which also listed the name as "Frances B. Frankling"]. Aged about 37 as noted in a 1779 deposition [Ref: DD-708, which listed the name as "Francis Boucher Franklin"].

FRANKLIN, Hezekiah. Private, Militia, 26th Battalion, Capt. Hezekiah Garner's Company, 1777 [Ref: M-163]. Took the Oath of Allegiance in 1778 [Ref: L-16, AA-641].

FRANKLIN, John. Private, Militia, Capt. Francis Mastin's Company, 26th Battalion, March 19, 1776 [Ref: M-158, K-1814]. Private, 1st Maryland Line, enrolled and passed on July 27, 1776 [Ref: D-31]. Private, Militia, 26th Battalion, Capt. Hezekiah Garner's Company, 1777 [Ref: M-163]. Took the Oath of Allegiance in 1778 [Ref: L-16]. Resident of Port Tobacco East Hundred in 1778 [Ref: Q-I:297].

FRANKLIN, Mary. See "Francis Clinkscales," q.v.

FRANKLIN, Priscilla. Rendered patriotic service by providing wheat for the use of the military in October 1781 and May 1783 [Ref: N-449, N-598, which also spelled the first name as "Presilia"].

FRANKLIN, Richard. Took the Oath of Allegiance in 1778 [Ref: L-16].

FRANKLIN, Robert. Private, Militia, 26th Battalion, Capt. Hezekiah Garner's Company, 1777 [Ref: M-163].

FRANKLIN, Thomas. Private, Militia, 12th Battalion, Capt. Walter Hanson's Company, 1777 [Ref: M-159]. Private (recruit), 1st Maryland Line, by Sept. 11, 1778 [Ref: D-330].

FRANKLIN, William. Private, 1st Maryland Line, enrolled and passed on July 27, 1776 [Ref: D-31]. Corporal, Militia, 26th Battalion, Capt. Hezekiah Garner's Company, 1777 [Ref: M-162]. Rendered patriotic service by providing wheat for the use of the military in November 1781 [Rcf: N-455].

FRANKLIN, William (1714-   ). Took the Oath of Allegiance in 1778 [Ref: AA-641]. Aged about 64 as noted in a 1778 deposition [Ref: DD-708].

FRANKLIN, William Jr. Took the Oath of Allegiance in 1778 [Ref: AA-641].

FRANKLIN, William Robertson. Private, 3rd Maryland Line, enrolled by Capt. Joseph Marbury by May 24, 1780 [Ref: D-333, F-181].

FRANKLIN, Zephaniah. Ensign, Militia, 26th Battalion, Capt. Hezekiah Garner's Company, 1777 [Ref: M-162]. Took the Oath of Allegiance in 1778 [Ref: L-16, AA-641]. Rendered patriotic service by providing wheat for the use of the military in September and October 1781, April 1782, and May 1783 [Ref: N-437, N-449, N-499, N-598, which listed the name as "Frankling"].

FRAZIER, James. Took the Oath of Allegiance in 1778 [Ref: L-16, AA-641, which listed the name as "Frasher"]. Resident of Port Tobacco Upper Hundred in 1778 [Ref: Q-I:297].

FRAZIER, John. Took the Oath of Allegiance in 1778 [Ref: AA-641, which listed the name as "Frazer"]. Resident of Port Tobacco West Hundred in 1778 [Ref: Q-I:297].

FREEMAN, Moab. Private, Militia, 12th Battalion, Capt. Walter Hanson's Company, 1777 [Ref: M-159]. Resident of Port Tobacco East Hundred in 1778 [Ref: Q-I:297].

FREEMAN, Nathaniel (1733-   ). Private, Militia, 12th Battalion, Capt. Walter Hanson's Company, 1777 [Ref: M-159]. Took the Oath of Allegiance in 1778 [Ref: AA-641]. Resident of Port Tobacco East Hundred in 1778 [Ref: Q-I:297]. Aged about 42 as noted in a 1775 deposition [Ref: DD-708].

FRENCH, James. Private, Militia, 12th Battalion, Capt. Jonathan Yates' Company, 1777 [Ref: X-70, but was omitted from the list in Reference M-162]. Took the Oath of Allegiance in 1778 [Ref: L-16, AA-641]. Resident of William & Mary Lower Hundred in 1778 [Ref: Q-I:297].

FRESH, Stephen. Private (substitute for 3 years), 1st Maryland Line, by Sept. 11, 1778 [Ref: D-330].

FULLER, William. Private, 3rd Maryland Line, 1780, enrolled in Charles County for Capt. Joseph Marbury's Company [Ref: D-333].

FURRY, Rachael. See "Rachael Flurry," q.v.

GABARD, John. Took the Oath of Allegiance in 1778 [Ref: AA-641].

GALES, James. Private, Militia, 26th Battalion, Capt. Samuel Smallwood's Company, 1777 [Ref: M-165].

GAMBLE, Edward. See "Jonathan Kidwell," q.v.

GAMBRA (GAMBRO), Richard. Took the Oath of Allegiance in 1778 [Ref: L-16]. Rendered patriotic service by providing wheat for the use of the military in December 1782 [Ref: N-575]. Resident of Port Tobacco West Hundred in 1778 [Ref: Q-I:297].

GARCENY, Abraham. Private (substitute during the war), 1st Maryland Line, by Sept. 11, 1778 [Ref: D-330].

GARDINER, Charles. Ensign, Militia, July 27, 1776 [Ref: M-77, B-127]. Ensign, Militia, 26th Battalion, Capt. Richard Bennett Mitchell's Company, 1777 [Ref: M-164].

GARDINER, Henry. Private, Militia, 12th Battalion, Capt. Alexander McPherson's Company, 1777 [Ref: M-160]. Took the Oath of Allegiance in 1778 [Ref: L-16]. Resident of Benedict Hundred in 1778 [Ref: Q-I:297, which listed the name as "Garner"].

GARDINER, Hugh. On Nov. 8, 1776 a letter was sent by General John Dent and Capt. John Parnham to the Maryland Council of Safety, as follows: "Mr. Hugh Gardner [sic] of Charles County being desirous of serving the American States in the Military wars, we beg leave to recommend him to your Honorable Board, from a thorough knowledge of Mr. Gardner, his strong attachment to the interest of his Country, the Zeal he has always shown in the common cause, his defatigable assiduity and application to and knowledge of Military affairs. We can assure that his merit wou'd well entitle him to the command of a Company or indeed to a higher commission, but as he is sensible that there are men of merit who have been some time in the service and who ought to be preferred, all that he at present aspires to is Lieutenancy, and I believe he would be glad of being in the Mattross Service. We wou'd therefore propose him as first Lieutenant in the Company of Mattrosses now raising for this Town, to the command of which company from the good opinion we entertain of his abilities, we hope Mr. William Campbell may be preferred." [Ref: B-432].

GARDINER, Ignatius. Private, Militia, 12th Battalion, Capt. John Thomas' Company, 1777 [Ref: M-161, which listed the name as "Gardner"]. Rendered patriotic service by providing wheat for the use of the military in September 1782 [Ref: N-556, which listed the name as "Gardener"]. Resident of Bryan Town Hundred in 1778 [Ref: Q-I:297]. "Ignatius Francis Gardiner" took the Oath of Allegiance in 1778 [Ref: L-16].

GARDINER, Jane. See "Richard Miles," q.v.

GARDINER, John. First Lieutenant, Militia, 12th Battalion, Capt. John Thomas' Company, 1777 [Ref: M-161, which listed the name as "Gardner"]. Took the Oath of Allegiance in 1778 [Ref: L-16]. Captain, commissioned on Jan. 19, 1781 [Ref: M-77, G-280]. Resident of Benedict Hundred in 1778 [Ref: Q-I:297].

GARDINER, John G. Private, Militia, 12th Battalion, Capt. John Hanson's Company, 1777 [Ref: M-159, which listed the name as "Gardner"]. Private (furnished by class for 9 months), 1st Maryland Line, by Sept. 11, 1778 [Ref: D-330].

GARDINER, Joseph Benedict (c1758-1829). Corporal, Militia, 12th Battalion, Capt. Alexander McPherson's Company, 1777 [Ref: M-160]. Took the Oath of Allegiance in 1778 [Ref: L-16]. He married Ann Dorothea Edelen (1770-1857) on April 14, 1793 and had children, including sons Joseph Benedict Gardiner, Jr., and Thomas Samuel Gardiner (1806-1859). [Ref: S-3122, S-3128, S-3158, which sources give three different birth years, 1757, 1758 and 1759, for the soldier].

GARDINER, Luke. Private, 1st Maryland Line, enrolled and passed on July 20, 1776 [Ref: D-33].

GARDINER, Mary. See "William Gardiner," q.v.

GARDINER, Philip. Took the Oath of Allegiance in 1778 [Ref: L-16, which listed the name as "Gardner"]. Resident of William & Mary Lower Hundred in 1778 [Ref: Q-I:297].

GARDINER, Richard. Private, Militia, 12th Battalion, Capt. Alexander McPherson's Company, 1777 [Ref: M-160, which listed the name as "Gardner"]. Took the Oath of Allegiance in 1778 [Ref: L-16].

GARDINER, Richard Jr. Took the Oath of Allegiance in 1778 [Ref: L-16]. Resident of Bryan Town Hundred in 1778 [Ref: Q-I:297].

GARDINER, Thomas S. See "Joseph Benedict Gardiner," q.v.

GARDINER, William (1745-1836). Private, Militia, 12th Battalion, Capt. Alexander McPherson's Company, 1777 [Ref: M-160]. Took the Oath of Allegiance in 1778 [Ref: L-16]. William's first wife was Ann Mattingly (1756-1795) and their daughter Mary Gardiner married Leonard Mudd (1772-1822) in 1795 at Bryantown, Maryland [Ref: S-3064, citing the *Mudd Family of the United States* by Dr. Richard D. Mudd]. Resident of Benedict Hundred in 1778 [Ref: Q-I:297, which listed the name as "Garner"].

GARNER, Benjamin. Private, Militia, 26th Battalion, Capt. Benjamin Cawood's Company, 1777 [Ref: M-162]. Benjamin Garner and Benjamin Garner, Sr., were residents of Port Tobacco East Hundred in 1778 [Ref: Q-I:297].

GARNER, Charles. Took the Oath of Allegiance in 1778 [Ref: L-16]. Resident of Port Tobacco West Hundred in 1778 [Ref: Q-I:297].

GARNER, Clement. Private, Militia, 12th Battalion, Capt. John Thomas' Company, 1777 [Ref: M-161, which listed the name as "Gardner"]. Took the Oath of Allegiance in 1778 [Ref: L-16, which listed the name as "Gardiner"]. Resident of Bryan Town Hundred in 1778 [Ref: Q-I:297, which listed the name as "Garner"].

GARNER, Francis. Ensign, Militia, 12th Battalion, Capt. Alexander McPherson's Company, July 5, 1777 [Ref: M-160, which listed the name as "Francis Garner" and M-77, which listed the name as "Francis Gardner"]. Resident of Benedict Hundred in 1778 [Ref: Q-I:297]. Second Lieutenant, Militia, 12th Battalion, Capt. Henry Boarman's Company, commissioned on Jan. 19, 1781 [Ref: M-77, G-280, which listed the name as "Francis J. Gardner"].

GARNER, Henry. See "Henry Gardiner," q.v.

GARNER, Hezekiah. Captain, Militia, 26th Battalion, 1777 [Ref: M-162]. Took the Oath of Allegiance in 1778 [Ref: L-16]. Rendered patriotic service by providing wheat for the use of the military in May 1783 [Ref: N-598].

GARNER, James. Took the Oath of Allegiance in 1778 [Ref: L-16].

GARNER, John. Took the Oath of Allegiance in 1778 [Ref: L-16, AA-641, which latter source listed the name "John Garner (Porto.)"]. One John Garner was a resident of Bryan Town Hundred and another John Garner was a resident of Benedict Hundred in 1778 [Ref: Q-I:297]. "John Gardiner (Garner), son of Joseph" was aged about 45 as noted in a 1774 deposition [Ref: DD-709].
GARNER, Joseph (1725-   ). Took the Oath of Allegiance in 1778 [Ref: AA-641, L-16, which latter source listed the name as "Ganner"]. Aged about 54 as noted in a 1779 deposition [Ref: DD-709]. Resident of Benedict Hundred in 1778 [Ref: Q-I:297].
GARNER, Peter. Private, Militia, 26th Battalion, Capt. Benjamin Cawood's Company, 1777 [Ref: M-162].
GARNER, Philip. Private, Militia, 12th Battalion, Capt. Jonathan Yates' Company, 1777 [Ref: X-70, but was omitted from the list in Reference M-162].
GARNER, Richard. Rendered patriotic service by providing clothing for the use of the military in February 1778 [Ref: Y-II:234]. Resident of Benedict Hundred in 1778 [Ref: Q-I:297].
GARNER, Sarah. See "Thomas Delozier," q.v.
GARNER, Walter. Took the Oath of Allegiance in 1780 [Ref: O-111].
GARNER, William. Took the Oath of Allegiance in 1778 [Ref: L-16]. One William Garner was a resident of Port Tobacco West Hundred and another John Garner was a resident of Benedict Hundred in 1778 [Ref: Q-I:297]. See "William Gardiner," q.v.
GARRETT, John Foley. Took the Oath of Allegiance in 1778 [Ref: L-16].
GARTIN, William. Rendered patriotic service by providing wheat for the use of the military in November 1782 [Ref: N-565].
GARVEY, William. Private (substitute for 3 years), 1st Maryland Line, by Sept. 11, 1778 [Ref: D-330].
GARVIN, Nancy. See "Jesse Boswell," q.v.
GARY, Francis. Took the Oath of Allegiance in 1778 [Ref: L-16, AA-641].
GARY, William. Took the Oath of Allegiance in 1778 [Ref: L-16].
GASKINS, William. Took the Oath of Allegiance in 1778 [Ref: L-16]. Resident of Durham Lower Hundred in 1778 [Ref: Q-I:297, which listed the name as "Gerskons"].
GATES, James. Took the Oath of Allegiance in 1778 [Ref: L-16, AA-641]. Resident of Port Tobacco Upper Hundred in 1778 [Ref: Q-I:297].
GATES, James Jr. Took the Oath of Allegiance in 1778 [Ref: L-16]. Resident of Port Tobacco Upper Hundred in 1778 [Ref: Q-I:297].

GATES, John (1731-   ). Took the Oath of Allegiance in 1778 [Ref: L-16]. Aged about 32 as noted in a 1763 deposition [Ref: DD-709]. Resident of Bryan Town Hundred in 1778 [Ref: Q-I:297].

GATES, Joseph. Took the Oath of Allegiance in 1778 [Ref: L-16, AA-641]. Resident of Bryan Town Hundred in 1778 [Ref: Q-I:297].

GATES, Leonard. Private, Militia, 26th Battalion, Capt. William McPherson's Company, 1777 [Ref: M-163]. Private (substitute for 3 years), 1st Maryland Line, by Sept. 11, 1778 [Ref: D-330]. Took the Oath of Allegiance in 1778 [Ref: L-16, AA-641]. Resident of Bryan Town Hundred in 1778 [Ref: Q-I:297].

GATES, Robert. Took the Oath of Allegiance in 1778 [Ref: L-16]. Resident of Bryan Town Hundred in 1778 [Ref: Q-I:297].

GATES, William. Private (furnished by class for 9 months), 1st Maryland Line, by Sept. 11, 1778 [Ref: D-330]. Private, 3rd Maryland Line, enrolled by Capt. Joseph Marbury by May 24, 1780 [Ref: D-333, F-181]. Resident of Bryan Town Hundred in 1778 [Ref: Q-I:297].

GATTON, Richard E. Private (substitute for 9 months), 1st Maryland Line, by Sept. 11, 1778 [Ref: D-330, which listed the name as "Gattin"].

GATTON, Silvester. Private (drafted and joined the army), 1st Maryland Line, by Sept. 11, 1778 [Ref: D-330, which listed the name as "Gatten"].

GAUGH, Thomas. Private, 1st Maryland Line, enrolled and passed on July 19, 1776 [Ref: D-31].

GERMAN, Stephen. Gave a deposition in 1781 pertaining to his inability to perform military service due to family obligations [Ref: Z-208].

GERSKONS, William. See "William Gaskins," q.v.

GIBBONS, George. Took the Oath of Allegiance in 1778 [Ref: L-16]. Resident of Bryan Town Hundred in 1778 [Ref: Q-I:297].

GIBBONS, Jeremiah. Took the Oath of Allegiance in 1778 [Ref: L-16]. Resident of Bryan Town Hundred in 1778 [Ref: Q-I:297].

GIBBONS, Nehemiah. Ensign, Militia, 26th Battalion, Capt. William Winter's Company, Feb. 26, 1776 [Ref: M-78, A-186, A-206, Y-II:23]. Private(?), Militia, 12th Battalion, Capt. Alexander McPherson's Company, 1777 [Ref: M-160, which listed the name as "Gibbins"]. Took the Oath of Allegiance in 1778 [Ref: L-16]. Resident of Bryan Town Hundred in 1778 [Ref: Q-I:297].

GIBBONS, Stephen. Private, Militia, 12th Battalion, Capt. Alexander McPherson's Company, 1777 [Ref: M-160, which listed the name as "Gibbins"].

GIBBONS, Thomas Sr. Took the Oath of Allegiance in 1778 [Ref: L-16]. "Thomas Gibbons, son of George" was aged about 46 as noted in a 1773

113

deposition [Ref: DD-709]. Resident of Bryan Town Hundred in 1778 [Ref: Q-I:297].
GIBBONS, William. Private, Militia, 12th Battalion, Capt. Alexander McPherson's Company, 1777 [Ref: M-160, which listed the name as "Gibbins"]. Resident of Bryan Town Hundred in 1778 [Ref: Q-I:297].
GIBSON, John. Sergeant, Militia, 12th Battalion, Capt. John Thomas' Company, 1777 [Ref: M-161]. Resident of Bryan Town Hundred in 1778 [Ref: Q-I:297].
GIBSON, John Jr. Took the Oath of Allegiance in 1778 [Ref: L-17]. Resident of Bryan Town Hundred in 1778 [Ref: Q-I:297].
GILDINGS (GELDINGS), Thomas. Took the Oath of Allegiance in 1778 [Ref: AA-641]. Rendered patriotic service by providing wheat for the use of the military in October 1782 [Ref: N-563, which listed the name as "Giddings"]. Resident of Pomonkey Hundred in 1778 [Ref: Q-I:297].
GILL, Adam. Private, Militia, 12th Battalion, Capt. Henry Clarkson's Company, 1777 [Ref: M-159]. Took the Oath of Allegiance in 1778 [Ref: L-17]. Resident of Newport East Hundred in 1778 [Ref: Q-I:297].
GILL, Charles (c1755-1838). Private, Militia, 12th Battalion, Capt. Peter Wood's Company, 1777 [Ref: M-161]. Took the Oath of Allegiance in 1778 [Ref: L-17]. Resident of Benedict Hundred in 1778 [Ref: Q-I:297]. One Charles Gill married Rebecca ---- and died in Virginia before June 25, 1838 [Ref: J-II:1160].
GILL, Henrietta. See "Richard Mudd," q.v.
GILL, John. Private, Militia, 12th Battalion, Capt. John Parnham's Company, 1777 [Ref: M-161]. Took the Oath of Allegiance in 1778 [Ref: L-17]. Resident of Newport East Hundred in 1778 [Ref: Q-I:297].
GILL, Jonathan (1757-1797). Private, Militia, 12th Battalion, Capt. John Parnham's Company, 1777 [Ref: M-161]. Jonathan Gill married Anne Fairfax and served as a matross in the Maryland Artillery during the war [Ref: J-II:1161].
GILL, Rebecca. See "Charles Gill," q.v.
GILL, Robert Jr. Private, Militia, 12th Battalion, Capt. Peter Wood's Company, 1777 [Ref: M-161]. Took the Oath of Allegiance in 1778 [Ref: L-17]. Resident of Benedict Hundred in 1778 [Ref: Q-I:297].
GILL, Robert Sr. (c1725-1778). Took the Oath of Allegiance in 1778 [Ref: L-17]. Resident of Benedict Hundred in 1778 [Ref: Q-I:297]. Robert Gill married Lydia Musgrave on Nov. 19, 1749 in Trinity Parish and died testate in May 1778 [Ref: J-II:1161, GG-210, EE-6, which latter source listed the name as "Jr."].
GILLAM, Thomas. Private, Militia, 12th Battalion, Capt. Henry Clarkson's Company, 1777 [Ref: M-159]. Private, 1st Maryland Line, drafted from

the Charles County militia on July 27, 1781 and discharged on Dec. 11, 1781 [Ref: G-569, D-408, D-377, I-18, which sources also listed the name as "Gillum" and "Gillsim"].

GILPIN, Benjamin Notley. Private, Militia, 12th Battalion, Capt. Walter Hanson's Company, 1777 [Ref: M-159]. "Benjamin Notley Gilpin" took the Oath of Allegiance in 1778 [Ref: AA-641]. "Notley Gilpin" was a resident of Port Tobacco East Hundred in 1778 [Ref: Q-I:297].

GILPIN, Leonard. Private, Militia, 26th Battalion, Capt. Robert Sinnett's Company, 1777 [Ref: M-164]. Took the Oath of Allegiance in 1778 [Ref: L-17]. Resident of Port Tobacco West Hundred in 1778 [Ref: Q-I:297].

GILPIN, Thomas. Private, Militia, 12th Battalion, Capt. Walter Hanson's Company, 1777 [Ref: M-159]. Took the Oath of Allegiance in 1778 [Ref: L-17, AA-641]. Resident of Port Tobacco East Hundred in 1778 [Ref: Q-I:297].

GITTINGS, Elenor. See "Richard Mudd," q.v.

GLADDEN (GLADEN), Robert (1713-   ). Took the Oath of Allegiance in 1778 [Ref: L-17, AA-641, which latter source listed the name as "Gladen"]. Aged about 45 as noted in a 1758 deposition [Ref: DD-709, which listed the name as "Glading"]. Resident of Benedict Hundred in 1778 [Ref: Q-I:297].

GLASCOCK, Elizabeth. See "Ledstone Noland," q.v.

GLASGOW (GLASSCO), John. Private, Militia, 26th Battalion, Capt. Benjamin Cawood's Company, 1777 [Ref: M-162, which listed the name as "John Glassco(?)"]. Took the Oath of Allegiance in 1778 [Ref: AA-641, which spelled the name as "Glascoe"]. Resident of Port Tobacco East Hundred in 1778 [Ref: Q-I:297, which listed the name as "Glasgow"].

GLASGOW (GLASSCO), Thomas. Private, Militia, 26th Battalion, Capt. Benjamin Cawood's Company, 1777 [Ref: M-162]. Resident of Port Tobacco East Hundred in 1778 [Ref: Q-I:297].

GLASGOW (GLASSCO), Walter. Private, 3rd Maryland Line, enrolled and passed on July 18, 1776, and still in the service by May 24, 1780 [Ref: D-32, F-181, which listed the name as "Glascow"].

GLASGOW (GLASSCO), William. Private (substitute for 3 years), 1st Maryland Line, enrolled Sept. 11, 1778 [Ref: D-330, which listed the name as "Glasgoe"]. Private, 1st Maryland Line, drafted from the Charles County militia and in service on June 11 or 12, 1781 and discharged on Dec. 3, 1781 [Ref: D-376, which listed the name as "Glassgow" and I-11, which listed the name as "Glascow"]. Rendered patriotic service by providing wheat for the use of the military in December 1782 [Ref: N-575, which listed the name as "Glasgoe"].

GLOVER, Philip. Took the Oath of Allegiance in 1778 [Ref: AA-641]. Resident of William & Mary Upper Hundred in 1778 [Ref: Q-I:297].
GODDARD, John. Private, 3rd Maryland Line, enrolled by Capt. Joseph Marbury by May 24, 1780 [Ref: F-181].
GODFREY, George (deceased by February 1779). Took the Oath of Allegiance in 1778 [Ref: L-17, AA-641]. Resident of Port Tobacco West Hundred in 1778 [Ref: Q-I:297].
GODFREY, Joseph Jr. (Colonel). Took the Oath of Allegiance in 1778 [Ref: L-17].
GODFREY, Lansdale. Private, Militia, 12th Battalion, Capt. Walter Hanson's Company, 1777 [Ref: M-159, which listed the first name as "Landsdale"]. Resident of Port Tobacco West Hundred in 1778 [Ref: Q-I:297].
GODFREY, Lansdale. Took the Oath of Allegiance in 1778 [Ref: L-17, AA-641, which sources listed the first name as "Lansdale"]. Resident of Port Tobacco East Hundred in 1778 [Ref: Q-I:297].
GODGRACE, William, of Robert. Private, Militia, 26th Battalion, Capt. Richard Bennett Mitchell's Company, 1777 [Ref: M-164].
GODY, Henry. Took the Oath of Allegiance in 1778 [Ref: AA-641]. Resident of William & Mary Lower Hundred in 1778 [Ref: Q-I:297].
GODY, Matthew. Took the Oath of Allegiance in 1778 [Ref: AA-641]. Resident of William & Mary Lower Hundred in 1778 [Ref: Q-I:297].
GOLDEN, Robert. Private, Militia, 26th Battalion, Capt. Hezekiah Garner's Company, 1777 [Ref: M-163]. "Robert Golding" took the Oath of Allegiance in 1778 [Ref: AA-641].
GOLDSBERRY, Charles. Private, 3rd Maryland Line, enrolled by Capt. Joseph Marbury by May 24, 1780 [Ref: F-181].
GOLDSMITH, Elizabeth. See "Samuel McPherson," q.v.
GOLEY, Thomas. Private, 1st Maryland Line, enrolled and passed on July 27, 1776 [Ref: D-31, which listed the name as "Goley (Goaley)"]. Private, Militia, 26th Battalion, Capt. Robert Sinnett's Company, 1777 [Ref: M-164, which listed the name as "Goly"]. Took the Oath of Allegiance in 1778 [Ref: L-17, which listed the name as "Goldy"]. Resident of Port Tobacco West Hundred in 1778 [Ref: Q-I:297].
GOOD, Roswell (Rosel). Private, Militia, 12th Battalion, Capt. Henry Clarkson's Company, 1777 [Ref: M-159]. Took the Oath of Allegiance in 1778 [Ref: L-17, which misspelled the first name as "Rafel" and AA-641, which spelled the first name as "Rosel"].
GOOD, William. Took the Oath of Allegiance in 1778 [Ref: L-17]. Resident of Bryan Town Hundred in 1778 [Ref: Q-I:297].
GOODEN, Alexander. See "William Lomax," q.v.

GOODEN, Tabitha. See "William Lomax," q.v.

GOODRICK (GOODRICH), Aaron. Private, Militia, 12th Battalion, Capt. Jonathan Yates' Company, 1777 [Ref: M-162]. Took the Oath of Allegiance in 1778 [Ref: L-17, AA-641, which listed the name as "Goodrich"]. Resident of William & Mary Lower Hundred in 1778 [Ref: Q-I:297].

GOODRICK (GOODRICH), Charles. Private, Militia, 12th Battalion, Capt. Walter Hanson's Company, 1777 [Ref: M-159]. Took the Oath of Allegiance in 1778 [Ref: L-17]. Rendered patriotic service by providing wheat for the use of the military in September 1781 [Ref: N-437, which listed the name as "Goodrich"]. Resident of Port Tobacco East Hundred in 1778 [Ref: Q-I:297].

GOODRICK (GOODRICH), Francis. See "George Goodrick," q.v.

GOODRICK (GOODRICH), George. Private, Militia, 12th Battalion, Capt. Walter Hanson's Company, 1777 [Ref: M-159]. Took the Oath of Allegiance in 1778 [Ref: L-17, which listed the name as "Goodrich"]. Resident of William & Mary Lower Hundred in 1778 [Ref: Q-I:297]. "George Goodrick, son of Francis" was aged about 32 as noted in a 1762 deposition [Ref: DD-710].

GOODRICK (GOODRICH), James. Took the Oath of Allegiance in 1778 [Ref: L-17, which listed the name as "Goodrich"].

GOODRICK (GOODRICH), Joseph. Private, Militia, 12th Battalion, Capt. Jonathan Yates' Company, 1777 [Ref: X-70, but was omitted from the list in Reference M-162]. Resident of William & Mary Lower Hundred in 1778 [Ref: Q-I:297].

GOODRICK (GOODRICH), Richard. Took the Oath of Allegiance in 1778 [Ref: L-17, which listed the name as "Goodwick"]. Resident of Port Tobacco East Hundred in 1778 [Ref: Q-I:297]. Rendered patriotic service by providing wheat for the use of the military in October 1782 [Ref: N-559, which listed the name as "Goodrich"].

GOODRICK (GOODRICH), Walter. Private, Militia, 12th Battalion, Capt. Jonathan Yates' Company, 1777 [Ref: M-162]. Took the Oath of Allegiance in 1778 [Ref: AA-641]. Resident of William & Mary Lower Hundred in 1778 [Ref: Q-I:297].

GOOMES, Emanuel. Private (furnished by class for 9 months), 1st Maryland Line, by Sept. 11, 1778 [Ref: D-330].

GORDON, James. See "Robert Gordon," q.v.

GORDON, Robert (1722-   ). Took the Oath of Allegiance in 1778 [Ref: L-17]. Aged about 49 as noted in a 1771 deposition which mentioned his father Robert and brother James [Ref: DD-710]. Resident of Pomonkey Hundred in 1778 [Ref: Q-I:297].

GRAHAM, James. Took the Oath of Allegiance in 1778 [Ref: L-17, AA-641].

GRAHAM Margaret. See "Gustavus Richard Brown," q.v.
GRAHAM, Patrick. This petition was presented to the Maryland Convention in August 1775, as follows (verbatim): "The humble Petition of Patrick Graham of Port Tobacco in Charles County sheweth, that some time ago he very justly incurred the displeasure and resentment of the County & the censure of the Committee of Charles County for a breach of the Resolves of the Honourable Continental Congress, by aiding a certain John Baillie secretly to land and dispose of sundry goods imported by him contrary to these Resolves; Your Petitioner sincerely laments his imprudence & ill conduct, & being deeply sensible of his offence, with contrition for the same, and his most solemn promise & assurance never more to do, or encourage any thing inimical to American Freedom, he most humbly solicits this Convention, that he may be restored to his former rights as a Citizen, as he has already suffered greatly, not only in his own Person, Property and reputation, but should he continue much longer in the present situation, his Offence must reduce an innocent wife & four young children to beggary & ruin. We the Subscribers being satisfied of the hearty repentance of Patrick Graham set forth in the above Petition, do recommend him to the consideration & clemency of the Honourable Convention." [Ref: A-10, A-35, A-36].
GRAHAM, Samuel. Private, Militia, 12th Battalion, Capt. John Parnham's Company, 1777 [Ref: M-161, which listed the name as "Grayham"]. Took the Oath of Allegiance in 1778 [Ref: L-17].
GRAHAM, William (1727-   ). Took the Oath of Allegiance in 1778 [Ref: AA-641]. Aged about 43 as noted in a 1770 deposition [Ref: DD-711, which listed the name as "Grayham"]. Resident of Bryan Town Hundred in 1778 [Ref: Q-I:297].
GRANT, Christian. See "Josias Smoot," q.v.
GRANT, Elizabeth. See "Peter Farnandis," q.v.
GRANT, John. Memorialist and Militiaman, Pomonkey Company, 1776. Ensign, Militia, Pomonkey Company, 1776. Ensign, Militia, 26th Battalion, Capt. Thomas H. Marshall's Company, Feb. 26, 1776. First Lieutenant, Militia, Capt. George Dent's Company, commissioned May 9, 1778 [Ref: M-80, M-158, M-163, A-186, A-206, E-72, Y-II:23, Y-II:26]. Took the Oath of Allegiance in 1778 [Ref: L-17]. Resident of Pomonkey Hundred in 1778 [Ref: Q-I:297]. Rendered patriotic service by providing wheat for the use of the military in June 1782 and May 1783 [Ref: N-523, N-597].
GRAY, Andrew (1745-   ). Private, Militia, 26th Battalion, Capt. William Winter's Company, 1777 [Ref: M-165]. Took the Oath of Allegiance in 1778 [Ref: AA-641, L-17, which latter source misspelled the name as "Govey"]. An "orphan aged 13 next May," he was bound to Notley Dutton

in August 1757 [Ref: DD-710]. Resident of Durham Lower Hundred in 1778 [Ref: Q-I:297].

GRAY, Ann. See "George Gray" and "James Gray" and "William Gray," q.v.

GRAY, Anthony Collins (1744-   ). Private, Militia, 26th Battalion, Capt. Hezekiah Garner's Company, 1777 [Ref: M-162, which listed the name as "Anthony C. Gray"]. Took the Oath of Allegiance in 1778 [Ref: AA-641]. Aged about 35 as noted in a 1779 deposition [Ref: DD-710, which listed the name as "Anthony Collins Gray"].

GRAY, Benjamin. Private, Militia, 26th Battalion, Capt. Richard Bennett Mitchell's Company, 1777; listed as an invalid (disabled) soldier [Ref: M-164]. Resident of Pomonkey Hundred in 1778 [Ref: Q-I:297]. One Benjamin Gray was deceased by August 1778 (date of inventory). [Ref: GG-209].

GRAY, Edward. Private, Militia, 26th Battalion, Capt. Hezekiah Garner's Company, 1777 [Ref: M-162]. Took the Oath of Allegiance in 1780 [Ref: O-111]. Rendered patriotic service by providing wheat for the use of the military in November 1781, January 1782, and May 1783 [Ref: N-457, N-470, N-598].

GRAY, George. Private, 1st Maryland Line, enrolled and passed on July 27, 1776 [Ref: D-31]. Two men by this name were privates in the militia in 1777: one in the 26th Battalion, Capt. Hezekiah Garner's Company, and one in the 12th Battalion, Capt. John Branham's Company [Ref: M-161, M-162]. One took the Oath of Allegiance in 1778 and another took the oath in 1780 [Ref: AA-641, L-17, O-111]. "George Gray" was a resident of Newport East Hundred and "George Grey" was a resident of Port Tobacco Town Hundred in 1778 [Ref: Q-I:297]. One George Gray was born on Oct. 15, 1752, son of William and Ann Gray [Ref: EE-7]. One George Gray rendered patriotic service by providing clothing for the use of the military in February 1778, and one rendered patriotic service by providing wheat for the use of the military in May 1783 [Ref: Y-II:234 N-599]. On Feb. 12, 1820, the Treasurer of Maryland was directed to pay to one "George Gray, of Charles County, for life, quarterly, half pay of a private, for his services during the Revolutionary War." [Ref: Q-II:348].

GRAY, George Sr. Took the Oath of Allegiance in 1780 [Ref: O-111].

GRAY, Henry Jr. Private, Militia, 26th Battalion, Capt. Hezekiah Garner's Company, 1777 [Ref: M-162].

GRAY, James. Private, Militia, 12th Battalion, Capt. John Parnham's Company, 1777 [Ref: M-160]. Took the Oath of Allegiance in 1778 [Ref: L-17]. One James Gray was an "orphan aged 15 next December" when bound to William Lindsay in August 1757 [Ref: DD-710]. One James Gray was born on Dec. 8, 1750, son of William and Ann Gray [Ref: EE-7]. One

James Gray was a resident of Newport East Hundred in 1778 [Ref: Q-I:297].

GRAY, Jeremiah. Sergeant, Militia, 26th Battalion, Capt. Hezekiah Garner's Company, 1777 [Ref: M-162]. Took the Oath of Allegiance in 1778 [Ref: L-17, AA-641]. Rendered patriotic service by providing wheat for the use of the military in December 1782 [Ref: N-577].

GRAY, John. Took the Oath of Allegiance in 1778 [Ref: L-17]. Gave a deposition in 1781 pertaining to his inability to perform military service (reason not stated, but the most common reasons given by others were either family obligations or poor health). [Ref: Z-208].

GRAY, John Jr. Took the Oath of Allegiance in 1778 [Ref: L-17].

GRAY, John N. Private, Militia, 26th Battalion, Capt. Hezekiah Garner's Company, 1777 [Ref: M-162]. Rendered patriotic service by providing wheat for the use of the military in November 1781 [Ref: N-458].

GRAY, Joseph. Two men by this name were privates in the militia in 1777: one in the 12th Battalion, Capt. John Parnham's Company, and one in the 26th Battalion, Capt. Hezekiah Garner's Company [Ref: M-160, M-162]. One took the Oath of Allegiance in 1778 [Ref: AA-641]. Resident of Newport East Hundred in 1778 [Ref: Q-I:297]. One Joseph Gray was born on Feb. 14, 1755, a son of William and Ann Gray [Ref: EE-9].

GRAY, Joseph, of John. Took the Oath of Allegiance in 1778 [Ref: L-17]. See "Joseph Gray," q.v.

GRAY, Moses (1713-   ). Took the Oath of Allegiance in 1780 [Ref: O-111]. Rendered patriotic service by providing wheat for the use of the military in May 1783 [Ref: N-598]. Aged about 67 as noted in a 1780 deposition [Ref: DD-710].

GRAY, Rachel. See "James Muncaster," q.v.

GRAY, Richard. Took the Oath of Allegiance in 1778 [Ref: L-17]. Resident of Pomonkey Hundred in 1778 [Ref: Q-I:297].

GRAY, Richard, of Richard. Private, Militia, 26th Battalion, Capt. Richard Bennett Mitchell's Company, 1777 [Ref: M-165].

GRAY, William. Two men by this name were privates in the 26th Battalion of Militia in 1777: one in Capt. John Parnham's Company, and one in Capt. Richard Bennett Mitchell's Company [Ref: M-161, M-165]. "William Gray, son of James" was aged about 31 as noted in a 1775 deposition [Ref: DD-710].

GRAY, William. Ensign, Militia, 26th Battalion, Capt. Francis Mastin's Company, 1777 [Ref: M-163]. Took the Oath of Allegiance in 1778 [Ref: L-17]. Resident of Newport East Hundred in 1778 [Ref: Q-I:297].

GRAY, William Jr. Private, Militia, 26th Battalion, Capt. Francis Mastin's Company, 1777 [Ref: M-164].

GRAY, William Sr. Took the Oath of Allegiance in 1778 [Ref: L-17]. Resident of Newport East Hundred in 1778 [Ref: Q-I:297]. See "James Gray" and "George Gray" and "Joseph Gray," q.v.

GRAY, William Mc. (Hill?). Took the Oath of Allegiance in 1778 [Ref: L-17, which listed the middle name as "Hill" and AA-641, which listed the middle name to be what looked like "Mc."].

GRAY, Wilson. Private, 1st Maryland Line, enrolled and passed on July 19, 1776 [Ref: D-31].

GRAYER, James. Private, Militia, 12th Battalion, Capt. Peter Wood's Company, 1777 [Ref: M-161].

GREEN, Benjamin. Took the Oath of Allegiance in 1778 [Ref: L-17]. Private (substitute for 9 months), 1st Maryland Line, by Sept. 11, 1778 [Ref: D-330].

GREEN, Charles. Took the Oath of Allegiance in 1778 [Ref: L-17, AA-641]. Resident of Port Tobacco Upper Hundred in 1778 [Ref: Q-I:297].

GREEN, Chloe. See "John Reeder," q.v.

GREEN, Edward. Rendered patriotic service by providing clothing for the use of the military in February 1778 [Ref: Y-II:234]. Took the Oath of Allegiance in 1778 [Ref: L-17, AA-641]. Rendered patriotic service by providing wheat for the use of the military in December 1782 and May 1783 [Ref: N-576, N-599]. Resident of Port Tobacco Upper Hundred in 1778 [Ref: Q-I:297].

GREEN, Edward Jr. Took the Oath of Allegiance in 1778 [Ref: L-17, AA-641]. Resident of Port Tobacco Upper Hundred in 1778 [Ref: Q-I:297].

GREEN, Elijah. Private, Militia, 26th Battalion, Capt. Richard Bennett Mitchell's Company, 1777 [Ref: M-164].

GREEN, Giles Jr. Took the Oath of Allegiance in 1778 [Ref: L-17, AA-641]. Resident of Port Tobacco Upper Hundred in 1778 [Ref: Q-I:297]. Rendered patriotic service by providing wheat for the use of the military in November 1781 [Ref: N-457].

GREEN, Giles Sr. (1698-   ). Took the Oath of Allegiance in 1778 [Ref: L-17, AA-641]. Aged about 64 as noted in a 1762 deposition [Ref: DD-711]. Resident of Port Tobacco West Hundred in 1778 [Ref: Q-I:297].

GREEN, Henry. Private, Militia, 26th Battalion, Capt. William McPherson's Company, 1777 [Ref: M-163]. Took the Oath of Allegiance in 1778 [Ref: L-17]. Resident of Port Tobacco East Hundred in 1778 [Ref: Q-I:297].

GREEN, Hugh. Took the Oath of Allegiance in 1778 [Ref: AA-641]. Resident of William & Mary Upper Hundred in 1778 [Ref: Q-I:297].

GREEN, James. Took the Oath of Allegiance in 1778 [Ref: L-17]. Resident of Benedict Hundred in 1778 [Ref: Q-I:297].

GREEN, John. Took the Oath of Allegiance in 1778 [Ref: L-17]. Resident of Port Tobacco East Hundred in 1778 [Ref: Q-I:297].
GREEN, Joshua. Private, Militia, 26th Battalion, Capt. William McPherson's Company, 1777 [Ref: M-163].
GREEN, Lucinda. See "Gerrard Dyson," q.v.
GREEN, Mary Jane. See "Elijah Athey," q.v.
GREEN, Nicholas. Took the Oath of Allegiance in 1778 [Ref: L-17, AA-641]. Resident of Port Tobacco Upper Hundred in 1778 [Ref: Q-I:297].
GREEN, Peter. First Lieutenant, Militia, 26th Battalion, Capt. William McPherson's Company, Feb. 26, 1776 [Ref: M-80, M-163, A-186, A-206, Y-II:23]. Took the Oath of Allegiance in 1778 [Ref: L-17]. Rendered patriotic service by providing wheat for the use of the military in December 1782 [Ref: N-575]. Resident of Port Tobacco Upper Hundred in 1778 [Ref: Q-I:297].
GREEN, Robert. Took the Oath of Allegiance in 1778 [Ref: L-17]. Resident of Port Tobacco West Hundred in 1778 [Ref: Q-I:297].
GREEN, Samuel Jr. Private (furnished by class for 9 months), 1st Maryland Line, by Sept. 11, 1778 [Ref: D-330]. Resident of Durham Lower Hundred in 1778 [Ref: Q-I:297].
GREEN, Samuel Sr. Took the Oath of Allegiance in 1778 [Ref: AA-641]. Resident of Durham Lower Hundred in 1778 [Ref: Q-I:297].
GREEN, Sarah. See "Simon Reeder," q.v.
GREEN, Thomas Jr. Second Lieutenant, Militia, 26th Battalion, Capt. William McPherson's Company, Feb. 26, 1776 [Ref: M-80, M-163, A-186, A-206, Y-II:23]. Resident of Port Tobacco Upper Hundred in 1778 [Ref: Q-I:297].
GREEN, Thomas Sr. Took the Oath of Allegiance in 1778 [Ref: L-17]. Resident of Port Tobacco Upper Hundred in 1778 [Ref: Q-I:297].
GREEN, Thomas Melchisdick. Corporal, Militia, 26th Battalion, Capt. William McPherson's Company, 1777 [Ref: M-163, which listed the name as "Thomas M. Green"]. Took the Oath of Allegiance in 1778 [Ref: L-17, which listed the name as "Tom Melchisdick Green" and AA-641, which listed the name as "Tom Melcd. Green"]. Resident of Port Tobacco East Hundred in 1778 [Ref: Q-I:297, which listed the name as "T. Melchizedeck Green"].
GREEN, Thomas, of Ed. Took the Oath of Allegiance in 1778 [Ref: L-17, AA-641].
GREEN, William (1739-1822). Private, 1st Maryland Line, Col. John H. Stone's Regiment. Invalid pensioner, "disability caused by rheumatic pains, can't get information when nor where disabled." His pension commenced Jan. 11, 1780 and was still on pension as of Oct. 11, 1789,

aged 50 [Ref: D-629]. Private, Revolutionary Army, Charles County, pensioned from March 4, 1789 under the Act of June 7, 1785 at $40 per annum and from April 24, 1816 at $64 per annum. He died in 1822 [Ref: Q-II:348, R-12].

GREENFIELD, Jane. See "Josias Hawkins," q.v.

GREENLEAVES, Simon. Private, Militia, 26th Battalion, Capt. Francis Mastin's Company, 1777 [Ref: M-163, which listed the name as "Simond Greenleaves"]. Took the Oath of Allegiance in 1778 [Ref: L-17, which listed the name as "Simon Greenlease" and AA-641, which listed the name as "Simon Greenleeves"]. Resident of Durham Lower Hundred in 1778 [Ref: Q-I:297]. Died by January 1779 (date of inventory). [Ref: GG-271].

GREER, James. Private, 1st Maryland Line, enrolled and passed on July 20, 1776 [Ref: D-33]. Took the Oath of Allegiance in 1778 [Ref: AA-641, which listed the name as "Greear"].

GREY, Elizabeth. See "Hezekiah Cooksey," q.v.

GREY, George. See "George Gray," q.v.

GRIFFIN, James. Sergeant, Militia, 12th Battalion, Capt. John Hanson's Company, 1777 [Ref: M-158]. Took the Oath of Allegiance in 1778 [Ref: L-17, AA-641]. Resident of Port Tobacco East Hundred in 1778 [Ref: Q-I:297]. See "Thomas Hussey Luckett," q.v.

GRIFFIN, John. Ensign, Militia, 12th Battalion, Capt. John Hanson's Company, Feb. 26, 1776 [Ref: M-80, M-158, A-186, A-206, Y-II:23]. Took the Oath of Allegiance in 1778 [Ref: L-17]. Resident of Port Tobacco East Hundred in 1778 [Ref: Q-I:297].

GRIFFIN, Mary. See "Thomas Hussey Luckett," q.v.

GRIFFIN, Peter. Sergeant, Militia, 12th Battalion, Capt. John Hanson's Company, 1777 [Ref: M-158]. Took the Oath of Allegiance in 1778 [Ref: L-17]. Resident of Port Tobacco East Hundred in 1778 [Ref: Q-I:297]. Constable, 1778 [Ref: CC-709].

GRIFFIN, Sarah. Rendered patriotic service by providing wheat for the use of the military in October 1781 [Ref: N-451]. See "Thomas Hussey Luckett," q.v.

GRIFFIN, William. Private (furnished by class for 9 months), 1st Maryland Line, by Sept. 11, 1778 [Ref: D-330].

GRIFFIS, Thomas. Private, Militia, 26th Battalion, Capt. William McPherson's Company, 1777 [Ref: M-163]. Took the Oath of Allegiance in 1778 [Ref: L-17, AA-641]. Resident of Port Tobacco Upper Hundred in 1778 [Ref: Q-I:297].

GROVES, John. Private, Militia, 26th Battalion, Capt. William Winter's Company, 1777 [Ref: M-165]. Resident of Durham Lower Hundred in 1778 [Ref: Q-I:297].

GROVES, William. Private, Militia, 26th Battalion, Capt. William Winter's Company, 1777 [Ref: M-165]. Resident of Durham Lower Hundred in 1778 [Ref: Q-I:297].
GUY, John. Private, Militia, 26th Battalion, Capt. William McPherson's Company, 1777 [Ref: M-163]. Took the Oath of Allegiance in 1778 [Ref: AA-641]. Rendered patriotic service by providing wheat for the use of the military in December 1782 [Ref: N-573]. Resident of Port Tobacco Upper Hundred in 1778 [Ref: Q-I:297].
GUY, John Sr. Took the Oath of Allegiance in 1778 [Ref: L-17, which listed the name as "John Grey, Sr." and AA-641, which listed the name as "John Guy, Sr."]. One John Guy "aged 16 last August" was bound to Matthew Pope in 1748 or 1749 [Ref: DD-711].
GUY, Moses. Private, Militia, 12th Battalion, Capt. Jonathan Yates' Company, 1777 [Ref: M-162]. Took the Oath of Allegiance in 1778 [Ref: L-17].
GUY, William Jr. Private, Militia, 26th Battalion, Capt. William McPherson's Company, 1777 [Ref: M-163]. Resident of Port Tobacco Upper Hundred in 1778 [Ref: Q-I:297].
GUY, William Sr. Took the Oath of Allegiance in 1778 [Ref: AA-641]. Rendered patriotic service by providing wheat for the use of the military in December 1782 [Ref: N-573]. Resident of Port Tobacco Upper Hundred in 1778 [Ref: Q-I:297].
GWINN, Edward. Corporal, Militia, 26th Battalion, Capt. William McPherson's Company, 1777 [Ref: M-163, which listed the name as "Guinn"]. Took the Oath of Allegiance in 1778 [Ref: L-17, AA-641]. Resident of Port Tobacco Upper Hundred in 1778 [Ref: Q-I:297].
GWINN, John. First Lieutenant, Militia, Capt. George Swann's Company, Feb. 26, 1776 [Ref: M-81, A-186, A-206, Y-II:23]. Resident of Port Tobacco Town Hundred in 1778 [Ref: Q-I:297].
GWINN, John. Took the Oath of Allegiance in 1778 [Ref: L-17, which listed the name as "Gwynn" and AA-641, which listed the name as "Gwyn"]. Resident of Port Tobacco Upper Hundred in 1778 [Ref: Q-I:297].
GWINN, John Jr. Took the Oath of Allegiance in 1778 [Ref: AA-641]. Resident of William & Mary Lower Hundred in 1778 [Ref: Q-I:297].
GWINN, Joseph (1699-1778). Took the Oath of Allegiance in 1778 [Ref: AA-641]. Rendered patriotic service by providing clothing for the use of the military in February 1778 [Ref: Y-II:234]. Aged about 55 as noted in a 1754 deposition [Ref: DD-711]. Resident of William & Mary Upper Hundred in 1778 [Ref: Q-I:297]. Died testate in August 1778 [Ref: GG-205].
HAGAN, Ann. See "Raphael Hagan," q.v.

HAGAN, Basil. See "Raphael Hagan," q.v.
HAGAN, Benjamin. Private, Militia, 12th Battalion, Capt. Alexander McPherson's Company, 1777 [Ref: M-160, which listed the name as "Hagon"]. Took the Oath of Allegiance in 1778 [Ref: L-17]. Resident of Bryan Town Hundred in 1778 [Ref: Q-I:297].
HAGAN, Charles. Cooper's Mate aboard the State Ship *Defence* from Feb. 12, 1777 to Dec. 31, 1777 [Ref: D-657].
HAGAN, Elizabeth. See "Raphael Hagan," q.v.
HAGAN, Francis. See "Raphael Hagan," q.v.
HAGAN, Henry. Took the Oath of Allegiance in 1778 [Ref: L-17]. Rendered patriotic service by providing wheat for the use of the military in December 1781, and October and December 1782 [Ref: N-462, N-563, N-573, which also listed the name as "Hagon"]. Resident of Port Tobacco Upper Hundred in 1778 [Ref: Q-I:297].
HAGAN, Jacob. Took the Oath of Allegiance in 1778 [Ref: L-17, which listed the name as "Hager"].
HAGAN, James (1754-1829). Private, Militia, 26th Battalion, Capt. Benjamin Cawood's Company, 1777 [Ref: M-162, which listed the name as "Hagon"]. Resident of Bryan Town Hundred in 1778 [Ref: Q-I:297]. "Jas. Hagen" was a corporal in Capt. William Adams' Company, 2nd Maryland Line, by Jan. 1, 1782 [Ref: D-445]. One James Hagan married Monacy Fenwick and migrated to Kentucky where he died on Dec. 30, 1829 [Ref: J-II:1263].
HAGAN, John (1727-). Took the Oath of Allegiance in 1778 [Ref: L-17]. Aged about 26 as noted in a 1753 deposition [Ref: DD-8]. Resident of Bryan Town Hundred in 1778 [Ref: Q-I:297].
HAGAN, Joseph (c1740-1809). Took the Oath of Allegiance in 1778 [Ref: AA-641]. Joseph Hagan married Mary Anne King and migrated to Missouri where he died before July 8, 1809 [Ref: J-II:1263]. See "Raphael Hagan," q.v.
HAGAN, Joseph, of Ignatius. Took the Oath of Allegiance in 1778 [Ref: AA-641]. Resident of Bryan Town Hundred in 1778 [Ref: Q-I:297].
HAGAN, Joseph, of William. Took the Oath of Allegiance in 1778 [Ref: L-17]. Resident of Bryan Town Hundred in 1778 [Ref: Q-I:297].
HAGAN, Leonard. Private, 1st Maryland Line, 1780, who died on Dec. 17, 1782 [Ref: D-539].
HAGAN, Nathaniel. Took the Oath of Allegiance in 1778 [Ref: L-17]. Resident of Port Tobacco East Hundred in 1778 [Ref: Q-I:297].
HAGAN, Nicholas. Private, 1st Maryland Line, drafted from the Charles County militia and reported sick or not in service on July 27, 1781 [Ref: D-377].

HAGAN, Raphael or Ralph (1757-1826). Private, Militia, 12th Battalion, Capt. Alexander McPherson's Company, 1777 [Ref: M-160, which listed the name as "Raphael Hagon"]. Resident of Bryan Town Hundred in 1778 [Ref: Q-I:297, which listed the name as "Ralph Hagan"]. Private (furnished by class for 9 months), 1st Maryland Line, by Sept. 11, 1778 [Ref: D-330]. Corporal, 1st Maryland Line, who was reported missing after the Battle of Camden in South Carolina on Aug. 16, 1780 [Ref: D-118]. On Nov. 6, 1844, in Spencer County, Kentucky, his surviving children were Basil Hagan, Joseph Hagan, Theresa Lilly, and Susannah Aud. They stated that "Raphael or Ralph Hagan" died in August 1826 and his widow Rebecca died on Feb. 27, 1844 (pension W8907). They had married in 1778 and had these children: Theresa Hagan 1st (born Jan. 1, 1783, died young), Elizabeth Hagan (born April 10, 1785), Susannah Hagan (born June 15, 1787), Theresa Hagan 2nd (born Sept. 20, 1789), Ann Hagan (born Jan. 8, 1792), Francis Hagan (born Aug. 26, 1794), Vestor Hagan 1st (born in September 1796, died in infancy), Vestor Hagan 2nd (born March 10, 1798), Basil Hagan (born in July 1800), and Nancy Hagan (born July 10, 1803). [Ref: V-II:1467]. Ralph Hagan was born in 1757, married Rebecca Lavielle, and migrated to Kentucky where he died in August 1826 [Ref: J-II:1263]. *Ed. Note:* Joseph Hagan, son of Raphael, was not listed with the other children above. Since Raphael was married in 1778 and the first listed child was not born until 1783, it is probable that Joseph was the first child born around 1780.

HAGAN, Rebecca. See "Raphael Hagan," q.v.

HAGAN, Susannah. See "Raphael Hagan," q.v.

HAGAN, Theresa. See "Raphael Hagan," q.v.

HAGAN, Vestor. See "Raphael Hagan," q.v.

HAGAN, Walter. Private, 1st Maryland Line, 1780; discharged on Feb. 23, 1783 [Ref: D-539].

HAGAN, William. Took the Oath of Allegiance in 1778 [Ref: L-17]. One William Hagan was aged about 71 as noted in a 1767 deposition [Ref: DD-8].

HAISLIP, Henry. See "John Haislip, of Henry," q.v.

HAISLIP, John. Took the Oath of Allegiance in 1778 [Ref: AA-641]. Resident of Port Tobacco West Hundred in 1778 [Ref: Q-I:297].

HAISLIP, John Jr. Took the Oath of Allegiance in 1778 [Ref: AA-641].

HAISLIP, John, of Henry. Private, Militia, 26th Battalion, Capt. Richard Bennett Mitchell's Company, 1777 [Ref: M-164]. Henry Haislip was aged about 71 in a 1777 deposition [Ref: CC-581].

HAISLIP, John, of Robert. Private, Militia, 26th Battalion, Capt. Richard Bennett Mitchell's Company, 1777 [Ref: M-164]. Resident of Port Tobacco West Hundred in 1778 [Ref: Q-I:297].

HAISLIP, John Boucher. Private, 3rd Maryland Line, enrolled by Capt. Joseph Marbury by May 24, 1780 [Ref: D-333, which listed the name as "Haislope" and F-181, which listed the name as "John B. Haslip"].

HAISLIP, Jonathan. Private, Militia, 26th Battalion, Capt. Francis Mastin's Company, 1777 [Ref: M-164].

HAISLIP, Laban (c1754-1816). Corporal, Militia, 26th Battalion, Capt. Richard Bennett Mitchell's Company, 1777 [Ref: M-164]. Took the Oath of Allegiance in 1778 [Ref: L-17, AA-641]. Resident of Port Tobacco West Hundred in 1778 [Ref: Q-I:297]. "Leban Haislip" married first to Ellener Williams, second to Rebecca Welch, and migrated to Alabama where he died on Dec. 14, 1816 [Ref: J-II:1266].

HAISLIP, Robert Sr. (1705-c1795). Took the Oath of Allegiance in 1778 [Ref: AA-641]. Aged about 57 as noted in a 1762 deposition [Ref: DD-8, which listed the name as "Robert Haislop"]. Resident of Port Tobacco West Hundred in 1778 [Ref: Q-I:297]. He married (wife's name not known) and died before 1795 [Ref: J-II:1266].

HAISLIP, Samuel. Private, Militia, 26th Battalion, Capt. Richard Bennett Mitchell's Company, 1777 [Ref: M-164]. Took the Oath of Allegiance in 1778 [Ref: AA-641]. Resident of Port Tobacco West Hundred in 1778 [Ref: Q-I:297].

HAISLIP, William. Private, Militia, 26th Battalion, Capt. Richard Bennett Mitchell's Company, 1777 [Ref: M-164]. Took the Oath of Allegiance in 1778 [Ref: AA-641]. Resident of Port Tobacco West Hundred in 1778 [Ref: Q-I:297].

HALKERSTON, John. Second Lieutenant, 1st Independent Maryland Company under the command of Capt. Rezin Beall, Jan. 2, 1776 [Ref: D-20, A-415]. Took the Oath of Allegiance in 1778 [Ref: AA-641, L-17, which listed the name as "Holkerston"]. Rendered patriotic service by providing clothing for the use of the military in February 1778 [Ref: Y-II:234, which listed the name as "Halkerstone"]. Resident of Port Tobacco Town Hundred in 1778 [Ref: Q-I:297, which listed the name as "Halkinton"].

HALKERSTON, Robert (1754-1825). Sergeant, 3rd Maryland Line, Feb. 5, 1777 to Jan. 9, 1780 (discharged). Ensign, 4th Maryland Line, commissioned Jan. 26, 1780. Lieutenant, 4th Maryland Line, April 25, 1781, and 1st Maryland Line, Jan. 1, 1783 [Ref: D-120, D-364, D-380, D-476]. In November 1811, the Treasurer of Maryland was directed to pay to "Robert Halkerstone of Charles County, or his order, the sum of $125 annually, during life, in quarterly payments, out of any unappropriated monies in the treasury." In December 1817, the Treasurer was directed to pay to "Robert Halkerston of Charles County, an old revolutionary officer, quarterly, the half pay of a lieutenant for life, instead of the sum allowed him by a resolution passed Jan. 6, 1812." He was placed on the pension rolls of Charles County as of Oct. 1, 1819 (retroactive to April 2, 1818) and died on Feb. 17, 1825 [Ref: Q-II:349, Q-II:350, R-33]. He received bounty land warrant #1053-200-21 in September 1789, and also applied for a federal pension (S34917) on April 2, 1818, aged 64. His name was spelled in three ways: Halkerstone, Halkuston, and Halkerston. In 1820 he had a wife (not named) aged 50 and two orphaned relatives (not named) were living with them: (a niece aged 22 and a nephew aged 6). [Ref: V-II:1475].

HALL, Clark. Memorialist and Militiaman, Pomonkey Company, after March 6, 1776 [Ref: M-158, Y-II:26].

HALL, Frederick (1736-c1833). Private, 3rd Maryland Line, 1780, enrolled in Charles County for Capt. Joseph Marbury's Company [Ref: D-333]. He applied for a pension (R7569) on Sept. 24, 1832, aged 97, in Washington, D. C., stating he was born March 6, 1736 at Port Tobacco in Charles County, Maryland and lived in Virginia at the time of his enlistment. Since the war he lived most of the time in Fairfax County, Virginia and then moved to Washington, D. C. [Ref: V-II:1479].

HALL, Hannah. See "James Craik," q.v.

HALL, John. Private, Militia, 26th Battalion, Capt. Richard Bennett Mitchell's Company, 1777 [Ref: M-164]. Took the Oath of Allegiance in 1778 [Ref: L-17]. Resident of Port Tobacco West Hundred in 1778 [Ref: Q-I:297].

HALL, Robert Clerk. Corporal, Militia, 26th Battalion, Capt. Thomas H. Marshall's Company, 1777 [Ref: M-163]. Took the Oath of Allegiance in 1778 [Ref: L-17]. Rendered patriotic service by providing wheat for the use of the military in May 1783 [Ref: N-598]. "Robert Clark Hall" was aged about 52 as noted in a 1772 deposition [Ref: DD-8]. Resident of Pomonkey Hundred in 1778 [Ref: Q-I:297].

HALL, Stephen. Mate aboard the State Ship *Defence* in 1777 [Ref: D-657]. Resident of William & Mary Upper Hundred in 1778 [Ref: Q-I:297].

HALL, William. Private, Militia, 26th Battalion, Capt. Thomas H. Marshall's Company, 1777 [Ref: M-163]. Took the Oath of Allegiance in 1778 [Ref: L-17]. Resident of Pomonkey Hundred in 1778 [Ref: Q-I:297].

HALLEY, John. Took the Oath of Allegiance in 1778 [Ref: L-17, which listed the name as "Haley" and X-1778, which listed the name as "Hally"].

HALLEY, Nathaniel. Took the Oath of Allegiance in 1778 [Ref: L-17]. Resident of Pomonkey Hundred in 1778 [Ref: Q-I:297, which listed the name as "Haly"].

HAMILL, Sarah. See "William Poston," q.v.

HAMILTON, Ann. See "Patrick Hamilton," q.v.

HAMILTON, Baptist. Private, Militia, 12th Battalion, Capt. John Parnham's Company, 1777 [Ref: M-160]. Resident of Port Tobacco East Hundred in 1778 [Ref: Q-I:297].

HAMILTON, Bennett. Private, Militia, 26th Battalion, Capt. William McPherson's Company, 1777 [Ref: M-163]. "Bennett Hamilton" took the Oath of Allegiance in 1778 [Ref: L-17, AA-641]. "Burnett Hamilton" was a resident of Port Tobacco Upper Hundred in 1778 [Ref: Q-I:297].

HAMILTON, Burdit. Second Lieutenant, Militia, 26th Battalion, Capt. William Winter's Company, Feb. 26, 1776 [Ref: A-186, A-206, M-82, X-87, Y-II:23, M-165, which latter source listed the name as "Burd.(?) Hamilton"]. Took the Oath of Allegiance in 1778 [Ref: L-17]. First Lieutenant, 26th Battalion, commissioned May 9, 1778 [Ref: M-82, E-72, which listed the name as "Hamelton"]. Resident of Durham Lower Hundred in 1778 [Ref: Q-I:297].

HAMILTON, Burnett. See "Bennett Hamilton," q.v.

HAMILTON, Edward. Private, Militia, 26th Battalion, Capt. William McPherson's Company, 1777 [Ref: M-163].

HAMILTON, Frances. See "John Carroll," q.v.

HAMILTON, Hamidathy. Private, Militia, 26th Battalion, Capt. William Winter's Company, 1777 [Ref: M-165].

HAMILTON, Ignatius (1760-1808). Private, Militia, 12th Battalion, Capt. John Hanson's Company, 1777 [Ref: M-159]. Resident of Port Tobacco East Hundred in 1778 [Ref: Q-I:297]. Petitioned the Council of Maryland in 1783 stating that he had not taken the Oath of Allegiance due to any disaffection with the government, but from a variety of incidents, and was unjustly penalized as a non-juror and fined unfairly; therefore, he asked the Council to consider ordering the County Justices to remit the fines they imposed on him and others who signed the petition. The Council of Maryland, after reviewing his case, indicated they believed the truth of the facts stated in the petition and ordered a remission of the fines and penalties on Sept. 17, 1783 [Ref: I-454]. Ignatius Hamilton was born in Virginia in 1760, served in the war in Maryland, married Ann Catherine Bush, and migrated to Louisiana where he died before 1808 [Ref: J-II:1286].

HAMILTON, John B. Private, Militia, 12th Battalion, Capt. Walter Hanson's Company, 1777 [Ref: M-159]. "John Bagehot Hambleton" took the Oath of Allegiance in 1778 [Ref: L-17].

HAMILTON, Lawrence. Took the Oath of Allegiance in 1778 [Ref: L-17, AA-641].

HAMILTON, Leonard. Ensign, Militia, 26th Battalion, Capt. William McPherson's Company, Feb. 26, 1776 [Ref: M-82, M-163, A-186, A-206, Y-II:23]. Took the Oath of Allegiance in 1778 [Ref: L-17, AA-641]. Rendered patriotic service by providing wheat for the use of the military in September and December 1782 [Ref: N-556, N-575, which also listed the name as "Hamelton"]. Resident of Port Tobacco Upper Hundred in 1778 [Ref: Q-I:297].

HAMILTON, Marmaduke (1749-1801). "Duke Hamilton" was a private in the militia, 26th Battalion, Capt. William McPherson's Company, in 1777 [Ref: M-163]. "Marmaduke Hamilton" rendered patriotic service by providing wheat for the use of the military in May 1783 [Ref: N-597]. Resident of Port Tobacco West Hundred in 1778 [Ref: Q-I:297]. Marmaduke Hamilton served as a private, married Mary ----, and died before February 1801 [Ref: J-II:1288].

HAMILTON, Mary. See "Marmaduke Hamilton," q.v.

HAMILTON, Patrick (1717-1790). Took the Oath of Allegiance in 1778 [Ref: L-17, AA-641]. Rendered patriotic service by providing wheat for the use of the military in December 1781 [Ref: N-464]. Aged about 45 as noted in a 1762 deposition [Ref: DD-9]. Resident of Port Tobacco Upper Hundred in 1778 [Ref: Q-I:297]. Patrick Hamilton married Ann ---- and died in 1790 [Ref: J-II:1288].

HAMILTON, Samuel. Rendered patriotic service by providing wheat for the use of the military in September and October 1782 [Ref: N-552, N-556, N-559, which also listed the name as "Hamelton"].

HAMILTON, Thomas (1716-   ). Took the Oath of Allegiance in 1778 [Ref: L-17]. "Thomas Hambleton" was aged about 40 as noted in a 1756 deposition [Ref: DD-8].

HAMILTON, William. Private, Militia, 26th Battalion, Capt. Thomas H. Marshall's Company, 1777 [Ref: M-163]. Took the Oath of Allegiance in 1778 [Ref: L-17]. Private, 3rd Maryland Line, enrolled in Charles County for Capt. Joseph Marbury's Company by May 24, 1780 [Ref: D-333, which listed the name as "Hamelton" and F-181, which listed the name as "Hambleton"]. Resident of Pomonkey Hundred in 1778 [Ref: Q-I:297].

HAMMERSLEY, Ann. See "John Digges," q.v.

HAMMERSLEY, Francis. Took the Oath of Allegiance in 1778 [Ref: L-17, which listed the name as "Hamersly"]. Rendered patriotic service by providing wheat for the use of the military in September and December 1782 [Ref: N-548, N-577, which also listed the name as "Hammoursly" and "Hamersley"]. Francis Hammersley was a brother of Ann Hammersley who married "John Digges," q.v.

HAMMERSLEY, Henry. Private, Militia, 12th Battalion, Capt. Jonathan Yates' Company, 1777 [Ref: M-162, which listed the name as "Hamsly"]. Rendered patriotic service by providing clothing for the use of the military in February 1778 [Ref: Y-II:234, which listed the name as "Hammersly"]. Took the Oath of Allegiance in 1778 [Ref: L-17, AA-641, which source listed the name as "Hamersly"]. Resident of William & Mary Lower Hundred in 1778 [Ref: Q-I:297]. Rendered patriotic service by providing wheat for the use of the military in January 1782 [Ref: N-476, which listed the name as "Hermesley"]. Henry Hammersley was a brother of Ann Hammersley who married "John Digges," q.v.

HAMMOND, Nicholas. Took the Oath of Allegiance in 1778 [Ref: AA-641]. Resident of Bryan Town Hundred in 1778 [Ref: Q-I:297].

HANCOCK, Abraham. Private, Militia, 12th Battalion, Capt. Benjamin Lusby Corry's Company, 1777 [Ref: M-160]. Resident of Newport West Hundred in 1778 [Ref: Q-I:297].

HANCOCK, Ann. See "Benjamin Dent," q.v.

HANCOCK, John. Private, Militia, 12th Battalion, Capt. Benjamin Lusby Corry's Company, 1777 [Ref: M-160]. Resident of Newport West Hundred in 1778 [Ref: Q-I:297].

HANCOCK, Thomas (c1753-1799). Private, Militia, 12th Battalion, Capt. Benjamin Lusby Corry's Company, 1777 [Ref: M-160]. Took the Oath of Allegiance in 1778 [Ref: L-17, AA-641]. Resident of Newport West Hundred in 1778 [Ref: Q-I:297]. Thomas Hancock married Elizabeth Latimer and died before Feb. 5, 1799 [Ref: J-II:1296].

HANCOCK, William. Private, Militia, 12th Battalion, Capt. Benjamin Lusby Corry's Company, 1777 [Ref: M-160]. Took the Oath of Allegiance in 1778 [Ref: L-17, AA-641]. Rendered patriotic service by providing wheat for the use of the military in December 1781 [Ref: N-461]. Resident of Newport West Hundred in 1778 [Ref: Q-I:297].

HAND, Benjamin. Took the Oath of Allegiance in 1778 [Ref: L-17].

HANNAH, Gabriel. See "William Hannon," q.v.

HANNAH, William. See "William Hannon," q.v.

HANNON, Mary. See "William Hannon," q.v.

HANNON, Robert. See "William Hannon," q.v.

HANNON, William (1761-1846). He applied for a pension (R4579) in Greenup County, Kentucky on Oct. 20, 1842, stating he was born in Charles County, Maryland on Feb. 28, 1761. He lived there at the time of his enlistment in the Revolutionary War at the age of 16. William died on March 31, 1846 in Kentucky, having moved there from Henry County, Virginia (no date was given). He had married (name of wife not stated) and left two children: Gabriel Hannon (aged 52 in 1843, lived in Greenup County, and died by 1851, leaving ten children) and Mary Anglin (lived in Carter County, Kentucky in 1851). Mentioned also in 1842 was Mary Hannon, widow of William's deceased brother Robert Hannon [Ref: V-II:1510, T-42. It must be noted that the first source stated "his mother was Sarah Rigg" while the other source noted that the "affidavit of Joseph Shelton stated that he had heard the mother of his wife, Sarah Rigg, state that the said William Hannon had served in the revolution. Gabriel Hannon, aged 52, mentioned his father William Hannon and Charles Riggs *[sic]* had served together in the war." The record also listed his name as Hanna or Hannah, as well as Hannon. However, although Charles Rigg was a Maryland soldier, William Hannon is not found in the "Muster Rolls of Maryland Line in the American Revolution, 1775-1783," *Archives of Maryland, Volume 18*]. Additional research may be necessary before drawing conclusions.

HANSON, Ann (Anne). See "Samuel Hanson, of Samuel" and "Walter Hanson" and "Samuel Hanson" and "John Nathan Smoot," q.v.

HANSON, Charity. See "Samuel Hanson, Jr.," q.v.

HANSON, Chloe. See "George Lee" and Samuel Hanson" and "Philip Briscoe," q.v.

HANSON, Dorothy. See "Richard Harrison" and "William Harrison" and "Robert Hanson Harrison," q.v.

HANSON, Eleanor. Sec "Henry Chapman" and "Samuel Hanson," q.v.

HANSON, Elizabeth. See "Samuel Hanson" and "Walter Hanson" and "Thomas McPherson" and "William Barton Smoot," q.v.

HANSON, Heloise. See "Walter Hanson," q.v.

HANSON, Henry. Rendered patriotic service by providing wheat for the use of the military in September and December 1781 [Ref: N-437, N-463].

HANSON, Henry Massey (1747-c1815). First Lieutenant, Militia, 12th Battalion, Capt. John Hanson's Company, Feb. 26, 1776 [Ref: A-186, A-206, B-126, M-84, M-158, Y-II:23]. Took the Oath of Allegiance in 1778 [Ref: L-17, AA-641, which latter source listed the name as "Henry Ms. Hanson"]. Aged about 32 as noted in a 1779 deposition [Ref: DD-9, which listed the name as "Henry M. Hanson"]. Resident of Port Tobacco East Hundred in 1778 [Ref: Q-I:297].

HANSON, Hoskins (c1745-1796). Sergeant, Militia, 12th Battalion, Capt. Walter Hanson's Company, 1777 [Ref: M-159]. Rendered patriotic service by providing clothing for the use of the military in February 1778 [Ref: Y-

II:234]. Resident of Port Tobacco East Hundred in 1778 [Ref: Q-I:297]. Second Lieutenant, May 28, 1779 [Ref: M-84, F-427]. Took the Oath of Allegiance in 1778 [Ref: AA-641]. Appointed a Justice of the Peace on Nov. 19, 1779 and Jan. 17, 1782 [Ref: F-19, I-45]. Hoskins Hanson married Catherine Queen Thompson and died intestate by September 1796 [Ref: J-II:1302]. See "Walter Hanson" and "William Thompson," q.v.

HANSON, Isaac Kay. See "Samuel Hanson, of Samuel," q.v.

HANSON, John (1721-1783). Captain, Militia, 12th Battalion, Feb. 26, 1776 [Ref: M-84, M-158, Y-II:23, B-125, A-186, A-206, which latter source listed the name as "John Hanson (youngest)"]. Resident of Port Tobacco East Hundred in 1778 [Ref: Q-I:297]. John Hanson was born on April 3, 1721, served as President of the United States in Congress Assembled in 1781, and died on November 22, 1783 [Ref: HH-1997, citing William Dougherty's *The Hanson Family* (1912), pp. 14, 17]. See "Samuel Hanson, of Samuel," q.v.

HANSON, John (1710-1795). Took the Oath of Allegiance in 1778 [Ref: L-17]. Aged about 69 in a 1779 deposition [Ref: BB-469]. Resident of Port Tobacco East Hundred in 1778 [Ref: Q-I:297].

HANSON, John Beall. See "Samuel Hanson, Jr.," q.v.

HANSON, Louisa. See "Samuel Hanson, of Samuel," q.v.

HANSON, Margaret. See "Walter Hanson" and "Samuel Hanson, Jr.," q.v.

HANSON, Maria. See "Samuel Hanson, of Samuel," q.v.

HANSON, Mary. See "Michael Jenifer Stone" and "Samuel Hanson, Jr." and "Daniel Jenifer Adams," q.v.

HANSON, Mildred. See "Samuel Hanson," q.v.

HANSON, Nancy. See "Samuel Hanson," q.v.

HANSON, Samuel (1716-1794). Son of Samuel Hanson and Elizabeth Storey, he was born on Dec. 20, 1716 and died in 1794. He married twice, first to Anne Hawkins and second to Anne Brown (widow of both Samuel Clagett and Robert Horner) in August 1774. His children were as follows: Thomas Hawkins Hanson (1750-1810); Samuel Hanson, of Samuel (c1752-1830); Chloe Hanson (married "George Lee," q.v.); Mildred Hanson (married William Baker); Sarah Hawkins Hanson (married Dr. William Beans); Nancy Hanson (married John Addison); Eleanor Hanson (married Henry Henley Chapman); Anne Hanson (married Nicholas Lingan); and, Elizabeth Hanson (married John Anderson). [Ref: P-I:407, W-115]. Samuel Hanson rendered the following patriotic services: Sheriff of Charles County, 1744-1750. County Justice, 1755-1778. Delegate to the Maryland Convention in 1775. Served in the Lower House of the Maryland Legislature, 1778-1780. Appointed an Election Judge for Charles County by the Maryland Convention on July 3, 1776 [Ref: Y-I:35].

133

Rendered patriotic service by providing clothing for the use of the military in February 1778 [Ref: Y-II:234]. Took the Oath of Allegiance in 1778 [Ref: L-17]. Resident of Port Tobacco Upper Hundred in 1778 [Ref: Q-I:297]. Justice who administered (and took) the Oath of Allegiance in 1778 [Ref: AA-641]. Appointed a Justice of the Peace on Nov. 21, 1778 [Ref: E-249]. Judge of the Orphans Court, 1777-1778, and Judge of the Court of Appeals, 1778. Subscription Officer, Continental Loan Office, 1779 [Ref: P-I:408]. *Ed. Note:* There were several men named Samuel Hanson. Additional research will be necessary before drawing conclusions. See "Samuel Hanson, Jr." and "Samuel Hanson, of Samuel" and "George Lee," q.v.

HANSON, Samuel Jr. (c1738-1817). Son of Major Samuel Hanson (1705-1749) and Mary Fendall, he was married first by 1759 to Margaret ---- (died 1792) and second by 1793 to Sarah Beall (widow of Basil Beall). He had these children by his first wife: Dr. Samuel Hanson (married Elizabeth Marshall Fendall), John Beall Hanson (married Elizabeth Marshall), Margaret Beall Hanson (married John Fendall Beall), Charity Fendall Noble Hanson, Mary Fendall Hanson (married ---- Cawood), and Elizabeth Beall Hanson (married ---- McPherson). [Ref: S-3123, P-I:408]. Delegate to the Maryland Convention from July 26 to Aug. 14, 1775 [Ref: A-3, Y-I:4]. Captain, Militia, 1775, and Second Major, Militia, 26th Battalion, from Jan. 6, 1776 until June 17, 1778 (resigned) [Ref: M-84, E-138, P-I:408]. Appointed a Judge of the Orphans Court of Charles County on June 4, 1777 and May 15, 1778 [Ref: C-274, E-84, which listed the name without the "Jr."]. Took the Oath of Allegiance in 1778 [Ref: L-17]. Resident of Port Tobacco Upper Hundred in 1778 [Ref: Q-I:297]. Appointed a Judge of the Court of Appeals for Charles County on May 20, 1778 [Ref: E-97]. Appointed a Justice of the Peace on Nov. 19, 1779 and Jan. 17, 1782 [Ref: F-19, I-45, which latter source mistakenly listed the name as "Samuel Hanson Jenifer" rather than "Samuel Hanson Junior"]. Rendered patriotic service by providing wheat for the use of the military in September 1782 [Ref: N-544]. *Ed. Note:* There were several men named Samuel Hanson; therefore, additional research will be necessary before drawing conclusions. See "Samuel Hanson" and "Samuel Hanson, of Samuel" and "Samuel Hanson, of John" and "William Hanson McPherson," q.v.

HANSON, Samuel, of John. Took the Oath of Allegiance in 1778 [Ref: L-17]. One "Samuel Hanson" was appointed an Ensign in the Maryland Line on Sept. 4, 1781, date of rank to be determined [Ref: G-600]. Additional research may be necessary before drawing conclusions.

HANSON, Samuel, of Samuel (c1752-1830). Son of Samuel Hanson (1716-1794) and Anne Hawkins, he married circa 1777 to Mary Key (or Kay), of Philadelphia, and had these children: Samuel Hanson (married Matilda Calloway Hickman and moved to Kentucky by 1807), Isaac Kay Hanson (married Maria H. Jones), Thomas Hanson, John Hanson, Maria Hanson, Ann Hanson, and Louisa Serena Hanson (married Roger Chew Weightman). [Ref: P-I:409]. Samuel served in the Maryland Legislature between 1775 and 1782, and as a County Justice between 1779 and 1786. Lieutenant Colonel, Militia, 26th Battalion, from Jan. 6, 1776 through at least Oct. 17, 1777 [Ref: M-84, P-I:409, C-399, C-485, Y-II:23, which latter two sources listed him as "Col. Samuel Hanson of the Marching Militia"]. Took the Oath of Allegiance in 1778 [Ref: L-17, AA-641]. Resident of Port Tobacco Upper Hundred in 1778 [Ref: Q-I:297]. Rendered patriotic service by providing wheat for the use of the military in September 1782 [Ref: N-556]. *Ed. Note:* There were several Samuel Hansons; therefore, additional research will be necessary before drawing conclusions. See Harry Wright Newman's *Charles County Gentry*, pp. 291-261. Also see "Samuel Hanson" and "Samuel Hanson, Jr." and "Samuel Hanson, of Walter" and "Samuel Hanson, of John," q.v.

HANSON, Samuel, of Walter (c1750-1810). Private, Militia, 26th Battalion, Capt. Robert Sinnett's Company, 1777 [Ref: M-164]. Took the Oath of Allegiance in 1778 [Ref: L-17]. Private ("voluntair"), 1st Maryland Line, by Sept. 11, 1778 [Ref: D-330]. He died intestate by February 13, 1810 (date of inventory). [Ref: P-I:409]. See "Walter Hanson," q.v.

HANSON, Sara. See "John Baptist Wathen," q.v.

HANSON, Sarah Hawkins. See "Samuel Hanson," q.v.

HANSON, Theophilus (1743-1808). Private, Militia, 26th Battalion, Capt. Robert Sinnett's Company, 1777 [Ref: M-164]. Took the Oath of Allegiance in 1778 [Ref: L-17, which misspelled the name as "Hannon"]. Appointed the Surveyor of Charles County on Jan. 22, 1784 in the room of Thomas McPherson, deceased [Ref: I-514]. Aged about 27 as noted in a 1770 deposition which mentioned his father William Hanson [Ref: DD-9]. Resident of Port Tobacco West Hundred in 1778 [Ref: Q-I:297].

HANSON, Thomas (1737-   ). Captain, 1st Maryland Line, July 1776 [Ref: D-31]. Rendered patriotic service by providing wheat for the use of the military in May 1781 [Ref: N-401]. Aged about 39 as noted in a 1776 deposition which mentioned his father William Hanson [Ref: DD-9]. Resident of Port Tobacco Upper Hundred in 1778 [Ref: Q-I:297]. See "Samuel Hanson, of Samuel" and "Thomas Hawkins Hanson," q.v.

HANSON, Thomas Hawkins (1750-1808). Private, Militia, 26th Battalion, Capt. William McPherson's Company, 1777 [Ref: M-163]. He married Mrs.

Rebecca Dulaney Anderson (daughter of Walter Dulaney) and died before April 4, 1808 [Ref: J-II:1303, P-I:407]. He was a brother of "Samuel Hanson," q.v. *Ed. Note:* Harry Wright Newman's *Charles County Gentry* (page 256) states that Thomas Hawkins Hanson was in command of a company of the Flying Camp at the beginning of the war, saw active service in New York, and died intestate in 1810. See "Thomas Hanson," q.v. Additional research may be necessary before drawing conclusions.
HANSON, Violetta. See "Walter Hanson," q.v.
HANSON, Walter (1711-1794). Son of Samuel Hanson and Elizabeth Storey, he married first by 1740 to Elizabeth Hoskins and second in 1783 to Elizabeth Hanson. His children were: Hoskins Hanson (married Catherine Queen Thompson and died in 1796), Samuel Hanson (died in 1810), William Hanson (married Sarah Sinnett and died in 1796), Walter Hanson, Elizabeth Hoskins Hanson (married William Barton Smoot), Violetta Hanson (married Henry Barnes), Anne Hanson (married first to Hugh Mitchell and second to Samuel Stone), Heloise Hanson, and Margaret Hanson (married John Muschett). [Ref: P-I:409, HH-1997, citing William Dougherty's *The Hanson Family* (1912), p. 13, which stated Walter married Jane Hoskins]. Walter Hoskins was Sheriff of Charles County, 1738-1741, Deputy Commissary, 1740-1751, 1767-1773, 1776-1777, Quartermaster, 26th Battalion, by Jan. 6, 1776, Court Justice, 1741-1794, Committee of Observation, 1774, Judge of the Court of Appeals, 1778, and Justice of the Orphans Court, 1779-1789 [Ref: P-I:409, P-I:410, M-84, J-II:1303]. Having been recommended to the Maryland Convention "as a Genius in the mechanical Way & as a Person that may be of Service to this Province in gaining a proper Knowledge of erecting and working Powder Mills or some other useful and necessary Manufacture," the Maryland Convention on April 17, 1776 "ordered that the Treasurer of the Western Shore to pay to Mr. Walter Hanson of Charles County thirty five pounds currency to defray his Expences in attending the Powder Mills in Pennsylvania, or elsewhere, for Instruction; which said sum Mr. Hanson agrees to refund in case he does not erect a Powder Mill in this Province." [Ref: A-337, A-341]. Captain, Militia, 12th Battalion, 1777 [Ref: M-159]. Rendered patriotic service by providing clothing for the use of the military in February 1778 [Ref: Y-II:234]. Took the Oath of Allegiance in 1778 [Ref: L-17, which listed the name as "Sr."]. Resident of Port Tobacco West Hundred in 1778 [Ref: Q-I:297]. Appointed a Judge of the Court of Appeals for Charles County on May 20, 1778 and Nov. 19, 1779 [Ref: E-97, F-19]. Justice who administered the Oath of Allegiance in 1778 [Ref: AA-641]. Appointed a Justice of the Peace on Nov. 21, 1778 and Nov. 19, 1779 and Jan. 17, 1782 [Ref: E-249, F-19, I-45]. Licensed by the Council

of Maryland to act as Deputy Assistant Commissary of Purchases for Charles County on Dec. 11, 1779 (commissioned on Nov. 13, 1779). [Ref: F-35]. Appointed a Judge of the Orphans Court on Dec. 29, 1779 and Jan. 17, 1782 [Ref: F-42, I-46]. Rendered patriotic service by providing wheat for the use of the military in October and November 1782 [Ref: N-559, N-564]. See "Walter Hanson, Jr." and "Walter Hanson, of John" and "Thomas Pickerel," q.v.

HANSON, Walter Jr. (c1750-1791). Took the Oath of Allegiance in 1778 [Ref: L-17]. Resident of Port Tobacco West Hundred in 1778 [Ref: Q-I:297]. "Walter Hanson Junr Esqr" was commissioned Contractor for Horses in Charles County on Sept. 6, 1780 [Ref: F-278]. He was accused, but not officially charged, however, of concealing his horses from Daniel Jenifer, Contractor of Horses in Charles County, in June 1781 [Ref: H-324]. See "Walter Hanson," q.v.

HANSON, Walter, of John. Captain, Militia, 26th Battalion, Feb. 26, 1776 [Ref: M-84, A-186, A-206, Y-II:23]. Resident of Port Tobacco East Hundred in 1778 [Ref: Q-I:297]. One "Walter Hanson" was appointed an ensign in the Maryland Line on Sept. 4, 1781, "date of rank to be determined." [Ref: G-600]. One "Walter Hanson (1760-1792)" was a captain and married Sarah Hatch Maddox [Ref: J-II:1303]. Additional research may be necessary before drawing conclusions. See Harry Wright Newman's *Charles County Gentry*, pp. 219-261].

HANSON, Walter Warren (c1750-1838). Private, 1st Maryland Line, drafted from the Charles County militia on July 27, 1781 [Ref: D-377, which listed the name as "Hannon" and G-469, which listed the name as "Harmon"].

HANSON, William. Private, 1st Maryland Line, enrolled and passed on July 19, 1776 [Ref: D-31]. Resident of Port Tobacco East Hundred in 1778 [Ref: Q-I:297]. Ensign, 4th Maryland Line by Jan. 1, 1782 [Ref: D-460]. See "Walter Hanson" and "Theophilus Hanson" and "Thomas Hanson," q.v.

HANSON, William Jr. "William Hanson, of William" was a sergeant in the militia, 12th Battalion, Capt. Walter Hanson's Company, 1777 [Ref: M-159]. "William Hanson, Jr." took the Oath of Allegiance in 1778 [Ref: L-17]. Resident of Port Tobacco East Hundred in 1778 [Ref: Q-I:297].

HANSON, William Sr. Took the Oath of Allegiance in 1778 [Ref: L-17].

HARBERT, Anne. See "George Dent" and "George Dent, Jr.," q.v.

HARBIN, Allen (1746-   ). Born on Jan. 5, 1746, son of Elisha and Elizabeth Harbin [Ref: EE-1, which listed the name as "Allen Hearbin"]. Private, Militia, 12th Battalion, Capt. Peter Wood's Company, 1777 [Ref: M-161, which listed the name as "Allan Harben"]. Took the Oath of Allegiance in 1778 [Ref: AA-641, L-17, which latter source mistakenly listed the name as "Arn Harnin"]. Resident of Bryan Town Hundred in 1778 [Ref: Q-I:297].

HARBIN, Elisha (1725-). Took the Oath of Allegiance in 1778 [Ref: AA-641]. Aged about 46 as noted in a 1771 deposition [Ref: DD-10]. Resident of Bryan Town Hundred in 1778 [Ref: Q-I:297]. See "Allen Harbin," q.v.

HARBIN, Elizabeth. See "Allen Harbin" and "Joshua Harbin," q.v.

HARBIN, John. "John Harbin" was a resident of Bryan Town Hundred in 1778 [Ref: Q-I:297]. "John Harbin" was constable in 1778 [Ref: CC-709]. "John Hardin" was a private (substitute during the war) in the Maryland Line on Sept. 11, 1778 [Ref: D-330].

HARBIN, Joshua. Private, 1st Maryland Line. He married Elizabeth ---- and died before June 16, 1792 [Ref: J-II:1304].

HARBIN, William. Private, Militia, 12th Battalion, Capt. Peter Wood's Company, 1777 [Ref: M-161, which listed the name as "Harben"]. Resident of Bryan Town Hundred in 1778 [Ref: Q-I:297].

HARBIN, Zephaniah W. Took the Oath of Allegiance in 1778 [Ref: AA-641, L-17, which latter source listed the name as "Zepheniah W. Harbord"]. Resident of Bryan Town Hundred in 1778 [Ref: Q-I:297].

HARDIN, John. See "John Harbin," q.v.

HARDMAN, Ignatius (1739-). Private, Militia, 12th Battalion, Capt. Benjamin Lusby Corry's Company, 1777 [Ref: M-160]. Aged about 40 as noted in a 1779 deposition [Ref: DD-10]. One Ignatius Hardman was a resident of Newport East Hundred and another Ignatius Hardman was a resident of Newport West Hundred in 1778 [Ref: Q-I:297].

HARDY, Thomas Dent (c1755-1781). Served in the naval service, was was captured by the British in 1780, taken prisoner to New York, and died there in the spring of 1781. By his will written on February 25, 1780, he devised his land on Piscataway Creek to his uncle "Thomas Dent," q.v. [Ref: Harry Wright Newman's *Charles County Gentry*, p. 31].

HARMON, Grace. See "William Marbury Smallwood," q.v.

HARGRAVES, George. Took the Oath of Allegiance in 1778 [Ref: L-17, which listed the name as "Hargreaves"]. Rendered patriotic service by providing wheat for the use of the military in September and December 1782 [Ref: N-548, N-573, which also listed the name as "Hargrave"]. Resident of Port Tobacco East Hundred in 1778 [Ref: Q-I:297, which listed the name as "Hardgraves"].

HAROY, William. Private, Militia, 12th Battalion, Capt. John Hanson's Company, 1777 [Ref: M-159].

HARRIS, Benjamin. Private, Militia, 26th Battalion, Capt. William McPherson's Company, 1777 [Ref: M-163]. Took the Oath of Allegiance in 1778 [Ref: L-17]. Resident of Port Tobacco Upper Hundred in 1778 [Ref: Q-I:297].

HARRIS, Charles. Took the Oath of Allegiance in 1778 [Ref: L-17].

HARRIS, John 2nd. Second Major, Militia, 12th Battalion, Jan. 6, 1776 [Ref: M-84].

HARRIS, Mary Thomas. Rendered patriotic service by providing clothing for the use of the military in February 1778 [Ref: Y-II:234]. See "Ellis Thomas," q.v.

HARRIS, Thomas. Captain, Militia, 1775. Major, Feb. 26, 1776. Lieutenant Colonel, Jan. 19, 1781 [Ref: M-84, M-85, A-186, G-280, Y-II:23]. Assisted the Purchaser of Clothing in Charles County in February 1778 [Ref: Y-II:235]. Took the Oath of Allegiance in 1778 [Ref: AA-641]. Resident of William & Mary Lower Hundred in 1778 [Ref: Q-I:297]. "Col. Thomas Harris" rendered patriotic service by providing wheat for the use of the military in December 1781 and December 1782 [Ref: N-464, N-577].

HARRISON, Ann Warren. See "William Harrison," q.v.

HARRISON, Benjamin. Rendered patriotic service in December 1781 by making a proposal via Hezekiah Reeder, Commissary of Purchases for Charles County, to the Governor of Maryland, regarding "the manufacture of wheat." [Ref: N-461].

HARRISON, Charles. Took the Oath of Allegiance in 1778 [Ref: L-17].

HARRISON, Dorothy Hanson. See "Joseph Hanson Harrison" and "John Courts Jones," q.v.

HARRISON, Elizabeth. See "William Elgin, Sr.," q.v.

HARRISON, George. Private, 1st Maryland Line, enrolled and passed on July 20, 1776 [Ref: D-33].

HARRISON, Grace. See "William Harrison," q.v.

HARRISON, Joseph. Took the Oath of Allegiance in 1778 [Ref: L-17]. See "Richard Harrison" and "Joseph Hanson Harrison," q.v.

HARRISON, Joseph Hanson (1722-1785). Son of Joseph Harrison and Verlinda Stone, he married Mary ---- by 1763 and had these children: Joseph White Harrison, Richard Harrison, Dorothy Harrison, and Mary Harrison (who married George Hutchinson). He served in the Lower House of the Maryland Legislature, 1768-1780. Delegate to the Maryland Conventions, 1774-1776. Court Justice, 1759-1773. Committee of Observation, 1774 [Ref: P-I:417, Y-I:28]. Aged about 50 as noted in a 1772 deposition [Ref: DD-10]. Resident of Durham Lower Hundred in 1778 [Ref: Q-I:297]. See "Samuel Wright" and "Joseph Hanson Harrison," q.v.

HARRISON, Joseph White. Son of "Joseph Hanson Harrison," q.v. Second Lieutenant, Militia, 26th Battalion, Capt. Walter Hanson's Company, Feb. 26, 1776 [Ref: M-85, A-186, A-206, P-I:417, Y-II:23]. Took the Oath of

Allegiance in 1778 [Ref: L-17]. Resident of Port Tobacco Town Hundred in 1778 [Ref: Q-I:297].

HARRISON, Mary. See "Joseph Hanson Harrison," q.v.

HARRISON, Rebecca. See "William Harrison," q.v.

HARRISON, Richard (1716-1780). Son of Joseph Harrison and Verlinda Stone, he married first by 1745 to Dorothy Hanson and second to Elizabeth Dent (widow of William Penn). His sons were: (1) Hon. Robert Hanson Harrison (who died in 1790 and was Military Secretary to George Washington and a Chief Judge of the Maryland General Court); (2) Col. William Harrison; and, (3) Rev. Walter Hanson Harrison. His stepsons were "Jezreal Penn," q.v., and William Penn [Ref: P-I:417, P-I:418, P-I:498, FF-84]. Richard was a captain in 1747, colonel in 1754, and a court justice from 1741 to 1769. Took the Oath of Allegiance in 1778 [Ref: L-17, P-I:418]. Rendered patriotic service by providing clothing for the use of the military in February 1778 [Ref: Y-II:234, which listed the name as "Col. Richard Harrison"]. Aged about 41 as noted in a 1757 deposition which also referred to him as "Col. Richard Harrison." [Ref: DD-10]. Resident of Durham Lower Hundred in 1778 [Ref: Q-I:297]. See "Joseph Hanson Harrison" and "Robert Hanson Harrison" and "Thomas Harrison," q.v.

HARRISON, Robert Hanson (1745-1790). Son of Richard Harrison and Dorothy Hanson, he was Military Secretary to George Washington and a Chief Judge of the Maryland General Court. The obituary of Robert Hanson Harrison appeared in the *Maryland Gazette* on June 17, 1790, stating he "died the 2nd instant, at his seat on the Potomac River, Charles County, in his 45th year. He was Chief Judge of the General Court of Maryland. He served the U. S. in the late war. Walter H. Harrison is administrator." [Ref: FF-84, P-I:417]. See "Richard Harrison" and "John Courts Jones" and "William Harrison," q.v.

HARRISON, Thomas (1760-   ). Private, 1st Maryland Line, enrolled and passed on July 19, 1776 [Ref: D-31]. Thomas Harrison, son of Richard, deceased, was aged 19 on June 2, 1779 [Ref: GG-275].

HARRISON, Walter Hanson. See "Richard Harrison" and "Robert Hanson Harrison," q.v.

HARRISON, William (1747-1789). Son of Richard Harrison and Dorothy Hanson, he married first to Rebecca Dent and second to Ann Jordan. His children were William Dent Harrison, Ann Warren Harrison, Rebecca Harrison, Grace Harrison, and probably Robert Hanson Harrison. William Harrison was born on Oct. 24, 1747 and died on July 21, 1789 [Ref: J-II:1330, P-I:419]. He served on the Committee of Observation, 1775, as a Delegate to the Maryland Convention from July 26 to Aug. 14, 1775 and in June 1776, Court Justice, 1778-1788, and Maryland Senate, 1786-1791 [Ref: A-3, P-I:420, Y-I:3, Y-I:28]. Captain, Militia, 1775, and Colonel, 26th Battalion, Jan. 6, 1776 [Ref: M-85, Y-II:23]. Justice who administered (and took) the Oath of Allegiance in 1778 [Ref: AA-641]. Resident of Durham Lower Hundred in 1778 [Ref: Q-I:297]. Appointed a Justice of the Peace on Nov. 21, 1778 and Nov. 19, 1779 and Jan. 17, 1782 [Ref: E-249, F-19, I-45]. Rendered patriotic service by providing wheat for the use of the military in December 1782 [Ref: N-577]. See "Richard Harrison," q.v.

HARRISON, William. Private, Militia, 12th Battalion, Capt. Henry Clarkson's Company, 1777 [Ref: M-159]. Took the Oath of Allegiance in 1778 [Ref: AA-641]. Resident of Newport East Hundred in 1778 [Ref: Q-I:297].

HARRISON, William Dent. See "William Harrison," q.v.

HARROLD, John. Private, Militia, 26th Battalion, Capt. Thomas H. Marshall's Company, 1777 [Ref: M-163].

HARRY, Elizabeth Anne. See "George Dent, of John," q.v.

HART, Michael. Took the Oath of Allegiance in 1778 [Ref: AA-641]. Resident of Port Tobacco West Hundred in 1778 [Ref: Q-I:297].

HARVEY, Elizabeth. See "George Walls," q.v.

HARVEY, Moses. Private, Militia, 26th Battalion, Capt. Thomas H. Marshall's Company, 1777 [Ref: M-163]. "Moses Harvey" took the Oath of Allegiance in 1778 [Ref: L-17, AA-641]. "Moses Harvin" was a resident of Port Tobacco Upper Hundred in 1778 [Ref: Q-I:297].

HARVIN, Annanias. Private, Militia, 26th Battalion, Capt. Benjamin Cawood's Company, 1777 [Ref: M-162].

HARVIN, Edward D. (1757-c1834). Private, Militia, 26th Battalion, Capt. Benjamin Cawood's Company, 1777 [Ref: M-162]. Edward Harvin applied for a pension (S18014) in Loudoun County, Virginia on Oct. 14, 1833, aged 76 years and 9 months, stating he was born in Montgomery County, Maryland in 1757 and lived in Charles County at the time of his enlistment. After the war he lived in Maryland and Virginia [Ref: V-II:1551].

HARVIN, John. See "John Harbin," q.v.

HARVIN, Moses. See "Moses Harvey," q.v.

HARVIN, Thomas Jr. Private, Militia, 26th Battalion, Capt. Benjamin Cawood's Company, 1777 [Ref: M-162].

HASKINS, Bennett. Private, Militia, 12th Battalion, Capt. Benjamin Lusby Corry's Company, 1777 [Ref: M-160, which listed the name as "Hoskins"]. Took the Oath of Allegiance in 1778 [Ref: AA-641, L-17, which latter

source misspelled the name as "Hadkins"]. Resident of Bryan Town Hundred in 1778 [Ref: Q-I:297].
HASKINS, Josiah. Colonel, Militia, 12th Battalion, Jan. 6, 1776 [Ref: M-85].
HATCHER, John. Private, 1st Maryland Line, enrolled and passed on July 27, 1776 [Ref: D-31, which listed the name as "Hatchen"]. Resident of Port Tobacco Upper Hundred in 1778 [Ref: Q-I:297].
HAW, Mary. See "Samuel Love," q.v.
HAW, Thomas. Took the Oath of Allegiance in 1778 [Ref: AA-641]. Resident of Port Tobacco Upper Hundred in 1778 [Ref: Q-I:297].
HAWKINS, Alexander. "Alexander Hawkins" took the Oath of Allegiance in 1778 [Ref: L-17, AA-641]. "Alexander S. W. Hawkins" was a corporal in the militia, 12th Battalion, Capt. Walter Hanson's Company, 1777 [Ref: M-159]. Resident of Port Tobacco East Hundred in 1778 [Ref: Q-I:297].
HAWKINS, Anne. See "Samuel Hanson" and "Samuel Hanson, of Samuel," q.v.
HAWKINS, Caleb. See "Josias Hawkins," q.v.
HAWKINS, Catharine. Rendered patriotic service by providing wheat for the use of the military in November 1781 [Ref: N-453].
HAWKINS, Eleanor. See "George Dent" and "George Dent, Jr." and "Josias Hawkins," q.v.
HAWKINS, Elizabeth. See "William Barton Smoot," q.v.
HAWKINS, Francis. See "Josias Hawkins," q.v.
HAWKINS, Henry. See "Josias Hawkins," q.v.
HAWKINS, Henry Smith (1727-   ). Rendered patriotic service by providing clothing for the use of the military in January and February 1778 [Ref: Y-II:230, Y-II:234]. Took the Oath of Allegiance in 1778 [Ref: L-17]. Resident of Port Tobacco East Hundred in 1778 [Ref: Q-I:297]. Aged about 52 as noted in a 1779 deposition [Ref: BB-469]. Appointed the Inspector of Tobacco at Chandlers Point on Aug. 30, 1780 [Ref: F-271]. Rendered patriotic service by providing wheat for the use of the military in November and December 1782 [Ref: N-567, N-576].
HAWKINS, John. Took the Oath of Allegiance in 1778 [Ref: L-17]. John Hawkins married Dorothy Wood on July 19, 1761 [Ref: EE-8].
HAWKINS, Josias (c1735-1789). Son of Henry Holland Hawkins and Jane Greenfield, he married Ann Warring by 1777 and had these children: Thomas Hawkins, Francis Waring Hawkins, Henry Holland Hawkins, Caleb Hawkins, Samuel Hawkins, Martha Porteus Hawkins, Eleanor Hawkins, and Mary Holliday Hawkins [Ref: P-I:425, P-I:426, J-II:1359]. Josias was a Delegate to the Maryland Convention, 1774-1776, a Court Justice, 1770-1777, member of the Committee of Observation, 1774, Commissioner of the Tax, 1777-1783, and Judge of the Court of Appeals

for Tax Assessment, 1786 [Ref: Y-I:1, Y-I:28, P-I:420]. Captain, Militia, 1775, and Colonel, 12th Battalion, from Jan. 3, 1776 through Sept. 29, 1783 [Ref: Y-II:23, M-86, which latter source listed the name as both "Josiah" and "Josias"]. Took the Oath of Allegiance in 1778 [Ref: AA-641, L-17, which latter source mistakenly listed the name as "Jonas"]. Resident of Port Tobacco East Hundred in 1778 [Ref: Q-I:297]. Rendered patriotic service by providing wheat for the use of the military in December 1781, and June, October, and November 1782 [Ref: N-461, N-526, N-561, N-564].

HAWKINS, Martha. See "Josias Hawkins," q.v.

HAWKINS, Mary. See "Josias Hawkins," q.v.

HAWKINS, Samuel. See "Josias Hawkins," q.v.

HAWKINS, Smith. Private, Militia, 12th Battalion, Capt. Walter Hanson's Company, 1777 [Ref: M-159]. Took the Oath of Allegiance in 1778 [Ref: L-17]. See "Thomas Pickerel," q.v.

HAWKINS, Susanna. Rendered patriotic service by providing clothing for the use of the military in February 1778 [Ref: Y-II:234]. See "John Baptist Wathen," q.v.

HAWKINS, Thomas. Private, Militia, 12th Battalion, Capt. Walter Hanson's Company, 1777 [Ref: M-159]. See "Josias Hawkins," q.v.

HAY, David. Took the Oath of Allegiance in 1778 [Ref: L-17]. Resident of Port Tobacco Town Hundred in 1778 [Ref: Q-I:297].

HAYS, Elextius. Private, Militia, 26th Battalion, Capt. Benjamin Cawood's Company, 1777 [Ref: M-162].

HAYS, Thomas. Took the Oath of Allegiance in 1778 [Ref: L-17, which listed the name as "Hayes"]. Private, Militia, 12th Battalion, Capt. John Thomas' Company, 1777 [Ref: M-161, which listed the name as "Thos. Have(?)," and X-65, which listed the name as "Hase"]. Resident of Port Tobacco East Hundred in 1778 [Ref: Q-I:297].

HAYS, William Sr. Private, Militia, 26th Battalion, Capt. Benjamin Cawood's Company, 1777 [Ref: M-162]. Rendered patriotic service by providing wheat for the use of the military in September 1782 [Ref: N-548, which listed the name as "Hais"]. Resident of Port Tobacco East Hundred in 1778 [Ref: Q-I:297].

HAYS, William, of William. Private, Militia, 26th Battalion, Capt. Benjamin Cawood's Company, 1777 [Ref: M-162].

HAYWOOD, Samuel. Took the Oath of Allegiance in 1778 [Ref: AA-641].

HAZARD, Michael. Private, Militia, 12th Battalion, Capt. Peter Wood's Company, 1777 [Ref: M-161]. Took the Oath of Allegiance in 1778 [Ref: AA-641]. Resident of Benedict Hundred in 1778 [Ref: Q-I:297].

HEABARD, Priscilla. See "William Smallwood," q.v.

HEARD, John. Took the Oath of Allegiance in 1778 [Ref: AA-641]. Resident of Newport West Hundred in 1778 [Ref: Q-I:297, which listed the name as "Herd"].
HEATHER, William. Took the Oath of Allegiance in 1778 [Ref: AA-641].
HELMSLEY, John. Private (substitute for 3 years), 1st Maryland Line, by Sept. 11, 1778 [Ref: D-330].
HEMASTY, Henry. Rendered patriotic service by providing wheat for the use of the military in December 1782 [Ref: N-577].
HEMSLEY, Francis. Sergeant, Militia, 12th Battalion, Capt. John Parnham's Company, 1777 [Ref: M-160]. See "Francis Hammersley," q.v.
HENNICAN, John. Drummer, Militia, 12th Battalion, Capt. Benjamin Lusby Corry's Company, 1777 [Ref: M-160, which listed the name as "John Hinckin (Henekin?), Drummer(?)"]. Took the Oath of Allegiance in 1778 [Ref: L-17, AA-641]. Resident of Newport West Hundred in 1778 [Ref: Q-I:297].
HENRY, John. Took the Oath of Allegiance in 1778 [Ref: L-17].
HENRY, William. Private, 1st Maryland Line, enrolled and passed on July 19, 1776 [Ref: D-31].
HERMSLEY, Henry. Rendered patriotic service by providing wheat for the use of the military in December 1782 [Ref: N-577]. See "Henry Hammersly," q.v.
HEWIN, John. Private, 3rd Maryland Line, enrolled by Capt. Joseph Marbury by March 24, 1780 [Ref: F-119, F-181].
HICKEY, Basil. Private, Militia, 12th Battalion, Capt. John Thomas' Company, 1777 [Ref: M-161]. Took the Oath of Allegiance in 1778 [Ref: AA-641]. Resident of Benedict Hundred in 1778 [Ref: Q-I:297].
HICKEY, Bayne. Took the Oath of Allegiance in 1778 [Ref: L-17, which listed the first name as "Bane"].
HICKEY, Francis. Private, Militia, 12th Battalion, Capt. Peter Wood's Company, 1777. Private (furnished by class for 9 months), 1st Maryland Line, enlisted May 16, 1778 and discharged Feb. 14, 1779 [Ref: M-161, D-118, D-330, which listed the name as "Hicky"]. One Francis Hickey was deceased by May 1778 (date of inventory). [Ref: GG-156].
HICKEY, Leonard. Private, 1st Maryland Line, enrolled and passed on July 20, 1776 [Ref: D-33]. Private, 1st Maryland Line, enlisted on Dec. 10, 1776, promoted to corporal on June 3, 1778, reduced to private on Nov. 5, 1779, and reportedly "deserted" on July 27, 1780 [Ref: D-117]. See "Thomas Mayhew," q.v.
HICKMAN, Matilda C. See "Samuel Hanson, of Samuel," q.v.
HICKS, Robert. Private, Militia, 26th Battalion, Capt. Samuel Smallwood's Company, 1777 [Ref: M-165]. Took the Oath of Allegiance in 1778 [Ref:

L-17, AA-641]. Resident of Port Tobacco Upper Hundred in 1778 [Ref: Q-I:297].

HICKS, Thomas Jr. Private, Militia, 26th Battalion, Capt. Samuel Smallwood's Company, 1777 [Ref: M-165, which listed the name without the "Jr."]. Resident of Port Tobacco Upper Hundred in 1778 [Ref: Q-I:297].

HICKS, Thomas Sr. Took the Oath of Allegiance in 1778 [Ref: L-17, AA-641, which listed the name without the "Sr."]. Resident of Port Tobacco Upper Hundred in 1778 [Ref: Q-I:297].

HIGDON, Benedict Leonard. See "Leonard Higdon," q.v.

HIGDON, Benjamin (1733-   ). Born on Dec. 4 or 11, 1733, son of William and Jane Higdon [Ref: EE-2]. Took the Oath of Allegiance in 1778 [Ref: AA-641, L-17, which latter source misspelled the name as "Bery Hydon"]. Resident of Newport West Hundred in 1778 [Ref: Q-I:297].

HIGDON, Francis. Private, Militia, 12th Battalion, Capt. Benjamin Lusby Corry's Company, 1777 [Ref: M-160, which listed the name as "Frans. Higden"]. Took the Oath of Allegiance in 1778 [Ref: AA-641]. Resident of Newport East Hundred in 1778 [Ref: Q-I:297].

HIGDON, Ignatius (1740-   ). Born on Aug. 12, 1740, son of William and Jane Higdon [Ref: EE-2]. Private, Militia, 26th Battalion, Capt. Robert Sinnett's Company, 1777 [Ref: M-164]. Took the Oath of Allegiance in 1778 [Ref: L-17]. Resident of Port Tobacco West Hundred in 1778 [Ref: Q-I:297]. Rendered patriotic service by providing wheat for the use of the military in May 1783 [Ref: N-598].

HIGDON, Jane. See "Benjamin Higdon" and "Leonard Higdon" and "Ignatius Higdon," q.v.

HIGDON, John Baptist. Private, Militia, 12th Battalion, Capt. John Parnham's Company, 1777 [Ref: M-160, which listed the name as "John Bts. Higdon"]. Resident of Newport East Hundred in 1778 [Ref: Q-I:297]. Petitioned the Council of Maryland in 1783 stating that he had not taken the Oath of Allegiance due to any disaffection with the government, but from a variety of incidents, and was unjustly penalized as a non-juror and fined unfairly; therefore, he asked the Council to consider ordering the County Justices to remit the fines they imposed on him and others who signed the petition. The Council of Maryland, after reviewing his case, indicated they believed the truth of the facts stated in the petition and ordered a remission of the fines and penalties on Sept. 17, 1783 [Ref: I-454].

HIGDON, Joseph (1759-1836). Private, 1st Maryland Line. He was born in Charles County, lived and enlisted in Montgomery County, Maryland, moved to North Carolina in 1784 and to Barren County, Kentucky in

1801. For more information see Henry C. Peden, Jr.'s *Revolutionary Patriots of Montgomery County, Maryland, 1775-1783*, p. 158].

HIGDON, Leonard. Private, Militia, 12th Battalion, Capt. Benjamin Lusby Corry's Company, 1777 [Ref: M-160]. Took the Oath of Allegiance in 1778 [Ref: AA-641, L-17, which latter source misspelled the name as "Hydon"]. "Leonard Higdon" was a resident of Newport West Hundred in 1778 [Ref: Q-I:297]. "Benedict Leonard Higdon" was born on Aug. 6, 1738, a son of William and Jane Higdon [Ref: EE-2].

HIGDON, William (1708-   ). Took the Oath of Allegiance in 1778 [Ref: AA-641]. "William Higdon, Sr." was aged about 71 as noted in a 1779 deposition [Ref: BB-487]. See "Benjamin Higdon" and "Leonard Higdon" and "Ignatius Higdon," q.v.

HIGDON, William Jr. Private, Militia, 12th Battalion, Capt. Benjamin Lusby Corry's Company, 1777 [Ref: M-160]. Private (substitute for 9 months), 1st Maryland Line, by Sept. 11, 1778 [Ref: D-118, D-330, which mistakenly listed the name as "Higoon"]. Resident of Newport West Hundred in 1778 [Ref: Q-I:297].

HIGDON, William, of Benjamin. Private, Militia, 12th Battalion, Capt. Benjamin Lusby Corry's Company, 1777 [Ref: M-160]. Took the Oath of Allegiance in 1778 [Ref: L-17, which mistakenly listed the name as "William Hydon, of Bery"].

HIGGS, George. Private, Militia, 12th Battalion, Capt. John Parnham's Company, 1777 [Ref: M-161]. Private (draught who had not yet joined the army), 1st Maryland Line, by Sept. 11, 1778 [Ref: D-330]. Took the Oath of Allegiance in 1778 [Ref: AA-641]. Resident of Newport East Hundred in 1778 [Ref: Q-I:297].

HIGGS, Jonathan. Took the Oath of Allegiance in 1778 [Ref: AA-641]. Resident of William & Mary Upper Hundred in 1778 [Ref: Q-I:297].

HIGHFIELD, Jeremiah (c1750-1805). Private, Militia, 12th Battalion, Capt. John Parnham's Company, 1777 [Ref: M-161, which listed the name as "Nisfield(?)," and X-64, which listed the name as "Nyfield"]. Resident of Newport East Hundred in 1778 [Ref: Q-I:297]. Rendered patriotic service by providing wheat for the use of the military in September 1782 [Ref: N-556, which listed the name as "Hifield"]. Petitioned the Council of Maryland in 1783 stating that he had not taken the Oath of Allegiance due to any disaffection with the government, but from a variety of incidents, and was unjustly penalized as a non-juror and fined unfairly; therefore, he asked the Council to consider ordering the County Justices to remit the fines they imposed on him and others who signed the petition. The Council of Maryland, after reviewing his case, indicated they believed the truth of the facts stated in the petition and ordered a remission of the fines and penalties on Sept. 17, 1783 [Ref: I-454, which listed the name as "Hughfield"]. Jeremiah Highfield married Sabra ---- and migrated to Kentucky where he died before 1805 [Ref: J-II:1418].

HIGHFIELD, Jonathan. Took the Oath of Allegiance in 1778 [Ref: AA-641].

HIGHFIELD, Leonard. Private, Militia, 12th Battalion, Capt. Henry Clarkson's Company, 1777 [Ref: M-159].

HIGHFIELD, Sabra. See "Jeremiah Highfield," q.v.

HIGHFIELD, Thomas. Private, Militia, 26th Battalion, Capt. Robert Sinnett's Company, 1777 [Ref: M-164]. Took the Oath of Allegiance in 1778 [Ref: AA-641, which spelled the name as "Hiefield"]. Resident of Port Tobacco West Hundred in 1778 [Ref: Q-I:297, which listed the name as "Hyfield"].

HILL, Clement Sr. (1707-1782). Took the Oath of Allegiance in 1778 [Ref: L-17]. Resident of Port Tobacco Upper Hundred in 1778 [Ref: Q-I:297]. He was born on Jan. 4, 1707, married Mary Digges, and died on Feb. 12, 1782 [Ref: J-II:1421].

HILL, Clement Jr. (1743-1807). Second lieutenant, 1st Maryland Line. He was born on Nov. 6, 1743, married Eleanor Brent, and died on Feb. 6, 1807 [Ref: J-II:1421].

HILL, Francis. Private, Militia, 12th Battalion, Capt. John Hanson's Company, 1777 [Ref: M-159]. Took the Oath of Allegiance in 1778 [Ref: L-17]. Resident of Port Tobacco East Hundred in 1778 [Ref: Q-I:297].

HILL, Joseph. Private, Militia, 26th Battalion, Capt. Samuel Smallwood's Company, 1777 [Ref: M-165].

HILL, Leonard. Private, Militia, 26th Battalion, Capt. Samuel Smallwood's Company, 1777 [Ref: M-165]. Took the Oath of Allegiance in 1778 [Ref: L-17]. Resident of Port Tobacco Upper Hundred in 1778 [Ref: Q-I:297].

HILL, Margit. See "Zephaniah Murphy," q.v.

HILL, Thomas. Private, Militia, 26th Battalion, Capt. Samuel Smallwood's Company, 1777 [Ref: M-165]. Private, 1st Maryland Line, drafted from the Charles County militia and reported sick with the flux in June 1781; discharged on Dec. 3, 1781 [Ref: D-376, I-11].

HILL, William. Took the Oath of Allegiance in 1778 [Ref: AA-641]. Resident of Port Tobacco West Hundred in 1778 [Ref: Q-I:297].

HILL, William. Took the Oath of Allegiance in 1780 [Ref: O-113].

HILLER, Sarah A. See "Cornelius Wells," q.v.

HILTON, Andrew (1757-). Private, Militia, 12th Battalion, Capt. Henry Clarkson's Company, 1777 [Ref: M-159]. He applied for a pension (S32316) in Monroe County, Illinois on June 3, 1833, stating he was born in 1757 in Charles County, Maryland and lived there at the time of his enlistment. He later lived in Rowan County, North Carolina for 17 years

and then moved to Warren County, Kentucky and later to Washington County, Kentucky and finally to Monroe County, Illinois [Ref: V-II:1645].
HINDS, John. Private (substitute during the war), 1st Maryland Line, by Sept. 11, 1778 [Ref: D-330].
HINDS, Thomas G. Private (substitute for 3 years), 1st Maryland Line, by Sept. 11, 1778 [Ref: D-330].
HINE, Ann. See "Charles Somerset Smith," q.v.
HINECK, Thomas. Rendered patriotic service by providing wheat for the use of the military in December 1782 [Ref: N-577].
HOBART, Edward. Took the Oath of Allegiance in 1778 [Ref: AA-641]. Resident of William & Mary Upper Hundred in 1778 [Ref: Q-I:297].
HOBART, Moses (1710-1782). Rendered patriotic service by providing clothing for the use of the military in February 1778 [Ref: Y-II:234]. Took the Oath of Allegiance in 1778 [Ref: AA-641]. Served as Coroner of Charles County until his death in 1782 [Ref: I-149]. Aged about 66 as noted in a 1776 deposition [Ref: DD-11]. Resident of William & Mary Upper Hundred in 1778 [Ref: Q-I:297].
HODGKINS, Samuel. Private, 1st Maryland Line, enrolled and passed on July 8, 1776 [Ref: D-32, which listed the name as "Hodskin (Hodgkins)"].
HODGSON, Richard. Took the Oath of Allegiance in 1778 [Ref: L-17].
HODSON, George. Private, 1st Maryland Line, discharged on Dec. 3, 1781 [Ref: I-10].
HOLDING, James. Private, Militia, 12th Battalion, Capt. Walter Hanson's Company, 1777 [Ref: M-159]. Took the Oath of Allegiance in 1778 [Ref: L-17, AA-641]. Resident of Port Tobacco East Hundred in 1778 [Ref: Q-I:297].
HOLLOWAY, Nancy. See "John Williams," q.v.
HOLM (HOLME, HOLMES), John. Took the Oath of Allegiance in 1778 [Ref: AA-641, L-17, which listed the name as "Holmes"]. Rendered patriotic service by providing clothing for the use of the military in February 1778 [Ref: Y-II:234, which listed the name as "Holm"]. Resident of William & Mary Lower Hundred in 1778 [Ref: Q-I:297]. "John Holme" died by November 1778 (date of inventory). [Ref: GG-204].
HOOE, Catharine. See "William Winter, Jr.," q.v.
HOOE, Robert Townshend (1743-1809). Deputy County Surveyor, 1766. Committee of Observation, 1774. Delegate to the Maryland Convention from April 24 to May 3, 1775 and July 26 to Aug. 14, 1775 and in June 1776 [Ref: A-3, Y-I:1, Y I:3, Y-I:28, P-I:454]. First Major, Militia, 12th Battalion, Jan. 6, 1776. Lieutenant Colonel, 1776, and Colonel by 1781. Appointed by the Maryland Convention on Feb. 2, 1776 to be one of the Collectors of Gold & Silver Coin in Charles County [Ref: A-132]. Owned

privateers during the Revolutionary War [Ref: M-88, P-I:455]. On March 14, 1776, the Maryland Convention "Ordered, that Mr. Robert Townsend Hooe be requested immediately to load the sloop *Molly*, Captain Conway, with Tobacco, Corn, Flour, and Staves on Account and Risk of this Province upon the best and most reasonable Terms & that he apply to the Council of Safety for sailing Orders of her when ready." [Ref: A-245]. The obituary of Robert Townshend Hooe appeared in the *Maryland Gazette* on March 29, 1809, stating that he "departed this life at Alexandria, on Thursday evening, 16th instant, in his 66th year. At an early period of his life, he was selected as a member of the Maryland Convention. In 1776 he received from the Convention the appointment of Lieutenant Colonel in the 12th Battalion." [Ref: FF-93].

HOOPER, Thomas (1730-   ). Private, Militia, 26th Battalion, Capt. Thomas H. Marshall's Company, 1777 [Ref: M-163]. Took the Oath of Allegiance in 1778 [Ref: AA-641]. Aged about 46 as noted in a 1776 deposition [Ref: DD-11]. Resident of Pomonkey Hundred in 1778 [Ref: Q-I:297].

HOPEWELL, John. Private, 1st Maryland Line, Smallwood's Regiment, enlisted Feb. 19, 1777 and discharged Feb. 21, 1780 [Ref: D-120]. See "Thomas Pickerel," q.v.

HOPEWELL, Thomas. Private, Militia, 12th Battalion, Capt. Walter Hanson's Company, 1777 [Ref: M-159, which listed the name as "Hopwell"]. Took the Oath of Allegiance in 1778 [Ref: L-17]. Resident of Port Tobacco East Hundred in 1778 [Ref: Q-I:297]. Rendered patriotic service by providing wheat for the use of the military in November 1781 and May 1783 [Ref: N-455, N-598]. See "Thomas Pickerel," q.v.

HOPEWELL, Thomas G. Private, Militia, 12th Battalion, Capt. Walter Hanson's Company, 1777 [Ref: M-159].

HOPKINS, Elizabeth. On Sept. 16, 1780, the Council of Maryland "ordered that the Issuing Commissary deliver to Eliza. Hopkins, a soldier's wife, 4 days rations to enable her to proceed to Charles County." [Ref: F-293].

HORNER, Robert. See "Samuel Hanson," q.v.

HOSKINS, Daniel (Mrs.). In August 1778, she received support from the county because she was a widow and her son (not named) was away "in the regular service." [Ref: CC-711]. One Daniel Hoskins was alive and aged about 64 as noted in a 1776 deposition [Ref: CC-578, DD-10, which latter source listed the name as "Haskins"].

HOSKINS, Jane. See "Walter Hanson," q.v.

HOSKINS, Randolph. Private, Militia, 12th Battalion, Capt. Benjamin Lusby Corry's Company, 1777 [Ref: M-160, which misspelled the name as "Hopkins"]. Private (substitute for 9 months), 1st Maryland Line, by Sept.

11, 1778; reenlisted Feb. 2, 1779 and served through at least November 1780 [Ref: D-118, D-330].

HOWARD, Baker (c1735-1790). Private, Militia, 12th Battalion, Capt. Jonathan Yates' Company, 1777 [Ref: M-162]. Took the Oath of Allegiance in 1778 [Ref: L-17, AA-641]. Rendered patriotic service by providing clothing for the use of the military in February 1778 [Ref: Y-II:234]. Resident of William & Mary Lower Hundred in 1778 [Ref: Q-I:297]. Baker Howard was born circa 1735, married second to Anne Phillips (first wife unknown) and died before Aug. 18, 1790 [Ref: J-II:1501].

HOWARD, Eleanor. See "John Douglas," q.v.

HOWARD, Gadshall. See "Thomas Godshall Howard," q.v.

HOWARD, Jeremiah. Private, Militia, 26th Battalion, Capt. Francis Mastin's Company, 1777 [Ref: M-164].

HOWARD, John. Private, Militia, Capt. Francis Mastin's Company, 26th Battalion, March 19, 1776 [Ref: M-158, K-1814]. Resident of Durham Lower Hundred in 1778 [Ref: Q-I:297].

HOWARD, Michael. Private, Militia, 12th Battalion, Capt. Walter Hanson's Company, 1777 [Ref: M-159]. Took the Oath of Allegiance in 1778 [Ref: AA-641]. Resident of Port Tobacco East Hundred in 1778 [Ref: Q-I:297].

HOWARD, Rachel. See "John Compton" and "Edmund Compton," q.v.

HOWARD, Thomas Godshall. "Thomas Goodale Howard" was a sergeant in the militia, 26th Battalion, Capt. Richard Bennett Mitchell's Company, 1777 [Ref: M-164]. "Thomas Godshall Howard" took the Oath of Allegiance in 1778 [Ref: AA-641]. "Gadshall Howard" was a resident of Port Tobacco West Hundred in 1778 [Ref: Q-I:297].

HOWARD, Thomas J. Rendered patriotic service by providing wheat for the use of the military in December 1782 [Ref: N-576].

HOWARD, William. Private, Militia, 26th Battalion, Capt. Richard Bennett Mitchell's Company, 1777 [Ref: M-164]. Took the Oath of Allegiance in 1778 [Ref: AA-641]. Resident of Port Tobacco West Hundred in 1778 [Ref: Q-I:297].

HOWELL, Mary. Rendered patriotic service by providing wheat for the use of the military in January 1782 [Ref: N-476].

HOWELL, Samuel. Private, Militia, 12th Battalion, Capt. John Hanson's Company, 1777 [Ref: M-159]. Resident of Port Tobacco East Hundred in 1778 [Ref: Q-I:297].

HOWELL, Thomas. Rendered patriotic service by providing wheat for the use of the military in November 1781 and December 1782 [Ref: N-457, N-576].

HOYE, Martha. See "Caesar Richards," q.v.

HOYE, Robert. See "Robert Townsend Hooe," q.v.

HUDSON, Caleb. Private, Militia, 26th Battalion, Capt. William Winter's Company, 1777 [Ref: M-165, which listed the first name as "Coleb"]. Resident of Durham Lower Hundred in 1778 [Ref: Q-I:297]. See "Samuel Wright," q.v.

HUDSON, George. Private, Militia, 12th Battalion, Capt. Jonathan Yates' Company, 1777 [Ref: X-70, but was omitted from the list in Reference M-162]. Resident of William & Mary Lower Hundred in 1778 [Ref: Q-I:297]. Private, 1st Maryland Line, drafted from the Charles County militia on July 27, 1781 [Ref: D-377, G-569].

HUDSON, Thomas. Private, Militia, 12th Battalion, Capt. Henry Clarkson's Company, 1777 [Ref: M-159]. Resident of Newport East Hundred in 1778 [Ref: Q-I:297]. Private (furnished by class for 9 months), 1st Maryland Line, by Sept. 11, 1778 [Ref: D-330]. One Thomas Hudson married Benedicta Coffer on Dec. 24, 1794 in Charles County [Ref: W-116].

HUDSON, William. Took the Oath of Allegiance in 1778 [Ref: AA-641].

HUGHES, John. Private (furnished by class for 9 months), 1st Maryland Line, by Sept. 11, 1778 [Ref: D-330]. Private, 3rd Maryland Line, enrolled by Capt. Joseph Marbury by May 24, 1780 [Ref: D-333, F-181].

HUGHS, John. Took the Oath of Allegiance in 1778 [Ref: AA-641].

HUGHS, William Jr. Private, Militia, 26th Battalion, Capt. Benjamin Cawood's Company, 1777 [Ref: M-162].

HUNGERFORD, Thomas (of Baltimore County). Took the Oath of Allegiance in February 1778 [Ref: AA-620]. Resident of William & Mary Upper Hundred in 1778 [Ref: Q-I:297].

HUNT, Ann. See "Luke Davis," q.v.

HUNT, Basil. Took the Oath of Allegiance in 1778 [Ref: AA-641]. Resident of Bryan Town Hundred in 1778 [Ref: Q-I:297].

HUNT, Benjamin. Private, Militia, 12th Battalion, Capt. Peter Wood's Company, 1777 [Ref: M-161]. Took the Oath of Allegiance in 1778 [Ref: AA-641]. Resident of Benedict Hundred in 1778 [Ref: Q-I:297, which misspelled the name as "Hernt"].

HUNT, Gladden. Private, 1st Maryland Line, enrolled and passed on July 20, 1776 [Ref: D-32]. Corporal, Militia, 12th Battalion, Capt. John Thomas' Company, 1777 [Ref: M-161, which listed the name as "Glaven(?) Hunt"]. Took the Oath of Allegiance in 1778 [Ref: L-17]. Resident of Benedict Hundred in 1778 [Ref: Q-I:297, which listed the name as "Gladen Hunt"].

HUNT, James. Private (furnished by class for 9 months), 1st Maryland Line, by Sept. 11, 1778 [Ref: D-330].

HUNT, John Stone. Private, 1st Maryland Line, who enlisted from Charles County for 3 years and was in service on June 11 or 12, 1781 [Ref: D-376].

HUNT, Joseph. Took the Oath of Allegiance in 1778 [Ref: AA-641, L-17]. Rendered patriotic service by providing wheat for the use of the military in January 1782 [Ref: N-476]. Resident of Port Tobacco East Hundred in 1778 [Ref: Q-I:297].
HUNT, Shadrach (Shadrick). Private, Militia, 12th Battalion, Capt. Henry Clarkson's Company, 1777 [Ref: M-159]. Resident of Newport East Hundred in 1778 [Ref: Q-I:297].
HUNT, Thomas. Took the Oath of Allegiance in 1778 [Ref: AA-641, L-17]. Resident of Benedict Hundred in 1778 [Ref: Q-I:297, which misspelled the name as "Hernt"].
HUNT, Thomas Jr. Private, Militia, 12th Battalion, Capt. Peter Wood's Company, 1777 [Ref: M-161].
HUNT, William. Private, Militia, 12th Battalion, Capt. John Thomas' Company, 1777 [Ref: M-161].
HUNTER, George (died testate in June 1779). Took the Oath of Allegiance in 1778 [Ref: L-17]. Rendered patriotic service by providing clothing for the use of the military in February 1778 [Ref: Y-II:234, which listed the name as "Rev. George Hunter"]. Resident of Port Tobacco East Hundred in 1778 [Ref: Q-I:297].
HUNTINGTON, John. Private, Militia, 12th Battalion, Capt. John Parnham's Company, 1777 [Ref: M-161]. Resident of Newport East Hundred in 1778 [Ref: Q-I:297]. Private, 1st Maryland Line, drafted from the Charles County militia and reported sick on July 27, 1781 [Ref: D-377].
HUNTINGTON, Luke. Private, Militia, 12th Battalion, Capt. John Parnham's Company, 1777 [Ref: M-161].
HUNTINGTON, Luke (1713-   ). Took the Oath of Allegiance in 1778 [Ref: AA-641]. Aged about 58 as noted in a 1771 deposition [Ref: DD-12]. Resident of Newport East Hundred in 1778 [Ref: Q-I:297].
HURRY, John. Private, Militia, 26th Battalion, Capt. Richard Bennett Mitchell's Company, 1777 [Ref: M-165]. Took the Oath of Allegiance in 1778 [Ref: AA-641].
HURRY, William. Took the Oath of Allegiance in 1778 [Ref: AA-641].
HUSE, Jacob. Took the Oath of Allegiance in 1778 [Ref: AA-641].
HUSK, Edward Jr. Private, Militia, 26th Battalion, Capt. Thomas H. Marshall's Company, 1777 [Ref: M-163]. Took the Oath of Allegiance in 1778 [Ref: L-17, which listed the name as "Hush"]. Resident of Pomonkey Hundred in 1778 [Ref: Q-I:297].
HUSK, Edward Sr. Memorialist and Militiaman, Pomonkey Company, after March 6, 1776 [Ref: M-158, Y-II:26, which listed the name as "Hust"].

Took the Oath of Allegiance in 1778 [Ref: L-17, which listed the name as "Hush"]. Resident of Pomonkey Hundred in 1778 [Ref: Q-I:297].

HUSSY, William. Private, Militia, Capt. Francis Mastin's Company, 26th Battalion, March 19, 1776 [Ref: M-158, K-1814].

HUTCHINSON, George. Took the Oath of Allegiance in 1778 [Ref: L-17, AA-641, which latter source listed the name as "Hutchison"]. Rendered patriotic service by providing wheat for the use of the military in November 1782 [Ref: N-566]. See "Joseph Hanson Harrison," q.v.

HUTCHISON, William. Private, Militia, 26th Battalion, Capt. Robert Sinnett's Company, 1777 [Ref: M-164]. Took the Oath of Allegiance in 1778 [Ref: L-17].

HYTON, Joseph. Private, Militia, 26th Battalion, Capt. Samuel Smallwood's Company, 1777 [Ref: M-165, which listed the name as "Hiton"]. Took the Oath of Allegiance in 1778 [Ref: L-17, which listed the name as "Hayton" and AA-641, which listed the name as "Huyton"]. Resident of Port Tobacco Upper Hundred in 1778 [Ref: Q-I:297].

IHANIETZ(?), Walter. See "Walter Kaniety(?)," q.v.

IMESON, Edy, Elizabeth, and Elkanah. See "John Imeson," q.v.

IMESON, John (1748-1822). Private, 1st Maryland Line. In November 1803, the Treasurer of Maryland was directed to pay to "John Imeson, a soldier in the Revolutionary War, fifteen pounds in current money, annually, during the remainder of his life, in quarterly payments." He was placed on the pension rolls of Charles County as of March 5, 1819 (retroactive to March 5, 1819) and died on Aug. 16, 1822 [Ref: Q-II:358, R-33]. He also applied for a federal pension (S34934) in Prince George's County on June 2, 1818, aged 70, but was a resident of Charles County at the time. In 1820 he had a wife Edy, aged 37 *[sic]* and two children, Elizabeth Imeson (aged 14) and Elkanah Imeson (aged 8). John died on Aug. 16, 1822 and Thomas Smitson, the administrator of his estate, received final payment on July 5, 1839 [Ref: V-II:1796].

INNIS, Charles. Private, Militia, 26th Battalion, Capt. Samuel Smallwood's Company, 1777 [Ref: M-165, which listed the name as "Inness"]. Took the Oath of Allegiance in 1778 [Ref: AA-641, which listed the name as "Innes"]. Resident of Port Tobacco Upper Hundred in 1778 [Ref: Q-I:297].

INNIS, George. Private (substitute for 3 years), 1st Maryland Line, by Sept. 11, 1778 [Ref: D-330, which listed the name as "Ennes"].

INNIS, James. Private, Militia, 26th Battalion, Capt. Samuel Smallwood's Company, 1777 [Ref: M-165, which listed the name as "Innes"]. Resident of Port Tobacco Upper Hundred in 1778 [Ref: Q-I:297].

JACKSON, John. Private, Militia, 26th Battalion, Capt. Benjamin Cawood's Company, 1777 [Ref: M-162]. Took the Oath of Allegiance in 1778 [Ref:

L-17, AA-641]. Resident of Port Tobacco East Hundred in 1778 [Ref: Q-I:297].

JACKSON, Robert. Took the Oath of Allegiance in 1778 [Ref: L-17, AA-641].

JACKSON, Thomas. Private, Militia, 26th Battalion, Capt. William Winter's Company, 1777 [Ref: M-165]. Took the Oath of Allegiance in 1778 [Ref: L-17, AA-641]. Resident of Bryan Town Hundred in 1778 [Ref: Q-I:297].

JACKSON, William. Took the Oath of Allegiance in 1778 [Ref: AA-641]. Resident of Bryan Town Hundred in 1778 [Ref: Q-I:297].

JAMES, George. Private, Militia, 12th Battalion, Capt. Jonathan Yates' Company, 1777 [Ref: M-162]. Took the Oath of Allegiance in 1778 [Ref: L-17, AA-641]. Rendered patriotic service by providing clothing for the use of the military in February 1778 [Ref: Y-II:234]. Resident of William & Mary Lower Hundred in 1778 [Ref: Q-I:297].

JAMES, Thomas (Doctor). Took the Oath of Allegiance in 1778 [Ref: L-17]. Rendered patriotic service by providing clothing for the use of the military in February 1778 [Ref: Y-II:234]. Rendered patriotic service by providing wheat for the use of the military in December 1782 [Ref: N-577]. Resident of William & Mary Lower Hundred in 1778 [Ref: Q-I:297].

JAMES, Thomas. Private, 1st Maryland Line, who was drafted from the Charles County militia and was in service by June 11, 1781 [Ref: D-376]. Took the Oath of Allegiance in 1778 [Ref: AA-641].

JAMESON, Benjamin Jr. Private, Militia, 12th Battalion, Capt. Alexander McPherson's Company, 1777 [Ref: M-160, which listed the name as "Jamison"].

JAMESON, Benjamin Sr. (1723-   ). Rendered patriotic service by providing clothing for the use of the military in January 1778 [Ref: Y-II:230]. Took the Oath of Allegiance in 1778 [Ref: L-17]. Rendered patriotic service by providing wheat for the use of the military in June 1782 [Ref: N-525, which listed the name as "Jameston"]. Aged about 50 as noted in a 1773 deposition [Ref: DD-12]. Resident of Bryan Town Hundred in 1778 [Ref: Q-I:297].

JAMESON, Benjamin, of James. Took the Oath of Allegiance in 1778 [Ref: L-17].

JAMESON, Benjamin, of Joseph. Took the Oath of Allegiance in 1778 [Ref: AA-641].

JAMESON, Henry Joshua (1739-   ). Private, Militia, 12th Battalion, Capt. Benjamin Lusby Corry's Company, 1777 [Ref: M-160, which listed the name as "Jamison"]. Took the Oath of Allegiance in 1778 [Ref: L-17]. Aged about 40 as noted in a 1779 deposition [Ref: DD-12]. Resident of Newport

West Hundred in 1778 [Ref: Q-I:297, which misspelled the name as "Henry I. Jamison"].

JAMESON, John. Private, Militia, 12th Battalion, Capt. Walter Hanson's Company, 1777 [Ref: M-159, which listed the name as "Jameston"]. Took the Oath of Allegiance in 1778 [Ref: L-17, AA-641]. Resident of Port Tobacco East Hundred in 1778 [Ref: Q-I:297].

JAMESON, Leonard. Private, Militia, 12th Battalion, Capt. Alexander McPherson's Company, 1777 [Ref: M-160, which listed the name as "Jamison"]. Took the Oath of Allegiance in 1778 [Ref: AA-641].

JAMESON, Thomas (1725-   ). Took the Oath of Allegiance in 1778 [Ref: L-17]. "Thomas Jameson, Jr." was aged about 30 as noted in a 1755 deposition and "Thomas Jeamson" was aged about 51 as noted in a 1775 deposition [Ref: DD-12]. Resident of Newport West Hundred in 1778 [Ref: Q-I:297].

JAMESON, Walter. Private, Militia, 12th Battalion, Capt. Alexander McPherson's Company, 1777 [Ref: M-160, which listed the name as Jamison"].

JEFFERSON, John. Private, Militia, 12th Battalion, Capt. John Thomas' Company, 1777 [Ref: M-161].

JEFFERSON, Thomas. See "George Dent, of John," q.v.

JENIFER, Daniel (1727-1795). Son of Dr. Daniel Jenifer and Elizabeth Mason, and brother of Daniel of St. Thomas Jenifer. He married first to Elizabeth Hanson (died in 1757) and second to Mary Hanson (who was possibly the widow of John Briscoe). Their children were Dr. Walter Hanson Jenifer, Dr. Daniel Jenifer, Daniel of St. Thomas Jenifer, and Warren Dent Jenifer [Ref: P-II:484, J-II:1589, FF-101]. Resident of Port Tobacco Town Hundred in 1778 [Ref: Q-I:297]. Daniel Jenifer held many important offices, as did his brother Daniel of St. Thomas Jenifer: Delegate to the Maryland Convention from April 24 to May 3, 1775 [Ref: A-3, Y-I:1]. Appointed a Judge of the Orphans Court of Charles County on June 4, 1777 and May 15, 1778 and Jan. 17, 1782 [Ref: C-274, E-84, I-46]. Appointed by the Council of Maryland as "Collector of Cloathing for the American Army in Charles County" on Nov. 27, 1777 [Ref: C-426]. Appointed Purchaser of Provisions in Charles County before April 22, 1778 [Ref: E-51, which referred to him as "Esq."]. Appointed a Judge of the Court of Appeals for Charles County on May 20, 1778 [Ref: E-97]. Justice who administered (and took) the Oath of Allegiance in 1778 [Ref: AA-641]. Appointed a Justice of the Peace on Nov. 21, 1778 and Nov. 19, 1779 and Jan. 17, 1782 [Ref: E-249, F-19, I-45]. Appointed Commissary of Purchases for Charles County on July 8, 1780 [Ref: F-215]. Commissioner of Loans for Charles County before September 1780 [Ref: F-278, which listed the name as "Esq."]. Appointed Purchaser of Cloathing on June 5, 1781 [Ref: G-462]. Rendered patriotic service by providing wheat for the use of the military in August 1782 [Ref: N-535, N-536]. Aged about 47 as noted in a 1774 deposition [Ref: DD-12]. See "Daniel of St. Thomas Jenifer" and "Walter Hanson Jenifer" and "Jesse Taylor" and "John Muschett" and "Thomas Crackels" and "Samuel Mitchell" and "Walter Hanson, Jr." and "George Kent" and "William Leigh" and "Benjamin Burroughs" and "John Hoskins Stone," q.v.

JENIFER, Daniel of St. Thomas (1723-1790). Son of Dr. Daniel Jenifer and Elizabeth Mason, and brother of Daniel Jenifer. He never married and died without progeny [Ref: P-II:485]. Daniel of St. Thomas Jenifer, like his brother Daniel, held many important offices: Lower House of the Maryland Legislature, 1754-1757. Upper House, 1771-1774. State Senate, 1776-1781. Senate President, 1777-1781. Provincial Court Justice, 1766-1773. Justice, Assize Court, 1766-1768. Rent Roll Keeper of the Western Shore, 1768. Executive Council, 1771-1776. Council of Safety, 1775-1777. Unsuccessful candidate for Governor of Maryland in 1782 and 1785. Delegate to the Continental Congress, 1778-1781. Delegate to the Federal Convention that formed the Constitution, 1787. Referred to as Major in 1765, but held no rank during the Revolutionary War, even though he was instrumental in raising supplies for the Continental Army [Ref: P-II:485, P-II:486, FF-100]. Rendered patriotic service by providing wheat for the use of the military in October 1781 [Ref: N-451]. See "Daniel Jenifer," q.v.

JENIFER, Elizabeth. See "John Hoskins Stone" and "Michael Jenifer Stone" and "Thomas Stone," q.v.

JENIFER, Walter Hanson (1751-1785). Son of Daniel Jenifer and Elizabeth Hanson, he was a doctor who assisted the Purchaser of Clothing in Charles County in February 1778 [Ref: P-II:484, Y-II:235]. Justice who administered (and took) the Oath of Allegiance in 1778 [Ref: AA-641]. Resident of Port Tobacco Town Hundred in 1778 [Ref: Q-I:297]. Appointed a Justice of the Peace on Nov. 21, 1778 and Nov. 19, 1779 and Jan. 17, 1782 [Ref: E-249, F-19, I-45]. Appointed a Judge of the Orphans Court on Dec. 29, 1779 [Ref: F-42]. Rendered patriotic service by providing wheat for the use of the military in August 1782 [Ref: N-536, N-538]. On Aug. 17, 1780, "W. H. Jenifer of Portobacco" wrote to Governor Lee stating, in part, "My father [name not stated here, but in another entry Daniel Jenifer referred to his son, Dr. Jenifer], who is extremely ill, has desired that I would return your Excellency the general Account of his Purchases of Provision in this County ... and also to request that some other person may be appointed Commissary of Purchases in his stead, as from his present ill State of Health he is apprehensive that it will not be in his power to execute the Office as it ought to be. He would wish that Mr. Gerard B. Causin and Mr. John Muschett could be jointly appointed. They are Gentlemen of Integrity and Industry and most fervently attached to the Cause of America ... His [father's] illness has been brought on by the great Fatigue he had undergone in endeavoring to procure supplies for the Army." [Ref: G-53, H-324].

JENIFER, Warren Dent. See "Daniel Jenifer," q.v.

JENKINS, Edward. Clerk, Militia, 26th Battalion, Capt. Benjamin Cawood's Company, 1777 [Ref: M-162]. Resident of Durham Lower Hundred in 1778 [Ref: Q-I:297]. Private, 1st Maryland Line, enlisted March 22, 1777 and discharged March 22, 1780 [Ref: D-125].

JENKINS, Edward. Took the Oath of Allegiance in 1778 [Ref: L-17]. Resident of Port Tobacco East Hundred in 1778 [Ref: Q-I:297].

JENKINS, Elizabeth. See "Leonard Boarman," q.v.

JENKINS, George. Private, Militia, 26th Battalion, Capt. Richard Bennett Mitchell's Company, 1777 [Ref: M-165]. Private, 1st Maryland Line, enlisted Feb. 20, 1777 and discharged Feb. 20, 1780 [Ref: D-125]. One George Jenkins was aged about 51 as noted in a 1774 deposition [Ref: DD-13].

JENKINS, Henrietta. See "Thomas Semmes," q.v.

JENKINS, Jason. Corporal, 1st Maryland Line, 1778, and sergeant, March 1, 1779; discharged on Dec. 27, 1779 [Ref: D-125].

JENKINS, Thomas. Took the Oath of Allegiance in August 1778 [Ref: AA-707]. Resident of William & Mary Upper Hundred in 1778 [Ref: Q-I:297].

JENKINS, Phil. Private, 1st Maryland Line, enlisted Dec. 10, 1776, taken prisoner Sept. 16, 1778, released and discharged Dec. 27, 1779 [Ref: D-125].

JENKINS, Thomas (Captain). Rendered patriotic service by providing wheat for the use of the military in December 1782 [Ref: N-576]. Took the Oath of Allegiance in 1778 [Ref: AA-641, which listed the name without the "Captain"].

JENKINS, Thomas. Private, 1st Maryland Line, enlisted May 22, 1778 and discharged April 5, 1779 [Ref: D-125].

JENKINS, William. Private, Militia, 12th Battalion, Capt. Jonathan Yates' Company, 1777 [Ref: X-70, but was omitted from the list in Reference M-162]. Took the Oath of Allegiance in 1778 [Ref: L-17, AA-641]. Resident of Pomonkey Hundred in 1778 [Ref: Q-I:297]. Rendered patriotic service by providing wheat for the use of the military in January 1782 [Ref: N-476].

JERNINGHAME, Katherine. Rendered patriotic service by providing clothing for the use of the military in February 1778 [Ref: Y-II:234].

JEWELL, George. Memorialist and Militiaman, Pomonkey Company, after March 6, 1776 [Ref: M-158, Y-II:26].

JOHNSON, Archibald (c1750-1818). Took the Oath of Allegiance in 1778 [Ref: AA-641, L-17, which latter source listed the name as "Johnston"]. Resident of Port Tobacco West Hundred in 1778 [Ref: Q-I:297]. Private, 1st Maryland Line, May 23, 1779; corporal, Jan. 1, 1780; sergeant, June 15, 1780; sergeant, 3rd Company, 3rd Maryland Line, by Aug. 28, 1781, and sergeant, 9th Company, Jan. 1, 1783 to Nov. 15, 1783 [Ref: D-126, D-358, D-393, D-497, D-541]. In November 1812, the Treasurer of Maryland was directed to pay to "Archibald Johnson, of Charles County, a sergeant in the Revolutionary War, half pay of a sergeant, as a further remuneration for his services in the Revolutionary War." He was placed on the pension rolls of Charles County as of Jan. 7, 1819, retroactive to April 1, 1818 [Ref: Q-II:359, Q-II:360, R-33]. The federal pension (S34938) for which he applied on April 1, 1818, stated he died on Aug. 20, 1818, leaving no widow, but left two children: Pamelia Johnson (who married and was the widow of John Dixon, of Charles County) and Thomas Johnson (of Frederick County). They applied for his pension on Oct. 6, 1828 and their affidavits were witnessed by Ignatius N. and Mary Ann Clements [Ref: V-II:1841].

JOHNSON, Archibald Jr. Private, Militia, 26th Battalion, Capt. Richard Bennett Mitchell's Company, 1777 [Ref: M-164].

JOHNSON, Benjamin. "Benjamin Johnson" was a resident of Port Tobacco Upper Hundred in 1778 [Ref: Q-I:297]. "Benjamin Colbert Johnson" was a private in the Maryland Line who was drafted from the Charles County militia and was in service on June 11, 1781. He was discharged on Dec. 3, 1781 [Ref: D-376, I-11].

JOHNSON, Daniel. Private, Militia, 26th Battalion, Capt. William Winter's Company, 1777 [Ref: M-165]. Resident of Durham Lower Hundred in 1778 [Ref: Q-I:297].

JOHNSON, Dradon. See "Zephaniah King," q.v.

JOHNSON, Gerrard. Private, 1st Maryland Line, enrolled and passed on July 8, 1776 [Ref: D-32]. Took the Oath of Allegiance in 1778 [Ref: L-17, AA-641].

JOHNSON, Henry. Private, 3rd Maryland Line, enrolled by Capt. Joseph Marbury by May 24, 1780 [Ref: F-181].

JOHNSON, Hezekiah (1730-1811). Private, Militia, 26th Battalion, Capt. William McPherson's Company, 1777 [Ref: M-163]. Took the Oath of Allegiance in 1778 [Ref: L-17]. Rendered patriotic service by providing wheat for the use of the military in September 1782 [Ref: N-556]. Resident of Port Tobacco Upper Hundred in 1778 [Ref: Q-I:297].

Hezekiah Johnson was born in January 1730, married first to Hepzabah (Beall) Ford, married second to Frances Smoot, and died in October 1811 [Ref: J-II:1605].

JOHNSON, Huett Jr. Took the Oath of Allegiance in 1778 [Ref: AA-641].

JOHNSON, Huett. Private, Militia, 12th Battalion, Capt. Peter Wood's Company, 1777 [Ref: M-161]. Took the Oath of Allegiance in 1778 [Ref: L-17]. Private (furnished by class for 9 months), 1st Maryland Line, by Sept. 11, 1778 [Ref: D-330, which listed the first name as "Hewit"]. Resident of Benedict Hundred in 1778 [Ref: Q-I:297].

JOHNSON, Jacob. Private, 1st Maryland Line, enrolled and passed on July 27, 1776 [Ref: D-31]. Private, Militia, 26th Battalion, Capt. Hezekiah Garner's Company, 1777 [Ref: M-163].

JOHNSON, James. Private, Militia, 12th Battalion, Capt. Henry Clarkson's Company, 1777 [Ref: M-159].

JOHNSON, James (1717-). Took the Oath of Allegiance in 1778 [Ref: L-17, AA-641]. Aged about 50 as noted in a 1767 deposition [Ref: DD-13]. Resident of Newport East Hundred in 1778 [Ref: Q-I:297].

JOHNSON, John. Private, Militia, 12th Battalion, Capt. Alexander McPherson's Company, 1777 [Ref: M-160]. Resident of Bryan Town Hundred in 1778 [Ref: Q-I:297]. See "Samuel Barker Davis," q.v.

JOHNSON, John (1701-). Took the Oath of Allegiance in 1778 [Ref: L-17, AA-641]. Aged about 77 as noted in a 1778 deposition [Ref: CC-705, DD-13]. Resident of Newport East Hundred in 1778 [Ref: Q-I:297].

JOHNSON, John Hugh. Took the Oath of Allegiance in 1778 [Ref: L-17].

JOHNSON, Jonathan. Private, Militia, 12th Battalion, Capt. Peter Wood's Company, 1777 [Ref: M-161].

JOHNSON, Joseph. Private, Militia, 12th Battalion, Capt. Peter Wood's Company, 1777 [Ref: M-161]. Took the Oath of Allegiance in 1778 [Ref: L-17]. Resident of Benedict Hundred in 1778 [Ref: Q-I:297].

JOHNSON, Josias (Josiah). "Josiah Johnson" was a private in the militia, 12th Battalion, Capt. Peter Wood's Company, 1777 [Ref: M-161]. "Josias Johnson" took the Oath of Allegiance in 1778 [Ref: L-17, AA-641]. "Jonias Johnson" was a resident of Bryan Town Hundred in 1778 [Ref: Q-I:297].

JOHNSON, Matthew. Private, 1st Maryland Line, enrolled and passed on July 18, 1776 [Ref: D-32]. Private (furnished by class for 9 months), 1st Maryland Line, by Sept. 11, 1778 [Ref: D-330]. Took the Oath of Allegiance in 1778 [Ref: AA-641]. Resident of Bryan Town Hundred in 1778 [Ref: Q-I:297].

JOHNSON, Nelson. Private, 1st Maryland Line, drafted from the Charles County militia, in service on June 11 or 12, 1781, and discharged on Dec.

3, 1781 [Ref: D-376, I-11]. Resident of Benedict Hundred in 1778 [Ref: Q-I:297].
JOHNSON, Pamelia. See "Archibald Johnson," q.v.
JOHNSON, Thomas. See "Archibald Johnson," q.v.
JOHNSON, Walter. Private, Militia, 26th Battalion, Capt. Richard Bennett Mitchell's Company, 1777 [Ref: M-164]. Took the Oath of Allegiance in 1778 [Ref: L-17, AA-641].
JOHNSON, William. Private, 1st Maryland Line, enrolled and passed on July 25, 1776 [Ref: D-32]. Took the Oath of Allegiance in 1778 [Ref: AA-641].
JOHNSON, Zachariah. Private, Militia, 12th Battalion, Capt. Peter Wood's Company, 1777 [Ref: M-161]. Took the Oath of Allegiance in 1778 [Ref: L-17]. Resident of Benedict Hundred in 1778 [Ref: Q-I:297].
JOHNSTON, Daniel. Took the Oath of Allegiance in 1778 [Ref: L-18].
JOHNSTON, John. Private, Militia, 26th Battalion, Capt. Hezekiah Garner's Company, 1777 [Ref: M-163].
JONES, Benjamin. Private, Militia, 26th Battalion, Capt. Francis Mastin's Company, 1777 [Ref: M-164]. Resident of Durham Lower Hundred in 1778 [Ref: Q-I:297].
JONES, Charles. Took the Oath of Allegiance in 1778 [Ref: L-18].
JONES, James. See "William Jones, Sr.," q.v.
JONES, John Courts (1754-1802). Born in Prince George's County, he married Dorothy Hanson Harrison (daughter of Robert Hanson Harrison) and died intestate in Charles County in 1802. During the Revolutionary War he was second lieutenant in the Flying Camp, first lieutenant in the 7th Maryland Line, captain in the 4th and 1st Maryland Lines from 1777 to 1781, and was aide-de-camp to Gen. William Smallwood until 1783 when retired from service. He also served in the Lower House of the Maryland Legislature in 1785 and was Naval Officer of the First District in 1786 [Ref: P-II:497, P-II:498]. John Courts Jones was born on Sept. 11, 1754 and died on May 20, 1802 [Ref: J-II:1623].
JONES, Lillias M. See "Samuel Jones," q.v.
JONES, Maria H. See "Samuel Hanson, of Samuel," q.v.
JONES, Samuel (1755-1804). Second Lieutenant, 1st Maryland Line, Capt. Thomas Hanson's Company, July 1776, and Lieutenant, 3rd Maryland Line, Dec. 10, 1776. Captain, Aug. 6, 1777 until Feb. 11, 1780 (resigned). [Ref: D-31, D-127]. Took the Oath of Allegiance in 1778 [Ref: AA-641]. Resident of William & Mary Upper Hundred in 1778 [Ref: Q-I:297]. Appointed Inspector of Tobacco at Lower Cedar Point on Aug. 30, 1780 [Ref: F-271]. The obituary of Major General Samuel Jones appeared in the *Maryland Gazette* on Feb. 2, 1804, stating he "died 15th ultimate, in Port Tobacco, in his 49th year, a member of the General Assembly of

Maryland, from Charles County. At an early period of his life he entered into the army at the commencement of the American struggle for liberty, and served as an officer until very near the end of the war, when circumstances forced him to retire. He has for some time past held the commission of Major-General in the Militia of the State, and for the last four years has been a member of the House of Delegates." [Ref: FF-104]. In March 1828, the Register of the Land Office was directed to issue to "Lillias M. Jones, of Charles County, daughter of Capt. Samuel Jones, an officer of the Maryland Line during the Revolutionary War, a common warrant for 200 acres of vacant land to the westward of Fort Cumberland in Allegany County, and patent without payment of composition therefor." [Ref: Q-II:360].

JONES, Thomas (1755-   ). Took the Oath of Allegiance in 1778 [Ref: L-18]. Resident of Benedict Hundred in 1778 [Ref: Q-I:297]. He applied for a pension (R20304) in Prince George's County on Dec. 6, 1833, aged 78, stating that he had lived in Charles County at the time of his enlistment in the Maryland Line [Ref: V-II:1883].

JONES, William. Ensign, Militia, Capt. Francis Mastin's Company, 26th Battalion, March 19, 1776 [Ref: M-158, K-1814, A-426]. Took the Oath of Allegiance in 1778 [Ref: L-18, AA-641]. Resident of Durham Lower Hundred in 1778 [Ref: Q-I:297]. See "William Jones, Sr.," q.v.

JONES, William. Private, Militia, 12th Battalion, Capt. Benjamin Lusby Corry's Company, 1777 [Ref: M-160]. Took the Oath of Allegiance in 1778 [Ref: AA-641, which listed the name as "Will Jones"]. Resident of Port Tobacco Upper Hundred in 1778 [Ref: Q-I:297]. See "William Jones, Sr.," q.v.

JONES, William Sr. Rendered patriotic service by providing wheat for the use of the military in September 1782 [Ref: N-545]. One William Jones, aged about 48, and his brother James Jones, aged about 50, were deposed in 1779 and stated their father was William Jones [Ref: BB-480, DD-13]. One William Jones gave a deposition in 1781 pertaining to his inability to perform military service due to family obligations [Ref: Z-208]. Resident of Newport West Hundred in 1778 [Ref: Q-I:297].

JORDAN, Ann. See "William Harrison," q.v.

JORDAN, Thomas. Private, 1st Maryland Line, enrolled and passed on July 19, 1776 [Ref: D-31].

JOYE, Joseph. Rendered patriotic service by providing wheat for the use of the military in December 1782 [Ref: N-577]. Took the Oath of Allegiance in 1778 [Ref: AA-641, which listed the name as "Josh. Joy"].

JUPIN, Mary. See "Hugh Lemaster," q.v.

KANE, Harriet R. See "Cornelius Wells," q.v.

KANIETY(?), Walter. Sergeant, Militia, 12th Battalion, Capt. John Parnham's Company, 1777 [Ref: M-160, which questionably listed the name as "Walter Ihanietz(?,)" and X-63, which questionably indexed and listed the name as "Walter Kaniety(?)"]. *Ed. Note:* Since the name is so illegible and there is no such surname as "Ihanietz" or "Kaniety," it is possible that it could have been "Kennedy" (or even "Karricks" or "Kerricks" if the "y" at the end of the name was actually an "s"). A search of the Charles County Census of 1778 revealed no other possibility except for "Walter Kerrick," q.v. Additional research will be necessary before drawing conclusions.

KEARTON, Anthony. Private, Militia, 12th Battalion, Capt. Jonathan Yates' Company, 1777 [Ref: M-162, which listed the name as "Aly (Aty?) Kearton"]. "Anthony Kearton" took the Oath of Allegiance in 1778 [Ref: AA-641]. "Anthony Kerton" was a resident of William & Mary Upper Hundred in 1778 [Ref: Q-I:297].

KEECH, Ann. See "James Keech," q.v.

KEECH, George (1741-   ). Private, Militia, 12th Battalion, Capt. Walter Hanson's Company, 1777 [Ref: M-159]. Took the Oath of Allegiance in 1778 [Ref: L-18]. Rendered patriotic service by providing wheat for the use of the military in June 1782 [Ref: N-525]. Aged about 35 as noted in a 1776 deposition [Ref: DD-13]. Resident of Port Tobacco East Hundred in 1778 [Ref: Q-I:297].

KEECH, James (1745-c1790). Private, 1st Maryland Line, enrolled and passed on July 18, 1776 [Ref: D-32]. James Keech married Ann Estep and died after 1790 in St. Mary's County. Ann Keech died in 1822. A son James Keech married Clarissa Sotheron (1782-1844) in 1804 [Ref: S-714, S-715, J-II:1641]. James Keech, the soldier, may have been the son of James Keech (died by October 1778) who was aged about 42 as noted in a 1765 deposition [Ref: DD-14].

KEECH, John J. S. (1760-1825). Private, 1st Maryland Line, 1777. He applied for a pension (S36671) in Nelson County, Kentucky on Aug. 19, 1818, aged 58, stating he had enlisted in Charles County, Maryland and served under Capt. William Bell in the 6th Maryland Line. He had no wife or children and died on May 15, 1825 [Ref: V-II:1901, T-59]. *Ed. Note:* "John Keech" served in the 3rd Maryland Line and "John Keitch" served from Prince George's County. There is no record of "John J. S. Keech" from Charles County in the 6th Maryland Line in "Muster Rolls of the Maryland Line in the American Revolution, 1775-1783" in *Archives of Maryland, Volume 18*].

KEECH, Samuel. Private, 1st Maryland Line, enlisted Dec. 10, 1776 and died April 10, 1777 [Ref: D-129].

KEECH, Walter. Private, 2nd Maryland Line, 1780; discharged on Aug. 1, 1783 [Ref: D-443, D-543].
KEENE, Sarah. See "Richard Tubman, Sr.," q.v.
KEITH, Duncan. Private, 1st Maryland Line, 1778, and corporal on July 1, 1779 [Ref: D-130].
KEITH, Ignatius. Took the Oath of Allegiance in 1778 [Ref: AA-641, which listed the name as "Keeth"].
KEITH, Richard. Took the Oath of Allegiance in 1778 [Ref: AA-641, which listed the name as "Keeth"].
KELOUGH (KELER), Mary. See "Jesse Boswell," q.v.
KELLOW, Thomas Jr. Private, Militia, 12th Battalion, Capt. John Hanson's Company, 1777 [Ref: M-159, which mistakenly listed the name as "Kellon"]. Resident of Port Tobacco East Hundred in 1778 [Ref: Q-I:297].
KELLOW, Thomas Sr. (1694-   ). Took the Oath of Allegiance in 1778 [Ref: AA-641]. Resident of Port Tobacco East Hundred in 1778 [Ref: Q-I:297]. Aged about 86 as noted in a 1780 deposition [Ref: DD-14].
KELLOW, William. Private, Militia, 12th Battalion, Capt. John Hanson's Company, 1777 [Ref: M-159, which listed the name as "Kellow"]. Private (furnished by class for 9 months), 1st Maryland Line, by Sept. 11, 1778 [Ref: D-330, which listed the name as "Killow"]. Took the Oath of Allegiance in 1778 [Ref: AA-641]. Resident of Port Tobacco East Hundred in 1778 [Ref: Q-I:297]. Sergeant, 1st Maryland Line, 1780, reported killed on March 15, 1781 [Ref: D-543, which listed the name as "Kello"].
KENNEDY, Clement. Took the Oath of Allegiance in 1778 [Ref: L-18]. Resident of Durham Lower Hundred in 1778 [Ref: Q-I:297].
KENNEDY, Walter. See "Walter Kaniety(?)," q.v.
KENT, George. On June 30, 1781, Daniel Jenifer, Contractor of Horses in Charles County, wrote to Governor Lee stating, in part, "a valuable horse belonging to Mr. George Kent (who is a good whig) I shou'd be glad to have orders to return as he was the only horse his wife cou'd ride, when I took him I thought the case urgent and that no time was to be lost or I shou'd not have taken him." [Ref: H-324].
KERBERT, Thomas. See "Thomas Keyberd," q.v.
KERRICK, Edward. Private, Militia, 12th Battalion, Capt. John Hanson's Company, 1777 [Ref: M-159]. Took the Oath of Allegiance in 1778 [Ref: L-18, AA-641]. On Aug. 23, 1781, the Council of Maryland ordered "that the Treasurer pay to Edward Kerrick sixty Pounds of the Emission of the money appropriated to be delivered over to Hezekiah Reeder, Commissary of Charles County." [Ref: G-576]. Rendered patriotic service by dressing cattle for the use of the military in October 1781 [Ref: N-449].

KERRICK, James. Private, Militia, 26th Battalion, Capt. Robert Sinnett's Company, 1777 [Ref: M-164]. Took the Oath of Allegiance in 1778 [Ref: L-18].
KERRICK, Joseph. Corporal, 1st Maryland Line, 1780, who died on Dec. 27, 1782 [Ref: D-543].
KERRICK, Walter. Took the Oath of Allegiance in 1778 [Ref: AA-641, which listed the name as "Karrick"]. Resident of Newport East Hundred in 1778 [Ref: Q-I:297]. Constable, 1778 [Ref: CC-709]. See comments under "Walter Kaniety(?)," q.v.
KERTON, Anthony. See "Anthony Kearton," q.v.
KEY, James (died testate in June 1779). Took the Oath of Allegiance in 1778 [Ref: L-18, which listed the name as "Keye"]. Resident of Port Tobacco Upper Hundred in 1778 [Ref: Q-I:297].
KEYBERD (KIBERD), John (1730-   ). Rendered patriotic service by providing clothing for the use of the military in February 1778 [Ref: Y-II:234]. Aged about 42 as noted in a 1772 deposition which mentioned his father Thomas and spelled their name as "Kiberd" [Ref: DD-14]. Resident of Durham Lower Hundred in 1778 [Ref: Q-I:297].
KEYBERD (KIBERD), Thomas. Private, Militia, 26th Battalion, Capt. William Winter's Company, 1777 [Ref: M-165, which listed the name as "Keibert"]. Took the Oath of Allegiance in 1778 [Ref: L-18, which listed the name as "Keibeard"]. Resident of Durham Lower Hundred in 1778 [Ref: Q-I:297]. Rendered patriotic service by providing wheat for the use of the military in November 1782 [Ref: N-566, which listed the name as "Kibord"]. See "John Keyberd," q.v.
KIDGATE, Thomas H. See "Thomas Haw (How) Ridgate," q.v.
KIDWELL, Benjamin. Private, 3rd Maryland Line, enlisted May 26, 1778 and still in service in November 1780 [Ref: D-130].
KIDWELL, James. Private, Lower Battalion, Prince George's County, 1776 [Ref: D-35]. Private, Charles County Militia, 26th Battalion, Capt. Samuel Smallwood's Company, 1777 [Ref: M-165].
KIDWELL, John. Private, Militia, 26th Battalion, Capt. Samuel Smallwood's Company, 1777 [Ref: M-165].
KIDWELL, Jonathan (1750-c1835). Private, North Carolina Line. He applied for a pension (S2706) on Sept. 8, 1833 in Henry County, Kentucky, stating he was born in 1750 in Charles County, Maryland and married Rebecca ---- in 1770. They moved to Rowan County, North Carolina in 1777 and he enlisted there in the Revolutionary War in September 1779. He served under Quartermaster General Edward Gamble and was discharged on Sept. 22, 1781. In 1784 he moved to (now) Madison County, Kentucky and in 1828 went to Henry County, Kentucky.

In 1833 he was aged 86 and his wife was aged 83 [Ref: V-II:1940, T-48, T-49].

KIDWELL, Matthew (1752-1842). Private, Militia, 26th Battalion, Capt. Samuel Smallwood's Company, 1777 [Ref: M-165]. Private (draught who had not yet joined the army), 1st Maryland Line, by Sept. 11, 1778 [Ref: D-330]. Resident of Port Tobacco Upper Hundred in 1778 [Ref: Q-I:297]. He applied for a pension (S30523) in Monroe County, Kentucky on Oct. 2, 1832, stating that he was born in Charles County, Maryland on June 8, 1752 and lived there at the time of his enlistment in the Revolutionary War. He lived in Maryland until the age of 30 and then moved to Frederick County, Virginia for 2 years, then to Pendleton County, Virginia for 15 years, then to White County, Tennessee for only 2 months, and then to Kentucky [Barren County, now Monroe County]. Matthew Kidwell married Martha ---- on May 21, 1778 and she was aged 81 in 1833 [Ref: T-62, V-II:1940. It must be noted, however, that a Matthew Kidwell married Priscilla Moore (More) on Dec. 25, 1781 in Charles County. See Robert W. Barnes' *Maryland Marriages, 1778-1800* (p. 127). Additional research may be necessary before drawing conclusions]. Matthew Kidwell is buried in the Old Mulkey Meeting House Cemetery in Monroe County, Kentucky, noting that he was a private in Hanson's Maryland Regiment and died in 1842 [Ref: Eva Coe Peden's *Monroe County, Kentucky Cemetery Records, Volume 2* (1975), p. 51].

KIDWELL, Rebecca. See "Jonathan Kidwell," q.v.

KIELS (RIELS?), Benjamin. Took the Oath of Allegiance in 1778 [Ref: AA-641].

KING, Anne. See "Jesse Doyne," q.v.

KING, Asa. Private, Militia, 12th Battalion, Capt. Jonathan Yates' Company, 1777 [Ref: M-162]. Took the Oath of Allegiance in 1778 [Ref: AA-641]. Resident of William & Mary Lower Hundred in 1778 [Ref: Q-I:297].

KING, Benjamin. Corporal, Militia, 12th Battalion, Capt. Jonathan Yates' Company, 1777 [Ref: M-162]. Took the Oath of Allegiance in 1778 [Ref: L-18, AA-641]. Resident of William & Mary Lower Hundred in 1778 [Ref: Q-I:297].

KING, Charles. Private, 1st Maryland Line, drafted from the Charles County militia on July 27, 1781 and discharged on Dec. 3, 1781 [Ref: D-377, G-569, I-11]. See "Edward Miles," q.v.

KING, Draden. See "James Waters," q.v.

KING, Elisha. Memorialist and Militiaman, Pomonkey Company, after March 6, 1776 [Ref: M-158, Y-II:26]. Private, Militia, 26th Battalion, Capt. Thomas H. Marshall's Company, 1777 [Ref: M-163]. Took the Oath of

Allegiance in 1778 [Ref: AA-641]. Resident of Pomonkey Hundred in 1778 [Ref: Q-I:297].
KING, James. Took the Oath of Allegiance in 1778 [Ref: L-18]. Resident of Pomonkey Hundred in 1778 [Ref: Q-I:297].
KING, John. Took the Oath of Allegiance in 1778 [Ref: L-18]. Resident of Pomonkey Hundred in 1778 [Ref: Q-I:297].
KING, Joseph. Took the Oath of Allegiance in 1778 [Ref: L-18]. See "Zephaniah King," q.v.
KING, Leonard. Private, Militia, 12th Battalion, Capt. Peter Wood's Company, 1777 [Ref: M-161].
KING, Leonard Ogdon. Took the Oath of Allegiance in 1778 [Ref: AA-641]. Resident of Bryan Town Hundred in 1778 [Ref: Q-I:297].
KING, Mary Anne. See "Joseph Hagan," q.v.
KING, Moses. Took the Oath of Allegiance in 1778 [Ref: L-18].
KING, Priscilla. See "Edward Miles," q.v.
KING, Rebeckah. Rendered patriotic service by providing clothing for the use of the military in February 1778 [Ref: Y-II:234].
KING, Richard. Took the Oath of Allegiance in 1778 [Ref: L-18]. Resident of Bryan Town Hundred in 1778 [Ref: Q-I:297].
KING, Robert. Private, Militia, 12th Battalion, Capt. John Parnham's Company, 1777 [Ref: M-161]. Took the Oath of Allegiance in 1778 [Ref: L-18]. Resident of Newport East Hundred in 1778 [Ref: Q-I:297].
KING, Thomas. Private, 1st Maryland Line, Capt. John S. Belt's Company, before Jan. 1, 1782 [Ref: D-437]. One Thomas King was "an orphan aged 17" when he chose Benjamin Gray as his guardian in 1755 [Ref: DD-14]. The obituary of one Thomas King appeared in the *Maryland Gazette* on March 29, 1832, stating he was "a Revolutionary soldier, died yesterday morning, in his 76th year." [Ref: FF-108]. Additional research will be necessary before drawing conclusions.
KING, Townley. Private, Militia, 12th Battalion, Capt. John Parnham's Company, 1777 [Ref: M-161]. Took the Oath of Allegiance in 1778 [Ref: L-18, AA-641]. Resident of Newport East Hundred in 1778 [Ref: Q-I:297].
KING, William. Private, Militia, 12th Battalion, Capt. John Parnham's Company, 1777 [Ref: M-161]. Took the Oath of Allegiance in 1778 [Ref: L-18]. See "Thomas Pickerel" and "Charles Smith," q.v.
KING, Williamson. Took the Oath of Allegiance in 1778 [Ref: AA-641]. Resident of Newport East Hundred in 1778 [Ref: Q-I:297].
KING, Zephaniah (1759-   ). Born on July 1, 1759, a son of Joseph King and Dradon Johnson who were married in Trinity Parish on June 7, 1756 [Ref: EE-15, EE-16]. Private, Militia, 12th Battalion, Capt. Henry Clarkson's Company, 1777 [Ref: M-159]. Took the Oath of Allegiance in 1778 [Ref:

L-18, AA-641]. Resident of Bryan Town Hundred in 1778 [Ref: Q-I:297]. Another source stated Zephaniah King was born circa 1734, married Draden Clarke, served as a private, rendered patriotic service, and died after 1778 [Ref: J-II:1688]. Additional research may be necessary before drawing conclusions.

KINNICK, Ann. See "John Kinnick," q.v.

KINNICK, John (c1755-1833). Took the Oath of Allegiance in 1778 [Ref: AA-641]. Resident of Bryan Town Hundred in 1778 [Ref: Q-I:297, which listed the name as "Kennich"]. John Kinnick married Ann ---- and migrated to North Carolina where he died before August 1833 [Ref: J-II:1693].

KINNICK, Joseph. Took the Oath of Allegiance in 1778 [Ref: L-18, which listed the name as "Kimmick"].

KINNICK, Richard. Private, 1st Maryland Line, enrolled and passed on July 20, 1776 [Ref: D-33, which listed the name as "Kinnick"].

KINNICK, Sarah. See "William Kinnick," q.v.

KINNICK, William (c1735-1785). Took the Oath of Allegiance in 1778 [Ref: L-18]. Resident of Bryan Town Hundred in 1778 [Ref: Q-I:297, which listed the name as "Kennich"]. William Kinnick was born circa 1735 in Holland, married Sarah ----, served as a sergeant major during the war, and died before April 18, 1785 [Ref: J-II:1693].

KINNIMAN, John. Private, Militia, 12th Battalion, Capt. Henry Clarkson's Company, 1777 [Ref: M-159, which listed the name as "Kinneman"].

KINNIMAN, Philip. Private, Militia, 12th Battalion, Capt. Henry Clarkson's Company, 1777 [Ref: M-159]. Took the Oath of Allegiance in 1778 [Ref: AA-641, which listed the name as "Kinnaman"].

KIRBY, James. See "Charles Smith," q.v.

KIRKPATRICK, William. Took the Oath of Allegiance in 1778 [Ref: AA-641]. Resident of William & Mary Upper Hundred in 1778 [Ref: Q-I:297, which listed the name as "Kerpatrick"].

KITCHEN, William. Private, Militia, 26th Battalion, Capt. William Winter's Company, 1777 [Ref: M-165, which listed the name as "Willm. Citchen"]. Resident of Durham Lower Hundred in 1778 [Ref: Q-I:297].

KNOTT, Francis. Took the Oath of Allegiance in 1778 [Ref: L-18].

KNOTT, James. Private, 1st Maryland Line, enlisted May 22, 1779 and taken prisoner by January 1780, when "struck off" muster rolls [Ref: D-129].

KNOTT, Jesse. Rendered patriotic service by providing wheat for the use of the military in May 1783 [Ref: N-598, which listed the name as "Nott"]. Resident of Port Tobacco East Hundred in 1778 [Ref: Q-I:297].

KNOTT, John. "John Knott" took the Oath of Allegiance in 1778 [Ref: L-18]. "John Filbut Nott" was a resident of Port Tobacco Upper Hundred in 1778 [Ref: Q-I:297].
KNOTT, Justinian. Private, Militia, 12th Battalion, Capt. Walter Hanson's Company, 1777 [Ref: M-159, which listed the name as "Jestinion Nott"]. Rendered patriotic service by providing wheat for the use of the military in November 1781 [Ref: N-457]. Took the Oath of Allegiance in 1778 [Ref: AA-641].
KNOTT, Mary. See "Richard Mudd," q.v.
KNOTT, Nathaniel. Private, 3rd Maryland Line, enrolled by Capt. Joseph Marbury by May 24, 1780 and discharged by Nov. 15, 1783 [Ref: F-181, D-543].
KNOX, Robert. Corporal, Militia, 26th Battalion, Capt. William Winter's Company, 1777 [Ref: M-165]. Took the Oath of Allegiance in 1778 [Ref: AA-641, L-18, which latter source mistakenly listed the name as "Knott"].
KNOX, Robert (Captain). Rendered patriotic service by providing clothing for the use of the military in February 1778 [Ref: Y-II:234]. Resident of Durham Lower Hundred in 1778 [Ref: Q-I:297].
KNOX, Rose T. Rendered patriotic service by providing wheat for the use of the military in May 1783 [Ref: N-598].
LADYMAN, William. Private, Militia, 12th Battalion, Capt. John Thomas' Company, 1777 [Ref: M-161, which listed the name as "Ladamon"]. Took the Oath of Allegiance in 1778 [Ref: L-18]. Resident of Benedict Hundred in 1778 [Ref: Q-I:297].
LAMASTER, Richard. See "Richard Lemaster," q.v.
LAMBERT, John. Private, Militia, 26th Battalion, Capt. Thomas H. Marshall's Company, 1777 [Ref: M-163].
LAMBETH, John B. Took the Oath of Allegiance in 1778 [Ref: L-18, AA-641]. Resident of Pomonkey Hundred in 1778 [Ref: Q-I:297].
LAMMONT, John. Took the Oath of Allegiance in 1778 [Ref: L-18].
LANCASTER, John. First Lieutenant, Militia, 12th Battalion, Capt. Jonathan Yates' Company, 1777 [Ref: M-162]. Rendered patriotic service by providing clothing for the use of the military in February 1778 [Ref: Y-II:234]. Resident of William & Mary Lower Hundred in 1778 [Ref: Q-I:297]. Justice who administered (and took) the Oath of Allegiance in 1778 [Ref: AA-641]. Appointed a Justice of the Peace on Nov. 21, 1778 [Ref: E-249]. Captain, Militia, commissioned on Jan. 19, 1781 [Ref: M-96, G-280]. Rendered patriotic service by providing wheat for the use of the military in December 1782 [Ref: N-577].
LANCASTER, John Jr. Ensign, Militia, 12th Battalion, May 7, 1777 [Ref: M-96]. First Lieutenant, May 28, 1779 [Ref: E-427]. Took the Oath of

Allegiance in 1778 [Ref: L-18, AA-641]. Resident of William & Mary Lower Hundred in 1778 [Ref: Q-I:297].

LANCASTER, Joseph. Took the Oath of Allegiance in 1778 [Ref: L-18]. Resident of Port Tobacco East Hundred in 1778 [Ref: Q-I:297].

LANCASTER, Thomas. Private, Militia, 12th Battalion, Capt. Jonathan Yates' Company, 1777 [Ref: X-70, but was omitted from the list in Reference M-162]. Took the Oath of Allegiance in 1778 [Ref: L-18, AA-641]. Resident of William & Mary Lower Hundred in 1778 [Ref: Q-I:297].

LANDSDALE, Charles. Rendered patriotic service for the Committee of Observation in Charles County by delivering money "to apply to the Account of Subsistance of that part of Captain Beall's Company Stationed at Port Tobacco" on July 19, 1776 [Ref: B-79, B-80].

LANGLEY, James. Private, 3rd Maryland Line, 1780, enrolled in Charles County for Capt. Joseph Marbury's Company [Ref: D-333].

LANGLEY, Juliana. See "James Montgomery, Jr.," q.v.

LANGLEY, William. Private, 1st Maryland Line, 1777 [Ref: D-131]. Took the Oath of Allegiance in 1778 [Ref: L-18, AA-641]. Resident of Bryan Town Hundred in 1778 [Ref: Q-I:297].

LANHAM, Elizabeth. See "John Lanham," q.v.

LANHAM, John (c1750-1801). Private, 1st Maryland Line, who received a disability pension (S25073) from Sept. 4, 1789 and died in Charles County in 1801. His estate was administered by his widow Susannah Lanham in 1802. She lived in Annapolis in 1827 and died on May 15, 1838, leaving a son John Lanham (aged 45) and a daughter Elizabeth or Betsy Lanham (who married Robert Bier); all lived in Baltimore. Also, in 1838, Tabitha Brown (wife of William Brown, aged 86, of Washington, D. C.) was aged about 90 and stated she was a relative of John Lanham, the soldier (exact relationship not stated, probably his sister). They all lived in Charles County before and during the Revolutionary War [Ref: V-II:2012].

LANHAM, Susannah. See "John Lanham," q.v.

LARMAN, John C. See "John Christopher Layman," q.v.

LARY, William. Private, 1st Maryland Line, drafted from the Charles County militia and in service on June 11 or 12, 1781 [Ref: D-376].

LASHER, John. See "John Lusher," q.v.

LATIMER, Ann. See "Marcus Latimer," q.v.

LATIMER, Benjamin (1743-1785). Private, Militia, 26th Battalion, Capt. Francis Mastin's Company, 1777 [Ref: M-164, which listed the name as "Benj. Lattemore"]. Took the Oath of Allegiance in 1778 [Ref: AA-641]. Benjamin Latimer was born on June 14, 1743, married Louisa Cazey, and died on May 5, 1785 [Ref: J-II:1748].

LATIMER, Elizabeth. See "Thomas Hancock," q.v.

LATIMER, Isaac Smoot. Private, Militia, 12th Battalion, Capt. Walter Hanson's Company, 1777 [Ref: M-159]. See "Thomas Pickerel," q.v.
LATIMER, Jacob (1714-1784). Resident of Port Tobacco East Hundred in 1778 [Ref: Q-I:297]. Took the Oath of Allegiance in 1778 [Ref: AA-641; however, he was not included in the Charles County oaths listed in Reference L-18]. Jacob Latimer's first wife was ---- Brandt; he married second to Judith Swann in 1748. A son Thomas Latimer (1750-1826) married Ann Ford (1764-1825) in 1786. Another son Randolph Brandt Latimer married Catharine Rutland and died in 1805. Jacob died in August 1784 [Ref: S-3053, P-II:518, J-II:1749]. See "Thomas Latimer" and "Randolph Brandt Latimer," q.v.
LATIMER, James. Corporal, Militia, 12th Battalion, Capt. John Hanson's Company, 1777 [Ref: M-158].
LATIMER, James B. See "Randolph Brandt Latimer," q.v.
LATIMER, John Ford. See "Thomas Latimer," q.v.
LATIMER, Marcus (c1740-1790). Rendered patriotic service by providing clothing for the use of the military in February 1778 [Ref: Y-II:234, which misspelled the first name as "Marius"]. Took the Oath of Allegiance in 1778 [Ref: AA-641]. Resident of William & Mary Upper Hundred in 1778 [Ref: Q-I:297]. Marcus Latimer married Ann [Cox] and died in 1790 [Ref: J-II:1749]. See "Thomas Hussey Luckett," q.v.
LATIMER, Mark. Private, Militia, 12th Battalion, Capt. Walter Hanson's Company, 1777 [Ref: M-159]. Took the Oath of Allegiance in 1778 [Ref: AA-641]. Resident of Port Tobacco East Hundred in 1778 [Ref: Q-I:297].
LATIMER, Mary. See "Randolph Brandt Latimer" and "Thomas Hussey Luckett," q.v.
LATIMER, Priscilla R. See "Randolph Brandt Latimer," q.v.
LATIMER, Randolph Brandt (c1755-1805). Son of Jacob Latimer and Judith Swann, he married Catharine Rutland and had these children: Randolph W. Latimer, James B. Latimer, William K. Latimer, Mary C. Latimer, Susanna W. Latimer, Priscilla R. Latimer, and Rebecca H. Latimer [Ref: P-II:518]. Private, Militia, 12th Battalion, Capt. John Hanson's Company, 1777 [Ref: M-159]. Appointed an ensign in the Maryland Line on Sept. 4, 1781, with date of rank to be determined [Ref: G-600, which listed the name as "R. B. Lattimer"]. Served as Deputy Auditor, 1782-1789, and on the Executive Council, 1789-1792. Later removed to Baltimore and became a Justice of the Orphans' Court in 1799 and a Notary Public in 1800. Suffered severe financial hardships, died in 1805, and litigation over his heavy indebtedness continued until 1820 [Ref: P-II:518, P-II:519]. See "Jacob Latimer," q.v.
LATIMER, Randolph W. See "Randolph Brandt Latimer," q.v.

LATIMER, Rebecca H. See "Randolph Brandt Latimer," q.v.
LATIMER, Samuel. Private, Militia, 26th Battalion, Capt. William McPherson's Company, 1777 [Ref: M-163]. Took the Oath of Allegiance in 1778 [Ref: AA-641, L-18, which latter source misspelled the name as "Larimer"]. Resident of Port Tobacco Upper Hundred in 1778 [Ref: Q-I:297].
LATIMER Susanna W. See "Randolph Brandt Latimer," q.v.
LATIMER, Thomas (1750-1826). Private, Militia, 12th Battalion, Capt. John Hanson's Company, 1777 [Ref: M-159]. Took the Oath of Allegiance in 1778 [Ref: L-18, AA-641]. Resident of Port Tobacco East Hundred in 1778 [Ref: Q-I:297]. Rendered patriotic service by providing wheat for the use of the military in May 1782 [Ref: N-511, which listed the name as "Lattamore"]. Thomas was a son of Jacob Latimer and Judith Swann. He married Ann Ford (1764 - March 16, 1825) on April 6, 1786, and died in Prince George's County on Sept. 23, 1826. Their son John Ford Latimer (1792-1835) married Susan Burch and lived in Prince George's County [Ref: S-3053, J-II:1749]. See "Jacob Latimer," q.v.
LATIMER, William K. See "Randolph Brandt Latimer," q.v.
LAVIELLE, Rebecca. See "Raphael or Ralph Hagan," q.v.
LAVIGNE, Michael. Private, 3rd Maryland Line, enrolled by Capt. Joseph Marbury by May 24, 1780 [Ref: D-333, F-181, which latter source listed the name as "Lavigna"].
LAWLOR, John. Took the Oath of Allegiance in 1778 [Ref: L-18].
LAWLOR, William. Took the Oath of Allegiance in 1778 [Ref: L-18].
LAWSON, Michael. Private, Militia, 12th Battalion, Capt. Walter Hanson's Company, 1777 [Ref: M-159]. Private (furnished by class for 9 months), 1st Maryland Line, by Sept. 11, 1778 [Ref: D-330].
LAWSON, Robert. Rendered patriotic service by providing wheat for the use of the military in November 1781 and September 1782 [Ref: N-453, N-548].
LAYMAN, Christopher. Private, Militia, 26th Battalion, Capt. Richard Bennett Mitchell's Company, 1777; listed as an invalid (disabled) soldier [Ref: M-165, which listed the name as "Chist. Layman"].
LAYMAN, John Christopher. Took the Oath of Allegiance in 1778 [Ref: L-18]. Resident of Port Tobacco Town Hundred in 1778 [Ref: Q-I:297, which misspelled the name as "John C. Larmon"].
LAYMAN, William. Ensign, Militia, Capt. George Swann's Company, Feb. 26, 1776 [Ref: M-96, A-186, A-206, Y-II:23, which also listed the name as "Laman"]. Ensign, 1st Maryland Line, April 10, 1777 and lieutenant, June 4, 1779 (resigned). [Ref: D-132]. Recruiting Officer for Charles County, 1779-1780 [Ref: F-54].

LAYMAN, William. Private, 1st Maryland Line, enrolled and passed on July 8, 1776 [Ref: D-32].
LEACH, John. Private, Militia, 12th Battalion, Capt. John Thomas' Company, 1777 [Ref: M-161]. Resident of Benedict Hundred in 1778 [Ref: Q-I:297].
LEACH, Samuel. Private, 1st Maryland Line, enrolled and passed on July 19, 1776 [Ref: D-31]. Private, Militia, 12th Battalion, Capt. John Parnham's Company, 1777 [Ref: M-161, which listed the name as "Leech"].
LEE, Ann. See "Philip Thomas Lee," q.v.
LEE, Eleanor. See "Philip Thomas Lee" and "Philip Richard Fendall," q.v.
LEE, George (1736-1807). Born in Prince George's County, he lived there and in Charles County alternately through 1794. He married Chloe Hanson, daughter of "Samuel Hanson," q.v., of Charles County. They had at least two daughters (names were not given). George was a Justice of Charles County between 1764-1770 and 1784-1795, a Justice of Prince George's County, 1779-1781, Sheriff of Charles County, 1771-1774, and Associate Justice, First District, 1791-1792. Served as Surveyor General of the Western Shore, 1768-1771, and attended the Maryland Conventions, 1774-1775. He rejected a commission in the Lower Battalion of Prince George's County in 1776. He died in the District of Columbia in 1807 and is buried with his wife at "Green Hill" in Charles County [Ref: P-II:525, P-II:526]. See "Samuel Hanson," q.v.
LEE, James. Private, Militia, Capt. Francis Mastin's Company, 26th Battalion, March 19, 1776 [Ref: M-158, K-1814].
LEE, Margaret Russell. See "Philip Thomas Lee," q.v.
LEE, Philip Thomas (1738-1778). Son of Richard Lee and Grace Ashton, he married his first cousin Ann Russell and had these children: Russell Lee (1776-1793); Sarah Russell Lee (married Benjamin Contee); Ann Lee; Eleanor Lee (married Dr. William Dawson); and, Margaret Russell Lee (married her cousin James Clerk who changed his name to James Clerk-Lee in 1804). Philip Thomas Lee served in the Upper House of the Maryland Legislature, 1773-1774, Executive Council, 1773-1776, Provincial Court Justice, 1773, and Naval Officer of North Potomac, 1774-1777. He was taxed as a loyalist until he took the Oath of Allegiance in 1778 and allegedly died over the distress of his native country's break with England [Ref: P-II:527, L-18, AA-641, FF-112]. Resident of William & Mary Upper Hundred in 1778 [Ref: Q-I:297].
LEE, Richard (1707-1787). Rendered patriotic service by providing clothing for the use of the military in February 1778 [Ref: Y-II:234]. Took the Oath of Allegiance in 1778 [Ref: AA-641]. Resident of William & Mary Upper Hundred in 1778 [Ref: Q-I:297]. His obituary appeared in the *Maryland*

Gazette on Feb. 15, 1787, stating "Hon. Richard Lee, Esq., died at Blenheim, Charles County, on Jan. 26th, in his 81st year." [Ref: FF-112]. See "Philip Thomas Lee," q.v.

LEE, Russell. See "Philip Thomas Lee," q.v.

LEE, Sarah Lettice. See "Philip Richard Fendall," q.v.

LEE, Sarah Russell. See "Philip Thomas Lee," q.v.

LEE, William. Took the Oath of Allegiance in 1778 [Ref: L-18]. Resident of Pomonkey Hundred in 1778 [Ref: Q-I:297].

LEFNAR (LITTNER), John Jochim. "John Jochim Lefnar" took the Oath of Allegiance in 1778 [Ref: AA-641]. "John I. Littner" was a resident of William & Mary Lower Hundred in 1778 [Ref: Q-I:297].

LEIGH, William. Rendered patriotic service by providing clothing for the use of the military in February 1778 [Ref: Y-II:234]. Resident of Port Tobacco East Hundred in 1778 [Ref: Q-I:297]. On June 30, 1781, Daniel Jenifer, Contractor of Horses for Charles County, wrote to Governor Lee stating, in part, that "Mr. William Leigh is to deliver a well fixt Waggon and geers at any place your Excellency shall order in hire of an *[sic]* Horse, the Waggon he is to purchase up the Country." [Ref: H-325]. Rendered patriotic service by providing wheat for the use of the military in May 1783 [Ref: N-597]. One William Leigh was Surgeon's Master on the State Ship *Defence* in 1777 [Ref: D-658].

LEMASTER, Hugh (1750-1837). Private, 1st Maryland Line. He applied for a pension in Shelby County, Kentucky on Jan. 18, 1834, stating he was born on May 27, 1750 in Charles County, Maryland, lived in Washington County at the time of his enlistment, and moved to Kentucky in 1796. On July 3, 1845 his widow Mary Lemaster applied for pension (W2951) in Shelby County, aged 78, stating Hugh had died on May 9, 1837 [Ref: V-II:2053]. Hugh Lemaster married second to Mary Jupin (first wife's name not known). [Ref: J-II:1780].

LEMASTER, Mary. See "Hugh Lemaster," q.v.

LEMASTER, Richard (1711-). Took the Oath of Allegiance in 1778 [Ref: L-18, AA-641, which latter source listed the name as "Lamaster"]. Aged about 65 as noted in a 1776 deposition [Ref: DD-14]. Resident of Port Tobacco East Hundred in 1778 [Ref: Q-I:297].

LEMASTER, William. Took the Oath of Allegiance in 1778 [Ref: L-18, AA-641, which latter source listed the name as "Lamaster"]. Resident of Port Tobacco East Hundred in 1778 [Ref: Q-I:297].

LEMMON (LEMON), John. Marine on the State Ship *Defence*, 1776-1777 [Ref: D-607, D-658]. Resident of Port Tobacco East Hundred in 1778 [Ref: Q-I:297].

LETCHWORTH, Leonard. Private, Militia, 12th Battalion, Capt. Peter Wood's Company, 1777 [Ref: M-161]. Second Lieutenant, May 7, 1777 [Ref: M-97]. Took the Oath of Allegiance in 1778 [Ref: L-18, AA-641, which latter source listed the name as "Litchworth"]. Resident of Benedict Hundred in 1778 [Ref: Q-I:297].
LEWIS, Benjamin. Took the Oath of Allegiance in 1778 [Ref: AA-641]. Resident of William & Mary Upper Hundred in 1778 [Ref: Q-I:297].
LEWIS, Isaac. Private, Militia, 12th Battalion, Capt. Alexander McPherson's Company, 1777 [Ref: M-160]. Took the Oath of Allegiance in 1778 [Ref: L-18].
LEWIS, John. Took the Oath of Allegiance in 1778 [Ref: L-18].
LEWIS, Thomas Jr. Took the Oath of Allegiance in 1778 [Ref: L-18, which mistakenly listed the name as "Lens"]. Resident of Port Tobacco Upper Hundred in 1778 [Ref: Q-I:297].
LILLY, Theresa. See "Raphael Hagan," q.v.
LINDSAY, David. Rendered patriotic service by providing wheat for the use of the military in November 1782 [Ref: N-564, which listed the name as "Linsey"].
LINDSAY, William. Took the Oath of Allegiance in 1778 [Ref: L-18, which listed the name as "Lyndsay"]. Gave a deposition in 1781 pertaining to his inability to perform military service due to family obligations [Ref: Z-208]. One "William Lindsey" was aged about 53 as noted in a 1770 deposition [Ref: DD-15], and died testate in February 1779. See "James Gray," q.v.
LINGAN, Nicholas. See "Samuel Hanson," q.v.
LINKINS, James. Rendered patriotic service by providing wheat for the use of the military in September 1781 [Ref: N-432]. Resident of Port Tobacco West Hundred in 1778 [Ref: Q-I:297].
LITTNER, John I. See "John Jochim Lefnar," q.v.
LIVERS, James. Took the Oath of Allegiance in 1778 [Ref: AA-641].
LOCK, Mary. See "Isaac Smoot," q.v.
LOGAN, John V. Private, Militia, 26th Battalion, Capt. Benjamin Cawood's Company, 1777 [Ref: M-162]. Took the Oath of Allegiance in 1778 [Ref: AA-641].
LOMAX, Amy. See "William Lomax," q.v.
LOMAX, Benjamin. Private, Militia, 12th Battalion, Capt. Walter Hanson's Company, 1777 [Ref: M-159].
LOMAX, Benjamin (1704-   ). Took the Oath of Allegiance in 1778 [Ref: AA-641]. Rendered patriotic service by providing clothing for the use of the military in February 1778 [Ref: Y-II:234]. Aged about 60 as noted in a 1764 deposition [Ref: DD-15]. Resident of Port Tobacco East Hundred in 1778 [Ref: Q-I:297].

LOMAX, Benjamin Thomas. Took the Oath of Allegiance in 1778 [Ref: L-18].
LOMAX, Cornelius. See "William Lomax," q.v.
LOMAX, John (1754-1824). Private, 1st Maryland Line, June 6, 1777; taken prisoner in January 1780; discharged on Jan. 6, 1781 as a sergeant [Ref: D-132, D-544]. He was placed on the pension rolls of Charles County as of April 11, 1821 (retroactive to Nov. 17, 1820) and died on June 21, 1824 [Ref: R-33]. He also applied for a federal pension (S34966) on Nov. 17, 1820, aged 66 [Ref: V-II:2107].
LOMAX, John A. See "William Lomax," q.v.
LOMAX, Luke. Private, Militia, 26th Battalion, Capt. Richard Bennett Mitchell's Company, 1777 [Ref: M-164]. Took the Oath of Allegiance in 1778 [Ref: L-18, AA-641]. Resident of Port Tobacco West Hundred in 1778 [Ref: Q-I:297].
LOMAX, Nancy. See "William Lomax," q.v.
LOMAX, Polly. See "William Lomax," q.v.
LOMAX, Seth. Private, Militia, Capt. Francis Mastin's Company, 26th Battalion, March 19, 1776 [Ref: M-158, K-1814]. Private, Militia, 26th Battalion, Capt. Francis Mastin's Company, 1777 [Ref: X-78, and M-164, which listed the name as "---- Lomox"]. Took the Oath of Allegiance in 1778 [Ref: AA-641].
LOMAX, Stephen (1737-   ). Private, Militia, 26th Battalion, Capt. Richard Bennett Mitchell's Company, 1777 [Ref: M-164]. Took the Oath of Allegiance in 1778 [Ref: L-18, AA-641]. Aged about 27 as noted in a 1764 deposition [Ref: DD-15]. Resident of Port Tobacco West Hundred in 1778 [Ref: Q-I:297].
LOMAX, Tabitha. See "William Lomax," q.v.
LOMAX, Thomas. Two men by this name were privates in the militia in 1777: one in the 26th Battalion, Capt. Francis Mastin's Company [Ref: M-164, which listed the name as "Thos. Lomox"], and one in the 12th Battalion, Capt. Walter Hanson's Company [Ref: M-159]. One rendered patriotic service by providing wheat for the use of the military in January 1782 [Ref: N-470]. Took the Oath of Allegiance in 1778 [Ref: AA-641].
LOMAX, Walter. Private, Militia, 26th Battalion, Capt. Richard Bennett Mitchell's Company, 1777 [Ref: M-164, which listed the name as "Walter West(?) Lomax"].
LOMAX, West or Wesley. See "William Lomax," q.v.
LOMAX, William (1754-1835). Private, North Carolina Line. He applied for a pension in May 1819 in Rowan County, North Carolina, stating he was born on Jan. 12, 1754 in Charles County, Maryland and at the age of 16 he moved to Guilford County, North Carolina. There he enlisted in the

Revolutionary War and a few years after the war he moved to Montgomery County. He married Tabitha Gooden or Goodin on Dec. 26, 1783 at her father Alexander's home in Montgomery County. William died on Nov. 6, 1835. His widow Tabitha Lomax applied for pension (W5028) on Oct. 19, 1838 in Davidson County, North Carolina. She was born on Nov. 4, 1769 and died on Feb. 15, 1856. Their children were: John A. Lomax (born Nov. 6, 1794 and died some time between 1857 and 1877); Amy Lomax (born Oct. 16, 1796); Nancy Lomax (born Jan. 20, 1799); Polly Lomax (born June 19, 1801); William Lomax (born June 20, 1803); Cornelius Lomax (born March 8, 1806); and, West or Wesley Lomax (born May 31, 1809). [Ref: V-II:2108].

LONG, Jonathan. Private, Militia, 26th Battalion, Capt. Thomas H. Marshall's Company, 1777 [Ref: M-163].

LONG, Thomas. Took the Oath of Allegiance in 1778 [Ref: L-18].

LOVE, Charles. Private, Militia, 12th Battalion, Capt. John Parnham's Company, 1777 [Ref: M-161]. Took the Oath of Allegiance in 1778 [Ref: L-18].

LOVE, Elizabeth. See "Samuel Love," q.v.

LOVE, Mary. See "Samuel Love," q.v.

LOVE, Samuel (1745/6-1781). Born on Feb. 20, 1745/6, son of Samuel Love, Jr., and Mary Haw, he married Elizabeth ---- by 1769 and died in 1781. Samuel attended the Maryland Conventions, 1774-1775, and was a County Court Justice, 1769-1776, and served on the Committee of Observation, 1775. He was appointed by the Maryland Convention on Feb. 2, 1776 to be one of the Collectors of Gold & Silver Coin in Charles County [Ref: P-II:547, P-II:548, A-132, EE-7]. Took the Oath of Allegiance in 1778 [Ref: AA-641]. Among the proceedings of the Council of Maryland there is a letter dated July 18, 1781 in which the Clerk of the Charles County Court requested that the original will of Samuel Love, late of Charles County, deceased, be produced by the Keeper of the Records for a trial in the case of Samuel Love, executor of Samuel Love vs. Thomas Reeder, Jr. [Ref: H-359].

LOVELESS, Elias (1755-1834). Private (furnished by class for 9 months), 1st Maryland Line, by Sept. 11, 1778 [Ref: D-330, which listed the name as "Lovless"]. One "Elias Lovelace" was born on Jan. 27, 1755 in Maryland, married Ann Roby, served in the North Carolina troops, and migrated to Kentucky where he died on Dec. 23, 1834 [Ref: J-II:1846].

LOVELESS, Elisha. Private, 1st Maryland Line, enlisted May 22, 1778 and reported dead on Jan. 16, 1779 [Ref: D-132].

LOVELESS, Ignatius. Private, Militia, 26th Battalion, Capt. Benjamin Cawood's Company, 1777 [Ref: M-162].

LOVELESS, James. Private, Militia, 26th Battalion, Capt. Benjamin Cawood's Company, 1777 [Ref: M-162].

LOVELESS, John. Two men by this name were privates in the militia in 1777: one in the 26th Battalion, Capt. Benjamin Cawood's Company, and one in the 12th Battalion, Capt. John Hanson's Company [Ref: M-159, M-162].

LOVELESS, Samuel. "Samuel Lovelass" took the Oath of Allegiance in 1778 [Ref: AA-641]. "Samuel Lovelace" was a resident of Port Tobacco East Hundred in 1778 [Ref: Q-I:297].

LOVELESS, William (1747-1815). Private, Militia, 12th Battalion, Capt. John Hanson's Company, 1777 [Ref: M-159]. Took the Oath of Allegiance in 1778 [Ref: L-18, AA-641]. Private (substitute for 9 months), 1st Maryland Line, by Sept. 11, 1778 [Ref: D-330, which listed the name as "Lovless"]. Resident of Port Tobacco East Hundred in 1778 [Ref: Q-I:297]. One "William Lovelace" was born on July 29, 1747 in Maryland, married Margery Beall, served in the Maryland and North Carolina troops, and migrated to Georgia where he died in August 1815 [Ref: J-II:1846].

LOVELIN, George. Took the Oath of Allegiance in 1778 [Ref: AA-641]. Resident of William & Mary Upper Hundred in 1778 [Ref: Q-I:297].

LOVELIN (LOVELY), William. Took the Oath of Allegiance in 1778 [Ref: AA-641, which listed the name sa "Lovelin"]. Resident of William & Mary Upper Hundred in 1778 [Ref: Q-I:297]. Private, 1st Maryland Line, drafted from the Charles County militia on July 27, 1781 [Ref: G-569, D-377, D-410, which latter sources listed the name as "Lovely, or Lovelin"]. Discharged on Dec. 3, 1781 [Ref: I-10, which listed the name as "Lovely"].

LOWRIE, John. Private, 1st Maryland Line, drafted from the Charles County militia and in service on June 11 or 12, 1781 [Ref: D-376].

LUCHIE, Charles. Private, Militia, 26th Battalion, Capt. William Winter's Company, 1777 [Ref: M-165, which listed the name as "Luchie(?)" and X-87, which listed the name as "Luckee"].

LUCKETT, Benjamin. Corporal, Militia, 12th Battalion, Capt. John Hanson's Company, 1777 [Ref: M-158]. Took the Oath of Allegiance in 1778 [Ref: AA-641]. Resident of Port Tobacco East Hundred in 1778 [Ref: Q-I:297].

LUCKETT, David. Private, Militia, Capt. Francis Mastin's Company, 26th Battalion, March 19, 1776 [Ref: M-158, K-1814]. Ensign, 1st Maryland Line, Jan. 26, 1780 [Ref: D-132].

LUCKETT, Francis Ware. Corporal, 1st Maryland Line, enlisted Dec. 10, 1776 and died April 16, 1778 [Ref: D-132].

LUCKETT, George. Took the Oath of Allegiance in 1778 [Ref: L-18]. Resident of Port Tobacco Town Hundred in 1778 [Ref: Q-I:297].

LUCKETT, Henry. Private, 1st Maryland Line, enrolled and passed on July 18, 1776 [Ref: D-32].

LUCKETT, Ignatius Jr. Private, Militia, Capt. Francis Mastin's Company, 26th Battalion, March 19, 1776 [Ref: M-158, K-1814]. "Ignatius Luckett" was a private in the Maryland Line, enrolled and passed on July 27, 1776 [Ref: D-31]. "Ignatius Luckett, Jr." took the Oath of Allegiance in 1778 [Ref: L-18]. Resident of Port Tobacco West Hundred in 1778 [Ref: Q-I:297].

LUCKETT, Ignatius Sr. (1726-1783). Took the Oath of Allegiance in 1778 [Ref: L-18, AA-641]. Aged about 46 as noted in a 1772 deposition [Ref: DD-15]. Resident of Durham Lower Hundred in 1778 [Ref: Q-I:297]. Ignatius Luckett married Margaret ---- and died before June 11, 1783 [Ref: J-II:1856]. Rendered patriotic service by providing wheat for the use of the military in November 1781 and April 1782 [Ref: N-454, N-457, N-504].

LUCKETT, Ignatius, of John. Took the Oath of Allegiance in 1778 [Ref: L-18]. Resident of Port Tobacco Town Hundred in 1778 [Ref: Q-I:297].

LUCKETT, Jannet. See "Pryor Posey," q.v.

LUCKETT, John (1726-   ). Took the Oath of Allegiance in 1778 [Ref: L-18]. Aged about 53 as noted in a 1779 deposition [Ref: BB-470, DD-16]. Resident of Port Tobacco Town Hundred in 1778 [Ref: Q-I:297].

LUCKETT, Joseph. See "William Rhody Luckett," q.v.

LUCKETT, Mary. See "Thomas Hussey Luckett," q.v.

LUCKETT, Mary Eleanor. See "Thomas Noland," q.v.

LUCKETT, Notley (1734-   ). Private, Militia, 12th Battalion, Capt. Walter Hanson's Company, 1777 [Ref: M-159, which listed the name as "Luckitt"]. Took the Oath of Allegiance in 1778 [Ref: L-18, AA-641]. Resident of Port Tobacco East Hundred in 1778 [Ref: Q-I:297]. Aged about 45 as noted in a 1779 deposition [Ref: BB-469]. See "Thomas Pickerel," q.v.

LUCKETT, Priscilla. See "John Baptist Wathen," q.v.

LUCKETT, Samuel. Sergeant, 1st Maryland Line, enlisted Dec. 10, 1776 and discharged Dec. 27, 1779 [Ref: D-132].

LUCKETT, Samuel. Sergeant, Militia, Capt. Francis Mastin's Company, 26th Battalion, March 19, 1776. Second Lieutenant, 1777 [Ref: M-158, M-163, K-1814]. Took the Oath of Allegiance in 1778 [Ref: L-18, AA-641]. Resident of Durham Lower Hundred in 1778 [Ref: Q-I:297]. Captain, Militia, commissioned on Jan. 19, 1781 [Ref: M-98, G-280]. See "Thomas Hussey Luckett" and "George Dunnington," q.v.

LUCKETT, Thomas (1724-   ). Took the Oath of Allegiance in 1778 [Ref: AA-641]. Rendered patriotic service by providing wheat for the use of the military in December 1782 [Ref: N-575]. Aged about 43 as noted in a 1767 deposition [Ref: DD-16]. Resident of Port Tobacco East Hundred in 1778 [Ref: Q-I:297]. See "Thomas Semmes" and "Thomas Hussey Luckett," q.v.

LUCKETT, Thomas Hussey. Private, Militia, 12th Battalion, Capt. Walter Hanson's Company, 1777 [Ref: M-159, which listed the name as "Luckitt"]. Took the Oath of Allegiance in 1778 [Ref: L-18]. Resident of Port Tobacco East Hundred in 1778 [Ref: Q-I:297]. Rendered patriotic service by providing wheat for the use of the military in May 1783 [Ref: N-598]. "Mary Griffin Luckett went to Washington County, Kentucky from Charles County, Maryland between 1797 and 1803. Mary Griffin was the daughter of James and Sarah Griffin, of Charles County. This is verified by the will of James Griffin (Charles County Wills, Volume AE#6, pp. 7-8, Aug. 3, 1767, CR49153 HR) in which he refers to his daughter Mary Luckett and to his wife Sarah, and the account of Sarah Griffin (Charles County Inventories & Accounts, 1776, F 329-30, CR39587 HR) in which a representative is Mary Luckett. To prove that Mary Griffin married Thomas Hussey Luckett [son of Samuel], when Thomas Luckett died Aug. 10, 1795, his children named in the certificate of "All Dispute" (Land Office, Certificates, Patented, Charles County, #62 31 July 1 [sic], 1790, MdHR 40009-62) are the same as those of Mary Luckett who died in Washington County, Kentucky in 1803. Mary Griffin Luckett died in Kentucky in 1803; her will was filed May 2, 1803 (Wills of Washington County, Kentucky, 1792-1858, Book A, page 247). All her children went to Kentucky except her son Thomas Luckett who married Mary Latimer, daughter of Marcus Latimer and Ann Cox." [Ref: Information compiled by Dorothy Murray Brault, of Rockville, Maryland, in 1997]. It appears that there were also two other men named Thomas Hussey Luckett, both of whom were from Maryland and died in Virginia: one married Elizabeth Noland and died in 1786 and the other married Eleanor Douglas and died in 1800 [Ref: J-II:1856]. Additional research will be necessary before drawing conclusions. See "William Rhody Luckett," q.v.

LUCKETT, William (1747-1820). Took the Oath of Allegiance in 1778 [Ref: L-18]. William Luckett married Clarissa Nelson and died in May 1820 [Ref: J-II:1856].

LUCKETT, William Rhody (c1720-1779). Resident of Port Tobacco Upper Hundred in 1778 [Ref: Q-I:297]. William Rhody Luckett married Mary Anne Semmes, rendered patriotic service during the war, and died testate before Feb. 9, 1779 [Ref: J-II:1856]. His sons named in his will were William Rhody Luckett, Thomas Hussey Luckett (born Nov. 25, 1770), and Joseph Luckett (born Oct. 14, 1764). [Ref: GG-276].

LUSHER, John (1750-   ). Private, 1st Maryland Line. He applied for a pension (R6527) in Carroll County, Indiana on Oct. 18, 1832, aged 82, stating he had enlisted at Port Tobacco, Maryland [Ref: V-II:2146]. *Ed. Note:* Although his pension application was rejected, it is interesting to note that there was a "John Lasher" who was a private in the 1st Maryland Line, 1779-1780 [Ref: D-132].

LYON, Henry. Second Lieutenant, Militia, 12th Battalion, Capt. John Thomas' Company, July 27, 1776 [Ref: M-99, M-161]. Took the Oath of Allegiance in 1778 [Ref: AA-641, L-18, which latter source listed the name as "Lyons"]. Resident of Benedict Hundred in 1778 [Ref: Q-I:297]. Died testate in May 1778 [Ref: GG-153].

LYON, Henry Jr. Ensign, Militia, 12th Battalion, July 5, 1777 [Ref: M-99]. Constable, Benedict Hundred, 1778 [Ref: Q-I:300, CC-709, which latter source listed the name without the "Jr."]. Appointed Inspector of Tobacco at Benedict Town on Aug. 30, 1780 [Ref: F-271]. First Lieutenant, Militia, Capt. John Gardner's Company, commissioned on Jan. 19, 1781 [Ref: M-99, G-280].

LYON, Isaac. Private (substitute for 3 years), 1st Maryland Line, by Sept. 11, 1778 [Ref: D-330].

LYON, James. Private, Militia, 12th Battalion, Capt. Henry Clarkson's Company, 1777 [Ref: M-159]. Took the Oath of Allegiance in 1778 [Ref: L-18]. Resident of Bryan Town Hundred in 1778 [Ref: Q-I:297].

LYON, John. Private, Militia, 12th Battalion, Capt. Peter Wood's Company, 1777 [Ref: M-161]. Took the Oath of Allegiance in 1778 [Ref: AA-641, L-18, which latter source listed the name as "Lyons"]. Resident of Benedict Hundred in 1778 [Ref: Q-I:297].

LYON, Joseph. Private, Militia, 12th Battalion, Capt. John Thomas' Company, 1777 [Ref: M-161]. Took the Oath of Allegiance in 1778 [Ref: L-18, which listed the name as "Lyons"]. Resident of Benedict Hundred in 1778 [Ref: Q-I:297].

LYON, Mark. Took the Oath of Allegiance in 1778 [Ref: L-18, which listed the name as "Leon"].

LYON, Walter. Private, Militia, 12th Battalion, Capt. Henry Clarkson's Company, 1777 [Ref: M-159]. Took the Oath of Allegiance in 1778 [Ref: L-18]. Resident of Bryan Town Hundred in 1778 [Ref: Q-I:297].

LYON, Zachariah. Sergeant, Militia, 12th Battalion, Capt. John Thomas' Company, 1777 [Ref: M-161]. Took the Oath of Allegiance in 1778 [Ref: AA-641, L-18, which latter source listed the name as "Lyons"]. Resident of Benedict Hundred in 1778 [Ref: Q-I:297].

MACKAY (MACKEY), John. Took the Oath of Allegiance in 1778 [Ref: AA-641]. Resident of William & Mary Upper Hundred in 1778 [Ref: Q-I:297].

MACONCHIE, William. See "William McConky," q.v.

MADDEN, John. Rendered patriotic service by providing wheat for the use of the military in December 1782 [Ref: N-577].

MADDOCKE, James. See "James Maddox," q.v.

MADDOX, Aaron. Private, 1st Maryland Line, enrolled and passed on July 25, 1776 [Ref: D-32].

MADDOX, Allison. Private, 1st Maryland Line, drafted from the Charles County militia and in service on June 11 or 12, 1781 [Ref: D-376].

MADDOX, Benjamin. Two men by this name were privates in the militia, 12th Battalion, in 1777: one in Capt. Walter Hanson's Company, and one in Capt. Francis Mastin's Company [Ref: M-159, M-164]. One took the Oath of Allegiance in 1778 [Ref: AA-641, L-18, which latter source mistakenly listed the name as "Berry Maddox"].

MADDOX, Charles. Private, Militia, 26th Battalion, Capt. Samuel Smallwood's Company, 1777 [Ref: M-165].

MADDOX, Cleon. See "John Maddox," q.v.

MADDOX, Cornelius (1730-   ). Private, Militia, 12th Battalion, Capt. Walter Hanson's Company, 1777 [Ref: M-159]. Took the Oath of Allegiance in 1778 [Ref: L-18, AA-641]. Aged about 42 as noted in a 1772 deposition [Ref: DD-16]. Resident of Port Tobacco East Hundred in 1778 [Ref: Q-I:297].

MADDOX, Elizabeth. See "Rhody Maddox," q.v.

MADDOX, Francis. Took the Oath of Allegiance in 1778 [Ref: L-18, AA-641].

MADDOX, George. Private, Militia, 12th Battalion, Capt. Jonathan Yates' Company, 1777 [Ref: X-70, but was omitted from the list in Reference M-162]. Took the Oath of Allegiance in 1778 [Ref: AA-641]. Resident of William & Mary Lower Hundred in 1778 [Ref: Q-I:297, which listed the name as "Maddocke"].

MADDOX, George. Private, Militia, 26th Battalion, Capt. Francis Mastin's Company, 1777 [Ref: M-164]. Took the Oath of Allegiance in 1778 [Ref: L-18]. Private, 1st Maryland Line, drafted from the Charles County militia to serve from July 27, 1781 to Dec. 10, 1781, he was discharged on April 6, 1782 [Ref: D-377, G-569, I-123, which latter source listed the name as "Maddux"].

MADDOX, Henry. Private, Militia, 12th Battalion, Capt. John Hanson's Company, 1777 [Ref: M-159, which listed the name as "Maddocke"]. Took the Oath of Allegiance in 1778 [Ref: L-18, which listed the name as "Maddox" and AA-641, which listed the name as "Maddocks"]. Resident of Port Tobacco East Hundred in 1778 [Ref: Q-I:297].

MADDOX, Ignatius. Private, Militia, Capt. Francis Mastin's Company, 26th Battalion, March 19, 1776 [Ref: M-158, K-1814]. Resident of Bryan Town Hundred in 1778 [Ref: Q-I:297].

MADDOX, James (1734-c1799). Took the Oath of Allegiance in 1778 [Ref: AA-641]. Aged about 45 as noted in a 1779 deposition [Ref: BB-466, DD-16, which listed the name as "Maddocke"]. Resident of Bryan Town Hundred in 1778 [Ref: Q-I:297]. James Maddox married twice (names of wives not given) and died after Nov. 26, 1798 [Ref: J-II:1875].

MADDOX, James Jr. Private, Militia, 12th Battalion, Capt. Jonathan Yates' Company, 1777 [Ref: M-162, which listed the name without the "Jr."]. Resident of Bryan Town Hundred in 1778 [Ref: Q-I:297].

MADDOX, James, of Notley. Took the Oath of Allegiance in 1778 [Ref: AA-641, which listed the name as "James Maddocke, of Notley"]. Resident of William & Mary Lower Hundred in 1778 [Ref: Q-I:297].

MADDOX, John (c1708-c1788). Rendered patriotic service by providing wheat for the use of the military in September and November 1781 [Ref: N-440, N-456]. One John Maddox married Mary Dyson and died in Virginia in October 1785 [Ref: J-II:1875]. However, a suit filed on May 10, 1808 in Charles County stated that John Maddox, Jr., died some time before June 24, 1788 in Charles County, the son of John Maddox, also deceased, of the same county. The heirs at law of John Maddox, Jr., were Joseph Maddox (administrator), Cleon Maddox (now deceased, without issue), Nancy Maddox (now deceased, wife of Isaac Brawner and mother of Polly Taylor and Betsy Brawner), and Molly Maddox. In 1810 Isaac Brawner stated that John Maddox, Jr., died before John Maddox, Sr. [Ref: HH-1997, citing Chancery Court Papers 5046]. Additional research may be necessary before drawing conclusions.

MADDOX, John (1755-1811). Private, 1st Maryland Line. He married Sarah Farnandis and died in Maryland on July 9, 1811 [Ref: J-II:1875].

MADDOX, Joseph. See "John Maddox," q.v.

MADDOX, Leonard. Took the Oath of Allegiance in 1780 [Ref: O-115].

MADDOX, Molly. See "John Maddox," q.v.

MADDOX, Nancy. See "John Maddox," q.v.

MADDOX, Nathan (c1760-1829). Private, Militia, 12th Battalion, Capt. John Thomas' Company, 1777 [Ref: M-161]. Nathan Maddox married Michel Robey and died in Ohio before Nov. 12, 1829 [Ref: J-II:1875].

MADDOX, Noah. Private, Militia, Capt. Francis Mastin's Company, 26th Battalion, March 19, 1776 [Ref: M-158, M-164, K-1814, which listed the name as "Maddocks"]. Private, 1st Maryland Line, enrolled and passed on July 27, 1776 [Ref: D-31]. Took the Oath of Allegiance in 1778 [Ref: L-18, AA-641].

MADDOX, Notley (1714-   ). Took the Oath of Allegiance in 1778 [Ref: AA-641]. Aged about 63 as noted in a 1778 deposition [Ref: CC-696]. Rendered patriotic service by providing wheat for the use of the military in February 1778 [Ref: Y-II:234]. "Notley Maddox, son of James Maddocke" *[sic]* was aged about 65 as noted in a 1779 deposition [Ref: BB-468, DD-16]. Notley Maddox was born in 1714, married (wife's name not known), and died in Maryland after Nov. 1, 1779 [Ref: J-II:1875].

MADDOX, Notley Jr. (1731-1820). Took the Oath of Allegiance in 1778 [Ref: L-18, AA-641]. Private, Militia, 12th Battalion, Capt. John Hanson's Company, 1777 [Ref: M-159, which listed the name as "Maddocke"]. Rendered patriotic service by providing clothing for the use of the military in December 1782 [Ref: N-575]. Resident of Port Tobacco East Hundred in 1778 [Ref: Q-I:297]. Notley Maddox was born on April 13, 1731 in Maryland, married Susannah Burch, served in Virginia during the war, and died in Kentucky on March 11, 1820. His children were: Mary Ann Maddox (born Jan. 4, 1759), Justinian Maddox (born Dec. 16, 1759), Sarah Maddox (born March 13, 1761), Samuel Maddox (born June 1, 1763), Susannah Maddox (born Aug. 12, 1765), Nancy Maddox (born July 7, 1770), Notley Maddox (born March 28, 1773), Elizabeth Maddox (born Dec. 19, 1775), John Maddox (born April 13, 1778), and Bennett Maddox (born May 4, 1780). [Ref: HH-1997, citing Maddox family information in Filing Case "A" at the Maryland Historical Society contributed by Mrs. Walter (Josie Mae) Matthews, of Lexington, Kentucky, a Maddox descendant, in 1920].

MADDOX, Notley Warren. Born in Maryland, married Frances Dillard, served in Virginia during the war, and died in Tennessee before Dec. 27, 1816 [Ref: J-II:1875].

MADDOX, Rhody (c1758-1828). Private, Militia, 26th Battalion, Capt. Francis Mastin's Company, 1777 [Ref: M-164]. Resident of Durham Lower Hundred in 1778 [Ref: Q-I:297]. Rhody Maddox married Elizabeth ---- and died in Maryland in 1828 [Ref: J-II:1875].

MADDOX, Richard. Took the Oath of Allegiance in 1778 [Ref: L-18, AA-641].

MADDOX, Samuel. Private, Militia, 26th Battalion, Capt. Francis Mastin's Company, 1777 [Ref: M-163, which listed the name as "Saml. Madox"].

MADDOX, Samuel (c1728-1798). Took the Oath of Allegiance in 1778 [Ref: L-18, AA-641]. Gave a deposition in 1781 pertaining to his inability to perform military service due to family obligations [Ref: Z-208]. Samuel Maddox married Lydia Turner and died in 1798 in Maryland [Ref: J-II:1875].

MADDOX, Sarah. Rendered patriotic service by providing wheat for the use of the military in April 1783 [Ref: N-593].
MADDOX, Sarah Hatch. See "Walter Hanson, of John," q.v.
MADDOX, Thomas. Private, Militia, 26th Battalion, Capt. Robert Sinnett's Company, 1777 [Ref: M-164]. Took the Oath of Allegiance in 1778 [Ref: L-18, AA-641, which listed the name as "Maddock"].
MADDOX, Townley. Private, Militia, 12th Battalion, Capt. Jonathan Yates' Company, 1777 [Ref: M-162]. Took the Oath of Allegiance in 1778 [Ref: L-18, AA-641].
MADDOX, William. Private, Militia, 12th Battalion, Capt. Jonathan Yates' Company, 1777 [Ref: M-162]. Took the Oath of Allegiance in 1778 [Ref: L-18, AA-641]. Resident of William & Mary Lower Hundred in 1778 [Ref: Q-I:297].
MADDOX, William. Private, Militia, Capt. Francis Mastin's Company, 26th Battalion, March 19, 1776 [Ref: M-158, K-1814]. Private, Militia, 26th Battalion, Capt. William Winter's Company, 1777 [Ref: M-165]. Resident of Port Tobacco East Hundred in 1778 [Ref: Q-I:297].
MADDOX, William (1725-   ). Took the Oath of Allegiance in 1778 [Ref: AA-641]. Aged about 52 as noted in a January 1776 deposition [Ref: DD-16]. Resident of Durham Lower Hundred in 1778 [Ref: Q-I:297].
MADKIN, John. See "John Mankin," q.v.
MAGRUDER, Anne. See "John Dent," q.v.
MAGRUDER, Mary Anne. See "Benjamin Murdock," q.v.
MAHOMEY (MAHORNEY), John. See "Walter Sutherland," q.v.
MAHONEY, Ignatius. Memorialist and Militiaman, Pomonkey Company, after March 6, 1776 [Ref: M-158, Y-II:26]. Sergeant, Militia, 26th Battalion, Capt. Thomas H. Marshall's Company, 1777 [Ref: M-163, which listed the name as "Igns. Mahaney"]. Took the Oath of Allegiance in 1778 [Ref: L-18]. "Ignatius McHoney" was a resident of Pomonkey Hundred in 1778 [Ref: Q-I:297].
MALONE, James. Took the Oath of Allegiance in 1778 [Ref: L-18, AA-641]. Resident of Bryan Town Hundred in 1778 [Ref: Q-I:297].
MALONE, William. Private, Militia, 12th Battalion, Capt. Benjamin Lusby Corry's Company, 1777 [Ref: M-160, which listed the name as "Milone"]. Took the Oath of Allegiance in 1778 [Ref: L-18]. Resident of Bryan Town Hundred in 1778 [Ref: Q-I:297].
MANERY, Ignatius. Private, Militia, 12th Battalion, Capt. Walter Hanson's Company, 1777 [Ref: M-159]. Took the Oath of Allegiance in 1778 [Ref: AA-641]. "Ignatius Manrey" was a resident of Port Tobacco East Hundred in 1778 [Ref: Q-I:297].

MANERY, John. Took the Oath of Allegiance in 1778 [Ref: L-18]. "John Manrey" was a resident of Port Tobacco West Hundred in 1778 [Ref: Q-I:297].

MANKIN, Charles. Private, Militia, 12th Battalion, Capt. Walter Hanson's Company, 1777 [Ref: M-159]. Took the Oath of Allegiance in 1778 [Ref: AA-641, L-18, which latter source misspelled the name as "Mankie"]. Resident of Port Tobacco East Hundred in 1778 [Ref: Q-I:297]. Served as the Auctioneer at Benedict regarding the sale of land in Calverton Manor in October 1781 [Ref: N-447]. Elected Sheriff of Charles County in October 1782 [Ref: I-294].

MANKIN, James. Private, Militia, 26th Battalion, Capt. Hezekiah Garner's Company, 1777 [Ref: M-163]. Took the Oath of Allegiance in 1780 [Ref: O-115].

MANKIN, James (1716-   ). Took the Oath of Allegiance in 1778 [Ref: L-18]. Aged about 56 as noted in a 1772 deposition [Ref: DD-17].

MANKIN, John. Two men by this name were privates in the militia, 26th Battalion, in 1777: one in Capt. Hezekiah Garner's Company, and one in Capt. Robert Sinnett's Company [Ref: M-163, M-164]. One took the Oath of Allegiance in 1780 [Ref: O-115]. John Mankin, of Durham, petitioned the Council of Maryland in 1783 stating that he had not taken the Oath of Allegiance due to any disaffection with the government, but from a variety of incidents, and was unjustly penalized as a non-juror and fined unfairly; therefore, he asked the Council to consider ordering the County Justices to remit the fines they imposed on him and others who signed the petition. The Council of Maryland, after reviewing his case, indicated they believed the truth of the facts stated in the petition and ordered a remission of the fines and penalties on Sept. 17, 1783 [Ref: I-454]. Gave a deposition in 1781 pertaining to his inability to perform military service due to family obligations [Ref: Z-208]. One "John Madkin" was a resident of Port Tobacco East Hundred in 1778 [Ref: Q-I:297].

MANKIN, Joseph. Private, Militia, 26th Battalion, Capt. Robert Sinnett's Company, 1777 [Ref: M-164]. Took the Oath of Allegiance in 1780 [Ref: O-115]. "Joseph Mankins" was a resident of Port Tobacco West Hundred in 1778 [Ref: Q-I:297].

MANKIN, Richard. Private, Militia, 26th Battalion, Capt. Robert Sinnett's Company, 1777 [Ref: M-164]. Took the Oath of Allegiance in 1778 [Ref: AA-641]. "Richard T. Mankins" was a resident of Port Tobacco West Hundred in 1778 [Ref: Q-I:297].

MANKIN, William (1725-   ). Petitioned the Council of Maryland in 1783 stating that he had not taken the Oath of Allegiance due to any disaffection with the government, but from a variety of incidents, and was

unjustly penalized as a non-juror and fined unfairly; therefore, he asked the Council to consider ordering the County Justices to remit the fines they imposed on him and others who signed the petition. The Council of Maryland, after reviewing his case, indicated they believed the truth of the facts stated in the petition and ordered a remission of the fines and penalties on Sept. 17, 1783 [Ref: I-454]. Aged about 49 as noted in a 1774 deposition and aged about 51 as noted in a January 1777 deposition [Ref: DD-17, CC-581, which also listed the name as "Mankins"].
MANN, Mary. See "John Hoskins Stone," q.v.
MANNING, John (1714-   ). Took the Oath of Allegiance in 1778 [Ref: AA-641]. Aged about 64 as noted in a 1778 deposition which mentioned his brother "Joseph Manning," q.v. [Ref: CC-701, DD-17]. Resident of Port Tobacco West Hundred in 1778 [Ref: Q-I:297]. See "Joseph Manning," q.v.
MANNING, John (c1745-1814 or 1815). Private, 1st Maryland Line. He married Susan Wimsatt and migrated to Missouri where he died in 1814 or 1815 [Ref: J-II:1887].
MANNING, Joseph (1749-c1790). Private, 1st Maryland Line, enrolled and passed on July 27, 1776 [Ref: D-31]. Private, Militia, 26th Battalion, Capt. Robert Sinnett's Company, 1777 [Ref: M-164]. Joseph Manning married Elizabeth Dunnington and died after 1790 in Maryland [Ref: J-II:1888].
MANNING Joseph (1712-   ). Took the Oath of Allegiance in 1778 [Ref: AA-641]. Aged about 48 as noted in a 1760 deposition which mentioned his father John Manning [Ref: DD-17]. Resident of Port Tobacco West Hundred in 1778 [Ref: Q-I:297]. See "John Manning," q.v.
MANNING, Mary. See "Joseph Manning Dent," q.v.
MANNING, Walter. Private, Militia, 26th Battalion, Capt. Robert Sinnett's Company, 1777 [Ref: M-164]. Took the Oath of Allegiance in 1778 [Ref: L-18]. Resident of Port Tobacco West Hundred in 1778 [Ref: Q-I:297].
MANREY, Ignatius. See "Ignatius Manery," q.v.
MARBURY, Francis H. Rendered patriotic service by providing wheat for the use of the military in May, October, and December 1782 [Ref: N-507, N-563, N-576].
MARBURY, Henry. Memorialist and Militiaman, Pomonkey Company, after March 6, 1776 [Ref: M-158, Y-II:26]. Private, Militia, 26th Battalion, Capt. Richard Bennett Mitchell's Company, 1777 [Ref: M-165]. Took the Oath of Allegiance in 1778 [Ref: L-18]. Resident of Pomonkey Hundred in 1778 [Ref: Q-I:297]. Rendered patriotic service by providing wheat for the use of the military in January 1782 [Ref: N-471].
MARBURY, Joseph (1746-   ). Captain, 3rd Maryland Line, by Jan. 11, 1780, at which time he was paid for recruiting services [Ref: F-54]. Aged about 26 as noted in a 1772 deposition [Ref: DD-17].

MARBURY, William. Took the Oath of Allegiance in 1778 [Ref: L-18]. Resident of Pomonkey Hundred in 1778 [Ref: Q-I:297]. Rendered patriotic service by providing wheat for the use of the military in December 1782 [Ref: N-576, which listed the name as "Marbry"].

MARLOW, Acton. Resident of Port Tobacco Upper Hundred in 1778 [Ref: Q-I:297]. Private, Militia, 26th Battalion, Capt. Samuel Smallwood's Company, 1777 [Ref: X-85, which listed the name as "Acton Morlore" and M-165, which listed the name as "Aiton Morlere"].

MARLOW, Butler. Resident of Port Tobacco Upper Hundred in 1778 [Ref: Q-I:297]. Took the Oath of Allegiance in Charles County in 1778 [Ref: AA-641]. Enrolled in the Maryland Line (substitute) in Prince George's County in 1781 [Ref: D-382].

MARLOW, Henry Acton. Took the Oath of Allegiance in 1778 [Ref: AA-641].

MARLOW, James. Private, Militia, 26th Battalion, Capt. Samuel Smallwood's Company, 1777 [Ref: X-85, which listed the name as "Morlore" and M-165, which listed the name as "Morlere"]. Took the Oath of Allegiance in 1778 [Ref: L-18, AA-641].

MARLOW, James Sr. Resident of Port Tobacco Upper Hundred in 1778 [Ref: Q-I:297]. Rendered patriotic service by providing wheat for the use of the military in December 1782 [Ref: N-573].

MARLOW, Richard. Private, Militia, 26th Battalion, Capt. Samuel Smallwood's Company, 1777 [Ref: M-165, which listed the name as "Marlor"]. Took the Oath of Allegiance in 1778 [Ref: L-18].

MARLOW, William. Resident of Port Tobacco Upper Hundred in 1778 [Ref: Q-I:297]. Took the Oath of Allegiance in Charles County in 1778 [Ref: L-18]. Another William Marlow, aged 16, enrolled in the Maryland Line in Prince George's County in 1781 [Ref: D-381].

MARR, Daniel. Private, Militia, 26th Battalion, Capt. Francis Mastin's Company, 1777 [Ref: M-164].

MARR, John. Private, Militia, 26th Battalion, Capt. Francis Mastin's Company, 1777 [Ref: M-164].

MARR, Martin. Petitioned the Council of Maryland in 1783 stating that he had not taken the Oath of Allegiance due to any disaffection with the government, but from a variety of incidents, and was unjustly penalized as a non-juror and fined unfairly; therefore, he asked the Council to consider ordering the County Justices to remit the fines they imposed on him and others who signed the petition. The Council of Maryland, after reviewing his case, indicated they believed the truth of the facts stated in the petition and ordered a remission of the fines and penalties on Sept. 17, 1783 [Ref: I-454].

MARSHALL, Ann. See "Thomas Hanson Marshall," q.v.

MARSHALL, Benjamin. Rendered patriotic service by providing wheat for the use of the military in December 1782 [Ref: N-577]. Took the Oath of Allegiance in 1778 [Ref: AA-641, L-18, which latter source mistakenly listed the name as "Berry Marshall"]. Resident of Newport West Hundred in 1778 [Ref: Q-I:297].

MARSHALL, Elizabeth. See "Samuel Hanson, Jr." and "Thomas Hanson Marshall," q.v.

MARSHALL, George. See "Thomas Hanson Marshall," q.v.

MARSHALL, John (1726-1802). Captain, Militia, 1775, and First Major, 12th Battalion, Jan. 6, 1776 [Ref: M-101, Y-II:23]. Rendered patriotic service by providing clothing for the use of the military in February 1778 [Ref: Y-II:234]. Took the Oath of Allegiance in 1778 [Ref: AA-641, L-18]. Resident of William & Mary Upper Hundred in 1778 [Ref: Q-I:297]. Rendered patriotic service by providing wheat for the use of the military in October 1781 and October 1782 [Ref: N-451, N-559]. John Marshall was born in 1726, married (wife's name not known), served as a major in the war, and died in 1802 [Ref: J-II:1901].

MARSHALL, John. Private, Militia, 26th Battalion, Capt. Thomas H. Marshall's Company, 1777 [Ref: M-163]. Resident of Pomonkey Hundred in 1778 [Ref: Q-I:297].

MARSHALL, Mary. See "Thomas Hanson Marshall," q.v.

MARSHALL, Philip. Ensign, Militia, 12th Battalion, Capt. Benjamin Philpott's Company, Feb. 26, 1776 [Ref: M-101, Y-II:23]. Took the Oath of Allegiance in 1778 [Ref: AA-641]. Resident of William & Mary Upper Hundred in 1778 [Ref: Q-I:297].

MARSHALL, Richard. Private, Militia, 26th Battalion, Capt. Robert Sinnett's Company, 1777 [Ref: M-164]. Took the Oath of Allegiance in 1778 [Ref: AA-641]. Resident of William & Mary Upper Hundred in 1778 [Ref: Q-I:297]. Rendered patriotic service by providing wheat for the use of the military in October 1782 [Ref: N-559].

MARSHALL, Robert. Took the Oath of Allegiance in 1778 [Ref: L-18]. Resident of William & Mary Upper Hundred in 1778 [Ref: Q-I:297].

MARSHALL, Samuel. Took the Oath of Allegiance in 1778 [Ref: L-18].

MARSHALL, Sarah. See "John Dent" and "George Dent, of John" and "William Marshall Wilkinson," q.v.

MARSHALL, Thomas. Took the Oath of Allegiance in 1778 [Ref: L-18]. Resident of William & Mary Upper Hundred in 1778 [Ref: Q-I:297].

MARSHALL, Thomas. Rendered patriotic service by providing wheat for the use of the military in October 1782 [Ref: N-563]. Resident of

Pomonkey Hundred in 1778 [Ref: Q-I:297]. See "Thomas Hanson Marshall," q.v.

MARSHALL, Thomas Hanson (1731-1801). Son of Thomas Marshall and Elizabeth Batie, he married Rebecca Dent in 1756 and had these children: Dr. Thomas Marshall (1757-1829, and was blinded in the Revolutionary War); George Dent Marshall (1763-1764); George Hanson Marshall (1770-1775); Ann Marshall (1759-1789, and married Dr. Benjamin Fendall); Elizabeth Marshall (married first to John Forbes and second to Samuel Bond); and, Mary Marshall (1767-1789, and married Gen. Philip Stuart of Virginia). Thomas served as a Court Justice in Prince George's County, 1764-1769, and on the Committee of Observation in 1774. Attended the Maryland Convention as a representative of Charles County in 1775. Judge of the Court of Appeals for Tax Assessment in Charles County, 1786. Captain, Militia, Pomonkey Company, 26th Battalion, Charles County, 1776 [Ref: P-II:575, P-II:576, A-186, A-206, M-101, M-158, Y-II:26, M-163, Y-II:23]. Rendered patriotic service by providing clothing for the use of the military in January 1778 [Ref: Y-II:230]. Took the Oath of Allegiance in 1778 [Ref: L-18]. Resident of Pomonkey Hundred in 1778 [Ref: Q-I:297]. Rendered patriotic service by providing wheat for the use of the military in April 1782 [Ref: N-498]. Thomas Hanson Marshall was born on April 9, 1731 and died on March 8, 1801 [Ref: J-II:1902].

MARSHALL, Thomas, of Richard. Took the Oath of Allegiance in 1778 [Ref: AA-641].

MARSHALL, Thomas, of Thomas. Private, Militia, 26th Battalion, Capt. Thomas H. Marshall's Company, 1777 [Ref: M-163]. See "Thomas Hanson Marshall," q.v.

MARSHALL, William. Private, Militia, 12th Battalion, Capt. John Hanson's Company, 1777 [Ref: M-159]. Rendered patriotic service by providing clothing for the use of the military in February 1778 [Ref: Y-II:234]. Took the Oath of Allegiance in 1778 [Ref: AA-641, L-18, which mistakenly listed the name as "Marstell"]. Resident of Port Tobacco East Hundred in 1778 [Ref: Q-I:297].

MARSHALL, William (1735-1793). Took the Oath of Allegiance in 1778 [Ref: AA-641]. Resident of William & Mary Upper Hundred in 1778 [Ref: Q-I:297]. Rendered patriotic service by providing wheat for the use of the military in December 1782 [Ref: N-573]. William Marshall was born in March 1735, married Susan Whitler, and died in 1793 [Ref: J-II:1903].

MARSTON, Osborn. Took the Oath of Allegiance in 1778 [Ref: L-18].

MARTIN, Francis. Took the Oath of Allegiance in 1778 [Ref: AA-641, L-18]. Resident of William & Mary Upper Hundred in 1778 [Ref: Q-I:297].

MARTIN, Huse. See "Huse Mastin," q.v.

MARTIN, Ignatius. Private, 1st Maryland Line, enrolled and passed on July 8, 1776 [Ref: D-32].
MARTIN, John. See "Michael Martin," q.v.
MARTIN, Leonard. Private, Militia, 12th Battalion, Capt. John Hanson's Company, 1777 [Ref: M-159]. Private (drafted and joined the army), 1st Maryland Line, by Sept. 11, 1778 [Ref: D-330]. Resident of Port Tobacco East Hundred in 1778 [Ref: Q-I:297].
MARTIN, Michael. Private, Militia, 12th Battalion, Capt. John Hanson's Company, 1777 [Ref: M-159]. Resident of Port Tobacco East Hundred in 1778 [Ref: Q-I:297].
MARTIN, Michael (1712-   ). Took the Oath of Allegiance in 1778 [Ref: AA-641, L-18, which latter source misspelled the name as "Masters"]. Aged about 59 as noted in a 1771 deposition which mentioned his father John Martin [Ref: DD-17].
MARTIN, Robert. "Robert Martin" was a private in the militia, 26th Battalion, Capt. William Winter's Company, 1777 [Ref: M-165, which listed the name as "Martain"]. "Robert Mastin" was a resident of Durham Lower Hundred in 1778 [Ref: Q-I:297].
MARTIN, Zachariah. Private, Militia, 26th Battalion, Capt. Hezekiah Garner's Company, 1777 [Ref: M-162]. Took the Oath of Allegiance in 1778 [Ref: AA-641]. Rendered patriotic service by providing wheat for the use of the military in July 1782 [Ref: N-531].
MARTINDALE, John (1756-   ). Private (substitute for 3 years), 1st Maryland Line, by Sept. 11, 1778 [Ref: D-330]. Took the Oath of Allegiance in 1778 [Ref: L-18, AA-641]. Resident of William & Mary Lower Hundred in 1778 [Ref: Q-I:297, which listed the name as "Martingdale"]. Drummer, 2nd Company, 1st Maryland Line, Capt. Edward Prall's Company, Jan. 1, 1782 [Ref: D-431]. Fifer, 1st Maryland Line, Col. John H. Stone's Regiment. Burned on the left hand at the Battle of James Island on Feb. 28, 1783. Invalid (disability) pension commenced on Nov. 15, 1783, aged 27, and he was still on pension as of Aug. 15, 1789 [Ref: D-629].
MASON, Andrew. Took the Oath of Allegiance in 1778 [Ref: L-18].
MASON, Andrew Sr. Took the Oath of Allegiance in 1778 [Ref: L-18].
MASON, Elizabeth. See "Daniel Jenifer" and "Daniel of St. Thomas Jenifer" and "Philip Briscoe," q.v.
MASON, George (Colonel). Rendered patriotic service by providing wheat for the use of the military in July, November, and December 1782 [Ref: N-531, N-568, N-576].
MASON, Ignatius. Took the Oath of Allegiance in 1778 [Ref: L-18].
MASON, Lott. Took the Oath of Allegiance in 1778 [Ref: AA-641].

MASON, Richard. Resident of Newport West Hundred in 1778 [Ref: Q-I:297]. Rendered patriotic service by providing wheat for the use of the military in December 1782 [Ref: N-575].

MASON, William (Captain). Rendered patriotic service by providing wheat for the use of the military in October and December 1782 [Ref: N-563, N-575].

MASON, William (Colonel). Rendered patriotic service by providing wheat for the use of the military in May 1783 [Ref: N-597].

MASSEY, Margaret. See "Francis Speake," q.v.

MASTERS, Michael. See "Michael Martin," q.v.

MASTIN, Alexander. Took the Oath of Allegiance in 1778 [Ref: AA-641, L-18, which latter source listed the name as "Masten"]. Resident of Durham Lower Hundred in 1778 [Ref: Q-I:297].

MASTIN, Elizabeth. Rendered patriotic service by providing clothing for the use of the military in January 1778 [Ref: Y-II:230].

MASTIN, Francis. Captain, Militia, 26th Battalion, from March 19, 1776 to Jan. 19, 1781 [Ref: A-426, G-280, M-101, M-158, M-163, K-1814]. Resident of Durham Lower Hundred in 1778 [Ref: Q-I:297]. Rendered patriotic service by providing clothing for the use of the military in February 1778 [Ref: Y-II:234].

MASTIN, Huse. "Huse Mastin" took the Oath of Allegiance in 1778 [Ref: AA-641]. "Huse Martin" was a resident of William & Mary Upper Hundred in 1778 [Ref: Q-I:297].

MASTIN, Leonard. Took the Oath of Allegiance in 1778 [Ref: AA-641, L-18, which latter source listed the name as "Mastten"].

MASTIN, Robert. See "Robert Martin," q.v.

MASTIN, Sarah (1713-   ). Rendered patriotic service by providing wheat for the use of the military in July 1782 [Ref: N-531, which listed the name as "Masten"]. Aged about 40 as noted in a 1753 deposition [Ref: DD-18].

MATTHEWS, Catherine. See "Samuel Amery," q.v.

MATTHEWS, Elizabeth. See "Thomas Matthews" and "Thomas Reed Cooksey," q.v.

MATTHEWS, Ignatius (Reverend). On July 30, 1782, the Council of Maryland ordered "that the Treasurer pay to Revd. Ignatius Matthews six thousand six hundred and fifty six pounds nett Tobacco in Nanjemoy or any other Warehouse in Charles County due him for Tobacco lent the State in 1780 per Certificate adjusted and passed." [Ref: I-225]. Rendered patriotic service by providing wheat for the use of the military in May and September 1781, April, September, and December 1782, and May 1783 [Ref: N-400, N-437, N-498, N-503, N-548, N-576, N-597].

MATTHEWS, James. Private, Militia, 12th Battalion, Capt. Henry Clarkson's Company, 1777 [Ref: M-159, which listed the name as "Matthew"]. Took the Oath of Allegiance in 1778 [Ref: L-18, AA-641]. Resident of Newport East Hundred in 1778 [Ref: Q-I:297]. Gave a deposition in 1781 pertaining to his inability to perform military service due to family obligations and financial responsibilities [Ref: Z-208].
MATTHEWS, Jane. Rendered patriotic service by providing clothing for the use of the military in February 1778 [Ref: Y-II:234].
MATTHEWS, John. Assisted the Purchaser of Clothing in Charles County in February 1778 [Ref: Y-II:235].
MATTHEWS, Joseph. Private, Militia, 12th Battalion, Capt. Walter Hanson's Company, 1777 [Ref: M-159]. Took the Oath of Allegiance in 1778 [Ref: AA-641]. Resident of Port Tobacco East Hundred in 1778 [Ref: Q-I:297].
MATTHEWS, Josie Mae. See "Notley Maddox, Jr.," q.v.
MATTHEWS, Luke Francis. See "Gerard Blackstone Causin," q.v.
MATTHEWS, Martha. Rendered patriotic service by providing clothing for the use of the military in February 1778 [Ref: Y-II:234].
MATTHEWS, Mary. Rendered patriotic service by providing wheat for the use of the military in April and December 1782 [Ref: N-503, N-576]. See "Benjamin Burch," q.v.
MATTHEWS, Thomas (1755-1796). Born on June 3, 1755, son of William and Elizabeth Matthews, he married Anne Poston on Dec. 24, 1780 in Trinity Parish and died on Dec. 25, 1796 [Ref: EE-8, EE-18, J-II:1924]. Sergeant, Militia, 12th Battalion, Capt. Benjamin Lusby Corry's Company, 1777 [Ref: M-160]. Took the Oath of Allegiance in 1778 [Ref: L-18]. Resident of Newport West Hundred in 1778 [Ref: Q-I:297].
MATTHEWS, Walter. See "Notley Maddox, Jr.," q.v.
MATTHEWS, William. See "Thomas Matthews," q.v.
MATTINGLY, Ann. See "William Gardiner," q.v.
MATTINGLY, Charles. Private, 3rd Maryland Line, enrolled by Capt. Joseph Marbury by May 24, 1780 [Ref: F-181, which listed the name as "Mattenly"].
MATTINGLY, Zachariah. Private, Militia, 12th Battalion, Capt. John Parnham's Company, 1777 [Ref: M-161]. Took the Oath of Allegiance in 1778 [Ref: AA-641]. Resident of Newport East Hundred in 1778 [Ref: Q-I:297].
MAXWELL, Elizabeth. Rendered patriotic service by providing clothing for the use of the military in February 1778 [Ref: Y-II:234].
MAY, Richard. Private, Militia, 12th Battalion, Capt. Jonathan Yates' Company, 1777 [Ref: M-162]. Private (furnished by class for 9 months),

1st Maryland Line, by Sept. 11, 1778 [Ref: D-330]. Took the Oath of Allegiance in 1778 [Ref: AA-641, L-18, which latter source misspelled the name as "Reid May"].
MAY, William. Private, Militia, 26th Battalion, Capt. Hezekiah Garner's Company, 1777 [Ref: M-162].
MAYHEW, Henry. Private, Militia, 12th Battalion, Capt. John Thomas' Company, 1777 [Ref: M-161].
MAYHEW, Thomas. Private (furnished by class for 9 months), 1st Maryland Line, by Sept. 11, 1778 [Ref: D-330, which listed the name as "Mahew"]. Private, 1st Maryland Line, enlisted Dec. 10, 1776 and "Exchd. for L. Hickey" [Ref: D-137].
McATEE, Edmond. Private, Militia, 26th Battalion, Capt. William Winter's Company, 1777 [Ref: M-165]. Took the Oath of Allegiance in 1778 [Ref: L-18, AA-641, which listed the name as "Macatee"]. Resident of Durham Lower Hundred in 1778 [Ref: Q-I:297]. See "Thomas McAtee," q.v.
McATEE, Elizabeth. Rendered patriotic service by providing wheat for the use of the military in April 1783 [Ref: N-593].
McATEE, George. Sergeant, Militia, 26th Battalion, Capt. William McPherson's Company, 1777 [Ref: M-163]. Took the Oath of Allegiance in 1778 [Ref: AA-641, L-18, which listed the name as "Macatee"]. Resident of Port Tobacco Upper Hundred in 1778 [Ref: Q-I:297].
McATEE, Henry. Two men by this name were privates in the militia, 26th Battalion, in 1777: one in Capt. Richard Bennett Mitchell's Company (who was listed as an invalid (disabled) soldier), and one in Capt. William McPherson's Company [Ref: M-163, M-165]. One took the Oath of Allegiance in 1778 [Ref: L-18]. One "Henry Macatee" was aged about 45 as noted in a 1777 deposition [Ref: DD-16]. Resident of Pomonkey Hundred in 1778 [Ref: Q-I:297]. See "Henry McAtee, Jr.," q.v.
McATEE, Henry Jr. Took the Oath of Allegiance in 1778 [Ref: AA-641]. Resident of Port Tobacco Upper Hundred in 1778 [Ref: Q-I:297]. See "Henry McAtee," q.v.
McATEE, Henry, of James. Private, Militia, 26th Battalion, Capt. Samuel Smallwood's Company, 1777 [Ref: M-165].
McATEE, James. Private, Militia, 26th Battalion, Capt. William McPherson's Company, 1777 [Ref: M-163]. Resident of Port Tobacco Upper Hundred in 1778 [Ref: Q-I:297]. See "Thomas McAtee," q.v.
McATEE, James, of James. Took the Oath of Allegiance in 1778 [Ref: AA-641, L-18, which latter source listed the name as "Macatee"].
McATEE, James, of Patrick. Took the Oath of Allegiance in 1778 [Ref: AA-641, L-18, which latter source listed the name as "Macatee"]. Resident of Port Tobacco Upper Hundred in 1778 [Ref: Q-I:297].

McATEE, John (1706-   ). Took the Oath of Allegiance in 1778 [Ref: L-18]. Aged about 72 as noted in a 1778 deposition [Ref: CC-699, DD-18, which listed the name as "McCatee"]. Rendered patriotic service by providing wheat for the use of the military in September and December 1782 [Ref: N-556, N-576, which listed the name as "Macatee"].

McATEE, John Jr. (1731-   ). Private, Militia, 26th Battalion, Capt. William McPherson's Company, 1777 [Ref: M-163, which listed the name without the "Jr."]. Took the Oath of Allegiance in 1778 [Ref: AA-641]. Aged 46 in a 1777 deposition [Ref: CC-581, which listed the name as "Macattee"]. Resident of Port Tobacco Upper Hundred in 1778 [Ref: Q-I:297].

McATEE, Samuel. Memorialist and Militiaman, Pomonkey Company, after March 6, 1776 [Ref: M-158, Y-II:26, which listed the name as "Maccattee"].

McATEE, Thomas (1735/6-   ). Recommended to be Second Lieutenant, Militia, Capt. Thomas H. Marshall's Company, Feb. 26, 1776, but was not selected [Ref: Y-II:23, which listed the name as "McAtie"]. First Sergeant, Militia, 12th Battalion, Capt. John Thomas' Company, 1776, and then promoted to Second Lieutenant [Ref: M-161, which listed the name as "McAtee," and Y-II:26 which listed the name as "Macattee"]. Took the Oath of Allegiance in 1778 [Ref: L-18, AA-641]. Rendered patriotic service by providing wheat for the use of the military in November 1781 [Ref: N-455]. Aged about 35 or 36 as noted in a 1772 deposition which mentioned his father Edmond (deceased), brother William, and uncle James McAtee [Ref: DD-18]. Resident of Pomonkey Hundred in 1778 [Ref: Q-I:297].

McATEE, Walter (1755-   ). Private, Flying Camp, Capt. Bowie's Company, enrolled July 17, 1776; native of Charles County, aged 21, height 6' 1/4" [Ref: D-36]. Took the Oath of Allegiance in 1778 [Ref: AA-641]. Resident of Port Tobacco Upper Hundred in 1778 [Ref: Q-I:297]. Rendered patriotic service by providing wheat for the use of the military in December 1782 and May 1783 [Ref: N-577, N-597].

McATEE, William. Private, Militia, 26th Battalion, Capt. William McPherson's Company, 1777 [Ref: M-163]. See "Thomas McAtee," q.v.

McATEE, William Sr. Took the Oath of Allegiance in 1778 [Ref: AA-641, L-18, which latter source listed the name as "Macatee"]. Resident of Port Tobacco East Hundred in 1778 [Ref: Q-I:297].

McBANE, William. Took the Oath of Allegiance in 1778 [Ref: L-18]. Resident of Port Tobacco West Hundred in 1778 [Ref: Q-I:297, which listed the name as "McBayne"].

McCANN, Francis. Private, 1st Maryland Line, drafted from the Charles County militia and in service on June 11 or 12, 1781 [Ref: D-376, G-569, which listed the name as "McCan"].

McCANN, Joseph. Private, 1st Maryland Line, enrolled and passed on July 25, 1776 [Ref: D-32, which listed the name as "Mcant"].
McCANN, Thomas. Private, 1st Maryland Line, enrolled and passed on July 8, 1776 [Ref: D-32, which listed the name as "Maccan"]. Private, Militia, 12th Battalion, Capt. Benjamin Lusby Corry's Company, 1777 [Ref: M-160]. Took the Oath of Allegiance in 1778 [Ref: L-18]. Resident of Newport West Hundred in 1778 [Ref: Q-I:297, which listed the name as "Mecan"].
McCAY, Hugh. See "Hugh McCoy," q.v.
McCAY, John. See "John McCoy," q.v.
McCLAIN, John. Private, Militia, 12th Battalion, Capt. John Thomas' Company, 1777 [Ref: M-161]. On April 15, 1780, General William Smallwood wrote to Governor Lee: "Sir, This will be addressed by Serjeant MacLain who has inlisted four fine Fellows for Soldiers all Natives, who he carries up to Annapolis to get cloathed & to obtain Blankets if possible for himself and them, complaining he has been obliged to give four Dollars per night for lodging for each oftentimes for want of Blankets, you will therefore be so obliging to order their Cloathing and by all means Blankets if to be had, as they will be very essential for the Recruits. You will also please order the Serjeant to be dispatched as soon as possible, as there is a prospect of his enlisting more men, for which purpose it wou'd be necessary to order him a further supply of Money, with which he may be trusted." [Ref: F-471, F-472]. "John McLean" was a resident of Benedict Hundred in 1778 [Ref: Q-I:297].
McCLANAHAN, Agnes. See "Samuel Elgin," q.v.
McCONCHIE, William. Second Lieutenant, Militia, 26th Battalion, Capt. Robert Sinnett's Company, from Feb. 26, 1776 through at least Oct. 17, 1777 [Ref: M-102 and M-164 listed the name as "Maconchie," A-206 listed the name as "McConchie," C-399 listed the name as "McCondree," and Y-II:23 listed the name as "McConhie"]. Took the Oath of Allegiance in 1778 [Ref: AA-641, which listed the name as "McConchie"]. Rendered patriotic service by providing wheat for the use of the military in October 1782 [Ref: N-558, which listed the name as "McConky"].
McCOY, Hugh. Private, Militia, 26th Battalion, Capt. Robert Sinnett's Company, 1777 [Ref: M-164]. Took the Oath of Allegiance in 1778 [Ref: AA-641, which listed the name as "MacCoy" and L-18, which misspelled the name as "McCary"]. Resident of Port Tobacco West Hundred in 1778 [Ref: Q-I:297, which listed the name as "McCay"].
McCOY, John (1700-   ). Took the Oath of Allegiance in 1778 [Ref: L-18, AA-641]. Aged about 52 as noted in a 1752 deposition [Ref: DD-18]. One John McCay (or McCoy?) was a resident of Port Tobacco West Hundred

and another was a resident of Port Tobacco Upper Hundred in 1778 [Ref: Q-I:297].

McCOY, Johnson. Private, Militia, 26th Battalion, Capt. Robert Sinnett's Company, 1777 [Ref: M-164]. Took the Oath of Allegiance in 1778 [Ref: AA-641, which listed the name as "Macoy" and L-18, which listed the name as "Johnston McKay"].

McCRAE (MACRAE, McCRAY), Jesse. Private, Militia, 12th Battalion, Capt. John Hanson's Company, 1777 [Ref: M-158].

McCRAE (McRAE, McCRAY), Philip. "Philip McCrae" (or McRae) took the Oath of Allegiance in 1778 [Ref: AA-641, L-18]. "Philip McCray" was a resident of Port Tobacco East Hundred in 1778 [Ref: Q-I:297].

McCURDY, D. See "Jeremiah Mudd," q.v.

McCURDY, Mary. See "Jeremiah Mudd," q.v.

McDANIEL, Allen (Allan). Private, Militia, 12th Battalion, Capt. John Hanson's Company, 1777 [Ref: M-159]. Took the Oath of Allegiance in 1778 [Ref: AA-641, L-18, which latter source listed the name as "MacDonald"].

McDANIEL, Daniel. Private, Militia, 12th Battalion, Capt. John Hanson's Company, 1777 [Ref: M-158]. "Daniel McDaniel" took the Oath of Allegiance in 1778 [Ref: AA-641]. "Daniel McDonald" was a resident of Port Tobacco East Hundred in 1778 [Ref: Q-I:297].

McDANIEL, Isaac. Private, Militia, 12th Battalion, Capt. John Hanson's Company, 1777 [Ref: M-159]. Took the Oath of Allegiance in 1778 [Ref: L-18]. "Isaac McDonald" was a resident of Port Tobacco East Hundred in 1778 [Ref: Q-I:297].

McDANIEL, James. Private, 1st Maryland Line, drafted from the Charles County militia on July 27, 1781 [Ref: D-377].

McDANIEL, Jonathan. "Jonathan McDaniel" was a private in the militia, 26th Battalion, Capt. Benjamin Cawood's Company, 1777 [Ref: M-162]. "Jonathan McDonald" was a resident of Port Tobacco East Hundred in 1778 [Ref: Q-I:297].

McDANIEL, Patrick. Resident of Durham Lower Hundred in 1778 [Ref: Q-I:297]. Took the Oath of Allegiance in 1778 [Ref: AA-641, which listed the name as "McDonald" and L-18, which listed the name as "MacDonald"].

McDANIEL, Thomas. Ensign, Militia, 26th Battalion, Capt. Benjamin Cawood's Company, 1777 [Ref: M-162].

McDANIEL, Zachariah. "Zachariah McDaniel" was a private in the militia, 26th Battalion, Capt. Robert Sinnett's Company, 1777 [Ref: M-164]. "Zachariah McDonald" was a resident of Port Tobacco West Hundred in 1778 [Ref: Q-I:297].

McDAVIS, James. Private, Militia, 26th Battalion, Capt. Francis Mastin's Company, 1777 [Ref: M-164].

McDOLAND, James. Private, Militia, 26th Battalion, Capt. Francis Mastin's Company, 1777 [Ref: M-164].

McDONALD, Alexander. Private, Militia, 26th Battalion, Capt. Thomas H. Marshall's Company, 1777 [Ref: M-163, which listed the name as "Alex. Mcdonold"]. Took the Oath of Allegiance in 1778 [Ref: L-18].

McDONALD, Charles. Private, 1st Maryland Line, drafted from the Charles County militia on July 27, 1781 [Ref: D-377, G-569].

McDONALD, Jonathan. Took the Oath of Allegiance in 1778 [Ref: AA-641]. See "Jonathan McDaniel," q.v.

McDONALD, Milly. See "Samuel Carrington," q.v.

McDONALD, Patrick. See "Patrick McDaniel," q.v.

McDONALD, Zachariah. Took the Oath of Allegiance in 1778 [Ref: L-18]. Rendered patriotic service by providing wheat for the use of the military in April 1783 [Ref: N-594, which listed the name as "Zacariah McDonal"]. See "Zachariah McDaniel," q.v.

McDONOGHT, Morris James. Private, Militia, 26th Battalion, Capt. Robert Sinnett's Company, 1777 [Ref: M-164, which listed the name as "Morris Jas. McDon..." and X-80, which listed the name as "Morris James McDono"]. Took the Oath of Allegiance in 1778 [Ref: L-18, which listed the name as "Morris James McDonoght" and AA-641, which listed the name as "Morris James McDonogh"]. Rendered patriotic service by providing wheat for the use of the military in December 1782 [Ref: N-575, which listed the name as "Morris J. McDonnow"]. "M. James McDono" was a resident of Port Tobacco West Hundred in 1778 [Ref: Q-I:297].

McGACHANON, James. Private, Militia, 26th Battalion, Capt. Francis Mastin's Company, 1777 [Ref: M-164, which listed the name as "James McGachanon(?)" and X-78, which listed the name as "Jamise McCactanon"].

McGLEW, Patrick. Private, Militia, 12th Battalion, Capt. John Parnham's Company, 1777 [Ref: M-161]. Took the Oath of Allegiance in 1778 [Ref: AA-641]. "Patrick McGlue" was a resident of Newport East Hundred in 1778 [Ref: Q-I:297].

McGREGOR, Ann. See "Hezekiah Dunnington," q.v.

McHONEY, Ignatius. See "Ignatius Mahoney," q.v.

McINTIRE, William. Took the Oath of Allegiance in 1778 [Ref: L-18, which listed the name as "Maccontire"].

McKAY, Mary. See "Stephen Penn," q.v.

McLAMAR, Dennis. Rendered patriotic service by providing wheat for the use of the military in April 1783 [Ref: N-593]. Took the Oath of Allegiance in 1778 [Ref: AA-641, which listed the name as "McLemar" and L-18, which mistakenly listed the name as "McLenian"]. Resident of Port Tobacco Upper Hundred in 1778 [Ref: Q-I:297].

McLAMAR, Elizabeth. See "Henry Miles," q.v.

McLANNON, John. Took the Oath of Allegiance in 1778 [Ref: L-18, AA-641, which listed the name as "McLannan"].

McLEAN, James. Private, Militia, 26th Battalion, Capt. William Winter's Company, 1777 [Ref: M-165].

McLEAN, John. See "John McClain," q.v.

McLEAN, William. Private, Militia, 26th Battalion, Capt. William Winter's Company, 1777 [Ref: M-165].

McMILLAN, William. Took the Oath of Allegiance in 1778 [Ref: AA-641, which listed the name as "Mackmillion"].

McNESS, George. Private, 1st Maryland Line, drafted from the Charles County militia on July 27, 1781 and discharged on Dec. 8, 1781 [Ref: D-377, I-17, which also listed the name as "McNass"].

McPHERSON, Alexander (1738-1805). Son of William McPherson and Barbara Acton, he married Mary Weems in 1776 and had eight children, viz., Alexander McPherson, John Weems McPherson, Mary Ann McPherson (married John Adams, Jr.), Sarah McPherson, Elizabeth McPherson, Eartheldry McPherson, Rachel McPherson, and Catherine McPherson. Alexander served in the Lower House of the Maryland Legislature, 1777-1778, as County Coroner, 1773, a Court Justice, 1787-1805, and Commissioner of the Tax, 1793-1798 [Ref: P-II:591]. Captain, Militia, 12th Battalion, from July 26, 1776 to Feb. 9, 1781 [Ref: M-103, M-160, G-307, B-125, C-403]. Resident of Bryan Town Hundred in 1778 [Ref: Q-I:297]. Alexander McPherson was born in August 1738, married Mary Weems, and died on Aug. 27, 1805 [Ref: J-II:1985]. See "Mark McPherson" and "John McPherson," q.v.

McPHERSON, Basil. Took the Oath of Allegiance in 1778 [Ref: AA-641, L-18, which latter source listed the name as "Mac Pherson"]. Resident of Port Tobacco West Hundred in 1778 [Ref: Q-I:297]. Rendered patriotic service by providing wheat for the use of the military in April 1783 [Ref: N-593].

McPHERSON, Catherine. See "Alexander McPherson," q.v.

McPHERSON, Chloe. Rendered patriotic service by providing wheat for the use of the military in September 1782 [Ref: N-556].

McPHERSON, Daniel. Private, Militia, 26th Battalion, Capt. William McPherson's Company, 1777 [Ref: M-163]. Took the Oath of Allegiance in 1778 [Ref: L-18, AA-641]. Resident of Durham Lower Hundred in 1778 [Ref: Q-I:297]. Rendered patriotic service by providing wheat for the use of the military in September 1781, February 1782, and April and May 1783 [Ref: N-435, N-593, N-598, I-81].

McPHERSON, Daniel Jr. Took the Oath of Allegiance in 1778 [Ref: AA-641]. Resident of Port Tobacco West Hundred in 1778 [Ref: Q-I:297].

McPHERSON, Eartheldry. See "Alexander McPherson," q.v.

McPHERSON, Elizabeth. See "Samuel Hanson, Jr." and "Thomas Cooksey" and "Alexander McPherson," q.v.

McPHERSON, Henry. See "Mark McPherson," q.v.

McPHERSON, John. Took the Oath of Allegiance in 1778 [Ref: L-18, AA-641]. Resident of Port Tobacco Upper Hundred in 1778 [Ref: Q-I:297]. See the other "John McPherson," q.v.

McPHERSON, John. Took the Oath of Allegiance in 1778 [Ref: L-18, AA-641]. Rendered patriotic service by providing wheat for the use of the military in October 1781 [Ref: N-451]. One John McPherson was aged about 62 as noted in a 1776 deposition and aged about 49 as noted in a 1765 deposition which mentioned his father Alexander McPherson [Ref: DD-19]. One John McPherson was born on April 5, 1742, son of William and Elinor McPherson, of Trinity Parish [Ref: EE-11]. One John McPherson was a resident of Port Tobacco West Hundred in 1778 [Ref: Q-I:297]. One John McPherson "died on March 19, 1785, aged between 50 and 60. While on his way to his residence near Benedict, his horse ran against a tree." Also, a Col. John McPherson died in Frederick Town in December 1829 [Ref: FF-120]. Additional will be necessary before drawing conclusions. See "John McPherson, Jr.," q.v.

McPHERSON, John Jr. Rendered patriotic service by providing clothing for the use of the military in January 1778 [Ref: Y-II:230]. Took the Oath of Allegiance in 1778 [Ref: L-18, AA-641]. Resident of Port Tobacco West Hundred in 1778 [Ref: Q-I:297]. Rendered patriotic service by providing wheat for the use of the military in December 1781 [Ref: N-462]. See "John McPherson," q.v.

McPHERSON, John B. See "Mark McPherson," q.v.

McPHERSON, John Weems. See "Alexander McPherson," q.v.

McPHERSON, Lydia. See "Mark McPherson," q.v.

McPHERSON, Mark (1754-1847). Private, 1st Maryland Line, March 6, 1776. Sergeant, 1st Maryland Line, Dec. 10, 1776. Discharged on Dec. 27, 1779. Commissioned an ensign by Aug. 1, 1780 and returned to service. Promoted to lieutenant, 2nd Maryland Line, on Jan. 1, 1781. Lieutenant, 4th Maryland Line, 1782-1783 [Ref: D-7, D-137, D-353, D-363, D-379, D-456]. Mark McPherson migrated to Lincoln County, Kentucky and married Mary Middleton on Nov. 27, 1795 (marriage bond signed by a Henry Middleton). [Ref: V-II:2307, W-119, which latter source states they were married "circa 1785 in Charles County, Maryland"]. Mark applied for a pension on Aug. 17, 1820, aged 67, stating he had a wife Mary McPherson (aged 45 or 46) and four children living with him, viz., Walter McPherson (aged 19), Henry McPherson (aged 9), John Dell McPherson (aged 7), and Mark McPherson (aged 5). The soldier died on Feb. 8, 1847 and his widow applied for a pension (W2144) on April 18, 1850, aged 73, and named their children as follows: Lydia McPherson (born Feb. 1, 1796), Alexander McPherson (March 14, 1798 - June 27, 1819), Samuel McPherson (born Jan. 12, 1800), Walter McPherson (born April 6, 1802), William McPherson (born April 14, 1807), Henry McPherson (born Feb. 20, 1810), John Bailey McPherson (born June 30, 1812), and Mark McPherson (born May 9, 1815). [Ref: V-II:2307, T-110, which latter source contains a petition signed by 50 men in Lincoln County, Kentucky on Feb. 15, 1826, recommending Mark McPherson, a Revolutionary War pensioner, for a special Act of Congress]. Mark McPherson was born on Feb. 14, 1754 in Maryland, married Mary Middleton, served as a lieutenant and adjutant in the Revolutionary War, and died in Kentucky on Feb. 8, 1847 [Ref: J-II:1986].

McPHERSON, Mary Ann. See "Alexander McPherson," q.v.

McPHERSON, Rachel. See "Alexander McPherson," q.v.

McPHERSON, Samuel (1739-1808). Cadet, 1st Maryland Line, Jan. 3, 1776. Lieutenant, Dec. 10, 1776. Captain-Lieutenant and Adjutant, April 7, 1780. Captain, 2nd Maryland Line, April 25, 1781. On duty in the Southern Army until June 1783, when retired [Ref: D-5, D-137, D-356, D-364, D-379, D-443, D-479]. Samuel McPherson was born on June 11, 1739, married second to Elizabeth Goldsmith (first wife's name not known), and died on Sept. 4, 1808 [Ref: J-II:1986]. See "Mark McPherson," q.v.

McPHERSON, Sarah. See "Alexander McPherson," q.v.

McPHERSON, Thomas. Took the Oath of Allegiance in 1778 [Ref: L-18, AA-641]. Resident of Port Tobacco West Hundred in 1778 [Ref: Q-I:297]. Aged about 51 or 53 as noted in two 1778 depositions [Ref: BB-469, DD-19]. Surveyor of Charles County in 1783; deceased by Jan. 22, 1784, when Theophilus Hanson was appointed due to Thomas' death [Ref: N-603, I-514]. One Thomas McPherson was born on Dec. 16, 1729, married Elizabeth Hanson, rendered patriotic service, and died on Aug. 22, 1793 [Ref: J-II:1986]. Additional research may be necessary before drawing conclusions. See "William Hanson McPherson," q.v.

McPHERSON, Walter. Memorialist and Militiaman, Pomonkey Company, after March 6, 1776 [Ref: M-158, Y-II:26]. Corporal, Militia, 12th Battalion, Capt. Walter Hanson's Company, 1777 [Ref: M-159]. Took the Oath of Allegiance in 1778 [Ref: L-18]. Resident of Pomonkey Hundred in 1778 [Ref: Q-I:297]. Constable, 1778 [Ref: Q-I:304, which listed the name only as "W. McPherson"]. Rendered patriotic service by providing wheat for the use of the military in May 1783 [Ref: N-597]. See "Mark McPherson," q.v.

McPHERSON, Walter Jr. Private, Militia, 26th Battalion, Capt. Thomas H. Marshall's Company, 1777 [Ref: M-163, which listed the name without the "Jr."]. Took the Oath of Allegiance in 1778 [Ref: AA-641, L-18, which latter source listed the name as "Mac Pherson Jr."].

McPHERSON, William (1740-1809). Captain, Militia, 26th Battalion, Feb. 26, 1776 [Ref: A-186, A-206, M-103, M-163, Y-II:23]. Resident of Newport West Hundred in 1778 [Ref: Q-I:297]. Rendered patriotic service by providing wheat for the use of the military in December 1782 [Ref: N-573]. William McPherson was born on Sept. 23, 1740, married Mary Smoot, served as a captain in the war, and died on Jan. 18, 1809 [Ref: J-II:1986]. See "Mark McPherson" and "Alexander McPherson," q.v.

McPHERSON, William Jr. Took the Oath of Allegiance in 1778 [Ref: L-18]. Resident of Port Tobacco West Hundred in 1778 [Ref: Q-I:297]. Nephew of "William Hanson McPherson," q.v.

McPHERSON, William Sr. (1708-   ). Took the Oath of Allegiance in 1778 [Ref: AA-641]. Aged about 69 as noted in a 1776 deposition [Ref: DD-19]. Resident of Port Tobacco West Hundred in 1778 [Ref: Q-I:297]. William McPherson married Eliner Wilkinson on Aug. 13, 1737 in Trinity Parish [Ref: EE-11].

McPHERSON, William Hanson (c1755-1815). Son of Thomas McPherson, he married first to Elizabeth Rutland in 1785 (widow of Nicholas Worthington), and probably second to Elizabeth Beall (daughter of Samuel Hanson, Jr.). Took the Oath of Allegiance in 1778 [Ref: L-18]. Served as Assistant Clerk to the Auditor General in 1778 and was in the Lower House of the Maryland Legislature, 1786-1810. Major, 43rd Regiment, 1794-1798 [Ref: P-II:592].

McWILLIAMS, William. Private, 5th Maryland Line, 1776-1779 [Ref: D-227]. Resident of William & Mary Upper Hundred in 1778 [Ref: Q-I:297].

MEAD, William. Private, Militia, 12th Battalion, Capt. Walter Hanson's Company, 1777 [Ref: M-159]. Took the Oath of Allegiance in 1778 [Ref: L-18, AA-641]. Resident of Port Tobacco East Hundred in 1778 [Ref: Q-I:297].

MEEK, John B. "John Bigger Meeke or Meeks" took the Oath of Allegiance in 1778 [Ref: L-18, AA-641]. "John B. Meeks" was a resident of Durham Lower Hundred in 1778 [Ref: Q-I:297]. "John Meek" was a drummer in the 7th Maryland Line on Jan. 20, 1776 [Ref: D-15]. "John Meeks" was a soldier in the Maryland Line who was reported killed on March 15, 1781

[Ref: D-391]. "John Meek" was a private during the war in Maryland, married Margaret ----, and died in Kentucky before December 1803. "John Booker Meek" rendered patriotic service in Maryland, married Virlinda Thomas, and died after June 5, 1800 in Maryland [Ref: J-II:1996]. Additional research will be necessary before drawing conclusions. See "John Robertson," q.v.

MEEK, Margaret. See "John B. Meek," q.v.

MEEKE, Richard. Private, 1st Maryland Line, drafted from the Charles County militia and reported "at sea" on July 27, 1781 [Ref: D-377].

MERCER, Julius. Private, 3rd Maryland Line, enrolled by Capt. Joseph Marbury by May 24, 1780 [Ref: D-333, F-181].

MERRICK, Walter. Took the Oath of Allegiance in 1778 [Ref: L-18].

MICHALL, Perry. Private, 1st Maryland Line, enrolled and passed on July 20, 1776 [Ref: D-33].

MICKUM, Henrietta. See "Henry Dixon," q.v.

MICKUM, Samuel. See "Henry Dixon," q.v.

MICKUM, William. See "Henry Dixon," q.v.

MIDDLETON, Ann. See "Belain Posey," q.v.

MIDDLETON, Henry. See "Mark McPherson," q.v.

MIDDLETON, Horatio. Sergeant, Militia, 26th Battalion, Capt. Thomas H. Marshall's Company, 1777 [Ref: M-163]. Ensign, Militia, Capt. George Dent's Company, commissioned May 9, 1778 [Ref: M-102, E-72]. Took the Oath of Allegiance in 1778 [Ref: L-18]. Resident of Pomonkey Hundred in 1778 [Ref: Q-I:297]. Rendered patriotic service by providing wheat for the use of the military in January, October, and December 1782 [Ref: N-471, N-563, N-575].

MIDDLETON, Hugh. Memorialist and Militiaman, Pomonkey Company, after March 6, 1776 [Ref: M-158, Y-II:26, which listed the name as "Middletown"]. Private, Militia, 26th Battalion, Capt. Thomas H. Marshall's Company, 1777 [Ref: M-163]. *Ed. Note:* There was a Hugh Middleton (c1715-1803), son of William Middleton of Charles County, Maryland, who migrated to McCormick County, South Carolina (date not given). [Ref: P-II:595].

MIDDLETON, Isaac Smallwood. First Lieutenant, Militia, 26th Battalion, Capt. Samuel Smallwood's Company, commissioned May 9, 1778 [Ref: M-103, M-165, E-72]. Took the Oath of Allegiance in 1778 [Ref: L-18]. Resident of Port Tobacco Upper Hundred in 1778 [Ref: Q-I:297].

MIDDLETON, James. Took the Oath of Allegiance in 1778 [Ref: L-18]. Resident of Port Tobacco East Hundred in 1778 [Ref: Q-I:297]. Private, 1st Maryland Line, 1781 [Ref: D-420, D-422].

MIDDLETON, James H. A. See "Belain Posey," q.v.

MIDDLETON, Mary. See "Mark McPherson," q.v.

MIDDLETON, Samuel. Private, Militia, 26th Battalion, Capt. Thomas H. Marshall's Company, 1777 [Ref: M-163].

MIDDLETON, Theodore. Took the Oath of Allegiance in 1778 [Ref: L-18].

MIDDLETON, William. See "Hugh Middleton," q.v.

MILES, Edward (1762-   ). Private, 1st Maryland Line, who was drafted from the Charles County militia and reported "sick or not in service" on July 27, 1781 [Ref: D-377]. He applied for pension (S11069) in Washington, D. C. on May 4, 1833, aged 71, stating he was born in Charles County and enlisted there with Nicholas Miles [relationship not stated, but probably his brother]. He also mentioned Priscilla King, wife of Charles King, who was the daughter of John Clements (a Revolutionary War soldier) and the niece of Benedict Clements (a Revolutionary War soldier and brother of John). [Ref: V-II:2345].

MILES, Edward (1730-   ). Took the Oath of Allegiance in 1778 [Ref: L-18]. Resident of Port Tobacco East Hundred in 1778 [Ref: Q-I:297]. Aged about 49 as noted in a 1779 deposition [Ref: BB-470, DD-19]. Rendered patriotic service by providing flour barrels for the use of the military in July 1782 [Ref: I-225].

MILES, Henry (1716-   ). Took the Oath of Allegiance in 1778 [Ref: AA-641]. Aged about 48 as noted in a 1764 deposition [Ref: DD-19]. Resident of Port Tobacco East Hundred in 1778 [Ref: Q-I:297].

MILES, Henry (1752-1796). Captain, 1st Maryland Line. He was born in November 1752, married Elizabeth McLamar, and died before June 21, 1796 [Ref: J-II:2020].

MILES, Henry. Private, 1st Maryland Line, enrolled and passed on July 18, 1776 [Ref: D-32].

MILES, Henry, of John. Took the Oath of Allegiance in 1778 [Ref: L-18].

MILES, Henry, of Joseph. Private, 1st Maryland Line, enrolled and passed on July 18, 1776 [Ref: D-32]. Corporal, Militia, 26th Battalion, Capt. Benjamin Cawood's Company, 1777 [Ref: M-162].

MILES, James. Private, Lower Battalion, Prince George's County, 1776 [Ref: D-35]. Took the Oath of Allegiance in Charles County in 1778 [Ref: AA-641]. Resident of Newport West Hundred in 1778 [Ref: Q-I:297].

MILES, Joseph. Private, Militia, 26th Battalion, Capt. Benjamin Cawood's Company, 1777 [Ref: M-162]. Resident of Port Tobacco East Hundred in 1778 [Ref: Q-I:297].

MILES, Joseph Sr. Took the Oath of Allegiance in 1778 [Ref: L-18]. Resident of Port Tobacco East Hundred in 1778 [Ref: Q-I:297].

MILES, Nicholas. Private, 1st Maryland Line, drafted from the Charles County militia on July 27, 1781 and discharged on Dec. 3, 1781 [Ref: D-377, G-569, I-11]. See "Edward Miles," q.v.

MILES, Richard (1760-1817). Private, 1st Maryland Line. He married Jane Gardiner and died before June 4, 1817 [Ref: J-II:2021].

MILES, Stephen, of Henry. Private, Militia, 26th Battalion, Capt. Benjamin Cawood's Company, 1777 [Ref: M-162].

MILES, William. Private, Militia, 26th Battalion, Capt. Benjamin Cawood's Company, 1777 [Ref: M-162]. Resident of Port Tobacco East Hundred in 1778 [Ref: Q-I:297].

MILLER, Christian (Christopher). "Christian Miller" took the Oath of Allegiance in 1778 [Ref: AA-641, L-18]. "Christopher Millar" was a resident of Port Tobacco East Hundred in 1778 [Ref: Q-I:297].

MILLER, Jacob. Private, Militia, 12th Battalion, Capt. Walter Hanson's Company, 1777 [Ref: M-159]. Private (furnished by class for 9 months), 1st Maryland Line, by Sept. 11, 1778 [Ref: D-330]. Took the Oath of Allegiance in 1778 [Ref: L-18, AA-641]. Rendered patriotic service by providing wheat for the use of the military in May 1783 [Ref: N-597].

MILLER, James. Took the Oath of Allegiance in 1778 [Ref: L-18].

MILLER, John (1734-   ). Took the Oath of Allegiance in 1778 [Ref: L-18, AA-641]. Resident of Port Tobacco East Hundred in 1778 [Ref: Q-I:297]. Aged about 44 as noted in a 1778 deposition [Ref: CC-697, DD-19, which sources listed the name as "Millar"].

MILLIT, George. Private, 3rd Maryland Line, enrolled by Capt. Joseph Marbury by May 24, 1780 [Ref: F-181].

MILLS, John Baptist. Private (furnished by class for 9 months), 1st Maryland Line, by Sept. 11, 1778 [Ref: D-330]. Private, 3rd Maryland Line, 1780, enrolled in Charles County for Capt. Joseph Marbury's Company [Ref: D-333].

MILSTEAD, Edward. Private, Militia, 26th Battalion, Capt. Hezekiah Garner's Company, 1777 [Ref: M-162]. Took the Oath of Allegiance in 1778 [Ref: L-18, AA-641, which latter source listed the name as "Melstead"].

MILSTEAD, Elizabeth. See "John Milstead," q.v.

MILSTEAD, John. Corporal, Militia, 26th Battalion, Capt. Hezekiah Garner's Company, 1777 [Ref: M-162]. Took the Oath of Allegiance in 1778 [Ref: L-18, AA-641, which latter source listed the name as "Melstead"]. This might be the John Milstead who served in the Maryland Line, married Elizabeth Purnell in December 1798, and died in Burke County, North Carolina on Dec. 6, 1836. His widow Elizabeth Milstead received pension W5317 in 1852 [Ref: V-II:2370].

MILSTEAD, John Sr. Took the Oath of Allegiance in 1778 [Ref: L-18, AA-641, which latter source listed the name as "Melstead"]. Resident of Durham Lower Hundred in 1778 [Ref: Q-I:297].
MILSTEAD, Jonathan. Private, 1st Maryland Line, Capt. Edward Prall's Company, Jan. 1, 1782, and noted as being a Guard for General William Smallwood [Ref: D-432].
MILSTEAD, Matthew. Took the Oath of Allegiance in 1778 [Ref: L-18, AA-641, which listed the name as "Melstead"].
MILSTEAD, Samuel. Private, Militia, 26th Battalion, Capt. Hezekiah Garner's Company, 1777 [Ref: M-162]. Took the Oath of Allegiance in 1778 [Ref: L-18, AA-641, which listed the name as "Melstead"].
MILSTEAD, Thomas. Private, 1st Maryland Line, enrolled and passed on July 19, 1776 [Ref: D-31].
MILSTEAD, William. Second Lieutenant, Militia, 26th Battalion, Capt. Hezekiah Garner's Company, 1777 [Ref: M-162]. Took the Oath of Allegiance in 1778 [Ref: L-18]. Rendered patriotic service by providing wheat for the use of the military in December 1782 [Ref: N-569].
MINITREE, Andrew. Private, Militia, 12th Battalion, Capt. Jonathan Yates' Company, 1777 [Ref: M-162]. Took the Oath of Allegiance in 1778 [Ref: AA-641, L-19, which latter source mistakenly listed the name as "A. Ministre"]. "Andrew Minetree" was a resident of William & Mary Lower Hundred in 1778 [Ref: Q-I:297]. One "Jacob Andrew Minitree" was aged about 55 as noted in a 1760 deposition [Ref: DD-20].
MINITREE, Gilferd. Private, 1st Maryland Line, enrolled and passed on July 8, 1776 [Ref: D-32, D-313, which sources listed the name as "Gilferd Minetree" and "Gifford Minitree"]. Private, 1st Maryland Line, Jan. 29, 1780 through November 1780 [Ref: D-138, which listed the name as "Gueld'd Menitry"].
MINITREE, Jacob Andrew. See "Andrew Minitree," q.v.
MINITREE, Paul. Private, 1st Maryland Line, enrolled and passed on July 8, 1776 [Ref: D-32]. Private, Militia, 12th Battalion, Capt. Jonathan Yates' Company, 1777 [Ref: M-162]. "Paul Minetree" was a resident of William & Mary Lower Hundred in 1778 [Ref: Q-I:297]. On Feb. 19, 1819, the Treasurer of Maryland was directed to pay to pay to "Paul Minitree, an old revolutionary soldier of Charles County, half pay of a private, for his Revolutionary War services." [Ref: Q-II:375].
MITCHELL, Hugh. See "Walter Hanson," q.v.
MITCHELL, Peregrine. Private, Militia, 12th Battalion, Capt. Henry Clarkson's Company, 1777 [Ref: M-159]. See "Perry Michall," q.v.
MITCHELL, Rachel. Rendered patriotic service by providing wheat for the use of the military in May 1783 [Ref: N-598].

MITCHELL, Richard. Sergeant, Militia, 26th Battalion, Capt. Richard Bennett Mitchell's Company, 1777 [Ref: M-164]. Took the Oath of Allegiance in 1778 [Ref: L-19]. Resident of Port Tobacco West Hundred in 1778 [Ref: Q-I:297].

MITCHELL, Richard Bennett. Captain, Militia, 26th Battalion, July 19, 1776 [Ref: B-83, B-127, M-104, M-164]. Rendered patriotic service by providing clothing for the use of the military in February 1778 [Ref: Y-II:234]. Took the Oath of Allegiance in 1778 [Ref: L-19, which mistakenly listed the name as "Richard Benjamin Mitchell"]. Resident of Port Tobacco West Hundred in 1778 [Ref: Q-I:297].

MITCHELL, Samuel. Took the Oath of Allegiance in 1778 [Ref: L-19]. Resident of Port Tobacco West Hundred in 1778 [Ref: Q-I:297]. He was accused, but not officially charged, however, of concealing his horses from Daniel Jenifer, Contractor of Horses for Charles County, in June 1781 [Ref: H-324].

MITCHELL, Sarah. See "Francis Mudd," q.v.

MOBLEY, William. Private, Militia, 26th Battalion, Capt. Benjamin Cawood's Company, 1777 [Ref: M-162]. Resident of Port Tobacco East Hundred in 1778 [Ref: Q-I:297].

MOLAHARN, Thomas. Rendered patriotic service by providing wheat for the use of the military in December 1782 [Ref: N-576].

MONEY, Isaac. Resident of William & Mary Upper Hundred in 1778 [Ref: Q-I:297]. Petitioned the Council of Maryland in 1783 stating that he had not taken the Oath of Allegiance due to any disaffection with the government, but from a variety of incidents, and was unjustly penalized as a non-juror and fined unfairly; therefore, he asked the Council to consider ordering the County Justices to remit the fines they imposed on him and others who signed the petition. The Council of Maryland, after reviewing his case, indicated they believed the truth of the facts stated in the petition and ordered a remission of the fines and penalties on Sept. 17, 1783 [Ref: I-454].

MONROE, Daniel. Took the Oath of Allegiance in 1778 [Ref: L-19, AA-641, which latter source listed the name as "Monrowe"].

MONROE, John. Memorialist and Militiaman, Pomonkey Company, after March 6, 1776 [Ref: M-158, Y-II:26, which sources listed the name as "Monnow" or "Monrow(?)"]. Private, Militia, 26th Battalion, Capt. Thomas H. Marshall's Company, 1777 [Ref: M-163, which listed the name as "Munroe"]. Took the Oath of Allegiance in 1778 [Ref: AA-641, which listed the name as "Monrowe"]. Resident of Pomonkey Hundred in 1778 [Ref: Q-I:297].

MONROE, Thomas. Private, Militia, 26th Battalion, Capt. Thomas H. Marshall's Company, 1777 [Ref: M-163, which listed the name as "Munroe"]. Took the Oath of Allegiance in 1778 [Ref: AA-641, which listed the name as "Monrowe"]. Resident of Pomonkey Hundred in 1778 [Ref: Q-I:297]. Rendered patriotic service by providing wheat for the use of the military in October 1782 [Ref: N-562].

MONTGOMERY, Basil. Private, Militia, 12th Battalion, Capt. Alexander McPherson's Company, 1777 [Ref: M-160]. Took the Oath of Allegiance in 1778 [Ref: L-19]. Resident of Bryan Town Hundred in 1778 [Ref: Q-I:297].

MONTGOMERY, Charles. Private, Militia, 12th Battalion, Capt. John Parnham's Company, 1777 [Ref: M-161]. Took the Oath of Allegiance in 1778 [Ref: L-19]. Assisted the Purchaser of Clothing in Charles County in February 1778 [Ref: Y-II:235]. Resident of Bryan Town Hundred in 1778 [Ref: Q-I:297].

MONTGOMERY, Christina. See "Caesar Richards," q.v.

MONTGOMERY, Elizabeth. See "James Montgomery, Jr." and "Thomas Dent," q.v.

MONTGOMERY, Francis. Private, Militia, 12th Battalion, Capt. Benjamin Lusby Corry's Company, 1777 [Ref: M-160]. Son of Peter Montgomery and brother of "Richard Montgomery," q.v.

MONTGOMERY, Francis (1710-   ). Took the Oath of Allegiance in 1778 [Ref: L-19]. Aged about 47 as noted in a 1757 deposition [Ref: DD-20]. Resident of Newport West Hundred in 1778 [Ref: Q-I:297].

MONTGOMERY, George. Private, 1st Maryland Line, enrolled and passed on July 8, 1776 [Ref: D-32, which listed the name as "Mountgomery"].

MONTGOMERY, Ignatius. Private, Militia, 12th Battalion, Capt. Alexander McPherson's Company, 1777 [Ref: M-160]. Took the Oath of Allegiance in 1778 [Ref: L-19]. Resident of Bryan Town Hundred in 1778 [Ref: Q-I:297]. Private, 1st Maryland Line, drafted from the Charles County militia on July 27, 1781, and discharged on Dec. 10, 1781 [Ref: D-377, I-7].

MONTGOMERY, James Jr. (c1755-1820). Private, 1st Maryland Line, enrolled and passed on July 18, 1776 [Ref: D-32]. Private, Militia, 26th Battalion, Capt. Benjamin Cawood's Company, 1777 [Ref: M-162]. Took the Oath of Allegiance in 1778 [Ref: AA-641]. Resident of Port Tobacco East Hundred in 1778 [Ref: Q-I:297]. Rendered patriotic service by providing wheat for the use of the military in April 1783 [Ref: N-593]. A son of James and Mary Montgomery, he married Elizabeth ---- and died in February 1820. She died in August 1845. Their son John Montgomery (1780-1848) married Juliana Langley (1797-1870) on Jan. 7, 1822 [Ref: S-

3010, J-II:2056, which latter source states he was born before 1756 and died before Feb. 12, 1820].

MONTGOMERY, James Sr. (1716-1781). Took the Oath of Allegiance in 1778. He married Mary ---- in Charles County [Ref: L-19, S-3010, J-II:2056, which latter source states he was born circa 1735 and died before April 1, 1780]. Resident of Port Tobacco East Hundred in 1778 [Ref: Q-I:297].

MONTGOMERY, John. See "James Montgomery, Jr.," q.v.

MONTGOMERY, Joseph. Private, Militia, 12th Battalion, Capt. Alexander McPherson's Company, 1777 [Ref: M-160]. Took the Oath of Allegiance in 1778 [Ref: L-19]. Resident of Bryan Town Hundred in 1778 [Ref: Q-I:297]. One Joseph Montgomery was born on Nov. 12, 1737, married Mary Ann Hagan, and died in Kentucky between 1797 and 1808 [Ref: J-II:2056].

MONTGOMERY, Joshua. Private, Militia, 26th Battalion, Capt. Benjamin Cawood's Company, 1777 [Ref: M-162]. Resident of Port Tobacco East Hundred in 1778 [Ref: Q-I:297].

MONTGOMERY, Mary. Rendered patriotic service by providing wheat for the use of the military in November 1782 [Ref: N-565, which listed the name as "Mungumry"]. See "James Montgomery" and "James Montgomery, Jr.," q.v.

MONTGOMERY, Peter. Private, Militia, 26th Battalion, Capt. Benjamin Cawood's Company, 1777 [Ref: M-162]. Resident of Port Tobacco East Hundred in 1778 [Ref: Q-I:297]. See "Richard Montgomery" and "Francis Montgomery," q.v.

MONTGOMERY, Richard (1722-   ). Took the Oath of Allegiance in 1778 [Ref: L-19]. Aged about 31 as noted in a 1753 deposition which mentioned his brother Peter and their father Francis [Ref: DD-20]. Resident of Port Tobacco East Hundred in 1778 [Ref: Q-I:297].

MONTGOMERY, William. Sergeant, Militia, 12th Battalion, Capt. Alexander McPherson's Company, 1777 [Ref: M-160]. Assisted the Purchaser of Clothing in Charles County in February 1778 [Ref: Y-II:235]. Resident of Bryan Town Hundred in 1778 [Ref: Q-I:297].

MONTGOMERY, William, of Peter. Took the Oath of Allegiance in 1778 [Ref: L-19].

MOORE, Elijah. Second Lieutenant, Militia, 26th Battalion, Capt. Benjamin Cawood's Company, 1777 [Ref: M-162].

MOORE (MOOR), Elizabeth. See "James Moore," q.v.

MOORE, George. Private, Militia, 26th Battalion, Capt. Benjamin Cawood's Company, 1777 [Ref: M-162]. Resident of Port Tobacco East Hundred in 1778 [Ref: Q-I:297, which misspelled the name as "Moone"].

MOORE, Hezekiah. Private, Militia, 26th Battalion, Capt. Benjamin Cawood's Company, 1777 [Ref: M-162]. "Hezekiah More" was a resident of Port Tobacco East Hundred in 1778 [Ref: Q-I:297].

MOORE, James. Rendered patriotic service by providing wheat for the use of the military in May 1782 [Ref: N-515]. Resident of Port Tobacco East Hundred in 1778 [Ref: Q-I:297]. "James Moor" was born on Aug. 27, 1752, son of "James Moor" and Elizabeth Dement, of Trinity Parish, who were married on Dec. 8, 1747 [Ref: EE-9].

MOORE, Matthew Jr. Drummer, Militia, 26th Battalion, Capt. Benjamin Cawood's Company, 1777 [Ref: M-162, which listed the name as "Mathew More Junr."]. Resident of Port Tobacco Upper Hundred in 1778 [Ref: Q-I:297].

MOORE, Matthew Sr. Took the Oath of Allegiance in 1778 [Ref: AA-641]. Resident of Port Tobacco East Hundred in 1778 [Ref: Q-I:297, which misspelled the name as "Moone"].

MOORE, Peter. Took the Oath of Allegiance in August 1778 [Ref: AA-707].

MOORE, Priscilla. See "Matthew Kidwell," q.v.

MORAN, Andrew Jr. Private, Militia, 12th Battalion, Capt. Peter Wood's Company, 1777 [Ref: M-161]. Took the Oath of Allegiance in 1778 [Ref: AA-641]. Resident of Benedict Hundred in 1778 [Ref: Q-I:297].

MORAN, Andrew Sr. Took the Oath of Allegiance in 1778 [Ref: L-19, AA-641]. Rendered patriotic service by providing wheat for the use of the military in November 1782 [Ref: N-566]. Resident of Benedict Hundred in 1778 [Ref: Q-I:297].

MORAN, Gabriel (1730-c1810). Private, Militia, 12th Battalion, Capt. Alexander McPherson's Company, 1777 [Ref: M-160, which listed the name as "Gabril Morran"]. Took the Oath of Allegiance in 1778 [Ref: L-19]. Resident of Benedict Hundred in 1778 [Ref: Q-I:297]. Gabriel Moran was born on June 30, 1730, married Margaret Wood, and died after Sept. 20, 1810 [Ref: J-II:2070].

MORAN, James. Took the Oath of Allegiance in 1778 [Ref: L-19]. Resident of Benedict Hundred in 1778 [Ref: Q-I:297].

MORAN, John Jr. Private, Militia, 12th Battalion, Capt. Peter Wood's Company, 1777 [Ref: M-161]. Took the Oath of Allegiance in 1778 [Ref: L-19]. Resident of Benedict Hundred in 1778 [Ref: Q-I:297]. Private, 2nd Maryland Line, Capt. Samuel McPherson's Company, by Jan. 1, 1782 [Ref: D-445, which listed the name without the "Jr."].

MORAN, John Sr. Took the Oath of Allegiance in 1778 [Ref: L-19]. Resident of Benedict Hundred in 1778 [Ref: Q-I:297].

MORAN, Jonathan. Private, Militia, 12th Battalion, Capt. Peter Wood's Company, 1777 [Ref: M-161]. Took the Oath of Allegiance in 1778 [Ref: L-19, AA-641]. Resident of Benedict Hundred in 1778 [Ref: Q-I:297].
MORAN, Luke. Private, Militia, 12th Battalion, Capt. Alexander McPherson's Company, 1777 [Ref: M-160, which listed the name as "Morran"].
MORAN, Meverel. Took the Oath of Allegiance in 1778 [Ref: L-18, which listed the name as "Marran"]. Private, Militia, 12th Battalion, Capt. Peter Wood's Company, 1777 [Ref: M-161, which questionably listed the name as "Murrel(?) Morgan," and X-67, which listed the name as "Meveril Moran"]. Resident of Bryan Town Hundred in 1778 [Ref: Q-I:297].
MORAN, Samuel. Private, Militia, 12th Battalion, Capt. Alexander McPherson's Company, 1777 [Ref: M-160, which listed the name as "Morran"].
MORAN, William. Sergeant, Militia, 12th Battalion, Capt. Peter Wood's Company, July 5, 1777. First Lieutenant, Militia, Capt. William Wilkinson's Company, commissioned May 9, 1778 [Ref: E-72, M-105, M-161]. Took the Oath of Allegiance in 1778 [Ref: L-19]. Resident of Benedict Hundred in 1778 [Ref: Q-I:297].
MORELAND, Isaac. Private, Militia, 26th Battalion, Capt. Samuel Smallwood's Company, 1777 [Ref: M-165, which listed the name as "Morland"]. Resident of Port Tobacco Upper Hundred in 1778 [Ref: Q-I:297].
MORELAND, Jacob. Private, Militia, 12th Battalion, Capt. John Hanson's Company, 1777 [Ref: M-159]. Resident of Port Tobacco East Hundred in 1778 [Ref: Q-I:297]. Petitioned the Council of Maryland in 1783 stating that he had not taken the Oath of Allegiance due to any disaffection with the government, but from a variety of incidents, and was unjustly penalized as a non-juror and fined unfairly; therefore, he asked the Council to consider ordering the County Justices to remit the fines they imposed on him and others who signed the petition. The Council of Maryland, after reviewing his case, indicated they believed the truth of the facts stated in the petition and ordered a remission of the fines and penalties on Sept. 17, 1783 [Ref: I-454].
MORELAND, James. Private, Militia, 26th Battalion, Capt. Samuel Smallwood's Company, 1777 [Ref: M-165].
MORELAND, John. Private, Militia, 26th Battalion, Capt. Benjamin Cawood's Company, 1777 [Ref: M-162, which listed the name as "Morland"]. Resident of Port Tobacco East Hundred in 1778 [Ref: Q-I:297].

MORELAND, Leddy. Rendered patriotic service by providing wheat for the use of the military in October 1782 [Ref: N-562, which listed the name as "Molin"].

MORELAND, Patrick. Private, Militia, 26th Battalion, Capt. Samuel Smallwood's Company, 1777 [Ref: M-165]. Resident of Port Tobacco Upper Hundred in 1778 [Ref: Q-I:297]. Rendered patriotic service by providing wheat for the use of the military in December 1782 [Ref: N-573, which listed the name as "Partuck Morland"].

MORELAND, Philip. Private (draught who had not yet joined the army), 1st Maryland Line, by Sept. 11, 1778 [Ref: D-330, which listed the name as "Morland"]. Two men by this name were privates in the militia, 26th Battalion, in 1777: one in Capt. Benjamin Cawood's Company [Ref: M-162, which listed the name as "Morland"], and one in Capt. Samuel Smallwood's Company [Ref: M-165]. One rendered patriotic service by providing wheat for the use of the military in October 1782 [Ref: N-562, which listed the name as "Molin"]. Resident of Port Tobacco East Hundred in 1778 [Ref: Q-I:297].

MORELAND, Richard. Resident of Port Tobacco East Hundred in 1778 [Ref: Q-I:297]. Petitioned the Council of Maryland in 1783 stating that he had not taken the Oath of Allegiance due to any disaffection with the government, but from a variety of incidents, and was unjustly penalized as a non-juror and fined unfairly; therefore, he asked the Council to consider ordering the County Justices to remit the fines they imposed on him and others who signed the petition. The Council of Maryland, after reviewing his case, indicated they believed the truth of the facts stated in the petition and ordered a remission of the fines and penalties on Sept. 17, 1783 [Ref: I-454].

MORELAND, Samuel (1751-1817). Private, Militia, 26th Battalion, Capt. Samuel Smallwood's Company, 1777 [Ref: M-165]. Samuel Moreland married Sarah Notley [Ref: J-II:2071].

MORELAND, Stephen. Private, Militia, 26th Battalion, Capt. Benjamin Cawood's Company, 1777 [Ref: M-162, which listed the name as "Morland"]. Resident of Port Tobacco East Hundred in 1778 [Ref: Q-I:297]. Gave a deposition in 1781 pertaining to his inability to perform military service due to family obligations [Ref: Z-208]. Petitioned the Council of Maryland in 1783 stating that he had not taken the Oath of Allegiance due to any disaffection with the government, but from a variety of incidents, and was unjustly penalized as a non-juror and fined unfairly; therefore, he asked the Council to consider ordering the County Justices to remit the fines they imposed on him and others who signed the petition. The Council of Maryland, after reviewing his case, indicated they believed the truth of the facts stated in the petition and ordered a remission of the fines and penalties on Sept. 17, 1783 [Ref: I-454]. Took the Oath of Allegiance in 1778 [Ref: AA-641].

MORELAND, Walter. Private, Militia, 12th Battalion, Capt. Henry Clarkson's Company, 1777 [Ref: M-159]. Rendered patriotic service by providing clothing for the use of the military in January 1778 [Ref: Y-II:230]. Took the Oath of Allegiance in 1778 [Ref: L-19, AA-641]. Resident of Port Tobacco East Hundred in 1778 [Ref: Q-I:297]. Rendered patriotic service by providing wheat for the use of the military in December 1782 [Ref: N-576, which listed the name as "Moalen"].

MORELAND, William. Private, Militia, 26th Battalion, Capt. Benjamin Cawood's Company, 1777 [Ref: M-162, which listed the name as "Wm. Morland"]. Resident of Port Tobacco East Hundred in 1778 [Ref: Q-I:297]. Rendered patriotic service by providing wheat for the use of the military in September and December 1782 [Ref: N-548, N-573, which source also spelled the name as "Molin"].

MORELAND, Zachariah. Private, Militia, 26th Battalion, Capt. Benjamin Cawood's Company, 1777 [Ref: M-162, which listed the name as "Zachh. Morland"]. Resident of Port Tobacco East Hundred in 1778 [Ref: Q-I:297].

MORETON, Anne. See "Daniel Murphy, Jr." and "Samuel Murphy" and "William Murphy," q.v.

MORRIS, Ann. Rendered patriotic service by providing wheat for the use of the military in May 1783 [Ref: N-597].

MORRIS, Jacob (1731-   ). Private, Militia, 12th Battalion, Capt. Walter Hanson's Company, 1777 [Ref: M-159]. Took the Oath of Allegiance in 1778 [Ref: L-19, AA-641]. Aged about 48 as noted in a 1779 deposition [Ref: DD-20]. Resident of Port Tobacco East Hundred in 1778 [Ref: Q-I:297, which listed the name as "Morriss"].

MORRIS, James. Private, Militia, 12th Battalion, Capt. John Parnham's Company, 1777 [Ref: M-160, which listed the name as "Morriss"]. Took the Oath of Allegiance in 1778 [Ref: L-19]. Resident of Newport East Hundred in 1778 [Ref: Q-I:297].

MORRIS, Joshua. Private, Militia, 12th Battalion, Capt. John Hanson's Company, 1777 [Ref: M-159]. Took the Oath of Allegiance in 1778 [Ref: L-19]. Resident of Bryan Town Hundred in 1778 [Ref: Q-I:297].

MORRIS, Nicholas. Took the Oath of Allegiance in 1778 [Ref: L-19].

MORRIS, Richard. Took the Oath of Allegiance in 1778 [Ref: AA-641, which listed the name as "Mooris"]. Resident of Newport West Hundred in 1778 [Ref: Q-I:297, which listed the name as "Morriss"].

MORRIS, Walter. Private, Militia, 12th Battalion, Capt. Walter Hanson's Company, 1777 [Ref: M-159]. Resident of Port Tobacco East Hundred in 1778 [Ref: Q-I:297, which listed the name as "Morriss"].
MORRIS, William. Took the Oath of Allegiance in 1778 [Ref: AA-641]. Resident of Port Tobacco East Hundred in 1778 [Ref: Q-I:297, which listed the name as "Morriss"].
MORRISON, John. Private (substitute for 3 years), 1st Maryland Line, by Sept. 11, 1778 [Ref: D-330].
MORRISON, William (1745-   ). Private, Militia, 26th Battalion, Capt. Robert Sinnett's Company, 1777 [Ref: M-164]. Private, 1st Maryland Line, Col. John H. Stone's Regiment. Wounded in the hand and head at the Battle of Camden in South Carolina on Aug. 16, 1780, his invalid (disability) pension commenced on Nov. 17, 1780 and he was still on pension as of Sept. 17, 1789, aged 44 [Ref: D-629].
MORTON (MORETON), Anne. See "Daniel Murphy, Jr.," q.v.
MORTON, George. Private, Militia, 12th Battalion, Capt. Peter Wood's Company, 1777 [Ref: M-161]. Took the Oath of Allegiance in 1778 [Ref: AA-641]. Resident of Bryan Town Hundred in 1778 [Ref: Q-I:297].
MORTON, John. Private, Militia, 12th Battalion, Capt. Peter Wood's Company, 1777 [Ref: M-161]. Assisted the Purchaser of Clothing in Charles County in February 1778 [Ref: Y-II:235]. Resident of Benedict Hundred in 1778 [Ref: Q-I:297]. Appointed a Justice of the Peace on Nov. 19, 1779 and Jan. 17, 1782 [Ref: F-19, I-45].
MORTON, Joseph. Private, Militia, 12th Battalion, Capt. Peter Wood's Company, 1777 [Ref: M-161]. Took the Oath of Allegiance in 1778 [Ref: AA-641]. Resident of Bryan Town Hundred in 1778 [Ref: Q-I:297].
MOSELY, William. See "Samuel Barker Davis," q.v.
MUDD, Ann. See "Bennett Mudd," q.v.
MUDD, Barbara. See "Jeremiah Mudd," q.v.
MUDD, Benjamin. Private, 1st Maryland Line, enrolled and passed on July 8, 1776 [Ref: D-32]. Took the Oath of Allegiance in 1778 [Ref: AA-641, L-19, which latter source mistakenly listed the name as "Bery Mudd"].
MUDD, Bennett (1719-1778). Took the Oath of Allegiance in 1778 [Ref: L-19]. Bennett Mudd married Mary Blandford and was deceased by September 1778 (date of inventory). [Ref: GG-218, J-II:2101, which latter source stated he was deceased by January 1804].
MUDD, Bennett (1760-1830). Private, Militia, 12th Battalion, Capt. Benjamin Lusby Corry's Company, 1777 [Ref: M-160]. "Bennett Mudd" was a private (substitute for 9 months), 1st Maryland Line, by Sept. 11, 1778 [Ref: D-330]. "Burnett Mudd" was a resident of Bryan Town Hundred in 1778 [Ref: Q-I:297]. Sergeant, 3rd Company, 3rd Maryland

Line, Aug. 28, 1781 [Ref: D-393]. On Feb. 19, 1819, the Treasurer of Maryland was directed to pay to "Bennett Mudd, of Charles County, an old soldier, during life, half pay of a sergeant." He was placed on the pension rolls of Charles County on March 6, 1819 (retroactive to Nov. 15, 1818). On March 10, 1835, the Treasurer was directed to pay to "Ann Mudd, $24.17, the balance of pension due her husband at the time of his death, and which was forfeited to the State by Resolution No. 26, of 1823." On June 4, 1836, the Treasurer was directed to pay to "Ann Mudd, widow of Bennett Mudd, late a sergeant in the Revolutionary War, quarterly, during life, half pay of a sergeant, for the services of her said husband in the said revolution." [Ref: Q-II:377, R-33]. He also applied for a federal pension on March 25, 1818, aged 58, in Georgetown, D. C., and in 1820 lived in Charles County with his wife Ann Mudd (aged about 43) and six children (3 boys and 3 girls, but no names were given). Ann Brown, aged 61, made affidavit in 1838 that she was married on Jan. 12, 1792 and Ann Swain [Swann] married Bennett Mudd "some four months and a few days later." Ann Mudd applied for a pension (W26283) in Washington, D. C. on Oct. 30, 1838, aged 60, stating she had married Bennett in 1792 and he died on Aug. 23, 1830 [Ref: V-II:2447]. See "Jeremiah Mudd," q.v.

MUDD, Clement (1726-   ). Took the Oath of Allegiance in 1778 [Ref: L-19]. Aged about 46 as noted in a 1772 deposition [Ref: DD-20].

MUDD, Edward. See "Jeremiah Mudd," q.v.

MUDD, Electious. See "Richard Mudd," q.v.

MUDD, Elenor. See "Richard Mudd," q.v.

MUDD, Elizabeth. See "Jeremiah Mudd" and "Richard Mudd," q.v.

MUDD, Francis (1746-1779). He married Sarah Mitchell, rendered patriotic service during the war, and died on July 3, 1779 [Ref: J-II:2101].

MUDD, Henrietta. See "Richard Mudd," q.v.

MUDD, Henry Jr. Private, 1st Maryland Line, enrolled and passed on July 19, 1776. Private, Militia, 12th Battalion, Capt. Alexander McPherson's Company, 1777 [Ref: D-31, M-160, which sources listed the name without the "Jr."]. Took the Oath of Allegiance in 1778 [Ref: L-19]. Resident of Bryan Town Hundred in 1778 [Ref: Q-I:297].

MUDD, Henry Sr. (c1731-1808) Took the Oath of Allegiance in 1778 [Ref: L-19]. Aged about 48 as noted in a 1779 deposition [Ref: BB-480, which listed the name without the "Sr."]. Resident of Bryan Town Hundred in 1778 [Ref: Q-I:297]. Henry Mudd, Sr., was born in 1727, married Blanch (Alice) Spaulding, served as a corporal, rendered patriotic service during the war, and died in 1808 [Ref: J-II:2101].

MUDD, Henry Thomas. Private, Militia, 12th Battalion, Capt. Alexander McPherson's Company, 1777 [Ref: M-160]. Took the Oath of Allegiance in 1778 [Ref: L-19].

MUDD, Hezekiah. Private, 1st Maryland Line, drafted from the Charles County militia on July 27, 1781 and discharged on Dec. 3, 1781 [Ref: D-377, G-569, I-11].

MUDD, Ignatius. Private, Militia, 12th Battalion, Capt. Alexander McPherson's Company, 1777 [Ref: M-160]. Took the Oath of Allegiance in 1778 [Ref: AA-641]. Resident of Bryan Town Hundred in 1778 [Ref: Q-I:297].

MUDD, Ignatius Ward. Took the Oath of Allegiance in 1778 [Ref: L-19].

MUDD, James. Private, Militia, 26th Battalion, Capt. Richard Bennett Mitchell's Company, 1777; listed as an invalid (disabled) soldier [Ref: M-164]. Took the Oath of Allegiance in 1778 [Ref: AA-641]. Resident of Port Tobacco West Hundred in 1778 [Ref: Q-I:297]. James Mudd married Anne Swann circa 1785 [Ref: W-119]. See "Jeremiah Mudd," q.v.

MUDD, James, of James (1715-   ). Took the Oath of Allegiance in 1778 [Ref: AA-641, L-19, which latter source listed the name as "James Mudd, Sr., of James"]. Resident of Port Tobacco West Hundred in 1778 [Ref: Q-I:297]. Aged about 65 as noted in a 1780 deposition [Ref: DD-20].

MUDD, Jeremiah. Took the Oath of Allegiance in 1778 [Ref: L-19]. Resident of Port Tobacco West Hundred in 1778 [Ref: Q-I:297].

MUDD, Jeremiah Jr. (c1755-1815). Private, Militia, 26th Battalion, Capt. Richard Bennett Mitchell's Company, 1777 [Ref: M-164]. Jeremiah Mudd was a sergeant in the 2nd Maryland Line commanded by Col. John Gunby. He lost his left arm at the Battle of Ninety-Six in South Carolina on June 17, 1781, and his invalid (disability) pension commenced on Aug. 5, 1783 in Prince George's County. He was still on pension as of June 5, 1789 in Charles County, aged 30 [Ref: D-461, D-629]. Barbara Mudd, widow of Jeremiah, applied for a federal pension (W9212) in Washington, D. C. on April 10, 1838, aged 83, stating she was the former Barbara Swan [Swann] daughter of Edward Swan [Swann], late of Charles County, and she had married Jeremiah Mudd "less than 2 years after Cornwallis' surrender" [which would have been in 1783; source W-119 mistakenly stated it was in 1785]. Barbara Swann had four brothers and three sisters, and two of her sisters, Elizabeth and Anne Swan [Swann], married two of her husband's ten brothers, Smith and James Mudd (and they only had one sister). Jeremiah and Barbara had twin sons (one died young and the other died about 2 years before his father whose date of death she could not remember). An affidavit in 1848 by one D. McCurdy stated that Jeremiah Mudd received an invalid's pension and died in 1815, aged 60 or more. Barbara Mudd was about the same age and died in 1838, aged 83. He also mentioned Edward Mudd, a cousin of Mary McCurdy "by father's and mother's side" who was aged 50 in 1838. Jeremiah's son Bennett Mudd was born in 1784 and was "some four years older" than this D. McCurdy, who also stated that Edward Mudd said that he was born on March 30, 1788 and served in the War of 1812. His widow was born on Feb. 29, 1796 and Mary McCurdy was a daughter of Bennett Mudd, one of the twin sons of Jeremiah Mudd. She applied for a pension in 1849. Edward Mudd, son of Smith and Elizabeth Mudd, made affidavit on April 19, 1838 in Washington, D. C. that Jeremiah Mudd had died on July 10, 1815 and his widow had died on Sept. 14, 1838 [Ref: V-II:2447].

MUDD, Jerome. See "Richard Mudd," q.v.

MUDD, John. Private, 1st Maryland Line, enrolled and passed on July 8, 1776 [Ref: D-32]. Private, Militia, 26th Battalion, Capt. Richard Bennett Mitchell's Company, 1777 [Ref: M-164]. Took the Oath of Allegiance in 1778 [Ref: L-19]. Resident of Port Tobacco West Hundred in 1778 [Ref: Q-I:297].

MUDD, John, of James. Resident of Bryan Town Hundred in 1778 [Ref: Q-I:297]. Took the Oath of Allegiance in 1778 [Ref: L-19, AA-641, which listed the name as "John Mudd, of James"].

MUDD, Joshua (c1740-1813). Corporal, Militia, 12th Battalion, Capt. John Thomas' Company, 1777 [Ref: M-161]. Took the Oath of Allegiance in 1778 [Ref: L-19]. Resident of Bryan Town Hundred in 1778 [Ref: Q-I:297]. Rendered patriotic service by providing clothing for the use of the military in February 1778 [Ref: Y-II:234]. Deputy Sheriff of Charles County in June 1778 [Ref: CC-709]. Joshua Mudd was born circa 1740, married Ann Neale Smith, served as a corporal in the war, and died on Sept. 15, 1813 [Ref: J-II:2101].

MUDD, Julian (Julia Ann). See "Richard Mudd," q.v.

MUDD, Leonard. See "William Gardiner," q.v.

MUDD, Luke (1737-1816). Rendered patriotic service in Maryland during the war, married (wife's name unknown), and migrated to Kentucky where he died in 1816 [Ref: J-II:2102].

MUDD, Mary. See "Richard Mudd," q.v.

MUDD, Matilda. See "Richard Mudd," q.v.

MUDD, Melinda. See "William Shercliff," q.v.

MUDD, Peter. Took the Oath of Allegiance in 1778 [Ref: L-19].

MUDD, Richard (c1759-1828). Private, Militia, 26th Battalion, Capt. Richard Bennett Mitchell's Company, 1777, and listed as an invalid (disabled) soldier at that time [Ref: M-164]. Took the Oath of Allegiance in 1778 [Ref: L-19]. Resident of Bryan Town Hundred in 1778 [Ref: Q-

I:297]. Private (furnished by class for 9 months), 1st Maryland Line, by Sept. 11, 1778 [Ref: D-330]. Sergeant, 1st Maryland Line, discharged Jan. 7, 1782 [Ref: D-136]. Mary Mudd, widow of Richard Mudd, applied for a pension (W8476) in Washington County, Kentucky on Jan. 30, 1841, aged 71, stating that she was his second wife (first wife's name not given). She was the former Mary Berry, daughter of Jeremiah Berry, and they were married at her father's home in Montgomery County, Maryland in November 1792 [although source W-119 indicated November 1793]. Richard died in Washington County, Kentucky on May 26, 1828. His two children by his first wife were Electious Mudd (born Feb. 27, 1787) and Mary Ann Mudd (born Aug. 13, 1789 and married ---- Alvey). His children by his second wife were: Elenor Mudd (born Oct. 20, 1794 and married ---- Gittings); Matilda Mudd (born Dec. 3, 1795, married ---- Sims and had children Elizabeth, Sarah E., Harriet F., Ann M., Robert, Emily, and Patrick Sims); Richard Mudd (born May 14, 1797); Jerome Mudd (twin of Mary, born Sept. 16, 1799); Mary Mudd (twin of Jerome, born Sept. 16, 1799, and married ---- Knott); Elizabeth Mudd (born March 23, 1801); Ann Sevilla Mudd (born March 29, 1803 and married ---- Thompson); Henrietta Mudd (born Nov. 29, 1804 and married ---- Gill); Walter Mudd (born Sept. 12, 1806); William B. Mudd (born May 20, 1808); and, Julian or Julia Ann Mudd (born Feb. 24, 1812). [Ref: V-II:2447, J-II:2102].

MUDD, Richard D. See "William Gardiner," q.v.

MUDD, Smith. Private, Militia, 26th Battalion, Capt. Richard Bennett Mitchell's Company, 1777; listed as an invalid (disabled) soldier [Ref: M-164]. Took the Oath of Allegiance in 1778 [Ref: L-19, AA-641]. Resident of Port Tobacco West Hundred in 1778 [Ref: Q-I:297]. Smith Mudd married Elizabeth Swann circa 1785 [Ref: W-119]. See "Jeremiah Mudd," q.v.

MUDD, Walter. See "Richard Mudd," q.v.

MUDD, William (1723-1804). Took the Oath of Allegiance in 1778 [Ref: L-19]. Resident of Port Tobacco West Hundred in 1778 [Ref: Q-I:297]. William Mudd married Elizabeth Clements and migrated to Kentucky where he died in 1804 [Ref: J-II:2102].

MUDD, William B. See "Richard Mudd," q.v.

MUGG, Peter. Private, Militia, 12th Battalion, Capt. John Parnham's Company, 1777 [Ref: M-161]. Resident of Newport West Hundred in 1778 [Ref: Q-I:297].

MUMFORT, Charles. Took the Oath of Allegiance in 1778 [Ref: L-19, AA-641].

MUNCASTER, Charles. Private, Militia, 26th Battalion, Capt. Robert Sinnett's Company, 1777 [Ref: M-164]. Took the Oath of Allegiance in 1778 [Ref: L-19].

MUNCASTER, James (1735-1805). Private, Militia, 26th Battalion, Capt. Robert Sinnett's Company, 1777 [Ref: M-164]. Rendered patriotic service by providing clothing for the use of the military in January 1778 [Ref: Y-II:230]. Took the Oath of Allegiance in 1778 [Ref: AA-641]. Rendered patriotic service by providing wheat for the use of the military in August 1782 [Ref: N-536]. James Muncaster was born in December 1735, married Rachel Gray, and died in Maryland in 1805 [Ref: J-II:2105].

MUNDELL, Robert. Rendered patriotic service by providing clothing for the use of the military in February 1778 [Ref: Y-II:234]. Resident of Port Tobacco Town Hundred in 1778 [Ref: Q-I:297].

MURDOCK, Benjamin (1753-1834). Second Lieutenant, 1st Maryland Line. Benjamin Murdock was born in January 1753, married Mary Anne Magruder, and died in June 1834 [Ref: J-II:2109].

MURDOCK, Godfrey. Took the Oath of Allegiance in 1778 [Ref: L-19]. "Godfree Mordock" was a resident of Durham Lower Hundred in 1778 [Ref: Q-I:297].

MURDOCK, James. Private, Militia, Capt. Francis Mastin's Company, 26th Battalion, March 19, 1776 [Ref: K-1814, M-158]. Private, Militia, 26th Battalion, Capt. Francis Mastin's Company, 1777 [Ref: X-78, and M-164, which listed the name as "Mordock"].

MURDOCK, Samuel. Private, Militia, 26th Battalion, Capt. Francis Mastin's Company, 1777 [Ref: M-164]. "Samuel Moredock" was a resident of Durham Lower Hundred in 1778 [Ref: Q-I:297].

MURDOCK, William. Private, Militia, 26th Battalion, Capt. William Winter's Company, 1777 [Ref: M-165]. "William Mondock" was a resident of Durham Lower Hundred in 1778 [Ref: Q-I:297].

MURPHY, Abraham. Private, Militia, 12th Battalion, Capt. Henry Clarkson's Company, 1777 [Ref: M-159]. Took the Oath of Allegiance in 1778 [Ref: L-19, AA-641]. Resident of Newport East Hundred in 1778 [Ref: Q-I:297]. "Abraham Murphey" married Elizabeth Boswell on Jan. 10, 1758 in Trinity Parish [Ref: EE-13].

MURPHY, Ann. See "William Murphy" and "Samuel Murphy," q.v.

MURPHY, Charles. See "Henry Dixon," q.v.

MURPHY, Daniel (1698-c1778). Took the Oath of Allegiance in 1778 [Ref: L-19, which listed the name as "Murphey"]. Aged about 69 as noted in a 1767 deposition [Ref: DD-21, which listed the name as "Daniel Murphy, Sr."]. Resident of Bryan Town Hundred in 1778 [Ref: Q-I:297]. Source J-II:2110 stated that Daniel Murphy married Mary ----, rendered patriotic service, and died in 1777. However, he took the oath and was still living in 1778.

MURPHY, Daniel Jr. (c1737-c1794) Took the Oath of Allegiance in 1778 [Ref: AA-641]. Resident of Newport West Hundred in 1778 [Ref: Q-I:297]. "Daniel Murphey, Jr." married Ann Moreton on Feb. 17, 1757 in Trinity Parish [Ref: EE-14]. "Daniel Murphy" was born circa 1737, married Anne Moreton, and died after June 10, 1794 [Ref: J-II:2110]. See "William Murphy" and "Samuel Murphy" and "Zephaniah Murphy," q.v.

MURPHY, Elizabeth Morton. See "Zephaniah Waters," q.v.

MURPHY, Francis J. See "Henry Dixon," q.v.

MURPHY, Hezekiah (1742-   ). Private, Militia, 12th Battalion, Capt. John Parnham's Company, 1777 [Ref: M-161, which listed the name as "Hezh. Murphey"]. Aged about 37 as noted in a 1779 deposition [Ref: BB-475, DD-21, which listed the name as "Murphey"]. One Hezekiah Murphy married Sarah Cotton on April 17, 1791 in Nelson County, Kentucky [Ref: W-120].

MURPHY, James (1744-   ). Took the Oath of Allegiance in 1778 [Ref: AA-641, which listed the name as "Murphey"]. Aged about 28 as noted in a 1772 deposition [Ref: DD-21]. Resident of William & Mary Upper Hundred in 1778 [Ref: Q-I:297].

MURPHY, Mary. See "Zephaniah Murphy" and "Daniel Murphy," q.v.

MURPHY, Samuel (1758-   ). Born on Oct. 15, 1758, a son of Daniel Murphy and Ann Moreton [Ref: EE-14]. Corporal, Militia, 12th Battalion, Capt. Henry Clarkson's Company, 1777 [Ref: M-159]. Took the Oath of Allegiance in 1778 [Ref: L-19, which listed the name as "Murphrey"]. Resident of Newport East Hundred in 1778 [Ref: Q-I:297].

MURPHY, William (1762-   ). Born on May 19, 1762, son of Daniel Murphy and Ann Moreton, of Trinity Parish [Ref: EE-11]. Private, 1st Maryland Line, discharged on Dec. 3, 1781 [Ref: I-11].

MURPHY, Zachariah. Private, Militia, 26th Battalion, Capt. Thomas H. Marshall's Company, 1777 [Ref: M-163, which listed the name as "Zacha. Murphey"]. Took the Oath of Allegiance in 1778 [Ref: L-19, which listed the name as "Murphey"]. Resident of Pomonkey Hundred in 1778 [Ref: Q-I:297]. Rendered patriotic service by providing wheat for the use of the military in December 1782 [Ref: N-576].

MURPHY, Zephaniah (1745-   ). Born on Jan. 20, 1745, son of Daniel and Mary Murphy [Ref: EE-3]. Private, Militia, 12th Battalion, Capt. John Parnham's Company, 1777 [Ref: M-161]. Took the Oath of Allegiance in 1778 [Ref: AA-641, which listed the name as "Murphey"]. Resident of Newport East Hundred in 1778 [Ref: Q-I:297]. Aged about 33 as noted in a 1779 deposition [Ref: BB-475, DD-21]. Zephaniah Murphey married

Margit [sic] Hill on Dec. 29, 1765, and Zephaniah Murphey married Eleanor Gray on Jan. 4, 1778, both in Trinity Parish [Ref: EE-12, EE-19].

MURRAY, James. Private (furnished by class for 9 months), 1st Maryland Line, by Sept. 11, 1778 [Ref: D-330, which listed the name as "Murrey"].

MURRAY, Philip Anderson. Private, Militia, 12th Battalion, Capt. John Hanson's Company, 1777 [Ref: M-159]. "Philip Anderson Murry" took the Oath of Allegiance in 1778 [Ref: L-19, AA-641]. "P. Andrew Murray" was a resident of Port Tobacco East Hundred in 1778 [Ref: Q-I:297].

MURROW, Richard. Rendered patriotic service by delivering three bushels of salt to Daniel Jenifer, Purchaser of Provisions for Charles County, on June 12, 1778 [Ref: E-132].

MUSCHETT, John. First Lieutenant, Militia, 26th Battalion, Capt. Robert Sinnett's Company, Feb. 26, 1776 [Ref: A-186, A-206, M-106, M-164, Y-II:23]. Rendered patriotic service by providing clothing for the use of the military in February 1778 [Ref: Y-II:234]. Resident of Port Tobacco West Hundred in 1778 [Ref: Q-I:297]. Rendered patriotic service by providing wheat for the use of the military in September 1781 [Ref: N-432, which listed the name as "Murshett"]. Appointed the Register of Wills for Charles County in the room of Daniel Jenifer (who resigned) on Oct. 8, 1781 [Ref: G-635, which misspelled the name as "Maschatt"]. See "Walter Hanson" and "Walter Hanson Jenifer," q.v.

MUSCHETT, Mungo. Took the Oath of Allegiance in 1778 [Ref: L-19]. Resident of Port Tobacco West Hundred in 1778 [Ref: Q-I:297]. Rendered patriotic service by providing wheat for the use of the military in September 1781 and December 1782 [Ref: N-571, N-432, which also listed the name as "Murshett"].

MUSCHETT, William. Took the Oath of Allegiance in 1778 [Ref: L-19]. Resident of Port Tobacco West Hundred in 1778 [Ref: Q-I:297].

MUSGRAVE, Lydia. See "Robert Gill, Sr.," q.v.

MUSGROVE, Mary Warren. See "John Stone," q.v.

NALLY, Anne. See "Gustavus Nally" and "Thomas Nally," q.v.

NALLY, Barnaba. Took the Oath of Allegiance in 1778 [Ref: AA-641, L-19, which listed the name as "Barnaba(?) Nalley"].

NALLY, Bernard. Private, Militia, 12th Battalion, Capt. Benjamin Lusby Corry's Company, 1777 [Ref: M-160].

NALLY, Dennis. Took the Oath of Allegiance in 1778 [Ref: L-19, AA-641]. Resident of Port Tobacco East Hundred in 1778 [Ref: Q-I:297]. Rendered patriotic service by providing wheat for the use of the military in November 1781 and April 1783 [Ref: N-453, which listed the name as "Dennis Nalley" and N-594, which listed the name as "Deney Natty"].

NALLY, Gustavus. Corporal, Militia, 12th Battalion, Capt. Benjamin Lusby Corry's Company, 1777 [Ref: M-160]. "Gustavus Nally" took the Oath of Allegiance in 1778 [Ref: AA-641]. "Rodolphea Gustavus Nalley" was born on Jan. 4, 1755, a son of Thomas and Anne Nalley, of Trinity Parish [Ref: EE-8].

NALLY, Ignatius. Private, Militia, 12th Battalion, Capt. Benjamin Lusby Corry's Company, 1777 [Ref: M-160]. Took the Oath of Allegiance in 1778 [Ref: L-19]. Resident of Newport West Hundred in 1778 [Ref: Q-I:297].

NALLY, John. Private, Militia, 26th Battalion, Capt. Hezekiah Garner's Company, 1777 [Ref: M-163].

NALLY, Leonard. Private, Militia, 12th Battalion, Capt. Alexander McPherson's Company, 1777 [Ref: M-160]. Took the Oath of Allegiance in 1778 [Ref: L-19, which listed the name as "Nalley"]. Resident of Port Tobacco East Hundred in 1778 [Ref: Q-I:297].

NALLY, Nathan. Sergeant, Militia, 26th Battalion, Capt. Richard Bennett Mitchell's Company, 1777 [Ref: M-164].

NALLY, Shadrick. Private, Militia, 26th Battalion, Capt. Samuel Smallwood's Company, 1777 [Ref: M-165]. Resident of Port Tobacco Upper Hundred in 1778 [Ref: Q-I:297].

NALLY, Thomas. "Thomas Nally" took the Oath of Allegiance in 1778 [Ref: L-19]. "Thomas Cooksey Nalley" was born on April 11, 1759, a son of Thomas and Anne Nalley, of Trinity Parish [Ref: EE-8]. See "Gustavus Nally," q.v.

NALLY, William (1709-   ). Took the Oath of Allegiance in 1778 [Ref: L-19]. Aged about 43 as noted in a 1752 deposition [Ref: DD-170]. Resident of Newport West Hundred in 1778 [Ref: Q-I:297].

NASH, Joseph. Took the Oath of Allegiance in 1778 [Ref: L-19].

NASH, Thomas (1701-   ). Took the Oath of Allegiance in 1778 [Ref: L-19, AA-641]. Aged about 62 as noted in a 1763 deposition [Ref: DD-170].

NATTY, Deney. See "Dennis Nally," q.v.

NAYLOR, Martha. See "George Walls," q.v.

NEALE, Benjamin (1702-   ). Took the Oath of Allegiance in 1778 [Ref: L-19, AA-641]. Aged about 35 as noted in a 1737 deposition [Ref: DD-170]. Resident of Port Tobacco West Hundred in 1778 [Ref: Q-I:297].

NEALE, Bennett. "Bennett Neall" was a private, 1st Maryland Line, who enlisted in Frederick County in July 1776 [Ref: D-45]. "Bennett Neale" took the Oath of Allegiance in Charles County in 1778 [Ref: AA-641]. Rendered patriotic service by providing clothing for the use of the military in February 1778 [Ref: Y-II:234]. Resident of William & Mary Lower Hundred in 1778 [Ref: Q-I:297].

NEALE, Henry. Born in Charles County in 1740, served as Third Lieutenant in the 5th Independent Maryland Company on Jan. 2, 1776, and married Eleanor Plowden in 1778. Their daughter Margaret Eleanor Neale (born 1784) married William Henry H. Pile [Ref: D-25, J-II:2124, *Maryland Directory, DAR, 1892-1965*, p. 540].

NEALE, James. Private, Militia, 12th Battalion, Capt. Jonathan Yates' Company, 1777 [Ref: M-162]. Rendered patriotic service by providing clothing for the use of the military in February 1778 [Ref: Y-II:234]. Took the Oath of Allegiance in 1778 [Ref: L-19, AA-641]. Resident of William & Mary Lower Hundred in 1778 [Ref: Q-I:297]. In November 1803, the Treasurer of Maryland was directed to pay to one "James Neale, on application, fifteen pounds current money, and the further sum of fifteen pounds like money annually, in quarterly payments, as a support to him in his infirm situation, and in consideration of his many services as a soldier in the late Revolutionary War, from the effects of which he has been rendered entirely unable to obtain a subsistence." [Ref: Q-II:377, Q-II:378]. It must be noted that there were men by this name in Charles County, Frederick County, and Washington County during the Revolutionary War [Ref: M-162, D-336, D-469, D-579, D-584]. One James Neale was born circa 1747, married Elizabeth Boarman, and died before April 29, 1800 [Ref: J-II:2124].

NEALE, John. Second Lieutenant, Militia, 12th Battalion, Capt. Jonathan Yates' Company, Feb. 26, 1776 [Ref: M-106, M-162, A-186, A-206, Y-II:23, which latter two sources listed the name as "Neal"]. Resident of William & Mary Lower Hundred in 1778 [Ref: Q-I:297]. First Lieutenant, Militia, Capt. John Lancaster's Company, commissioned on Jan. 19, 1781 [Ref: G-280, M-106].

NEALE, Joseph. Private, Militia, 12th Battalion, Capt. Jonathan Yates' Company, 1777 [Ref: X-70, but was omitted from the list in Reference M-162]. Took the Oath of Allegiance in 1778 [Ref: L-19, AA-641]. Resident of William & Mary Lower Hundred in 1778 [Ref: Q-I:297].

NEALE, Margaret Eleanor. See "Henry Neale," q.v.

NEALE, Mary. See "John Digges," q.v.

NEALE, Raphael (1745-   ). Took the Oath of Allegiance in 1778 [Ref: L-19]. Resident of Port Tobacco East Hundred in 1778 [Ref: Q-I:297]. Aged about 33 as noted in a 1778 deposition [Ref: CC-704, which listed the name as "Neal"]. "Raphael Neal" was an ensign in the St. Mary's County militia in 1779 [Ref: M-106, F-18]. Rendered patriotic service by providing wheat for the use of the military in Charles County in December 1781 [Ref: N-464, which mistakenly listed the name as "Nedle"]. "Ralph Neal" rendered patriotic service by providing wheat for the use of the military in December 1782 [Ref: N-577].

NEALE, William. Private, 1st Maryland Line, drafted (substitute) from the Charles County militia to served from July 27, 1781 to Dec. 10, 1781; discharged on April 6, 1782 [Ref: D-377, I-123].

NEALE, William F. Private, Militia, 12th Battalion, Capt. Jonathan Yates' Company, 1777 [Ref: M-162]. Resident of William & Mary Lower Hundred in 1778 [Ref: Q-I:297].

NELSON, Clarissa. See "William Luckett," q.v.

NELSON, John. Private, 1st Maryland Line, enrolled and passed on July 19, 1776 [Ref: D-31]. Took the Oath of Allegiance in 1778 [Ref: L-19, AA-641]. Resident of Port Tobacco West Hundred in 1778 [Ref: Q-I:297]. Ensign, 1st Maryland Line, Jan. 26, 1780 [Ref: D-146].

NELSON, John, of John. Private, Militia, 26th Battalion, Capt. Richard Bennett Mitchell's Company, 1777 [Ref: M-164]. Resident of Port Tobacco West Hundred in 1778 [Ref: Q-I:297].

NELSON, Joseph. Private, Militia, 26th Battalion, Capt. Richard Bennett Mitchell's Company, 1777 [Ref: M-164]. Took the Oath of Allegiance in 1778 [Ref: L-19, AA-641]. Rendered patriotic service by providing wheat for the use of the military in May 1783 [Ref: N-598]. Resident of Port Tobacco West Hundred in 1778 [Ref: Q-I:297].

NELSON, Penner. Private, 1st Maryland Line, enrolled and passed on July 19, 1776 [Ref: D-31].

NELSON, Richard (1745-   ). Took the Oath of Allegiance in 1778 [Ref: L-19]. Resident of Port Tobacco East Hundred in 1778 [Ref: Q-I:297]. Aged about 33 as noted in a 1778 deposition [Ref: DD-170]. See "William Nelson," q.v.

NELSON, Thomas. Private, Militia, 26th Battalion, Capt. Hezekiah Garner's Company, 1777 [Ref: M-163]. Petitioned the Council of Maryland in 1783 stating that he had not taken the Oath of Allegiance due to any disaffection with the government, but from a variety of incidents, and was unjustly penalized as a non-juror and fined unfairly; therefore, he asked the Council to consider ordering the County Justices to remit the fines they imposed on him and others who signed the petition. The Council of Maryland, after reviewing his case, indicated they believed the truth of the facts stated in the petition and ordered a remission of the fines and penalties on Sept. 17, 1783 [Ref: I-454].

NELSON, William (1700-   ). Took the Oath of Allegiance in 1778 [Ref: L-19, AA-641]. Resident of Port Tobacco West Hundred in 1778 [Ref: Q-I:297]. Aged about 53 as noted in a 1753 deposition (which mentioned his brother Richard Nelson), aged about 73 as noted in a 1773 deposition, and aged about 79 as noted in a 1778 deposition [Ref: DD-170].

NELSON, William, of Thomas. Private, Militia, 26th Battalion, Capt. Richard Bennett Mitchell's Company, 1777 [Ref: M-164].

NEVITT, Charles. Private, Militia, 26th Battalion, Capt. William Winter's Company, 1777 [Ref: M-165].

NEWBERRY, John. Private, 1st Maryland Line, drafted from the Charles County militia and reported sick on July 27, 1781 [Ref: D-377].

NEWBERRY, Joseph. Private, 1st Maryland Line, drafted from the Charles County militia and in service on June 11 or 12, 1781 [Ref: D-376, G-569, which latter source listed the name as "Newbury"].

NEWMAN, Butler (1735-c1790). Born in Charles County, he took the Oath of Allegiance in Prince George's County in 1778. He married Virlinda Stonestreet and their eldest son George Newman (born in 1760) served in the Flying Camp and saw active duty in New York with the Maryland Line during the war [Ref: Harry Wright Newman's *Charles County Gentry*, p. 272].

NEWMAN, Edward. Private, Militia, 12th Battalion, Capt. John Hanson's Company, 1777 [Ref: M-159]. Took the Oath of Allegiance in 1778 [Ref: AA-641].

NEWMAN, Eleanor. See "Walter Fearson," q.v.

NEWMAN, George. See "Butler Newman" and "Walter Fearson," q.v.

NEWMAN, Harry Wright. See "Benjamin Lusby Corry" and "George Clarke Smoot" and "John Alexander Smoot" and "Isaac Smoot" and "Edward Smoot" and "Thomas Smoot" and "Willoughby Smoot" and "Henry Smoot" and "Benjamin Dent" and "Joseph Manning Dent" and "Theodore Dent" and "Walter Dent, Jr." and "Benjamin Edelen" and "Clement Edelen" and "Edward Edelen" and "Joseph Edelen" and "Susannah Edelen" and "Samuel Hanson, of Samuel" and "Thomas Hawkins Hanson" and "Walter Hanson, of John" and "Butler Newman" and "Thomas Dent Hardy" and "Robert Rogers," q.v.

NEWMAN, Pricilla. See "Attwix Fearson," q.v.

NEWTON, Richard. See "Henry Woodward," q.v.

NISFIELD, Jeremiah. See "Jeremiah Highfield," q.v.

NOBLE, John. Private, 2nd Maryland Regiment, 1777, promoted to sergeant on June 1, 1778, and discharged on Jan. 1, 1780 [Ref: D-146].

NOBLE, Martin. Private, 2nd Maryland Line, enlisted June 26, 1779. Initially reported as missing after the Battle of Camden in South Carolina on Aug. 16, 1780, he was subsequently reported "died of wounds." [Ref: D-146].

NOBLE, Salome. See "Edward Edelen (Eadlin)" and "Joseph Edelen (Edelin)," q.v.

NOBLE, William F. Took the Oath of Allegiance in 1778 [Ref: L-19, AA-641].

NOLAND, Barbara. See "James Noland," q.v.

NOLAND, Elizabeth. See "Thomas Hussey Luckett," q.v.

NOLAND, Francis. See "James Noland," q.v.

NOLAND, James (1740-1833). Born in Charles County, Maryland, he moved with his father (not named) and family to Loudoun County, Virginia as a young man. He married Barbara Saunders on Dec. 26, 1774 and served in the Revolutionary War. They then moved to Rowan County, North Carolina where he served again in 1780 as a captain for about twelve months. His brother Jesse Noland also served. In 1812 James moved to Estill County, Kentucky where he died on Dec. 26, 1833. His widow applied for and received pension W9202 on Oct. 1, 1838, stating she was born on May 28, 1760. In 1844 she moved to LaPorte County, Indiana to live with her children: Stephen Noland (first child, born June 6, 1776); Silas Noland (born Oct. 11, 1778); Rasha Noland (son, born July 29, 1771); Francis Noland (born in 1785); John Noland (seventh child, born June 9, 1792), and James Noland (no birth date was given). [Ref: T-33, T-34, V-III:2507, J-II:2156]. See "Jesse Noland," q.v.

NOLAND, Jesse (1761-c1836). Born in Charles County, Maryland, he moved with his father (not named) and family to Loudon County, Virginia as a child. They later went to Rowan County, North Carolina, where Jesse enlisted in the militia in 1780 and served three years. During this time his father (name not given) died, leaving his mother a widow. Jesse moved to Kentucky in 1784 and applied for and received a pension (S14039) in Estill County on Nov. 19, 1832, aged 71. Jesse's brother James Noland (aged 92) verified his service during the war. Jesse Noland married first to Sarah ----, second to Abigail Whitacre, and died after Sept. 9, 1836 in Kentucky [Ref: T-33, V-III:2507, J-II:2156]. See "James Noland," q.v.

NOLAND, John. See "James Roland," q.v.

NOLAND, Ledstone (1750-1839). Private, North Carolina troops. He was born in Maryland in 1750, married first to Elizabeth Glascock, second to Mary Smallwood, lived in North Carolina, and migrated to Missouri where he died before July 6, 1839 [Ref: J-II:2156].

NOLAND, Mary. See "Stephen Noland," q.v.

NOLAND, Patrick. Private, 1st Maryland Line, enlisted Dec. 10, 1776 and discharged Dec. 27, 1779; apparently reenlisted in 1780 and was reported dead on Sept. 1, 1782 [Ref: D-549, D-146, which listed the name as "Patk. Nolan"].

NOLAND, Rasha. See "James Noland," q.v.
NOLAND, Sarah. See "Jesse Noland," q.v.
NOLAND, Silas. See "James Noland," q.v.
NOLAND, Stephen (c1741-c1792). Private, North Carolina troops. He was born in Maryland circa 1741, married Mary ----, and died in North Carolina before Aug. 11, 1792 [Ref: J-II:2156]. See "James Noland," q.v.
NOLAND, Thomas (1748-1811). Private, 1st Maryland Line. He was born in Virginia, married Mary Eleanor Luckett, served in the Maryland Line during the war, and died in Virginia on March 12, 1811 [Ref: J-II:2156].
NORRIS, Daniel. Private, Militia, 26th Battalion, Capt. Robert Sinnett's Company, 1777 [Ref: M-164, which listed the name as "Danl. Norriss"]. Took the Oath of Allegiance in 1778 [Ref: L-19, which listed the name as "Norriss"]. Resident of Port Tobacco West Hundred in 1778 [Ref: Q-I:297]. Gave a deposition in 1781 pertaining to his inability to perform military service due to poor health [Ref: Z-208].
NORRIS, Mark (c1759-c1840). Private, Flying Camp, Capt. Bowie's Company, enrolled July 16, 1776; native of Charles County, aged 17, height 5' 7 1/4" [Ref: D-36, which listed the name as "Norriss"]. Took the Oath of Allegiance in 1778 [Ref: AA-641, L-19, which latter source listed the name as "Norriss"]. Resident of Port Tobacco West Hundred in 1778 [Ref: Q-I:297]. "Marke Norris" was born circa 1753, married Martha Seaton, and migrated to Kentucky where he died before 1840 [Ref: J-II:2158].
NORRIS, William. Private, Militia, Capt. Francis Mastin's Company, 26th Battalion, March 19, 1776 through at least 1777 [Ref: M-158, M-164, K-1814]. Took the Oath of Allegiance in 1778 [Ref: L-19, AA-641, which listed the name as "Norrice"].
NORRY, Mark. Private, Militia, 26th Battalion, Capt. Richard Bennett Mitchell's Company, 1777 [Ref: M-164].
NORTON, John. Took the Oath of Allegiance in 1778 [Ref: L-19].
NORWOOD, Garner. Took the Oath of Allegiance in 1778 [Ref: AA-641]. Resident of William & Mary Upper Hundred in 1778 [Ref: Q-I:297].
NORWOOD, Gerard. Private, Militia, 12th Battalion, Capt. Jonathan Yates' Company, 1777 [Ref: M-162].
NOTAIRE, Michael. Private, 1st Maryland Line, enrolled and passed on July 25, 1776 [Ref: D-32].
NOTLEY, Sarah. See "Samuel Moreland," q.v.
NOTT, Jestinion. See "Justinian Knott," q.v.
NOTTINGHAM, Stephen. Private, Militia, 26th Battalion, Capt. Richard Bennett Mitchell's Company, 1777; listed as an invalid (disabled) soldier [Ref: M-165]. Took the Oath of Allegiance in 1778 [Ref: L-19, AA-641,

which latter source listed the name as "Nottinghame"]. Resident of Pomonkey Hundred in 1778 [Ref: Q-I:297].

NULE, Bennett. Rendered patriotic service by providing wheat for the use of the military in December 1782 [Ref: N-578].

OAKLEY, Elijah. Private, 4th Maryland Line, by Jan. 1, 1782 [Ref: D-461].

OAKLEY, John. Corporal, Militia, 12th Battalion, Capt. Jonathan Yates' Company, 1777 [Ref: M-162].

OAKLEY, John (1721-   ). Took the Oath of Allegiance in 1778 [Ref: L-19, AA-641]. Aged about 40 as noted in a 1761 deposition [Ref: DD-171]. Resident of William & Mary Lower Hundred in 1778 [Ref: Q-I:297].

OAKLEY, Robert. Private, Militia, 12th Battalion, Capt. Jonathan Yates' Company, 1777 [Ref: M-162]. Took the Oath of Allegiance in 1778 [Ref: AA-641]. Resident of William & Mary Lower Hundred in 1778 [Ref: Q-I:297].

OARD, Peter. Private, Lower Battalion, Prince George's County, 1776 [Ref: D-35]. Took the Oath of Allegiance in Charles County in 1778 [Ref: AA-641, L-19, which latter source listed the name as "Ord"]. Resident of Port Tobacco Upper Hundred in 1778 [Ref: Q-I:297].

OARD, William (1754-1833). Born in Charles County, Maryland on Sept. 22, 1754, he lived in St. Mary's County at the time of his enlistment in the Maryland Line. During the war he moved to Virginia and served in the Virginia Line. After the war he moved to Ohio and then to Indiana where he applied for a pension (S16496) in Parke County on May 11, 1833. He died on Sept. 15, 1833 [Ref: V-III:2527].

O'BRYAN, Cornelius. Private, Militia, 12th Battalion, Capt. Alexander McPherson's Company, 1777 [Ref: M-160]. Took the Oath of Allegiance in 1778 [Ref: L-19].

O'BRYAN, James. Took the Oath of Allegiance in 1778 [Ref: L-19].

O'BRYAN, Jonas. Took the Oath of Allegiance in 1778 [Ref: L-19].

O'BRYAN, Josias. Private, Militia, 12th Battalion, Capt. Alexander McPherson's Company, 1777 [Ref: M-160].

ODEN, Elias. Corporal, Militia, 12th Battalion, Capt. Alexander McPherson's Company, 1777 [Ref: M-160]. Resident of Bryan Town Hundred in 1778 [Ref: Q-I:297].

ODEN, Isaac. Private, Militia, 12th Battalion, Capt. Peter Wood's Company, 1777 [Ref: M-161].

ODEN, Sarah Biggs. See "Edward Lloyd Wales," q.v.

ODEN, Thomas. Corporal, Militia, 12th Battalion, Capt. Peter Wood's Company, 1777 [Ref: M-161, which listed the name as "Odan"]. Took the Oath of Allegiance in 1778 [Ref: AA-641]. Resident of Benedict Hundred in 1778 [Ref: Q-I:297].

ODEN, Vincent. Corporal, Militia, 12th Battalion, Capt. Peter Wood's Company, 1777 [Ref: M-161, which listed the name as "Odan"]. Took the Oath of Allegiance in 1778 [Ref: L-19, which listed the name as "Odin"]. Resident of Benedict Hundred in 1778 [Ref: Q-I:297].

OGDON, Benjamin. Sergeant, Militia, 12th Battalion, Capt. Peter Wood's Company, 1777 [Ref: M-161]. Ensign, Militia, Capt. William Wilkinson's Company, commissioned May 9, 1778 [Ref: M-108, E-72, which listed the name as "Ogden"]. Took the Oath of Allegiance in 1778 [Ref: L-19, AA-641]. Resident of Benedict Hundred in 1778 [Ref: Q-I:297].

OGDON, Henry. Took the Oath of Allegiance in 1778 [Ref: AA-641]. Resident of Bryan Town Hundred in 1778 [Ref: Q-I:297].

OGDON, Jonathan. Private, Militia, 26th Battalion, Capt. Benjamin Cawood's Company, 1777 [Ref: M-162, which listed the name as "Ogden"]. Took the Oath of Allegiance in 1778 [Ref: AA-641]. Resident of Port Tobacco East Hundred in 1778 [Ref: Q-I:297].

OGDON, Thomas. Private, Militia, 12th Battalion, Capt. Alexander McPherson's Company, 1777 [Ref: M-160]. Took the Oath of Allegiance in 1778 [Ref: AA-641]. Resident of Port Tobacco East Hundred in 1778 [Ref: Q-I:297].

OGDON, William Sr. Took the Oath of Allegiance in 1778 [Ref: AA-641]. Resident of Newport West Hundred in 1778 [Ref: Q-I:297].

OLIVER, William. Resident of Newport West Hundred in 1778 [Ref: Q-I:297]. Private, 1st Maryland Line, drafted from the Charles County militia on July 27, 1781, determined unfit for service and discharged on Oct. 30, 1781 [Ref: D-377, G-569, G-657].

O'NEALE, Andrew. Took the Oath of Allegiance in 1778 [Ref: L-19, which listed the name as "O'Nealle"].

O'NEALE, Anthony. Private, Militia, 26th Battalion, Capt. Samuel Smallwood's Company, 1777 [Ref: M-165]. Took the Oath of Allegiance in 1778 [Ref: AA-641]. Resident of Port Tobacco Upper Hundred in 1778 [Ref: Q-I:297].

OSBORN, David. "David Osborn" took the Oath of Allegiance in 1778 [Ref: L-19, AA-641]. "David Osbin" was a resident of Port Tobacco East Hundred in 1778 [Ref: Q-I:297].

OSBORN, Henry. Private, Militia, 26th Battalion, Capt. Benjamin Cawood's Company, 1777 [Ref: M-162, which listed the name as "Ozburne"]. Took the Oath of Allegiance in 1778 [Ref: L-19, AA-641]. Resident of Port Tobacco East Hundred in 1778 [Ref: Q-I:297].

OSBORN, John. Private, Militia, 26th Battalion, Capt. Benjamin Cawood's Company, 1777 [Ref: M-162, which listed the name as "Ozburne"].

OSBURN, Joseph. "Joseph Osburn" took the Oath of Allegiance in 1778 [Ref: AA-641]. "Joseph Osbin" was a resident of Port Tobacco East Hundred in 1778 [Ref: Q-I:297].

OSBURN, Thomas. Private, 1st Maryland Line, enrolled and passed on July 18, 1776 [Ref: D-32, which listed the name as "Ozburn"]. Took the Oath of Allegiance in 1778 [Ref: L-19]. Resident of Bryan Town Hundred in 1778 [Ref: Q-I:297].

OSBORN, Thomas Sr. Private, Militia, 12th Battalion, Capt. Alexander McPherson's Company, 1777 [Ref: M-160]. Resident of Port Tobacco East Hundred in 1778 [Ref: Q-I:297].

OSTRO, Thomas. Corporal, Militia, 26th Battalion, Capt. Richard Bennett Mitchell's Company, 1777 [Ref: M-164]. Resident of Port Tobacco West Hundred in 1778 [Ref: Q-I:297].

OSTROW, William. Private, 1st Maryland Line, enlisted June 17, 1777 and discharged Oct. 1, 1779. "Did not return to his furlough, discharged by G. Smallwood 20 April 1780." [Ref: D-148].

OWEN, Joseph. Sergeant, Militia, 26th Battalion, Capt. Benjamin Cawood's Company, 1777 [Ref: M-162]. Took the Oath of Allegiance in 1778 [Ref: AA-641].

OWEN, Richard. See "Richard Owens," q.v.

OWEN, Thomas (c1753-c1800). Private, Flying Camp, Capt. Bowie's Company, enrolled July 16, 1776; native of Charles County, aged 23, height 6' 1/2" [Ref: D-36]. Private, Militia, 26th Battalion, Capt. Robert Sinnett's Company, 1777 [Ref: M-164]. Resident of Port Tobacco West Hundred in 1778 [Ref: Q-I:297]. One Thomas Owen was born in Maryland in 1750, married Sally Farmer, served as a private in the war, and migrated to Kentucky where he died in 1800 [Ref: J-II:2203].

OWEN, Thomas Sr. Took the Oath of Allegiance in 1778 [Ref: L-19]. Resident of Port Tobacco West Hundred in 1778 [Ref: Q-I:297].

OWENS, Ewell. Private, Militia, 26th Battalion, Capt. Francis Mastin's Company, 1777 [Ref: M-164].

OWENS, Joseph. Private, 1st Maryland Line, drafted from the Charles County militia and reported sick on July 27, 1781 [Ref: D-377].

OWENS, Richard. Took the Oath of Allegiance in 1778 [Ref: L-19]. One "Richard Owen" was a resident of Port Tobacco West Hundred and another "Richard Owen" was a resident of Port Tobacco East Hundred in 1778 [Ref: Q-I:297].

OWINGS, Joseph. Private (furnished by class for 9 months), 1st Maryland Line, enlisted June 5, 1778 and discharged in February 1779 [Ref: D-148, D-330].

OWINGS, Samuel. Private (substitute for 3 years), 1st Maryland Line, by Sept. 11, 1778; subsequently mustered and joined the Maryland Line on April 1, 1780 [Ref: D-148, D-330].

PADGETT (PAGGETT), Aaron. Private, Militia, 26th Battalion, Capt. Samuel Smallwood's Company, 1777 [Ref: M-165]. Took the Oath of Allegiance in 1778 [Ref: L-19, AA-641]. Resident of Port Tobacco Upper Hundred in 1778 [Ref: Q-I:297].

PADGETT (PAGGETT), Benjamin. Took the Oath of Allegiance in 1778 [Ref: AA-641]. Resident of Port Tobacco Upper Hundred in 1778 [Ref: Q-I:297]. One "Benjn. Paget" was aged about 31 as noted in a 1726 deposition [Ref: DD-171].

PADGETT (PAGGETT), Benjamin Jr. Took the Oath of Allegiance in 1778 [Ref: L-19, AA-641]. "Benjamin Paggett, of Benjamin" was a private in the militia, 26th Battalion, Capt. Samuel Smallwood's Company, 1777 [Ref: M-165]. Resident of Port Tobacco Upper Hundred in 1778 [Ref: Q-I:297].

PADGETT (PAGGETT), Benjamin, of William. Private, Militia, 26th Battalion, Capt. Samuel Smallwood's Company, 1777 [Ref: M-165, which listed the name as "Benj Padgitt of Wm."]. Resident of Port Tobacco Upper Hundred in 1778 [Ref: Q-I:297].

PADGETT (PAGGETT), Henry. Took the Oath of Allegiance in 1778 [Ref: L-19, AA-641]. Rendered patriotic service by providing wheat for the use of the military in December 1782 [Ref: N-573]. Resident of Port Tobacco East Hundred in 1778 [Ref: Q-I:297].

PADGETT (PAGGETT), James. Private, Militia, 12th Battalion, Capt. John Hanson's Company, 1777 [Ref: M-159, which listed the name as "Padget"]. Took the Oath of Allegiance in 1778 [Ref: L-19, AA-641]. Resident of Port Tobacco Upper Hundred in 1778 [Ref: Q-I:297].

PADGETT (PAGGETT), Jonathan. Took the Oath of Allegiance in 1778 [Ref: AA-641]. Resident of Port Tobacco East Hundred in 1778 [Ref: Q-I:297].

PADGETT (PAGGETT), Joseph. Private, Militia, 26th Battalion, Capt. Benjamin Cawood's Company, 1777 [Ref: M-162]. Resident of Port Tobacco East Hundred in 1778 [Ref: Q-I:297]. Private, 1st Maryland Line, drafted from the Charles County militia and reported lame in June 1781 [Ref: D-376, which listed the name as "Pagett"].

PADGETT (PAGGETT), Thomas. Private, Militia, 12th Battalion, Capt. John Hanson's Company, 1777 [Ref: M-158, which listed the name as "Padget"]. Resident of Port Tobacco East Hundred in 1778 [Ref: Q-I:297].

PADGETT (PAGGETT), William. Corporal, Militia, 26th Battalion, Capt. Thomas H. Marshall's Company, 1777 [Ref: M-163]. Rendered patriotic service by providing wheat for the use of the military in October 1782 [Ref: N-562, which listed the name as "Pagett"].

PADGETT (PAGGETT), William. Took the Oath of Allegiance in 1778 [Ref: L-19]. Resident of Pomonkey Hundred in 1778 [Ref: Q-I:297]. Died testate in July 1778 [Ref: GG-187].

PAGE, Walter. Private, Militia, 26th Battalion, Capt. Richard Bennett Mitchell's Company, 1777 [Ref: M-165].

PALMER, James. Took the Oath of Allegiance in 1778 [Ref: L-19].

PARK, Thomas. Took the Oath of Allegiance in 1778 [Ref: L-19].

PARKER, Abraham Jr. Private, Militia, 12th Battalion, Capt. Peter Wood's Company, 1777 [Ref: M-161]. Took the Oath of Allegiance in 1778 [Ref: AA-641]. Resident of Benedict Hundred in 1778 [Ref: Q-I:297].

PARKER, Abraham Sr. Took the Oath of Allegiance in 1778 [Ref: L-19]. Resident of Benedict Hundred in 1778 [Ref: Q-I:297].

PARKER, Jonathan. Private, Militia, 12th Battalion, Capt. Peter Wood's Company, 1777 [Ref: M-161]. Took the Oath of Allegiance in 1778 [Ref: L-19]. Resident of Benedict Hundred in 1778 [Ref: Q-I:297].

PARKER, Paul. Private, 1st Maryland Line, enrolled and passed on July 19, 1776 [Ref: D-31].

PARMER, James. Private, Militia, 26th Battalion, Capt. Thomas H. Marshall's Company, 1777 [Ref: M-163]. Resident of Pomonkey Hundred in 1778 [Ref: Q-I:297].

PARMER, Thomas. Private, 3rd Maryland Line, May 21, 1779 until discharged and transferred to the Invalids Corps on Dec. 22, 1779. Reportedly "deserted" on June 21, 1780 [Ref: D-152].

PARNHAM, Eleanor Ann Hawkins Dent. See "John Parnham," q.v.

PARNHAM, Francis (doctor). See "John Parnham," q.v.

PARNHAM, George Dent. See "John Parnham," q.v.

PARNHAM, John (c1748-1813). Son of Dr. Francis Parnham, he married Ann Dent and had these children: George Dent Parnham; John Pile Parnham; Mary Parnham; Eleanor Ann Hawkins Dent Parnham; and, Susannah Ann Parnham. John attended the Maryland Convention in 1776 and served in the Lower House of the Maryland Legislature, 1787-1799, 1808-1810. Committee of Observation, 1776. Court Justice, 1777-1796. Maryland Senate Elector between 1791 and 1806 [Ref: P-II:635, P-II:636]. Captain, Militia, 12th Battalion, from July 26, 1776 through March 20, 1781 or April 6, 1781. Served as chief surgeon of Gen. William Smallwood's Regiment during the entire war [Ref: B-125, B-126, B-269, G-379, H-136, P-II:636, M-110, M-160, which latter source misspelled the name as "Barnham"]. Justice who administered (and took) the Oath of Allegiance in 1778 [Ref: AA-641]. Resident of Newport West Hundred in

1778 [Ref: Q-I:297]. Appointed a Justice of the Peace on Nov. 21, 1778 and Nov. 19, 1779 and Jan. 17, 1782 [Ref: E-249, F-19, I-45].
PARNHAM, John Pile. See "John Parnham," q.v.
PARNHAM, Mary. See "John Parnham," q.v.
PARNHAM, Susannah Ann. See "John Parnham," q.v.
PARSONS, Jeremiah. Private (substitute for 9 months), 1st Maryland Line, by Sept. 11, 1778 [Ref: D-330].
PATTERSON, Hezekiah. Private (substitute for 9 months), 1st Maryland Line, by Sept. 11, 1778 [Ref: D-330]. Took the Oath of Allegiance in 1778 [Ref: L-19, AA-641].
PATTERSON, John. "John Paterson" took the Oath of Allegiance in 1778 [Ref: L-19, AA-641]. "John Pattison" was a resident of Bryan Town Hundred in 1778 [Ref: Q-I:297]. See "Perry Patterson," q.v.
PATTERSON, Perry. Private (substitute for 3 years), 1st Maryland Line, by Sept. 11, 1778 [Ref: D-330]. Took the Oath of Allegiance in 1778 [Ref: AA-641, which listed the name as "Perry Pattison" and L-19, which mistakenly listed the name as "Persy Patterson"]. "Perry Pattison" was aged about 50 as noted in a 1772 deposition (which mentioned his father John) and "Perry Patterson" was aged about 61 as noted in a 1778 deposition [Ref: DD-171]. "Perry Pattison" was a resident of Durham Lower Hundred in 1778 [Ref: Q-I:297].
PATTERSON, Thomas. Private, 1st Maryland Line, enrolled and passed on July 25, 1776 [Ref: D-32].
PAYNE (PAINE), Ebenezer. Private, Militia, 26th Battalion, Capt. Samuel Smallwood's Company, 1777 [Ref: M-165].
PAYNE (PAINE), Francis. Private, Militia, 26th Battalion, Capt. Samuel Smallwood's Company, 1777 [Ref: M-165]. Resident of Port Tobacco Upper Hundred in 1778 [Ref: Q-I:297].
PAYNE (PAINE), Francis Jr. Took the Oath of Allegiance in 1778 [Ref: L-19, which listed the name as "Pain" and AA-641, which listed the name as "Paine"]. Resident of Port Tobacco Upper Hundred in 1778 [Ref: Q-I:297].
PAYNE (PAINE), Ignatius. Private, Militia, 26th Battalion, Capt. Samuel Smallwood's Company, 1777 [Ref: M-165]. Took the Oath of Allegiance in 1778 [Ref: L-19]. Resident of Port Tobacco Upper Hundred in 1778 [Ref: Q-I:297].
PAYNE (PAINE), Jest. or Josh. Private, Militia, 26th Battalion, Capt. Francis Mastin's Company, 1777 [Ref: M-164, which listed the name as "Jest. Payne" and X-78, which listed the name as "Josh. Payne"].
PAYNE (PAINE), Josias. Took the Oath of Allegiance in 1778 [Ref: AA-641].

PEARSON, Dennis. Private (substitute for 3 years), 1st Maryland Line, by Sept. 11, 1778 [Ref: D-330].
PEARSON, Edward. Private, 1st Maryland Line, enrolled and passed on July 19, 1776 [Ref: D-31].
PECK, Sarah. Rendered patriotic service by providing wheat for the use of the military in September 1781 [Ref: N-432].
PEDEN, Eva Coe. See "Matthew Kidwell," q.v.
PEDEN, Henry C. See "Joseph Higdon" and "Ralph Briscoe," q.v.
PEEK (PEAK), John. "John Peek" is listed twice among those who took the Oath of Allegiance in 1780 [Ref: O-117]. One "John Peak" was a resident of Port Tobacco West Hundred in 1778 [Ref: Q-I:297].
PEEK (PEAKE), Nathan. Private, 1st Maryland Line, Capt. Edward Prall's Company, by 1782, and "certified by Ensign B. Burgess that his time of service expired 17 Nov 1782." [Ref: D-149, D-432, D-550, which latter source referred to him as "Serjt."].
PENN, Elizabeth. See "Stephen Penn," q.v.
PENN, Jezreal. Private, Militia, 12th Battalion, Capt. Jonathan Yates' Company, 1777 [Ref: M-162, which listed the name as "Jezrul Penn"]. Rendered patriotic service by providing clothing for the use of the military in February 1778 [Ref: Y-II:234, which listed the name as "Jezreel Penn"]. Took the Oath of Allegiance in 1778 [Ref: L-19, which listed the name as "Jez Penn" and AA-641, which listed the name as "Jezreel Penn"]. Resident of William & Mary Lower Hundred in 1778 [Ref: Q-I:297, which misspelled the name as "Zezreel Penn"]. Rendered patriotic service by providing wheat for the use of the military in April and December 1782, and May 1783 [Ref: N-504, N-577, N-599, which mistakenly listed the name as "Teyreell Penn" and "Teyeerl Penn"]. See "Richard Harrison," q.v.
PENN, John. Private (substitute for 9 months), 1st Maryland Line, by Sept. 11, 1778 [Ref: D-330]. On Feb. 16, 1820, the Treasurer of Maryland was directed to pay to "John Penn, of Charles County, during life, half pay of a private for his Revolutionary War services." [Ref: Q-II:381]. See "Benjamin Dent" and "Stephen Penn," q.v.
PENN, John (1718-   ). Took the Oath of Allegiance in 1778 [Ref: AA-641]. Aged about 32 as noted in a 1750 deposition [Ref: DD-172]. Rendered patriotic service by providing wheat for the use of the military in August 1781 [Ref: N-421].
PENN, Mary. See "Stephen Penn," q.v.
PENN, Stephen (1760-1839). Private, Militia, 12th Battalion, Capt. Peter Wood's Company, 1777 [Ref: M-161]. Private (substitute for 9 months), 1st Maryland Line, by Sept. 11, 1778 [Ref: D-330]. Took the Oath of Allegiance in Charles County in 1778 [Ref: AA-641]. He applied for a

pension on Aug. 20, 1832 in Lawrence County, Alabama, stating that he was born on Jan. 25, 1760 and married Mary McKay (born May 3, 1767) on Feb. 18, 1786 by license issued in Charles County, Maryland. He enlisted in the Maryland Line in St. Mary's County. His widow Mary Penn applied for a pension (W6858) on July 18, 1843, in Alabama, stating that he had died on March 9, 1839 and their children were as follows: Sary Penn (born Nov. 30, 1786); William Penn (born May 3, 1797); Stephen Penn (born May 5, 1800); Elizabeth Penn (born Sept. 22, 1802); and, John Penn (born Oct. 4, 1806). [Ref: V-III:2653, J-III:2273].

PENN, Sary. See "Stephen Penn," q.v.

PENN, William. See "Stephen Penn" and "Richard Harrison," q.v.

PERMILLIAN, Benjamin. See "Benjamin Vermillion," q.v.

PERRY, Francis. Private, Militia, 26th Battalion, Capt. William Winter's Company, 1777 [Ref: M-165]. Took the Oath of Allegiance in 1778 [Ref: L-19]. Rendered patriotic service by providing wheat for the use of the military in September 1781 [Ref: N-438].

PERRY, Hugh (1747-   ). Private, Militia, 12th Battalion, Capt. Peter Wood's Company, 1777 [Ref: M-161, which listed the name as "Perrie"]. Aged about 26 as noted in a 1773 deposition which mentioned his father John Perry [Ref: DD-172]. Took the Oath of Allegiance in 1778 [Ref: L-19, AA-641]. Resident of Benedict Hundred in 1778 [Ref: Q-I:297].

PERRY, John. Private, Militia, 26th Battalion, Capt. Thomas H. Marshall's Company, 1777 [Ref: M-163, which listed the name as "John Pemy(?)" and X-76, which listed the name as "John Perry"]. Private (substitute during the war), 1st Maryland Line, by Sept. 11, 1778 [Ref: D-330, which listed the name as "John Perrie"]. Resident of Durham Lower Hundred in 1778 [Ref: Q-I:297].

PERRY, John Jr. Private, Militia, 26th Battalion, Capt. William Winter's Company, 1777 [Ref: M-165].

PERRY, John Sr. (1702-   ). Rendered patriotic service by providing wheat for the use of the military in May 1783 [Ref: N-598]. Aged about 40 as noted in a 1742 deposition [Ref: DD-172, which listed the name as "John Perrie"]. Resident of Pomonkey Hundred in 1778 [Ref: Q-I:297]. See "Hugh Perry," q.v.

PERRY, Margaret E. See "Francis Dunnington," q.v.

PERRY, Samuel. Private, Militia, 12th Battalion, Capt. John Thomas' Company, 1777 [Ref: M-161]. Resident of Bryan Town Hundred in 1778 [Ref: Q-I:297].

PERRY, Simon. Private (substitute for 3 years), 1st Maryland Line, by Sept. 11, 1778 [Ref: D-330, which listed the name as "Perrie"]. Private, 1st Maryland Line, Capt. Edward Prall's Company, Jan. 1, 1782 [Ref: D-432].

Private, 1st Maryland Line, Col. John H. Stone's Regiment. Wounded. Cause of disability unknown. Invalid (disability) pension commenced on Nov. 15, 1783 and he was still on pension as of Aug. 15, 1786. He reportedly "removed out of the State" in October 1786 [Ref: D-629].

PERRY, Thomas Jr. Private, 1st Maryland Line, enrolled and passed on July 25, 1776 [Ref: D-32, which listed the name without the "Jr."]. Sergeant, Militia, 26th Battalion, Capt. William Winter's Company, 1777 [Ref: M-165]. Resident of Durham Lower Hundred in 1778 [Ref: Q-I:297]. Gave a deposition in 1781 pertaining to his inability to perform military service due to family obligations [Ref: Z-208].

PERRY, Thomas Sr. Took the Oath of Allegiance in 1778 [Ref: AA-641].

PETER, Richard. Took the Oath of Allegiance in 1778 [Ref: L-19].

PEVER, Thomas. Took the Oath of Allegiance in 1778 [Ref: L-19].

PHERSON, Attwix. See "Attwix Fearson," q.v.

PHILBERT, John. Took the Oath of Allegiance in 1778 [Ref: L-19].

PHILBERT, Joseph. Private, 1st Maryland Line, enrolled and passed on July 18, 1776 [Ref: D-32]. Private (furnished by class for 9 months), 1st Maryland Line, by Sept. 11, 1778 [Ref: D-330]. Resident of Port Tobacco East Hundred in 1778 [Ref: Q-I:297].

PHILLIPS, Anne. See "Baker Howard," q.v.

PHILLIPS, James (1741-   ). Private, Militia, 12th Battalion, Capt. John Hanson's Company, 1777 [Ref: M-159, which listed the name as "Philips"]. Took the Oath of Allegiance in 1778 [Ref: L-19]. Aged about 30 as noted in a 1771 deposition [Ref: DD-173]. Resident of Port Tobacco East Hundred in 1778 [Ref: Q-I:297].

PHILLIPS, John. Private, 1st Maryland Line, enrolled and passed on July 27, 1776 [Ref: D-31, which listed the name as "Philops (Phillips)"].

PHILLIPS, Thomas Hambleton (Hamilton). Drummer, Militia, 12th Battalion, Capt. John Parnham's Company, 1777 [Ref: M-160]. Took the Oath of Allegiance in 1778 [Ref: L-19, which listed the name as "Thomas Hambleton Phillips" and AA-641, which listed the name as "Thomas Hamilton Philips"]. See "Thomas Pickerel," q.v.

PHILPOTT (PHILPOT), Benjamin. Captain, Militia, 12th Battalion, from Feb. 26, 1776 to Feb. 9, 1781 [Ref: A-186, A-206, M-111, G-307, Y-II:23]. Rendered patriotic service by providing clothing for the use of the military in February 1778 [Ref: Y-II:234]. Rendered patriotic service by providing wheat for the use of the military in December 1782 [Ref: N-577]. Resident of William & Mary Upper Hundred in 1778 [Ref: Q-I:297].

PICKIN, John. Private, Militia, 26th Battalion, Capt. William Winter's Company, 1777 [Ref: M-165].

PICKRELL (PICKELL, PICKRALL), John. Private, Militia, 12th Battalion, Capt. John Hanson's Company, 1777 [Ref: M-159]. Took the Oath of Allegiance in 1778 [Ref: AA-641]. "John Pickell" was a resident of Port Tobacco East Hundred in 1778 [Ref: Q-I:297].

PICKRELL (PICKELL, PICKRON), Joseph (1723-   ). Took the Oath of Allegiance in 1778 [Ref: L-19]. Aged about 57 as noted in a 1780 deposition [Ref: DD-173]. "Joseph Pickell" was a resident of Port Tobacco East Hundred in 1778 [Ref: Q-I:297]. "Joseph Pickron" rendered patriotic service by providing wheat for the use of the military in May 1783 [Ref: N-597].

PICKRELL (PICKELL, PICKRON), Thomas. "Thomas Pickell" took the Oath of Allegiance in 1778 [Ref: AA-641]. Resident of Port Tobacco East Hundred in 1778 [Ref: Q-I:297]. On June 16, 1781, "Thomas Pickerel" petitioned the Governor and Council of Maryland stating "that your Petitioner was draughted on Monday the 11th Instant to serve as a Regular Soldier to the 10th of December 1781. Your Petitioner is therefore under the Necessity of Shewing your Excellency & Honours that he has been Subject to a Grievous Complaint in his Breast for several years past, for remedy of which he has been under the hands of Doctor Gustavus R. Brown these two years past, as will appear by the Doctor's Certificate. Your Petitioner further begs Leave to shew that he was Draughted in the month of June 1778, but being then subject to the same Complaint was discharged by the Court of Appeals appointed by Law to enquire into and Determine such Cases -- shall therefore submit it to your Great Judgment whether a person who has been in a declining State for several years and Weakening every day can be fit for the service of his Country. And therefore Prays you would take the matter into Consideration and Grant such relief as in your Great wisdom seem meet -- and your Petitioner as in duty Bound will Ever Pray." Also, the certification by Dr. G. R. Brown on June 12, 1781 stated "Thomas Pickerel hath been subject to a complaint in the Breast for two years, which very often terminates in Consumption, and I am of the opinion that the fatigues incident to a military life are such as he will never be able to bear, but at the extreme hazzard of life." The condition of Thomas Pickerel was further attested by twenty-three of his fellow Charles Countians (apparently most were soldiers themselves) who were acquainted with his health problems on June 16, 1781 and signed their names: Jacob Ware, Thomas Hopewell, John Hopewell, Notly Lucket, John M. Crismond, Francis Ware, William King, F. H. [T. H.?] Phillips, Francis Sewall, Smith Hawkins, Joseph Dixson, Isaac Lattimore, William Tear Jr., Isaac Latemore, Hugh Cox, John Dodson, Raphael Tear, Francis Tiar, Joseph

Tiar, William B. Smoot, John Cox, Walter Hanson Sr., and William B. Dodson [Ref: H-294, H-295]. Gave a deposition in 1781 pertaining to his inability to perform military service due to family obligations [Ref: Z-208, which source questionably listed the name as "Thomas Proherrele?"]. "Thomas Pickrin" was a private in the militia, 12th Battalion, Capt. Walter Hanson's Company, 1777 [Ref: M-159].

PILE, Mary. See "Henry Boarman," q.v.

PILE, Mrs. Rendered patriotic service by providing clothing for the use of the military in February 1778 [Ref: Y-II:234].

PILE, William Henry H. See "Henry Neale," q.v.

PLOWDEN, Eleanor. See "Henry Neale," q.v.

POLAND, William. Private (substitute for 3 years), 1st Maryland Line, by Sept. 11, 1778 [Ref: D-330]. Private, 1st Maryland Line, Capt. Edward Prall's Company, Jan. 1, 1782 [Ref: D-432, which listed the name as "Wm. Poling"].

POMPY, Luke. Took the Oath of Allegiance in 1778 [Ref: AA-641]. Resident of William & Mary Upper Hundred in 1778 [Ref: Q-I:297].

POORE, William. Rendered patriotic service by providing wheat for the use of the military in February 1782 [Ref: N-480].

POPE, Jane. See "Gerard Blackstone Causin," q.v.

POPE, Matthew. See "John Guy," q.v.

PORTEUS, Martha. Rendered patriotic service by providing clothing for the use of the military in February 1778 [Ref: Y-II:234].

POSEY, Belain (1737-1791). Captain, Militia, Jan. 27, 1776 [Ref: D-31, M-112, B-141, A-111, which latter source misspelled his first name as "Belam"]. Took the Oath of Allegiance in 1778 [Ref: AA-641]. Resident of William & Mary Upper Hundred in 1778 [Ref: Q-I:297]. Rendered patriotic service by providing wheat for the use of the military in April 1782 and May 1783 [Ref: N-504, N-597]. Belain Posey was born on May 2, 1737 and married Margaret Corry on Nov. 5 or 11, 1777 in Charles County. On Oct. 11, 1838 the widow Margaret Posey, aged 80, applied for a pension (W9238) and stated that Belain died on June 5, 1791, leaving several children (no names were given). A grandson Washington Posey was mentioned in 1836, as were Mrs. Ann Middleton and James H. A. Middleton (who was a Justice of the Peace in Charles County), but no relationship was stated. Margaret Posey was deceased by 1844 [Ref: V-III:2737, W-121, J-III:2345]. See "William Campbell," q.v.

POSEY, Benjamin (1760-1826). Private, Militia, 12th Battalion, Capt. Benjamin Lusby Corry's Company, 1777 [Ref: M-160]. Private, 1st Maryland Line, enlisted March 9, 1777 and discharged March 7, 1780 [Ref: D-149]. Resident of Port Tobacco East Hundred in 1778 [Ref: Q-

I:297]. Rendered patriotic service by providing wheat for the use of the military in October 1781 [Ref: N-448]. Benjamin applied for a pension (S36238) on Sept. 12, 1818, aged 58, at Alexandria in the District of Columbia and in 1820 had a wife Mary (aged 50) and children Eliza Posey (aged 18), William Posey (aged 15), Sarah Posey (aged 11), and Benjamin Posey (aged 8). On May 5, 1826, James Posey was the administrator of the estate of Benjamin Posey at Alexandria in Washington, D. C. [Ref: V-III:2738]. See "Francis Posey," q.v.

POSEY, Bennett. Private (furnished by class for 9 months), 1st Maryland Line, enlisted June 5, 1778 and discharged April 5, 1779 [Ref: D-150, D-330].

POSEY, Charles Francis. See "Thomas Posey, Sr.," q.v.

POSEY, Eliza. See "Benjamin Posey," q.v.

POSEY, Francis (c1701-c1782). Rendered patriotic service by providing wheat for the use of the military in November and December 1781 [Ref: N-458]. Aged about 70 as noted in a 1772 deposition (which mentioned his brother Benjamin) and aged about 73 as noted in a 1773 deposition [Ref: DD-173]. See "Thomas Posey, Sr.," q.v.

POSEY, Francis (c1740-1785). Private, Militia, 26th Battalion, Capt. Francis Mastin's Company, 1777 [Ref: M-164]. Private (drafted and joined the army), 1st Maryland Line, by Sept. 11, 1778 [Ref: D-330]. Took the Oath of Allegiance in 1778 [Ref: AA-641, L-19, which latter source listed the name as "Posy"]. Francis Posey was born circa 1740, married Elizabeth Simpson, and died before August 1785 [Ref: J-III:2345].

POSEY, Francis. Second Lieutenant, Militia, 12th Battalion, Capt. Benjamin Lusby Corry's Company, 1777 [Ref: M-160].

POSEY, George. Private, Militia, 26th Battalion, Capt. Francis Mastin's Company, 1777 [Ref: M-164].

POSEY, Henrietta. See "Thomas Posey," q.v.

POSEY, Hezekiah (1751-c1844). Private, South Carolina Line. He applied for a pension (S14192) on July 9, 1834 in Benton County, Alabama, stating that he was born on March 20, 1751 in Charles County, Maryland and lived in the part of 96 District that later became Abbeville District, South Carolina. There he lived at the time of his enlistment in the Revolutionary War. He married twice (first wife's name not known), second wife was Ruth ----. In 1796 they moved to Tennessee and in 1817 they migrated to Alabama where he died after Oct. 14, 1844 [Ref: V-III:2738, J-III:2345].

POSEY, Humphrey Jr. Corporal, Militia, 26th Battalion, Capt. Francis Mastin's Company, March 19, 1776 [Ref: K-1814 and M-158, which listed the name as "Dossy(?)" without the "Jr.," and X-78 which listed the name as "Hump: Posey," and M-164 which listed the name as "Nehmp:(?) Posey"]. Took the Oath of Allegiance in 1778 [Ref: AA-641, L-19, which listed the name with the "Jr."]. Second Lieutenant, Militia, Capt. Samuel Luckett's Company, commissioned on March 24, 1781 [Ref: M-112, G-361, H-136 which listed the name without the "Jr."].

POSEY, Humphrey Sr. Took the Oath of Allegiance in 1778 [Ref: L-19, AA-641]. Rendered patriotic service by providing wheat for the use of the military in May 1783 [Ref: N-598].

POSEY, James. Private, 1st Maryland Line, enlisted Feb. 18, 1777 [Ref: D-149]. See "Benjamin Posey," q.v.

POSEY, John. Private, 1st Maryland Line, enrolled and passed on July 8, 1776 [Ref: D-32]. Private, Militia, 26th Battalion, Capt. Francis Mastin's Company, 1777 [Ref: M-164].

POSEY, John, of John. Private, Militia, 26th Battalion, Capt. Francis Mastin's Company, 1777 [Ref: M-164].

POSEY, Margaret. See "Belain Posey," q.v.

POSEY, Mary. See "Benjamin Posey," q.v.

POSEY, Pryor (c1753-1782). Private, Militia, 26th Battalion, Capt. Francis Mastin's Company, 1777 [Ref: X-78, M-164, which mistakenly listed the name as "Price Posey"]. Took the Oath of Allegiance in 1778 [Ref: L-19, which mistakenly listed the name as "Pryn Posey" and AA-641, which listed the name as "Pryor Posey"]. Pryor Posey was born circa 1753, married Jannet Luckett, and died before Dec. 14, 1782 [Ref: J-III:2345].

POSEY, Rhody. Private, Militia, Capt. Francis Mastin's Company, 26th Battalion, March 19, 1776 [Ref: M-158, K-1814]. Took the Oath of Allegiance in 1778 [Ref: L-19, AA-641]. Resident of Durham Lower Hundred in 1778 [Ref: Q-I:297].

POSEY, Rhody Jr. Private, Militia, 26th Battalion, Capt. Francis Mastin's Company, 1777 [Ref: M-164].

POSEY, Richard. Private, Militia, 26th Battalion, Capt. Francis Mastin's Company, 1777 [Ref: M-164]. Resident of Durham Lower Hundred in 1778 [Ref: Q-I:297].

POSEY, Roger. Private, 1st Maryland Line, drafted from the Charles County militia on June 11, 1781 to serve until Dec. 10, 1781; discharged on April 6, 1782 [Ref: D-376, I-123].

POSEY, Ruth. See "Hezekiah Posey," q.v.

POSEY, St. Laurence. Private, 1st Maryland Line, enrolled and passed on July 8, 1776 [Ref: D-32].

POSEY, Sarah. See "Benjamin Posey," q.v.

POSEY, Thomas (1758-   ). Born on July 10, 1758, a son of Thomas and Henrietta Posey [Ref: GG-138]. Private, 1st Maryland Line, enrolled and passed on July 27, 1776 [Ref: D-32]. Private, Militia, 26th Battalion, Capt. Robert Sinnett's Company, 1777 [Ref: M-164]. Took the Oath of Allegiance in 1778 [Ref: L-19]. Rendered patriotic service by providing wheat for the use of the military in January and April 1782 [Ref: N-474, N-497].

POSEY, Thomas Sr. (1730-1778). Took the Oath of Allegiance in 1778 [Ref: L-19, AA-641]. Resident of Port Tobacco East Hundred in 1778 [Ref: Q-I:297]. "Thomas Posey, Sr." was aged about 45 as noted in a 1775 deposition which mentioned his father Francis Posey. "Thomas Posey, of Nanjemy" was deceased by April 25, 1778 (date of final account, naming his wife Henrietta Posey and sons Thomas Posey (born July 10, 1758) and Charles Francis Posey (born Dec. 13, 1761), among other children [Ref: GG-137, GG-138, DD-173].

POSEY, Uzziah. Private, Militia, 26th Battalion, Capt. William Winter's Company, 1777 [Ref: M-165]. Constable, Durham Lower Hundred, 1778 [Ref: CC-709, Q-I:297].

POSEY, Walter. Private, Militia, Capt. Francis Mastin's Company, 26th Battalion, March 19, 1776 [Ref: M-158, K-1814]. Took the Oath of Allegiance in 1778 [Ref: L-19]. Died by May 1778 (date of inventory). [Ref: GG-155].

POSEY, Washington. See "Belain Posey," q.v.

POSEY, William. See "Benjamin Posey," q.v.

POSEY, Zachariah. Private, 1st Maryland Line, drafted from the Charles County militia to serve from June 2, 1781 to Dec. 10, 1781; discharged on April 6, 1782 [Ref: D-377, G-569, I-123].

POSTON, Anne. See "William Poston" and "Thomas Matthews," q.v.

POSTON, Barton. Private, Militia, 12th Battalion, Capt. Henry Clarkson's Company, 1777 [Ref: M-159].

POSTON, Benjamin. Private, 1st Maryland Line, enrolled and passed on July 8, 1776 [Ref: D-32, which listed the name as "Postin"]. Corporal, Militia, 12th Battalion, Capt. Henry Clarkson's Company, 1777 [Ref: M-159]. "Benjamin Poston" took the Oath of Allegiance in 1778 [Ref: L-19, AA-641]. "Benjamin Paston" was a resident of Bryan Town Hundred in 1778 [Ref: Q-I:297].

POSTON, Catherine. See "Hezekiah Dent," q.v.

POSTON, Chloe. See "Philip Davis," q.v.

POSTON, Edward (1725-). Took the Oath of Allegiance in 1778 [Ref: L-19, AA-641]. Aged about 39 as noted in a 1764 deposition which mentioned his deceased father John Poston [Ref: DD-173]. "Edward Paston" was a resident of Bryan Town Hundred in 1778 [Ref: Q-I:297].

PRALL, Edward. Although not a native Charles Countian, he was Captain, 2nd Company, 1st Maryland Line, on Jan. 1, 1782 and many Charles Countians served under his command [Ref: D-150, D-431].

PRALL, Richard D. See "John Compton," q.v.

PRICE, Ann. See "Rhody Bowye," q.v.

PRICE, James. Private, Militia, 12th Battalion, Capt. Walter Hanson's Company, 1777 [Ref: M-159]. Took the Oath of Allegiance in 1778 [Ref: L-19, AA-641].

PRICE (PRICESS), Louisa. See "Charles Smith," q.v.

PRICE, Richard. Sergeant, Militia, 26th Battalion, Capt. Hezekiah Garner's Company, 1777 [Ref: M-162]. Took the Oath of Allegiance in 1778 [Ref: L-19]. Rendered patriotic service by providing wheat for the use of the military in October 1782 and May 1783 [Ref: N-561, N-598].

PRICE, Thomas. A letter dated July 23, 1776 from General John Dent to the Council of Safety in Charles County stated, in part, that he had received an order "from your Honours appointing Major Thomas Price to the command." [Ref: B-107].

PRICE, William. Private, Militia, Capt. Francis Mastin's Company, 26th Battalion, March 19, 1776 [Ref: M-158, K-1814]. Private, Militia, 26th Battalion, Capt. Hezekiah Garner's Company, 1777 [Ref: M-163]. Took the Oath of Allegiance in 1778 [Ref: L-19, AA-641].

PROCTER, Benjamin. Took the Oath of Allegiance in 1778 [Ref: AA-641]. Resident of William & Mary Upper Hundred in 1778 [Ref: Q-I:297].

PROCTER, Charles. Private (furnished by class for 9 months), 1st Maryland Line, by Sept. 11, 1778 [Ref: D-330]. Took the Oath of Allegiance in 1778 [Ref: L-19, AA-641]. Resident of Port Tobacco Upper Hundred in 1778 [Ref: Q-I:297].

PROCTER, Charles Sr. Took the Oath of Allegiance in 1778 [Ref: L-19, which listed the name as "Charles Proctor, Sr."]. Resident of Bryan Town Hundred in 1778 [Ref: Q-I:297].

PROCTER, Francis. Took the Oath of Allegiance in 1778 [Ref: AA-641]. Resident of Bryan Town Hundred in 1778 [Ref: Q-I:297].

PROCTER, Henry. Took the Oath of Allegiance in 1778 [Ref: AA-641]. Took the Oath of Allegiance in 1778 [Ref: AA-641]. Resident of Bryan Town Hundred in 1778 [Ref: Q-I:297]. Private, 1st Maryland Line, drafted from the Charles County militia on July 27, 1781 and discharged on Dec. 3, 1781 [Ref: D-377, G-569, I-10, which listed the name as "Proctor"].

PROCTER, Leonard. Took the Oath of Allegiance in 1778 [Ref: L-19].

PROCTER, Richard. Private, 3rd Maryland Line, June 4, 1777, and 1st Maryland Line, Capt. Samuel McPherson's Company, Aug. 1, 1780 to Jan. 1, 1781 [Ref: D-152, D-357]. On Jan. 6, 1812 the Treasurer of Maryland

POSTON, John. Private, Militia, 12th Battalion, Capt. Henry Clarkson's Company, 1777 [Ref: M-159]. See "Edward Poston," q.v.
POSTON, Judith. See "Hatch Dent," q.v.
POSTON, Priscilla. Rendered patriotic service by providing wheat for the use of the military in July 1781, July and December 1782, and April 1783 [Ref: N-408, N-533, N-573, N-593, which also listed the name as "Posten"]. She was the wife of "William Poston," q.v., of Trinity Parish [Ref: EE-15].
POSTON, Solomon. Private, Militia, 12th Battalion, Capt. Henry Clarkson's Company, 1777 [Ref: M-159]. "Solomon Poston" took the Oath of Allegiance in 1778 [Ref: L-19, AA-641]. "Solomon Paston" was a resident of Bryan Town Hundred in 1778 [Ref: Q-I:297].
POSTON, William (1760-1823). Private, Militia, 12th Battalion, Capt. Henry Clarkson's Company, 1777 [Ref: M-159]. Born on Oct. 6, 1760, twin of Anne, and son of William and Priscilla Poston, of Trinity Parish, William Poston married Sarah Hamill and migrated to Virginia after the war. He died before July 15, 1823 [Ref: EE-15, J-III:2347].
POSTON, William (1719-1778). Took the Oath of Allegiance in 1778 [Ref: L-19]. Aged about 50 as noted in a 1769 deposition [Ref: DD-173]. William Poston, of Trinity Parish, married Priscilla ---- by 1745 and died before Nov. 3, 1778 (date of final account). [Ref: EE-15, GG-246]. See "Priscilla Poston," q.v.
POWER, Jesse (1761-1834). Private, 1st Maryland Line, 1780, and discharged on July 19, 1783 [Ref: D-551]. He applied for a pension (S35030) on May 12, 1818, aged about 57, in St. Mary's County, stating that he lived in Charles County at the time of his enlistment. In 1820 "Jesse Power" received a state pension of $40 per year and had a wife aged 35 and three daughters, aged 21, 15 and 10 (no names were given). [Ref: V-III:2751]. "Jesse Powers" was born in 1761, married Millie ----, received a pension, and died on Dec. 4, 1834 [Ref: J-III:2356].
POWER, John. Took the Oath of Allegiance in 1778 [Ref: AA-641]. Resident of Pomonkey Hundred in 1778 [Ref: Q-I:297]. Rendered patriotic service by providing wheat for the use of the military in May 1783 [Ref: N-597, which listed the name as "Powre"].
POWER, Joseph. Took the Oath of Allegiance in 1778 [Ref: AA-641]. Resident of Port Tobacco East Hundred in 1778 [Ref: Q-I:297].
POWER, Millie. See "Jesse Power," q.v.
POWER, Walter. Private, Lower Battalion, Prince George's County, 1776 [Ref: D-35]. Private, Charles County Militia, 12th Battalion, Capt. John Hanson's Company, 1777 [Ref: M-159]. Took the Oath of Allegiance in Charles County in 1778 [Ref: AA-641]. Resident of Port Tobacco East Hundred in 1778 [Ref: Q-I:297].

was directed to pay to "Richard Proctor, late a private in the Revolutionary War, belonging to the Maryland Line, quarterly, the half pay of a private, as a provision to him in his indigent situation and advanced life, and as a further remuneration to him for those services by which his country has been so essentially benefitted." [Ref: Q-II:383].

PROCTER, Thomas. Took the Oath of Allegiance in 1778 [Ref: AA-641]. Resident of Bryan Town Hundred in 1778 [Ref: Q-I:297].

PROCTER, Walter. Private (furnished by class for 9 months), 1st Maryland Line, by Sept. 11, 1778 [Ref: D-330]. Took the Oath of Allegiance in 1778 [Ref: AA-641].

PROCTER, William. Took the Oath of Allegiance in 1778 [Ref: AA-641].

PROSKER, Frederick. Took the Oath of Allegiance in 1778 [Ref: L-19].

PRYOR, Benjamin. Private (furnished by class for 9 months), 1st Maryland Line, by Sept. 11, 1778 [Ref: D-330].

PURCELL, Edward. Took the Oath of Allegiance in 1778 [Ref: L-19].

PURNELL, Elizabeth. See "John Milstead," q.v.

PYE, Walter (1743/4-   ). Second Lieutenant, Militia, 26th Battalion, Capt. George Dent's Company, commissioned May 9, 1778 [Ref: M-113, E-72]. Rendered patriotic service by providing clothing for the use of the military in February 1778 [Ref: Y-II:235]. Took the Oath of Allegiance in 1778 [Ref: AA-641]. Resident of Pomonkey Hundred in 1778 [Ref: Q-I:297]. Aged about 39 or 40 as noted in a 1783 deposition [Ref: DD-174].

QUADE, Ignatius. Private, Militia, 26th Battalion, Capt. Robert Sinnett's Company, 1777 [Ref: M-164, which listed the name as "Igns. Quaid"]. Took the Oath of Allegiance in 1778 [Ref: L-19, AA-641]. Resident of Port Tobacco West Hundred in 1778 [Ref: Q-I:297].

QUADE, John. Took the Oath of Allegiance in 1778 [Ref: L-19, which misspelled the name as "Quake"]. Resident of Port Tobacco West Hundred in 1778 [Ref: Q-I:297].

QUALLS, Whorton. Private, 1st Maryland Line, enrolled and passed on July 19, 1776 [Ref: D-31].

QUEEN, Anne. See "Thomas Semmes," q.v.

QUEEN, Catharine. See "Joseph Bowling" and "Hoskins Hanson" and "Joseph Edelen," q.v.

QUEEN, Elizabeth. See "Marsham Queen," q.v.

QUEEN, Francis (c1755-c1804). Second Lieutenant, Militia, 12th Battalion, Capt. Alexander McPherson's Company, July 5, 1777 [Ref: M-113, M-160]. Took the Oath of Allegiance in 1778 [Ref: L-19]. Resident of Bryan Town Hundred in 1778 [Ref: Q-I:297]. Rendered patriotic service by providing wheat for the use of the military in July 1782 [Ref: N-533]. Francis Queen was born circa 1755, married Anna Boarman, and died after Nov. 16, 1804

[Ref: J-III:2390]. He was the brother of Anne Queen, wife of "Thomas Semmes," q.v.

QUEEN, Henry. Memorialist and Militiaman, Pomonkey Company, after March 6, 1776 [Ref: M-158, Y-II:26]. Private, Militia, 26th Battalion, Capt. Richard Bennett Mitchell's Company, 1777 [Ref: X-83, and M-165, which mistakenly listed the name as "Heny Queen"]. Took the Oath of Allegiance in 1778 [Ref: L-19]. Resident of Pomonkey Hundred in 1778 [Ref: Q-I:297].

QUEEN, Marsham (1756-1839). On March 13, 1832, the Treasurer of Maryland was directed to pay to "Marsham Queen, of Charles County, during life, half yearly, half pay of a private, in consideration of his services during the Revolutionary War." [Ref: Q-II:383]. On Feb. 7, 1854, at Baltimore, the children of Marsham Queen applied for his pension (R8542), viz., Thomas M. Queen (aged 42), Sarah M. R. Queen (aged 45), Elizabeth J. Queen (aged 40), Mary Ann Queen Bowen (aged 38). Marsham Queen had died on Oct. 10, 1839, aged 83, leaving no widow [Ref: V-III:2794]. It must be noted, however, that Marsham Queen is not listed in the "Muster Rolls of Maryland Line in the American Revolution, 1775-1783" in *Archives of Maryland, Volume 18*, nor in Clements & Wright's *Maryland Militia in the Revolutionary War*. There was also a Marsham Queen who was aged about 45 as noted in a 1758 deposition [Ref: DD-174].

QUEEN, Richard (c1725-c1794). He rendered patriotic service in Maryland, married (wife's name not known), and died before Oct. 7, 1794 [Ref: J-II:2390].

QUEEN, Sarah M. R. See "Marsham Queen," q.v.

QUEEN, Thomas M. See "Marsham Queen," q.v.

QUEEN, William. Rendered patriotic service by providing clothing for the use of the military in January 1778 [Ref: Y-II:230]. Took the Oath of Allegiance in 1778 [Ref: L-19]. Resident of Bryan Town Hundred in 1778 [Ref: Q-I:297]. Brother of Anne Queen, wife of "Thomas Semmes," q.v.

RAGAN, Thomas. Private, 3rd Maryland Line, enrolled by Capt. Joseph Marbury by May 24, 1780 [Ref: F-181].

RAINES, Mancy. See "Isaac Stewart," q.v.

RATCLIFF, Burdit. Private, Militia, 26th Battalion, Capt. William Winter's Company, 1777 [Ref: M-165, which listed the name as "Ratliff"]. Took the Oath of Allegiance in 1778 [Ref: AA-641, L-19, which latter source listed the name as "Burdit Ratleff"]. Resident of Durham Lower Hundred in 1778 [Ref: Q-I:297]. See "Samuel Wright," q.v.

RATCLIFF, David. Private, Militia, 12th Battalion, Capt. Jonathan Yates' Company, 1777 [Ref: M-162].

RATCLIFF, Ignatius. Private, Militia, 26th Battalion, Capt. William Winter's Company, 1777 [Ref: M-165, which listed the name as "Ratliff"]. Took the Oath of Allegiance in 1778 [Ref: L-19, AA-641].

RATCLIFF, James. Private, Militia, 26th Battalion, Capt. Francis Mastin's Company, 1777 [Ref: M-164]. Took the Oath of Allegiance in 1778 [Ref: L-19, AA-641].

RATCLIFF, John Jr. Took the Oath of Allegiance in 1778 [Ref: AA-641, L-19, which latter source listed the name as "Ratcliffe"].

RATCLIFF, John Sr. (1714-   ). Took the Oath of Allegiance in 1778 [Ref: AA-641, L-19, which latter source listed the name as "Ratcliffe"]. Aged about 52 as noted in a 1757 deposition [Ref: DD-174]. Resident of William & Mary Upper Hundred in 1778 [Ref: Q-I:297].

RATCLIFF, Joseph Sr. (1705-1778). Rendered patriotic service by providing clothing for the use of the military in January 1778 [Ref: Y-II:230]. Took the Oath of Allegiance in 1778 [Ref: L-19, AA-641]. Aged about 52 as noted in a 1757 deposition [Ref: DD-174]. Resident of Durham Lower Hundred in 1778 [Ref: Q-I:297]. He died testate in October 1778 [Ref: GG-253].

RATCLIFF, Joseph Jr. Took the Oath of Allegiance in 1778 [Ref: AA-641, L-19, which latter source listed the name without the "Jr."].

RATCLIFF, Mary Ann. See "Thomas Semmes," q.v.

RATCLIFF, Rhody. Private, Militia, 26th Battalion, Capt. William Winter's Company, 1777 [Ref: M-165, which listed his first name "Rhoday Ratliff"]. Resident of Durham Lower Hundred in 1778 [Ref: Q-I:297]. Took the Oath of Allegiance in 1780 [Ref: O-118, which listed the name as "Ratcliffe"].

RATCLIFF, Richard. Took the Oath of Allegiance in 1778 [Ref: AA-641, L-19, which listed the name as "Ratcliffe"]. Resident of William & Mary Upper Hundred in 1778 [Ref: Q-I:297].

RATCLIFF, Townley. Private, 1st Maryland Line, enrolled by Aug. 5, 1776 [Ref: D-31].

RAWLINGS, Benjamin. Private (furnished by class for 9 months), 1st Maryland Line, by Sept. 11, 1778 [Ref: D-330, which listed the name as "Rollings"].

RAWLINGS, David. Took the Oath of Allegiance in 1778 [Ref: L-20, which listed the name as "Rollings"]. Assisted the Purchaser of Clothing in Charles County in February 1778 [Ref: Y-II:235, which listed the name as "Rawlings"]. Resident of Bryan Town Hundred in 1778 [Ref: Q-I:297].

RAWLINGS, Elias. Private, 1st Maryland Line, drafted from the Charles County militia and reported sick or not in service in June 1781;

determined unfit for service and discharged on Oct. 30, 1781 [Ref: D-376, G-656, which latter source listed the name as "Rollins"].
RAWLINGS, Elijah. "Elijah Rollings" was a private in the militia, 12th Battalion, Capt. John Thomas' Company, 1777 [Ref: M-161]. "Elisha Rawlings" was a resident of Bryan Town Hundred in 1778 [Ref: Q-I:297].
RAWLINGS, Isaac. Private (furnished by class for 9 months), 1st Maryland Line, by Sept. 11, 1778 [Ref: D-330, which listed the name as "Rollings"].
RAY, Charles. Took the Oath of Allegiance in 1778 [Ref: AA-641]. Resident of Port Tobacco West Hundred in 1778 [Ref: Q-I:297]. Rendered patriotic service by providing wheat for the use of the military in September 1781 and December 1782 [Ref: N-441, N-576].
RAY, James. Took the Oath of Allegiance in 1780 [Ref: O-118]. Resident of Port Tobacco West Hundred in 1778 [Ref: Q-I:297].
RAZIN, Henry. Rendered patriotic service by providing wheat for the use of the military in December 1782 [Ref: N-577].
READ, Sarah Foster. See "Edmund H. Compton," q.v.
READ, Thomas. Took the Oath of Allegiance in 1778 [Ref: L-19].
REARDON, James. Took the Oath of Allegiance in 1778 [Ref: L-19].
REARDON, John. Private, Militia, 26th Battalion, Capt. Robert Sinnett's Company, 1777 [Ref: M-164, which listed the name as "Reardan"].
REDBURN, Henry. Took the Oath of Allegiance in 1778 [Ref: L-19].
REDMAN, Henry. Private, Militia, 12th Battalion, Capt. Henry Clarkson's Company, 1777 [Ref: M-159]. Resident of Bryan Town Hundred in 1778 [Ref: Q-I:297].
REED, Thomas. Sergeant, Militia, 26th Battalion, Capt. William Winter's Company, 1777 [Ref: M-165]. Resident of Durham Lower Hundred in 1778 [Ref: Q-I:297].
REEDER, Benjamin. See "Richard Robert Reeder," q.v.
REEDER, Hezekiah (1726-   ). Took the Oath of Allegiance in 1778 [Ref: L-19, AA-641]. Commissary of Purchases for Charles County in 1781 [Ref: N-453, G-545]. Aged about 50 as noted in a 1776 deposition [Ref: DD-174]. See "Edward Kerrick," q.v.
REEDER, John (1759-   ). Corporal, Militia, 26th Battalion, Capt. Richard Bennett Mitchell's Company, 1777 [Ref: M-164]. Took the Oath of Allegiance in 1778 [Ref: L-19, AA-641]. Resident of Port Tobacco West Hundred in 1778 [Ref: Q-I:297]. John Reeder was born in 1759, married Chloe Green, and died after 1790 [Ref: J-III:2428].
REEDER, Richard H. Private, Militia, 26th Battalion, Capt. Robert Sinnett's Company, 1777 [Ref: M-164].
REEDER, Richard Robert (1721-   ). Took the Oath of Allegiance in 1778 [Ref: AA-641, L-19, which latter source listed the name as "Richard

Robert Reader"]. Aged about 56 as noted in a January 1778 deposition [Ref: CC-623, which listed the name as "Richard Robert Reeder" and DD-174, which listed the name as "Richard Robins Reeder" and mentioned his father Benjamin Reeder]. Resident of Port Tobacco West Hundred in 1778 [Ref: Q-I:297]. Rendered patriotic service by providing wheat for the use of the military in November 1781 and April 1783 [Ref: N-456, N-594, which also listed the name as "Richard R. Reder" and "Richard R. Reeder"].

REEDER, Simon (1724-   ). He rendered patriotic service, married Sarah Green, and died after 1790 [Ref: J-III:2429].

REEDER, Thomas Jr. Took the Oath of Allegiance in 1778 [Ref: L-19]. Resident of Newport East Hundred in 1778 [Ref: Q-I:297]. See "Joseph Thompson" and "Samuel Love," q.v.

REEN, John. See "John Rhenn," q.v.

REEVES, Elizabeth. See "William Thomas, Sr.," q.v.

REEVES, Hezekiah. Private, Militia, 26th Battalion, Capt. Benjamin Cawood's Company, 1777 [Ref: M-162]. Took the Oath of Allegiance in 1778 [Ref: L-19]. Resident of Port Tobacco East Hundred in 1778 [Ref: Q-I:297].

REEVES, James. Two men by this name were privates in the militia, 12th Battalion, in 1777: one in Capt. Jonathan Yates' Company, and one in Capt. Walter Hanson's Company [Ref: M-162, M-159, which also listed the name as "Reaves"]. One took the Oath of Allegiance in 1778 [Ref: AA-641]. One rendered patriotic service by providing clothing for the use of the military in February 1778 [Ref: Y-II:235]. Resident of Port Tobacco East Hundred in 1778 [Ref: Q-I:297].

REEVES, Mary. See "Samuel Reeves," q.v.

REEVES, Samuel (1749-   ). Born on April 9, 1749, a son of Thomas and Mary Reeves [Ref: EE-5]. Private, Militia, 12th Battalion, Capt. John Parnham's Company, 1777 [Ref: M-161, which listed the name as "Saml. Reives"]. Took the Oath of Allegiance in 1778 [Ref: L-19]. Resident of Newport East Hundred in 1778 [Ref: Q-I:297].

REEVES, Thomas. Private, Militia, 12th Battalion, Capt. Jonathan Yates' Company, 1777 [Ref: M-162].

REEVES, Thomas (1697-   ). Took the Oath of Allegiance in 1778 [Ref: AA-641, L-19, which latter source listed the name as "Reaves"]. Aged about 79 as noted in a 1776 deposition which mentioned his father Ubgate Reeves [Ref: DD-174]. Resident of William & Mary Lower Hundred in 1778 [Ref: Q-I:297]. See "Samuel Reeves," q.v.

REEVES, Thomas Courtney. Private, Militia, 12th Battalion, Capt. Alexander McPherson's Company, 1777 [Ref: M-160]. Took the Oath of

Allegiance in 1778 [Ref: L-19]. One "Thomas Reeves" was deceased by Aug. 25, 1778 (date of final account). [Ref: GG-212].
REEVES, Ubgate. See "Thomas Reeves" and "Upget Reeves," q.v.
REEVES, Upget (Upgate). "Upget Reeves" took the Oath of Allegiance in 1778 [Ref: AA-641]. "Upgate Reeves" was a resident of William & Mary Upper Hundred in 1778 [Ref: Q-I:297]. One "Ubgate Reeves" was aged about 57 as noted in a 1726 deposition [Ref: DD-174]. See "Thomas Reeves," q.v.
RHENN (REEN), John. "John Rhenn" was a private in the militia, 26th Battalion, Capt. Francis Mastin's Company, 1777 [Ref: M-164]. "John Reen" was a resident of Durham Lower Hundred in 1778 [Ref: Q-I:297].
RICE, William. Took the Oath of Allegiance in 1778 [Ref: L-19].
RICHARDS, Caesar (1758-1813). Private, Militia, 26th Battalion, Capt. Benjamin Cawood's Company, 1777 [Ref: M-162, which listed the name as "Cigger(?) Richard"]. Resident of Port Tobacco East Hundred in 1778 [Ref: Q-I:297]. He rendered patriotic service by providing wheat for the use of the military in October 1781 and November 1782 [Ref: N-443, N-564]. A son of Thomas Richards and Martha Hoye, Caesar was born in 1758 in Charles County, married Priscilla ----, and died on Dec. 14, 1813. She died on March 19, 1822. Their son Leonard R. Richards (1787-1830) married Christina Montgomery (1786-1858) and lived in Bryantown, Maryland [Ref: S-3138, J-III:2452].
RICHARDS, Clement. Private, Militia, drafted into the Continental Army in 1781 [Ref: D-411]. The obituary of Clement Richards appeared in the *Maryland Gazette* on Aug. 11, 1808, stating he "died on Sunday morning last, an old Revolutionary soldier. He was buried on Monday afternoon, with the honors of war." [Ref: FF 152].
RICHARDS, John. Private, 3rd Maryland Line, 1780, enrolled in Charles County for Capt. Joseph Marbury's Company [Ref: D-333].
RICHARDS, Leonard. See "Caesar Richard," q.v.
RICHARDS, Priscilla. See "Caesar Richards," q.v.
RICHARDS, Thomas. Private, Militia, 12th Battalion, Capt. John Thomas' Company, 1777 [Ref: M-161]. Resident of Bryan Town Hundred in 1778 [Ref: Q-I:297]. See "Caesar Richards," q.v.
RICHARDS, William. Private, Militia, 12th Battalion, Capt. John Thomas' Company, 1777 [Ref: M-161]. Resident of Bryan Town Hundred in 1778 [Ref: Q-I:297].
RICHARDSON, Mark. Private, Militia, 26th Battalion, Capt. Samuel Smallwood's Company, 1777 [Ref: M-165].
RICHARDSON, Thomas. Although he was from Montgomery County, his service as Assistant Deputy Commissary of Purchases included Charles

County, St. Mary's County, and Prince George's County. He was appointed by the Council of Maryland on Sept. 10, 1779 [Ref: E-518].

RICHARDSON, William. Took the Oath of Allegiance in 1778 [Ref: L-19, AA-641]. Resident of Port Tobacco Upper Hundred in 1778 [Ref: Q-I:297]. Rendered patriotic service by providing wheat for the use of the military in April 1783 [Ref: N-593].

RIDER, Thomas. Private, Militia, 12th Battalion, Capt. John Parnham's Company, 1777 [Ref: M-161].

RIDGATE, Thomas How (1734-1790). Rendered patriotic service by providing clothing for the use of the military in February 1778 [Ref: Y-II:235]. Took the Oath of Allegiance in 1778 [Ref: L-19, AA-641]. Resident of Port Tobacco Town Hundred in 1778 [Ref: Q-I:297, which mistakenly listed the name as "Thomas H. Kidgate"]. Gave (or perhaps sold) some "trifling goods" for the use of the military in June 1781, including some hats of which "the felts are only fit for small boys [and] the others may do for soldiers." [Ref: H-324]. His name was also listed in a record of the Council of Maryland dated Feb. 4, 1783 [Ref: I-354]. The obituary of Thomas How Ridgate appeared in the *Maryland Gazette* on July 1, 1790, stating, in part, that he "died Friday, March 26th, in his 56th year, a merchant in Port Tobacco. Elizabeth Ridgate is the administratrix." [Ref: FF-153]. See "Maurice Simons," q.v.

RIDGELY, Justinian. Private, Militia, 26th Battalion, Capt. Francis Mastin's Company, 1777 [Ref: M-164, which listed the name as "Jest. Ridgley"].

RIDGLEY, Martha. See "Lancelot Chunn, Jr.," q.v.

RIELEY, William. Although not a native Charles Countian, he was a Captain in the 1st Maryland Line by Jan. 1, 1782 and a number of Charles Countians served under his command [Ref: D-433].

RIELS, Benjamin. See "Benjamin Kiels (Riels?)," q.v.

RIGG, Charles (1756-1839). Private, 1st Maryland Line, enlisted March 27, 1777, and was a corporal when discharged on Feb. 1, 1779 (or March 28, 1780?). [Ref: D-155]. He applied for and received a pension (S32484) in Greenup County, Kentucky on Nov. 25, 1832, aged 76 on January 8 (or June 8?), and stated he had lived near Hoe's Ferry on the Potomac River in Charles County, Maryland. By 1837 he was in Wabash County, Illinois by which time his wife was deceased. He had seven children, including four sons (no names were given), and a Samuel Riggs was living in Illinois in 1837. Charles Rigg (or Riggs) was born in Maryland on June 8, 1756, married Elizabeth Andrus, and died in Illinois on Feb. 24, 1839 [Ref: V-III:2889, T-42, J-III:2468]. See "William Hannon," q.v.

RIGG, Matthew (c1750-1779). Sergeant, Militia, 26th Battalion, Capt. Robert Sinnett's Company, 1777 [Ref: M-164]. Took the Oath of Allegiance in 1778 [Ref: L-19, AA-641]. Resident of Port Tobacco West Hundred in 1778 [Ref: Q-I:297].

RIGG, Sarah. See "William Hannon," q.v.

RIGG, Thomas. Private, Militia, 12th Battalion, Capt. Jonathan Yates' Company, 1777 [Ref: M-162]. Rendered patriotic service by providing clothing for the use of the military in February 1778 [Ref: Y-II:234]. Took the Oath of Allegiance in 1778 [Ref: AA-641, L-19, which latter source listed the name as "Riggs"]. Resident of William & Mary Lower Hundred in 1778 [Ref: Q-I:297]. One Thomas Rigg was aged about 48 as noted in a 1753 deposition [Ref: DD-174].

RIGGIN, Charles. Private, 1st Maryland Line, enrolled and passed on July 27, 1776 [Ref: D-31].

RIGGS, Charles. See "Charles Rigg," q.v.

RIGGS, Samuel. See "Charles Rigg," q.v.

RIGHT, John. Private, Militia, 12th Battalion, Capt. John Thomas' Company, 1777 [Ref: M-161]. Resident of Port Tobacco East Hundred in 1778 [Ref: Q-I:297]. See "John Wright," q.v.

RIGHT, Samuel. Private, Militia, 12th Battalion, Capt. John Thomas' Company, 1777 [Ref: M-161]. Rendered patriotic service by providing wheat for the use of the military in November 1782 [Ref: N-564]. Resident of Port Tobacco East Hundred in 1778 [Ref: Q-I:297]. See "Samuel Wright," q.v.

RINEY, Henrietta. See "John Baptist Wathen," q.v.

RINEY, Thomas. See "John Baptist Wathen," q.v.

RIPPITH, William. Private, 1st Maryland Line, enrolled and passed on July 19, 1776 [Ref: D-31].

RISON (RESIN), Chandler. Private, Militia, 26th Battalion, Capt. William Winter's Company, 1777 [Ref: M-165, which misspelled the name as "Kyson"]. "Chandlee Resin" was a resident of Durham Lower Hundred in 1778 [Ref: Q-I:297]. "Chandler Rising" took the Oath of Allegiance in 1780 [Ref: O-118].

RISON (RESIN), Gerard. Private, Militia, 26th Battalion, Capt. Francis Mastin's Company, 1777 [Ref: M-164]. Rendered patriotic service by providing wheat for the use of the military in May 1783 [Ref: N-597, which listed the first name as "Garrard"]. "Jarot Resin" was a resident of Durham Lower Hundred in 1778 [Ref: Q-I:297].

RISTON, James. Took the Oath of Allegiance in 1778 [Ref: L-19].

RISTON (RISON, RESIN), Philip. Private, Militia, 26th Battalion, Capt. William Winter's Company, 1777 [Ref: M-165, which listed the name as

"Phillip Risten(?)"]. "Philip Resin" was a resident of Durham Lower Hundred in 1778 [Ref: Q-I:297].

ROBERSON, Elijah. See "Elijah Robinson," q.v.

ROBERSON, William. Constable, 1778 [Ref: CC-709]. Resident of William & Mary Upper Hundred in 1778 [Ref: Q-I:297].

ROBERTS, Richard. Resident of William & Mary Upper Hundred in 1778 [Ref: Q-I:297]. One Richard Roberts enlisted as a private in the 1st Maryland Line on April 23, 1778 and was reported dead in August 1778 [Ref: D-155].

ROBERTSON, Charles. Private (substitute for 3 years), 1st Maryland Line, by Sept. 11, 1778 [Ref: D-330].

ROBERTSON, John. Private, Militia, Capt. Francis Mastin's Company, 26th Battalion, March 19, 1776 [Ref: M-158, K-1814]. Private, 1st Maryland Line, enrolled and passed on July 20, 1776 [Ref: D-33]. Took the Oath of Allegiance in 1778 [Ref: L-19]. Resident of Port Tobacco West Hundred in 1778 [Ref: Q-I:297]. This or perhaps another John Robertson was a private in the militia, 26th Battalion, Capt. Robert Sinnett's Company, in 1777 [Ref: M-164]. One John Robertson petitioned the Governor and Council of Maryland on July 31, 1781, stating that he had been drafted and since he was incapable of rendering service due to disease, he requested that he may be discharged from the service. Doctor G. R. Brown certified that John Robertson "hath laboured under a rheumatic complaint upward of four years which appeared to be immovable by remedies, and I am of opinion the disease is such as to render him utterly unfit for military duty." Ignatius Byass, Andrew Baillie, and John B. Meek, three of his neighbors in Nanjemoy, further verified that John Robertson "had several severe attacks of rheumatism [and] we have been witnesses to swellings in his wrists at several times which appeared to be very painful and have often heard him complain of being afflicted with the same pain in different parts of his body." [Ref: H-375, H-376].

ROBERTSON, Richard. Private, Militia, Capt. Francis Mastin's Company, 26th Battalion, March 19, 1776 [Ref: M-158, K-1814]. Took the Oath of Allegiance in 1778 [Ref: L-20, AA-641, which latter source listed the name as "Roberson"].

ROBERTSON, William. Private, 1st Maryland Line, enrolled and passed on July 8, 1776 [Ref: D-32]. Resident of Port Tobacco Upper Hundred in 1778 [Ref: Q-I:297].

ROBINSON, Elijah (1753-   ). Private, Militia, 26th Battalion, Capt. Samuel Smallwood's Company, 1777 [Ref: M-165]. "Elijah Robinson" took the Oath of Allegiance in 1780 [Ref: O-118]. "Elijah Roberson" was aged about 21 as noted in a 1774 deposition [Ref: DD-174].

ROBINSON, Richard. Private, Militia, 26th Battalion, Capt. Francis Mastin's Company, 1777 [Ref: M-164].

ROBINSON, William. Ensign, Militia, 12th Battalion, Capt. Benjamin Philpott's Company, May 28, 1779 [Ref: M-117, E-427]. Took the Oath of Allegiance in 1778 [Ref: L-20, AA-641].

ROBY (ROBEY), Acton. Private (furnished by class for 9 months), 1st Maryland Line, by Sept. 11, 1778 [Ref: D-330].

ROBY (ROBEY), Alexander. Took the Oath of Allegiance in 1778 [Ref: L-20, AA-641]. Resident of Port Tobacco East Hundred in 1778 [Ref: Q-I:297].

ROBY (ROBEY), Ann. See "Elias Loveless," q.v.

ROBY (ROBEY), Aquilla (1760-   ). Private, 1st Maryland Line. He applied for a pension (R8918) on Nov. 19, 1833 in Lewis County, Virginia, stating that he was born on Sept. 8, 1760 in Charles County, Maryland. He served in the Revolutionary War and in 1790 moved to Pendleton County, Virginia, then to Randolph County, and in 1819 to Lewis County [Ref: V-III:2927].

ROBY (ROBEY), Basil. Private, Militia, 12th Battalion, Capt. John Hanson's Company, 1777 [Ref: M-159]. Took the Oath of Allegiance in 1778 [Ref: L-20, AA-641]. Resident of Port Tobacco East Hundred in 1778 [Ref: Q-I:297]. Rendered patriotic service by providing wheat for the use of the military in September 1782 [Ref: N-552].

ROBY (ROBEY), Benjamin. Took the Oath of Allegiance in 1778 [Ref: L-20, AA-641].

ROBY (ROBEY), Benjamin, of Richard. Private, Militia, 12th Battalion, Capt. John Hanson's Company, 1777 [Ref: M-159]. Resident of Port Tobacco East Hundred in 1778 [Ref: Q-I:297].

ROBY (ROBEY), Benjamin, of Samuel. Private, Militia, 12th Battalion, Capt. John Hanson's Company, 1777 [Ref: M-159].

ROBY (ROBEY), John. Private, 1st Maryland Line, enlisted May 13, 1778; prisoner in January 1780; reenlisted; discharged Jan. 9, 1782 [Ref: D-155].

ROBY (ROBEY), John. Rendered patriotic service by providing wheat for the use of the military in November 1781 [Ref: N-453, N-458].

ROBY (ROBEY), John A. Rendered patriotic service by providing wheat for the use of the military in May and September 1782 [Ref: N-551, N-556].

ROBY (ROBEY), John H. Private, Militia, 26th Battalion, Capt. William McPherson's Company, 1777 [Ref: M-163]. Resident of Port Tobacco Upper Hundred in 1778 [Ref: Q-I:297].

ROBY (ROBEY), John Nally. Took the Oath of Allegiance in 1778 [Ref: AA-641]. Resident of Port Tobacco East Hundred in 1778 [Ref: Q-I:297]. Rendered patriotic service by providing wheat for the use of the military in December 1782 [Ref: N-573].
ROBY (ROBEY), John, of Richard. Took the Oath of Allegiance in 1778 [Ref: L-20]. Resident of Port Tobacco East Hundred in 1778 [Ref: Q-I:297].
ROBY (ROBEY), Joseph. Private, Militia, 12th Battalion, Capt. John Hanson's Company, 1777 [Ref: M-159]. Took the Oath of Allegiance in 1778 [Ref: AA-641]. Resident of Port Tobacco East Hundred in 1778 [Ref: Q-I:297]. Private, 1st Maryland Line, enlisted June 14, 1779; fifer, Oct. 1, 1779; died Sept. 23, 1780 [Ref: D-155].
ROBY (ROBEY), Joseph. Took the Oath of Allegiance in 1778 [Ref: AA-641]. Resident of Bryan Town Hundred in 1778 [Ref: Q-I:297].
ROBY (ROBEY), Josias. Rendered patriotic service by providing wheat for the use of the military in November 1782 [Ref: N-565].
ROBY (ROBEY), Leonard. Took the Oath of Allegiance in 1778 [Ref: AA-641]. Resident of Port Tobacco East Hundred in 1778 [Ref: Q-I:297].
ROBY (ROBEY), Leonard Jr. Private, Militia, 12th Battalion, Capt. John Hanson's Company, 1777 [Ref: M-159].
ROBY (ROBEY), Mary. See "John Boswell," q.v.
ROBY (ROBEY), Michael Hines. Private, Militia, 26th Battalion, Capt. Benjamin Cawood's Company, 1777 [Ref: M-162].
ROBY (ROBEY), Michel. See "Nathan Maddox," q.v.
ROBY (ROBEY), Peter H. Private, Militia, 12th Battalion, Capt. Walter Hanson's Company, 1777 [Ref: M-159, which listed the name as "Robey"]. Took the Oath of Allegiance in 1778 [Ref: AA-641, L-20, which latter source listed the name without the "H."]. Resident of Port Tobacco East Hundred in 1778 [Ref: Q-I:297]. Rendered patriotic service by providing wheat for the use of the military in July 1782 [Ref: N-530].
ROBY (ROBEY), Richard. Private, Militia, 26th Battalion, Capt. William McPherson's Company, 1777 [Ref: M-163]. Resident of Port Tobacco East Hundred in 1778 [Ref: Q-I:297]. Private, 1st Maryland Line, drafted from the Charles County militia on July 27, 1781 [Ref: D-377, which listed the name as "Robey," and G-569 which listed the name as "Robie"]. Rendered patriotic service by providing wheat for the use of the military in September 1781 [Ref: N-441].
ROBY (ROBEY), Richard Sr. Took the Oath of Allegiance in 1778 [Ref: AA-641]. One "Richard Robey, son of John" was aged about 65 as noted in a 1764 deposition [Ref: DD-175].

253

ROBY (ROBEY), Richard, of Richard. Took the Oath of Allegiance in 1778 [Ref: L-20].

ROBY (ROBEY), Samuel. Rendered patriotic service by providing wheat for the use of the military in November 1781 [Ref: N-457, which listed the name as "Robey" and AA-641, which listed the name as "Robey, Sr."]. Resident of Port Tobacco East Hundred in 1778 [Ref: Q-I:297].

ROBY (ROBEY), Samuel Jr. Private, Militia, 12th Battalion, Capt. John Hanson's Company, 1777 [Ref: M-159]. Took the Oath of Allegiance in 1778 [Ref: AA-641].

ROBY (ROBEY), Samuel, of John. Drummer, Militia, 12th Battalion, Capt. John Hanson's Company, 1777 [Ref: M-158]. Took the Oath of Allegiance in 1778 [Ref: L-20]. Resident of Port Tobacco East Hundred in 1778 [Ref: Q-I:297].

ROBY (ROBEY), Stephen. Private, Militia, 12th Battalion, Capt. Alexander McPherson's Company, 1777 [Ref: M-160]. Took the Oath of Allegiance in 1778 [Ref: AA-641]. Resident of Bryan Town Hundred in 1778 [Ref: Q-I:297].

ROBY (ROBEY), Thomas. Private, Militia, 12th Battalion, Capt. John Hanson's Company, 1777 [Ref: M-159]. Took the Oath of Allegiance in 1778 [Ref: AA-641]. Resident of Port Tobacco East Hundred in 1778 [Ref: Q-I:297]. Rendered patriotic service by providing wheat for the use of the military in August 1782 [Ref: N-539].

ROBY (ROBEY), Thomas Sr. Took the Oath of Allegiance in 1778 [Ref: AA-641]. Resident of Port Tobacco East Hundred in 1778 [Ref: Q-I:297].

ROBY (ROBEY), William Sr. Took the Oath of Allegiance in 1778 [Ref: L-20, AA-641]. Resident of Bryan Town Hundred in 1778 [Ref: Q-I:297].

ROBY (ROBEY), William. Private, Militia, 12th Battalion, Capt. Henry Clarkson's Company, 1777 [Ref: M-159]. Took the Oath of Allegiance in 1778 [Ref: L-20].

ROBY (ROBEY), William, of Benjamin. Private, Militia, 12th Battalion, Capt. John Hanson's Company, 1777 [Ref: M-159]. Resident of Port Tobacco East Hundred in 1778 [Ref: Q-I:297].

ROBY (ROBEY), William, of Richard. Took the Oath of Allegiance in 1778 [Ref: L-20]. Assisted the Purchaser of Clothing in Charles County in February 1778 [Ref: Y-II:235]. William Roby, of Richard, married Susannah Dement (daughter of William Dement) on Dec. 12, 1762 in Trinity Parish [Ref: EE-18].

ROBY (ROBEY), William, of William. Private, Militia, 12th Battalion, Capt. John Hanson's Company, 1777 [Ref: M-159]. Resident of Port Tobacco East Hundred in 1778 [Ref: Q-I:297].

ROBY (ROBEY), Zachariah. Private, Militia, 12th Battalion, Capt. John Hanson's Company, 1777 [Ref: M-159]. Took the Oath of Allegiance in 1778 [Ref: AA-641]. Resident of Port Tobacco East Hundred in 1778 [Ref: Q-I:297].

ROCK, James. Took the Oath of Allegiance in 1778 [Ref: AA-641]. Resident of William & Mary Upper Hundred in 1778 [Ref: Q-I:297].

ROCK, William. Took the Oath of Allegiance in 1778 [Ref: AA-641]. Resident of William & Mary Upper Hundred in 1778 [Ref: Q-I:297].

ROGERS, Robert. Corporal, Militia, 12th Battalion, Capt. John Hanson's Company, 1777 [Ref: M-158]. Took the Oath of Allegiance in 1778 [Ref: AA-641]. Resident of Port Tobacco East Hundred in 1778 [Ref: Q-I:297]. Constable, 1778 [Ref: CC-709]. Rendered patriotic service by providing wheat for the use of the military in May 1783 [Ref: N-599]. Robert Rogers married Joanna Warren, daughter of Notley and Sarah Warren, prior to 1784 and moved to Fauquier County, Virginia after 1790 [Ref: Harry Wright Newman's *Charles County Gentry*, p. 303].

ROLAND, George. Memorialist and Militiaman, Pomonkey Company, after March 6, 1776 [Ref: M-158, Y-II:26]. "George Roland" was aged about 56 as noted in a 1771 deposition, and "George Rowland" was aged about 44 as noted in a 1767 deposition [Ref: DD-175].

ROLAND, Gorden. Memorialist and Militiaman, Pomonkey Company, after March 6, 1776 [Ref: M-158, Y-II:26]. Corporal, Militia, 26th Battalion, Capt. Thomas H. Marshall's Company, 1777 [Ref: M-163].

ROLAND, Thomas. Private, Militia, 26th Battalion, Capt. William McPherson's Company, 1777 [Ref: M-163]. Took the Oath of Allegiance in 1778 [Ref: L-20, AA-641]. "Thomas Rowland" was a resident of Port Tobacco Upper Hundred in 1778 [Ref: Q-I:297]. Rendered patriotic service by providing wheat for the use of the military in December 1781 [Ref: N-461].

ROLLINGS, David. See "David Rawlings," q.v.

ROSE, Benjamin (1761-1838). Private, Virginia Line. He applied for a pension on May 3, 1834 in Mercer County, Kentucky, stating that he was born on March 1, 1761 in Charles County, Maryland, but was raised in King George County, Virginia. He married Susannah Rutherford on March 30, 1816 in Garrard County, Kentucky and died on Dec. 9, 1838. His widow applied for a pension (W11162) in April 1853, aged 56, in Johnson County, Indiana. Susannah Rose and son George Rose were still living in 1856, apparently in Garrard County, Kentucky [Ref: V-III:2950].

ROSE, George. See "Benjamin Rose," q.v.

ROSE, Susannah. See "Benjamin Rose," q.v.

ROSE, William. Private, 1st Maryland Line, enlisted June 10, 1779; sergeant, Aug. 14, 1779; sergeant major, Dec. 25, 1779; still in service as of Nov. 1, 1780 [Ref: D-155].
ROSIER, Henry. Rendered patriotic service by providing wheat for the use of the military in April and December 1782 [Ref: N-498, N-577].
ROWE, Anthony. Private, Militia, 26th Battalion, Capt. Thomas H. Marshall's Company, 1777 [Ref: M-163]. Took the Oath of Allegiance in 1778 [Ref: L-20]. Resident of Pomonkey Hundred in 1778 [Ref: Q-I:297].
ROWE, John. Took the Oath of Allegiance in 1778 [Ref: L-20]. Resident of Pomonkey Hundred in 1778 [Ref: Q-I:297].
ROWE, John Jr. Private, Militia, 26th Battalion, Capt. Richard Bennett Mitchell's Company, 1777 [Ref: M-165, which misspelled the name as "Bowe"]. Took the Oath of Allegiance in 1778 [Ref: L-20]. Resident of Pomonkey Hundred in 1778 [Ref: Q-I:297]. Rendered patriotic service by providing wheat for the use of the military in October 1782 [Ref: N-563].
ROWE, William. Memorialist and Militiaman, Pomonkey Company, after March 6, 1776 [Ref: M-158, Y-II:26]. Private, Militia, 26th Battalion, Capt. Thomas H. Marshall's Company, 1777 [Ref: M-163]. Took the Oath of Allegiance in 1778 [Ref: L-20]. Resident of Pomonkey Hundred in 1778 [Ref: Q-I:297].
RULES, Benjamin. "Benjamin Rules" took the Oath of Allegiance in 1778 [Ref: L-20]. "Benjamin Lewis Rules" was a resident of Port Tobacco East Hundred in 1778 [Ref: Q-I:297].
RUMMELHART, Dave. See "Cornelius Bryan," q.v.
RUPELL, James. See "James Russell," q.v.
RUSSELL, Ann. See "Philip Thomas Lee," q.v.
RUSSELL, Henry (c1754-1836). Private (substitute for 3 years), 1st Maryland Line, by Sept. 11, 1778 [Ref: D-330]. Took the Oath of Allegiance in 1778 [Ref: AA-641]. Henry Russell was born circa 1754 in Maryland, served as a private in the war, married Chloe Smallwood, and migrated to Indiana where he died on Dec. 10, 1836 [Ref: J-III:2539].
RUSSELL, James. Second Lieutenant, Militia, 12th Battalion, Capt. John Hanson's Company, Feb. 26, 1776 [Ref: M-118, M-158, A-186, A-206, Y-II:23]. Took the Oath of Allegiance in 1778 [Ref: L-20]. "James Rupell" [Russell?] was a resident of Port Tobacco East Hundred in 1778 [Ref: Q-I:297].
RUSSELL, John. Private, Militia, 26th Battalion, Capt. Hezekiah Garner's Company, 1777 [Ref: M-163]. Took the Oath of Allegiance in 1778 [Ref: AA-641, L-19, which latter source listed the name as "Rissell"].

RUSSELL, Thomas. Private, Militia, 12th Battalion, Capt. John Hanson's Company, 1777 [Ref: M-159]. Took the Oath of Allegiance in 1778 [Ref: L-20].

RUTHERFORD, Susannah. See "Benjamin Rose," q.v.

RUTLAND, Catharine. See "Randolph Brandt Latimer" and "Jacob Latimer" and "Thomas Latimer," q.v.

RUTLAND, Elizabeth. See "William Hanson McPherson," q.v.

RUTTER, Hezekiah. Private, Militia, 12th Battalion, Capt. John Thomas' Company, 1777 [Ref: M-161, which listed the name as "Ruter"]. Took the Oath of Allegiance in 1778 [Ref: L-20]. Resident of Bryan Town Hundred in 1778 [Ref: Q-I:297].

RUTTER, Joseph. Private, Militia, 12th Battalion, Capt. John Thomas' Company, 1777 [Ref: M-161, which listed the name as "Ruter"]. Resident of Bryan Town Hundred in 1778 [Ref: Q-I:297].

RYON, Ignatius (1729-   ). Sergeant, Militia, 26th Battalion, Capt. William Winter's Company, 1777 [Ref: M-165]. Took the Oath of Allegiance in 1778 [Ref: L-20]. Resident of Bryan Town Hundred in 1778 [Ref: Q-I:297]. Aged about 49 as noted in a 1778 deposition [Ref: DD-175, which listed the name as "Ryan"].

RYE, Rolly. "Rolly Rye" took the Oath of Allegiance in 1778 [Ref: AA-641]. "Royle Rye" was a resident of Durham Lower Hundred in 1778 [Ref: Q-I:297].

RYE, Samuel. Took the Oath of Allegiance in 1778 [Ref: AA-641]. Resident of Durham Lower Hundred in 1778 [Ref: Q-I:297].

RYE, Walter. Rendered patriotic service by providing wheat for the use of the military in April, August, and September 1782 [Ref: N-538, N-548, N-549, N-503].

RYE, Warren. Took the Oath of Allegiance in 1778 [Ref: AA-641]. Resident of Durham Lower Hundred in 1778 [Ref: Q-I:297].

SALISBURY, Thomas. Private (recruit), 1st Maryland Line, by Sept. 11, 1778 [Ref: D-330, which listed the name as "Salsbury"]. Took the Oath of Allegiance in 1778 [Ref: L-20, AA-641].

SANDERS (SAUNDERS), Barbara. See "James Noland," q.v.

SANDERS, Benedict. Corporal, Militia, 26th Battalion, Capt. Samuel Smallwood's Company, 1777 [Ref: M-165]. Took the Oath of Allegiance in 1778 [Ref: L-20, AA-641].

SANDERS, Benjamin. Rendered patriotic service by providing clothing for the use of the military in February 1778 [Ref: Y-II:235]. Gave a deposition in 1781 pertaining to his inability to perform military service due to family obligations [Ref: Z-208].

SANDERS, Bennett. "Bennit Sanders" was a private (furnished by class for 9 months) in the Maryland Line, by Sept. 11, 1778 [Ref: D-330]. "Burnett Sanders" was a resident of Port Tobacco Upper Hundred in 1778 [Ref: Q-I:297].

SANDERS, Edward (1741-   ). Private, Militia, 26th Battalion, Capt. Robert Sinnett's Company, 1777 [Ref: M-164]. Took the Oath of Allegiance in 1778 [Ref: L-20]. Resident of Port Tobacco West Hundred in 1778 [Ref: Q-I:297]. Aged about 37 as noted in a 1778 deposition [Ref: CC-704, DD-175]. Rendered patriotic service by providing wheat for the use of the military in October 1781, and February and September 1782 [Ref: N-450, N-480, N-549].

SANDERS, John (1721-   ). Took the Oath of Allegiance in 1778 [Ref: L-20]. Aged about 37 as noted in a 1758 deposition [Ref: DD-176].

SANDERS, John (1730-   ). Justice who administered (and took) the Oath of Allegiance in 1778 [Ref: AA-641]. Resident of Port Tobacco West Hundred in 1778 [Ref: Q-I:297]. Rendered patriotic service by providing wheat for the use of the military in April 1783 [Ref: N-594]. Aged about 44 as noted in a 1774 deposition [Ref: DD-176].

SANDERS, John Foreguis R. (1756/7-   ). Private, Flying Camp, Capt. Bowie's Company, enrolled July 16, 1776; native of Charles County, aged about 20, height 5' 11" [Ref: D-36, which mistakenly listed the name as "John F. K. Sanders"]. Private, Militia, 26th Battalion, Capt. Robert Sinnett's Company, 1777 [Ref: M-164, which listed the name as "J. F. R. Sanders"]. Took the Oath of Allegiance in 1778 [Ref: L-20, which listed the name as "John F. R. Sanders"]. Aged about 21 as noted in a 1778 deposition [Ref: CC-704, DD-176]. "J. Foreguis Sanders" was a resident of Port Tobacco West Hundred in 1778 [Ref: Q-I:297].

SANDERS, Jorden. Private, Militia, 26th Battalion, Capt. Hezekiah Garner's Company, 1777 [Ref: M-163, which listed the first name as "Jardin"]. Took the Oath of Allegiance in 1778 [Ref: L-20, AA-641].

SANDERS, Joseph. Private, Militia, 12th Battalion, Capt. Alexander McPherson's Company, 1777 [Ref: M-160, which listed the name as "Joseph Sanders" and X-61, which listed the name as "Joseph Sandey"]. Took the Oath of Allegiance in 1778 [Ref: L-20]. Resident of Port Tobacco West Hundred in 1778 [Ref: Q-I:297].

SANDERS, Joshua (1730-   ). Took the Oath of Allegiance in 1778 [Ref: L-20]. Appointed a Justice of the Peace on Nov. 21, 1778 and Nov. 19, 1779 and Jan. 17, 1782 [Ref: E-249, F-19, I-45]. Resident of Bryan Town Hundred in 1778 [Ref: Q-I:297]. Aged about 45 as noted in a 1775 deposition [Ref: DD-176].

SANDERS, Thomas (1725/6-). Took the Oath of Allegiance in 1778 [Ref: L-20, AA-641]. Aged about 30 as noted in a 1756 deposition and aged about 50 as noted in a 1775 deposition [Ref: DD-176].

SANDERS, Thomas (1737-). Private, 1st Maryland Line, Col. John H. Stone's Regiment. Wounded in the hand and head at the Battle of Camden on Aug. 16, 1780. Invalid (disability) pension commenced on July 29, 1781 and still on pension as of Aug. 29, 1789, aged 52 [Ref: D-629]. Resident of Port Tobacco West Hundred in 1778 [Ref: Q-I:297].

SANDERS, Thomas Jr. (1758-). Private, Flying Camp, Capt. Bowie's Company, enrolled July 17, 1776; native of Charles County, aged 18, height 5' 8 1/2" [Ref: D-36, which did not include the "Jr."]. Private, Militia, 26th Battalion, Capt. Robert Sinnett's Company, 1777 [Ref: M-164, which did include the "Jr."].

SANDEFORD, Thomas. "Thomas Sandeford" took the Oath of Allegiance in 1778 [Ref: L-20, AA-641]. "Thomas Sandyford" was a resident of Port Tobacco East Hundred in 1778 [Ref: Q-I:297].

SANQUEHART, Peter. Private, 3rd Maryland Line, enrolled by Capt. Joseph Marbury by May 24, 1780 [Ref: D-333, F-181, which latter source listed the name as "Sanguehart"].

SAUSER, Benjamin. Took the Oath of Allegiance in 1778 [Ref: AA-641].

SAVOY, Archibald. Took the Oath of Allegiance in 1778 [Ref: AA-641].

SAVOY, Arthur. Took the Oath of Allegiance in 1778 [Ref: L-20]. Resident of Newport West Hundred in 1778 [Ref: Q-I:297].

SAVOY, Philip. Private, 1st Maryland Line, enlisted May 20, 1778, taken prisoner, and discharged Jan. 25, 1780 [Ref: D-160].

SAVOY, Thomas. Took the Oath of Allegiance in 1778 [Ref: AA-641]. Resident of Bryan Town Hundred in 1778 [Ref: Q-I:297].

SAVOY, William. Took the Oath of Allegiance in 1778 [Ref: AA-641]. Resident of Newport West Hundred in 1778 [Ref: Q-I:297].

SCALLION, John. Took the Oath of Allegiance in 1778 [Ref: AA-641]. Resident of Newport East Hundred in 1778 [Ref: Q-I:297].

SCALLION, Jonathan. Private, Militia, 12th Battalion, Capt. John Parnham's Company, 1777 [Ref: M-161].

SCALLION, Peter. Private, Militia, 12th Battalion, Capt. Henry Clarkson's Company, 1777 [Ref: M-159]. Resident of Newport East Hundred in 1778 [Ref: Q-I:297, which listed the name as "Scattian"].

SCONE, George. Corporal, 1st Maryland Line, Capt. William Rieley's Company, before Jan. 1, 1782 [Ref: D-433].

SCONE, William. Private, Militia, 26th Battalion, Capt. William McPherson's Company, 1777 [Ref: M-163, which listed the name as "Sone"].

SCOTT, Charles. Private (substitute for 3 years), 1st Maryland Line, by Sept. 11, 1778 [Ref: D-330].
SCOTT, David. Private, Militia, 26th Battalion, Capt. Hezekiah Garner's Company, 1777 [Ref: M-163].
SCOTT, James. Private, 1st Maryland Line, enrolled and passed on July 27, 1776 [Ref: D-31]. Two men by this name were privates in the militia in 1777: one in the 26th Battalion, Capt. Hezekiah Garner's Company, and one in the 12th Battalion, Capt. John Parnham's Company [Ref: M-161, M-162]. One took the Oath of Allegiance in 1778 [Ref: L-20, AA-641]. Resident of Newport East Hundred in 1778 [Ref: Q-I:297].
SCOTT, John. Private, Militia, 12th Battalion, Capt. Jonathan Yates' Company, 1777 [Ref: X-70, but was omitted from the list in Reference M-162]. Took the Oath of Allegiance in 1778 [Ref: L-20]. Private, 3rd Maryland Line, enrolled by Capt. Joseph Marbury by May 24, 1780 [Ref: D-333, F-181]. Resident of William & Mary Upper Hundred in 1778 [Ref: Q-I:297].
SCOTT, John. Took the Oath of Allegiance in 1778 [Ref: AA-641, which listed the name as "John Scott, Cob Neck" and L-20, which mistakenly listed the name as "Col. John Scott"]. One John Scott was aged about 49 as noted in a 1776 deposition [Ref: DD-176]. John Scott and John Scott, Jr. were residents of William & Mary Upper Hundred in 1778 [Ref: Q-I:297]. One John Scott married Sarah Edgar on Nov. 14, 1754 in Trinity Parish [Ref: EE-11].
SCOTT, John Day. Private, Militia, 26th Battalion, Capt. Francis Mastin's Company, March 19, 1776. Private, Militia, 26th Battalion, Capt. Robert Sinnctt's Company, 1777 [Ref: M-158, M-164, K-1814, which sources listed the name as "John D. Scott"]. Took the Oath of Allegiance in August 1778 [Ref: AA-710].
SCOTT, Robert. Private, Militia, 26th Battalion, Capt. Hezekiah Garner's Company, 1777 [Ref: M-163]. Took the Oath of Allegiance in 1778 [Ref: L-20, AA-641].
SCOTT, Thomas. Private, Militia, 12th Battalion, Capt. John Parnham's Company, 1777 [Ref: M-160].
SCOTT, William. Took the Oath of Allegiance in 1778 [Ref: L-20, AA-641]. Resident of Newport East Hundred in 1778 [Ref: Q-I:297].
SCROGIN, Barton. Took the Oath of Allegiance in 1778 [Ref: AA-641]. Resident of William & Mary Upper Hundred in 1778 [Ref: Q-I:297].
SCROGIN, John. Took the Oath of Allegiance in 1778 [Ref: AA-641, L-20]. Resident of William & Mary Lower Hundred in 1778 [Ref: Q-I:297]. Rendered patriotic service by providing clothing for the use of the military in February 1778 [Ref: Y-II:234]. "John Scroggin" was aged about 25 as

noted in a 1750 deposition which mentioned his father John Scroggin [Ref: DD-176].

SCROGIN, Obediah. Private, Militia, 12th Battalion, Capt. Walter Hanson's Company, 1777 [Ref: M-159]. Took the Oath of Allegiance in 1778 [Ref: AA-641]. Resident of Port Tobacco East Hundred in 1778 [Ref: Q-I:297].

SCROGIN, Sarah. Rendered patriotic service by providing clothing for the use of the military in February 1778 [Ref: Y-II:234].

SCROGIN, Walter. Private, Militia, 12th Battalion, Capt. John Parnham's Company, 1777 [Ref: M-161]. Took the Oath of Allegiance in 1778 [Ref: L-20, which misspelled the name as "Scoggen"]. Resident of Newport East Hundred in 1778 [Ref: Q-I:297].

SEAGAR, Nathaniel (1759-). Private, 1st Maryland Line. He applied for a pension (S11365) on Oct. 26, 1832 in Washington, D. C., stating that he was born in St. Mary's County on Oct. 8, 1759 and lived in Charles County at the time of his enlistment. He moved to Washington, D. C. in 1802 [Ref: V-III:3055].

SEAMANS, Joseph. Took the Oath of Allegiance in 1778 [Ref: L-20].

SEARS, Susannah M. See "Cornelius Wells," q.v.

SEATON, Martha. See "Mark Norris," q.v.

SEGO, Benjamin. Private, Militia, 12th Battalion, Capt. Henry Clarkson's Company, 1777 [Ref: M-159].

SEMMES, Alexius (1704-). "Alexius Semmes" took the Oath of Allegiance in 1778 [Ref: L-20]. "Alexius Simmes" was aged about 31 as noted in a 1735 deposition [Ref: DD-177].

SEMMES, Anne. See "Thomas Semmes" and "Ignatius Simpson," q.v.

SEMMES, Catherine. See "Thomas Semmes," q.v.

SEMMES, Edward. Second Lieutenant, Militia, 12th Battalion, Capt. Alexander McPherson's Company, 1777. First Lieutenant, Militia, Capt. Henry Boarman's Company, commissioned on Jan. 19, 1781 [Ref: M-119, M-160, G-280, which latter source listed the name as "Semms"]. Took the Oath of Allegiance in 1778 [Ref: L-20]. One Edward Semmes, son of "Thomas Semmes," q.v., was born in 1759. "Dr. Edward Simms" was a resident of Bryan Town Hundred in 1778 [Ref: Q-I:297]. Also see "Edward Simms," q.v.

SEMMES, Edward Jr. Took the Oath of Allegiance in 1778 [Ref: L-20]. "Edward Simms, Jr." was a resident of Port Tobacco Upper Hundred in 1778 [Ref: Q-I:297].

SEMMES, Elizabeth. See "Thomas Semmes," q.v.

SEMMES, Francis (1747-). Born on Oct. 28, 1747, a son of Francis Semmes and Lucretia Chapman [Ref: EE-4]. Private, Militia, 12th

Battalion, Capt. Benjamin Lusby Corry's Company, 1777 [Ref: M-160, which listed the name as "Simms"].

SEMMES, Francis (1707-   ). "Francis Seems" married Lucretia Chapman in Trinity Parish on Jan. 14, 1733 [Ref: EE-4]. "Francis Simmes" took the Oath of Allegiance in 1778 [Ref: L-20]. "Francis Simes" was aged about 67 as noted in a 1767 deposition [Ref: DD-177]. See "Joseph Semmes" and "Marmaduke Semmes" and "Ignatius Semmes," q.v.

SEMMES, Ignatius (1745-1779). Born on Sept. 5, 1745, a son of Francis Semmes and Lucretia Chapman [Ref: EE-4, which listed the name as "Seems"]. Private, Militia, 26th Battalion, Capt. William McPherson's Company, 1777 [Ref: M-163, which listed the name as "Simmes"]. Private, 1st Maryland Line, May 19, 1777 until July 17, 1779 when he was reported dead [Ref: D-160, which listed the name as "Simms"].

SEMMES, Ignatius. "Ignatius Simms" was a resident of Port Tobacco Upper Hundred in 1778 [Ref: Q-I:297]. Took the Oath of Allegiance in 1778 [Ref: L-20, which listed the name as "Simms"]. Rendered patriotic service by providing wheat for the use of the military in December 1782 [Ref: N-573]. See "Thomas Semmes," q.v.

SEMMES, James. Private, Militia, 12th Battalion, Capt. John Parnham's Company, 1777 [Ref: M-161]. Sergeant, 3rd Maryland Line, 1778, reduced to a private in June 1779, and discharged on Sept. 21, 1779 [Ref: D-165, which listed the name as "Simms"]. "James Semmes," son of "Thomas Semmes," q.v., was born in 1755. "James Sims" was a resident of Durham Lower Hundred in 1778 [Ref: Q-I:297].

SEMMES, James. Quartermaster Lieutenant, 1st Maryland Line, April 17, 1777. Lieutenant, 4th Maryland Line, May 27, 1778 [Ref: D-160, D-364, which listed the name as "Simmes"]. "James Simms" was a resident of Newport West Hundred in 1778 [Ref: Q-I:297]. In November 1812, the Treasurer of Maryland was directed to pay to "James Semmes, of Charles County, late a second lieutenant in the Revolutionary War, or order, annually in quarterly payments, during his life, a sum of money equal to the half pay of a second lieutenant." [Ref: Q-II:389].

SEMMES, Jean. See "Thomas Semmes," q.v.

SEMMES, Jesse. Private, 3rd Maryland Line, enrolled by Capt. Joseph Marbury by May 24, 1780 [Ref: D-333, which listed the name as "Semms (Simmes)" and F-181, which listed the name as "Semms"].

SEMMES, John. Private, Militia, 12th Battalion, Capt. Benjamin Lusby Corry's Company, 1777 [Ref: M-160]. Resident of Newport West Hundred in 1778 [Ref: Q-I:297]. See "John Simms," q.v.

SEMMES, Joseph (1738/9-   ). Born on March 3, 1738/9, a son of Francis Semmes and Lucretia Chapman [Ref: EE-4, which listed the name as

"Seems"]. Private, 1st Maryland Line, enrolled and passed on July 19, 1776 [Ref: D-31, which listed the name as "Simms"]. Private, Militia, 26th Battalion, Capt. Robert Sinnett's Company, 1777 [Ref: M-164]. Took the Oath of Allegiance in 1778 [Ref: L-20]. Rendered patriotic service by providing wheat for the use of the military in November 1781 [Ref: N-457]. "Joseph Simmes" was a resident of Durham Lower Hundred in 1778 [Ref: Q-I:297]. "Joseph Simms" married Elizabeth Dent on Sept. 8, 1760 in Trinity Parish [Ref: EE-11]. "Joseph Simmes" rendered patriotic service by providing wheat for the use of the military in February 1782 [Ref: N-480, which listed the name as "Simmes"].

SEMMES, Joseph Jr. Private, Militia, 26th Battalion, Capt. Francis Mastin's Company, 1777 [Ref: M-164].

SEMMES, Joseph Milburn. See "Thomas Semmes," q.v.

SEMMES, Lucretia. See "Francis Semmes," q.v.

SEMMES, Mark. Took the Oath of Allegiance in 1778 [Ref: L-20, which listed the name as "Simms"].

SEMMES, Marmaduke (1741-   ). Born on May 23, 1741, a son of Francis Semmes and Lucretia Chapman [Ref: EE-4]. Private, Militia, 12th Battalion, Capt. John Hanson's Company, 1777 [Ref: M-159]. Rendered patriotic service by providing wheat for the use of the military in May 1783 [Ref: N-598].

SEMMES, Marmaduke (1700-   ). Took the Oath of Allegiance in 1778 [Ref: L-20, AA-641, which latter source listed the name as "Mard. Simms"]. Aged about 69 as noted in a 1779 deposition [Ref: DD-177]. Resident of Port Tobacco East Hundred in 1778 [Ref: Q-I:297]. See "Thomas Semmes," q.v.

SEMMES, Martha. See "Thomas Semmes," q.v.

SEMMES, Mary. See "Thomas Semmes," q.v.

SEMMES, Robert Doyne. Ensign, Militia, 26th Battalion, Capt. William Winter's Company, commissioned May 9, 1778 [Ref: M-119, E-72]. Took the Oath of Allegiance in 1778 [Ref: L-20, AA-641, which latter source listed the name as "Robert D. Simms"].

SEMMES, Roger (1755-   ). Private, Flying Camp, Capt. Bowie's Company, enrolled July 16, 1776; native of Charles County, aged 21, height 5' 8 1/2" [Ref: D-36]. Took the Oath of Allegiance in 1778 [Ref: L-20, which listed the name as "Simmes"]. "Roger Simms" was a resident of Port Tobacco West Hundred in 1778 [Ref: Q-I:297].

SEMMES, Susanna. See "Thomas James Boarman, Jr.," q.v.

SEMMES, Thomas (c1732-c1827). Son of Marmaduke Semmes (1701-1772) and Henrietta Jenkins, he married Anne Queen by 1755 and had these children: James Semmes (born 1755); Henrietta Semmes (born 1757 and married Aquila Scott); Edward Semmes (born 1759); Anne Semmes (born 1760 and moved to Georgia); Jean Semmes (born 1762); Mary Semmes (born 1764); Joseph Milburn Semmes (born 1766 and moved to Georgia); Dr. Ignatius Semmes (born 1768 and moved to Georgia); Catherine Semmes (born 1770); Elizabeth Semmes (born 1772 and married Thomas Luckett); and, Martha Semmes (born 1774). Attended the Maryland Convention in 1776 and served in the Lower House of the Maryland Legislature, 1777-1778 [Ref: P-II:721, P-II:722]. First Lieutenant, Militia, 12th Battalion, Capt. Walter Hanson's Company, Feb. 26, 1776 [Ref: M-119, M-159, A-186, A-206, Y-II:23, which latter source listed the name as "Simms"]. Took the Oath of Allegiance in 1778 [Ref: L-20, AA-641, which latter source listed the name as "Thomas Simms"]. Resident of Bryan Town Hundred in 1778 [Ref: Q-I:297]. Rendered patriotic service by providing clothing for the use of the military in February 1778 [Ref: Y-II:235]. He was attacked while serving as Tobacco Inspector in 1785, severely beaten in the head, and never recovered his mental faculties. He moved with his family to Wilkes County, Georgia after 1789 and died there in 1827 [Ref: P-II:722]. However, another source states Thomas Semmes was born in Maryland in 1748, married Ann Queen, rendered patriotic service in Maryland, and migrated to Georgia where he died on June 14, 1832. This same source states Thomas Semmes was born in 1758, married first to Mrs. Mary Ann (Ratcliff) Branner, married second to Mary Semmes, served in the war as a first lieutenant, and died in Georgia on June 16, 1824 [Ref: J-III:2612]. With such discrepancies in the records, additional research will be necessary before drawing conclusions.

SEMMES, William. Took the Oath of Allegiance in 1778 [Ref: AA-641, which listed the name as "Simmes"]. Rendered patriotic service by providing wheat for the use of the military in November 1781 [Ref: N-457].

SERAT, Alphonsus. See "Alphonsus Sorat," q.v.

SEWELL (SEWALL), Charles (1754-c1820). Private, Flying Camp, Capt. Bowie's Company, enrolled July 12, 1776; native of Charles County, aged 22, height 5' 10" [Ref: D-36, which listed the name as "Chas. Sewele (Sewall)"]. Took the Oath of Allegiance in 1778 [Ref: L-20. AA-641]. Resident of Port Tobacco East Hundred in 1778 [Ref: Q-I:297]. Ensign, 1st Maryland Line, placed on the pension rolls of Charles County as of Oct. 9, 1818 and was subsequently reported dead, but no date was given [Ref: R-33]. He also received a federal pension (S35064) for which he applied on March 31, 1818. In 1820 he was aged 67 [Ref: V-III:3073].

SEWELL (SEWALL), Francis. Private, Militia, 12th Battalion, Capt. Walter Hanson's Company, 1777 [Ref: M-159]. Took the Oath of

Allegiance in 1778 [Ref: L-20]. Resident of Port Tobacco East Hundred in 1778 [Ref: Q-I:297]. See "Thomas Pickerel," q.v.

SEWELL (SEWALL), Lewis (1760-c1832). Private, Militia, 12th Battalion, Capt. Walter Hanson's Company, 1777 [Ref: M-159]. Took the Oath of Allegiance in 1778 [Ref: L-20]. Lewis Sewall was born on Feb. 2, 1760 in Maryland, married Elizabeth Howard Wailes, served as a private during the war, and migrated to Alabama where he died after July 4, 1832 [Ref: J-III:2615].

SEWELL (SEWALL), Nicholas. "Nicholas Sewell" took the Oath of Allegiance in 1778 [Ref: L-20]. "Nicholas H. Sewall" was a corporal in the militia, 12th Battalion, Capt. Walter Hanson's Company, 1777 [Ref: M-159].

SHAW, Benjamin (1730/1-). Private, Militia, 12th Battalion, Capt. Walter Hanson's Company, 1777 [Ref: M-159]. Took the Oath of Allegiance in 1778 [Ref: AA-641]. Aged about 45 as noted in a 1776 deposition which mentioned his brother Ralph and their father Ralph Shaw, and aged about 50 as noted in a 1780 deposition which mentioned his father Ralph Shaw, deceased [Ref: CC-578, DD-176]. Resident of Port Tobacco East Hundred in 1778 [Ref: Q-I:297].

SHAW, Benjamin. Private, 1st Maryland Line, drafted from the Charles County militia and in service on June 11 or 12, 1781 [Ref: D-376].

SHAW, Elizabeth. See "Joseph Fearson," q.v.

SHAW, John (1760-). Corporal, Militia, 12th Battalion, Capt. Jonathan Yates' Company, 1777 [Ref: M-162]. Took the Oath of Allegiance in 1778 [Ref: AA-641]. Resident of William & Mary Upper Hundred in 1778 [Ref: Q-I:297]. He applied for a pension (R9440) on Nov. 23, 1836, aged 77, in Orange County, North Carolina, stating that he was born in Charles County, Maryland on Oct. 6, 1760 and lived there at the time of his enlistment [Ref: V-III:3088].

SHAW, Joseph. Sergeant, Militia, 12th Battalion, Capt. Jonathan Yates' Company, 1777 [Ref: M-162]. Took the Oath of Allegiance in 1778 [Ref: L-20, AA-641]. Resident of William & Mary Lower Hundred in 1778 [Ref: Q-I:297]. Ensign, Militia, Capt. John Lancaster's Company, commissioned on Jan. 19, 1781 [Ref: M-120, G-280].

SHAW, Ralph. See "Benjamin Shaw," q.v.

SHAW, William. Private, Militia, 12th Battalion, Capt. Jonathan Yates' Company, 1777 [Ref: M-162]. Took the Oath of Allegiance in 1778 [Ref: L-20, AA-641]. Resident of William & Mary Lower Hundred in 1778 [Ref: Q-I:297].

SHEID, Eleanor. See "Theodore Dent," q.v.

SHEID, Martha. See "Theodore Dent," q.v.

SHELDON, William (1712-   ). "William Sheldon" took the Oath of Allegiance in 1778 [Ref: L-20]. "William Shelton" was aged about 29 as noted in a 1741 deposition [Ref: DD-177].
SHEPPARD, John. "John Shepheard" took the Oath of Allegiance in 1778 [Ref: L-20, AA-641]. "John Sheppard" was a resident of Durham Lower Hundred in 1778 [Ref: Q-I:297].
SHEPPARD, Valinda. See "Rezin Beall," q.v.
SHERCLIFF, Joseph (1755-   ). Private, Flying Camp, Capt. Bowie's Company, enrolled July 16, 1776; native of Charles County, aged 22, height 5' 11" [Ref: D-36, which listed the name as "Shutliff (Shiercliff)"]. Private, Militia, 26th Battalion, Capt. Robert Sinnett's Company, 1777 [Ref: M-164, which listed the name as "Shirclift"].
SHERCLIFF, Thomas (1727-   ). "Thomas Shercliff" took the Oath of Allegiance in 1778 [Ref: AA-641]. "Thomas Sherckliff" was aged about 51 as noted in a 1778 deposition [Ref: DD-177]. "Thomas Shercliff" was a resident of Port Tobacco East Hundred in 1778 [Ref: Q-I:297].
SHERCLIFF, William (c1750-1808). First Lieutenant, 1st Maryland Line. He married Melinda Mudd and died on Jan. 13, 1808 [Ref: J-III:2653, which listed his name as "Shircliff"].
SHETTLEWORTH, John. Took the Oath of Allegiance in 1778 [Ref: AA-641]. Resident of Bryan Town Hundred in 1778 [Ref: Q-I:297].
SHIELDS, Thomas. Took the Oath of Allegiance in 1778 [Ref: AA-641].
SHIERBURN (SHURBIN), Richard (1751-   ). "Richard Shierburn" took the Oath of Allegiance in 1778 [Ref: AA-641]. "Richard Shurbin" was aged about 27 as noted in a 1778 deposition [Ref: DD-177].
SHIRBIN, Mary. Rendered patriotic service by providing clothing for the use of the military in February 1778 [Ref: Y-II:235].
SHIRCLIFF, William. See "William Shercliff," q.v.
SIMMONS, Aaron (c1760-1832). Private, 1st Maryland Line, Light Infantry Company, from Aug. 1, 1780 until discharged in July 1781 [Ref: D-359, D-603]. On Feb. 19, 1819, the Treasurer of Maryland was directed to pay to "Aaron Simmons, late a revolutionary soldier, or order, quarterly during life, half pay of a private." On March 4, 1834, the Treasurer was directed to pay to "Sarah Simmons, of Charles County, during life, quarterly, half pay of a private, for the services rendered by her husband during the Revolutionary War." [Ref: Q-II:391]. Sarah applied for a federal pension (W9293) on Dec. 23, 1839, aged about 82, stating that she married Aaron Simmons on Jan. 30, 1783 in Charles County and he died there on March 1, 1832 [Ref: V-III:3134, W-122].
SIMMONS, John. Private, 1st Maryland Line, enrolled and passed on July 8, 1776 [Ref: D-32].

SIMMONS, Samuel. Took the Oath of Allegiance in 1778 [Ref: L-20]. Resident of Bryan Town Hundred in 1778 [Ref: Q-I:297].

SIMMONS, Sarah. See "Aaron Simmons," q.v.

SIMMS, Charles. See "Charles Timms," q.v.

SIMMS, Edward. Ensign, 1st Maryland Regiment of Continental Troops, appointed on Sept. 11, 1779 and a commission was requested from the Board of War [Ref: E-521]. See "Edward Semmes," q.v.

SIMMS, John. Took the Oath of Allegiance in 1778 [Ref: L-20, AA-641]. Gave a deposition in 1781 pertaining to his inability to perform military service due to family obligations [Ref: Z-208]. Resident of Durham Lower Hundred in 1778 [Ref: Q-I:297].

SIMMS, Joseph, of Ignatius. Took the Oath of Allegiance in August 1778 [Ref: AA-710].

SIMMS, Joseph, of James. Took the Oath of Allegiance in 1778 [Ref: L-20, AA-641].

SIMMS, Joshua Jr. Private, Militia, 26th Battalion, Capt. Francis Mastin's Company, 1777 [Ref: M-164, which listed the name as "Josh. Simms, Junr." and X-78, which listed the name as "Joshua Simons, Jr."].

SIMMS, Marmaduke. See "Marmaduke Semmes," q.v.

SIMMS, Matilda. See "Richard Mudd," q.v.

SIMMS, William. See "William Semmes," q.v.

SIMONS, Maurice. On Feb. 4, 1783, the Council of Maryland "ordered that the Western Shore Treasurer deliver to Thomas How Ridgate for the use of Maurice Simons five hogsheads of Tobacco weighing four thousand eight hundred and ten pounds at Nanjemoy and Chaptico Warehouses in Charles County in lieu of the like Quantity for which Mr. Simons had an Order in March 1782, and did not receive." [Ref: I-354].

SIMPSON, Andrew (1730-   ). Took the Oath of Allegiance in 1778 [Ref: L-20]. Aged about 48 as noted in a 1778 deposition [Ref: DD-177]. Resident of Newport East Hundred in 1778 [Ref: Q-I:297].

SIMPSON, Anne. See "Clement Edelen," q.v.

SIMPSON, Charles. Corporal, Militia, 12th Battalion, Capt. Benjamin Lusby Corry's Company, 1777 [Ref: M-160]. Took the Oath of Allegiance in 1778 [Ref: L-20]. Resident of Newport West Hundred in 1778 [Ref: Q-I:297]. Rendered patriotic service by providing wheat for the use of the military in September 1782 [Ref: N-556].

SIMPSON, Elizabeth. See "Francis Posey," q.v.

SIMPSON, Henry (1730-   ). Corporal, Militia, 26th Battalion, Capt. Robert Sinnett's Company, 1777 [Ref: M-164]. Took the Oath of Allegiance in 1778 [Ref: L-20]. Aged about 49 as noted in a 1779 deposition which

mentioned his brother William and their father Ignatius Simpson [Ref: DD-177]. Resident of Port Tobacco West Hundred in 1778 [Ref: Q-I:297].
SIMPSON, Henry Jr. Private, Militia, 12th Battalion, Capt. Benjamin Lusby Corry's Company, 1777 [Ref: M-160, which listed the name without the "Jr."]. Took the Oath of Allegiance in 1778 [Ref: L-20]. Resident of Newport West Hundred in 1778 [Ref: Q-I:297].
SIMPSON, Ignatius (1708-   ). Took the Oath of Allegiance in 1778 [Ref: L-20]. Aged about 44 as noted in a 1752 deposition which mentioned his father Thomas Simpson, Sr. [Ref: DD-177]. See "Henry Simpson," q.v.
SIMPSON, Ignatius (c1760-1793). Sergeant, Militia, 26th Battalion, Capt. Robert Sinnett's Company, 1777 [Ref: M-164]. Resident of Port Tobacco West Hundred in 1778 [Ref: Q-I:297]. Ignatius Simpson married Anne Semmes and died in 1793 [Ref: J-III:2674].
SIMPSON, Ignatius. Private, Militia, 12th Battalion, Capt. Benjamin Lusby Corry's Company, 1777 [Ref: M-160]. Resident of Newport West Hundred in 1778 [Ref: Q-I:297].
SIMPSON, James. Two men by this name were privates in the militia in 1777: one in the 12th Battalion, Capt. Benjamin Lusby Corry's Company, and one in the 26th Battalion, Capt. Robert Sinnett's Company [Ref: M-160, M-164]. Another was a corporal in the 26th Battalion, Capt. Robert Sinnett's Company, in 1777 [Ref: M-164]. One took the Oath of Allegiance in 1778 [Ref: L-20]. One rendered patriotic service by providing wheat for the use of the military in September 1782 [Ref: N-556]. One James Simpson, son of Thomas Simpson, was aged about 41 as noted in a 1778 deposition and had a brother Thomas, aged about 56 [Ref: CC-627, DD-177]. Resident of Newport West Hundred in 1778 [Ref: Q-I:297].
SIMPSON, John Lowe. Took the Oath of Allegiance in 1778 [Ref: L-20]. Resident of Newport West Hundred in 1778 [Ref: Q-I:297].
SIMPSON, Joseph. Corporal, Militia, 26th Battalion, Capt. Samuel Smallwood's Company, 1777 [Ref: M-165]. Rendered patriotic service by providing wheat for the use of the military in January and November 1782 [Ref: N-470, N-565].
SIMPSON, Lawrence (1762-1843). Private, 1st Maryland Line, drafted from the Charles County militia and in service in June 1781 [Ref: D-376]. Private, 1st Maryland Line, Capt. Edward Prall's Company, until discharged Jan. 8, 1782 [Ref: D-433]. He married Sarah Carrico circa 1795 in Charles County [Ref: W-123]. In December 1816, the Treasurer of Maryland was directed to pay to "Lawrence Simpson, of Charles County, an old revolutionary soldier, quarterly, the half pay of a private soldier, as a further remuneration for his services in the Revolutionary War." He was placed on the pension rolls of Charles County as of April 1, 1820

(retroactive to Dec. 17, 1819). On Feb. 27, 1843, the Treasurer was directed to pay to "Peter W. Crain, for the widow of Lawrence Simpson, the balance due said Lawrence Simpson, a revolutionary pensioner, at his death." [Ref: Q-II:391, R-33]. He also applied for a federal pension on Dec. 17, 1819, aged 57, and in 1821 had a wife Sarah (aged about 56) and a daughter (aged 17, name not given) living at home. Aaron died on Feb. 2, 1843 and his widow applied for a pension (W26443) on July 7, 1852 in Washington, D. C. Their only child was a daughter Mary Burk who was aged 52 in 1853 and stated her parents married in 1798 (the widow had stated 1799). Her mother's maiden name was Carrico and she died on Aug. 13, 1853. Also mentioned in 1852 was a Peter Burk, but no relationship was stated [Ref: V-III:3143].

SIMPSON, Sarah. See "Lawrence Simpson," q.v.

SIMPSON, Thomas (1722-   ). Rendered patriotic service by providing wheat for the use of the military in November 1782 [Ref: N-565]. Aged about 56 as noted in a 1778 deposition which mentioned his brother James and their father Thomas Simpson, now deceased [Ref: CC-627, DD-178]. Resident of Newport West Hundred in 1778 [Ref: Q-I:297].

SIMPSON, Thomas Sr. (1751-   ). Private, Flying Camp, Capt. Bowie's Company, enrolled July 16, 1776; native of Charles County, aged 25, height 6' [Ref: D-36].

SIMPSON, Thomas Jr. (1759-   ). Private, Flying Camp, Capt. Bowie's Company, enrolled July 16, 1776; native of Charles County, aged 17, height 6' [Ref: D-36].

SIMPSON, William (1730-   ). Private, Militia, 12th Battalion, Capt. Jonathan Yates' Company, 1777 [Ref: M-162]. Aged about 35 as noted in a 1765 deposition [Ref: DD-178]. Resident of Newport West Hundred in 1778 [Ref: Q-I:297]. See "Henry Simpson," q.v.

SIMPSON, William Jr. Took the Oath of Allegiance in 1778 [Ref: L-20]. Resident of Newport West Hundred in 1778 [Ref: Q-I:297].

SIMPSON, William Sr. (c1700-1784). Took the Oath of Allegiance in 1778 [Ref: L-20, AA-641]. Aged about 52 as noted in a 1752 deposition (which mentioned his father Thomas Simpson, Sr.), aged about 66 as noted in a 1765 deposition (which mentioned his brother Thomas Simpson, now deceased), and aged about 82 as noted in a 1779 deposition [Ref: DD-178]. Resident of William & Mary Lower Hundred in 1778 [Ref: Q-I:297]. William Simpson was born circa 1700, married (wife's name not known), and died before Dec. 11, 1784 [Ref: J-III:2675].

SIMS, Matilda. See "Richard Mudd," q.v.

SINNETT, Robert (1745-   ). Captain, Militia, 26th Battalion, from Feb. 26, 1776 through at least Oct. 17, 1777 [Ref: M-121, M-164, A-186, A-206, C-

399, Y-II:23]. Took the Oath of Allegiance in 1778 [Ref: AA-641, L-20, which latter source listed the name as "Sennett"]. Resident of Port Tobacco West Hundred in 1778 [Ref: Q-I:297]. "Robert Sinnett" was aged about 33 as noted in a 1778 deposition. There was also a "Robert Sinnet" who was aged about 59 as noted in a 1761 deposition [Ref: CC-705, DD-178].

SINNETT, Sarah. See "Walter Hanson," q.v.

SISSEL, Nicholas. Private, 3rd Maryland Line, enrolled by Capt. Joseph Marbury by May 24, 1780 [Ref: F-181].

SKINNER, Edward. Private, Militia, 26th Battalion, Capt. Francis Mastin's Company, 1777 [Ref: M-164].

SKINNER, George. Private, Militia, 26th Battalion, Capt. Hezekiah Garner's Company, 1777 [Ref: M-162].

SKINNER, Hezekiah. "Hezekiah Skinner" took the Oath of Allegiance in 1778 [Ref: AA-641]. "Ezekiah Skinner" was a resident of Durham Lower Hundred in 1778 [Ref: Q-I:297].

SKINNER, James Jr. Private, Militia, 26th Battalion, Capt. Francis Mastin's Company, 1777 [Ref: M-164].

SKINNER, James Sr. Private, Militia, 26th Battalion, Capt. Francis Mastin's Company, 1777 [Ref: M-164]. Resident of Durham Lower Hundred in 1778 [Ref: Q-I:297].

SKINNER, Jeremiah. Took the Oath of Allegiance in 1778 [Ref: L-20]. Resident of Durham Lower Hundred in 1778 [Ref: Q-I:297].

SKINNER, John Jr. Private, Militia, 26th Battalion, Capt. Francis Mastin's Company, 1777 [Ref: X-78, M-164, which latter source mistakenly listed the name as "John Minner Jur"].

SKINNER, John Sr. Took the Oath of Allegiance in 1778 [Ref: AA-641].

SKINNER, Manning. Took the Oath of Allegiance in 1778 [Ref: AA-641].

SKINNER, Thomas, of Thomas. Private, Militia, Capt. Francis Mastin's Company, 26th Battalion, March 19, 1776 through at least 1777 [Ref: M-158, M-164, K-1814]. Resident of Durham Lower Hundred in 1778 [Ref: Q-I:297].

SKINNER, William. Private, Militia, 26th Battalion, Capt. Francis Mastin's Company, 1777 [Ref: M-164]. Resident of Durham Lower Hundred in 1778 [Ref: Q-I:297].

SLATER, James. Sergeant, Militia, 26th Battalion, Capt. William McPherson's Company, 1777 [Ref: M-163]. Took the Oath of Allegiance in 1778 [Ref: L-20, AA-641].

SLATER, John. Private, Militia, 26th Battalion, Capt. William McPherson's Company, 1777 [Ref: M-163]. Took the Oath of Allegiance in 1778 [Ref: L-20, AA-641]. Rendered patriotic service by providing wheat for the use of the military in August 1781 [Ref: N-421, which listed the name as "Slator"]. Resident of Port Tobacco Upper Hundred in 1778 [Ref: Q-I:297].

SLATER, Nehemiah. Private, Militia, 26th Battalion, Capt. William McPherson's Company, 1777 [Ref: M-163]. Resident of Port Tobacco Upper Hundred in 1778 [Ref: Q-I:297].

SLATER, Richard Jr. Private, Militia, 26th Battalion, Capt. William McPherson's Company, 1777 [Ref: M-163, which listed the name without the "Jr."]. Took the Oath of Allegiance in 1778 [Ref: L-20, AA-641]. Resident of Port Tobacco Upper Hundred in 1778 [Ref: Q-I:297].

SLATER, Richard Sr. Took the Oath of Allegiance in 1778 [Ref: L-20, AA-641]. "Richard Slader" was aged about 57 as noted in a 1767 deposition and "Richard Slater" was aged about 44 as noted in a 1763 deposition [Ref: DD-178]. Resident of Port Tobacco Upper Hundred in 1778 [Ref: Q-I:297].

SLYE, Clare. Rendered patriotic service by providing wheat for the use of the military in September and November 1781, February, July, and November 1782, and May 1783 [Ref: N-441, N-453, N-479, N-532, N-536, N-566, N-597].

SLYE, Eleanor. See "Robert Slye," q.v.

SLYE, John. See "Robert Slye," q.v.

SLYE, Robert (1745-   ). Born on Nov. 15, 1745, son of John and Eleanor Slye [Ref: EE-9]. Private, Militia, 12th Battalion, Capt. John Parnham's Company, 1777 [Ref: M-160, which listed the name as "Sly"]. Took the Oath of Allegiance in 1778 [Ref: L-20]. Resident of Newport East Hundred in 1778 [Ref: Q-I:297].

SMALLWOOD, Ann. Rendered patriotic service by providing wheat for the use of the military in December 1782 [Ref: N-576].

SMALLWOOD, Bayne (c1742-c1820). Private, Lower Battalion, Prince George's County, 1776 [Ref: D-35]. Memorialist and Militiaman, Pomonkey Company, Charles County, 1776 [Ref: M-158, Y-II:26]. Private, Charles County Militia, 26th Battalion, Capt. Thomas H. Marshall's Company, 1777 [Ref: M-163]. Took the Oath of Allegiance in 1778 [Ref: L-20]. Resident of Pomonkey Hundred in 1778 [Ref: Q-I:297]. Rendered patriotic service by providing wheat for the use of the military in May 1783 [Ref: N-598]. Bayne Smallwood was born circa 1742 in Maryland, married first to Mary Wynn, married second to Marsilva Coe, and died after 1820 in Virginia [Ref: J-III:2694]. See "William Smallwood," q.v.

SMALLWOOD, Chloe. See "Henry Russell," q.v.

SMALLWOOD, Heabard. Second Lieutenant, Militia, Capt. Francis Mastin's Company, 26th Battalion, March 19, 1776 [Ref: A-426, M-127, M-158, K-1814, which latter sources listed the first name as "Keabard"].

Brother of Gen. William Smallwood, he served in the war and died in Virginia in 1780 without progeny [Ref: P-II:741].

SMALLWOOD, Henry. Took the Oath of Allegiance in 1778 [Ref: L-20, AA-641]. Resident of Port Tobacco Upper Hundred in 1778 [Ref: Q-I:297].

SMALLWOOD, Hezekiah. Memorialist and Militiaman, Pomonkey Company, after March 6, 1776 [Ref: M-158, Y-II:26]. Private, Militia, 26th Battalion, Capt. Thomas H. Marshall's Company, 1777 [Ref: M-163]. Resident of Pomonkey Hundred in 1778 [Ref: Q-I:297].

SMALLWOOD, James. "James Smallwood" was a private in the militia, 26th Battalion, Capt. Samuel Smallwood's Company, 1777 [Ref: M-165]. "James Smallwood, of John" was a resident of Port Tobacco Upper Hundred in 1778 [Ref: Q-I:297].

SMALLWOOD, James Jr. "James Smallwood, Jr." took the Oath of Allegiance in 1778 [Ref: L-20, AA-641]. "James Smallwood, of James" was a resident of Port Tobacco East Hundred in 1778 [Ref: Q-I:297].

SMALLWOOD, James Sr. (1700-1778). "James Smallwood" took the Oath of Allegiance in 1778 [Ref: L-20, AA-641]. "James Smallwood, Sr." was aged about 45 as noted in a 1745 deposition [Ref: DD-179]. "James Smallwood" died by May 1778 [Ref: GG-167].

SMALLWOOD, James Boyden. Ensign, Militia, 26th Battalion, Capt. Samuel Smallwood's Company, 1777 [Ref: M-165]. Took the Oath of Allegiance in 1778 [Ref: L-20, which listed the name as "James B. Smallwood" and AA-641, which listed the name as "James Byden Smallwood"]. Resident of Port Tobacco Upper Hundred in 1778 [Ref: Q-I:297]. "James Boyden Smallwood" died by September 1778 (date of inventory). [Ref: GG-220, GG-221].

SMALLWOOD, John (1705-). Took the Oath of Allegiance in 1778 [Ref: L-20]. Aged about 45 as noted in a 1745 deposition [Ref: DD-179]. Resident of Port Tobacco West Hundred in 1778 [Ref: Q-I:297].

SMALLWOOD, John Jr. Private, Militia, 26th Battalion, Capt. Thomas H. Marshall's Company, 1777 [Ref: M-163, which listed the name without the "Jr."]. Took the Oath of Allegiance in 1778 [Ref: L-20]. Resident of Pomonkey Hundred in 1778 [Ref: Q-I:297].

SMALLWOOD, John, of Ledstone. Took the Oath of Allegiance in 1778 [Ref: AA-641, L-20, which latter source listed the name as "of Leadston"].

SMALLWOOD, Ledstone. Private, Lower Battalion, Prince George's County, 1776 [Ref: D-35]. Took the Oath of Allegiance in Charles County in 1778 [Ref: AA-641, L-20, which latter source listed the name as "Leadston"]. Resident of Port Tobacco East Hundred in 1778 [Ref: Q-I:297]. See "Lydestone Smallwood," q.v.

SMALLWOOD, Luke. Sergeant, Militia, 26th Battalion, Capt. Samuel Smallwood's Company, 1777 [Ref: M-165]. Took the Oath of Allegiance in 1778 [Ref: L-20, AA-641]. Resident of Port Tobacco Upper Hundred in 1778 [Ref: Q-I:297].

SMALLWOOD, Lydestone. Private, Militia, 26th Battalion, Capt. Samuel Smallwood's Company, 1777 [Ref: M-165, which listed the name as "Lyde Stone"]. Took the Oath of Allegiance in 1778 [Ref: L-20, which listed the name as "Lydestone" and AA-641, which listed the name as "Ledstone"]. Resident of Port Tobacco Upper Hundred in 1778 [Ref: Q-I:297, which listed the name as "Ledstone"]. See "Ledstone Smallwood," q.v.

SMALLWOOD, Mary. Rendered patriotic service by providing wheat for the use of the military in May 1783 [Ref: N-597]. See "Ledstone Noland," q.v.

SMALLWOOD, Priscilla. Rendered patriotic service by providing clothing for the use of the military in February 1778 [Ref: Y-II:235]. Rendered patriotic service by providing wheat for the use of the military in May 1782 [Ref: N-515, which listed the first name as "Presila"].

SMALLWOOD, Prior (1731-   ). Rendered patriotic service by providing wheat for the use of the military in April 1783 [Ref: N-593]. Aged about 40 as noted in a 1771 deposition [Ref: DD-179]. Resident of Port Tobacco East Hundred in 1778 [Ref: Q-I:297].

SMALLWOOD, Pryor. Private, Militia, 26th Battalion, Capt. Thomas H. Marshall's Company, 1777 [Ref: M-163]. Resident of Pomonkey Hundred in 1778 [Ref: Q-I:297].

SMALLWOOD, Robert. Took the Oath of Allegiance in 1778 [Ref: L-20].

SMALLWOOD, Samuel. Captain, Militia, 26th Battalion, commissioned May 9, 1778 [Ref: M-122, M-165, E-72]. Took the Oath of Allegiance in 1778 [Ref: L-20, AA-641]. Resident of Port Tobacco Upper Hundred in 1778 [Ref: Q-I:297]. Constable, 1778 [Ref: CC-709]. Rendered patriotic service by providing wheat for the use of the military in April 1783 [Ref: N-594].

SMALLWOOD, Thomas. Two men by this name were privates in the militia, 26th Battalion, in 1777: one in Capt. William McPherson's Company, and one in Capt. Thomas H. Marshall's Company [Ref: M-163]. One took the Oath of Allegiance in 1778 [Ref: L-20]. One rendered patriotic service by providing wheat for the use of the military in May 1783 [Ref: N-598]. "Thomas Smallwood, Sr." was a resident of Pomonkey Hundred in 1778 [Ref: Q-I:297]. One "Thomas Smallwood" died testate in August 1778 [Ref: GG-209]. *Ed. Note:* Some of this information could pertain to "Thomas Smallwood, Jr.," q.v. Additional research may be necessary before drawing conclusions.

SMALLWOOD, Thomas Jr. Took the Oath of Allegiance in 1778 [Ref: L-20, AA-641]. One Thomas Smallwood, Jr., was a resident of Pomonkey Hundred and another Thomas Smallwood, Jr., was a resident of Port Tobacco Upper Hundred in 1778 [Ref: Q-I:297]. See "Thomas Smallwood," q.v.

SMALLWOOD, William (1732-1792). Son of Bayne Smallwood and Priscilla Heabard, he never married and died without progeny. William Smallwood was a career military officer and held many civil and political offices, including Governor of Maryland, 1785-1788. He was a Delegate to the Maryland Convention from July 26 to Aug. 14, 1775, served in the Lower House of the Maryland Legislature, 1761-1774, and President of the Senate, 1791-1792 [Ref: P-II:741, A-3, Y-I:4]. He served in the French and Indian Wars, became a colonel in 1776, and was subsequently major general in the Maryland Line throughout the Revolutionary War. Smallwood's Maryland Regiment was well known for its bravery and heroics, notably at the Battle of Long Island in August 1776 [Ref: P-II:741, which contains much more detailed information on his illustrious career, and V-III:3166, which contains information on his heirs in 1816]. William Smallwood took the Oath of Allegiance in 1778 [Ref: AA-641]. He rendered patriotic service by providing clothing for the use of the military in February 1778, and by providing wheat for the use of the military in December 1782 [Ref: N-569, Y-II:235]. See "John Courts Jones" and "John Parnham" and "Heabard Smallwood" and "John Hoskins Stone," q.v. *Ed. Note:* A chapter of the Maryland Society, Sons of the American Revolution, was named in honor of General William Smallwood in 1968.

SMALLWOOD, William Jr. Took the Oath of Allegiance in 1778 [Ref: L-20]. *Ed. Note:* Probable family members: Lydia Egerton, daughter of William Smallwood, who was aged about 30 as noted in a 1779, and William Smallwood, Sr., who was aged about 59 as noted in a 1780 deposition which mentioned his parents, John and Mary Smallwood [Ref: BB-465, DD-179, DD-706].

SMALLWOOD, William Marbury (c1741-1809). "William M. Smallwood" took the Oath of Allegiance in 1778 [Ref: L-20, AA-641]. Resident of Port Tobacco Upper Hundred in 1778 [Ref: Q-I:297]. "William Marbury Smallwood" was born circa 1741, married Mrs. Grace Harmon, and died before Aug. 26, 1809 [Ref: J-III:2694].

SMITH, Ann Neale. See "Joshua Mudd," q.v.

SMITH, Basil. Corporal, Militia, 12th Battalion, Capt. Alexander McPherson's Company, 1777 [Ref: M-160]. Resident of Port Tobacco East Hundred in 1778 [Ref: Q-I:297].

SMITH, Basil. Took the Oath of Allegiance in 1778 [Ref: L-20]. Resident of Port Tobacco East Hundred in 1778 [Ref: Q-I:297].

SMITH, Charles (c1758-c1788). Private, 1st Maryland Line. Charles Smith married Mary Bowling on Jan. 19, 1782 and died in 1787 or 1788. His widow Mary applied for a pension (W25002) on Aug. 18, 1838. Mary's niece, Mrs. Louisa "Price or Pricess," subsequently made affidavit in Baltimore and stated that the widow died leaving no children, but her daughter Mary Smith had married Raphel W. Boarman by whom she had four children (grandchildren of the soldier Charles Smith): Mary Rose Boarman (married Horatio Dyer, of Prince George's County, and died in 1836); Marcelino Smith (married James P. Kirby and lived in Georgetown, D. C. in 1850); Ignatius W. Boarman (lived in Alabama in 1850); and, Charles E. Boarman (lived in Ohio in 1850). William King stated he buried Mary Smith on Oct. 19, 1843 [Ref: V-III:3174, W-123].

SMITH, Charles S. Private, Militia, 12th Battalion, Capt. Peter Wood's Company, 1777 [Ref: M-161]. Resident of Benedict Hundred in 1778 [Ref: Q-I:297].

SMITH, Charles Somerset (1733-c1780). Captain, Militia, 12th Battalion, from March 3, 1776 to Sept. 9, 1776 (resigned). [Ref: M-122]. Took the Oath of Allegiance in 1778 [Ref: L-20]. Charles Somerset Smith was born on Oct. 13, 1733, married Ann Hine, and died after Nov. 17, 1780 [Ref: J-III:2700].

SMITH, Clement. Private, Militia, 26th Battalion, Capt. Robert Sinnett's Company, 1777 [Ref: M-164]. Took the Oath of Allegiance in 1778 [Ref: L-20]. Resident of Port Tobacco West Hundred in 1778 [Ref: Q-I:297].

SMITH, Edward Miles. Private, 1st Maryland Line, enrolled and passed on July 18, 1776 [Ref: D-32].

SMITH, Elizabeth. See "Richard Smith," q.v.

SMITH, Henry. Private, Militia, 26th Battalion, Capt. Richard Bennett Mitchell's Company, 1777 [Ref: M-165].

SMITH, James. Private, Militia, 12th Battalion, Capt. Peter Wood's Company, 1777 [Ref: M-161]. Resident of William & Mary Upper Hundred in 1778 [Ref: Q-I:297].

SMITH, James. Took the Oath of Allegiance in 1778 [Ref: L-20, AA-641]. Resident of William & Mary Lower Hundred in 1778 [Ref: Q-I:297].

SMITH, James Jr. (1727-). Took the Oath of Allegiance in 1778 [Ref: AA-641]. Aged about 36 as noted in a 1763 deposition [Ref: DD-179]. Resident of Benedict Hundred in 1778 [Ref: Q-I:297].

SMITH, John. Private, Militia, 26th Battalion, Capt. William Winter's Company, 1777 [Ref: M-165]. Took the Oath of Allegiance in 1778 [Ref: L-20, AA-641]. Resident of Durham Lower Hundred in 1778 [Ref: Q-

I:297]. On Feb. 19, 1819, the Treasurer of Maryland was directed to pay to "John Smith, of Charles County, late a revolutionary soldier, quarterly during life, half pay of a private, for his revolutionary services." [Ref: Q-II:393].

SMITH, John Jr. Two men by the name of "John Smith, Jr." were privates in the Charles County militia, 12th Battalion, in 1777: one in Capt. John Thomas' Company and one in Capt. Alexander McPherson's Company [Ref: M-160, M-161]. One took the Oath of Allegiance in 1778 [Ref: L-20]. Resident of Bryan Town Hundred in 1778 [Ref: Q-I:297].

SMITH, John Sr. Took the Oath of Allegiance in 1778 [Ref: L-20]. Resident of Bryan Town Hundred in 1778 [Ref: Q-I:297].

SMITH, John (carpenter). Took the Oath of Allegiance in 1778 [Ref: AA-641]. Resident of Port Tobacco East Hundred in 1778 [Ref: Q-I:297].

SMITH, Joseph. Private, Militia, 26th Battalion, Capt. Robert Sinnett's Company, 1777 [Ref: M-164]. Resident of Port Tobacco West Hundred in 1778 [Ref: Q-I:297].

SMITH, Josias. Private (furnished by class for 9 months), 1st Maryland Line, by Sept. 11, 1778 [Ref: D-330]. Took the Oath of Allegiance in 1778 [Ref: L-20].

SMITH, Leonard. Private, 1st Maryland Line, enrolled and passed on July 18, 1776 [Ref: D-32].

SMITH, Levin. Private (furnished by class for 9 months), 1st Maryland Line, by Sept. 11, 1778 [Ref: D-330, which listed the first name as "Levine"].

SMITH, Mary. See "Charles Smith," q.v.

SMITH, Matthew. Private, Militia, 12th Battalion, Capt. Alexander McPherson's Company, 1777 [Ref: M-160]. Took the Oath of Allegiance in 1778 [Ref: L-20]. Private (furnished by class for 9 months), 1st Maryland Line, by Sept. 11, 1778 [Ref: D-330]. Resident of Port Tobacco East Hundred in 1778 [Ref: Q-I:297].

SMITH, Nathan. Private, 1st Maryland Line, discharged on Dec. 3, 1781 [Ref: I-11].

SMITH, Nicholas. Private, Militia, 12th Battalion, Capt. Alexander McPherson's Company, 1777 [Ref: M-160]. Took the Oath of Allegiance in 1778 [Ref: AA-641].

SMITH, Peter. Took the Oath of Allegiance in 1778 [Ref: AA-641]. Resident of William & Mary Upper Hundred in 1778 [Ref: Q-I:297].

SMITH, Richard (1755-1840). Private, 1st Maryland Line, enrolled and passed on July 18, 1776 [Ref: D-32]. He applied for a pension on May 20, 1833 in Rowan County, North Carolina, stating he was born in Charles County, Maryland in 1755 and lived there at the time of his enlistment.

He married Elizabeth ---- in January 1785, in Prince George's County and moved to North Carolina around 1812. Richard died on June 13, 1840 and his widow applied for a pension (W4073) on Jan. 2, 1844, aged 79 [Ref: V-III:3220]. Richard Smith married Elizabeth Church by license dated Jan. 12, 1785 [Ref: *Index of Marriage Licenses, Prince George's County, Maryland, 1777-1886*, by Helen W. Brown (1973), p. 199].

SMITH, Richard (1726-). Took the Oath of Allegiance in 1778 [Ref: AA-641]. Aged about 36 as noted in a 1762 deposition which mentioned his father Richard, deceased [Ref: DD-179]. Resident of William & Mary Upper Hundred in 1778 [Ref: Q-I:297].

SMITH, Simon. Took the Oath of Allegiance in 1778 [Ref: L-20]. Resident of Durham Lower Hundred in 1778 [Ref: Q-I:297].

SMITH, Thomas. Private, Militia, 26th Battalion, Capt. Benjamin Cawood's Company, 1777 [Ref: M-162]. "Thomas Smith, blacksmith" was a resident of Port Tobacco East Hundred in 1778 [Ref: Q-I:297].

SMITH, Walter. Sergeant, Militia, 26th Battalion, Capt. William McPherson's Company, 1777 [Ref: M-163]. Took the Oath of Allegiance in 1778 [Ref: L-20, AA-641]. Resident of Port Tobacco East Hundred in 1778 [Ref: Q-I:297].

SMITHSON (SMITSON), Thomas. See "John Imeson," q.v.

SMITHSON (SMITHTON), William E. "William E. Smithson" was a private in the militia, 12th Battalion, Capt. John Hanson's Company, 1777 [Ref: M-159]. "William E. Smithton" was a resident of Port Tobacco East Hundred in 1778 [Ref: Q-I:297]. "William Aton Smithton" took the Oath of Allegiance in 1778 [Ref: AA-641].

SMOOT, Abigail. See "Arthur Smoot" and "Thomas Smoot" and "Josias Smoot" and "John Alexander Smoot," q.v.

SMOOT, Arthur (1742-1797). Born on Aug. 16, 1742, son of Thomas and Abigail Smoot [Ref: EE-3]. Took the Oath of Allegiance in 1778 [Ref: L-20, AA-641]. Resident of Bryan Town Hundred in 1778 [Ref: Q-I:297].

SMOOT, Barton. See "Thomas Smoot" and "George Clarke Smoot," q.v.

SMOOT, Charles. See "William Barton Smoot, of Charles" and "John Nathan Smoot" and "Hendley Smoot" and "John Alexander Smoot" and "Josias Smoot," q.v.

SMOOT, Edward (1724-1795). Took the Oath of Allegiance in 1778 [Ref: L-20, AA-641]. Rendered patriotic service by providing clothing for the use of the military in February 1778 [Ref: Y-II:234]. Aged about 38 as noted in a 1762 deposition [Ref: DD-180]. Resident of William & Mary Lower Hundred in 1778 [Ref: Q-I:297]. Edward Smoot (son of John Smoot and Posthuma Ford) was born in 1724, married first to Ann Chandler, married second to Mary Magdalene Stoddert, and died before Feb. 24, 1795 (date of probate). [Ref: J-III:2729]. John Smoot, son of Edward Smoot and Ann Chandler, was born circa 1748, served as a captain in the Dorchester County militia during the Revolutionary War, married Elizabeth Douglas, settled at "Rehoboth" where he constructed Liberty Hall, a spacious Georgian mansion, and died in 1793 [Ref: Harry Wright Newman's *The Smoots of Maryland and Virginia* (1936), pp. 17-19]. See "Henry Smoot," q.v.

SMOOT, Eleanor. See "Thomas Smoot," q.v.

SMOOT, Elizabeth. Rendered patriotic service by providing wheat for the use of the military in September 1781 [Ref: N-438].

SMOOT, Frances. See "George Clarke Smoot" and "Hezekiah Johnson," q.v.

SMOOT, George Clarke. Took the Oath of Allegiance in 1778 [Ref: AA-641]. Resident of William & Mary Upper Hundred in 1778 [Ref: Q-I:297]. Son of Barton Smoot and Susannah Mackall Clarke, George married Sarah Fendall (widow of John Fendall) and died testate in October 1779. His children were Susannah Mackall Smoot, Wilks (Willoughby?) Smoot, John Alexander Smoot, George Clarke Smoot, Philip Barton Smoot, and Frances Smoot [Ref: Harry Wright Newman's *The Smoots of Maryland and Virginia* (1936), pp. 61-62].

SMOOT, Hendley (c1749-1811). Ensign, Militia, 12th Battalion, Capt. John Parnham's Company, from 1777 through at least May 28, 1779 [Ref: E-427, M-123, M-160, which latter source misspelled the first name as "Kendly"]. Took the Oath of Allegiance in 1778 [Ref: AA-641, L-20, which latter source listed the first name as "Hendlay"]. Resident of Newport West Hundred in 1778 [Ref: Q-I:297]. Hendley Smoot (son of Charles Smoot and Mary Brandt) was born circa 1749, married Eleanor Wilson Briscoe, and died intestate in 1811 [Ref: J-III:2729].

SMOOT, Henry (1759-1820). Private, Militia, 12th Battalion, Capt. Jonathan Yates' Company, 1777 [Ref: X-70, but was omitted from the list in Reference M-162]. Took the Oath of Allegiance in 1778 [Ref: AA-641]. Resident of William & Mary Lower Hundred in 1778 [Ref: Q-I:297]. Henry Smoot, son of Edward, was born on October 26, 1759, served as a private in Charles County and after settling in Dorchester County served as a lieutenant of the Upper Battalion in that county. He married Elizabeth Warren on December 23, 1781, raised a large family, and drowned while crossing the Nanticoke River on February 13, 1820 [Ref: Harry Wright Newman's *The Smoots of Maryland and Virginia* (1936), pp. 21-22]. However, another source states that Henry Smoot was born in 1761, married Elizabeth Douglass, and died on Feb. 24, 1820 [Ref: J-III:2729]. Additional research may be necessary before drawing conclusions.

SMOOT, Isaac (1745-1821). Ensign, Militia, 12th Battalion, Capt. Benjamin Lusby Corry's Company, 1777, and Capt. Alexander McPherson's Company, Oct. 22, 1777. Second Lieutenant, Militia, Capt. H. Dent's Company, May 28, 1779 [Ref: M-123, M-160, C-401, E-427]. Took the Oath of Allegiance in 1778 [Ref: L-20, AA-641]. Resident of Newport West Hundred in 1778 [Ref: Q-I:297]. Rendered patriotic service by providing wheat for the use of the military in September 1782 [Ref: N-544]. Isaac Smoot, son of Isaac, was born on December 2, 1745, married Mary Lock on October 28, 1779 (had no surviving children), and died in St. Mary's County before February 8, 1821 (date of inventory). [Ref: Harry Wright Newman's *The Smoots of Maryland and Virginia* (1936), p. 63].

SMOOT, John. Private, Militia, 12th Battalion, Capt. Jonathan Yates' Company, 1777 [Ref: M-162]. Took the Oath of Allegiance in 1778 [Ref: L-20, AA-641]. Resident of William & Mary Lower Hundred in 1778 [Ref: Q-I:297]. See "Edward Smoot," q.v.

SMOOT, John Alexander (c1760-1827). Private, Militia, 26th Battalion, Capt. Benjamin Cawood's Company, 1777 [Ref: M-162]. Son of George Clarke Smoot and Sarah Fendall, he married Abigail Hunter Tabbs on November 4, 1784 in St. Mary's County and raised a large family. They settled in Jefferson County, Kentucky between 1795 and 1798 and he was thereafter referred to as Alexander Smoot [Ref: Harry Wright Newman's *The Smoots of Maryland and Virginia* (1936), pp. 67-68]. See "George Clarke Smoot," q.v.

SMOOT, John Nathan (1744-1815). Quartermaster, 12th Battalion, Jan. 6, 1776, and possibly an Ensign, 1st Maryland Line, in March 1780 [Ref: M-123, F-121]. Took the Oath of Allegiance in 1778 [Ref: L-20, AA-641]. Resident of Newport West Hundred in 1778 [Ref: Q-I:297]. Aged about 35 as noted in a 1779 deposition [Ref: DD-180]. John Nathan Smoot (son of Charles Smoot and Mary Brandt) was born in 1744, married first to Ann Hanson, married second to Mary Briscoe, and died testate before Jan. 21, 1815 [Ref: J-III:2729].

SMOOT, John Weems. See "William Barton Smoot," q.v.

SMOOT, Josias or Josiah (c1750-1797). Private, Militia, 26th Battalion, Capt. Richard Bennett Mitchell's Company, 1777 [Ref: M-165]. Took the Oath of Allegiance in 1778 [Ref: L-20]. Resident of Newport West Hundred in 1778 [Ref: Q-I:297]. Rendered patriotic service by providing wheat for the use of the military in January 1782 [Ref: N-471]. Josiah Smoot, son of Thomas and Abigail Smoot, married first to Christian Grant, married second to Anne Douglas, and died testate before November 5, 1797 (date of probate). His sons were Charles Smith Smoot

(born 1774) and Samuel Smoot [Ref: Harry Wright Newman's *The Smoots of Maryland and Virginia* (1936), p. 84].
SMOOT, Margaretta. See "William Dent," q.v.
SMOOT, Mary. See "William McPherson," q.v.
SMOOT, Matthew. Private, 1st Maryland Line, drafted from the Charles County militia on July 27, 1781 [Ref: D-377, G-569].
SMOOT, Philip Barton. See "George Clarke Smoot," q.v.
SMOOT, Richard. Took the Oath of Allegiance in 1778 [Ref: AA-641].
SMOOT, Samuel (c1720-1792). Took the Oath of Allegiance in 1778 [Ref: L-20, AA-641]. Resident of Bryan Town Hundred in 1778 [Ref: Q-I:297]. Samuel Smoot was born circa 1720, married Elizabeth Davis, and died before Nov. 12, 1792 [Ref: J-III:2729]. See "Thomas Smoot, of Samuel" and "Josias Smoot," q.v.
SMOOT, Susannah Mackall. See "George Clarke Smoot," q.v.
SMOOT, Thomas (1697-1782). Took the Oath of Allegiance in 1778 [Ref: L-20, AA-641]. Resident of Benedict Hundred in 1778 [Ref: Q-I:297]. Son of Thomas Smoot and Elizabeth Barton, he married Abigail ---- and died testate by December 5, 1782 [Ref: Harry Wright Newman's *The Smoots of Maryland and Virginia* (1936), p. 82]. See "William Barton Smoot" and "Josias Smoot," q.v.
SMOOT, Thomas (1742-1783). Private, Militia, 12th Battalion, Capt. Jonathan Yates' Company, 1777 [Ref: M-162]. Sergeant, 3rd Maryland Line, enlisted April 23, 1777 and discharged Aug. 29, 1778 [Ref: D-163]. Resident of Port Tobacco West Hundred [Ref: Q-I:297]. Son of William and Eleanor Smoot, he married Elizabeth ----, settled in Prince William County, Virginia after 1778, and died testate by July 7, 1783 [Ref: Harry Wright Newman's *The Smoots of Maryland and Virginia* (1936), p. 64].
SMOOT, Thomas, of Samuel (c1750-1824). Resident of Bryan Town Hundred in 1778 [Ref: Q-I:297]. He may have been the Thomas Smoot who rendered patriotic service by providing wheat for the use of the military in June 1782 [Ref: N-523]. Thomas Smoot, son of Samuel Smoot and Elizabeth Davis, migrated to Fauquier County, Virginia and moved after 1800 to Rowan County, North Carolina [Ref: Harry Wright Newman's *The Smoots of Maryland and Virginia* (1936), pp. 89-90].
SMOOT, Wilks or Willoughby. During the Revolution he aided the cause by the manufacture of salt for the Army and subsequently settled in St. Mary's County where he died before 1800 [Ref: I-195, and Harry Wright Newman's *The Smoots of Maryland and Virginia* (1936), p. 67]. See "George Clarke Smoot," q.v.
SMOOT, William. Sergeant, 1st Maryland Line, enlisted Dec. 10, 1776 and discharged Dec. 27, 1779. Ensign, 1st Maryland Line, Jan. 26, 1780.

Lieutenant, 2nd Maryland Line, Capt. Samuel McPherson's Company, by Jan. 1, 1782 [Ref: D-159, D-161, D-443].

SMOOT, William (1751-1821). Private, Militia, 26th Battalion, Capt. Hezekiah Garner's Company, 1777 [Ref: M-163]. Took the Oath of Allegiance in 1778 [Ref: AA-641]. Born in Maryland in 1751 and died in Virginia in 1821 [Ref: J-III:2729, and refer to source V-III:3236 for the heirs of one William Smoot in 1827]. See "Thomas Smoot," q.v.

SMOOT, William Barton (c1755-1816). "William B. Smoot" was a corporal in the militia, 12th Battalion, Capt. John Parnham's Company, in 1777 [Ref: M-160]. Took the Oath of Allegiance in 1778 [Ref: L-20]. Resident of Port Tobacco East Hundred in 1778 [Ref: Q-I:297]. Rendered patriotic service by providing wheat for the use of the military in November 1782 [Ref: N-564]. "William Barton Smoot" was the son of Thomas and Eleanor Smoot, served as a corporal in the war, married Margaret Dodson, and died testate before Jan. 8, 1817 (date of probate). A son John Weems Smoot (1796-1861) married Elizabeth Eleanor Hawkins [Ref: J-III:2729, S-1409, S-1428, S-1516A, which latter source stated he was a sergeant]. See "Thomas Pickerel" and "Walter Hanson" and "William Barton Smoot, of Charles," q.v.

SMOOT, William Barton, of Charles (c1746-1822). Took the Oath of Allegiance in 1778 [Ref: L-20]. Private, Militia, 12th Battalion, Capt. Walter Hanson's Company, 1777 [Ref: M-159, which listed the name as "Smoote"]. Resident of Newport West Hundred in 1778 [Ref: Q-I:297]. Son of Charles Smoot and Mary Brandt, he married Elizabeth Hanson and died testate in 1821 [Ref: Harry Wright Newman's *The Smoots of Maryland and Virginia* (1936), pp. 110-111].

SORAT, Alphonsus. Private, Militia, 12th Battalion, Capt. John Thomas' Company, 1777 [Ref: M-161, X-66, which latter source listed the name as "Serat"]. Resident of Benedict Hundred in 1778 [Ref: Q-I:297].

SOTHERON, Clarissa. See "James Keech," q.v.

SOTHORON, John. Took the Oath of Allegiance in 1778 [Ref: L-20]. Resident of Bryan Town Hundred in 1778 [Ref: Q-I:297].

SOUTHERLAND, Alexander. Private, 2nd Maryland Line, 1778, and discharged Jan. 10, 1780 [Ref: D-162].

SOUTHERLAND, Ignatius. Private, Militia, 26th Battalion, Capt. Hezekiah Garner's Company, 1777 [Ref: M-162].

SOUTHERLAND, Robert. Private, Militia, 26th Battalion, Capt. Hezekiah Garner's Company, 1777 [Ref: M-163]. Took the Oath of Allegiance in 1778 [Ref: AA-641].

SOUTHWELL, John. Rendered patriotic service by providing wheat for the use of the military in October 1782 [Ref: N-559]. Resident of Port Tobacco Upper Hundred in 1778 [Ref: Q-I:297].
SPALDING, Basil (c1718-1791). Took the Oath of Allegiance in 1778 [Ref: L-20]. Resident of Port Tobacco Upper Hundred in 1778 [Ref: Q-I:297]. Rendered patriotic service by providing wheat for the use of the military in December 1782 [Ref: N-573, N-575, which listed the name as "Spalden"]. Basil Spalding, Sr., was born circa 1718, married Catherine ----, and died on Sept. 26, 1791 [Ref: J-III:2745].
SPALDING, Blanch. See "Henry Mudd, Sr.," q.v.
SPALDING, Catherine. See "Basil Spalding," q.v.
SPALDING, Ignatius. Took the Oath of Allegiance in 1778 [Ref: L-20]. Resident of Bryan Town Hundred in 1778 [Ref: Q-I:297].
SPALDING, Philip. Rendered patriotic service by providing wheat for the use of the military in April 1783 [Ref: N-593].
SPALDING, Richard. Private, Militia, 12th Battalion, Capt. Alexander McPherson's Company, 1777 [Ref: M-160]. Took the Oath of Allegiance in 1778 [Ref: L-20]. Resident of Bryan Town Hundred in 1778 [Ref: Q-I:297].
SPALDING, Thomas. Took the Oath of Allegiance in 1778 [Ref: L-20, AA-641]. Resident of Bryan Town Hundred in 1778 [Ref: Q-I:297].
SPALDING, William (1759-1778). Private, Flying Camp, Capt. Bowie's Company, enrolled July 17, 1776; native of Charles County, aged 17, height 5' 6 1/2" [Ref: D-36]. Private, Militia, 26th Battalion, Capt. William McPherson's Company, 1777 [Ref: M-163]. Resident of Port Tobacco Upper Hundred in 1778 [Ref: Q-I:297]. Private, 1st Maryland Line, reported dead on Nov. 26, 1778 [Ref: D-161].
SPEAKE, Francis. Rendered patriotic service by providing wheat for the use of the military in December 1782 [Ref: N-577, which listed the name as "Speak"]. One Francis Speake was born circa 1750, served as a naval captain during the war, married Margaret Massey, and died after 1790 [Ref: J-III:2750].
SPEAKE, George. Private, Militia, Capt. Francis Mastin's Company, 26th Battalion, March 19, 1776 [Ref: M-158, K-1814]. Private, 1st Maryland Line, enrolled and passed on July 27, 1776 [Ref: D-31].
SPEAKE, Henrietta. Rendered patriotic service by providing wheat for the use of the military in December 1782 [Ref: N-569, which listed the name as "Henerita Speak"].
SPEAKE, Henry. Private, Militia, 26th Battalion, Capt. Richard Bennett Mitchell's Company, 1777 [Ref: M-165]. Took the Oath of Allegiance in 1778 [Ref: L-20. AA-641]. Resident of Pomonkey Hundred in 1778 [Ref:

Q-I:297]. Rendered patriotic service by providing wheat for the use of the military in October 1781 [Ref: N-450, which listed the name as "Speak"], and in November 1781 and October 1782 [Ref: N-452, N-558, which listed the name as "Speake"].

SPEAKE, John (1712-   ). Took the Oath of Allegiance in 1778 [Ref: L-20, AA-641]. Aged about 62 as noted in a 1774 deposition [Ref: DD-180].

SPEAKE, Joseph. Rendered patriotic service by providing wheat for the use of the military in December 1782 [Ref: N-575, which listed the name as "Speak"].

SPEAKE, Lawson (c1759-c1804). Private, Militia, Capt. Francis Mastin's Company, 26th Battalion, March 19, 1776 through at least 1777 [Ref: M-158, M-163, K-1814, X-78]. Took the Oath of Allegiance in 1778 [Ref: L-20, which listed the name as "Speke"]. Lawson Speake was born circa 1759, married Mary ----, and died before Feb. 1, 1804 [Ref: J-III:2750].

SPEAKE, Mary. See "Lawson Speake," q.v.

SPEAKE, Richard. First Lieutenant, Militia, Capt. Francis Mastin's Company, 26th Battalion, 26th Battalion, March 19, 1776 through at least 1777 [Ref: M-123, M-158, M-163, K-1814, A-426, which also listed the name as "Speak"].

SPEAKE, Richard (died testate in November 1779). Took the Oath of Allegiance in 1778 [Ref: AA-641, L-20, which latter source listed the name as "Speke"].

SPEAKE, Thomas. Private, Militia, 26th Battalion, Capt. Benjamin Cawood's Company, 1777 [Ref: M-162].

SPICKNALL, Leonard. Rendered patriot service in Maryland. He was born in Virginia in 1752, married (wife's name not known), and died in Indiana in 1834 [Ref: J-III:2758].

SPICKNALL, Robert. Private, 1st Maryland Line, enrolled and passed on July 20, 1776 [Ref: D-33].

STAINS, Thomas. Took the Oath of Allegiance in 1778 [Ref: AA-641, L-20, which latter source listed the name as "Stainer"]. Resident of Bryan Town Hundred in 1778 [Ref: Q-I:297].

STALLIONS, Samuel. Private, Militia, 12th Battalion, Capt. Peter Wood's Company, 1777 [Ref: M-161]. Resident of Bryan Town Hundred in 1778 [Ref: Q-I:297].

STEEL (STEELE), George. Private, Militia, 12th Battalion, Capt. Jonathan Yates' Company, 1777 [Ref: M-162]. Resident of William & Mary Lower Hundred in 1778 [Ref: Q-I:297].

STEPHENS, Hugh. Private, Militia, 26th Battalion, Capt. Samuel Smallwood's Company, 1777 [Ref: M-165].

283

STEWART, Benjamin. Private, 3rd Maryland Line, 1780, enrolled in Charles County for Capt. Joseph Marbury's Company [Ref: D-333, which listed the name as "Steuart"].

STEWART, George. Private, Militia, 26th Battalion, Capt. Thomas H. Marshall's Company, 1777 [Ref: M-163, which listed the name as "Steward"]. Took the Oath of Allegiance in 1778 [Ref: L-20, which listed the name as "Stuart" and AA-641, which listed the name as "Stewart"]. Resident of Pomonkey Hundred in 1778 [Ref: Q-I:297].

STEWART, Henry. Memorialist and Militiaman, Pomonkey Company, after March 6, 1776 [Ref: M-158, Y-II:26, which sources listed the name as "Steward"]. Private, Militia, 26th Battalion, Capt. Thomas H. Marshall's Company, 1777 [Ref: M-163]. Took the Oath of Allegiance in 1778 [Ref: L-20, which listed the name as "Stuart" and AA-641, which listed the name as "Stewart"]. Resident of Port Tobacco Upper Hundred in 1778 [Ref: Q-I:297].

STEWART, Ignatius. Private, Militia, 26th Battalion, Capt. Samuel Smallwood's Company, 1777 [Ref: M-165, which listed the name as "Steward"]. Private, 1st Maryland Line, drafted from the Charles County militia on July 27, 1781 and discharged on Dec. 3, 1781 [Ref: D-377 which listed the name as "Stuart," D-412 which listed the name as "Ignatious Steward," G-569 which listed the name as "Stewart," and I-10 which listed the name as "Steward"].

STEWART, Isaac (1754-1837). Private, 1st Maryland Line, enrolled and passed on July 19, 1776 [Ref: D-31, which listed the name as "Steuart"]. Private, Militia, 26th Battalion, Capt. William McPherson's Company, 1777 [Ref: M-163, which listed the name as "Steward"]. Took the Oath of Allegiance in 1778 [Ref: L-20, AA-641]. Resident of Port Tobacco Upper Hundred in 1778 [Ref: Q-I:297]. He was placed on the pension rolls of Charles County on April 16, 1833 (retroactive to March 4, 1831). [Ref: R-47]. He also applied for a federal pension (S7624) on March 30, 1833, stating he was born in 1754 in Charles County. An inquiry by his son Linus Stewart, of Fresno, California, on April 11, 1888 stated that his father Isaac Stewart died in 1837. On April 8, 1888 a newspaper clipping showed the oldest Revolutionary War pensioner to be Mancy [sic] Raines, aged 96 (no relationship was stated). Isaac Stewart married Helen Dodson [Ref: V-III:3335, J-III:2806].

STEWART, James. Private, Militia, 26th Battalion, Capt. Hezekiah Garner's Company, 1777 [Ref: M-162, which listed the name as "Steward"]. Private, 3rd Maryland Line, 1780, enrolled in Charles County for Capt. Joseph Marbury's Company [Ref: D-333, which listed the name as "Steuart"]. Two men by this name took the Oath of Allegiance in 1778

[Ref: AA-641, L-20]. Resident of Port Tobacco East Hundred in 1778 [Ref: Q-I:297, which listed the name as "Steward"].

STEWART, John. Private, Militia, 12th Battalion, Capt. Henry Clarkson's Company, 1777 [Ref: M-159].

STEWART, Joshua. Private, 1st Maryland Line, drafted from the Charles County militia on July 27, 1781 [Ref: G-569, D-377, D-412, which latter sources listed the name as "Steward" and "Steuart"].

STEWART, Linus. See "Isaac Stewart," q.v.

STEWART, Walter. Private, Militia, 26th Battalion, Capt. Samuel Smallwood's Company, 1777 [Ref: M-165, which listed the name as "Steward"]. Took the Oath of Allegiance in 1778 [Ref: L-20, AA-641]. Resident of Port Tobacco Upper Hundred in 1778 [Ref: Q-I:297]. Rendered patriotic service by providing wheat for the use of the military in May 1783 [Ref: N-597].

STEWART, William. Private, Militia, 26th Battalion, Capt. Benjamin Cawood's Company, 1777 [Ref: M-162]. Resident of Port Tobacco Upper Hundred in 1778 [Ref: Q-I:297].

STEWART, William. Private, Militia, 26th Battalion, Capt. Hezekiah Garner's Company, 1777 [Ref: M-162, which listed the name as "Steward"]. Resident of Durham Lower Hundred in 1778 [Ref: Q-I:297].

STODDERT, Elizabeth. Rendered patriotic service by providing wheat for the use of the military in April 1782 [Ref: N-499]. She was probably the widow of William Truman Stoddert (1736-1770). [Ref: P-II:782]. Also see "William Truman Stoddert," q.v.

STODDERT, John. See "Kenhelm Truman Stoddert," q.v.

STODDERT, John Truman. See "William Truman Stoddert," q.v.

STODDERT, Kenhelm Truman (1739-1779). First Lieutenant, Militia, Pomonkey Company (in the room of Samuel Ward who had died), and subsequently promoted to First Major, 26th Battalion, on Jan. 6, 1776 [Ref: M-126, M-158, Y-II:26, which sources misspelled the name as "Henelin Truman Stoddart" and "Kenelin Trueman Stoddert"]. Took the Oath of Allegiance in 1778 [Ref: L-20]. Resident of Pomonkey Hundred in 1778 [Ref: Q-I:297]. "Kenelm Truman Stoddert" (son of John) was born on Sept. 11, 1739, married Letitia (Letty) Dent, and died by November 1779 (date of inventory). [Ref: J-III:2820, P-II:782]. See "Letty Stoddert," q.v.

STODDERT, Letty. Rendered patriotic service by providing wheat for the use of the military in April 1782 [Ref: N-498]. She was the wife of "Kenhelm Truman Stoddert," q.v.

STODDERT, Margaret. Rendered patriotic service by providing clothing for the use of the military in February 1778 [Ref: Y-II:235]. She was probably the widow of Walter Truman Stoddert (1747-1772). [Ref: P-II:782].
STODDERT, Mary Magdalene. See "Edward Smoot," q.v.
STODDERT, Sally. Rendered patriotic service by providing wheat for the use of the military in October 1782 [Ref: N-563, which listed the name as "Stodert"]. She was probably the wife of "William Truman Stoddert," q.v.
STODDERT, Walter Truman. See "Margaret Stoddert," q.v.
STODDERT, William. Private, Militia, Capt. Francis Mastin's Company, 26th Battalion, March 19, 1776 [Ref: M-158, K-1814]. Rendered patriotic service by providing wheat for the use of the military in August 1782 [Ref: N-538, which spelled the name as "Stodert"].
STODDERT, William Truman. "Major William Truman Stoddert" rendered patriotic service by providing wheat for the use of the military in December 1782 and May 1783 [Ref: N-577, N-598]. He was probably a son of John Truman Stoddert (1732-1765), married Sally ----, and died in 1793 [Ref: P-II:783]. "Lt. William Truman Stoddert" received bounty land warrant #2051-200-25 in September 1789 [Ref: V-III:3351]. See "Sally Stoddert" and "Elizabeth Stoddert," q.v.
STONE, Anne. See "John Hoskins Stone," q.v.
STONE, Barton. Took the Oath of Allegiance in 1778 [Ref: AA-641].
STONE, Barton Jr. Took the Oath of Allegiance in 1778 [Ref: L-20].
STONE, Barton Warren. See "John Stone," q.v.
STONE, Catharine. See "Charles Bryan," q.v.
STONE, Couden. See "John Hoskins Stone," q.v.
STONE, David. See "Michael Jenifer Stone" and "John Hoskins Stone" and "Thomas Stone," q.v.
STONE, Edward (1739-   ). Took the Oath of Allegiance in 1778 [Ref: L-20]. Aged about 33 as noted in a 1772 deposition which mentioned his father Edward Stone, deceased [Ref: DD-181]. See "John Stone," q.v.
STONE, Eleanor. See "Michael Jenifer Stone," q.v.
STONE, Elizabeth. See "Gerard Blackstone Causin" and "Michael Jenifer Stone," q.v.
STONE, Frederick. See "Thomas Stone," q.v.
STONE, Frederick Daniel. See "Michael Jenifer Stone," q.v.
STONE, John (1714-1775). In 1774 John Stone served as a member of the committee chosen in Charles County to execute the laws of the Continental Congress regarding the Non-Importation Act. His wife was Mary Warren and a son Matthew Stone was born in Port Tobacco on July 28, 1763. John died in 1775 and in 1779 his widow Mary moved the family to Pittsylvania County, Virginia and settled on the Dan River. Her older

sons (names not given) served in the army and Matthew Stone was on the payroll of Capt. Samuel Gilbert's Company, where he served for a time as messenger. The youngest son, Barton Warren Stone, who became a minister, wrote of that time: "I shall never forget the sorrows of my widowed mother when her sons shouldered their firelocks and marched away to join the army. Never will the impressions of my own grief be erased from the tablet of my memory when these scenes occurred. We knew that General Green and Lord Cornwallis would shortly meet in mortal combat not far from us. The whole country was in a state of great anxiety and bustle. Nothing was secure from the depredations of the Tories, and bands of thieves were worse than they. My mother had some valuable horses needed for use on the farm. To secure them from being taken by scouting parties she sent me with my two elder brothers to conceal them in a thicket of brushwood not far distant from the house. This was to me, even then, a gloomy day. It was the day when General Green and Lord Cornwallis met at Guilford Court House [1781] in North Carolina about thirty miles distant from us. We distinctly heard the roar of artillery and awfully feared the result." After the Revolutionary War, Matthew Stone moved to Georgia and in 1789 married Jane Duke, daughter of Thomas and Elizabeth Duke, who lived on an adjoining plantation. Matthew Stone was later an early settler in Rapids and Catahoula Parishes in Louisiana [Ref: "Matthew Stone," by Mrs. M. Earl Denham, *Louisiana Genealogical Register*, Vol. 24, No. 4 (1977), p. 301]. John Stone was born in 1714, married second to Mrs. Mary (Warren) Musgrove (first wife's name not known), and died after Aug. 6, 1775 in Maryland [Ref: J-III:2824].

STONE, John. Private, Militia, 26th Battalion, Capt. Richard Bennett Mitchell's Company, 1777 [Ref: M-165]. Resident of Pomonkey Hundred in 1778 [Ref: Q-I:297]. Rendered patriotic service by providing wheat for the use of the military in December 1782 and May 1783 [Ref: N-576, N-597]. "John Stone, son of Matthew" was aged about 55 as noted in a 1769 deposition.

STONE, John Hoskins (1750-1804). Son of David Stone (1709-1773) and Elizabeth Jenifer (daughter of Dr. Daniel Jenifer), he married Mary Couden in 1781 and was a well known lawyer before the Revolution. His children were as follows: Robert Couden Stone (married Mary Mann, of Annapolis, in 1805); Couden Stone (died young); Anne Stone (married John Turner); and, Elizabeth Stone (married Dr. Nathaniel Pope Causin in 1808). John Hoskins Stone had a distinguished political career, from serving as a Delegate to the Maryland Convention in 1775 to being Governor of Maryland, 1794-1797 [Ref: A-3, Y-I:4, P-II:784, P-II:785, which latter source should be consulted for more detailed information]. He was also a captain in the militia, 1775-1776, commissioned a captain in the 1st Maryland Line on Jan. 3, 1776, and was colonel in the Maryland Line until Aug. 1, 1779 (wounded and resigned). [Ref: M-126, C-483, D-5, D-160, D-628, Y-II:23]. Colonel John H. Stone was aged about 28 as noted in a 1779 deposition [Ref: BB-470]. On March 21, 1839, the Treasurer of Maryland was directed to pay to "Dr. N. P. Cousin *[sic]* for the use of Col. John Stone, a sum of money amounting to the half pay of a colonel in the Maryland Line between the periods of 1779 and 1782, for 2 years and 11 months; provided he shall be satisfied by competent evidence that the sum herein authorized to be paid, which is ordered under Act of 1778, Chapter 14, and Resolutions of 1779 and 1780, of this State, to be paid to the said heirs for the period of time intervening between the resignation of said Col. Stone, in August 1779, and the date of the first payment to him in 1782, has not been paid to Col. Stone, or his heirs, by the general government." [Ref: Q-II:397]. The obituary of General John Hoskins Stone appeared in the *Maryland Gazette* on Oct. 11, 1804, stating that he "departed this life on Friday last, in his 54th year of age. During the American Revolution he appeared as a captain [in] the celebrated regiment of Smallwood, and highly distinguished himself at the battles of Long Island, White Plains, and Princeton. At the battle of Germantown, he received a wound that deprived him of bodily activity for the remainder of life. As a representative of his native Charles County, and as a member of the Executive Council, he continued to serve his country. In 1794 he was elected Governor of Maryland." [Ref: FF-177]. See "Gerard Blackstone Causin," q.v.

STONE, John, of Edward (1726/9-). Took the Oath of Allegiance in 1778 [Ref: AA-641]. Aged about 43 as noted in a 1772 deposition and aged about 48 as noted in a 1774 deposition [Ref: DD-181].

STONE, Margaret. See "Thomas Stone" and "Zaccheus Davis," q.v.

STONE, Mary. Rendered patriotic service by providing clothing for the use of the military in February 1778 [Ref: Y-II:235]. Rendered patriotic service by providing wheat for the use of the military in November 1781 and September 1782 [Ref: N-456, N-549]. See "John Stone," q.v.

STONE, Matthew. Private, Militia, 12th Battalion, Capt. Henry Clarkson's Company, 1777 [Ref: M-159]. Took the Oath of Allegiance in 1778 [Ref: AA-641]. Resident of Bryan Town Hundred in 1778 [Ref: Q-I:297]. Rendered patriotic service by providing wheat for the use of the military in December 1782 [Ref: N-573]. See "John Stone," q.v.

STONE, Michael Jenifer (1747-1812). Son of David Stone and Elizabeth Jenifer, he married Mary Hanson Briscoe and had these children:

Frederick Daniel Stone (1796-1820); William Briscoe Stone (1797-1872); Dr. Michael Jenifer Stone (1806-1877); Elizabeth Stone; and, Eleanor Stone [Ref: P-II:785, P-II:786]. Michael served on the Committee of Observation in 1776, attended the Constitution Ratification Convention in 1778, and served in the Lower House of the Maryland Legislature from 1780 to 1783. He was a U. S. Congressman, 1789-1791, and Chief Judge of the 1st Judicial District of Maryland, 1791-1802 [Ref: P-II:786]. Took the Oath of Allegiance in 1778 [Ref: L-20, AA-641, which latter source listed the name as "M. J. Stone"]. Resident of Port Tobacco West Hundred in 1778 [Ref: Q-I:297]. Rendered patriotic service by providing wheat for the use of the military in December 1782 [Ref: N-573, which mistakenly listed the name as "Michael T. Stone"]. Second Lieutenant, Militia, Capt. George Swann's Company, March 7, 1776 [Ref: M-126, A-186, A-206, Y-II:23, which sources listed the name as "Michael Jenifer"]. Michael Jenifer Stone was born in 1747, married Mary Hanson Briscoe, and died before April 1, 1812 [Ref: J-III:2825].

STONE, Mildred. See "Thomas Stone," q.v.

STONE, Richard. Rendered patriotic service by providing clothing for the use of the military in January and February 1778 [Ref: Y-II:230, Y-II-235].

STONE, Robert Couden. See "John Hoskins Stone," q.v.

STONE, Samuel Sr. Took the Oath of Allegiance in 1778 [Ref: L-20, AA-641]. Died testate in May 1778 [Ref: GG-179]. See "Walter Hanson," q.v.

STONE, Samuel Jr. Ensign, Militia, 26th Battalion, Capt. Robert Sinnett's Company, Feb. 26, 1776 [Ref: M-126, M-164, A-186, A-206, Y-II:23; some sources listed the name without the "Jr."]. Took the Oath of Allegiance in 1778 [Ref: L-20, AA-641]. Rendered patriotic service by providing wheat for the use of the military in November 1782 [Ref: N-566].

STONE, Thomas (1742/3-1787). Son of David Stone and Elizabeth Jenifer, he married Margaret Brown (daughter of Dr. Gustavus Brown) and had these children: Frederick Stone (c1769-1793); Margaret Stone (1771-1809, married Dr. John Moncure Daniel); and, Mildred Stone (1771-1836, married Travers Daniel, Jr., brother of John). Delegate to the Continental Congress between 1774 and 1784. Elected to the First Council of Safety in 1775, but did not serve. Delegate to the Maryland Convention, 1775-1776. Served in the Maryland Senate, 1776-1780, 1781-1786, and in the Lower House of the Maryland Legislature, 1780. One of four Maryland Delegates to the Continental Congress who signed the Declaration of Independence [Ref: A-4, Y-I:1, Y-I:4, Y-I:28, P-II:786, P-II:787, P-II:788]. On Dec. 13, 1777, he reported to the Governor and Council of Maryland that the "enemy is between Boyd's Hob and Nanjemoy; if Virginia and Maryland could jointly attack, the British ships might flee; their *Phoenix* has run aground more than once; Col. Ware has served well as county lieutenant." [Ref: Y-I:83]. Took the Oath of Allegiance in 1778 [Ref: L-20, AA-641]. Resident of Port Tobacco West Hundred in 1778 [Ref: Q-I:297]. Rendered patriotic service by providing clothing for the use of the military in February 1778 [Ref: Y-II:235]. Thomas Stone died on Oct. 5, 1787 in Alexandria, Virginia and was buried at "Haber de Venture" in Charles County, Maryland [Ref: P-II:788, J-III:2827]. *Ed. Note:* A chapter of the Maryland Society, Sons of the American Revolution, was named in his honor in 1992.

STONE, Thomas. Private, Militia, 26th Battalion, Capt. Robert Sinnett's Company, 1777 [Ref: M-164].

STONE, Verlinda. See "Richard Harrison" and "Joseph Hanson Harrison," q.v.

STONE, William (1731-   ). Private, Militia, 26th Battalion, Capt. William McPherson's Company, 1777 [Ref: M-163]. Took the Oath of Allegiance in 1778 [Ref: L-20, AA-641]. Rendered patriotic service by providing wheat for the use of the military in November 1782 [Ref: N-566]. Aged about 42 as noted in a 1774 deposition [Ref: DD-181]. Resident of Port Tobacco Upper Hundred in 1778 [Ref: Q-I:297].

STONE, William Barton. Private, Militia, 26th Battalion, Capt. Robert Sinnett's Company, 1777 [Ref: M-164]. Took the Oath of Allegiance in 1778 [Ref: L-20, AA-641].

STONE, William Briscoe. See "Michael Jenifer Stone," q.v.

STONE, William Howard. Private, Militia, 26th Battalion, Capt. Robert Sinnett's Company, 1777 [Ref: M-164]. Took the Oath of Allegiance in 1778 [Ref: L-20, AA-641].

STONESTREET, Basil. Private, Militia, 26th Battalion, Capt. William McPherson's Company, 1777 [Ref: M-163]. Took the Oath of Allegiance in 1778 [Ref: L-20, AA-641]. Resident of Port Tobacco Upper Hundred in 1778 [Ref: Q-I:297].

STONESTREET, Butler (1748-   ). Born on Oct. 20, 1748, son of Butler and Elizabeth Stonestreet [Ref: EE-6]. "Butler Stoonstreet" was a private in the Charles County Militia, 12th Battalion, Capt. John Parnham's Company, in 1777 [Ref: M-160].

STONESTREET, Butler (1715-   ). Resident of Newport East Hundred in 1778 [Ref: Q-I:297]. Aged about 50 as noted in a 1765 deposition [Ref: DD-181]. He petitioned the Council of Maryland in 1783 stating that he had not taken the Oath of Allegiance due to any disaffection with the government, but from a variety of incidents, and was unjustly penalized as a non-juror and fined unfairly; therefore, he asked the Council to consider ordering the County Justices to remit the fines they imposed on him and others who signed the petition. The Council of Maryland, after reviewing his case, indicated they believed the truth of the facts stated in the petition and ordered a remission of the fines and penalties on Sept. 17, 1783 [Ref: I-454].

STONESTREET, Elizabeth. See "Butler Stonestreet," q.v.

STONESTREET, Leonard. Private, Militia, 12th Battalion, Capt. John Parnham's Company, 1777 [Ref: M-160, which listed the name as "Stoonstreet"].

STONESTREET, Mary. See "John Farrand," q.v.

STONESTREET, Sarah. See "Richard Edelen," q.v.

STONESTREET, Virlinda. See "Butler Newman," q.v.

STOREY, Elizabeth. See "Walter Hanson" and "Samuel Hanson," q.v.

STOREY, Walter. See "Samuel Hanson," q.v.

STORKE, Johannis. See "George Dent," q.v.

STROMATT, Babtist. "Babtist Stromatt" took the Oath of Allegiance in 1778 [Ref: L-20]. "Babtist Shomat" was a resident of Durham Lower Hundred in 1778 [Ref: Q-I:297].

STROMATT, John. Corporal, Militia, 26th Battalion, Capt. William Winter's Company, 1777 [Ref: M-165, which misspelled the name as "Shomatt"].

STROMATT, John (1710-   ). Took the Oath of Allegiance in 1778 [Ref: L-20]. Aged about 47 as noted in a 1757 deposition [Ref: DD-181, which listed the name as "Stromat"]. Resident of Durham Lower Hundred in 1778 [Ref: Q-I:297].

STROMATT, John B. Private, Militia, 26th Battalion, Capt. William Winter's Company, 1777 [Ref: M-165, which misspelled the name as "Shomatt"]. Gave a deposition in 1781 pertaining to his inability to perform military service due to family obligations and poor health [Ref: Z-208, which listed the name as "Stramatt"].

STUART, Ignatius. See "Ignatius Stewart," q.v.

STUART, Philip. See "Thomas Hanson Marshall," q.v.

SUIT (SUTE), Edward. Private, 2nd Maryland Line, enlisted July 8, 1779 and promoted to corporal on Feb. 1, 1780 [Ref: D-163].

SUIT (SUTE), Jesse. Sergeant, 2nd Maryland Line, Jan. 20, 1777, reduced to private on Oct. 7, 1779, and still in service as of Nov. 1, 1780 [Ref: D-161].

SUIT (SUTE), John. Took the Oath of Allegiance in 1778 [Ref: L-20, AA-641]. Resident of Bryan Town Hundred in 1778 [Ref: Q-I:297].

SUIT (SUTE), Thomas. Private, 1st Maryland Line, enrolled and passed on July 8, 1776 [Ref: D-32].

SUIT (SUTE), Walter. Private, Militia, 12th Battalion, Capt. Henry Clarkson's Company, 1777 [Ref: M-159]. Resident of Bryan Town Hundred in 1778 [Ref: Q-I:297].
SUIT (SUTE), William. Private, Militia, 12th Battalion, Capt. John Parnham's Company, 1777 [Ref: M-160].
SUMMERSET, Martha. See "William Tubb," q.v.
SUTHERLAND, Ann, et al. See "Walter E. Sutherland," q.v.
SUTHERLAND, Enos, et al. See "Walter E. Sutherland," q.v.
SUTHERLAND, John, et al. See "Walter E. Sutherland," q.v.
SUTHERLAND, Sarah, et al. See "Walter E. Sutherland," q.v.
SUTHERLAND, Traverse (1745-c1834). Private, Virginia Line, 1777. He applied for a pension (S31398) on Dec. 31, 1833, aged 88, in Henry County, Kentucky, stating he was born in Charles County, Maryland in 1745 and later moved to Virginia. He enlisted in Culpeper County in July 1777, and about 1808 moved to Shelby County, Kentucky. In September or October 1833 he moved to Henry County. The name of his wife was not given, but a daughter, Nancy Wilson, was living in 1833 [Ref: V-III:3393, T-49]. See "Walter E. Sutherland," q.v.
SUTHERLAND, Walter E. (1749-1837). Private, 1st Maryland Line, who enrolled and was passed on July 25, 1776 [Ref: D-32]. He applied for a pension in Henry County, Kentucky on Aug. 29, 1833, stating he was born in 1749 in Charles County, Maryland and lived there at the time of his enlistment. Around 1800 he moved to Clarke County, Kentucky and in 1828 went to Henry County. He married first to Ann ---- on July 30, 1780 and second to Sarah ---- on April 22, 1798. His brother was Traverse Sutherland. Walter died in March 1837 and his widow applied for an received a pension (W10266) on April 20, 1851, aged 77, in Henry County, Kentucky. Walter had several children as follows: Sarah Sutherland (born April 11, 1781), William M. Sutherland (born Sept. 11, 1784), Verlinda B. Sutherland (born Jan. 23, 1787), Elizabeth Sutherland (born Sept. 11, 1788), Thomas Sutherland (born March 4, 1799 and married Elizabeth Sutherland on Oct. 14, 1819), Enos Sutherland (born June 22, 1800 and married Sally ---- in Aug. 28, 1823), Travis Sutherland (born June 3, 1805), Luanor Sutherland (born March 20, 1807), Walter Sutherland (born Jan. 25, 1809), Elizabeth Sutherland (born Feb. 15, 1811), and Beldad Sutherland (born Feb. 13, 1813). Other family members, probably the children of son Enos Sutherland, were listed as follows: Therline Sutherland (born May 30, 1823), Lemly Jain Sutherland (born Nov. 8, 1824), Eliza Ann Sutherland (born July 9, 1826), Elisebeth Sutherland (born Oct. 16, 1828), Travis Sutherland (born April 2, 1831), Mary Sutherland (born Aug. 19, 1833), David Sutherland (born Aug. 10, 1836),

and John M. Sutherland (born June 9, 1842). Also, a John B. Sutherland married Rebecca ---- on Jan. 9, 1842. When Sarah Sutherland applied for and received bounty land on March 27, 1855 (warrant #24998-160-55) a William Sutherland and a John H. Mahomey (or Mahorney) gave their affidavits [Ref: V-III:3393, T-49, T-50].

SUTHERLAND, William. Private, 1st Maryland Line, 1778-1779 [Ref: D-160]. See "Walter Sutherland," q.v.

SWAIN, Ann. See "Bennett Mudd," q.v.

SWAIN, Thomas. Rendered patriotic service by providing wheat for the use of the military in May 1783 [Ref: N-598].

SWANN, Alexander. Private, 1st Maryland Line, enrolled and passed on July 19, 1776. Private, 3rd Maryland Line, enlisted Feb. 18, 1777 and reported missing at the Battle of Camden in South Carolina on Aug. 16, 1780 [Ref: D-31, D-163, F-181].

SWANN, Ann (Anne). See "James Mudd" and "Bennett Mudd" and "Jeremiah Mudd" and "Zedekiah Swann," q.v.

SWANN, Barbara. See "Jeremiah Mudd," q.v.

SWANN, Barton. Private, 1st Maryland Line, enlisted Sept. 7, 1777 and died on Sept. 20, 1778 [Ref: D-160].

SWANN, Basil. Private, 1st Maryland Line, enrolled and passed on July 8, 1776. Private, 3rd Maryland Line, enlisted March 18, 1777 and struck off the rolls in January 1780 [Ref: D-32, D-163].

SWANN, David. Took the Oath of Allegiance in 1778 [Ref: L-20].

SWANN, Edward. Took the Oath of Allegiance in 1778 [Ref: AA-641]. Resident of Newport East Hundred in 1778 [Ref: Q-I:297]. See "Jeremiah Mudd," q.v.

SWANN, Elizabeth. See "Smith Mudd," q.v.

SWANN, George. Captain, Militia, Feb. 26, 1776 [Ref: Y-II:23].

SWANN, James. Private, Militia, 12th Battalion, Capt. John Parnham's Company, 1777 [Ref: M-161]. Took the Oath of Allegiance in 1778 [Ref: AA-641]. Resident of Newport East Hundred in 1778 [Ref: Q-I:297]. Rendered patriotic service by providing wheat for the use of the military in May 1783 [Ref: N-597, which listed the name as "Swan"].

SWANN, James Jr. Private, 1st Maryland Line, enrolled and passed on July 8, 1776 [Ref: D-32]. Resident of Newport East Hundred in 1778 [Ref: Q-I:297].

SWANN, John. Private, 3rd Maryland Line, until discharged on April 1, 1779 [Ref: D-164].

SWANN, Jonathan (c1738-1786). Second Lieutenant, Militia, 12th Battalion, Capt. Henry Clarkson's Company, July 5, 1777 [Ref: M-127, M-159]. Took the Oath of Allegiance in 1778 [Ref: L-20]. Resident of

Newport East Hundred in 1778 [Ref: Q-I:297]. Jonathan Swann was born circa 1738, married Eleanor Amery, and died before December 1786 [Ref: J-III:2862].
SWANN, Judith. See "Jacob Latimer" and "Thomas Latimer" and "Randolph Brandt Latimer," q.v.
SWANN, Leonard. Private, 3rd Maryland Line, May 3, 1778 through at least November 1780 [Ref: D-164]. In December 1817, the Treasurer of Maryland was directed to pay to "Leonard Swann, an old soldier, quarterly during life, a sum of money equal to the half pay of a private." [Ref: Q-II:397].
SWANN, Margaret P. See "Elisha Burroughs," q.v.
SWANN, Richard. Took the Oath of Allegiance in 1778 [Ref: L-20, AA-641, which sources listed the name as "Swan"].
SWANN, Samuel. Private, Militia, 12th Battalion, Capt. John Parnham's Company, 1777 [Ref: M-161].
SWANN, Thomas. Sergeant, Militia, 12th Battalion, Capt. Henry Clarkson's Company, 1777 [Ref: M-159].
SWANN, Thomas Sr. Took the Oath of Allegiance in 1778 [Ref: L-20]. Resident of Newport East Hundred in 1778 [Ref: Q-I:297]. Thomas Swann married Ann Dent on Jan. 11, 1757 in Trinity Parish [Ref: EE-10]. See "Zedekiah Swann," q.v.
SWANN, Thomas Jr. Private, Militia, 12th Battalion, Capt. Henry Clarkson's Company, 1777 [Ref: M-159]. Took the Oath of Allegiance in 1778 [Ref: AA-641]. Resident of Newport East Hundred in 1778 [Ref: Q-I:297].
SWANN, William. Took the Oath of Allegiance in 1778 [Ref: AA-641]. Private, 3rd Maryland Line, 1780, enrolled in Charles County for Capt. Joseph Marbury's Company [Ref: D-333, F-181]. Drummer, 3rd Maryland Line, from April 13, 1780 to at least Nov. 1, 1780 [Ref: D-165].
SWANN, Zachariah. Private, Militia, 12th Battalion, Capt. Henry Clarkson's Company, 1777 [Ref: M-159, which listed the name as "Swan"]. Took the Oath of Allegiance in 1778 [Ref: AA-641]. Resident of Newport East Hundred in 1778 [Ref: Q-I:297].
SWANN, Zedekiah (1760-). Born on April 16, 1760, a son of Thomas and Ann Swann, of Trinity Parish [Ref: EE-12]. Private, Militia, 12th Battalion, Capt. Henry Clarkson's Company, 1777 [Ref: M-159].
SWANN, Zephaniah (1740-1816). Private, 1st Maryland Line, enrolled and passed on July 8, 1776 [Ref: D-32]. Private, Militia, 12th Battalion, Capt. John Parnham's Company, 1777 [Ref: M-161]. Zephaniah Swann was born in Maryland in 1740, married first to Mary Coats, married second to Mary

Beall, and migrated to North Carolina where he died in 1816 [Ref: J-III:2863].

SWEETMAN, Henry. Took the Oath of Allegiance in 1778 [Ref: AA-641, L-20, which latter source listed the name as "Henry Sweethan"].

TABBS, Abigail Hunter. See "John Alexander Smoot," q.v.

TAGG, William. See "William Fagg," q.v.

TALLMISE (TALMASH), James. "James Tallmise" was a private in the militia, 26th Battalion, Capt. William Winter's Company, 1777 [Ref: M-165]. "James Talmash" was a resident of Durham Lower Hundred in 1778 [Ref: Q-I:297].

TASKER, Benjamin. Private (substitute for 9 months), 1st Maryland Line, by Sept. 11, 1778 [Ref: D-330]. Took the Oath of Allegiance in 1778 [Ref: L-20].

TAYLOR, Edward. Private, Militia, 12th Battalion, Capt. John Thomas' Company, 1777 [Ref: M-161]. Resident of Benedict Hundred in 1778 [Ref: Q-I:297].

TAYLOR, Francis. Took the Oath of Allegiance in 1778 [Ref: L-20]. Resident of Durham Lower Hundred in 1778 [Ref: Q-I:297].

TAYLOR, Ignatius. Took the Oath of Allegiance in 1778 [Ref: L-20]. Resident of Benedict Hundred in 1778 [Ref: Q-I:297].

TAYLOR, James. Private, Militia, 12th Battalion, Capt. John Thomas' Company, 1777 [Ref: M-161].

TAYLOR, James. Private, Militia, 12th Battalion, Capt. Peter Wood's Company, 1777 [Ref: M-161].

TAYLOR, James. Private, 1st Maryland Line, drafted from the Charles County militia on July 27, 1781. On Feb. 19, 1782, the Council of Maryland ordered "James Taylor, a Draught from Capt. John Gardner's Company in the 12th Battalion of Charles County, discharged and his pay to be settled to the 10th Dec. last." [Ref: D-377, G-569, I-81].

TAYLOR, James. Three men by this name took the Oath of Allegiance in 1778, two named "James Tayler" and one "James Taler" [Ref: AA-641, L-20, which latter source only listed one "James Taylor"]. "James Taylor, son of John" was aged about 42 as noted in a 1765 deposition. "James Taylor" was aged about 56 as noted in a 1778 deposition [Ref: DD-270]. "James Taylor" was a resident of Durham Lower Hundred, "James Tayler" was a resident of Benedict Hundred, "James Taylor" was a resident of Port Tobacco East Hundred, and "James Tayler" was a resident of Bryan Town Hundred in 1778 [Ref: Q-I:297]. Additional research may be necessary before drawing conclusions.

TAYLOR, Jesse. On Sept. 4, 1781, the Council of Maryland ordered "that the Western Shore Treasurer pay to Jesse Taylor, Jr., seven hundred and forty pounds nine shillings and eight pence farthing of the Bills emitted under the Act for the Emission of Bills of Credit not exceeding 200,000 lbs. etc., of the money appropriated for the present Campaign to be delivered over to his father Jesse Taylor, Sr., for goods purchased of him by Daniel Jenifer, Esq., Purchaser of Clothing for Charles County." [Ref: G-599, G-600].

TAYLOR, John. Private (furnished by class for 9 months), 1st Maryland Line, by Sept. 11, 1778 [Ref: D-330]. Took the Oath of Allegiance in 1778 [Ref: L-20]. Rendered patriotic service by providing wheat for the use of the military in December 1781 [Ref: N-461].

TAYLOR, John, of Ignatius. Private, Militia, 12th Battalion, Capt. John Thomas' Company, 1777 [Ref: M-161]. Resident of Benedict Hundred in 1778 [Ref: Q-I:297].

TAYLOR, John, of Stafford. Private, Militia, 12th Battalion, Capt. John Thomas' Company, 1777 [Ref: M-161]. Resident of Benedict Hundred in 1778 [Ref: Q-I:297].

TAYLOR, Joseph. Private, 1st Maryland Line, enrolled and passed on July 8, 1776 [Ref: D-32, which listed the name as "Taylor (Talor)"]. Took the Oath of Allegiance in 1778 [Ref: AA-641].

TAYLOR, Polly. See "John Maddox," q.v.

TAYLOR, Robert. Private, Militia, 26th Battalion, Capt. Francis Mastin's Company, March 19, 1776 [Ref: M-158, M-164, K-1814, which sources listed the name as "Talor" and "Tailor"]. Took the Oath of Allegiance in 1778 [Ref: L-20, AA-641]. First Lieutenant, Militia, 26th Battalion, Capt. Samuel Luckett's Company, commissioned on March 24, 1781 [Ref: M-128, G-361, H-136, which latter source listed the name as "Tayler"].

TAYLOR, Samuel. Took the Oath of Allegiance in 1778 [Ref: AA-641]. Resident of Durham Lower Hundred in 1778 [Ref: Q-I:297].

TAYLOR, Stafford. Took the Oath of Allegiance in 1778 [Ref: L-20]. Resident of Benedict Hundred in 1778 [Ref: Q-I:297].

TAYLOR, William. Sergeant, Militia, Capt. Francis Mastin's Company, 26th Battalion, March 19, 1776 [Ref: M-158, K-1814].

TENCH (TINCH), Joshua. Took the Oath of Allegiance in 1778 [Ref: L-20]. Resident of Bryan Town Hundred in 1778 [Ref: Q-I:297]. Rendered patriotic service by providing wheat for the use of the military in December 1782 [Ref: N-573].

TENCH (TINCH), Leonard. Private, Militia, 12th Battalion, Capt. Alexander McPherson's Company, 1777 [Ref: M-160, which questionably listed the name as "Icrick (Terich?)"]. Took the Oath of Allegiance in 1778 [Ref: L-20]. Resident of Bryan Town Hundred in 1778 [Ref: Q-I:297].

TENCH (TINCH), William Jr. Took the Oath of Allegiance in 1778 [Ref: L-21]. Resident of Bryan Town Hundred in 1778 [Ref: Q-I:297].

TENCH (TINCH), William Sr. Took the Oath of Allegiance in 1778 [Ref: L-21]. Resident of Bryan Town Hundred in 1778 [Ref: Q-I:297].
TENNISON, Benjamin. Private, Militia, 12th Battalion, Capt. Alexander McPherson's Company, 1777 [Ref: M-160].
TENNISON, John. Private, Militia, 12th Battalion, Capt. John Hanson's Company, 1777 [Ref: M-159].
TERRY, Hugh. Took the Oath of Allegiance in 1778 [Ref: L-21].
THARLKILL, Robert. Private (furnished by class for 9 months), 1st Maryland Line, by Sept. 11, 1778 [Ref: D-330].
THOMAS, Absalom. Took the Oath of Allegiance in 1778 [Ref: L-21].
THOMAS, Allen. Private, Militia, 12th Battalion, Capt. John Thomas' Company, 1777 [Ref: M-161]. Private, 5th Maryland Line, 1777-1780 [Ref: D-251]. Resident of Benedict Hundred in 1778 [Ref: Q-I:297].
THOMAS, Caleb. Corporal, Militia, 12th Battalion, Capt. John Thomas' Company, 1777 [Ref: M-161, which spelled the first name as "Calib"]. Took the Oath of Allegiance in 1778 [Ref: L-21]. Resident of Benedict Hundred in 1778 [Ref: Q-I:297]. Private, 1st Maryland Line, drafted from the Charles County militia and reported sick with smallpox in June 1781 [Ref: D-376].
THOMAS, Clement. Private, Militia, 26th Battalion, Capt. Francis Mastin's Company, 1777 [Ref: M-164]. Took the Oath of Allegiance in 1778 [Ref: L-21, AA-641]. Resident of Durham Lower Hundred in 1778 [Ref: Q-I:297]. Rendered patriotic service by providing wheat for the use of the military in December 1782 [Ref: N-573].
THOMAS, Ellis. Took the Oath of Allegiance in 1778 [Ref: L-21, AA-641]. Died by July 1778 (date of inventory). [Ref: GG-198].
THOMAS, Ellis (1755-1839). Private, Militia, 26th Battalion, Capt. William McPherson's Company, 1777 [Ref: M-163]. Ellis Thomas was born in 1755, married Mary Harris, and died on Nov. 13, 1839 [Ref: J-III:2915].
THOMAS, George Salsbury. "George Salsbery Thomas" took the Oath of Allegiance in 1778 [Ref: AA-641, L-21, which latter source listed the name as "George S. Thomas"]. "George Salsbury Thomas" died before June 13, 1791 [Ref: J-III:2915]. "Salisbury Thomas" rendered patriotic service by providing wheat for the use of the military in December 1782 [Ref: N-573]. Resident of Durham Lower Hundred in 1778 [Ref: Q-I:297].
THOMAS, Giles (1763-1842). Private, 1st Maryland Line, 1782; discharged on July 25, 1783 [Ref: D-442, D-508]. He applied for a pension (S6226) in Montgomery County, Virginia on Aug. 6, 1832, aged 68, stating that he lived in Charles County, Maryland at the time of his enlistment [Ref: V-III:3463]. Giles Thomas was born on Nov. 30, 1763 in Maryland, married Anne Wheeler, and died in March 21, 1842 in Virginia [Ref: J-III:2915].

THOMAS, Henry. Took the Oath of Allegiance in 1778 [Ref: L-21]. Resident of Newport East Hundred in 1778 [Ref: Q-I:297].
THOMAS, Isaac. Private, Militia, 12th Battalion, Capt. John Thomas' Company, 1777 [Ref: M-161, X-62]. Private, 5th Maryland Line, 1778-1779 [Ref: D-251]. Resident of Benedict Hundred in 1778 [Ref: Q-I:297].
THOMAS, John. Captain, Militia, 12th Battalion, from 1777 to Jan. 19, 1781 [Ref: M-128, M-161, G-280]. Took the Oath of Allegiance in 1778 [Ref: L-21]. Resident of Port Tobacco East Hundred in 1778 [Ref: Q-I:297].
THOMAS, John. Private, 5th Maryland Line, 1779-1780 [Ref: D-252]. Resident of Benedict Hundred in 1778 [Ref: Q-I:297].
THOMAS, John Jr. Took the Oath of Allegiance in 1778 [Ref: L-21]. Resident of William & Mary Lower Hundred in 1778 [Ref: Q-I:297].
THOMAS, Jonathan. Second Lieutenant, Militia, 26th Battalion, Capt. William Winter's Company, Feb. 26, 1776 [Ref: M-128, A-186, A-206, Y-II:23].
THOMAS, Jonathan (c1730-1784). Took the Oath of Allegiance in 1778 [Ref: L-21]. Resident of Bryan Town Hundred in 1778 [Ref: Q-I:297]. Jonathan Thomas was born before 1735, married Catherine Burch, and died in 1784 [Ref: J-III:2917].
THOMAS, Peregrine. Took the Oath of Allegiance in 1778 [Ref: L-21].
THOMAS, Philip. Corporal, Militia, 12th Battalion, Capt. Jonathan Yates' Company, 1777 [Ref: M-162]. Took the Oath of Allegiance in 1778 [Ref: L-21, AA-641]. Resident of Benedict Hundred in 1778 [Ref: Q-I:297].
THOMAS, Philip. Private, Militia, 12th Battalion, Capt. John Thomas' Company, 1777 [Ref: M-161]. Took the Oath of Allegiance in 1778 [Ref: AA-641, L-21, which latter source listed the name as "Philips Thomas"]. Resident of William & Mary Lower Hundred in 1778 [Ref: Q-I:297].
THOMAS, Salisbury. See "George Salsbury Thomas," q.v.
THOMAS, Smallwood. Took the Oath of Allegiance in 1778 [Ref: L-21].
THOMAS, Thomas. Private, Militia, 12th Battalion, Capt. Alexander McPherson's Company, 1777 [Ref: M-160]. Resident of Bryan Town Hundred in 1778 [Ref: Q-I:297].
THOMAS, Thomas. Private, Militia, 12th Battalion, Capt. John Thomas' Company, 1777 [Ref: M-161]. Resident of Newport East Hundred in 1778 [Ref: Q-I:297].
THOMAS, Thomas. Took the Oath of Allegiance in 1778 [Ref: AA-641].
THOMAS, William. Private, 1st Maryland Line, 1780 [Ref: D-168].
THOMAS, William Jr. (1757-1815). Adjutant, 1st Maryland Line. He was born in 1757, married Catharine Boarman, and died in 1815 [Ref: J-III:2919].

THOMAS, William Sr. (1714-1795). Rendered patriotic service. He was born in 1714, married Elizabeth Reeves, and died in March 1795 [Ref: J-III:2919]. Resident of Benedict Hundred in 1778 [Ref: Q-I:297].
THOMAS, William, of John. Private, Militia, 12th Battalion, Capt. John Thomas' Company, 1777 [Ref: M-161].
THOMAS, William, of William. Private, Militia, 12th Battalion, Capt. John Thomas' Company, 1777 [Ref: M-161].
THOMPSON, Ann Sevilla. See "Richard Mudd," q.v.
THOMPSON, Benjamin. Took the Oath of Allegiance in 1780 [Ref: O-121].
THOMPSON, Benjamin Jr. Took the Oath of Allegiance in 1778 [Ref: L-21].
THOMPSON, Benjamin Sr. Took the Oath of Allegiance in 1778 [Ref: L-21].
THOMPSON, Catherine Queen. See "Walter Hanson" and "Hoskins Hanson," q.v.
THOMPSON, Charles. Private, Militia, 26th Battalion, Capt. William McPherson's Company, 1777 [Ref: M-163, which listed the name as "Thomson"].
THOMPSON, Cornelius. Private, 1st Maryland Line, Capt. William Rieley's Company, Jan. 1, 1782 [Ref: D-434].
THOMPSON, David. Took the Oath of Allegiance in 1778 [Ref: L-21].
THOMPSON, Elijah. Took the Oath of Allegiance in 1780 [Ref: O-121]. Resident of Durham Lower Hundred in 1778 [Ref: Q-I:297].
THOMPSON, Francis. Private, 1st Maryland Line, Capt. Edward Prall's Company, Jan. 1, 1782 [Ref: D-432].
THOMPSON, George. Private, Militia, 26th Battalion, Capt. William McPherson's Company, 1777 [Ref: M-163]. Took the Oath of Allegiance in 1778 [Ref: L-21]. Resident of Port Tobacco East Hundred in 1778 [Ref: Q-I:297].
THOMPSON, Henry. Took the Oath of Allegiance in 1778 [Ref: L-21, AA-641, which latter source listed the name as "Thomson"].
THOMPSON, James. Took the Oath of Allegiance in 1778 [Ref: AA-641]. Resident of Port Tobacco West Hundred in 1778 [Ref: Q-I:297].
THOMPSON, Jane. See "Joseph Thompson," q.v.
THOMPSON, John. Private, Militia, 12th Battalion, Capt. Jonathan Yates' Company, 1777 [Ref: M-162]. Took the Oath of Allegiance in 1778 [Ref: L-21, AA-641]. Resident of Durham Lower Hundred in 1778 [Ref: Q-I:297]. See "William Thompson," q.v.
THOMPSON, John. Took the Oath of Allegiance in 1780 [Ref: O-121]. Resident of Bryan Town Hundred in 1778 [Ref: Q-I:297].

THOMPSON, John Baptist. First lieutenant in the Flying Camp in Frederick County in 1776 [Ref: D-44, D-46]. Took the Oath of Allegiance in Charles County in 1778 [Ref: AA-641]. Resident of William & Mary Upper Hundred in 1778 [Ref: Q-I:297].

THOMPSON, Joseph (1720-   ). Took the Oath of Allegiance in 1778 [Ref: L-21]. Aged about 53 as noted in a 1773 deposition which mentioned his father Thomas Thompson [Ref: DD-271]. Resident of Durham Lower Hundred in 1778 [Ref: Q-I:297].

THOMPSON, Joseph. Private, 1st Maryland Line, enrolled and passed on July 8, 1776 [Ref: D-32]. Resident of Port Tobacco East Hundred in 1778 [Ref: Q-I:297]. Private and Drummer, 3rd Maryland Line, 1780, enrolled in Charles County for Capt. Joseph Marbury's Company [Ref: D-333, F-181, F-501]. On April 13, 1780 the Sheriff of Charles County was ordered to take into custody and to safe keep in his jail the bodies of Joseph Thompson (Drummer) and Jane Thompson (wife of Joseph) who stand committed on suspicion of being concerned in breaking open the house and desk of Mr. Thomas Reeder and stealing a silver watch, sundry papers, and a considerable sum of continental money [Ref: F-502]. Took the Oath of Allegiance in 1780 [Ref: O-121].

THOMPSON, Joseph Green. Private, Militia, 26th Battalion, Capt. William McPherson's Company, 1777 [Ref: M-163]. Took the Oath of Allegiance in 1778 [Ref: L-21, AA-641].

THOMPSON, Joseph, of William. Took the Oath of Allegiance in 1778 [Ref: L-21]. Resident of Newport East Hundred in 1778 [Ref: Q-I:297].

THOMPSON, Joshua. Private, Militia, 26th Battalion, Capt. William Winter's Company, 1777 [Ref: M-165].

THOMPSON, Joshua Sanders. Took the Oath of Allegiance in 1778 [Ref: AA-641, which listed the name as "Joshua Sanders Thomson" and L-21, which listed the name as "Joshua S. Tomson"].

THOMPSON, Leonard. Corporal, Militia, 26th Battalion, Capt. William McPherson's Company, 1777 [Ref: M-163]. Took the Oath of Allegiance in 1778 [Ref: L-21]. Rendered patriotic service by providing wheat for the use of the military in November 1781 [Ref: N-457].

THOMPSON, Matthew. Took the Oath of Allegiance in 1778 [Ref: L-21, which listed the name as "Tomson"].

THOMPSON, Richard. Private, 1st Maryland Line, enrolled and passed on July 19, 1776 [Ref: D-31]. Private, Militia, 26th Battalion, Capt. Richard Bennett Mitchell's Company, 1777 [Ref: M-165]. Took the Oath of Allegiance in 1778 [Ref: AA-641]. Private (furnished by class for 9 months), 1st Maryland Line, by Sept. 11, 1778 [Ref: D-330]. Resident of Durham Lower Hundred in 1778 [Ref: Q-I:297].

THOMPSON, Richard. Took the Oath of Allegiance in 1780 [Ref: O-121]. Resident of William & Mary Upper Hundred in 1778 [Ref: Q-I:297].
THOMPSON, Samuel. Private (furnished by class for 9 months), 1st Maryland Line, by Sept. 11, 1778 [Ref: D-330]. Resident of Durham Lower Hundred in 1778 [Ref: Q-I:297].
THOMPSON, Sarah. See "Aaron Simmons," q.v.
THOMPSON, Smallwood. Took the Oath of Allegiance in 1778 [Ref: AA-641]. Resident of Newport East Hundred in 1778 [Ref: Q-I:297].
THOMPSON, Thomas. Sergeant, Militia, 26th Battalion, Capt. Benjamin Cawood's Company, 1777 [Ref: M-162]. Took the Oath of Allegiance in 1778 [Ref: L-21]. Resident of Newport West Hundred in 1778 [Ref: Q-I:297]. See "Joseph Thompson," q.v.
THOMPSON, Thomas. Private, Militia, 26th Battalion, Capt. Hezekiah Garner's Company, 1777 [Ref: M-162]. Took the Oath of Allegiance in 1778 [Ref: L-21, which listed the name as "Tomson"]. Resident of Port Tobacco East Hundred in 1778 [Ref: Q-I:297]. Private, 3rd Maryland Line, enrolled by Capt. Joseph Marbury's Company by May 24, 1780 [Ref: D-333, F-181]. See "Joseph Thompson," q.v.
THOMPSON, Thomas Jr. (1734-   ). Took the Oath of Allegiance in 1778 [Ref: L-21]. Aged about 21 as noted in a 1745 deposition [Ref: DD-271]. Resident of Newport West Hundred in 1778 [Ref: Q-I:297].
THOMPSON, Thomas (mulatto). Took the Oath of Allegiance in 1778 [Ref: AA-641, which listed the name as "Thomas Thomson (mulo.)"].
THOMPSON, William (1705-   ). Took the Oath of Allegiance in 1778 [Ref: AA-641]. Aged about 57 as noted in a 1762 deposition (which mentioned his father John Thompson), and aged about 58 as noted in a 1763 deposition [Ref: DD-271]. Resident of Durham Lower Hundred in 1778 [Ref: Q-I:297].
THOMPSON, William. Took the Oath of Allegiance in 1780 [Ref: O-121]. On Aug. 5, 1781, he petitioned the Governor and Council of Maryland stating "that your Petitioner being at Sea in the month of April 1780, that on the 18th of said month he being at the Mast head in a Gale of Wind, the Mast head broke and he fell on deck by which fall he received so much hurt that three of his ribs and his Breast Bone was broke, which renders him very unfit to go through any hard labour or the fatigues of marching although he was drafted in June last. Therefore, he prays that your Excellency and Honours will take his Case to your mature Consideration and grant him such relief as you shall think fit, and your Petitioner as in duty Bound will ever pray." This petition was supported by Dr. G. R. Brown and Hoskins Hanson, the latter of whom stated that "William Thompson has lived with me ever since his misfortune at Sea. He had

many Infectuous Swellings in his Groins out of which Pieces of his Rib have come. They continue to rise on the least Fatigue. He is now in so ill of Health that I think he is not able to march ten miles." [Ref: H-391].
THOMPSON, Williamson. Private, Militia, 26th Battalion, Capt. Francis Mastin's Company, 1777 [Ref: M-164, which listed the name as "Thomson"].
THORN, Absolam. Private, Militia, 12th Battalion, Capt. John Parnham's Company, 1777 [Ref: M-161]. Took the Oath of Allegiance in 1778 [Ref: AA-641]. Resident of Newport East Hundred in 1778 [Ref: Q-I:297, which misspelled the name as "Thom"].
THORN, Barton. Ensign, Militia, 12th Battalion, Capt. Henry Clarkson's Company, 1777, and Capt. Alexander McPherson's Company, Oct. 23, 1777. First Lieutenant, Militia, Capt. Thomas A. Dyson's Company, commissioned on Jan. 19, 1781 [Ref: M-129, M-159, C-403, G-280]. Took the Oath of Allegiance in 1778 [Ref: AA-641]. Resident of Newport East Hundred in 1778 [Ref: Q-I:297, which misspelled the name as "Thom"].
THORN, Cassandra. See "Thomas Thorn," q.v.
THORN, Peregrine. Private, Militia, 12th Battalion, Capt. Henry Clarkson's Company, 1777 [Ref: M-159]. Took the Oath of Allegiance in 1778 [Ref: AA-641]. Resident of Newport East Hundred in 1778 [Ref: Q-I:297, which misspelled the name as "Thom"]. Rendered patriotic service by providing wheat for the use of the military in September 1782 [Ref: N-557].
THORN, Rachel. See "Thomas Thorne," q.v.
THORN, Thomas (c1730-c1788). Took the Oath of Allegiance in 1778 [Ref: L-21, which listed the name as "Thorne"]. Thomas Thorn was born circa 1730, married first to Rachel ----, married second to Cassandra ----, and died after Sept. 14, 1788 [Ref: J-III:2930].
THORNE, Walter. Took the Oath of Allegiance in 1778 [Ref: L-21].
THORNTON, George. Took the Oath of Allegiance in 1778 [Ref: L-21]. Resident of Port Tobacco East Hundred in 1778 [Ref: Q-I:297].
THORNTON, Thomas. "Thomas Thornton" took the Oath of Allegiance in 1778 [Ref: L-21]. "Rev. Thomas Thornton" was a resident of Port Tobacco East Hundred in 1778 [Ref: Q-I:297].
TIAR, Raphael. See "Raphael Tyer," q.v.
TILLARD, James or John (1755-   ). Private, 1st Maryland Line, Col. John H. Stone's Regiment. *James Tillard* lost his left arm at the Battle of Little York (no date given). Invalid (disability) pension commenced on Dec. 10, 1781, aged 26, and still on pension as of Aug. 10, 1789 [Ref: D-629]. On April 16, 1782, the Council of Maryland stated that "We are of Opinion that the Petitioner is entitled to Half Pay, during Life under the Act of Oct. Session 1778 Chap. 14 vide sect. 2 and 8, and that the

Orphan's Court of Charles County is authorized to draw on the Treasurer of the Western Shore for the Provision allowed thereby, and request the Court to draw accordingly. NB. The Petitioner *John Tillard*, lost his Arm. The Petition and Certificate sent to the Orphan's Court." [Ref: I-140]. *Ed.*

Note: Regardless of the mix-up in the first name of this soldier, neither John Tillard nor James Tillard are included among the pensioners listed in References Q-II:399 and V-III:3500.

TIMMS, Bennett (1741-   ). Took the Oath of Allegiance in 1778 [Ref: L-21]. Aged about 33 as noted in a 1774 deposition [Ref: DD-271].

TIMMS, Charles. Private, Militia, 26th Battalion, Capt. Robert Sinnett's Company, 1777 [Ref: M-164]. Took the Oath of Allegiance in 1778 [Ref: AA-641, L-20, which latter source listed the name as "Simms"].

TIMMS, Edward. Private, 1st Maryland Line, enlisted on Feb. 11, 1778 and discharged on July 10, 1781 [Ref: D-168, D-557].

TIMMS, John. Private, Militia, 26th Battalion, Capt. Robert Sinnett's Company, 1777 [Ref: M-164]. Rendered patriotic service by providing wheat for the use of the military in August 1782 [Ref: N-539, which listed the name as "Fimms"]. One John Timms died by May 1778 (date of account). [Ref: GG-180].

TIMMS, Joseph (1751-c1820). Private, 1st Maryland Line, enrolled and passed on July 19, 1776, promoted to corporal on Oct. 25, 1777, and discharged on Sept. 14, 1780 [Ref: D-31, D-168]. Joseph Timms was born in 1751, married Susan Douglas, and died in Virginia after 1820 [Ref: J-III:2945].

TIMMS, William. Private, Militia, 26th Battalion, Capt. Robert Sinnett's Company, 1777 [Ref: M-164].

TIMPSON, Benjamin. Private, Militia, 12th Battalion, Capt. Alexander McPherson's Company, 1777 [Ref: X-62]. Resident of Bryan Town Hundred in 1778 [Ref: Q-I:297].

TIMPSON, Thomas Sr. Took the Oath of Allegiance in 1778 [Ref: L-21, which listed the name as "Tympson" and AA-641, which listed the name as "Timson"]. Resident of Bryan Town Hundred in 1778 [Ref: Q-I:297].

TINCH, William. See "William Tench (Tinch)," q.v.

TOWNLEY, Joseph. Private, Militia, 26th Battalion, Capt. Richard Bennett Mitchell's Company, 1777; listed as an invalid (disabled) soldier [Ref: M-164, which listed the name as "Townly"]. See "Joseph Townslin," q.v.

TOWNLEY, Joseph. Sergeant, Militia, 12th Battalion, Capt. Alexander McPherson's Company, 1777 [Ref: M-160, which listed the name as Townly"]. See "Joseph Townslin," q.v.

TOWNSEND, Mary. See "Benjamin Burch," q.v.

303

TOWNSHEND, Rose. Rendered patriotic service by providing wheat for the use of the military in August 1782 [Ref: N-536].

TOWNSLIN, Joseph. "Joseph Townslin" took the Oath of Allegiance in 1778 [Ref: L-21]. "Joseph Townsen" took the Oath of Allegiance in 1780 [Ref: O-122]. "Joseph Townley" was a resident of Bryan Town Hundred in 1778 [Ref: Q-I:297].

TOWNSLIN, Thomas. "Thomas Townslin" took the Oath of Allegiance in 1778 [Ref: AA-641]. "Thomas Townley" was a resident of Bryan Town Hundred in 1778 [Ref: Q-I:297].

TRANOR, John. Private, Militia, 12th Battalion, Capt. Walter Hanson's Company, 1777 [Ref: M-159].

TRAVERSE, Nancy. See "Richard Tubman," q.v.

TRUMAN, Anne Magruder. See "George Dent, of John," q.v.

TRUMAN, James. See "George Dent, of John," q.v.

TUBB, William. Private, Militia, 12th Battalion, Capt. Alexander McPherson's Company, 1777 [Ref: M-160]. Took the Oath of Allegiance in 1778 [Ref: L-21]. "William Tub" married "Martha Summerset" on Jan. 1, 1774 in Trinity Parish [Ref: EE-16].

TUBMAN, Elinor. Rendered patriotic service by providing wheat for the use of the military in December 1782 [Ref: N-576].

TUBMAN, George (1729-). Clerk, Militia, 26th Battalion, Capt. Thomas H. Marshall's Company, 1777 [Ref: M-163]. Took the Oath of Allegiance in 1778 [Ref: L-21]. Rendered patriotic service by providing wheat for the use of the military in December 1782 and May 1783 [Ref: N-576, N-599]. Aged about 36 as noted in a 1765 deposition [Ref: DD-272]. Resident of Pomonkey Hundred in 1778 [Ref: Q-I:297].

TUBMAN, Henry (of St. Mary's County). Took the Oath of Allegiance which was recorded in the minutes of the Charles County Court in August 1778 [Ref: AA-708].

TUBMAN, Richard Jr. (1752-1813). Clerk, Militia, 26th Battalion, Capt. Samuel Smallwood's Company, 1777 [Ref: M-165]. Took the Oath of Allegiance in 1778 [Ref: L-21, AA-641]. Resident of Newport East Hundred in 1778 [Ref: Q-I:297]. Richard Tubman, Jr., was born in Maryland in 1752, married Nancy Traverse, served as a lieutenant during the war, and migrated to South Carolina where he died on Aug. 26, 1813 [Ref: J-III:2984].

TUBMAN, Richard Sr. (1717-1786). Rendered patriotic service by providing wheat for the use of the military in May 1783 [Ref: N-598]. Richard Tubman, Sr., was born in Maryland in 1717, married Sarah Keene, and died on Jan. 27, 1786 [Ref: J-III:2984].

TUBMAN, Samuel. Clerk, Militia, 12th Battalion, Capt. Walter Hanson's Company, 1777 [Ref: M-159]. Took the Oath of Allegiance in 1778 [Ref: L-21]. Resident of Port Tobacco East Hundred in 1778 [Ref: Q-I:297].
TUEL, Joseph. Took the Oath of Allegiance in 1778 [Ref: L-21, which listed the name as "Joseph Tuel(?)"].
TURNBULL, John. Took the Oath of Allegiance in 1778 [Ref: L-21, AA-641]. Resident of Port Tobacco West Hundred in 1778 [Ref: Q-I:297].
TURNER, Deborah. See "Zachariah Chunn," q.v.
TURNER, Edward. See "Randolph Turner" and "William Turner" and "Samuel Turner" and "Joseph Turner," q.v.
TURNER, Elinor. See "Randolph Turner" and "William Turner" and "Samuel Turner" and "Joseph Turner," q.v.
TURNER, John. Memorialist and Militiaman, Pomonkey Company, after March 6, 1776 [Ref: M-158, Y-II:26]. Took the Oath of Allegiance in 1778 [Ref: L-21]. See "John Hoskins Stone," q.v.
TURNER, John Beall. Ensign, Militia, 12th Battalion, Capt. Walter Hanson's Company, Feb. 26, 1776 [Ref: M-131, M-159, A-186, A-206, Y-II:23, which latter source listed the name as "John Beal Turner"].
TURNER, Joseph. Treasurer for Charles County in 1776 [Ref: A-415]. Took the Oath of Allegiance in 1778 [Ref: L-21]. Resident of Port Tobacco East Hundred in 1778 [Ref: Q-I:297]. One Joseph Turner was born on March 1, 1746/7, a son of Edward and Elinor Turner, of Trinity Parish [Ref: EE-4].
TURNER, Leonard. Private, 3rd Maryland Line, enrolled by Capt. Joseph Marbury by May 24, 1780 and still in service in November 1780 [Ref: F-181, D-171].
TURNER, Lydia. See "Samuel Maddox," q.v.
TURNER, Mary. See "Zephaniah Turner," q.v.
TURNER, Randolph. Private, Militia, 12th Battalion, Capt. Alexander McPherson's Company, 1777 [Ref: M-160]. Took the Oath of Allegiance in 1778 [Ref: L-21]. Rendered patriotic service by providing wheat for the use of the military in October 1781 and December 1782 [Ref: N-447, N-577]. "Randolph Turner" was a resident of Bryan Town Hundred in 1778 [Ref: Q-I:297]. "Randal Turner" was born on Sept. 20, 1739, a son of Edward and Elinor Turner, of Trinity Parish [Ref: EE-4].
TURNER, Robert. See "Zephaniah Turner," q.v.
TURNER, Samuel. Private, Militia, 12th Battalion, Capt. John Parnham's Company, 1777 [Ref: M-160]. One Samuel Turner was born on Oct. 7, 1733, son of Edward and Elinor Turner, and another Samuel Turner was born on June 9, 1752, a son of Samuel and Virlinda Turner [Ref: EE-4, EE-9]. One Samuel Turner was born circa 1752 in Maryland, married

Jane Vance, rendered patriotic service, and migrated to Ohio where he died on Sept. 4, 1823 [Ref: J-III:2993]. Additional research will be necessary before drawing conclusions. See "Zephaniah Turner," q.v.

TURNER, Virlinda. See "Zephaniah Turner" and "Virlinda Turner," q.v.

TURNER, William (1737-1801). Born on Dec. 14, 1737, a son of Edward and Elinor Turner, of Trinity Parish, William married Rhoda Dent on July 1, 1764 and died in December 1801 [Ref: EE-4, EE-12, J-III:2994]. Private, Militia, 12th Battalion, Capt. Alexander McPherson's Company, 1777 [Ref: M-160]. Took the Oath of Allegiance in 1778 [Ref: L-21]. Resident of Bryan Town Hundred in 1778 [Ref: Q-I:297].

TURNER, Zephaniah (1737-1794). Born on Sept. 19, 1737, a son of Samuel and Virlinda Turner, he married by 1771 to Mary ---- and probably had five children (three sons and two daughters), but the only ones known were Samuel Beal Turner and Robert Turner [Ref: P-II:844, EE-2]. Served on the Committee of Observation, 1774, and in the Lower House of the Maryland Legislature between 1777 and 1785. Treasurer of the Council of Safety in 1778 and Auditor, 1778-1783. Commissioner of the Tax in 1779 and 1781. Attended the Constitution Ratification Convention, 1788 [Ref: P-II:845]. Took the Oath of Allegiance in 1778 [Ref: L-21]. Resident of Port Tobacco East Hundred in 1778 [Ref: Q-I:297]. Appointed by the Maryland General Assembly to be Auditor General in the room of Uriah Forrest (who had resigned) on Feb. 9, 1781 [Ref: G-307, which listed the name as "Esq."].

TURNEY, William. Private, Militia, 26th Battalion, Capt. Hezekiah Garner's Company, 1777 [Ref: M-163].

TUSEN, Robert. Took the Oath of Allegiance in 1778 [Ref: L-21].

TYER, Charles. Private, Militia, 26th Battalion, Capt. Robert Sinnett's Company, 1777 [Ref: M-164, which listed the name as "Tyers"]. Took the Oath of Allegiance in 1778 [Ref: L-21, AA-641, which sources listed the name as "Tiar"]. Resident of Port Tobacco West Hundred in 1778 [Ref: Q-I:297, which listed the name as "Tyre"]. Rendered patriotic service by providing wheat for the use of the military in May and December 1782 [Ref: N-511, N-577, which listed the name as "Tiar" and "Tyan"].

TYER, Francis. See "Thomas Pickerel," q.v.

TYER, John. Private, Militia, 12th Battalion, Capt. Walter Hanson's Company, 1777 [Ref: M-159, which listed the name as "Tyre"]. Resident of Port Tobacco East Hundred in 1778 [Ref: Q-I:297]. Rendered patriotic service by providing wheat for the use of the military in December 1782 [Ref: N-577].

TYER, Joseph. Private, Militia, 12th Battalion, Capt. Walter Hanson's Company, 1777 [Ref: M-159, which listed the name as "Tyre"]. Took the

Oath of Allegiance in 1778 [Ref: L-20, which listed the name as "Tear" and AA-641, which listed the name as "Tiar"]. Resident of Port Tobacco East Hundred in 1778 [Ref: Q-I:297]. Rendered patriotic service by providing wheat for the use of the military in April and September 1782 [Ref: N-504, N-548, which listed the name as "Tyer" and "Tian"]. See "Thomas Pickerel," q.v.

TYER, Raphael. Private, Militia, 12th Battalion, Capt. Walter Hanson's Company, 1777 [Ref: M-159, which listed the name as "Raphael Tyre"]. Took the Oath of Allegiance in 1778 [Ref: AA-641, which listed the name as "Raphael Tiar"]. Rendered patriotic service by providing wheat for the use of the military in December 1782 [Ref: N-577, which listed the name as "Ralph Tyer"]. See "Thomas Pickerel," q.v.

TYER, William. Took the Oath of Allegiance in 1778 [Ref: AA-641, which listed the name as "Tyre"]. Resident of Port Tobacco East Hundred in 1778 [Ref: Q-I:297]. Rendered patriotic service by providing wheat for the use of the military in November 1782 [Ref: N-566, which listed the name as "Tian"].

TYER, William Jr. Private, Militia, 12th Battalion, Capt. Walter Hanson's Company, 1777 [Ref: M-159, which listed the name as "Tyre"]. Took the Oath of Allegiance in 1778 [Ref: L-21, which listed the name as "Tiar"]. Resident of Port Tobacco East Hundred in 1778 [Ref: Q-I:297]. See "Thomas Pickerel," q.v.

TYLER, Katrain. Took the Oath of Allegiance in 1778 [Ref: L-21].

TYLER, William. Private, Militia, 26th Battalion, Capt. Thomas H. Marshall's Company, 1777 [Ref: M-163]. Took the Oath of Allegiance in 1778 [Ref: AA-641]. Resident of Pomonkey Hundred in 1778 [Ref: Q-I:297]. Rendered patriotic service by providing clothing for the use of the military in January 1778 [Ref: Y-II:230]. Rendered patriotic service by providing wheat for the use of the military in December 1782 [Ref: N-576].

TYSER, Thomas. Private, 1st Maryland Line, enrolled and passed on July 20, 1776 [Ref: D-32].

VANCE, Jane. See "Samuel Turner," q.v.

VARDEN, Henrietta. See "Henry Dixon," q.v.

VARDEN, John. Private, Militia, 12th Battalion, Capt. Walter Hanson's Company, 1777 [Ref: M-159, which listed the name as "Verdin"]. Took the Oath of Allegiance in 1778 [Ref: AA-641, L-21, which latter source misspelled the name as "Warden"]. Resident of Port Tobacco East Hundred in 1778 [Ref: Q-I:297]. Paid by the Collector of the Tax for Charles County some money that was "due him agreeable to a certificate from the Commissary of Purchases" on Dec. 9, 1780 [Ref: F-239, which listed the name as "Verdin"]. Rendered patriotic service by collecting cattle for the use of the military in October 1781 [Ref: N-451, which listed the name as "Vardin"]. See "John Arms," q.v.

VARDEN, Joseph. See "Henry Dixon," q.v.

VARDEN, Richard. See "Henry Dixon" q.v.

VAYNE, John Jr. Private, Militia, 26th Battalion, Capt. Benjamin Cawood's Company, 1777 [Ref: M-162]. See "John Wayne," q.v.

VAYNE, William. Private, Militia, 26th Battalion, Capt. Benjamin Cawood's Company, 1777 [Ref: M-162, which listed the name as "Vayne"]. Rendered patriotic service by providing wheat for the use of the military in April 1783 [Ref: N-593, which listed the name as "Vain"]. See "William Wayne," q.v.

VENABLES, Ezekiel. Private, Militia, 12th Battalion, Capt. Peter Wood's Company, 1777 [Ref: M-161].

VENABLE (VENABLES), Lawrence. Private, Militia, 12th Battalion, Capt. Peter Wood's Company, 1777 [Ref: M-161]. Took the Oath of Allegiance in 1778 [Ref: AA-641]. Resident of Benedict Hundred in 1778 [Ref: Q-I:297].

VENABLE (VENABLES), Samuel. Private, Militia, 12th Battalion, Capt. Peter Wood's Company, 1777 [Ref: M-161]. Resident of Benedict Hundred in 1778 [Ref: Q-I:297].

VENABLE (VENABLES), Theodore Jr. Private, Militia, 12th Battalion, Capt. Peter Wood's Company, 1777 [Ref: M-161]. Resident of Benedict Hundred in 1778 [Ref: Q-I:297].

VENABLE (VENABLES), William. On March 2, 1782, the Council of Maryland "ordered that the Western Shore Treasurer pay to William Venables thirteen pounds, one shilling and five pence specie agreeable to the Act to adjust the Debts due from this State per Accounts pay roll and Certificates adjusted and passed." [Ref: I-89].

VERDIN, John. See "John Vardin," q.v.

VERDIN, Richard. Private, Militia, 12th Battalion, Capt. Walter Hanson's Company, 1777 [Ref: M-159]. On Jan. 26, 1781, the Council of Maryland ordered "the Armourer deliver to Richard Verdin two hundred pounds of powder and fifty muskets to be delivered over to Francis Ware, Esq., Lieutenant of Charles County, for the use of the militia of said county, and that the Issuing Commissary deliver to the said Richard Verdin one beeves hide to cover powder and arms sent to Colonel Ware." [Ref: G-289].

VERMILLION, Benjamin. Took the Oath of Allegiance in 1778 [Ref: L-21, which listed the name as "Vermillon" and AA-641, which listed the name as "Virmillion"]. Resident of Port Tobacco Upper Hundred in 1778 [Ref: Q-I:297, which misspelled the name as "Permillian"].

VERMILLION, Edward. Private, Militia, 26th Battalion, Capt. Thomas H. Marshall's Company, 1777 [Ref: M-163, which listed the name as "Virmillion"]. Resident of Pomonkey Hundred in 1778 [Ref: Q-I:297, which misspelled the name as "Permillian"].

VERMILLION, Francis. Private, Militia, 26th Battalion, Capt. Thomas H. Marshall's Company, 1777 [Ref: M-163, which listed the name as "Virmillion"].

VERMILLION, Giles. Memorialist and Militiaman, Pomonkey Company, after March 6, 1776 [Ref: M-158, Y-II:26]. Private, Militia, 26th Battalion, Capt. Thomas H. Marshall's Company, 1777 [Ref: M-163, which listed the name as "Virmillion"]. Took the Oath of Allegiance in 1778 [Ref: L-21, which listed the name as "Vermillon" and AA-641, which listed the name as "Virmillion"].

VERMILLION, Guy. Private, Militia, 26th Battalion, Capt. Thomas H. Marshall's Company, 1777 [Ref: M-163, which listed the name as "Virmillion"].

VERMILLION, John. Private, Militia, 26th Battalion, Capt. Thomas H. Marshall's Company, 1777 [Ref: M-163, which listed the name as "Virmillion"].

VERMILLION, Samuel (1755-1837). Private, Maryland and North Carolina Lines. He applied for a pension (S7790) in Macon County, North Carolina on April 11, 1832, stating that he was born on April 6, 1755 in Charles County, Maryland. He died on Feb. 8, 1837, leaving children, but no names were given [Ref: V-III:3614, J-III:3050].

VINCENT, John. Private, Lower Battalion, Prince George's County, 1776 [Ref: D-35, which listed the name as "Vinson"]. Sergeant, Charles County Militia, 12th Battalion, Capt. Jonathan Yates' Company, 1777 [Ref: M-162]. Took the Oath of Allegiance in 1778 [Ref: L-21, AA-641]. Resident of William & Mary Lower Hundred in Charles County in 1778 [Ref: Q-I:297]. Constable, 1778 [Ref: CC-709]. Second Lieutenant, Militia, Capt. John Lancaster's Company, commissioned on Jan. 19, 1781 [Ref: M-132, G-280]. *Ed. Note:* One John Vincent died in Charles County in July 1778 (date of inventory). Additional research may be necessary before drawing conclusions.

VINCENT, John Jr. Took the Oath of Allegiance in 1778 [Ref: L-21, AA-641]. Resident of William & Mary Lower Hundred in 1778 [Ref: Q-I:297].

VINCENT, Rhodes. Private, Militia, 26th Battalion, Capt. Benjamin Cawood's Company, 1777 [Ref: M-162, which listed the name as "Rhods(?) Vinson" and X-72, which listed it as "Rhoda Vinson"].

VINCENT, William Jr. Private, Militia, 12th Battalion, Capt. Jonathan Yates' Company, 1777 [Ref: M-162]. Took the Oath of Allegiance in 1778 [Ref: AA-641]. Resident of William & Mary Lower Hundred in 1778 [Ref: Q-I:297].
VINCENT, William Sr. Private, Militia, 12th Battalion, Capt. Jonathan Yates' Company, 1777 [Ref: M-162]. Took the Oath of Allegiance in 1778 [Ref: AA-641]. Resident of William & Mary Lower Hundred in 1778 [Ref: Q-I:297].
WADE, Lancelot. Took the Oath of Allegiance in 1778 [Ref: L-21].
WADE, Richard. Took the Oath of Allegiance in 1778 [Ref: L-21]. Resident of Pomonkey Hundred in 1778 [Ref: Q-I:297].
WADE, Zachariah. "Zachariah Meek Wade" was a private in the Lower Battalion of Prince George's County in 1776 [Ref: D-35]. "Zachariah Wade" was a Memorialist and Militiaman, Pomonkey Company, Charles County, in 1776 [Ref: M-158, Y-II:26]. Resident of Pomonkey Hundred in 1778 [Ref: Q-I:297]. Two men by this name were privates in the militia, 26th Battalion, in 1777: one in Capt. Francis Mastin's Company, and one in Capt. Thomas H. Marshall's Company [Ref: M-163, M-164].
WAKEFIELD, Able (1734-   ). Took the Oath of Allegiance in 1778 [Ref: AA-641]. Aged about 28 as noted in a 1762 deposition [Ref: DD-272]. Resident of William & Mary Upper Hundred in 1778 [Ref: Q-I:297].
WALES, Edward Lloyd (1758-1809). Ensign, 1st Maryland Line. "Edward Lloyd Wales" took the Oath of Allegiance in 1778 [Ref: AA-641]. "Loyd Wales" was a resident of Benedict Hundred in 1778 [Ref: Q-I:297]. Edward Lloyd Wales was born on Sept. 25, 1758 in Maryland, married Sarah Biggs Oden, served as an ensign in the Maryland Line, and migrated to Georgia where he died on Jan. 27, 1809 [Ref: J-III:3073].
WALKER, Archibald. Private, Militia, 12th Battalion, Capt. Benjamin Lusby Corry's Company, 1777 [Ref: M-160].
WALKER, George (1759-1826). Private (furnished by class for 9 months), 1st Maryland Line, by Sept. 11, 1778 [Ref: D-330]. George Walker was born on Oct. 17, 1759, married Ann Martha Bryan, and died on June 26, 1826 [Ref: J-III:2076].
WALKER, Peter. Took the Oath of Allegiance in 1778 [Ref: L-21]. Resident of Port Tobacco Upper Hundred in 1778 [Ref: Q-I:297].
WALKIN, Martin. Took the Oath of Allegiance in 1778 [Ref: L-21].
WALLACE, Alexander. Private, 1st Maryland Line, who was drafted from the Charles County militia and reported "sick or not in service" in June 1781 [Ref: D-376].
WALLACE, Anne Elizabeth. See "James Farnandis," q.v.

WALLACE (WALLIS), Basil. "Basil Wallis" took the Oath of Allegiance in 1778 [Ref: AA-641]. "Basell Wallace" was a resident of Benedict Hundred in 1778 [Ref: Q-I:297].
WALLACE (WALLIS), James. Corporal, Militia, 12th Battalion, Capt. Peter Wood's Company, 1777 [Ref: M-161]. "James Wallace" was a resident of Benedict Hundred in 1778 [Ref: Q-I:297]. "James Wallis" took the Oath of Allegiance in 1778 [Ref: AA-641].
WALLACE, John (1755-   ). Private, Flying Camp, Capt. Bowie's Company, enrolled July 16, 1776; native of Charles County, aged 21, height 5' 8 1/2" [Ref: D-36]. Private, Militia, 26th Battalion, Capt. Robert Sinnett's Company, 1777 [Ref: M-164]. Took the Oath of Allegiance in 1778 [Ref: L-21, AA-641]. Resident of Port Tobacco West Hundred in 1778 [Ref: Q-I:297]. Rendered patriotic service by providing wheat for the use of the military in May 1783 [Ref: N-599].
WALLACE, Richard. Private, Militia, 12th Battalion, Capt. Peter Wood's Company, 1777 [Ref: M-161]. Resident of Benedict Hundred in 1778 [Ref: Q-I:297].
WALLACE (WALLIS), William. "William Wallis" took the Oath of Allegiance in 1778 [Ref: AA-641]. "William Wallace" was a resident of Benedict Hundred in 1778 [Ref: Q-I:297].
WALLINGFORD, Martha Elliott. See "Charles Willett," q.v.
WALLS, Benjamin. See "George Walls," q.v.
WALLS, Elizabeth. See "George Walls," q.v.
WALLS, George (1752-1831). Private, 1st Maryland Line, enrolled and passed on July 20, 1776 [Ref: D-33]. Private, Militia, 12th Battalion, Capt. John Thomas' Company, 1777 [Ref: M-161]. Born on Feb. 14, 1752, he lived in Charles County at the time of his enlistment and married Martha Naylor on March 28, 1784 in Prince George's County. She applied for a pension (W8972) on June 21, 1845, stating that she was born on Feb. 14, 1762 and George died on May 11, 1831. Their children were: Margaret Baden Walls (born Jan. 30, 1787 and married Josiah Wilson on Jan. 30, 1817); Jane N. Walls (born May 23, 1791); William Batson Walls (July 3, 1793 - Jan. 29, 1823); George Naylor Walls (born Aug. 22, 1796 and married Sarah Club on Jan. 20, 1824); Naylor Davis Walls (Nov. 12, 1798 - Jan. 15, 1835); Benjamin Baden Walls (born July 6, 1801, married Elizabeth Harvey on July 30, 1835, and died Sept. 16, 1836); Elizabeth Ann Walls (born Nov. 11, 1803); and, Martha Ann Walls (born March 18, 1807). [Ref: V-III:3660].
WALLS, Jane N. See "George Walls," q.v.
WALLS, Martha. See "George Walls," q.v.
WALLS, Margaret. See "George Walls," q.v.

WALLS, Naylor Davis. See "George Walls," q.v.
WALLS, William. Private, 1st Maryland Line, enrolled and passed on July 20, 1776 [Ref: D-33]. See "George Walls," q.v.
WALTERS, Asenath. See "James Downing," q.v.
WAPLE, John. Took the Oath of Allegiance in 1778 [Ref: AA-641]. Resident of Durham Lower Hundred in 1778 [Ref: Q-I:297].
WAPLE, William. Private, 1st Maryland Line, enrolled and passed on July 27, 1776 [Ref: D-31, which listed the name as "Wapels (Waples)"]. Resident of Durham Lower Hundred in 1778 [Ref: Q-I:297].
WARD, Achilles (1713-   ). Took the Oath of Allegiance in 1778 [Ref: L-21, AA-641]. "Archillis Ward, son of John" was aged about 64 as noted in a 1777 deposition [Ref: CC-625]. "Archilus Ward" was a resident of Port Tobacco West Hundred in 1778 [Ref: Q-I:297]. Rendered patriotic service by providing wheat for the use of the military in May 1782 [Ref: N-511].
WARD, David Linsy. Private, Militia, 26th Battalion, Capt. Hezekiah Garner's Company, 1777 [Ref: M-163]. Took the Oath of Allegiance in 1778 [Ref: AA-641, which listed the name as "David L. Ward"].
WARD, Edward (1757-1840). Private, 1st Maryland Line, 1776-1778. He applied for a pension (R1115) on Nov. 14, 1833 in Perry County, Ohio, stating he was born in 1757 in Charles County, Maryland. His parents moved to Frederick County, Maryland when he was young and there he served in the Revolutionary War. In 1778 he moved near Cumberland, Maryland, married Lucy Wilson on Aug. 6, 1779, and moved to Ohio in 1811. Edward Ward died on Aug. 25, 1840 and Lucy Ward died on May 27, 1847. Their surviving children were John Ward, James Ward, William Ward, Jeremiah Ward, and Anna Burgess [Ref: V-III:3668, U-104, but not mentioned in *Archives of Maryland, Volume 18*].
WARD, George. Private, Militia, 26th Battalion, Capt. Richard Bennett Mitchell's Company, 1777 [Ref: M-165]. Private (substitute for 3 years), 1st Maryland Line, by Sept. 11, 1778 [Ref: D-330]. Resident of Port Tobacco West Hundred in 1778 [Ref: Q-I:297].
WARD, Henry. Recommended to be a captain in the militia on Feb. 26, 1776, but was not selected [Ref: Y-II:23]. Second Lieutenant, Militia, Pomonkey Company, commanded by Capt. Thomas H. Marshall, 1776, and was later promoted to captain [Ref: M-158, Y-II:26]. Resident of Pomonkey Hundred in 1778 [Ref: Q-I:297].
WARD, Ignatius. Rendered patriotic service by providing wheat for the use of the military in January 1782 and April 1783 [Ref: N-474, N-593].
WARD, James. See "Edward Ward," q.v.
WARD, Jeremiah. See "Edward Ward," q.v.

WARD, John. Memorialist and Militiaman, Pomonkey Company, after March 6, 1776 [Ref: M-158, Y-II:26]. Private, Militia, 26th Battalion, Capt. Thomas H. Marshall's Company, 1777 [Ref: M-163]. Took the Oath of Allegiance in 1778 [Ref: L-21]. Resident of Port Tobacco West Hundred in 1778 [Ref: Q-I:297]. Rendered patriotic service by providing wheat for the use of the military in December 1782 and April 1783 [Ref: N-576, N-593]. See "Edward Ward" and "Achilles Ward," q.v.

WARD, John, of Augustine. Took the Oath of Allegiance in 1778 [Ref: L-21]. Resident of Pomonkey Hundred in 1778 [Ref: Q-I:297].

WARD, Lancelot. Private (drafted and joined the army), 1st Maryland Line, by Sept. 11, 1778 [Ref: D-330].

WARD, Lucy. See "Edward Ward," q.v.

WARD, Samuel. Chosen to be first lieutenant in the militia, Pomonkey Company, Feb. 26, 1776, but died circa March 6, 1776 [Ref: M-158, Y-II:26].

WARD, Thomas. Private, Militia, 26th Battalion, Capt. Thomas H. Marshall's Company, 1777 [Ref: M-163]. Private (drafted and joined the army), 1st Maryland Line, by Sept. 11, 1778 [Ref: D-330].

WARD, William. Memorialist and Militiaman, Pomonkey Company, after March 6, 1776 [Ref: M-158, Y-II:26]. Private, Militia, 26th Battalion, Capt. Thomas H. Marshall's Company, 1777 [Ref: M-163]. Took the Oath of Allegiance in 1778 [Ref: L-21]. Resident of Pomonkey Hundred in 1778 [Ref: Q-I:297]. Rendered patriotic service by providing wheat for the use of the military in February 1782 [Ref: N-480]. See "Edward Ward," q.v.

WARD, Zeruia. See "Gustavus Boswell," q.v.

WARDEN, Elijah. Private, Militia, Capt. Francis Mastin's Company, 26th Battalion, March 19, 1776 through 1777 [Ref: M-158, M-163, K-1814, which also listed the name as "Wardin"]. Took the Oath of Allegiance in 1778 [Ref: AA-641]. Rendered patriotic service by providing wheat for the use of the military in May and July 1782 [Ref: N-509, N-531].

WARDEN, John. Took the Oath of Allegiance in 1778 [Ref: L-21]. One John Warden was aged about 63 as noted in a 1758 deposition [Ref: DD-273].

WARDEN, Richard Morse. "Richard Morse Worden" took the Oath of Allegiance in 1778 [Ref: L-21]. "Richard Warden" was a resident of Bryan Town Hundred in 1778 [Ref: Q-I:297].

WARDER, James. Private, Militia, 26th Battalion, Capt. Hezekiah Garner's Company, 1777 [Ref: M-162]. Took the Oath of Allegiance in 1778 [Ref: AA-641].

WARDER, Jesse. Private, Militia, 26th Battalion, Capt. Hezekiah Garner's Company, 1777 [Ref: M-163]. Private, 1st Maryland Line, drafted from

the Charles County militia and in service on June 11 or 12, 1781 [Ref: D-376].
WARDER, John. Private, 1st Maryland Line, enrolled and passed on July 19, 1776 [Ref: D-31, which listed the name as "Worder"]. Corporal, Militia, 26th Battalion, Capt. Hezekiah Garner's Company, 1777 [Ref: M-162].
WARDER, Joseph (1752-c1798). Private, Militia, 26th Battalion, Capt. Hezekiah Garner's Company, 1777 [Ref: M-162]. Took the Oath of Allegiance in 1778 [Ref: AA-641]. Rendered patriotic service by providing wheat for the use of the military in February 1782 [Ref: N-481]. Joseph Warder was born on Dec. 5, 1752, married Esther Ford, and died after 1798 [Ref: J-III:3097].
WARDER, Philip. Private, Militia, 26th Battalion, Capt. Hezekiah Garner's Company, 1777 [Ref: M-163]. Took the Oath of Allegiance in 1778 [Ref: AA-641].
WARDER, William (1698-   ). Took the Oath of Allegiance in 1778 [Ref: L-21]. Aged about 70 as noted in a 1768 deposition [Ref: DD-273]. Resident of Port Tobacco East Hundred in 1778 [Ref: Q-I:297].
WARE, Edward Scott (1740-   ). Private, Militia, 12th Battalion, Capt. Walter Hanson's Company, 1777 [Ref: M-159]. Took the Oath of Allegiance in 1778 [Ref: AA-641]. Aged about 39 as noted in a 1779 deposition [Ref: DD-273]. Resident of Port Tobacco East Hundred in 1778 [Ref: Q-I:297].
WARE, Francis (1732-   ). Captain, Militia, 1775. Lieutenant Colonel, Feb. 26, 1776. Colonel and County Lieutenant from July 1, 1777 to at least Jan. 17, 1782 [Ref: M-133, A-186, C-304, D-331, Y-II:23, I-53]. Delegate to the Maryland Convention from April 24 to May 3, 1775 [Ref: Y-I:1]. Aged about 42 as noted in a 1774 deposition which referred to him as Capt. Francis Ware (and also mentioned his father Francis, deceased). Aged about 47 as noted in a 1779 deposition. Aged about 48 as noted in a 1780 deposition which referred to him as Col. Francis Ware [Ref: CC-578, DD-273]. Took the Oath of Allegiance in 1778 [Ref: L-21, AA-641]. Resident of Port Tobacco East Hundred in 1778 [Ref: Q-I:297]. Rendered patriotic service by providing clothing for the use of the military in February 1778 [Ref: Y-II:235]. In November 1800, the Maryland Legislature passed Resolution No. 7 as follows (verbatim): "Francis Ware (who heretofore commanded the troops of this state, then the colony of Maryland, with distinguished bravery and fidelity, and who, during the late Revolutionary War, was lieutenant colonel of the 1st regiment raised by this state, from which service he was compelled to retire by the infirmities peculiarly incident to the military life in these climates), has, by reason of his said infirm health, and misfortunes arising from those acts of benevolence which the duties of society often render indispensable, and not by

imprudence or want of due economy, became reduced to extreme indigence in his advanced age; and it being unworthy (both in example & principle) of the citizens of a free republic, to desert, in their distress, those of their fellow-citizens who have rendered important services in distinguished stations, whilst high honours and great rewards attend public services in other forms of government; Resolved unanimously, That there be granted to the said Francis Ware half pay as lieutenant colonel (rated according to the establishment when he retired from the service) from date of this resolution, during the remainder of his life; Treasurer Western Shore pay same to said Francis Ware in quarterly payments." [Ref: Q-II:403]. See "Richard Verdin" and "Thomas Pickerel" and "Thomas Stone," q.v.

WARE, Francis Jr. "Francis Ware" was an ensign in Capt. John S. Belt's Company, 1st Maryland Line, on Jan. 1, 1782 [Ref: D-435]. "Francis Ware, Jr." was a resident of Port Tobacco East Hundred in 1778 [Ref: Q-I:297].

WARE, Francis, of Jacob. Private, Militia, 12th Battalion, Capt. Walter Hanson's Company, 1777 [Ref: M-159]. See "Francis Wier," q.v.

WARE, Jacob. Took the Oath of Allegiance in 1778 [Ref: AA-641]. Resident of Port Tobacco East Hundred in 1778 [Ref: Q-I:297]. See "Thomas Pickerel," q.v.

WARREN, Anne. See "Warren Dent," q.v.

WARREN, Basil. See "Basil Warring," q.v.

WARREN, Charles. See "John Warren," q.v.

WARREN, Edward. Sergeant, Militia, 12th Battalion, Capt. Jonathan Yates' Company, 1777 [Ref: M-162]. Took the Oath of Allegiance in 1778 [Ref: L-21, AA-641]. Rendered patriotic service by providing clothing for the use of the military in February 1778 [Ref: Y-II:234]. Ensign, Militia, Capt. Yates' Company, May 28, 1779 [Ref: M-134, E-427]. Resident of William & Mary Lower Hundred in 1778 [Ref: Q-I:297].

WARREN, Elizabeth. See "Henry Smoot," q.v.

WARREN, Joanna. See "Robert Rogers," q.v.

WARREN, John. Took the Oath of Allegiance in 1778 [Ref: AA-641]. Resident of Port Tobacco East Hundred in 1778 [Ref: Q-I:297].

WARREN, John (1759-c1850). Private, 5th Maryland Line, 1777-1779 [Ref: D-254]. Resident of William & Mary Lower Hundred in 1778 [Ref: Q-I:297]. John Warren applied for a pension (R11158) in Orange County, North Carolina on Nov. 23, 1836, stating that he was born on Oct. 21, 1759 in Charles County, Maryland. He lived there during the Revolutionary War and served in the Maryland Line. In 1796 he moved to North Carolina and died before 1851, at which time a son Charles S. Warren lived in Orange County [Ref: V-III:3684]. Orphans Court records in Charles County in 1778 stated that John Warren was aged 18 on Oct. 21, 1777 and Burford Cotterel (Cottrell) was his brother-in-law and guardian [Ref: GG-134].

WARREN, Mary. See "John Stone," q.v.

WARREN, Notley. See "Robert Rogers," q.v.

WARREN, Sarah. See "Robert Rogers," q.v.

WARREN, William. Private, Militia, 26th Battalion, Capt. Benjamin Cawood's Company, 1777 [Ref: M-162]. Private (drafted and joined the army), 1st Maryland Line, by Sept. 11, 1778 [Ref: D-330, which listed the name as "Warrin"]. Resident of Port Tobacco East Hundred in 1778 [Ref: Q-I:297].

WARRING, Ann. See "Basil Warring" and "Josias Hawkins," q.v.

WARRING, Basil. Took the Oath of Allegiance in 1778 [Ref: L-21]. Ensign, 3rd Maryland Line, 1781. Lieutenant, 2nd Maryland Line, Oct. 15, 1781 [Ref: D-450, D-476, D-480, which listed the name as "Waring"]. On March 4, 1834, the Treasurer of Maryland was directed to pay to "Ann Warring, widow of Basil Warring, during life, quarterly, half pay of a lieutenant in consideration of the services rendered by her husband during the Revolutionary War." [Ref: Q-II:403].

WARRINGTON, James. Private, 1st Maryland Line, drafted from the Charles County militia on July 27, 1781; determined unfit for service and discharged on Oct. 30, 1781 [Ref: D-377, G-569, G-656].

WASHINGTON, George. See "James Craik" and "Richard Harrison" and "Gustavus Richard Brown" and "Robert Hanson Harrison," q.v.

WATERS, Chloe. See "Joseph Waters, of James," q.v.

WATERS, Dyer. Private, 1st Maryland Line, enlisted May 6, 1782 [Ref: D-423, D-472].

WATERS, James (1737-1808). Born on Dec. 8, 1737, a son of James and Susanna Waters, he married first to Anne Dement, married second to Draden King on Sept. 12, 1780 in Trinity Parish, and died in 1808 [Ref: J-III:3115, EE-4, EE-18]. Rendered patriotic service by providing wheat for the use of the military in November 1781 [Ref: N-456]. Aged about 41 as noted in a 1779 deposition [Ref: BB-475, DD-274]. Resident of Bryan Town Hundred in 1778 [Ref: Q-I:297]. See "William Waters" and "John Cartwright Waters" and "Thomas Waters," q.v.

WATERS, James (1759-   ). Born on May 13, 1759, a son of Joseph and Katherine Waters, of Trinity Parish [Ref: EE-17]. Private, 1st Maryland Line, enlisted April 6, 1782 [Ref: D-422, D-471].

WATERS, Jediah or Jedidiah (1763-   ). Born on July 9, 1763, a son of Joseph and Katherine Waters, of Trinity Parish [Ref: EE-17]. Private, 1st

Maryland Line, drafted from the Charles County militia and reported "lame" in June 1781 [Ref: D-376].

WATERS, John Cartwright (c1742-c1812). Private, Militia, 12th Battalion, Capt. Alexander McPherson's Company, 1777 [Ref: M-160]. "John Cartwright Waters" took the Oath of Allegiance in 1778 [Ref: L-21, J-III:3115]. "John C. Waters" was a resident of Bryan Town Hundred in 1778 [Ref: Q-I:297]. One "John Waters" was born on March 8, 1742/3, a son of James and Mary Waters, of Trinity Parish [Ref: EE-6].

WATERS, Joseph. Took the Oath of Allegiance in 1778 [Ref: L-21]. Resident of Bryan Town Hundred in 1778 [Ref: Q-I:297]. See "Jediah or Jedidiah Waters" and "James Waters" and "Zephaniah Waters," q.v.

WATERS, Joseph, of James. Took the Oath of Allegiance in 1778 [Ref: L-21]. Joseph Waters, of James married Katherine Carrico on Aug. 6, 1764 and she died on Sept. 3, 1776. He married secondly to Chloe Dent on Feb. 17, 1767 [Ref: EE-17].

WATERS, Joseph, of Joseph. Took the Oath of Allegiance in 1778 [Ref: L-21].

WATERS, Katherine. See "Jediah or Jedidiah Waters" and "James Waters" and "Zephaniah Waters" and "Joseph Waters, of James," q.v.

WATERS, Mary. See "John Waters" and "Thomas Waters," q.v.

WATERS, Milesent. See "Abednego Downing," q.v.

WATERS, Susannah. See "James Waters" and "William Waters," q.v.

WATERS, Thomas (1745-   ). Born on Aug. 11, 1745, a son of James and Mary Waters [Ref: EE-7]. Took the Oath of Allegiance in 1778 [Ref: L-21]. Resident of Bryan Town Hundred in 1778 [Ref: Q-I:297].

WATERS, William (1745-   ). Born on Aug. 15, 1745, a son of James and Susanna Waters [Ref: EE-4]. Sergeant, Militia, 12th Battalion, Capt. Alexander McPherson's Company, 1777 [Ref: M-160]. Took the Oath of Allegiance in 1778 [Ref: L-21]. Resident of Bryan Town Hundred in 1778 [Ref: Q-I:297].

WATERS, Zephaniah (1757-   ). Born on Feb. 7, 1757, a son of Joseph and Katherine Waters [Ref: EE-17]. Took the Oath of Allegiance in 1778 [Ref: L-21]. Resident of Bryan Town Hundred in 1778 [Ref: Q-I:297]. Zephaniah Waters and Elizabeth Morton Murphy were married by Rev. Hatch Dent on Jan. 1, 1786 in Trinity Parish [Ref: EE-19].

WATHEN, Baker. Private, 1st Maryland Line, enrolled and passed on July 8, 1776 [Ref: D-32]. Took the Oath of Allegiance in 1778 [Ref: L-21, AA-641].

WATHEN, Barton. Private, Militia, 12th Battalion, Capt. Alexander McPherson's Company, 1777 [Ref: M-160]. Took the Oath of Allegiance in 1778 [Ref: L-21]. Resident of Newport West Hundred in 1778 [Ref: Q-

I:297]. Private, 1st Maryland Line, drafted from the Charles County militia and in service on June 11 or 12, 1781; determined unfit for service and discharged on Oct. 30, 1781 [Ref: D-376, G-656].

WATHEN, Bennett Jr. (1741-   ). Born in November 1741, a son of Hudson and Sarah Bennett [Ref: EE-6, which listed the birth date as "-- Nov 17--" after listing his brother Martin Wathen whose birth was in 1739]. Aged about 38 as noted in a 1779 deposition [Ref: DD-274]. Private, Militia, 12th Battalion, Capt. Benjamin Lusby Corry's Company, 1777 [Ref: M-160]. Took the Oath of Allegiance in 1778 [Ref: AA-641, L-21, which latter source mistakenly listed the name as "Watkins"]. Resident of Newport West Hundred in 1778 [Ref: Q-I:297].

WATHEN, Bennett Sr. (1729-   ). Private, Militia, 12th Battalion, Capt. Benjamin Lusby Corry's Company, 1777 [Ref: M-160]. Took the Oath of Allegiance in 1778 [Ref: AA-641]. Rendered patriotic service by providing wheat for the use of the military in September 1782 [Ref: N-556, which listed the name as "Bennet Worthen"]. Rendered patriotic service by providing wheat for the use of the military in December 1782 [Ref: N-575, which listed the name as "Bennett Warthen"]. Aged about 50 as noted in a 1779 deposition [Ref: DD-274]. Resident of Newport West Hundred in 1778 [Ref: Q-I:297].

WATHEN, Clement. Took the Oath of Allegiance in 1778 [Ref: AA-641, L-21, which latter source mistakenly listed the name as "Watkins"]. Resident of Newport West Hundred in 1778 [Ref: Q-I:297].

WATHEN, Francis. Private, 1st Maryland Line, enrolled and passed on July 18, 1776 [Ref: D-32, which listed the name as "Wathan"].

WATHEN, Francis, of Barton. Private, 1st Maryland Line, enrolled and passed on July 18, 1776 [Ref: D-32, which listed the name as "Wathan"].

WATHEN Henrietta. See "John Wathen," q.v.

WATHEN, Hudson. See "Bennett Wathen, Jr." and "Martin Wathen," q.v.

WATHEN, Ignatius. Private, Militia, 12th Battalion, Capt. Walter Hanson's Company, 1777 [Ref: M-159]. Took the Oath of Allegiance in 1778 [Ref: AA-641]. Resident of Port Tobacco East Hundred in 1778 [Ref: Q-I:297]. See "John Baptist Wathen," q.v.

WATHEN, John Baker. Private, Militia, 12th Battalion, Capt. Benjamin Lusby Corry's Company, 1777 [Ref: M-160]. Resident of Newport West Hundred in 1778 [Ref: Q-I:297].

WATHEN, John Baptist (c1721-1788). Private, Militia, 12th Battalion, Capt. Benjamin Lusby Corry's Company, 1777 [Ref: M-160]. Resident of Port Tobacco East Hundred in 1778 [Ref: Q-I:297]. John Baptist Wathen was born circa 1721, married first to Sara Hanson, married second to Priscilla Luckett, and died before Oct. 27, 1788 [Ref: J-III:3116].

WATHEN, John Baptist (1740-1810). "John Wathen" wsa a sergeant in the militia, 12th Battalion, Capt. John Hanson's Company, 1777 [Ref: M-158]. "John Wathen" was born circa 1740, married Henrietta ---- and migrated to Kentucky where he died on Dec. 12, 1810 [Ref: J-III:3116]. "John B. Wathen" took the Oath of Allegiance in 1778 [Ref: AA-641]. "John B. Wathen" was a resident of Newport West Hundred in 1778 [Ref: Q-I:297]. "John Baptist Wathen" was born in 1740, a son of Ignatius Wathen and Susannah Hawkins, and married circa 1761 to Henrietta Riney, daughter of Thomas Riney. John migrated to Kentucky and bought land on Cartwright's Creek in Washington County in 1799 [Ref: Information compiled in 1997 by Carolyn Huebner Collins of South Bend, Indiana].

WATHEN, Martin (1739-   ). Born on Feb. 2, 1739, a son of Hudson and Sarah Wathen, of Trinity Parish [Ref: EE-6]. Private, Militia, 12th Battalion, Capt. Benjamin Lusby Corry's Company, 1777 [Ref: M-160, which listed the first name as "Martain"]. Took the Oath of Allegiance in 1778 [Ref: AA-641, L-21, which latter source mistakenly listed the name as "Watkins"]. See "Bennett Wathen, Jr.," q.v.

WATHEN, Nicholas. Private, Militia, 12th Battalion, Capt. John Hanson's Company, 1777 [Ref: M-159]. Took the Oath of Allegiance in 1778 [Ref: AA-641]. Resident of Port Tobacco East Hundred in 1778 [Ref: Q-I:297].

WATHEN, Sarah. See "Bennett Wathen, Jr." and "Martin Wathen," q.v.

WATHEN, William. Private, Militia, 12th Battalion, Capt. Walter Hanson's Company, 1777 [Ref: M-159]. Took the Oath of Allegiance in Charles County in 1778 [Ref: L-21, AA-641]. William Wathen, of St. Mary's County, was aged about 63 as noted in a 1782 deposition [Ref: DD-274].

WATTS, Henry. Rendered patriotic service by providing wheat for the use of the military in October 1781 [Ref: N-451].

WAYNE, John. "John Wayne" took the Oath of Allegiance in 1778 [Ref: AA-641]. "John Wain" was a resident of Port Tobacco East Hundred in 1778 [Ref: Q-I:297]. See "John Vayne," q.v.

WAYNE, William. "William Wayne" took the Oath of Allegiance in 1778 [Ref: AA-641]. "William Wain" was a resident of Port Tobacco East Hundred in 1778 [Ref: Q-I:297]. See "William Vayne," q.v.

WEAKLING, Alexander. Private, 1st Maryland Line, enrolled and passed on July 8, 1776 [Ref: D-32].

WEDDING, Chloe. See "Benjamin Burch," q.v.

WEDDING, John. Private (furnished by class for 9 months), 1st Maryland Line, by Sept. 11, 1778 [Ref: D-330]. Took the Oath of Allegiance in 1778 [Ref: AA-641, which listed the name as "Widding"]. Resident of Port Tobacco East Hundred in 1778 [Ref: Q-I:297].

WEDDING, John, of Thomas. Corporal, Militia, 26th Battalion, Capt. Benjamin Cawood's Company, 1777 [Ref: M-162, which listed the name as "Weding"]. Resident of Port Tobacco East Hundred in 1778 [Ref: Q-I:297].
WEDDING, Philip. Private, Militia, 12th Battalion, Capt. John Hanson's Company, 1777 [Ref: M-159]. Took the Oath of Allegiance in 1778 [Ref: AA-641, which listed the name as "Widding"]. Resident of Port Tobacco East Hundred in 1778 [Ref: Q-I:297].
WEDDING, Thomas. Took the Oath of Allegiance in 1778 [Ref: AA-641, which listed the name as "Widding"]. Resident of Port Tobacco East Hundred in 1778 [Ref: Q-I:297]. Rendered patriotic service by providing wheat for the use of the military in August 1781 and February 1782 [Ref: N-421, N-480].
WEDDING, Thomas Jr. (1758-1838). Private, Militia, 26th Battalion, Capt. Benjamin Cawood's Company, 1777 [Ref: M-162, which listed the name as "Weding"]. Resident of Port Tobacco East Hundred in 1778 [Ref: Q-I:297]. Thomas Wedding, Jr., was born in 1758, married (wife's name not known), and migrated to Kentucky where he died on Aug. 16, 1838 [Ref: J-III:3135].
WEEDIN, Mary. See "William Etcheson," q.v.
WEIGHT, William. See "William Wright," q.v.
WEIGHTMAN, Roger Chew. See "Samuel Hanson, of Hanson," q.v.
WELCH, Edward. Private, Militia, 26th Battalion, Capt. Richard Bennett Mitchell's Company, 1777 [Ref: M-164]. Resident of Port Tobacco West Hundred in 1778 [Ref: Q-I:297].
WELCH, George. Private, Militia, 26th Battalion, Capt. Richard Bennett Mitchell's Company, 1777 [Ref: M-164]. Private (drafted and joined the army), 1st Maryland Line, by Sept. 11, 1778 [Ref: D-330].
WELCH, Rebecca. See "Laban Haislip," q.v.
WELCH (WELSH), William. "William Welsh" took the Oath of Allegiance in 1778 [Ref: AA-641]. Rendered patriotic service by providing wheat for the use of the military in May 1783 [Ref: N-597]. "William Welch" was a resident of Port Tobacco West Hundred in 1778 [Ref: Q-I:297].
WELLS, Cordelia. See "Cornelius Wells," q.v.
WELLS, Cornelius (1751-1844). Private, 1st Maryland Line. He applied for a pension on Dec. 11, 1826 in Washington, D. C., stating that he was born in St. Mary's County, Maryland in 1751 and enlisted at Port Tobacco in Charles County during the Revolutionary War. After the war he lived in Prince William County, Virginia and Fairfax County, Virginia before moving to Washington, D. C. His widow applied for a pension (W2503) on Aug. 20, 1853, aged 38 *[sic]*, stating that Cornelius had died on or about July 22, 1844. Cornelius Wells married Sarah A. Hiller on Nov. 8, 1839 in

Washington, D. C. His children by a former wife (name not stated) were Harriet R. Kane (born 1791), Susannah M. Sears (born 1796), and Thomas C. Wells (born 1808). The children of Cornelius and his second wife Sarah were Cornelia Wells (born Jan. 2, 1842) and Cordelia Wells (born Jan. 27, 1846) *[sic]*. Sarah Wells married John Young by 1857 and lived in Alexandria County, Virginia [Ref: V-III:3740].

WELLS, Sarah. See "Cornelius Wells," q.v.

WELLS, Thomas. See "Cornelius Wells," q.v.

WEST, Thomas. Private, Militia, 12th Battalion, Capt. Peter Wood's Company, 1777 [Ref: M-161].

WHEATLEY, Bennett (Burnett). "Bennett Wheatley" took the Oath of Allegiance in 1778 [Ref: L-21]. "Burnett Wheatley" was a resident of Bryan Town Hundred in 1778 [Ref: Q-I:297].

WHEATLEY, Francis (1724-   ). Took the Oath of Allegiance in 1778 [Ref: L-21]. Rendered patriotic service by providing wheat for the use of the military in July 1781 [Ref: N-411, which listed the name as "Wheatty"]. Aged about 57 as noted in a 1781 deposition [Ref: DD-275]. There was also a Francis Wheatley who was aged about 67 as noted in a 1767 deposition [Ref: DD-275]. Resident of Bryan Town Hundred in 1778 [Ref: Q-I:297].

WHEATLEY, John. Two men by this name were privates in the militia, 12th Battalion, in 1777: one in Capt. Peter Wood's Company, and one in Capt. Alexander McPherson's Company, 1777 [Ref: M-160, M-161, which listed the name as "Wheatly"]. One took the Oath of Allegiance in 1778 [Ref: L-21]. Resident of Bryan Town Hundred in 1778 [Ref: Q-I:297].

WHEATLEY, Richard. Private, Militia, 12th Battalion, Capt. Peter Wood's Company, 1777 [Ref: M-161, which listed the name as "Wheatly"].

WHEATLEY, Silvester. Took the Oath of Allegiance in 1778 [Ref: L-21, which listed the name as "Silvert Wheatley" and AA-641, which listed the name as "Selvester Whately"].

WHEATLEY, Thomas. Private, Militia, 12th Battalion, Capt. Peter Wood's Company, 1777 [Ref: M-161, which listed the name as "Wheatly"]. Resident of William & Mary Lower Hundred in 1778 [Ref: Q-I:297].

WHEATLEY, William. "William Wheatly" took the Oath of Allegiance in 1778 [Ref: L-21]. Resident of Benedict Hundred in 1778 [Ref: Q-I:297]. "William Whitely" was a private in the Maryland Line, enrolled and passed on July 20, 1776 [Ref: D-33].

WHEATON, Isaac. Took the Oath of Allegiance in 1778 [Ref: L-21].

WHEELER, Anne. See "Giles Thomas," q.v.

WHEELER, Basil. Private (furnished by class for 9 months), 1st Maryland Line, by Sept. 11, 1778 [Ref: D-330].

WHEELER, Benedict. Private, Militia, 26th Battalion, Capt. Richard Bennett Mitchell's Company, 1777 [Ref: M-164]. Took the Oath of Allegiance in 1778 [Ref: L-21]. Resident of Port Tobacco West Hundred in 1778 [Ref: Q-I:297]. Rendered patriotic service by providing wheat for the use of the military in May 1783 [Ref: N-598].

WHEELER, Benjamin. Private, Militia, 26th Battalion, Capt. Richard Bennett Mitchell's Company, 1777 [Ref: M-164]. Resident of Port Tobacco West Hundred in 1778 [Ref: Q-I:297]. Gave a deposition in 1781 pertaining to his inability to perform military service due to family obligations [Ref: Z-208].

WHEELER, Butler. Took the Oath of Allegiance in 1778 [Ref: L-21].

WHEELER, Clement. Private, Militia, 26th Battalion, Capt. Richard Bennett Mitchell's Company, 1777 [Ref: M-164]. Took the Oath of Allegiance in 1778 [Ref: L-21]. Resident of Port Tobacco West Hundred in 1778 [Ref: Q-I:297]. Rendered patriotic service by providing wheat for the use of the military in May 1783 [Ref: N-598].

WHEELER, Ignatius. Two men by this name took the Oath of Allegiance in 1778 [Ref: AA-641, L-21]. One was a resident of Port Tobacco West Hundred in 1778 [Ref: Q-I:297].

WHEELER, Ignatius, of Clement. Private, Militia, 26th Battalion, Capt. Richard Bennett Mitchell's Company, 1777 [Ref: M-164, which listed the name as "Igns. Wheeler, of Clems."].

WHEELER, Ignatius, of Richard. Private, Militia, 26th Battalion, Capt. Richard Bennett Mitchell's Company, 1777 [Ref: M-164].

WHEELER, Joseph. Memorialist and Militiaman, Pomonkey Company, after March 6, 1776 [Ref: M-158, Y-II:26]. Private, Militia, 26th Battalion, Capt. Richard Bennett Mitchell's Company, 1777 [Ref: M-164]. Took the Oath of Allegiance in 1778 [Ref: L-21]. Resident of Pomonkey Hundred in 1778 [Ref: Q-I:297].

WHEELER, Joshua. Took the Oath of Allegiance in 1778 [Ref: AA-641]. One Joshua Wheeler was a resident of Pomonkey Hundred and another was a resident of Port Tobacco West Hundred in 1778 [Ref: Q-I:297].

WHEELER, Leonard. Private, Militia, 26th Battalion, Capt. Robert Sinnett's Company, 1777 [Ref: M-164]. Took the Oath of Allegiance in 1778 [Ref: L-21]. Resident of Port Tobacco West Hundred in 1778 [Ref: Q-I:297].

WHEELER, Luke. Memorialist and Militiaman, Pomonkey Company, after March 6, 1776 [Ref: M-158, Y-II:26]. Private, Militia, 26th Battalion, Capt. Richard Bennett Mitchell's Company, 1777 [Ref: M-165]. Took the Oath of Allegiance in 1778 [Ref: L-21, AA-641]. Resident of Pomonkey Hundred in 1778 [Ref: Q-I:297]. Rendered patriotic service by providing wheat for the use of the military in April and October 1782 [Ref: N-499, N-563].

WHEELER, Thomas. Private, Militia, 26th Battalion, Capt. Richard Bennett Mitchell's Company, 1777; listed as an invalid (disabled) soldier [Ref: M-165]. Took the Oath of Allegiance in 1778 [Ref: L-21]. Resident of Port Tobacco West Hundred in 1778 [Ref: Q-I:297].

WHEELER, William. Private, Militia, 26th Battalion, Capt. Richard Bennett Mitchell's Company, 1777 [Ref: M-164]. Took the Oath of Allegiance in 1778 [Ref: L-21]. Resident of Port Tobacco West Hundred in 1778 [Ref: Q-I:297].

WHELAN, Ann. Rendered patriotic service by providing wheat for the use of the military in December 1782 [Ref: N-576].

WHELAN, Thomas. Rendered patriotic service by providing wheat for the use of the military in June 1782 [Ref: N-525].

WHELAN, William. Rendered patriotic service by providing wheat for the use of the military in April 1782 [Ref: N-498].

WHITACRE, Abigail. See "Jesse Noland," q.v.

WHITAKER, Aquilla. See "Cornelius Bryan," q.v.

WHITCOMB, John. Private, 4th Maryland Line, by Jan. 1, 1782 [Ref: D-461].

WHITCOMBE, Notley. Private, 1st Maryland Line, drafted from the Charles County militia and in service on June 11, 1781 [Ref: D-376, G-569]. Private, 1st Maryland Line, Capt. Edward Prall's Company, Jan. 1, 1782, and reported sick in Virginia [Ref: D-433, which listed the name as "Witcomb"].

WHITE, Isle of. See "Isle of Wight," q.v.

WHITE, Jonathan. Private, Militia, 12th Battalion, Capt. John Thomas' Company, 1777 [Ref: M-161]. Private (furnished by class for 9 months), 1st Maryland Line, by Sept. 11, 1778 [Ref: D-330]. Resident of Benedict Hundred in 1778 [Ref: Q-I:297].

WHITE, Richard. Private, Militia, 26th Battalion, Capt. Thomas H. Marshall's Company, 1777 [Ref: M-163].

WHITE, William. Private, Militia, 12th Battalion, Capt. John Thomas' Company, 1777 [Ref: M-161]. Resident of Port Tobacco East Hundred in 1778 [Ref: Q-I:297].

WHITE, William (1700-   ). Took the Oath of Allegiance in 1778 [Ref: L-21, AA-641]. Aged about 76 as noted in a 1776 deposition [Ref: DD-275]. Resident of Benedict Hundred in 1778 [Ref: Q-I:297].

WHITELY, William. See "William Wheatley," q.v.

WHITLER, Johanna. See "Thomas Davis," q.v.

WHITLER, Susan. See "William Marshall," q.v.

WHITTEN, Joannah. See "Thomas Davis," q.v.
WHITTER, Buckler. Took the Oath of Allegiance in 1778 [Ref: AA-641].
WHITTER, William. Took the Oath of Allegiance in 1778 [Ref: AA-641]. Resident of Port Tobacco East Hundred in 1778 [Ref: Q-I:297].
WIER, Francis. Private, 1st Maryland Line, enrolled and passed on July 19, 1776 [Ref: D-31]. See "Francis Ware," q.v.
WIGHT, Isle of. Took the Oath of Allegiance in 1778 [Ref: AA-641]. Resident of Port Tobacco East Hundred in 1778 [Ref: Q-I:297, which listed the name as "Isle of White"].
WIGHT, Isle of, Jr. Private, Militia, 26th Battalion, Capt. Benjamin Cawood's Company, 1777 [Ref: M-162, which listed the name as "Isle Wright (Whight?), Junr." and X-72, which listed the name as Isle Wight, Jr."]. Took the Oath of Allegiance in 1778 [Ref: AA-641]. Resident of Port Tobacco East Hundred in 1778 [Ref: Q-I:297, which listed the name as "Isle of White"].
WILDER, Benjamin. Took the Oath of Allegiance in 1778 [Ref: L-21]. Resident of William & Mary Lower Hundred in 1778 [Ref: Q-I:297].
WILDER, Edward. Took the Oath of Allegiance in 1778 [Ref: L-21]. Resident of William & Mary Lower Hundred in 1778 [Ref: Q-I:297]. Appointed the Coroner of Charles County on April 27, 1782, in the room of Moses Hobart, deceased [Ref: I-149]. Edward Wilder married Margaret [Marget] Compton on Jan. 31, 1769 [Ref: EE-13].
WILDER, James. Private, Militia, 12th Battalion, Capt. Jonathan Yates' Company, 1777 [Ref: M-162]. Took the Oath of Allegiance in 1778 [Ref: L-21, AA-641]. Resident of William & Mary Lower Hundred in 1778 [Ref: Q-I:297].
WILDER, John. Took the Oath of Allegiance in 1778 [Ref: AA-641]. Resident of William & Mary Lower Hundred in 1778 [Ref: Q-I:297]. Rendered patriotic service by providing clothing for the use of the military in February 1778 [Ref: Y-II:234].
WILDER, John B. Private, Militia, 12th Battalion, Capt. Jonathan Yates' Company, 1777 [Ref: M-162]. Took the Oath of Allegiance in 1778 [Ref: L-21, AA-641]. Resident of William & Mary Lower Hundred in 1778 [Ref: Q-I:297].
WILKERSTON, William. Took the Oath of Allegiance in 1778 [Ref: L-21, AA-641]. Resident of Benedict Hundred in 1778 [Ref: Q-I:297].
WILKINSON, Alexander. Private, Militia, 26th Battalion, Capt. Samuel Smallwood's Company, 1777 [Ref: M-165, which listed the name as "Wilkerson"]. Took the Oath of Allegiance in 1778 [Ref: L-21, which listed the name as "Wilkinson" and AA-641, which listed the name as "Wilkerson"]. Rendered patriotic service by providing wheat for the use of

the military in April 1783 [Ref: N-593, which listed the name as "Wilkenson"]. "Alex. Wilkenston" was a resident of Port Tobacco Upper Hundred in 1778 [Ref: Q-I:297].

WILKINSON, Barbara. See "William Mackall Wilkinson," q.v.

WILKINSON, Eliner. See "William McPherson," q.v.

WILKINSON, George. See "William Mackall Wilkinson," q.v.

WILKINSON, Jane. See "William Mackall Wilkinson," q.v.

WILKINSON, Sarah. See "William Mackall Wilkinson," q.v.

WILKINSON, Walter. Private, Militia, 26th Battalion, Capt. Samuel Smallwood's Company, 1777 [Ref: M-165, which listed the name as "Wilkerson"]. Took the Oath of Allegiance in 1778 [Ref: L-21, which listed the name as "Wilkinson" and AA-641, which listed the name as "Wilkerson"]. "Walter Wilkenson" was a resident of Port Tobacco Upper Hundred in 1778 [Ref: Q-I:297]. Rendered patriotic service by providing wheat for the use of the military in April 1783 [Ref: N-593].

WILKINSON, William Mackall (1752-1799). Son of William Wilkinson and Barbara Mackall, he married Ann Herbert Dent (1756-1813), daughter of Gen. John Dent and Sarah Marshall, and had these children: George Francis Wilkinson; William Wilkinson; Jane Wilkinson; Barbara Wilkinson; and, Sarah Marshall Wilkinson (1779-1853) married Dr. Edward Briscoe (1769-1815) in 1800 [Ref: P-II:890, S-3107, S-3134, S-3136, which latter sources have some variation in the dates of birth and death]. William M. Wilkinson was born on Feb. 12, 1752, married Ann Herbert Dent, and died on March 12, 1799 [Ref: J-III:3221]. Served in the Lower House of the Maryland Legislature, 1782-1783. Captain, Militia, 12th Battalion, commissioned May 9, 1778 [Ref: M-137, E-72, P-II:890]. See "John Dent," q.v.

WILLETT, Charles (c1742-1831). Private, 1st Maryland Line, drafted from the militia and in service on June 11 or 12, 1781 [Ref: D-376]. One Charles Willett was born circa 1742, married Martha Elliott Wallingford, and migrated to Kentucky where he died on April 15, 1831 [Ref: J-III:3223]. He may have been related to a "Charles Willet" who was aged about 23 as noted in a 1745 deposition in Charles County [Ref: DD-276]. It must also be noted that the muster rolls of the Maryland Line indicate that a Charles Willet died on Sept. 19, 1782 [Ref: D-561]. Additional research may be necessary before drawing conclusions.

WILLETT, Edward (1761-1837). Ensign, 1st Maryland Line. Edward Willett was born in 1761, married Eleanor Fisher, and migrated to Kentucky where he died on July 3, 1837 [Ref: J-III:3223].

WILLETT, George (1750-   ). Corporal, Militia, 26th Battalion, Capt. Samuel Smallwood's Company, 1777 [Ref: M-165, which listed the name as "Willitt"]. Took the Oath of Allegiance in 1778 [Ref: AA-641]. Aged about 24 as noted in a 1774 deposition [Ref: DD-276]. Resident of Port Tobacco Upper Hundred in 1778 [Ref: Q-I:297].

WILLETT, Richard. Took the Oath of Allegiance in 1778 [Ref: L-21]. Resident of Port Tobacco Upper Hundred in 1778 [Ref: Q-I:297]. Rendered patriotic service by providing wheat for the use of the military in February, May, and September 1782 [Ref: N-479, N-514, N-556, which also listed the name as "Willet"].

WILLIAMS, Ann. See "Thomas Williams," q.v.

WILLIAMS, Charles. Private, 3rd Maryland Line, enrolled by Capt. Joseph Marbury by May 24, 1780 [Ref: F-181].

WILLIAMS, Ellener. See "Laban Haislip," q.v.

WILLIAMS, Esther. See "Justinian Williams," q.v.

WILLIAMS, Hudson. Private, Militia, 26th Battalion, Capt. William Winter's Company, 1777 [Ref: M-165].

WILLIAMS, James. See "Justinian Williams," q.v.

WILLIAMS, John. Private, 1st Maryland Line, enrolled and passed on July 8, 1776 [Ref: D-32]. Private, Militia, 12th Battalion, Capt. John Hanson's Company, 1777 [Ref: M-159]. Took the Oath of Allegiance in 1778 [Ref: L-21, AA-641]. Private (furnished by class for 9 months), 1st Maryland Line, by Sept. 11, 1778 [Ref: D-330]. Rendered patriotic service by providing wheat for the use of the military in November and December 1781 [Ref: N-457, N-461]. "John Williams" was a resident of Port Tobacco East Hundred, "John Williams" was a resident of Pomonkey Hundred, and "John Williams, Sr." and "John Williams, Jr." were residents of Newport West Hundred in 1778 [Ref: Q-I:297]. Additional research may be necessary before drawing conclusions.

WILLIAMS, John (1761-1833). Private, Virginia Line. He applied for a pension in Surry County, Virginia on Sept. 24, 1832, aged 71, stating that he was born in Charles County, Maryland and lived in Surry County, Virginia at the time of his enlistment. He died on Aug. 9, 1833 and his widow Nancy Williams (nee Holloway) applied for a pension (W26060) on June 26, 1854, aged 79, stating they had married on Nov. 1, 1824 and John died leaving children Mary Ann Williams, Susanna Williams, and Nancy Williams [Ref: V-III:3861].

WILLIAMS, Justinian (1745/6-   ). Born on Jan. 19(?), 1745/6, son of James and Esther Williams, of Trinity Parish [Ref: EE-5]. Private, Militia, 12th Battalion, Capt. Benjamin Lusby Corry's Company, 1777 [Ref: M-160]. Took the Oath of Allegiance in 1778 [Ref: L-21].

WILLIAMS, Mary Ann. See "John Williams," q.v.

WILLIAMS, Nancy. See "John Williams," q.v.

WILLIAMS, Nathaniel. Took the Oath of Allegiance in 1778 [Ref: L-21]. See "Samuel Wright," q.v.

WILLIAMS, Samuel. Private, Militia, 12th Battalion, Capt. John Hanson's Company, 1777 [Ref: M-159].

WILLIAMS, Susanna. See "John Williams," q.v.

WILLIAMS, Thomas (1745-   ). Born on Aug. 2, 1745, twin of Elizabeth, and son of Thomas and Ann Williams, of Trinity Parish [Ref: EE-6]. One Thomas Williams was a corporal in the 1st Maryland Line, 1777-1778, and there were two men named Thomas Williams who were privates in the 4th Maryland Line, 1777-1778 [Ref: D-173, D-178, D-179]. Additional research will be necessary before drawing conclusions.

WILLIAMS, William. Private, Militia, 12th Battalion, Capt. Benjamin Lusby Corry's Company, 1777 [Ref: M-160].

WILLIAMS, William (1722-   ). Took the Oath of Allegiance in 1778 [Ref: L-21]. Aged about 41 as noted in a 1763 deposition [Ref: DD-276].

WILLIAMS, Zachariah. Private, Militia, 12th Battalion, Capt. Benjamin Lusby Corry's Company, 1777 [Ref: M-160].

WILLS, Edward. Private, Militia, 12th Battalion, Capt. John Parnham's Company, 1777 [Ref: M-161, which listed the name as "Edward Willis(?)"].

WILLS, John. Took the Oath of Allegiance in 1778 [Ref: L-21].

WILLS, John Baptist. Private, Militia, 26th Battalion, Capt. William McPherson's Company, 1777 [Ref: M-163]. Took the Oath of Allegiance in 1778 [Ref: AA-641]. Resident of Port Tobacco East Hundred in 1778 [Ref: Q-I:297].

WILMON, Edward. Private, 1st Maryland Line, enrolled and passed on July 19, 1776 [Ref: D-31].

WILSON, Abraham. Private, Militia, 12th Battalion, Capt. Peter Wood's Company, 1777 [Ref: M-161]. Resident of Benedict Hundred in 1778 [Ref: Q-I:297].

WILSON, Josiah. See "George Walls," q.v.

WILSON, Lucy. See "Edward Ward," q.v.

WILSON, Mary. See "Daniel Barron," q.v.

WILSON, Nancy. See "Traverse Sutherland," q.v.

WILSON, William Alexander. Private, Militia, 26th Battalion, Capt. Samuel Smallwood's Company, 1777 [Ref: M-165, which listed the name as "Wm. Alex Wilson"]. Resident of Port Tobacco Upper Hundred in 1778 [Ref: Q-I:297].

WIMSATT, Susan. See "John Manning," q.v.

WINNETT, Mark. Took the Oath of Allegiance in 1778 [Ref: L-21, AA-641]. Resident of Bryan Town Hundred in 1778 [Ref: Q-I:297].

WINSOR, Ignatius. Private, Militia, 26th Battalion, Capt. Samuel Smallwood's Company, 1777 [Ref: M-165].

WINSOR, Joseph Sr. Rendered patriotic service by providing wheat for the use of the military in September 1782 [Ref: N-555, which listed the name as "Winzor"]. Resident of Port Tobacco Upper Hundred in 1778 [Ref: Q-I:297, which listed the name as "Winson"].

WINSOR, Joseph Jr. Private, Militia, 26th Battalion, Capt. Samuel Smallwood's Company, 1777 [Ref: M-165]. Gave a deposition in 1781 pertaining to his inability to perform military service due to family obligations [Ref: Z-208]. Resident of Port Tobacco Upper Hundred in 1778 [Ref: Q-I:297, which listed the name as "Winson"].

WINTER, Charles. Rendered patriotic service by providing wheat for the use of the military in October 1781 [Ref: N-449].

WINTER, Elizabeth. See "Walter Winter," q.v.

WINTER, John. Took the Oath of Allegiance in 1778 [Ref: L-21]. See "Walter Winter," q.v.

WINTER, Walter (1745-   ). Captain, Militia, 26th Battalion, Feb. 26, 1776 [Ref: M-139, A-186, A-206, Y-II:23]. Took the Oath of Allegiance in 1778 [Ref: L-21]. "Walter Winters" was appointed a Justice of the Peace on Nov. 21, 1778 [Ref: E-249]. "Walter Winter" was aged about 34 as noted in a 1779 deposition [Ref: DD-276]. Resident of Newport West Hundred in 1778 [Ref: Q-I:297]. See the other "Walter Winter," q.v.

WINTER, Walter (1747-   ). Born on Nov. 7, 1747, a son of John and Elizabeth Winter, of Trinity Parish [Ref: EE-6]. Sergeant, Militia, Capt. Francis Mastin's Company, 26th Battalion, March 19, 1776 [Ref: M-158, K-1814]. "Walter Winters, of John" was appointed a Justice of the Peace on Nov. 19, 1779 and Jan. 17, 1782 [Ref: F-19, I-45]. See the other "Walter Winter," q.v.

WINTER, William Jr. Captain, Militia, 26th Battalion, Feb. 26, 1776 [Ref: M-139, M-165, A-186, A-206, Y-II:23]. Rendered patriotic service by providing clothing for the use of the military in February 1778 [Ref: Y-II:235]. Took the Oath of Allegiance in 1778 [Ref: L-21, AA-641]. William Winter, Jr., was born in 1760 *[sic]*, married Catharine Hooe, and died in 1787 [Ref: J-III:3264].

WINTER, William Sr. (1713-   ). Took the Oath of Allegiance in 1778 [Ref: L-21]. Rendered patriotic service by providing wheat for the use of the military in December 1782 [Ref: N-573]. Aged about 51 as noted in a 1764 deposition [Ref: DD-276].

WISEMAN, James. Private, Militia, 12th Battalion, Capt. John Parnham's Company, 1777 [Ref: M-160, which listed the name as "James Waseman(?)"]. Resident of Newport East Hundred in 1778 [Ref: Q-I:297].

WISEMAN, Thomas. Private, 4th Maryland Line, enlisted Jan. 12, 1776 [Ref: D-12]. Private, 1st Maryland Line, enlisted Dec. 10, 1776, and reportedly "deserted" at the Battle of Camden in South Carolina on Aug. 16, 1780 [Ref: D-173].

WITHERINGTON, Benjamin. "Benjamin Witherington" took the Oath of Allegiance in 1778 [Ref: AA-641]. "Benjamin Whitherington" was a resident of Bryan Town Hundred in 1778 [Ref: Q-I:297]. "Benjamin Wetherton" was a private in the militia, 12th Battalion, Capt. Henry Clarkson's Company, 1777 [Ref: M-159].

WITHERINGTON, Richard. "Richard Witherington" took the Oath of Allegiance in 1778 [Ref: AA-641]. "Richard Whitherington" was a resident of Bryan Town Hundred in 1778 [Ref: Q-I:297]. "Richard Weatherton" was a private in the militia, 12th Battalion, Capt. Henry Clarkson's Company, 1777 [Ref: M-159].

WITHERINGTON, Thomas (1731-   ). "Thomas Worthinton or Wortherington" took the Oath of Allegiance in 1778 [Ref: L-21, AA-641]. "Thomas Witherington" was aged about 44 as noted in a 1775 deposition [Ref: DD-276]. "Thomas Whitherington" was a resident of Bryan Town Hundred in 1778 [Ref: Q-I:297].

WITTELL, Richard. Took the Oath of Allegiance in 1778 [Ref: AA-641].

WOOD, Anne. See "Ralph Briscoe," q.v.

WOOD, Benjamin. Private, Militia, 12th Battalion, Capt. Peter Wood's Company, 1777 [Ref: M-159]. Took the Oath of Allegiance in 1778 [Ref: L-21]. Resident of Benedict Hundred in 1778 [Ref: Q-I:297].

WOOD, Benjamin. Private, Militia, 12th Battalion, Capt. Henry Clarkson's Company, 1777 [Ref: M-161]. Took the Oath of Allegiance in 1778 [Ref: L-21]. Resident of Bryan Town Hundred in 1778 [Ref: Q-I:297].

WOOD, Benjamin C. (1763-1838). Private, 1st Maryland Line. He applied for a pension (S11890) on Dec. 9, 1833 in Washington, D. C., stating that he was born in 1763 in Charles County, Maryland and lived there at the time of his enlistment. After the war he moved to Alexandria, Virginia and later to Washington, D. C. where he died on Feb. 18, 1838 [Ref: V-III:3925].

WOOD, Dorothy. See "John Hawkins," q.v.

WOOD, Gerard (1754-1822). Corporal, Militia, 12th Battalion, Capt. John Parnham's Company, 1777 [Ref: M-160]. Took the Oath of Allegiance in 1778 [Ref: L-21]. Resident of Newport East Hundred in 1778 [Ref: Q-I:297]. "Gerrard Wood" was a private in the Maryland Line, drafted from the Charles County militia and in service on June 11 or 12, 1781 [Ref: D-376]. "Gerad Wood" was born in 1754, served as a surgeon's mate, married Winifred Chunn, and died in November 1822 [Ref: J-III:3277].

WOOD, Henry (deceased by May 1779). Private, Militia, 26th Battalion, Capt. Richard Bennett Mitchell's Company, 1777 [Ref: M-165].
WOOD, Ignatius. Private, Militia, 26th Battalion, Capt. Richard Bennett Mitchell's Company, 1777 [Ref: M-165]. Took the Oath of Allegiance in 1778 [Ref: AA-641].
WOOD, James. Took the Oath of Allegiance in 1778 [Ref: AA-641]. Rendered patriotic service by providing wheat for the use of the military in May 1782 [Ref: N-507].
WOOD, James Greenfield. Took the Oath of Allegiance in 1778 [Ref: AA-641, L-21, which latter source listed the name as "Woods"]. Resident of Benedict Hundred in 1778 [Ref: Q-I:297].
WOOD, John Wilder. Private, 1st Maryland Line, enrolled and passed on July 8, 1776 [Ref: D-32].
WOOD, Leonard. Corporal, Militia, 12th Battalion, Capt. John Parnham's Company, 1777 [Ref: M-160]. Took the Oath of Allegiance in 1778 [Ref: L-21]. Resident of Newport East Hundred in 1778 [Ref: Q-I:297]. Rendered patriotic service by providing wheat for the use of the military in December 1782 [Ref: N-575].
WOOD, Margaret. See "Gabriel Moran," q.v.
WOOD, Peter. Captain, Militia, 12th Battalion, July 5, 1777 [Ref: M-139, M-161]. Resident of Benedict Hundred in 1778 [Ref: Q-I:297].
WOOD, Peter. Second Lieutenant, Militia, 12th Battalion, Capt. Peter Wood's Company, 1777 [Ref: M-161].
WOOD, Phillip. Took the Oath of Allegiance in 1778 [Ref: L-21]. Resident of Newport East Hundred in 1778 [Ref: Q-I:297].
WOODBURN, William. Private, 1st Maryland Line, enrolled and passed on July 20, 1776 [Ref: D-33].
WOODWARD, Henry. Private, Militia, 26th Battalion, Capt. Francis Mastin's Company, 1777 [Ref: M-163, which listed the name as "Woodword"].
WOODWARD, Henry (1706-   ). Took the Oath of Allegiance in 1780 [Ref: O-124, which listed the name as "Woodyard"]. Aged about 66 as noted in a 1772 deposition. An earlier deposition in 1758 mentioned his father John Woodward and stated that his mother (not named) was a daughter of Gerrard Brown and her first husband was Richard Newton. Also, his grandmother (not named) was the widow of Gerrard Brown when she married second to Dr. John Cornish [Ref: DD-277].
WOODWARD, James (deceased by October 1779). Private, Militia, Capt. Francis Mastin's Company, 26th Battalion, March 19, 1776 [Ref: M-158, K-1814].

WOODWARD, Jesse. Private, Militia, 26th Battalion, Capt. Francis Mastin's Company, 1777 [Ref: M-164, which listed the name twice on the rolls]. Private (furnished by class for 9 months), 1st Maryland Line, by Sept. 11, 1778 [Ref: D-330].
WOODWARD, John. See "Henry Woodward," q.v.
WOODWARD, Richard. Private, Militia, 26th Battalion, Capt. Francis Mastin's Company, 1777 [Ref: M-164].
WOODWARD, Richard (1727-   ). Took the Oath of Allegiance in 1778 [Ref: L-21, AA-641]. Resident of Durham Lower Hundred in 1778 [Ref: Q-I:297]. Aged about 45 as noted in a 1772 deposition [Ref: DD-277, which listed the name as "Woodyard"].
WOODWARD, Samuel. Private, Militia, 26th Battalion, Capt. William Winter's Company, 1777 [Ref: M-165]. Rendered patriotic service by providing wheat for the use of the military in October 1781 and May 1783 [Ref: N-450, N-598].
WOODYARD, Henry. See "Henry Woodward," q.v.
WOODYARD, Richard. See "Richard Woodward," q.v.
WORDEN, Richard. See "Richard Warden," q.v.
WORTHINGTON, Nicholas. See "William Hanson McPherson," q.v.
WRIGHT, Benjamin. Private (drafted and joined the army), 1st Maryland Line, by Sept. 11, 1778, when the muster roll noted he was "fined by court martial." [Ref: D-330].
WRIGHT, George. Took the Oath of Allegiance in 1778 [Ref: L-21].
WRIGHT, James. Private, 1st Maryland Line, drafted from the Charles County militia, in service on June 11 or 12, 1781 and discharged on Dec. 3, 1781 [Ref: D-376, G-569, I-10].
WRIGHT, John. Took the Oath of Allegiance in 1778 [Ref: AA-641]. Resident of Durham Lower Hundred in 1778 [Ref: Q-I:297].
WRIGHT, John Lugar. Corporal, Militia, 26th Battalion, Capt. William Winter's Company, 1777 [Ref: M-165]. "John Lugar Wright" took the Oath of Allegiance in 1778 [Ref: L-21]. "Lugar Wright" was a resident of Durham Lower Hundred in 1778 [Ref: Q-I:297]. Rendered patriotic service by providing wheat for the use of the military in February 1782 [Ref: N-478]. See "John Right," q.v.
WRIGHT, Robert. Private, Militia, 26th Battalion, Capt. William Winter's Company, 1777 [Ref: M-165]. Took the Oath of Allegiance in 1778 [Ref: L-21, AA-641]. Resident of Durham Lower Hundred in 1778 [Ref: Q-I:297].
WRIGHT, Samuel. Private, Militia, 26th Battalion, Capt. William Winter's Company, 1777 [Ref: M-165]. Took the Oath of Allegiance in 1778 [Ref: AA-641]. Resident of Durham Lower Hundred in 1778 [Ref: Q-I:297].

Samuel Wright was a private in the Maryland Line who was drafted from the Charles County militia and reported sick on July 27, 1781 [Ref: D-377]. In August 1781, Mary Wright petitioned the Governor and Council of Maryland stating "that your Petitioner being a Widdo who has five children to support being very poor, and that her son Samuel Wright who is all her dependance for Assistance was on the 27th of July last Drafted into the Continental Army. Also that he the said Samuel haveing been for some time past in a bad State of health therefore your petitioner Hopes your Honours will take her Destressed Condition into Your consideration and release her son Samuel Wright, Jr., the said Draft and she as in Duty bound will pray." Her petition was supported by Jo. H. Harrison, Nathaniel Williams, Caleb Hudson, Burdit Ratliff, and William Davies who "being acquainted with the petitioner hereby certify that the facts set fourth in the above petition is the truth." [Ref: H-464, H-465]. It must also be noted that the muster rolls of the Maryland Line indicate that a Samuel Wright died on Jan. 20, 1782 [Ref: D-561]. Additional research may be necessary before drawing conclusions. See "Samuel Right," q.v.

WRIGHT, William. Corporal, Militia, 26th Battalion, Capt. Benjamin Cawood's Company, 1777 [Ref: M-162, which listed the name as "Wm. Wright(?)" and X-72, which listed the name as "William Weight"].

WYNN, Mary. See "Bayne Smallwood," q.v.

YATES, Charles. Private, Militia, 12th Battalion, Capt. Jonathan Yates' Company, 1777 [Ref: X-70, but was omitted from the list in Reference M-162].

YATES, Elizabeth. See "George Dent" and "George Dent, Jr.," q.v.

YATES, John. Took the Oath of Allegiance in 1778 [Ref: L-21, AA-641]. On Oct. 17, 1781, the Council of Maryland ordered "that the Treasurer pay to John Yeates one thousand pounds ... to be delivered over to the Commissary of Charles County." [Ref: G-645]. Rendered patriotic service by providing wheat for the use of the military in November 1781 and December 1782 [Ref: N-457, N-577].

YATES, Jonathan. Captain, Militia, 12th Battalion, Feb. 26, 1776, and Major, Jan. 19, 1781 [Ref: M-140, M-162, A-186, A-206, G-280, Y-II:23]. Rendered patriotic service by providing clothing for the use of the military in February 1778 [Ref: Y-II:234]. Resident of William & Mary Lower Hundred in 1778 [Ref: Q-I:297]. Appointed a Justice of the Peace on Nov. 19, 1779 [Ref: F-19, which listed the name as "Yeates"].

YATES, Theophilus. Took the Oath of Allegiance in 1778 [Ref: AA-641]. Resident of William & Mary Upper Hundred in 1778 [Ref: Q-I:297].

YATES, Thomas. Private, 1st Maryland Line, 1781, who was paid for his services on April 6, 1782 [Ref: I-123, which listed the name as "Yeates"].

YOUNG, Robert. Private, Militia, 12th Battalion, Capt. John Hanson's Company, 1777 [Ref: M-159]. Resident of Port Tobacco East Hundred in 1778 [Ref: Q-I:297]. Justice who administered (and took) the Oath of Allegiance in 1778 [Ref: L-21, AA-641]. Rendered patriotic service by providing clothing for the use of the military in February 1778 [Ref: Y-II:234]. Appointed a Judge of the Orphans Court for Charles County on May 15, 1778 and Nov. 19, 1779 and Jan. 17, 1782 [Ref: E-84, F-19, F-42, I-46]. Appointed a Justice of the Peace on Nov. 21, 1778 and Nov. 19, 1779 and Jan. 17, 1782 [Ref: E-249, F-19, I-45].

YOUNG, John. See "Cornelius Wells," q.v.

Other books by the author:

A Closer Look at St. John's Parish Registers [Baltimore County, Maryland], 1701-1801
A Collection of Maryland Church Records
A Guide to Genealogical Research in Maryland: 5th Edition, Revised and Enlarged
Abstracts of the Ledgers and Accounts of the Bush Store and Rock Run Store, 1759-1771
Abstracts of the Orphans Court Proceedings of Harford County, 1778-1800
Abstracts of Wills, Harford County, Maryland, 1800-1805
Baltimore City [Maryland] Deaths and Burials, 1834-1840
Baltimore County, Maryland, Overseers of Roads, 1693-1793
Bastardy Cases in Baltimore County, Maryland, 1673-1783
Bastardy Cases in Harford County, Maryland, 1774-1844
Bible and Family Records of Harford County, Maryland Families: Volume V
Children of Harford County: Indentures and Guardianships, 1801-1830
Colonial Delaware Soldiers and Sailors, 1638-1776
Colonial Families of the Eastern Shore of Maryland
Volumes 5, 6, 7, 8, 9, 11, 12, 13, 14, and 16
Colonial Maryland Soldiers and Sailors, 1634-1734
Dr. John Archer's First Medical Ledger, 1767-1769, Annotated Abstracts
Early Anglican Records of Cecil County
Early Harford Countians, Individuals Living in Harford County, Maryland in Its Formative Years
Volume 1: A to K, Volume 2: L to Z, and Volume 3: Supplement
Harford County Taxpayers in 1870, 1872 and 1883
Harford County, Maryland Divorce Cases, 1827-1912: An Annotated Index
Heirs and Legatees of Harford County, Maryland, 1774-1802
Heirs and Legatees of Harford County, Maryland, 1802-1846
Inhabitants of Baltimore County, Maryland, 1763-1774
Inhabitants of Cecil County, Maryland, 1649-1774
Inhabitants of Harford County, Maryland, 1791-1800
Inhabitants of Kent County, Maryland, 1637-1787
Joseph A. Pennington & Co., Havre De Grace, Maryland Funeral Home Records:
Volume II, 1877-1882, 1893-1900
Maryland Bible Records, Volume 1: Baltimore and Harford Counties
Maryland Bible Records, Volume 2: Baltimore and Harford Counties
Maryland Bible Records, Volume 3: Carroll County
Maryland Bible Records, Volume 4: Eastern Shore
Maryland Deponents, 1634-1799
Maryland Deponents: Volume 3, 1634-1776
Maryland Public Service Records, 1775-1783: A Compendium of Men and Women of Maryland Who Rendered Aid in Support of the American Cause against Great Britain during the Revolutionary War
Marylanders to Carolina. Migration of Marylanders to North Carolina and South Carolina prior to 1800

Marylanders to Kentucky, 1775-1825
Methodist Records of Baltimore City, Maryland: Volume 1, 1799-1829
Methodist Records of Baltimore City, Maryland: Volume 2, 1830-1839
Methodist Records of Baltimore City, Maryland: Volume 3, 1840-1850 (East City Station)
More Maryland Deponents, 1716-1799
More Marylanders to Carolina: Migration of Marylanders to North Carolina and South Carolina prior to 1800
More Marylanders to Kentucky, 1778-1828
Outpensioners of Harford County, Maryland, 1856-1896
Presbyterian Records of Baltimore City, Maryland, 1765-1840
Quaker Records of Baltimore and Harford Counties, Maryland, 1801-1825
Quaker Records of Northern Maryland, 1716-1800
Quaker Records of Southern Maryland, 1658-1800
Revolutionary Patriots of Anne Arundel County, Maryland
Revolutionary Patriots of Baltimore Town and Baltimore County, 1775-1783
Revolutionary Patriots of Calvert and St. Mary's Counties, Maryland, 1775-1783
Revolutionary Patriots of Caroline County, Maryland, 1775-1783
Revolutionary Patriots of Cecil County, Maryland
Revolutionary Patriots of Delaware, 1775-1783
Revolutionary Patriots of Dorchester County, Maryland, 1775-1783
Revolutionary Patriots of Frederick County, Maryland, 1775-1783
Revolutionary Patriots of Harford County, Maryland, 1775-1783
Revolutionary Patriots of Kent and Queen Anne's Counties
Revolutionary Patriots of Lancaster County, Pennsylvania
Revolutionary Patriots of Maryland, 1775-1783: A Supplement
Revolutionary Patriots of Maryland, 1775-1783: Second Supplement
Revolutionary Patriots of Montgomery County, Maryland, 1776-1783
Revolutionary Patriots of Prince George's County, Maryland, 1775-1783
Revolutionary Patriots of Talbot County, Maryland, 1775-1783
Revolutionary Patriots of Worcester and Somerset Counties, Maryland, 1775-1783
Revolutionary Patriots of Washington County, Maryland, 1776-1783
St. George's (Old Spesutia) Parish, Harford County, Maryland: Church and Cemetery Records, 1820-1920
St. John's and St. George's Parish Registers, 1696-1851
Survey Field Book of David and William Clark in Harford County, Maryland, 1770-1812
The Crenshaws of Kentucky, 1800-1995
The Delaware Militia in the War of 1812
Union Chapel United Methodist Church Cemetery Tombstone Inscriptions, Wilna, Harford County, Maryland

www.ingramcontent.com/pod-product-compliance
Lightning Source LLC
Chambersburg PA
CBHW071314150426
43191CB00007B/617